THIRD EDITION

Teaching Language *in* Context

Alice Omaggio Hadley
University of Illinois at Urbana-Champaign

Technology information from Robert M. Terry,
University of Richmond

HEINLE & HEINLE

THOMSON LEARNING ™ Australia   Canada   Mexico   Singapore   Spain   United Kingdom   United States

HEINLE & HEINLE
THOMSON LEARNING

Dedication

To my husband Henry, with my deepest appreciation for his patience, encouragement, and support throughout this project.

Publisher:
Wendy Nelson

Developmental Editor:
Anne Besco

Marketing Manager:
Jill Garrett

Production Editor:
Jeffrey M. Freeland

Senior Manufacturing Coordinator:
Mary Beth Hennebury

Compositor:
dix!

Printer:
Malloy Lithographing, Inc.

Cover Designer:
Peter Blaiwas/Vernon Press

Illustrators:
Len Shalansky; Dave Sullivan

Library of Congress Catalog-in-Publication Data

Hadley, Alice Omaggio
Teaching Language in Context / Alice Omaggio Hadley.— 3rd ed.
p. cm.
Includes bibliographical references and index.
ISBN 0-8384-1705-1
1. Languages, Modern—Study and teaching. I. Title.

PB35 .H24 2000
418'.0071—dc21   00-044901

ASIA (including India):
Thomson Learning
60 Albert Street #15-01
Albert Complex
Singapore 189969
Tel 65 336-6411
Fax 65 336-7411

AUSTRALIA/NEW ZEALAND:
Nelson
102 Dodds Street
South Melbourne
Victoria 3205
Australia
Tel 61 (0)3 9685-4111
Fax 61 (0)3 9685-4199

LATIN AMERICA:
Thomson Learning
Seneca, 53
Colonia Polanco
11560 México D.F. México
Tel (525) 281-2906
Fax (525) 281-2656

CANADA:
Nelson
1120 Birchmount Road
Toronto, Ontario
Canada M1K 5G4
Tel (416) 752-9100
Fax (416) 752-8102

UK/EUROPE/MIDDLE EAST:
Thomson Learning
Berkshire House
168-173 High Holborn
London, WC1V 7AA
United Kingdom
Tel 44 (0)020 497-1422
Fax 44 (0)020 497-1426

SPAIN (includes Portugal):
Paraninfo
Calle Magallanes, 25
28015 Madrid
España
Tel 34 (0)91 446-3350
Fax 34 (0)91 445-6218

Contents

Epilogue: *Planning Instruction for the Proficiency-Oriented Classroom: Some Practical Guidelines*   456

Preface

As we begin a new century and a new millennium, it seems natural to look back over the past several years to see what we have accomplished and, at the same time, look forward to see what challenges lie ahead. In the language teaching profession, we have been both blessed and challenged by the substantial growth of knowledge that has taken place in our field in the past few decades. We have been blessed with a renewal of interest in language learning in this country and a greater recognition of its place in the curriculum of the future. We have been revitalized by the excitement generated as we pursue new directions in research and develop more creative ways to enhance learning in the classroom. Yet we are challenged by the many unanswered questions that our research efforts have only begun to address, and by the need to sort through the profusion of developments and ideas in our field and clarify for ourselves our own vision of the learning/teaching process.

Rod Ellis, in his excellent book, *Understanding Second Language Acquisition*,[1] argues that language teachers would greatly benefit from attempting to make explicit their own theories of how second-language acquisition occurs. This continuing struggle to understand, clarify, and articulate one's beliefs and practices is at the very heart of what it means to be a professional. We as teachers need to be able to choose wisely among the multitude of options that are presented in the professional literature and to know why we think these choices are best. At the same time, all of us need to be willing to be open to new ideas that lead to professional growth and positive change.

This book has been written in an attempt to assist readers interested in classroom language learning in the process of clarifying their own beliefs about language teaching and learning. I have chosen to organize this third edition of *Teaching Language in Context* around the set of hypothesized principles of language teaching that I presented in the first edition—principles derived in part

---

[1] Rod Ellis, *Understanding Second Language Acquisition* (Oxford: Oxford University Press, 1985).

from my own understanding of the concept of "proficiency," as described in the *ACTFL Proficiency Guidelines.*[2] These principles represent some of my own assumptions about teaching and are offered as one way to look at the issues before us. But the set of hypotheses is not meant to be prescriptive. As Strasheim[3] pointed out in 1976, we have moved out of the period of our professional history that was governed by absolutes. Neither are these hypothesized principles meant to define a particular methodology. Many practitioners reject the idea that one "true way" can be found for all learners, who bring a wide variety of personalities, cognitive styles, and learning preferences to our classrooms. Rather, the principles set forth in the third chapter of this new edition are derived from the theories explored in Chapters 1 and 2 and serve as an organizer for the discussion of theory and practice that unfolds in subsequent chapters.

Although the set of hypothesized principles is not new to this edition, there are a number of new topics that are reflected throughout the chapters of the book. First, the third edition includes a discussion of the *Standards for Foreign Language Learning*[4], which represent the efforts of a large group of professional organizations and individuals to outline goals for foreign language study in the twenty-first century. The standards movement has already had a strong influence on the thinking of the profession and promises to challenge us to work toward improving our language programs in significant ways in the years ahead.

A second topic that has been integrated throughout the third edition is that of the role of technology in language teaching. Most of this new material has been contributed by Robert M. Terry, whose expertise in this area far exceeds my own. I am grateful to him not only for contributing to the new edition in this way, but also for his help in reading and commenting on the entire manuscript and providing a number of ideas for classroom activities that are also new to this edition.

The third edition also includes an updated review of some of the literature in the fields of second-language acquisition and foreign language education. Some of the topics that are of special interest to researchers and practitioners today are the role of instruction in language learning and the importance of focusing, at least to some extent, on formal features of the language within a communicative approach. Additional topics of high interest include the integration of culture and language study and the development of alternative assessments to measure students' progress, particularly in light of the standards. The sheer volume of research that has taken place in the past several years in second-language acquisition and foreign language learning prohibits any comprehensive review of all of the relevant literature, but it is hoped that the new materials included

---

[2] *ACTFL Proficiency Guidelines* (Yonkers, NY: ACTFL, 1986, 1999).

[3] Lorraine Strasheim, "What Is a Foreign Language Teacher Today?" *Canadian Modern Language Review* 33 (1976):39–48.

[4] *Standards for Foreign Language Learning: Preparing for the 21st Century* (Yonkers, NY: National Standards in Foreign Language Education Project, 1996).

in this edition will lead readers to some interesting and helpful resources that treat the various topics in greater depth.

A brief summary of the chapter contents for this edition follows.

In Chapter 1, "On Knowing a Language: Communicative Competence, Proficiency, and the *Standards for Foreign Language Learning*," various theoretical and practical insights into what it means to be competent or proficient in a language are explored. This chapter, updated for this edition, extends the discussion of the first two editions about the nature of language proficiency, partly in response to the proliferation of ideas about this concept and its meaning since the first edition appeared in 1986. Most of us in the foreign- and second-language field consider teaching "for communication" or "for proficiency" our ultimate goal. Yet what do these terms mean precisely? In recent years, concepts such as "communicative competence" and "proficiency" have been used to refer to a wide variety of practices and approaches, and undoubtedly their meanings have been overextended and sometimes distorted. These concepts are considered in this first chapter, and various theoretical models of language competence are reviewed and discussed. The *ACTFL Proficiency Guidelines* are described briefly, and oral proficiency level descriptions are summarized. Research about levels of proficiency attained by students in high school and college programs is examined, and some misconceptions about proficiency are also discussed. In the last section of the chapter, the *Standards for Foreign Language Learning* are presented, and the five interrelated goal areas of communication, cultures, connections, comparisons, and communities are briefly outlined.

Chapter 2, "On Learning a Language: Some Theoretical Perspectives," deals with the question of how adult learners *develop* proficiency in a second language. Many new theoretical viewpoints have been advanced in the professional literature in the past two decades, and any approach to language teaching that we ultimately choose should be informed by these developments and the insights they provide. The sample of theoretical positions about the way in which adults acquire a second language has been chosen to reflect a continuum of perspectives from empiricist to rationalist views. Five theoretical viewpoints are reviewed and summarized in the chapter. Because learners are not alike, theoretical models of how learners acquire language should take into account the role that learner differences might play in the process of proficiency development. This important issue is therefore treated as well. The last section of the chapter considers how language learning theory can be related to classroom practice and how research interests and perspectives in the somewhat different fields of second-language acquisition (SLA) and foreign language learning/teaching can complement and inform one another.

In Chapter 3, a set of hypothesized principles for classroom teaching that are derived from the discussions in Chapters 1 and 2 is presented, and a rationale for each principle is given. The chapter then looks at a variety of methodological approaches, both from a historical perspective and in terms of current practices, analyzing their salient features. Underlying theoretical assumptions are explored, as well as teaching strategies and techniques that typically predominate in each approach.

Chapter 4 presents a review of the research, in both first- and second-language learning, regarding the role of context in the comprehension and production of discourse. The chapter ends with a discussion of content-based learning and the whole continuum of possibilities for including both cultural and interdisciplinary subject matter in the language classroom. Chapter 5 then offers suggestions for contextualizing listening and reading practice, as well as a rationale for incorporating such activities into classroom instruction. In this edition, new activities based on authentic materials have been included. The role of video and computer technology in fostering the development of listening and reading abilities is also discussed.

Chapters 6 and 7 provide guidelines for contextualizing practice in speaking and writing, as well as ideas for integrative activities involving listening, speaking, reading, writing, and culture. Creative language-use activities and formats for small-group communicative interaction are also presented. Some ideas for responding to specific learner problems in each of these skill areas are also highlighted.

Chapter 8 treats the teaching of culture, including various models for choosing cultural topics and materials and activities that integrate the teaching of language and culture.

Chapter 9 presents formats for proficiency-oriented classroom testing, as well as a description of oral proficiency testing techniques used in conjunction with the ACTFL and ILR proficiency guidelines. Item types for classroom tests of listening, reading, speaking, writing, and integrated skills are presented in contextualized, situational formats. Additional suggestions are included in this edition for the use of authentic materials in classroom tests and quizzes. The final section of the chapter reviews some of the literature on new types of assessments, including computer-adaptive testing, portfolios, and performance-based tasks.

The epilogue to this edition synthesizes the material in the preceding pages by illustrating how curricular planning can reflect a proficiency-oriented approach. Practical suggestions for goal setting, text selection, and lesson planning are discussed.

The appendices to the second edition include various practical resources for the language teacher. Appendix A includes the most recent *ACTFL Proficiency Guidelines* for speaking. The other appendices include additional illustrative material relating to evaluating multimedia programs (Appendix B) and providing feedback on students' writing (Appendix C).

The reader will notice that certain key ideas relating to the development of language proficiency recur throughout the book in cyclical fashion. For example, the concept of contextualized language use is presented in Chapter 1, where models of language competence are discussed. This concept recurs in the discussion of methodology in Chapter 3, is examined from the perspective of the researcher in Chapter 4, recurs in Chapters 5, 6, and 7 and in discussions of practical classroom techniques, appears again in Chapter 8 on teaching culture, and is central to the illustrations of testing procedures in Chapter 9. Important themes, or threads, are thus woven through the chapters to achieve an integrated perspective of language learning and teaching. Such an integrated framework is essential if we are to make reasoned and purposeful choices among the many approaches, strategies, and materials available to us as language teaching professionals.

This book is designed to address the needs and concerns of those whose primary interest is the teaching of second and foreign languages to adult learners in classroom settings. It does not attempt to treat issues relating to language acquisition in children or the acquisition of a second language by learners in informal or natural settings, although it may be possible for the reader to extrapolate some ideas for these situations from some of the chapters. It is designed to be used as a basic or supplementary text in methodology courses for pre- and in-service secondary teachers and university teaching assistants, or as an up-to-date reference and resource for experienced professionals and researchers. Novice teachers or teacher trainees will find practical ideas for teaching language and culture, as well as some background information to help them formulate their own hypotheses about language learning. The experienced practitioner will, hopefully, find some new teaching ideas or gain a new perspective on some familiar techniques or approaches. It is also hoped that this book will stimulate further research and contribute to the theory-building process, a process that must continue as our knowledge about language acquisition and learning grows in the years ahead.

Alice Omaggio Hadley
Urbana, Illinois
May 2000

Acknowledgments

I would like to express my sincere thanks and appreciation to all those colleagues and friends whose helpful comments, support, and encouragement have been invaluable to me in the preparation of this third edition. Specifically, I would like to thank the following people, who carefully read and reviewed part or all of the manuscript in its various stages: L. Kathy Heilenman, University of Iowa, who read the whole manuscript and gave me very helpful feedback and support; Robert M. Terry, who also read and reacted to the whole manuscript, provided sample teaching ideas, and wrote new material on technology for this edition. Thanks also to Teresa Pica, University of Pennsylvania; Larbi Oukada, Indiana University—Purdue University, Indianapolis; Mary Wildner-Bassett, University of Arizona; and Cindy Kendall, Michigan State University, who read and reviewed parts of the manuscript for this edition. I am also grateful to the following people who had input into the shaping of the third edition: Judith Frommer, Harvard University; Diana Adler, North Carolina State University; Gail Guntermann, Arizona State University; Katherine Kulick, College of William and Mary; Carol Klee, University of Minnesota; Margaret Azevedo, Stanford University; Helene Neu, University of Michigan; and Lydie Meunier, University of Tulsa.

I would also like to express my appreciation for the input and support of several of my colleagues at the University of Illinois at Urbana-Champaign: Peter Golato, who provided me with a number of useful resources on second-language acquisition research and whose helpful and thoughtful comments on the first draft of Chapter 2 was very much appreciated; and John Lalande and Andrea Golato, who graciously provided me with sample teaching activities in German for this edition.

I am also deeply grateful for the help and support of all those colleagues and friends who provided comments for the first two editions of this book. Their professional input and support were invaluable to me throughout the development of the project.

I would also like to thank Wendy Nelson, Publisher; Anne Besco, Developmental Editor; and Jeffrey M. Freeland, Production Editor at Heinle & Heinle for their careful work, support, and encouragement in the preparation of this third edition. I owe a special debt of gratitude to Anne Besco for her many hours of work and unending patience in the editing of the manuscript and her follow-through on two sets of page proofs. Special thanks are also due to Barbara Ames, who copyedited the manuscript, and Janet McCartney for her careful proofreading. I would also like to express my appreciation for the many hours of work that Henry H. Hadley and Robert M. Terry spent proofreading the manuscript. Finally, I want to thank Charles H. Heinle and Stanley J. Galek, who were open to the approach I wanted to take in this book, and for their unconditional support of the project throughout its development.

A. O. H.

1 ONE
On Knowing a Language: Communicative Competence, Proficiency, and the *Standards for Foreign Language Learning*

Introduction

As we enter the new millenium, the language teaching profession continues to experience substantial growth due to the rapid expansion of knowledge that has taken place in our field in the past few decades. There has been an abundance of creative new approaches, materials, teaching ideas, and technological innovations in recent years, and no lack of stimulating, scholarly debate about how best to use them. Never before in our professional history have we had so many choices; never before has the need for professionalism and critical judgment been clearer. The struggle to understand, clarify, and articulate one's beliefs and practices is at the very heart of what it means to be a professional.

This book has been written in an attempt to assist teachers, teacher educators, and students interested in classroom language learning in the process of clarifying their own beliefs about language learning and teaching, both in terms of theoretical issues and practical implications for classroom instruction. Its purpose is, therefore, not to promote a particular theory or methodology; rather, it seeks to review and summarize past and current language acquisition theories, examine various recent trends that have influenced teaching practice, and extract from our rich heritage of resources those elements that seem most relevant to the construction of viable models for teaching.

Consider for a moment the fundamental question: "How can we help students learning a second language in a classroom setting become proficient in that language?" As we explore that question further, at least three subquestions emerge:

1. What does *proficient* mean?
2. How does one become proficient in a language?

1

3. What characterizes a classroom environment in which opportunities to become proficient are maximized?

With each of these subquestions, a new area of inquiry is opened, raising issues that are equally difficult to resolve. Being proficient implies that one *knows* a language, but to what degree? A given student might *know* a little German, but not enough to really *do* anything with it. The student's knowledge of another foreign language, Spanish, will allow him or her to carry on a simple conversation and handle his or her needs as a tourist. But the student wouldn't say that he or she really knows Spanish. The individual certainly does not claim to be proficient in that language. What does *knowing a language* involve? How proficient can people become in a language other than their own? Is there a difference between the way people learn their native language and the way they learn a second one? What does *learn* mean? Can people become proficient in a second language in a formal classroom environment? Is the age at which a person begins to acquire a language a factor? To what degree or level can a person's competence develop in a second language if he or she begins study as an adult? What should be the goals of instruction? What curriculum and materials should a teacher choose? Should teachers embrace modern technological innovations and incorporate them into their teaching? Will technology make teachers more effective or students better learners?

These are only a few of the many questions that challenge us as language teachers. In this and subsequent chapters, some of the answers that have been proposed in recent years to questions such as these are explored. Chapter 1 looks at the issue of language proficiency and how that concept might be defined and understood. At the end of the chapter, the *Standards for Foreign Language Learning* (1996, 1999) are presented and briefly discussed. The *Standards* outline goals for learning that should help students become proficient *users* of the language beyond the limits of the classroom, as well as help them learn about the culture(s) of the people whose language they are learning and how culture and language are intertwined. Chapter 2 summarizes some of the theoretical approaches to the question of how adults become proficient in a second language. Chapter 3 then proposes a set of hypothesized principles of language teaching that are derived from the issues surrounding the concept of proficiency. These principles serve, in turn, as an organizer for the chapters that follow.

Defining Language Proficiency

What does it mean to be *proficient* in a language? What does one have to know in terms of grammar, vocabulary, sociolinguistic appropriateness, conventions of discourse, cultural understanding, and the like in order to know a language well enough to use it for some real-world purpose?

We might shed some light on these questions by considering first what *proficient* means in a more general context. Some common synonyms for the term *proficiency* include words like *expertise, ability,* or *competence,* implying a high level of *skill*, well-developed *knowledge*, or a polished *performance*. The terms *competence* and *performance* introduce yet another complication, especially for those familiar with the fields of languages and linguistics. These two terms, used for centuries by philosophers and scientists to characterize all types of knowledge (Brown 1980, 1987, 1994), were fundamental to Chomsky's (1965) theory of transformational-generative grammar. In his theory, Chomsky distinguished between an *idealized* native speaker's underlying *competence* (referring to one's implicit or explicit knowledge of the system of the language) and the individual's *performance* (or one's actual production and comprehension of language in specific instances of language use). Because the native speaker's performance is so often imperfect, due to such factors as memory limitations, distractions, errors, hesitations, false starts, repetitions, and pauses, Chomsky believed that actual performance did not properly reflect the underlying knowledge (competence) that linguistic theory sought to describe. Thus Chomsky felt that, for the purposes of developing a linguistic theory, it was important to make the competence-performance distinction. He also believed it was necessary to study and describe language through idealized abstractions rather than through records of natural speech, which was so often flawed.

From Grammatical Competence to Communicative Competence

Chomsky's competence-performance distinction served as the basis for the work of many other researchers interested in the nature of language acquisition. In an influential position paper published in 1980, Canale and Swain (1980a) reviewed and evaluated the various theoretical perspectives on competence and performance that had been articulated in response to Chomsky's work. According to their review, two of the most notable extensions to Chomsky's theory came from Hymes (1972) and Campbell and Wales (1970). Hymes felt that there are rules of language use that are neglected in Chomsky's view of language. He espoused a much broader view, in which grammatical competence is only one of the components of knowledge that native speakers possess. This broader notion of "communicative competence," a term he had introduced in the mid-1960s (Canale 1983a), incorporated sociolinguistic and contextual competence as well as grammatical competence. Campbell and Wales accepted Chomsky's methodological distinction between competence and actual performance, but they pointed out that Chomsky's conceptualization of these terms did not include any reference to either the *appropriateness* of an utterance to a particular situation or context or its *sociocultural significance*. For Campbell and Wales, the degree to which a person's production or understanding of the language is appropriate to the context in which it takes place is even more important than its grammaticality. They referred to Chomsky's very restricted view of competence as "grammatical competence," and to their more inclusive view as "communicative competence" (Campbell and Wales 1970, p. 249).

During the 1970s, some linguists and researchers, proceeding from the earlier work previously cited, began to refer to "communicative competence" as a notion that was distinct from "grammatical" or "linguistic" competence. As Canale and

Swain (1980a) point out, there was some disagreement in the literature of the 1970s about whether the notion of communicative competence included grammatical competence as one of its components:

> . . . it is common to find the term "communicative competence" used to refer exclusively to knowledge or capability relating to the rules of language use and the term "grammatical (or linguistic) competence" used to refer to the rules of grammar. . . . It is equally common to find these terms used in the manner in which Hymes (1972) and Campbell and Wales (1970) use them. . . . (p. 5).

Perhaps one of the best-known studies involving the concept of communicative competence in the early 1970s was that done by Savignon (1972) at the University of Illinois. In that study, Savignon sought to compare the effects of various types of practice on communicative skills development. Her definition of communicative competence did incorporate linguistic competence as one of its components: "*Communicative competence* may be defined as the ability to function in a truly communicative setting—that is, in a dynamic exchange in which *linguistic competence* must adapt itself to the total informational input, both linguistic and paralinguistic, of one or more interlocutors" (p. 8). She went on to point out that successful communication would depend largely on individuals' willingness to take risks and express themselves in the foreign language, and on their resourcefulness in using the vocabulary and structures under their control to make themselves understood. According to Savignon, the use of gestures, intonation, and facial expression also contributes to communication, but linguistic accuracy, though of some importance, should be considered as only one of the major constituents of a communicative exchange.

In later discussions of communicative competence, Savignon (1983, 1997) emphasizes again its dynamic nature, pointing out that it is an *"interpersonal. . .trait"* (1997, p. 14) that involves two or more persons negotiating meaning together, whether through oral or written communication. She further emphasizes the contextual dimension of language use and that one's success in communicating may vary from situation to situation:

> Communication takes place in an infinite variety of situations, and success in a particular role depends on one's understanding of the context and on prior experience of a similar kind. Success requires making appropriate choices of register *and* style *in terms of the situation and the other participants (Savignon 1997, p. 15).*

She distinguishes, as does Chomsky, between *competence* and *performance,* with competence being "defined as a *presumed underlying ability* and performance as the *overt manifestation of that ability*" (p. 15):

> Competence is what one knows. Performance is what one does. However, only performance is observable, and it is only through performance that competence can be developed, maintained, and evaluated (p. 15).

Because Savignon sees communicative competence as a *"relative, not absolute"* trait and because it "depends on the cooperation of all the participants," she adds that one should speak in terms of *"degrees* of communicative competence" (p. 15). As one considers these important points in her conceptualization of the term, one might conclude that "communicative competence" may be difficult to measure. The issues that Savignon raises should be kept in mind as we discuss later in this chapter ways in which language proficiency is described and assessed.

Most of the definitions of communicative competence discussed in Canale and Swain's (1980a) review include slightly different components or view the relationship or importance of components to be somewhat different. As mentioned earlier, the role of grammatical competence seems to be the most controversial. Munby (1978) contends that the term "communicative competence" should include the notion of grammatical competence. Failure to include it in the definition might lead one to conclude: (1) that grammatical competence and communicative competence need to be developed separately, usually with attention given first to grammar; and (2) "that grammatical competence is not an essential component of communicative competence" (Canale and Swain 1980a, p. 5). In terms of Munby's second point, Canale and Swain agree that both grammatical competence and sociolinguistic competence are important elements in any theoretical framework of communicative competence:

> *Just as Hymes (1972) was able to say that there are rules of grammar that would be useless without rules of language use, so we feel that there are rules of language use that would be useless without rules of grammar (p. 5).*

However, in reference to Munby's first point, Canale and Swain (1980a) maintain that even instructors who agree that grammatical competence is indeed an important part of communicative competence could still prefer to address some aspects of grammatical competence separately from or prior to the teaching of sociolinguistic rules of language use, especially in early stages of language learning. They add, however, that ". . . second language learning will proceed more effectively when grammatical usage is not abstracted from meaningful context" (p. 24), and that facilitating the integration of various competencies should be the primary goal of language teaching in any communicative approach, "an outcome that is not likely to result from overemphasis on one form of competence over the others throughout a second language programme" (p. 27).

In order to determine how one might best design communicative approaches to language teaching, Canale and Swain (1980a) felt it was necessary to clarify further the concept of "communicative competence." Drawing on the work of many scholars, including Campbell and Wales (1970), Hymes (1972), Savignon (1972), Charolles (1978), Munby (1978), and Widdowson (1978), they formulated a theoretical framework for communicative competence that, in the modified version described by Canale (1983a), consisted of four major components: (1) grammatical competence, (2) sociolinguistic competence, (3) discourse competence, and (4) strategic competence.[1]

In the Canale and Swain framework (1980a; Canale 1983a), *grammatical competence* refers to the degree to which the language user has mastered the linguistic code, including knowledge of vocabulary, rules of pronunciation and spelling, word formation, and sentence structure. Canale and Swain (1980b) maintain that such competence is an essential concern for any communicative approach that is oriented toward the eventual attainment of higher levels of proficiency, in which accuracy and precision of understanding and expression are important goals.

Sociolinguistic competence addresses the extent to which the second language can be used or understood appropriately in various contexts to convey specific communicative functions, such as describing, narrating, persuading, eliciting information, and the like. Such factors as topic, role of the participants, and setting will determine the appropriateness of the attitude conveyed by speakers and their choice of style or register. Brown (1980, 1987, 1994) uses the term "register" to refer to the many styles available to proficient speakers of a language. Speakers can vary their choice of vocabulary, syntax, pronunciation, intonation, and even nonverbal features to tailor their message for a particular person or social context. Registers range from very informal to very formal styles and apply to both spoken and written discourse. Brown points out that the skilled use of appropriate registers requires sensitivity to cross-cultural differences, making this type of competence especially difficult to attain.

Discourse competence, the third component of the Canale and Swain framework, involves the ability to combine ideas to achieve cohesion in form and coherence in thought. A person who has a highly developed degree of discourse competence will know how to use cohesive devices, such as pronouns and grammatical connectors (i.e., conjunctions, adverbs, and transitional phrases), to achieve unity of thought and continuity in a text. The competent language user will also be skilled in expressing and judging the relationships among the different ideas in a text (coherence). (See also Widdowson 1978; Hatch 1978, 1983, 1984, 1992; Brown and Yule 1983; and Larsen-Freeman and Long 1991 for further discussions of the role of discourse factors in language use.)

Strategic competence, the final component of the framework, involves the use of verbal and nonverbal communication strategies to compensate for gaps in the language user's knowledge of the code or for breakdown in communication because of performance factors. Canale (1983a, 1983b) adds that strategic competence can also be used to enhance the rhetorical effectiveness of one's communication. This component is qualitatively different from the other three in that it emphasizes the use of effective strategies in negotiating meaning. Students at

---

[1] The framework developed by Canale and Swain (1980a) first consisted of three major components: *grammatical competence, sociolinguistic competence* (including both sociocultural rules of use and rules of discourse), and *strategic competence.* The framework was later modified in Canale (1983a) to include *discourse competence* as a distinct component.

lower levels of proficiency can benefit from learning effective communication strategies such as paraphrasing through circumlocution or approximations, using gestures, and asking others to repeat or to speak more slowly.

Although Canale and Swain refer to their theoretical framework as a way of characterizing communicative competence, they acknowledge that the term "communicative competence" itself may be problematic, since there has been so much disagreement and confusion about what it means. Canale (1983a) maintains that "the distinction between communicative competence and actual communication remains poorly understood . . . in the second language field" (p. 5). He prefers the term "actual communication" to the earlier term "communicative performance" used in the 1980 version of the framework, since the latter term tends to lead to confusion with Chomsky's competence-performance distinction. Canale stresses, however, that his use of the term "communicative competence" refers to both underlying knowledge about language and communicative language use and skill, or how well an individual can perform with this knowledge base in actual communication situations.

The Canale and Swain framework has had a great deal of influence on the thinking of many scholars who are working toward a better understanding of what communicative language proficiency entails. Bachman (1990) has proposed a model for a theoretical framework of "communicative language ability" that incorporates some of the same components identified by Canale and Swain, but that is arranged and explained in a somewhat different fashion. His framework consists of three major components: (1) language competence, (2) strategic competence, and (3) psychophysiological mechanisms. The first component is made up of various kinds of knowledge that we use in communicating via language, whereas the second and third components include the mental capacities and physical mechanisms by which that knowledge is implemented in communicative language use. Bachman identifies the first component—*language competence*—as "knowledge of language" (p. 85) and relates it to other frameworks of communicative competence such as those described by Hymes (1972), Munby (1978), Canale and Swain (1980a), and Canale (1983b). The components of language competence are depicted in Illustration 1.1. In Bachman's description of *language competence*, two major types of abilities are included. The first is *organizational competence*, which relates to controlling the formal structure of language (*grammatical competence*) and knowing how to construct discourse (*textual competence*). The second type of ability is called *pragmatic competence*, which relates to the functional use of language (*illocutionary competence*) and knowledge of its appropriateness to the context in which it is used (*sociolinguistic competence*). Each of the four subcomponents of the model is further defined, as shown in Illustration 1.1. *Grammatical competence* includes control of vocabulary, morphology, syntax, and phonemic and graphemic elements; *textual competence* includes cohesion and rhetorical organization. *Illocutionary competence* comprises control of functional features of language, such as the ability to express ideas and emotions (*ideational functions*); to get things done (*manipulative functions*); to use language to teach, learn, and solve problems (*heuristic functions*); and to be creative (*imaginative functions*). Finally, *sociolinguis-*

Illustration 1.1
Components of Language
Competence

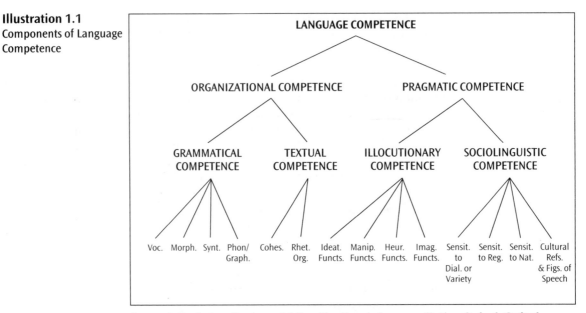

Source: L. Bachman, *Fundamental Considerations in Language Testing.* Oxford: Oxford University Press, 1990, p. 87. Reprinted by permission of the Oxford University Press.

tic competence includes such things as sensitivity to dialect and register, naturalness (or native-like use of language), and understanding of cultural referents and figures of speech (Bachman 1990, pp. 87–98).

Bachman's framework represents a promising alternative for looking at communicative language ability and for addressing the question: "What does it mean to know a language?"

The models of language ability described in this section have been derived from various theoretical perspectives about the nature of language and language use. In the next section, we will examine the development of a model of language ability that arose initially not from a particular theoretical perspective on language competence or performance but from a series of grass-roots initiatives originating among practitioners (Liskin-Gasparro 1984; Scebold 1992).

■ Communicative Competence and the Notion of Proficiency

In one sense, a focus on proficiency has always driven language learning and teaching. Obviously, no program has ever claimed to be oriented toward "non-proficiency" or incompetence. Yet it is only within the past two decades or so that practitioners have begun to use the term "proficiency" in a new light. Prior to the communicative language teaching movement of the 1970s, foreign language proficiency had been defined and conceptualized largely in terms of structural accuracy by many members of the academic community. In the past thirty years, many teachers have come to understand that language proficiency is not a monolithic concept representing an amorphous ideal that students rarely attain; rather it is comprised of a whole range of abilities that must be described in a graduated fashion in order to be meaningful.

With the definitions of "communicative competence" of the 1970s came new insights into the various components of language ability that needed to be developed in order to know a language well enough to use it. Yet most of these early models did not specify *levels* of competence in a way that could help practitioners measure their students' progress or articulate program goals. Across language learners and language programs, the degrees of proficiency needed, desired, or attained can vary considerably, depending on such factors as purpose, motivation for language study, or learning environment. Without a clear understanding of what we mean by "proficiency," communication about goals and outcomes and articulation among programs and settings can be difficult and frustrating. As Higgs and Clifford (1982) indicate, some specification about levels of proficiency and what they mean is needed to help refine the concept for practitioners:

> *A student cannot merely be declared competent in communication. The functions that he is competent to express must be specified. The degree of proficiency required to survive as a tourist or a student is not the same as that required to negotiate treaties. One finds that content areas and language functions needed for discussing abstract ideas differ from those used in telling about one's immediate needs or one's latest European vacation. . . . We must tell [our students] not that they are competent to speak German, but that they are competent to meet routine physical and social obligations in an environment where German is spoken (pp. 60–61).*

The *ACTFL Provisional Proficiency Guidelines*, published in November 1982, were the first attempt by the foreign language teaching profession to define and describe levels of functional competence for the academic context in a comprehensive fashion. The history of the development of these guidelines has been outlined by Liskin-Gasparro (1984), who traces the "quest for proficiency" from its antecedents in the ancient world to the modern conceptualizations of the 1970s (p. 13). It was during this decade that a convergence of events—the establishment of the President's Commission on Foreign Language and International Studies, the work in communicative syllabus design in Europe, the beginning of communicative language teaching movements in the United States, and the work of government agencies to refine the ways in which functional language ability was taught and tested—led to a series of projects that would give birth to a significant new movement in language education. Some of the events described in Liskin-Gasparro's comprehensive historical review are highlighted below. Readers should consult this source for more specific details.

The Move Toward National Standards: Defining and Assessing Proficiency

When I asked Ed Scebold, Executive Director of the American Council on the Teaching of Foreign Languages, to talk about how he became interested in the

ACTFL Proficiency Guidelines project, he began with his experiences writing curricular guidelines as a language teacher. He explained that, throughout the history of language teaching, instructors and curriculum specialists have attempted to set goals and define outcomes for language learning to foster greater articulation among levels of instruction and improve communication about what was being accomplished. For decades, these goal statements, articulated on the local or state level, had taken the form of long lists of topics to be "covered." Achievement tests were designed by individual teachers to see how well students had learned the designated material. Yet comprehensive lists of content and tests of discrete linguistic features seemed to have limited usefulness in shaping and changing language instruction in any significant way. By the late 1970s, it was becoming increasingly clear that the focus of curricular planning and testing would need to shift from a micro-analysis of what was being *taught* to a macro-analysis of what students could actually do with the language before any real progress could be made (Scebold 1992).

By the end of the decade, it had become increasingly apparent that a widely used, nationally approved procedure for assessing language proficiency was needed. It seemed that the academic community was ready to seek some consensus on defining more clearly than ever before proficiency goals and standards for second language programs. This interest in setting standards reflected the more general concern about excellence in education that was brewing on the national level. The need for standards in the area of foreign languages and international studies was pointed out by Paul Simon (Illinois) and other members of Congress, who, together with language professional organizations, urged the establishment of a special presidential commission. This initiative was supported by President Jimmy Carter, and in April 1978, the President's Commission on Foreign Language and International Studies was formed.

Among recommendations included in the commission's report was that a "National Criteria and Assessment Program" be established to "develop foreign language proficiency tests, and to report on, monitor, and assess foreign language teaching in the U.S." (*Strength through Wisdom*, 1979, p. 15, cited in Liskin-Gasparro 1984, p. 30). This recommendation paralleled other similar recommendations that had been made by the MLA-ACLS Language Task Force for the President's Commission in late 1978:

> **Recommendation 10.** Institutions and, where appropriate, state educational systems should be encouraged by the Modern Language Association to adopt *nationally recognized performance or proficiency standards*, and make such standards known widely to students and faculty.
>
> **Recommendation 12.** The Modern Language Association and the American Council on the Teaching of Foreign Languages should secure funding for the *revision and redevelopment of tests for the measurement of proficiencies in the four language skills in all the most commonly taught and wide-use languages*. Such tests should be developed by committees consisting of both secondary school and college teachers (Brod 1980, cited in Liskin-Gasparro 1984, p. 29).

At the same time that the MLA-ACLS task forces were making the above recommendations, the Educational Testing Service (ETS) was approaching the problem of proficiency testing from another perspective. As early as 1970, Protase Woodford of ETS had coined the term *Common Yardstick*, which would be used some ten years later to refer to a project attempting to define language proficiency levels for academic contexts using a scale parallel to the one used by federal government schools since World War II (Liskin-Gasparro 1984). The government scale had been developed in the early 1950s by linguists at one of the major government language schools, the Foreign Service Institute (FSI), in order to describe the speaking abilities of candidates for foreign service positions. It made provision for eleven major ranges of proficiency, beginning with 0 (no functional ability in the language) to 5 (proficiency equivalent to that of an educated native speaker), using "+" designations between levels.

In addition to the proficiency scale, FSI had developed an interview-based evaluation procedure for assigning a rating. This procedure was also of interest to the *Common Yardstick* project. During the 1970s, ETS cooperated with other organizations in Great Britain and Germany, representatives of the U.S. government, and business and academic groups to develop and refine the proficiency scales and the interview procedure for academic use (Liskin-Gasparro 1984). The outcome of this project was an adaptation of the government scale, currently known as the ILR (Interagency Language Roundtable) scale, involving an expansion of the lower levels to allow greater latitude and precision in describing proficiency below ILR Level 2.

The work begun by the *Common Yardstick* project was continued in 1981 by the American Council on the Teaching of Foreign Languages (ACTFL), in consultation with MLA, ETS, and other professional associations, under a grant entitled "A Design for Measuring and Communicating Foreign Language Proficiency." Some of the groundwork for this project had been laid by ACTFL in 1978 when a planning grant was obtained to begin work on the drafting of proficiency standards. The 1981 project brought together a large number of scholars who worked together to create both the generic and language-specific proficiency descriptions known as the *ACTFL Provisional Proficiency Guidelines,* which were disseminated in November of 1982. Since 1982 they have been reviewed and revised twice as new insights and knowledge have been incorporated. (See Liskin-Gasparro 1987 for specific details about revisions in the 1986 guidelines. The most recent [1999] generic descriptions for speaking are provided in Appendix A.)

As one reviews some of the history surrounding these developments, it becomes clear that the proficiency guidelines were essentially the product of a number of grass-roots initiatives. The projects were informed by literature reviews and consultation with scholars who had expertise in various theoretical perspectives of language learning. But rather than emerging from a particular theory of language learning, they came about primarily as a result of the perceived needs of practitioners in both government and academic settings who wanted to make a difference in the way languages were taught and to communicate more effectively about the results of that instruction. As Ed Scebold, Executive Director of

ACTFL, expressed it, the initiators of the proficiency projects used their many years of experience as teachers, their good sense, and trial and error to make the system come together (Scebold 1992). Yet in spite of the fact that the proficiency descriptions were not initiated from a particular theoretical perspective, they share many of the same components of other theoretically derived frameworks of communicative language ability, such as the one developed by Canale and Swain, described earlier. The congruence of these various frameworks will become clear as we look at the way in which proficiency is assessed using the *ACTFL Proficiency Guidelines*, to be discussed in the next section.

Assessing Language Proficiency Using the ACTFL Proficiency Guidelines

The *ACTFL Proficiency Guidelines* define and measure language ability in speaking, listening, reading, and writing. Global ratings are assigned by eliciting samples of performance and evaluating those samples using a set of interrelated criteria. It is important to understand that the scale is not linear in nature; rather, it is a multi-dimensional, expanding spiral (Liskin-Gasparro 1987). As one goes up the scale, progressively more language skill is needed to attain the next level. It might be helpful to think of the proficiency levels in terms of an inverted pyramid, such as the one depicted in Illustration 1.2.

One can see that relatively little positive change is needed to progress from the Novice level to the Intermediate, but that relatively more change is needed to make the leap from the Intermediate level to the Advanced, and so on up the scale. The Superior level of proficiency on the ACTFL scale corresponds to Levels 3, 4, and 5 on the government scale. As Liskin-Gasparro (1984) points out, the most difficult leap on the ILR scale is from Level 4 to Level 5. Indeed, it is unusual for nonnative speakers to attain the latter rating.

Levels of proficiency on the ACTFL scale can be distinguished by considering the four interrelated assessment criteria underlying the proficiency descriptions: **global tasks/functions, context/content, accuracy,** and **text type.** Illustration 1.3 presents the assessment criteria for speaking proficiency as they appear in the 1999 *ACTFL Oral Proficiency Interview Tester Training Manual* (Swender 1999). These criteria are interrelated in that "[t]he Oral Proficiency Interview is an integrative test, i.e., it addresses a number of abilities simultaneously and looks at them from a global perspective rather than from the point of view of the presence or absence of any given linguistic feature" (p. 21). One should therefore not think in terms of discrete points of grammar or discrete tasks or skills when considering a rating of a speech sample. Trained testers are skilled in their ability to use the assessment criteria to assign a global rating based on the overall communicative ability of the speaker.

A brief description of each of these criteria follows, as summarized from the *ACTFL Oral Proficiency Interview Tester Training Manual*:

- **Global tasks/functions** refers to real-world tasks that the speaker can do in the language. At the lowest level of the scale, functions such as naming various

Illustration 1.2
Inverted Pyramid
Representing ACTFL
Rating Scale with Major
Ranges and Sublevels

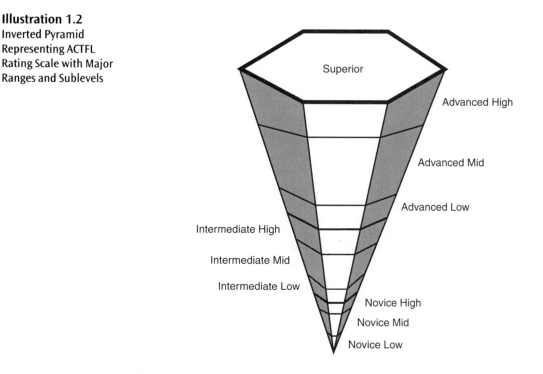

Source: Swender 1999, p. 12. Reprinted by permission of ACTFL.

objects or using basic greetings are typically within the ability of the persons interviewed. In the Intermediate range, interviewees can handle somewhat more challenging tasks such as responding to simple questions or asking for information. Persons rated as Advanced are capable of paragraph-length description and narration in different time frames. At the highest ranges of proficiency, interviewees are capable of quite complex tasks, such as developing an argument cogently and persuasively, supporting an opinion, or discussing a hypothetical situation extensively and with sophistication. As one's proficiency increases, the complexity of the language used to accomplish these tasks and the accuracy and precision with which the task can be accomplished also increase.

- **Context** "refers to circumstances or settings in which a person uses language" (Swender 1999, p. 23). At lower levels of proficiency, one can typically handle very predictable situations or "contexts which permit greater use of memorized or learned material because of the predictable, scripted nature of the settings and the concrete nature of interactions firmly based in the present" (p. 23). At the higher levels of proficiency, the context of conversation typically demands more of the participant due to the unpredictability of the situation and the need for flexibility in dealing with it.

ASSESSMENT CRITERIA—SPEAKING

Proficiency Level*	Global Tasks & Functions	Context/*Content*	Accuracy	Text Type
Superior	Discuss topics extensively, support opinions and hypothesize. Deal with a linguistically unfamiliar situation.	Most formal and informal settings / *Wide range of general interest topics and some special fields of interest and expertise.*	No pattern of errors in basic structures. Errors virtually never interfere with communication or distract the native speaker from the message.	Extended discourse
Advanced	Narrate and describe in major time frames and deal effectively with an unanticipated complication.	Most informal and some formal settings / *Topics of personal and general interest.*	Understood without difficulty by speakers unaccustomed to dealing with non-native speakers.	Paragraphs
Intermediate	Create with language, initiate, maintain, and bring to a close simple conversations by asking and responding to simple questions.	Some informal settings and a limited number of transactional situations / *Predictable, familiar topics related to daily activities.*	Understood, with some repetition, by speakers accustomed to dealing with non-native speakers.	Discrete sentences
Novice	Communicate minimally with formulaic and rote utterances, lists and phrases.	Most common informal settings / *Most common aspects of daily life.*	May be difficult to understand, even for speakers accustomed to dealing with non-native speakers.	Individual words and phrases

[* *A rating at any major level is arrived at by the sustained performance of the functions of the level, within the contexts and content areas for that level, with the degree of accuracy described for the level, and in the text type for the level. The performance must be sustained across ALL of the criteria for the level in order to be rated at that level.*]

Illustration 1.3
ACTFL Assessment
Criteria: Speaking
Proficiency

Source: Swender 1999, p. 31. Reprinted by permission of ACTFL.

The sophistication of language needed to argue one's point of view in a political discussion or to handle an unexpected problem in the foreign culture typically exceeds that needed to order food in a restaurant or to ask for a night's lodging.

- The **content** dimension of the assessment criteria, referring to topics or themes of conversation, "is the most variable element of the OPI" (Swender 1999, p. 23). Each oral interview is different, as the topics discussed depend on the interests and background of the person being interviewed. However, the content at the lower levels often centers on autobiographical information and personal experiences and interests, since these types of topics allow the interviewee to stay in "the here-and-now" and deal with concrete rather than abstract content. As one's proficiency increases, the range of topics one can discuss with facility increases. At the higher levels of proficiency, the range of content that the interviewee can discuss comfortably and with facility is as wide as that typically handled in the native language.

The **content** dimension of the assessment criteria should not be thought of as a hierarchical list of topics or themes. The same topic can usually be explored at virtually any level of proficiency. The following example serves to illustrate how a topic such as "the family" might be discussed differently at the various levels on the scale. *Novice* speakers might be able to enumerate the members of their families but say very little else about them. At the *Intermediate* level, speakers might give a brief description of family members or mention some of their activities or interests, whereas speakers at the *Advanced* level can talk about family members in detail, recount events that the family has shared together, or talk about future plans. At the *Superior* level, more abstract topics such as the societal forces that threaten family life, the issues surrounding family planning, or the role of the family in the target culture might be discussed. Thus it is not the topic or content per se, but rather the depth and breadth of the discussion and the precision and sophistication with which it is handled that will differ from one level of proficiency to the next.

- **Accuracy** "refers to the acceptability, quality and precision of the message conveyed" (Swender 1999, p. 25). Included among the features considered when assessing accuracy are *fluency, grammar, pronunciation, vocabulary, pragmatic competence,* and *sociolinguistic competence* (p. 25). Many Novice speakers tend to make errors in most or all of these areas, often rendering them incomprehensible to native speakers who are not used to dealing with foreigners. (However, it *is* possible for Novice speakers to be quite accurate, especially when using memorized material, although the amount of language they can use is extremely limited.) Generally, one can characterize speakers at the lower end of the scale as intelligible, but typically the native-speaking conversational partner bears the responsibility of negotiating communication. The OPI Tester Manual clarifies the process by which accuracy is assessed in an interview:

  > ***The degree to which the speaker relies on the listener for filling in gaps in the message due to imperfect control of the language is one way to assess accuracy.***

  > *As proficiency increases, the responsibility of the interlocutor for negotiating the message decreases. At the same time, the global tasks associated with higher levels of proficiency—describing, narrating, hypothesizing, supporting opinion and discussing topics concretely and abstractly—require more refined and elaborated use of grammatical, lexical and sociolinguistic rules as well as effective use of cohesive devices to transmit complex messages (Swender 1999, p. 25).*

- **Text type** in the set of assessment criteria refers to the structure of the discourse, i.e. **"the quantity and the organizational aspects of speech"** (Swender 1999, p. 29). Typically, speakers rated as Novice can produce mainly isolated words or phrases, whereas Intermediate-level speech is characterized by sentence-length discourse. To attain the rating of Advanced, speakers must demonstrate their ability to function in paragraph-length discourse, using appropriate connectors and transitional phrases. Finally, speakers rated Superior can speak extensively in an organized and sequenced fashion.

As more specific characteristics for each level of the ACTFL scale are outlined below, it becomes clear how the components of communicative competence described by Canale (1983a) and others can be measured on a hierarchical scale within the context of these four assessment criteria. Thus, the proficiency guidelines capture much of the current thinking about the nature of communicative competence and represent one way to quantify the various elements of that construct.

For those unfamiliar with the *ACTFL Proficiency Guidelines*, the following shorthand characteristics of each proficiency range in oral skills should prove helpful. They are synthesized from the *ETS Oral Proficiency Testing Manual* (Liskin-Gasparro 1982), the *Oral Proficiency Interview Tester Training Manual* (Buck, Byrnes, and Thompson 1989; Swender 1999), and various ACTFL proficiency workshops.

Novice (ILR Level 0/0+)

Individuals performing at the Novice level of proficiency, though perhaps capable of some limited expression in the language, have no real functional ability to communicate with what they know. Typically, their speech is characterized by the use of a few memorized words or phrases, with little or no syntactic variation beyond the scope of the prefabricated, familiar material at their disposal. They can often give short lists of vocabulary and/or answer simple questions relating to highly predictable common daily settings. Questions relating to names of basic objects, names of family members, weather expressions, days of the week, time of day, and the like will often elicit some sample of speech when all other attempts at conversation fail. This is not to say that every speaker rated at the Novice level can say something about these topics nor that these are the only content areas that such individuals can control. Rather, they are meant to suggest the *type* of speech one can expect to elicit at the lowest levels of oral proficiency.

Speakers rated at the Novice High (ILR 0+) level on the academic scale have considerably more memorized material within their control and some ability to communicate their own personal messages with that material. Although they show that they have some of the features of the Intermediate level, including creating with the language, they are not able to sustain conversation adequately at that level.

Intermediate (ILR Level 1/1+)

Individuals in the Intermediate range of oral proficiency have the following characteristics:

1. They can create with the language; that is, they can express their own thoughts without relying exclusively on prefabricated or memorized responses to get their meaning across.
2. They are capable of *asking* questions as well as answering them. Whereas

Novice-level speakers typically respond to questions with one or two words, Intermediate-level speakers answer with longer phrases or full sentences and are capable of holding up their own end of the conversation by making inquiries.

3. They have at least a minimal level of sociolinguistic competence in that they can handle everyday social encounters (such as greetings and leave-takings) with some degree of appropriateness.

4. They can handle a simple "survival situation" that one might expect to encounter while traveling or residing for a short time in the target culture. Finding lodging, food, transportation, obtaining directions, and the like are tasks that can generally be handled successfully by Intermediate-level speakers.

5. Their discourse is characterized by simple sentences or phrases, normally limited to present time, with little use of cohesive devices or embedded sentence structure. Intermediate-level speech is usually quite inaccurate, even in basic structures, and vocabulary is quite limited. However, Intermediate-level speakers are intelligible to native speakers who are *used to dealing with foreigners*.

At the Intermediate High (ILR 1+) level, speakers begin to take on some of the characteristics of the Advanced range of proficiency. However, they are unable to sustain performance at this higher level during the course of the interview and, therefore, do not meet the minimal threshhold characteristics for the Advanced level.

Advanced (ILR Level 2/2+)

Speakers in the Advanced range are capable of sustained conversation and can be characterized as follows:

1. They can narrate and describe in major time/aspect frames. In addition, their narrations and descriptions are sustained in longer discourse segments; that is, Advanced-level speakers generally speak in paragraphs rather than in short phrases or sentences.

2. They can talk about a wide range of concrete topics, including autobiographical details, daily routines at home, school, or workplace, current events, and the like. They can participate fully in casual conversations, expressing facts, giving instructions, describing places, people, and things, reporting on events, and providing narration about past, present, and future activities.

3. They can "live off the economy" of the target culture and can handle routine work requirements with facility. Faced with a "survival situation" in which a complication has arisen (such as a missed plane, an unsatisfactory hotel room, a flat tire, or a similar situation in which one must explain one's way out of trouble), Advanced-level speakers can get their message across successfully.

4. They show a greater degree of sociolinguistic competence in their speech than do speakers at the Intermediate level, including some sensitivity to register and to the appropriateness of certain expressions in a given context.
5. Their strategic competence is improved. Some ability to paraphrase and to cope in more complicated situations or in unforseen circumstances is one of the hallmarks of speakers in this proficiency range.
6. Their discourse competence is also improved as they continue to use longer and more complex sentence structure to express their meaning. There is growing evidence of the ability to use cohesive devices to unify discourse.
7. Although they still make errors in some basic structures, their control of the grammatical system is much improved over that of Intermediate-level speakers. They still display patterns of errors, however, and their linguistic system tends to break down when they are asked to perform functions that are controlled at the next higher level of proficiency. Nonetheless, Advanced-level speakers are comprehensible to native speakers who are *not used to dealing with foreigners*.

At the Advanced High level, speakers have many of the characteristics of the Superior range, although they cannot sustain performance at that level.

Superior (ILR Levels 3, 3+, 4, 4+, 5)

The ACTFL scale collapses under one proficiency range all of the government ranges above Level 3. The reason for this will soon become clear. Basically, Superior-level speakers can be characterized as follows:

1. They have, at the very minimum, a "professional" level of proficiency; that is, they can handle a broad range of topics and situations, give supported opinions, hypothesize, provide complicated explanations, describe in detail with a great deal of precision, and tackle virtually any practical, social, professional, or abstract topic that they can discuss in their native language.
2. Although they may make random errors in grammar, especially in the more complicated structures of the language, speakers at the Superior level rarely make errors that would interfere with comprehension or distract their conversational partner from the message being conveyed.
3. At the lower end of the Superior range (ILR Level 3), speakers may occasionally lack some precision in vocabulary, but they are rarely at a loss to express their meaning through paraphrase or circumlocution. Strategic competence is high at this level, as is discourse competence. Though the Level 3 speaker may be unfamiliar with some idiomatic expressions and unable to shift registers easily, sociolinguistic competence is continuously developing. At Levels 4 and 5, however, speakers are more able to systematically tailor their language to any audience in a totally appropriate fashion. At these higher levels, vocabulary also becomes much more precise, and speakers can choose from a wide range of synonyms in much the same manner as they do in their native language.

As stated previously, the brief descriptions of proficiency levels given here are summary statements, or shorthand characteristics, used to familiarize practitioners with the concepts relating to proficiency testing. Note that the level definitions do *not* specify particular grammatical structures or lexical items that need to be controlled but outline instead more generalized performance criteria that must be met at each level of proficiency. Performance within the levels of proficiency is not completely uniform; on the contrary, there is often quite a wide variation in the *details* of performance, especially in the Intermediate and Advanced ranges. The descriptions provided by the *ACTFL Guidelines* for speaking (see Appendix A) provide more complete information about the nature of the performance that might be expected within proficiency ranges. For the most complete description and discussion of oral proficiency testing, see Swender (1999).

As mentioned earlier, the components of language proficiency that underlie the ACTFL descriptions—functions or tasks, grammatical competence, sociolinguistic features, pragmatic competence, discourse competence, organizational abilities—correspond in many respects with those underlying various theoretically derived frameworks of communicative language ability. This is not to say that all of these frameworks are the same. There are some important differences in the way in which the components are arranged and the way in which tests are constructed. (Some of these issues are treated later in this chapter.) But despite these differences, there seems to be a basic agreement among the various frameworks about what aspects of knowledge and performance are important in describing language proficiency. As we in the language teaching profession continue to develop our understanding in the years ahead, we can attempt to reach greater consensus as we build on this common ground.

Proficiency and Language Acquisition Theory

As we have already seen, the proficiency guidelines generated through the ACTFL projects were meant to describe levels of competence in listening, speaking, reading, and writing, based largely on many years of observation and testing both in the government context and in the academic community. They were not designed to present a theoretical model of language competence nor to explain how language acquisition might occur. Yet there is a rather strong degree of compatibility between the *global* level descriptions of linguistic and functional features in the oral proficiency guidelines and the overall sequence of development that some language acquisition theorists describe. Ellis (1985), in his comprehensive review of language acquisition theory and research, concludes that four macrostages of linguistic development are probably universal:

> **Stage One:** Interlanguage forms resemble those of pidgin languages, with more or less standard word order, regardless of the target language. Parts of sentences are omitted, and learners use memorized chunks of discourse in their communication.

Stage Two: Learners begin to use word order that is appropriate to the target language and to include most of the required sentence constituents in their speech. Language production in these first two stages is often quite inaccurate, however, as learners begin to include target-language features in their speech, but not consistently as a native speaker would use them.

Stage Three: Learners begin to use grammatical morphemes systematically and meaningfully.

Stage Four: Learners acquire complex sentence structures, such as embedded clauses and relative constructions, and use them with greater facility and precision (summary based on pp. 62–63).

Ellis cautions that these four stages are not clear-cut but tend to blend into one another.

In discussing the functional and/or contextual aspects of language development, Ellis points out that early-stage learners, like children learning their first language, benefit from talking about the here-and-now. They seem to be most successful and accurate when they are presented with tasks that are cognitively simple and that allow for reference to concrete objects or events in the immediate environment (pp. 88–89). As one moves to more advanced stages of language development, one can begin to talk about more "displaced activity" (p. 89), such as events in more distant time frames or abstract situations or topics. If learners are pushed to produce language that is too cognitively complex for their level, however, they may experience a kind of linguistic breakdown. Ellis explains that this is due to the fact that when tasks present difficulties that are not linguistic in nature, they divert learners' attention from form. When this happens, learners cannot focus on those forms that are the most recently acquired and, thus, not fully automatized, leading to more error-ridden speech (p. 89). This phenomenon of linguistic breakdown is often observed in ACTFL oral proficiency interviews during the "probe" phase, when the level of the conversation is deliberately raised to see if the learner can function at the next highest level of proficiency. Ellis's observation supports the notion that linguistic breakdown is a reliable indicator of task difficulty and serves to identify those aspects of a learner's interlanguage that are still relatively unstable and, thus, not fully acquired.

The central premise of Ellis's view of language acquisition is that there are identifiable global stages of development that all language learners seem to follow. On a micro-level within these broad stages, much variability can be seen. To reconcile the claim that there are universal sequences of general development and that there is variability on the micro-level, Ellis proposes a distinction between the *sequence* of development and the *order* of development in language acquisition (p. 64). The four macro-stages described above relate to *sequence*, whereas the development of specific grammatical or morphosyntactic features of language relate to *order*. The order of linguistic development can vary from learner to learner, depending on such factors as native language background and individual preferences for approaching the learning task (p. 63). Following Hatch (1974), Ellis describes two very different approaches to language acquisition that might affect the order in which discrete linguistic features of the language are acquired within the four broad stages. Learners who are characterized as "data gatherers" emphasize the acquisition of vocabulary and fluency, often at the expense of grammatical accuracy. "Rule formers," on the other hand, are concerned with form and attempt to use the language accurately, sometimes at the expense of fluency. Differences such as these can contribute to different learner performance profiles on a micro-level, even though the students being evaluated are grouped in the same global level of proficiency.

As we consider the observations Ellis makes in evaluating the nature of language acquisition, much of which is based on studies of oral production, we begin to see a kind of intellectual fit between the developmental sequence that has been furnished through the insights and experience of practitioners and the one that research and theory describe. The global levels of oral proficiency (*Novice, Intermediate, Advanced, Superior*) as defined in the *ACTFL Proficiency Guidelines* are compatible, in terms of describing general linguistic development, with the four stages of development that Ellis outlines. Within those various proficiency levels, testing experience has shown that learner language can differ substantially on a micro-level. Thus the four global level designations of the guidelines seem to be capturing a continuum of development similar to the one that Ellis describes as universal, lending support to their usefulness as an overall organizational framework within which pedagogical choices can be made.

Some Research Findings about Oral Proficiency

What level of proficiency can students expect to reach at the end of a given program of study? What is the average proficiency level of classroom teachers in high school and college programs? How long does it take to reach the Superior level of proficiency in a given language? These and other questions have been addressed in recent years through the use of oral proficiency interviews and other kinds of tests administered in both government and academic settings.

In an early study reported by Carroll (1967), the foreign language proficiency of 2,784 college seniors majoring in French, German, Italian, Russian, and Spanish at 203 institutions was measured with a battery of tests. These tests included the MLA Foreign Language Proficiency Tests for Teachers and Advanced Students in all four skills, the Modern Language Aptitude Test, and two questionnaires administered to students and to the foreign language department chairmen, respectively. In an independent study, FSI personnel administered oral interviews to 127 French, Spanish, German, and Russian language teachers participating in NDEA Summer Institutes in 1965. The teachers also took the MLA skills tests at the end of their summer experience. Scores for listening and speaking on the MLA tests were then equated with the FSI ratings in speaking; scores on the reading and writing portions of the MLA battery were equated with the FSI ratings on reading. Carroll reports that the correlations between the FSI and MLA scores were substantial, especially when looking at corresponding skill areas. Based on this independent study, the FSI ratings were estimated for the college seniors who had taken the MLA tests. The study concluded that *"the median graduate with a foreign language major can speak and comprehend the language only at about an FSI Speaking rating of '2+'. . . ."* (p. 134). It is important to bear in mind that the students who were tested were foreign language *majors* at the end of their college program who had concentrated on both language and literature study for at least four years, who may have had additional coursework in high school, and who may have spent some time abroad. The teachers at the NDEA institutes who had actually been tested with both the FSI and MLA measures had mean scores comparable to those of the college seniors, with teachers in French and Spanish averaging an FSI speaking rating of "2+," those in German a "3," and those in Russian a "1+" (p. 145).

In a more informal study undertaken by ETS in 1979, approximately thirty first- and second-year high school students in Spanish were tested using the oral interview. Liskin-Gasparro (1984) reports that "although the students varied considerably in their ability to communicate orally, none of them reached Level 1. Some of them were rated 0+ but most would have rated a 0 on the ILR scale" (p. 27). This study confirmed the need to expand the lower ranges of the ILR scale if they were to be adapted for academic use, especially at the high school level.

Magnan (1986) conducted a study at the University of Wisconsin in which she interviewed forty students of French, randomly selected from course lists in the first through fourth years of college study. The oral interviews were rated independently by two certified testers at ETS. Interrater reliability was .72 using Cohen's kappa, a conservative correlation statistic. Rater differences (9 out of 40 cases) were all within a major level (such as Intermediate) and no more than one step apart.

Magnan found that students' proficiency increased from first to second year, with first-year students ranging from Novice Mid to Intermediate Mid/High on the scale, and second-year students ranging from Intermediate Low to Advanced. An increase was also seen from second to third years, as the third-year students' ratings ranged from Intermediate Mid/High to Advanced/Advanced High. There was not much difference in scores for the fourth-year students, with French majors ranging from Intermediate Mid to Advanced High at the end of their college course of study. It is not surprising to see such a plateau occurring between the third and fourth year, since students in these courses were, for the most part, at the Advanced level of proficiency. Magnan explains that this level of oral proficiency represents a broad range of ability and that the scale may, therefore, not be sensitive to real differences between third- and fourth-year levels.

In discussing the overlapping levels observed in her investigation, Magnan points out a very important aspect of the relationship between oral proficiency level and level of study. "Students at the same level of oral proficiency may be enrolled in different levels of study, and students of the same level of study may be at different levels of oral proficiency" (Magnan 1986, p. 430). It is also likely that students who have attained a given level of oral proficiency may be at an entirely different level of proficiency in the other skill modalities. Magnan explains the lack of congruence between course level and attained oral proficiency in terms of the many sources of variation that exist in language classrooms: students differ in abilities, motivation, learning strategies, commitment, and amount of prior language study in high school; and materials, teachers, and methods vary considerably as well. Placement procedures may also be tapping different language skills, as many large institutions do not test oral proficiency because of practical problems in test administration.

In spite of these areas of overlap, Magnan's study does show that oral proficiency increased with time and that some students in college course sequences were able to attain the Intermediate level of proficiency after just one year, even if they had had no previous experience with French in high school (p. 432).

In reviewing other studies similar to her own, Magnan found her results to be consistent with what other researchers had learned. Hirsch (1985) had found that students ranged from Novice High to Advanced High in the first two years of language study at Cabrillo College in California; studies by Kaplan (1984) and Cramer and Terrio (1985) reported small numbers of students tested in the third and fourth year at their institutions to be in the same ranges as those in the Wisconsin study—from Intermediate High to Advanced High; Wing and Mayewski (1984) found second-year French students at the University of New Hampshire to be generally in the Intermediate Mid range, while third-year students typically scored at the Intermediate High level. They also reported similar results in Spanish, German, and Russian. However, Wing and Mayewski caution that the ratings in their study were given by beginning testers involved in a training project, and that experienced testers lowered the ratings fifty-three percent of the time (p. 23). This tendency of inexperienced testers to inflate ratings was corroborated in a study by Levine, Haus, and Cort (1987). They asked eight high school French and Spanish teachers with an average of 14.5 years of teaching experience but with no proficiency assessment training to read the ACTFL scale descriptions and then predict the rating of four students randomly selected from their classes. When two certified testers then rated thirty of these students, they found that the teachers had consistently overrated pupil performance. The researchers maintain that an oral proficiency familiarization workshop might help teachers become more accurate in their judgments. They cite research by Adams (1978), Shohamy (1983), and Liskin-Gasparro (1984) that provides evidence of the benefits of training. However, they caution that familiarization workshops cannot "put the teachers at the competency level of trained and certified testers" (p. 50).

The need for training in order to become an accurate interviewer and rater is pointed out by Liskin-Gasparro (1987), who says that "there seems to be no shortcut around intensive training workshops that expose the participants to numerous speech samples and engage them in extensive discussion of the relationship between those speech samples and the words of the level descriptions" (p. 25). Therefore, we must be cautious in interpreting studies of oral proficiency levels attained by students when it is not clear whether certified raters/testers were involved in the assessment procedure.

Some recent studies of OPI ratings among students in various languages continue to add to the research base about attainable levels of oral proficiency among classroom learners. Tschirner and Heilenman (1998) report that OPI ratings ranged from Novice High to Intermediate Mid (with a median of Intermediate Low) in their study of twenty students of German completing their fourth semester of college study. Tschirner (1996) had also rated the oral proficiency of forty college students of German at the end of each of four semesters (ten students per semester) in 1993. In that study, he found a median of Intermediate Low after one year and Intermediate Mid after two years. In a study of students of Russian conducted by Thompson (1996), results on the OPI indicated median scores of Novice Mid after one year, Novice High/Intermediate Low after two years, Intermediate Mid/High after three years, Intermediate High/Advanced after four years, and Advanced/Advanced High after five years of study. Thompson's study also looked at measures of proficiency in reading, listening, and writing skills. She found that, just as in oral skills, there was no exact correspondence of proficiency level with years of study, although there was an overall progression with each additional year of study. She concluded that ". . . the picture of proficiency that emerged from this study is one of overlapping ranges of performances with no exact correspondence between levels of study and levels of proficiency in speaking, reading, listening, and writing" (p. 47). She also found that "correlations among the four skills were not particularly strong, suggesting that they follow different paths of development which do not always parallel each other" (p. 47).

Tschirner and Heilenman (1998) provide a very useful review of twelve recent studies gauging average OPI levels of high school and college students. Only three of the studies they reviewed (Magnan 1986; Thompson 1996; and Tschirner 1996) followed the standards for OPI testing established by ACTFL. In their own study, Tschirner and Heilenman also followed the accepted ACTFL procedure, whereby certified testers must be used for administering and/or rating the test, and a second certified tester assigns a second "blind" rating, i.e., without knowing the results of the first rating. In the other studies they reviewed, only one certified tester or, in some cases, uncertified testers were used to obtain ratings. Also, sample sizes were sometimes quite small at some class levels. The authors conclude that such studies "provide only rough estimates of representative OPI scores in relationship to length of instruction" (p. 148). However, the various studies do seem to show some interesting differences between languages, especially between French and Russian, in the time required to reach a given level of proficiency. Thompson (1996) noted that Russian students, at least in their first two years of study, lagged behind French students (as reported in Magnan 1986) by about two steps on the ACTFL scale. However, the gap between language groups seemed to narrow with additional study "so that after 4 years, Russian students were only slightly behind their French counterparts" (p. 56). As Tschirner and Heilenman note, these results in American colleges and universities tend to support the language difficulty hierarchy based on data collected by the Foreign Service Institute (see Illustration 1.4 on page 26). The data also support the notion that as students progress from semester to semester, they tend to become more heterogeneous in their language proficiency (Magnan 1986; Thompson 1986; Tschirner and Heilenman

1998). Thompson (1996), for example, found that after five years of study, students of Russian scored anywhere from Intermediate Mid to Advanced High in oral proficiency.

Most studies of college students to date have demonstrated the difficulty of reaching the Superior level of proficiency in an undergraduate program of studies. However, a Canadian study of high school graduates who had significant exposure to French showed that some of those students were able to achieve a Superior level of proficiency (Hamm 1988). One needs to interpret these results with some caution, however, because only one interviewer was used in the study, and it is not specified whether this interviewer was a certified tester. The study compared two groups of Ontario high school graduates. The French core group had been exposed to a daily period of French of approximately one hour from Grade 1 through high school graduation and had taken a six-week French language course in Quebec in the summer after graduating. The immersion group had taken either an early, middle, or late immersion program followed by twelve or thirteen credits in French in the high school. This group also had traveled to Quebec or a francophone country or had worked in a francophone environment. Results indicated that the median proficiency level of the French core group (with approximately 1,500 hours of instruction) was Intermediate High/Advanced and that of the immersion group (with between 3,000 and 7,000 hours of exposure) was Advanced/Advanced Plus. One student in the French core group was rated Superior, whereas six students in the immersion group attained that rating.

Hamm reports, however, that the general level of accuracy of the French core students who had attained the Advanced level was quite good and more consistent than that of their immersion counterparts. She points out that although the results cannot be generalized since the interviewees in her study were self-selected and represented a relatively small sample, the study reveals the effects of different programs on proficiency. In this study, immersion students with 3,000 to 7,000 hours of exposure to French had an advantage in terms of general communicative skills and ease of expression. On the other hand, core French students seemed to be more accurate, even when they had had at least 1,500 fewer hours of instruction. Hamm's Canadian study shows the advantages of having long sequences of language study in terms of building proficiency. It also indicates that the amount of time to reach a given level of competence can vary considerably with different learners and with different learning conditions.

The issue of the time needed to attain significant levels of oral proficiency is one that is of special interest to teachers, administrators, program designers, and students alike. Over a series of several years, FSI collected information for its own programs in training diplomatic personnel in order to determine the interaction of student ability level and the amount of time needed to reach the upper levels of oral proficiency. Illustration 1.4 reveals the results of their study in various languages.

It is important to keep in mind that the data given in Illustration 1.4 were collected in a very special context, that of intensive language training of adults at the Foreign Service Institute. The amount of time to reach a given level of proficiency

Illustration 1.4
Expected Levels of
Speaking Proficiency
in Languages Taught
at the Foreign Service
Institute

GROUP I:　Afrikaans, Danish, Dutch, French, Haitian Creole, Italian, Norwegian, Portuguese, Romanian, Spanish, Swahili, Swedish

Length of Training	Aptitude for Language Learning		
	Minimum	Average	Superior
8 weeks (240 hours)	1	1/1+	1+
16 weeks (480 hours)	1+	2	2+
24 weeks (720 hours)	2	2+	3

GROUP II:　Bulgarian, Dari, Farsi, German, Greek, Hindi, Indonesian, Malay, Urdu

Length of Training	Aptitude for Language Learning		
	Minimum	Average	Superior
16 weeks (480 hours)	1	1/1+	1+/2
24 weeks (720 hours)	1+	2	2+/3
44 weeks (1320 hours)	2/2+	2+/3	3/3+

GROUP III:　Amharic, Bengali, Burmese, Czech, Finnish, Hebrew, Hungarian, Khmer, Lao, Nepali, Philipino, Polish, Russian, Serbo-Croatian, Sinhala, Thai, Tamil, Turkish, Vietnamese

Length of Training	Aptitude for Language Learning		
	Minimum	Average	Superior
16 weeks (480 hours)	0+	1	1/1+
24 weeks (720 hours)	1+	2	2/2+
44 weeks (1320 hours)	2	2+	3

GROUP IV:　Arabic, Chinese, Japanese, Korean

Length of Training	Aptitude for Language Learning		
	Minimum	Average	Superior
16 weeks (480 hours)	0+	1	1
24 weeks (720 hours)	1	1+	1+
44 weeks (1320 hours)	1+	2	2+
80–92 weeks (2400–2760 hours)	2+	3	3+

Source: Judith E. Liskin-Gasparro. *ETS Oral Proficiency Testing Manual.* Princeton, N.J.: Educational Testing Service, 1982. Reprinted by permission.

will undoubtedly vary among students in this type of context as it does in high school or college programs. What this chart does indicate, however, when considered in conjunction with the research reported earlier in this section, is that we must amend our expectations for student attainment of oral proficiency to conform more closely to the realities of language study in formal classroom contexts. If it typically takes 720 hours of instruction under the rather ideal conditions of intensive study at the Foreign Service Institute for an adult with high aptitude to become proficient at the Superior level in French or Spanish, it is difficult to expect students in a four-year high school program or a four-semester college sequence to reach that same level of competence after 200 or 300 hours. On the other hand, we can be very encouraged when we find that students in programs such as the one in Wisconsin reported earlier (Magnan 1986) are able to function at the Intermediate level of proficiency after one year. This represents the ability to use the language creatively to meet one's needs on a daily basis in the target culture and to have conversations in the language about topics of personal interest. The attainment of Advanced and Advanced High ratings by students who had taken three or four years of course work in the studies reviewed in this section is also very encouraging. However, further studies need to be done to see if such findings can be generalized and supported.

Issues in Language Proficiency Assessment: Caveats, Clarifications, and New Directions

As we emphasized earlier in this chapter, the *ACTFL Proficiency Guidelines* and the oral interview procedure represent one possible way to define and measure proficiency. As with any new development in the field, the guidelines have been received with enthusiasm by some members of the profession and viewed with skepticism by others. In recent years, there have been several scholars who have criticized the ILR and ACTFL Guidelines and have questioned the appropriateness of the Oral Proficiency Interview for capturing adequately the construct of communicative language proficiency. This section presents some of the issues that have been raised since the guidelines appeared. The review of literature is not meant to be comprehensive, but represents the broader questions that need to be addressed in future research as well as suggestions that might be incorporated in any further revisions of the guidelines.

Questions Regarding Oral Proficiency Assessment

One of the earlier articles dealing with problems in proficiency assessment was written by Lantolf and Frawley (1985), who questioned the logic and validity of the *ACTFL Proficiency Guidelines* on philosophical grounds, objecting to their analytic approach to testing and the use of the "native-speaker yardstick" (p. 339). They assert that the definitions of proficiency levels are circular and not based on empirical reality. They also question whether the criteria used in oral proficiency testing are the same as those used by native speakers engaged in communication with nonnatives, where conversational partners cooperate in the negotiation of meaning. The authors seem to object to criterion-referenced testing of any type: "At best, criterion-referenced tests measure the extent to which the person performs with reference to analytically derived levels and nothing more" (p. 340).

Lantolf and Frawley also object to the use of "the educated native speaker" as the reference point against which performance is judged. They maintain that "the native speaker is not a theoretically interesting construct, since the construct is neither unitary nor reliable" (p. 343). Although the *ACTFL Proficiency Guidelines* no longer use the standard of the "educated native speaker" in the level descriptions, there are still implications in some of the definitions that a prototypical native speaker group exists (Bachman and Savignon 1986). This seems like a valid point that should be considered in any further revisions of the guidelines.

Lantolf and Frawley do not propose, however, any clear alternative to the guidelines or the oral testing procedure that would resolve some of the problems they have identified. Rather they suggest that the profession "delay any decision to implement guidelines of any nature until research is able to develop a clear understanding of what it means to be a proficient speaker of a language" (p. 344).

Other scholars, such as Bachman and Savignon (1986) and Clark and Lett (1988) disagree with this point of view, recommending instead that a research agenda be designed to address the questions and problems associated with current testing procedures. Bachman and Savignon affirm the usefulness of the development of guidelines and "common metric" tests for a wide range of language abilities and consider the current guidelines a good starting point. However, they suggest that some further development is needed to capture the full context of language use represented in theoretical frameworks of communicative language proficiency. They assert that in examining definitions of communicative competence and proficiency, they "are struck more by similarities than by differences" (p. 381). Differences seem to relate not to the components of language proficiency identified, but rather to the relative importance accorded to them in the assessment procedures.

One of their objections to the current guidelines is that they include both context and content descriptions in the scale definitions. In their view, this confounds language ability descriptions with test method and can create problems with comparability of test results across different contexts and settings. They propose that the specifications of language abilities be divorced from elicitation procedures and conditions, enabling interviews to be geared to the needs and interests of the particular candidate. This suggestion might be explored further in subsequent revisions of the guidelines. However, it would be useful to conduct research studies to determine whether skilled testers currently vary interviews to correspond to the special needs and interests of candidates in the way that Bachman and Savignon suggest. Tester training emphasizes that the content and context samples given in the guidelines are not meant as checklists of discrete points to be included in every conversation, but rather serve as indicators of the kinds of topics and situations that might be used to elicit a speech sample. Liskin-Gasparro (1987) suggests that inter-interviewer reliability studies be conducted to investigate whether two or more experienced testers elicit comparable speech samples from the same group of speakers, a suggestion that is also made by Shohamy (1987).

Clark and Lett (1988) propose a detailed research plan for looking at issues relating to the reliability and validity of the oral interview and make specific suggestions about ways in which the current guidelines could be refined and improved. In contrast to Lantolf and Frawley's view, Clark and Lett consider the development of the ILR scale and testing procedure to be "the most significant and most highly consequential measurement initiative in the proficiency testing field to have occurred in the last three decades" (p. 72). However, they point out that no one test can provide us with more than a small sample of language and cannot represent the full range of language-use situations that one might expect to encounter. The current oral interview procedure, in their view, constitutes a "highly realistic sample of polite, reasonably formal conversation between relative strangers" (p. 56) but does not sample language nearly so well from other sociolinguistic contexts requiring differing styles or registers. They suggest that in order to get a more comprehensive view of a person's language proficiency, a variety of measures that would test language use in different contexts and situations is needed.

Shohamy (1987) reports on a number of research studies that show that different speech styles and functions are tapped with different kinds of oral interactions. She found that performance in an oral interview such as the OPI does not accurately predict performance on another kind of oral task, such as reporting, role-play, or discussion (Shohamy 1983; Shohamy, Reves, and Bejerano 1986). She argues that more than one kind of oral interaction is needed to test oral proficiency in a valid way and that multiple tasks should be designed to obtain a more representative sample of speech, preferably conducted by different testers.

In regard to the question raised by Lantolf and Frawley (1985) about whether the hierarchy of oral proficiency levels inherent in the guidelines has any basis in reality, some preliminary research reported by Dandonoli and Henning (1990) suggests that it does. Statistical analyses performed on oral interviews in both English and French indicate that the difficulty continua associated with the level descriptions were upheld, with few exceptions. Interrater reliabilities for the OPI among certified tester/raters ranged from .85 to .98 in ESL and from .89 to .97 in French. A second validity check involved comparing ratings given to speech samples by experienced raters with those given to the same samples by untrained native speakers who were told to rank order the samples using whatever criteria they chose. Ratings of samples in both English and French showed a very high correlation: for English, the correlations ranged from 0.904 to 1.000 with a mean of 0.934; for French, correlations ranged from 0.857 to 1.000 with a mean of 0.929 (p. 20). This high correspondence of ratings by trained testers and untrained native speakers constitutes strong evidence of the face validity of the oral proficiency guidelines for both English and French.

A number of recent studies that have looked into the interrater reliability of testers using the Oral Proficiency Interview include those by Thompson (1995) and Halleck (1996). Thompson reviews previous studies, such as those done by Magnan (1986,1987) in French and by Dandonoli and Henning (1990) in French and ESL and states that "[t]hese small-scale studies of the ACTFL version of the OPI demonstrate high interrater reliabilities that are comparable to those of ILR testers" (p. 409). Thompson adds that, because these studies used a small number of testers and interviews, a larger and more representative sample was needed to see if the interrater reliabilities obtained were upheld. Her analysis for the 1995 study was based on a sample of 795 interviews (from Intermediate Mid to Superior) obtained from Language Testing International (LTI). Most of these were telephone interviews in French, Spanish, English, Russian, and German; one third of the Russian interviews were done by phone and the rest were face-to-face interviews. All the interviews were conducted by ACTFL-certified testers, and each interview was also rated by a second "blind" rater. A third rater was used when there was disagreement of more than one step apart between the first and second rater. Thompson found that interrater reliabilities were highly significant (p<.0001) and very similar across languages. Pearson correlation statistics ranged from the lowest of .839 in ESL to the highest of .897 in Russian. Thompson remarks that these ratings are lower than those obtained by Magnan (1986) and Dandonoli and Henning (1990), but she points out that the 174 raters in this study were widespread geographically and diverse in their level of experience as testers. Furthermore, the samples did not include interviews at the very lowest proficiency levels (Novice Low through Intermediate Low). Another caveat that Thompson mentions is the fact that we do not know if interrater reliability results on telephone interviews would apply as well to face-to-face OPIs.

In spite of these limitations, Thompson's study adds to the research base about the reliability of the OPI. One important result of the study was that some levels of proficiency seemed to be more difficult to rate than others: Overall, reliability was greatest for the Superior level, followed by Intermediate Mid, Advanced, Intermediate High, and Advanced High. Halleck (1996) also found this to be the case in her study with 31 graduate students who were trained in the use of the OPI in a series of semester-long testing seminars she conducted. The students rated 150 interviews she had conducted in ESL. Her study looked at whether trainee ratings would be within an acceptable margin of error (only one sublevel difference, without crossing a major border) when compared with her own ratings as a trained and certified tester. As in the Thompson (1995) study, the interviews ranged from the Intermediate Mid to the Superior level, and the most reliable ratings were made for the Superior level (97.3% acceptable agreement) and for Intermediate Mid (96.7%). Levels of acceptable agreement were lower in this study for Advanced High (66.1%), Advanced (72.2%), and Intermediate High (69.4%). Halleck cautions that when interpreting the results of her study, one needs to bear in mind that these were uncertified and inexperienced raters. "That these raters had difficulty with what seemed to them to be atypical samples does not mean that certified, experienced raters would be similarly troubled" (p. 232). She recommends that more study is needed to answer this question. Thompson (1995) also recommends further study to see what reliabilities exist "below the Intermediate Mid level, where most academic testing takes place" (p. 415).

Questions Regarding Proficiency Assessment in Other Skills

Thus far in our discussion of language proficiency, we have concentrated on oral skills and their measurement, since the oral interview procedure developed by the ILR and adapted for academic contexts by ETS and ACTFL has been widely discussed, disseminated, and debated in the past decade among language professionals. Research and critical commentary relative to the guidelines have not been limited to the oral proficiency scales. Dandonoli and Henning (1990) investigated the construct validity of the 1986 version of the guidelines in all four skill areas, as well as the Oral Interview procedure itself. Their results provided "strong support for the use of the Guidelines as a foundation for the development of proficiency tests and for the reliability and validity of the Oral Proficiency Interview" (p. 11). Their investigation also uncovered areas where additional research must be done to refine the guidelines and test procedures, especially in listening comprehension. The most problematic finding of the study was the relatively low level of validity exhibited by the French listening test. The tests used were developed specifically for the validation study of the guidelines, mainly because the existing proficiency tests in listening and other skill areas had not been developed from the criteria underlying the guidelines and did not span the entire scale (p. 13). Both multiple-choice and open-ended test methods were devised for listening and reading. The low level of construct validity in the French listening test may have been due either to the guidelines themselves or to the tests that were designed for the project (p. 20). The authors stress the need for further research to replicate the study's goals and to identify more clearly possible modifications needed in the guidelines or the tests used to measure proficiency in the different skill areas.

Lee and Musumeci (1988) have questioned the validity of the reading proficiency definitions, especially with respect to the issue of text types and the implied developmental progression of reading skills. In terms of the latter issue, the authors have inferred from their reading of the guidelines and the associated literature a developmental progression that would limit the use of a given reading skill (such as skimming, scanning, or making inferences) to a particular proficiency level. This inference, however, is not warranted, as the guidelines do not suggest that learners at any given level of proficiency will use one and only one process as they approach a given reading text. (For a discussion of this point, see Phillips 1988. See also Dandonoli 1988; Galloway 1988; Omaggio Hadley 1988; and Edwards 1996 for various critical comments on the design of the reading model used in this study.)

The issue of the specifications of text types within the level descriptions that Lee and Musumeci (1988) discuss was also investigated in a study by Allen, Bernhardt, Berry, and Demel (1988) involving high school readers in French, Spanish, and German. In both of these studies, results showed that text type was not a significant predictor of reading difficulty. However, several scholars have questioned the use of the genre of a text as a sole criterion for gauging the proficiency level at which it can be read successfully (see, for example, Dandonoli 1988 and Edwards 1996).

One should not conclude, though, that the question of the role of text type is not controversial. The use of text typologies has been debated and discussed for a number of years in the language testing community (see, for example, Child 1987, 1988 and Phillips 1988). Both Child and Phillips point out that the ILR and ACTFL reading guidelines consider both text type and tasks and also take into account the background knowledge and strategy use that readers may bring to any given text as they attempt to comprehend it. They recognize, however, that the hierarchical ordering of texts by "type" is a complex problem. Edwards (1996) reports on a study she conducted with students of French exploring Child's (1987) "pragmatic approach to text difficulty" and concluded that "the Child text hierarchy may indeed provide a sound basis for the development of FL reading tests when it is applied by trained raters and when such tests include an adequate sample of passages at each level to be tested" (Edwards 1996, p. 350). She cautions that more research is needed to see if these results are replicated with texts in other languages and with other populations.

The studies reviewed in this section indicate that further exploration of the second-language reading process, as well the development of the other language skills, is needed in the years ahead. Such research should prove to be invaluable in informing the efforts of the profession in test development and design.

▧ The Notion of Language Proficiency: Some Further Clarifications

Whether one uses the *ACTFL Proficiency Guidelines* or some other framework for describing language ability, it is important to bear in mind that these descriptions are meant to be used to *describe* and *measure* competence in a language, not to prescribe methods, materials, or approaches to language teaching and learning. As Bachman and Savignon (1986) point out, the terms "proficiency" and "communicative competence" have both been stretched far beyond their original meanings in the professional literature of the past two decades. The term "communicative competence," for example, has been used in so many different ways that "it has become an accretion of meanings, a beneficent chameleon that takes on whatever characteristics the user believes to be 'good' and 'right' " (Bachman and Savignon 1986, p. 381). The same can be said for the term "proficiency," which has suffered much the same fate in recent years. Elsewhere, I have listed some common misconceptions about proficiency that have surfaced in professional discussions in the 1980s (Omaggio Hadley 1988, 1990). It might be helpful at this point to clarify further what "proficiency" is by focusing briefly on what it is *not*.

1. **Proficiency is not a theory of language acquisition**. As seen in the discussions earlier in this chapter, the *ACTFL Proficiency Guidelines* do not outline a theory of language acquisition, nor are they derived from a particular theoretical perspective. Some congruence can be seen between the global stages of development that are inherent in the guidelines for oral proficiency and the overall developmental progression suggested by research and theory, as summarized in Ellis (1985). In addition, there are some parallels between the components of language proficiency inherent in the guideline descriptions and the aspects of language that have been described in various theoretical frameworks of competence and/or performance. This is not to say that the implications about language development in the guidelines are wholly accurate or that the level descriptions are free from

problems. We have reviewed some of the criticisms of the 1986 descriptions and have identified problems that need to be resolved as our knowledge about language proficiency in all skill areas continues to develop. In the years ahead the guidelines and associated testing procedures will undoubtedly continue to be modified to correspond to new insights provided by theory and research.

2. **Proficiency is not a method of language teaching.** As we have seen throughout this chapter, proficiency is focused on *measurement*, not method. There are no methodological prescriptions in the guidelines. The descriptions of what learners can *do* in functional terms can have an effect, however, on what methods and procedures we choose to use in our classrooms to help students attain certain goals. Instruction that fosters the growth of proficiency for all learners will need to be flexible in order to accommodate learners' differing needs and preferences. Rather than being prescriptive or restrictive in nature, proficiency-oriented instruction must embrace and reconcile many different approaches and points of view about language learning and teaching. Second and foreign language instruction can derive some direction and focus from a better understanding of the concept of proficiency as an organizing principle (Higgs 1984). Within that general framework, the language learning experience can be enriched by an integration of multiple perspectives that respond to the differing needs and interests of both students and their teachers. More will be said about ways in which the concept of "proficiency" can affect teaching methodology in Chapter 3.

3. **Proficiency is not a curricular outline or syllabus.** Because the proficiency descriptions are evaluative in nature and because they identify in a global way some stages through which language learners typically pass, they may have some interesting implications for curricular design. However, the guidelines neither provide a curricular outline nor imply that a particular kind of syllabus or sequence of instruction should be followed. The guidelines do not describe incremental or discrete steps in performance but provide holistic and integrative descriptions. Just as many different methods may lead to the development of language proficiency, many different curricular sequences can be derived from an intelligent and careful examination of the guidelines. As Galloway states, "the roads to proficiency are as many and varied as are the descriptions of the destinations themselves" (Galloway 1987, p. 36).

4. **Proficiency does not imply a preoccupation with grammar or error.** This misconception arises when one confuses the concept of proficiency itself (a way to measure language competence and performance) with various methods and approaches that individuals have advocated for developing proficiency. Because the higher levels of proficiency are characterized by accuracy and precision in the use of language, many practitioners and researchers believe that some attention must be paid to the development of accuracy in formal language teaching programs (see, for example, Canale

and Swain 1980; Higgs and Clifford 1982; Long 1983; Lightbown 1985, 1990; Swain 1985; Ellis 1990; Stern 1990; Lyster and Ranta 1997; Doughty and Williams 1998a, 1998b). However, the precise role and value of grammatical instruction and various kinds of "focus on form" in achieving this goal is currently the subject of lively debate. More will be said about this issue in Chapter 3.

Defining the Content of Instruction:
Standards for Foreign Language Learning

The development of the *ACTFL Proficiency Guidelines* constituted an important early step in the effort of the language teaching profession to reach a consensus about how to define proficiency goals and standards for second language programs. As discussed earlier in this chapter, the *Guidelines* projects attempted to define global levels of language proficiency and thus to help us *measure* second language users' abilities in communicating in a foreign/second language without reference to the specific context in which the language had been learned or acquired. Thus the *Guidelines* are not tied to any particular type or sequence of classroom instruction, nor do they attempt to specify the content that classroom language instruction should offer.

Yet what should be the content of the foreign language curriculum in grades K–12? At the time the proficiency projects were first undertaken in the late 1970s, a clear consensus for answering this question did not yet exist. It was only in the 1980s that a reform movement began that had as its purpose the articulation of goals and expectations across a range of academic disciplines. Davis (1997), citing Gagnon (1995), traces the history of the standards movement back to the Reagan administration's assessment of American education, described in *A Nation at Risk* (National Commission on Excellence in Education, 1983). In that report, the Commission wrote that

> . . . while we can take justifiable pride in what our schools and colleges have historically accomplished and contributed to the United States and the well-being of its people, the educational foundations of our society are presently being eroded by a rising tide of mediocrity that threatens our very future as a Nation and a people (p. 5).

Among the recommendations in the report was that state and local high school graduation requirements include, at a minimum, "the Five New Basics" of English (4 years), mathematics (3 years), science (3 years), social studies (3 years), and computer science (one-half year). In addition, the Commission made an important statement about foreign language study, a subject recommended for college-bound students:

Achieving proficiency in a foreign language *ordinarily requires from 4 to 6 years of study and should, therefore, be started in the elementary grades. We believe it is desirable that students achieve such proficiency because study of a foreign language introduces students to non-English-Speaking cultures, heightens awareness and comprehension of one's native tongue, and serves the Nation's needs in commerce, diplomacy, defense, and education (A Nation at Risk, 1983, pp. 25–26).*

Six years after the publication of the Commission's report, the Bush administration's America 2000 project was launched at the 1989 Educational Summit of the nation's governors in Charlottesville, Virginia. The Clinton administration renamed the project "Goals 2000" in 1994. Davis (1997) points out that foreign languages did not play a role in the America 2000 strategy for reforming education, as only five areas of the curriculum (English, math, science, history, and geography) were initially designated for national standards development. However, due to the collaborative work of ACTFL and several professional language associations (The American Association of Teachers of French, The American Association of Teachers of German, and The American Association of Teachers of Spanish and Portuguese), the process was begun in the fall of 1992 to set standards for foreign languages and make them part of the "core curriculum" (Lafayette and Draper 1996; Davis 1997). Federal funding for the project was received in early 1993, and "foreign language education became the seventh and final subject area . . . to develop national standards for students in kindergarten through twelfth grade" (*Standards for Foreign Language Learning* 1996, pp. 12–13).

The Standards Project, led by June Phillips as project director and Christine Brown as task force chair, involved a great number of individuals and organizations who worked to achieve consensus as they forged the document that would eventually be released to the public at the ACTFL Annual Meeting in Anaheim, California on November 18, 1995. The project team included a Board of Directors (representing the four collaborating organizations and two at-large members), an Advisory Council (with leaders of business and industry, government, education, and community organizations), a Board of Reviewers, and an eleven-member Task Force who, together with project staff and consultants, created the *Standards* document. The project was endorsed by 46 state, regional, and national language organizations and had input from "thousands of individuals who intensively examined the drafts of the standards and conscientiously communicated their reactions" (*Standards* . . . , 1996, p. 5). (For a more detailed history of the reform movement and the associated standards projects, see Jennings 1996; Phillips and Lafayette 1996; Lafayette and Draper 1996; and Davis 1997).

Like the standards-based projects in the other disciplines, *Standards for Foreign Language Learning* attempt to outline the *content* of instruction, with specific reference to grades four, eight, and twelve. As Phillips (1999) explains:

Content standards, upon which performance standards are assessed, lie at the heart of education reforms undertaken during these transitional years to the next century. The design of content standards for our discipline required that the profession articulate its best judgment of what students should know and be able to do *as a result of their study of world languages (pp. 1–2).*

The content standards for foreign language education are depicted in Illustration 1.5. They are arranged into five major goal areas (*Communication, Cultures, Connections, Comparisons,* and *Communities*), each with specific content standards subsumed under them. The 1996 *Standards* document also includes "*sample progress indicators*" for 4th, 8th, and 12th grades, as well as a set of sample "*learning scenarios,*" most of which were provided by teachers piloting the standards for a nine-month period (pp. 23–24). An expanded version of the *Standards* document (*Standards for Foreign Language Learning in the 21st Century*, 1999) includes the original standards plus a set of language-specific versions created by professional associations in 9 languages, most of which extend the descriptions to include the postsecondary level (i.e., K–16).

Before discussing in detail how the *Standards* can be used, the authors of the document are careful to point out what the *Standards* are *not:*

1. They "do not describe the current state of foreign language education in this country"; rather "they provide a gauge against which to measure improvement in foreign language education in the years to come" (p. 24).
2. They are not meant to be prescriptive, nor are they meant to serve as a curriculum guide:

   While this document suggests the types of content and curricular experience needed to enable students to achieve the standards, and supports the ideal of extended sequences of study, it does not describe specific course content, nor a recommended scope and sequence (Standards . . . 1996, p. 24).

3. They are not designed to be used alone, but in conjunction with state and local standards documents "to determine the best approaches and reasonable expectations for students in individual districts and schools" (*Standards . . . ,* 1996, p. 24).

Jennings (1996) emphasizes the voluntary and collaborative aspects of the various standards-based movements across the disciplines, describing them as "experiments searching for ways for the country to agree on what needs to be done and then using those agreements to encourage, not coerce, state and local actions" (p. 19). For the framers of the *Standards for Foreign Language Learning,* this emphasis on collaboration and local freedom and responsibility in designing curricula is extremely important. Thus the interrelationship among national, state, district, and local levels is envisioned as a dynamic one, with each contributing to the goal-setting process.

Phillips (1997) further states that "[t]he standards framework does not prescribe an instructional approach or methodology. Instead, it reflects more broadly conceived purposes and objectives for language study for all the nation's students" (p. xii). This resistance to prescribing particular teaching approaches is a

Illustration 1.5
Standards for
Foreign Language
Learning (1996)

Standards for Foreign Language Learning

COMMUNICATION

Communicate in Languages Other Than English

Standard 1.1: Students engage in conversations, provide and obtain information, express feelings and emotions, and exchange opinions.

Standard 1.2: Students understand and interpret written and spoken language on a variety of topics.

Standard 1.3: Students present information, concepts, and ideas to an audience of listeners or readers on a variety of topics.

CULTURES

Gain Knowledge and Understanding of Other Cultures

Standard 2.1: Students demonstrate an understanding of the relationship between the practices and perspectives of the culture studied.

Standard 2.2: Students demonstrate an understanding of the relationship between the products and perspectives of the cultures studied.

CONNECTIONS

Connect with Other Disciplines and Acquire Information

Standard 3.1: Students reinforce and further their knowledge of other disciplines through the foreign language.

Standard 3.2: Students acquire information and recognize the distinctive viewpoints that are only available through the foreign language and its cultures.

COMPARISONS

Developing Insight into the Nature of Language and Culture

Standard 4.1: Students demonstrate understanding of the nature of language through comparisons of the language studied and their own.

Standard 4.2: Students demonstrate understanding of the concept of culture through comparisons of the cultures studied and their own.

COMMUNITIES

Participate in Multilingual Communities at Home and Around the World

Standard 5.1: Students use the language both within and beyond the school setting.

Standard 5.2: Students show evidence of becoming life-long learners by using the language for personal enjoyment and enrichment.

Source: *Standards for Foreign Language Learning,* National Standards in Foreign Language Education Project (1996), p. 9. Reprinted by permission.

crucial point that has also been made in discussions surrounding language proficiency. Learners who differ in such factors as age, level of proficiency, learning preferences, reason for language study, and the like may find different approaches appropriate for their own situation and circumstances. What is effective with students in kindergarten and the early grades may not be equally so with students in college classrooms; approaches that seem most successful with beginning language students are not necessarily the ones that will work best in more advanced classes. Thus it seems that the goals outlined in the standards can be reached in a variety of ways, just as the "routes to proficiency" are many and varied.

The Five Cs: Integrated Goals for Foreign Language Learning

The *Standards for Foreign Language Learning* present a set of interconnected goals that emphasize using language for communication with other peoples, gaining understanding of other cultures, and accessing information in a wide range of disciplines. This vision of language study goes well beyond what has traditionally been the main focus of foreign language learning in the past: mastering the "code" or linguistic system. Although the advent of communicative and proficiency-based language teaching in the past few decades has helped us expand our curricular goals significantly to incorporate a greater emphasis on meaningful communication and cultural understanding, the current reality in language classrooms still falls far short of the vision represented in the standards document (*Standards . . .* , 1996, p. 24). One reason for this is certainly related to the small amount of time generally afforded for language study in most of our schools and postsecondary institutions. The vision of the *Standards* is based in part on the hope that longer sequences of language study, beginning in the elementary schools and extending through the college level, will become commonplace in the twenty-first century. Unfortunately, there are no guarantees that this will happen in American schools. This does not mean, however, that the descriptions of interrelated goals of foreign language study in the *Standards* cannot serve as a resource for improving language education as it exists now and for shaping our thinking as we design curricula and materials for the future.

As we look at the first of the five goal areas in Illustration 1.5, it is clear that the development of language competence or proficiency remains central to the mission of foreign language education in the schools. As we saw in the earlier parts of this chapter, there are a number of ways of organizing our thinking about the components of language competence. A skills-based perspective (focusing on listening, speaking, reading, and writing) can be useful when working on the subcomponents of language competence or in testing specific abilities; a modality-based perspective, such as we see in the *Standards,* reminds us of the ultimate use to which we will be putting the language skills we are learning. Both perspectives can be helpful in language teaching and will be useful for different purposes. As Phillips and Draper (1999) explain, the "four skills" of listening, speaking, reading, and writing "remain visible within the Framework of Communicative Modes, but they are viewed differently—not as separate skills, but within the context of communication" (p. 17). For example, "speaking" can be thought of as "interpersonal" in conversation, where "two-way communication and nego-tiation are occurring" (p. 17), but "presentational" when the speaker is addressing an audience. This latter use of the skill will entail a different style or register and may require a different set of abilities. The same is true when one considers writ-ten communication that is informal and interactive, as in e-mail correspondence, versus the type of writing involved in preparing a report or creating a piece of fic-tion. In the same way, the skills of listening and reading are implicit in the de-scription of the "interpretive" mode (Standard 1.2), but "interpretation" also implies that one can understand the cultural allusions, nuances, and other infor-mation that may be contained "between the lines" (*Standards . . .* , 1996, p. 33). A culturally authentic interpretation of texts, however, will not be easily achievable at early levels of language learning. As the authors of the *Standards* explain, the "interpretative" mode, which does not involve two-way negotiation of meaning, "requires a much more profound knowledge of culture from the outset. The more one knows about the other language and culture, the greater the chances of creat-ing the appropriate cultural interpretation of a written or spoken text" (p. 33). They add that "cultural literacy and the ability to read or listen between the lines are developed over time and through exposure to the language and culture" (p. 33).

The content standards for Culture (Standards 2.1 and 2.2) and Comparisons (Standards 4.1 and 4.2) emphasize the need for students to develop an awareness of the cultural framework or "perspectives" of the culture whose language they are studying. It is thus not enough to learn about "practices" and "products" in isolation of their cultural framework; rather, students need to begin to discover how they are viewed and understood from the point of view of the people who de-veloped them. Likewise, students need to develop a more general awareness of how languages and cultures work and how languages reflect the perspectives and cultural framework of the people who use them—perspectives that may be differ-ent from their own. A discussion of these standards and of the teaching of culture in general can be found in Chapter 8, as well as in various other sources (see, for example, Lafayette 1996; Phillips 1997; Phillips and Terry 1999; and Phillips and Draper 1999).

The standards associated with Connections (3.1 and 3.2) emphasize that there are "additional bodies of knowledge that are unavailable to monolingual English speakers" (*Standards . . .* , 1996, p. 27) and that the students' developing language skills can be used to access this knowledge. It has long been emphasized, for ex-ample, that access to the literature of another culture, though possible in transla-tion, is most complete and satisfying if done in the language of origin. Access to a whole range of authentic texts, both oral and written, is possible to those who have mastered the language in which they are written and have an understanding of the cultural implications within them. The "connections" standards articulate this type of access as an important part of the goals underlying the foreign lan-guage curriculum.

The Communities standards (5.1 and 5.2) likewise emphasize the use of the language beyond the traditional boundaries of the foreign language classroom to communicate with others in multilingual communities "in a variety of contexts and in culturally appropriate ways" (p. 27). Participation in multilingual communities is becoming easier as people travel more widely and have access to one another through new technologies, such as in Web-based communication. Yet the definition of "community" should be understood very broadly, according to Phillips and Draper (1999): "Participation in the community is not limited to students physically interacting with native speakers of the language. A community can be a community of learners of different ages or in different locations. The idea here is that the classroom provides the means so that students can interact beyond their classroom walls" (p. 68). Standard 5.2 helps us focus on ways to continue using the foreign language even when formal study has been completed. "The intent of the 'lifelong learning' standard is that students from the beginning develop the tools, the habits of mind, and the motivations that allow them to independently pursue activities using language throughout their lifetime" (Phillips and Draper 1999, p. 68).

As mentioned at the beginning of this section, the *Standards for Foreign Language Learning* outline descriptions of the *content* envisioned for study in foreign language classrooms. They do not provide ways to assess "how well" students are mastering that content. Development of assessment instruments is, therefore, one of the next steps that will need to be taken in continuing the work initiated by this project.

The authors of the *Standards* acknowledge the role that the proficiency projects have played in the development of the document. The guidelines projects have given the language teaching profession a "common metric" that is performance based; they can thus serve as a point of departure for developing new kinds of performance assessments reflecting the eleven content standards, particularly those in the area of communication. *The ACTFL Oral Proficiency Interview Tester Training Manual* elucidates further the potential relationship of the OPI to the *Standards:*

> *The interactive nature of the OPI, that is to say the use of active negotiation of meaning between the interviewer and interviewee to elicit a ratable speech sample, makes the OPI an effective, valid, and reliable means to assess Standard 1.1 as described in the Standards (Swender 1999, p. 6).*

In terms of establishing "performance standards" for each of the content standards, the authors of the standards document state that "[i]ndividual states and school districts hold the responsibility for determining performance standards for their students" (*Standards . . .* , 1996, p. 13). Although the guidelines and the associated literature surrounding them have had strong effects on instruction at all levels of schooling, their use for measuring performance seems most appropriate with adult language users. As Swender and Duncan (1998, 1999) observe, the ACTFL proficiency guidelines "assume a certain level of cognitive development with which the language user can perform language tasks and functions . . . " (1999, p. 1). They add that if language proficiency is to be assessed eventually for students at all levels of schooling, these guidelines would not be appropriate for younger learners. In response to the need for a model for measuring performance at younger ages, ACTFL has recently developed performance guidelines that are meant "to help foreign language educators better understand the developmental path that second language learning takes when it occurs within a school setting" (Swender and Duncan 1998, p. 480). These new performance guidelines are also designed to be used in conjunction with the *Standards,* as they are organized using the three modes of communication (Interpersonal, Interpretive, and Presentational) described in the standards document. Thus this new project may be helpful to states and school districts as they begin to develop and/or select ways to assess performance in all the goal areas. Chapter 9 will provide some discussion of classroom testing and "alternative assessments" (Liskin-Gasparro 1996) that will address these important issues.

The goals of language study, as outlined in the *Standards,* represent a challenging view of our mission as language teachers in the years ahead. Whether this conceptualization of language study will actually bring about changes in local schools is an open question; success in this endeavor will be dependent on a whole host of factors, from the availability of resources and funding to the attitudes of teachers and administrators as they respond to the proposed reforms and participate in the process of educational change. The reaction of the profession to the *Standards* and the impact of the document on language education are still largely unknown at this writing, as the *Standards* are still in the process of being more widely circulated and have been piloted at only a few sites thus far. (For some initial reactions from educators at both the K-12 and university levels, see Bartz and Singer 1996; Glisan 1996; Lange and Wieczorek 1997; James 1998; and Wells 1998.) Whatever their eventual impact on language teaching may be, the *Standards* document and the associated professional activity surrounding its development and dissemination reflect very positively on the foreign language teaching profession at the beginning of the new millennium. The degree of collaboration that has gone into this new intitiative and the level of involvement and energy are remarkable and unprecedented. This commitment to excellence should encourage us, even as it challenges us.

Summary: On Knowing a Language

In this chapter various definitions and theories of what it means to "know" a language have been examined. We have explored the concepts of competence and performance, studied various definitions of communicative competence, and traced the development of the notion of proficiency, especially as it is described in the *ACTFL Proficiency Guidelines*. The way in which various components of language ability can be integrated in a variety of different frameworks for describing and defining language proficiency has been illustrated. Some common misconceptions surrounding the use of the term "proficiency" have been discussed, most of which have arisen out of an improper extension of the term beyond its intended use for measurement and assessment. Although one can draw implications from the proficiency guidelines for making instructional decisions, "proficiency" is neither a method nor a specific blueprint for designing a curriculum.

The last part of the chapter describes the reform movement leading to the development of the *Standards for Foreign Language Learning* and describes the five integrated goals of *communication, cultures, connections, comparisons,* and *communities.* Thus it represents another type of framework for looking at the question of "what it means to know a language." All of the frameworks that have been reviewed in this chapter are valuable resources that can inform us: Each one gives us a particular perspective, new insights, and guidance as we seek effective ways to teach language in context.

In the next chapter, a number of theories about how adults become proficient in a second language will be considered. As we explore various perspectives on the language learning process, we can begin to trace the source of many teaching practices that have been advanced across the years. An understanding of language acquisition theory can thus inform the choices we make among these options and provide important insights into our own current beliefs and practices.

Activities for Review and Discussion

1. Write a brief paragraph describing what it means, in your opinion, to "know a language."

2. What components of language ability are common to the definitions of communicative competence, communicative language ability, and proficiency described in this chapter? Describe each of these components briefly.

3. Various theoretical frameworks of language ability include discussions of "grammatical competence." What does this term mean to you?

4. Give a brief description of the global levels of oral proficiency, as defined in the *ACTFL Proficiency Guidelines.* Then decide what level of oral proficiency you would assign to each of the following learner profiles:

   a. Sarah B. knows enough Spanish to speak simply, with some circumlocution, in casual conversations about concrete topics, such as her own background, her family, her interests at school, her travels, and various current events. She can express facts, give instructions, describe, and narrate in past, present, and future time. She handles elementary constructions with accuracy most of the time but still makes patterned errors, especially when trying to express an opinion or support her point of view.

   b. Sam R. has no practical speaking ability in Russian, although he does know a few isolated words and expressions. He can name the days of the week and the months of the year, name a few basic objects and colors, and use a few memorized expressions, such as "Hello," "How are you?"

and "Goodbye." However, he really can't use what he knows, even in a very simple conversation. Native speakers have a very difficult time understanding him because of his heavy American accent.

Advanced
(?)

c. Bill R. can converse in both formal and informal situations, resolve problems, deal with unfamiliar topics, describe in detail, and offer supported opinion in his second language, French. He is quite adept at talking about his special field of competence—political science—and is generally able to handle any topic of discussion he can handle in English. He has a slight accent and occasionally makes errors, but they never interfere with communication or disturb native speakers.

d. Gail P. knows enough German to cope with routine, daily situations in a German-speaking environment. She can create with the language, ask and answer questions, and participate in conversations dealing with everyday topics. Most native speakers understand what she is saying, though she is sometimes not comprehensible to people who aren't used to dealing with foreigners because she makes frequent errors in pronunciation and grammar. She can handle requests for services, like renting a room or ordering a meal, although she sometimes has to search for the appropriate words, which makes her speech a little hesitant.

e. Mary Anne T. speaks Chinese well enough to participate fully in casual conversations, especially when the discussion relates to topics such as her family, her work as a missionary, her travel experiences, and current events. She does have some difficulty expressing her point of view in Chinese, and her language tends to break down when the discussion gets too complex. Sometimes she miscommunicates, but most native speakers, including those who have never dealt with Americans, can understand her meaning. In her work in the mission field, which includes social ministry, Mary Anne is good at giving instructions, explaining and describing various health-related procedures, and talking with people about her past travels and her aspirations for the future.

5. Galloway (1987) has stated that the *ACTFL Proficiency Guidelines* are neither a curricular model nor a methodological prescription, but that one might be able to look for *implications* in the descriptions for making instructional decisions. What implications for instruction do you see in the guidelines? What kinds of goals might you set for students at the Novice level in any of the skill modalities (speaking, listening, reading, writing)? How might your goal statements differ for students at the Intermediate level? the Advanced level?

6. What is your reaction to the content specifications given in the *Standards for Foreign Language Learning?* Are there any other goals that you think should be added to the five Cs? Are there goals that you think should not be included? Are there goals that should take priority over others, or do you think all of the five areas should receive equal emphasis and attention? Explain your point of view.

References: Chapter 1

ACTFL Proficiency Guidelines. Hastings-on-Hudson, NY: American Council on the Teaching of Foreign Languages, 1986.

ACTFL Proficiency Guidelines—Speaking. Yonkers, NY: American Council on the Teaching of Foreign Languages, 1999.

ACTFL *Provisional Proficiency Guidelines.* Hastings-on-Hudson, NY: American Council on the Teaching of Foreign Languages, 1982.

Adams, Marianne L. "Measuring Foreign Language Speaking Proficiency: A Study of Agreement Among Raters." In John L. D. Clark, ed., *Direct Testing of Speaking Proficiency: Theory and Application.* Princeton, NJ: Educational Testing Service, 1978.

Allen, Edward D., Elizabeth B. Bernhardt, Mary Therese Berry, and Marjorie Demel. "Comprehension and Text Genre: An Analysis of Secondary School Foreign Language Readers." *The Modern Language Journal*, 72, ii (1988): 163–72.

Bachman, Lyle F. *Fundamental Considerations in Language Testing.* Oxford: Oxford University Press, 1990.

Bachman, Lyle F. and John L. D. Clark. "The Measurement of Foreign/Second Language Proficiency." *Annals of the American Academy of Political and Social Science* 490 (1987): 20–33.

Bachman, Lyle F. and Sandra J. Savignon. "The Evaluation of Communicative Language Proficiency: A Critique of the ACTFL Oral Interview." *The Modern Language Journal* 70, iv (1986): 380–90.

Bartz, Walter H. and Margaret Keefe Singer. "The Programmatic Implications of Foreign Language Standards." Pp. 139–67 in R. C. Lafayette, ed., *National Standards: A Catalyst for Reform.* The ACTFL Foreign Language Education Series. Lincolnwood, IL: National Textbook Company, 1996.

Brod, Richard I., ed. *Language Study for the 1980s: Reports of the MLA-ACLS Language Task Forces.* New York: Modern Language Association, 1980.

Brown, Gillian and George Yule. *Discourse Analysis.* Cambridge: Cambridge University Press, 1983.

Brown, H. D. *Principles of Language Learning and Teaching.* Englewood Cliffs, NJ: Prentice Hall, 1980. 2nd edition 1987. 3rd edition 1994.

Buck, Kathryn, Heidi Byrnes, and Irene Thompson, eds. *The ACTFL Oral Proficiency Interview Tester Training Manual.* Yonkers, NY: ACTFL, 1989.

Burn, Barbara. "The President's Commission on Foreign Language and International Studies: Its Origin and Work." *The Modern Language Journal* 64 (1980): 7–8.

Byrnes, Heidi and Michael Canale, eds. *Defining and Developing Proficiency: Guidelines, Implementations and Concepts.* The ACTFL Foreign Language Education Series. Lincolnwood, IL: National Textbook Company, 1987.

Campbell, R. and R. Wales. "The Study of Language Acquisition." In J. Lyons, ed., *New Horizons in Linguistics.* Harmondsworth, England: Penguin Books, 1970.

Canale, Michael. "From Communicative Competence to Communicative Language Pedagogy." In J. Richards and R. Schmidt, eds., *Language and Communication.* London: Longman, 1983a.

———. "On Some Dimensions of Language Proficiency." In J. W. Oller, Jr., ed., *Issues in Language Testing Research.* Rowley, MA: Newbury House, 1983b.

Canale, Michael and Merrill Swain. "Theoretical Bases of Communicative Approaches to Second Language Teaching and Testing." *Applied Linguistics* 1 (1980a): 1–47.

———. Introduction to the *Ontario Assessment Instrument Pool/French as a Second Language: Junior and Intermediate Divisions (Grades 6 and 9).* Toronto, Ontario: Ontario Ministry of Education, 1980b.

Carroll, John B. "Foreign Language Proficiency Levels Attained by Language Majors Near Graduation from College." *Foreign Language Annals* 1 (1967): 131–51.

Charolles, M. "Introduction aux problèmes de la cohérence des textes." *Langue française* 38 (1978): 7–41.

Child, James R. "Language Proficiency Levels and the Typology of Texts." Chapter 4 (pp. 97–106) in H. Byrnes and M. Canale, eds., *Defining and Developing Proficiency: Guidelines, Implementations and Concepts.* The ACTFL Foreign Language Education Series. Lincolnwood, IL: National Textbook Company, 1987.

———. "Reading Proficiency Assessment: Section 1: A Framework for Discussion." Pp. 125–35 in P. Lowe, Jr. and C. Stansfield, eds., *Second Language Proficiency Assessment: Current Issues. CAL/ERIC Language in Education: Theory and Practice 70.* Englewood Cliffs, NJ: Prentice Hall, 1988.

Chomsky, Noam. "A Review of B. F. Skinner's *Verbal Behavior.*" *Language* 35 (1959): 26–58.

———. *Aspects of the Theory of Syntax.* Cambridge, MA: M.I.T. Press, 1965.

Clark, John L. D. *Foreign Language Testing: Theory and Practice.* Philadelphia: Center for Curriculum Development, 1972.

Clark, John L. D. and John Lett. "A Research Agenda." Chapter 2 in P. Lowe, Jr. and C. W. Stansfield, eds., *Second Language Proficiency Assessment: Current Issues. CAL/ERIC Language in Education: Theory and Practice 70.* Englewood Cliffs, NJ: Prentice Hall, 1988.

Cramer, Hazel and Susan Terrio. "Moving from Vocabulary Acquisition to Functional Proficiency: Techniques and Strategies." *French Review* 59 (1985): 198–209.

Dandonoli, Patricia. "MLJ Readers' Forum." *The Modern Language Journal* 72 (1988): 450.

Dandonoli, Patricia and Grant Henning. "An Investigation of the Construct Validity of the ACTFL Proficiency Guidelines and Oral Interview Procedure." *Foreign Language Annals* 23, i (1990): 11–22.

Davis, James N. "Educational Reform and the Babel (Babble) of Culture: Prospects for the *Standards for Foreign Language Learning.*" *Modern Language Journal* 81, ii (1997): 151–63.

Doughty, Catherine and Jessica Williams, eds. *Focus on Form in Classroom Second Language Acquisition.* Cambridge: Cambridge University Press, 1998a.

———. "Pedagogical Choices in Focus on Form." Chapter 10 (pp. 197–261) in C. Doughty and J. Williams, eds., *Focus on Form in Classroom Second Language Acquisition.* Cambridge: Cambridge University Press, 1998b.

Edwards, Alison L. "Reading Proficiency Assessment and the ILR/ACTFL Text

Typology: A Reevaluation." *Modern Language Journal* 80, iii (1996): 350–61.

Ellis, Rod. *Understanding Second Language Acquisition.* Oxford: Oxford University Press, 1985.

———. *Instructed Second Language Acquisition.* Oxford: Basil Blackwell, 1990.

Galloway, Vicki. "From Defining to Developing Proficiency: A Look at the Decisions." Chapter 2 (pp. 25–73) in H. Byrnes and M. Canale, eds., *Defining and Developing Proficiency: Guidelines, Implementations and Concepts.* ACTFL Foreign Language Education Series. Lincolnwood, IL: National Textbook Company, 1987.

———. "MLJ Readers' Forum." *The Modern Language Journal* 72 (1988): 450–52.

Gass, Susan M. and Carolyn G. Madden, eds. *Input in Second Language Acquisition.* Cambridge, MA: Newbury House, 1985.

Glisan, Eileen. "A Collaborative Approach to Professional Development." Pp. 57–95 in R. C. Lafayette, ed., *National Standards: A Catalyst for Reform.* The ACTFL Foreign Language Education Series. Lincolnwood, IL: National Textbook Company, 1996.

Halleck, Gene B. "Interrater Reliability of the OPI: Using Academic Trainee Raters." *Foreign Language Annals* 29, ii (1996): 223–38.

Hamm, Christiane. "The ACTFL Oral Proficiency Interview in a Canadian Context: The French Speaking Proficiency of Two Groups of Ontario High-School Graduates." *Foreign Language Annals* 21, vi (1988): 561–67.

Harley, Birgit, Patrick Allen, Jim Cummins, and Merrill Swain, eds. *The Development of Second Language Proficiency.* Cambridge: Cambridge University Press, 1990.

Hatch, Evelyn. "Second Language Learning—Universals." *Working Papers in Bilingualism* 3 (1974): 1–17.

———. "Discourse Analysis and Second Language Acquisition." In E. Hatch, ed., *Second Language Acquisition: A Book of Readings.* Rowley, MA: Newbury House, 1978.

———. *Psycholinguistics: A Second Language Perspective.* Rowley, MA: Newbury House, 1983.

———. "Theoretical Review of Discourse and Interlanguage." In A. Davies, C. Criper, and A. Howatt, eds., *Interlanguage.* Edinburgh: Edinburgh University Press, 1984.

———. *Discourse and Language Education.* Cambridge: Cambridge University Press, 1992.

Higgs, Theodore V. "Language Teaching and the Quest for the Holy Grail." In T.V. Higgs, ed., *Teaching for Proficiency: The Organizing Principle.* The ACTFL Foreign Language Education Series, Vol. 15. Lincolnwood, IL: National Textbook Company, 1984.

———. "Proficiency Assessment and the Humanities." *ADFL Bulletin* 18, i (1986): 6–8.

Higgs, Theodore V. and Ray Clifford. "The Push toward Communication." Chapter 1 in T. V. Higgs, ed., *Curriculum, Competence, and the Foreign Language Teacher.* The ACTFL Foreign Language Education Series, vol. 13. Lincolnwood, IL: National Textbook Company, 1982.

Hirsch, Bette. "A Proficiency-Based French Conversation Course." *French Review* 59 (1985): 210–18.

Hymes, Dell. "On Communicative Competence." In J. B. Pride and J. Holmes, eds., *Sociolinguistics*. Harmondsworth, England: Penguin Books, 1972.

James, Dorothy. "The Impact on Higher Education of Standards for Foreign Language Learning: Preparing for the 21st Century." *ACTFL Newsletter,* XI, i (Fall 1998): 11–14.

Jennings, John F. "Using Standards to Improve Education: A Way to Bring About Truth in Teaching and Learning." Pp. 9–21 in R. C. Lafayette, ed., *National Standards: A Catalyst for Reform.* The ACTFL Foreign Language Education Series. Lincolnwood, IL: National Textbook Company, 1996.

Kaplan, Isabelle. "Oral Proficiency Testing and the Language Proficiency Curriculum: Two Experiments in Curricular Design for Conversation Courses." *Foreign Language Annals* 17 (1984): 491–98.

Lafayette, Robert C., ed. *National Standards*: *A Catalyst for Reform.* The ACTFL Foreign Language Education Series. Lincolnwood, IL: National Textbook Company, 1996.

Lafayette, Robert C. and Jamie B. Draper. "Introduction: National Standards: A Catalyst for Reform." Pp. 1–8 in R. C. Lafayette, ed., *National Standards: A Catalyst for Reform.* The ACTFL Foreign Language Education Series. Lincolnwood, IL: National Textbook Company, 1996.

Lange, Dale and Joseph Wieczorek. "Reflections on the Collaborative Projects: Two Perspectives, Two Professionals." Pp. 243–72 in J. K. Phillips, ed., *Collaborations: Meeting New Goals, New Realities.* Northeast Conference on the Teaching of Foreign Languages. Lincolnwood, IL: National Textbook Company, 1997.

Lantolf, James P. and William Frawley. "Oral Proficiency Testing: A Critical Analysis." *The Modern Language Journal* 69 (1985): 337–45.

Larsen-Freeman, Diane and Michael H. Long. *An Introduction to Second Language Acquisition Research.* White Plains, NY: Longman, 1991.

Lee, James F. and Diane Musumeci. "On Hierarchies of Reading Skills and Text Types." *The Modern Language Journal* 72 (1988): 173–87.

Levine, Martin G., George J. Haus, and Donna Cort. "The Accuracy of Teacher Judgment of the Oral Proficiency of High School Foreign Language Students." *Foreign Language Annals* 20, i (1987): 45–50.

Lightbown, Patsy M. "Can Language Acquisition be Altered by Instruction?" In K. Hyltenstam and M. Pienemann, eds. *Modelling and Assessing Second Language Acquisition.* Clevedon, Avon: Multilingual Matters, 1985.

———. "Process-Product Research on Second Language Learning in Classrooms." Chapter 6 in Birgit Harley, Patrick Allen, Jim Cummins, and Merrill Swain, eds., *The Development of Second Language Proficiency.* Cambridge: Cambridge University Press, 1990.

Liskin-Gasparro, Judith E. *ETS Oral Proficiency Testing Manual.* Princeton, NJ: Educational Testing Service, 1982.

———. "The ACTFL Proficiency Guidelines: A Historical Perspective." In T. V. Higgs, ed., *Teaching for Proficiency: The Organizing Principle.* The ACTFL Foreign Language Education Series, vol. 15. Lincolnwood, IL: National Textbook Company, 1984.

———. "The ACTFL Proficiency Guidelines: An Update." In A. Valdman, ed., *Proceedings of the Symposium on the Evaluation of Foreign Language Proficiency.* Bloomington, IN: Indiana University, 1987.

————. "Assessment: From Content Standards to Student Performance." Pp. 169–96 in R. C. Lafayette, ed., *National Standards: A Catalyst for Reform*. The ACTFL Foreign Language Education Series. Lincolnwood, IL: National Textbook Company, 1996.

Long, Michael. "Does Second Language Instruction Make a Difference? A Review of the Research." *TESOL Quarterly* 17 (1983): 359–82.

Lowe, Pardee Jr. *Manual for Language School Oral Interview Workshops*. Washington, DC: Defense Language Institute/Language School Joint Oral Interview Transfer Project, 1982.

Lowe, Pardee Jr. and Charles Stansfield, eds. *Second Language Proficiency Assessment: Current Issues. CAL/ERIC Language in Education: Theory and Practice 70*. Englewood Cliffs, NJ: Prentice Hall, 1988.

Lyster, Roy and Leila Ranta. "Corrective Feedback and Learner Uptake: Negotiation of Form in Communicative Classrooms." *Studies in Second Language Acquisition* 19, i (1997): 37–66.

Magnan, Sally S. "Assessing Speaking Proficiency in the Undergraduate Curriculum: Data from French." *Foreign Language Annals* 19, v (1986): 429–37.

Munby, J. *Communicative Syllabus Design*. Cambridge: Cambridge University Press, 1978.

A Nation at Risk: The Imperative for Education Reform. A Report to the Nation and the Secretary of Education, United States Department of Education. The National Commission on Excellence in Education, April 1983. (Reprinted by the American Council on the Teaching of Foreign Languages [ACTFL], October 1983.)

Omaggio Hadley, Alice. "Proficiency-Based Instruction: Implications for Methodology." *IDEAL* 3 (1988): 25–37.

————. "MLJ Readers' Forum." *The Modern Language Journal* 72 (1988): 452–54.

————. "Le concept de compétence fonctionnelle et son impact sur les programmes et l'enseignement des langues étrangères." *Etudes de linguistique appliquée* 77 (1990): 85–96.

Phillips, June K. "Reading Proficiency Assessment: Section 2: Interpretations and Misinterpretations." Pp. 136–48 in P. Lowe Jr. and C. Stansfield, eds., *Second Language Proficiency Assessment: Current Issues. CAL/ERIC Language in Education: Theory and Practice 70*. Englewood Cliffs, NJ: Prentice Hall, 1988.

————. ed., *Collaborations: Meeting New Goals, New Realities*. Northeast Conference on the Teaching of Foreign Languages. Lincolnwood, IL: National Textbook Company, 1997.

————. "Introduction: Standards for World Languages—On a Firm Foundation." Pp. 1–14 in J. K. Phillips and R. M. Terry, eds., *Foreign Language Standards: Linking Research, Theories, and Practices*. The ACTFL Foreign Language Education Series. Lincolnwood, IL: National Textbook Company, 1999.

Phillips, June K. and Jamie C. Draper. *The Five Cs: The Standards for Foreign Language Learning Work Text*. Boston, MA: Heinle & Heinle, 1999.

Phillips, June K. and Robert C. Lafayette. "Reactions to the Catalyst: Implications for Our New Professional Structure." Pp. 197–209 in R. C. Lafayette, ed., *National Standards: A Catalyst for Reform*. The ACTFL Foreign Language Education Series. Lincolnwood, IL: National Textbook Company, 1996.

Phillips, June K. and R. M. Terry, eds. *Foreign Language Standards: Linking Research, Theories, and Practices*. The ACTFL Foreign Language Education Series. Lincolnwood, IL: The National Textbook Company, 1999.

Savignon, Sandra J. *Communicative Competence: An Experiment in Foreign Language Teaching*. Philadelphia: Center for Curriculum Development, 1972.

———. *Communicative Competence: Theory and Practice*. Reading, MA: Addison-Wesley Publishing Company, 1983.

———. *Communicative Competence: Theory and Practice*, 2nd edition: New York: McGraw Hill, 1997.

Scebold, C. Edward. Personal communication, 1992.

Shohamy, Elana. "Rater Reliability of the Oral Interview Speaking Test." *Foreign Language Annals* 16 (1983): 219–22.

———. "Reactions to Lyle Bachman's Paper 'Problems in Examining the Validity of the ACTFL Oral Proficiency Interview.' " In A. Valdman, ed., *Proceedings of the Symposium on the Evaluation of Foreign Language Proficiency*. Bloomington, IN: Indiana University, 1987.

Shohamy, Elana, T. Reves, and Y. Bejerano. "Introducing a New Comprehensive Test of Oral Proficiency." *English Language Teaching Journal* 40 (1986): 212–22.

Standards for Foreign Language Learning in the 21st Century. Yonkers, NY: National Standards in Foreign Langue Education Project, 1999.

Standards for Foreign Language Learning: Preparing for the 21st Century. Yonkers, NY: National Standards in Foreign Language Education Project, 1996.

Stern, H. H. "Analysis and Experience as Variables in Second Language Pedagogy." Chapter 7 in Birgit Harley, Patrick Allen, Jim Cummins, and Merrill Swain, eds., *The Development of Second Language Proficiency*. Cambridge: Cambridge University Press, 1990.

Strength through Wisdom: A Critique of U.S. Capability. A Report to the President from the President's Commission on Foreign Language and International Studies. Washington, DC: U.S. Government Printing Office, 1979. (Reprinted in *The Modern Language Journal* 64 [1980]: 9–57.)

Swain, Merrill. "Communicative Competence: Some Roles of Comprehensible Input and Comprehensible Output in its Development." Chapter 14 in S. Gass and C. Madden, eds., *Input in Second Language Acquisition*. Cambridge, MA: Newbury House, 1985.

Swender, Elvira, ed. *ACTFL Oral Proficiency Interview Tester Training Manual*. Yonkers, NY: American Council on the Teaching of Foreign Languages, 1999.

Swender, Elvira and Greg Duncan. "ACTFL Performance Guidelines for K–12 Learners." *Foreign Language Annals* 31, iv (1998): 479–91.

———, eds. *ACTFL Performance Guidelines for K–12 Learners*. Yonkers, NY: American Council on the Teaching of Foreign Languages, 1999.

Thompson, Irene. "A Study of Interrater Reliability of the ACTFL Oral Proficiency Interview in Five European Languages: Data from ESL, French, German, Russian, and Spanish." *Foreign Language Annals* 28, iii (1995): 407–22.

———. "Assessing Foreign Language Skills: Data from Russian." *The Modern Language Journal* 80, i (1996): 47–63.

Tschirner, Erwin. "Scope and Sequence: Rethinking Beginning Foreign Language Instruction." *The Modern Language Journal* 80, i (1996): 1–14.

Tschirner, Erwin and L. Kathy Heilenman. "Reasonable Expectations: Oral Proficiency Goals for Intermediate-Level Students of German." *The Modern Language Journal* 82, ii (1998): 147–58.

Wells, Elizabeth. "Standards for Foreign Language Learning: Implications and Perceptions." *ACTFL Newsletter* XI, i (Fall 1998): 7–9.

Widdowson, H. G. *Teaching Language as Communication.* Oxford: Oxford University Press, 1978.

Wing, Barbara and Sandi Mayewski. *Oral Proficiency Testing in College-Level Foreign Language Programs.* Hastings-on-Hudson, NY: ACTFL Materials Center, 1984.

2 TWO
On Learning a Language: Some Theoretical Perspectives

Introduction

In Chapter 1, various ways to define and describe language competence were explored, and components of language that were thought to be important in designing models of "communicative competence" and "language proficiency" were identified and considered. We saw that many of the same components (grammatical, lexical, phonological, pragmatic, sociolinguistic, and discourse features) were included in the various models that have been proposed. Although we have not reached complete consensus on the question of what it means to know a language, the profession is in basic agreement about the features of language that are relevant to that question.

This chapter addresses another fundamental question that concerns language researchers and practitioners: How do adults become proficient in a second language? Consensus about this question may be far more difficult to achieve. Ellis (1985) comments that there has been a great deal of theorizing about second-language acquisition (SLA), especially since the early 1970s, and that "the research literature abounds in approaches, theories, models, laws, and principles" (p. 248). He speculates that perhaps the profession has generated far too many theories, agreeing with Schouten (1979) that "too many models have been built and taken for granted too soon, and this has stifled relevant research" (p. 4, cited in Ellis 1985, p. 248). Spolsky (1989) argues for the development of a unified macro-theory—a new general theory of second-language learning—and outlines seventy-four separate "conditions" that would need to be integrated into such a comprehensive model. McLaughlin (1987) takes the view that although micro-theories, which try to deal with a smaller range of phenomena and are limited in scope, may be "intrinsically more satisfactory" (p. 9), a theory must be comprehensive enough to explain more than a very limited range of phenomena: "A satisfactory theory of adult second-language learning must go beyond accounting for how people form relative clauses" (pp. 9–10). He adds that, given the relatively early stage of the development of knowledge in the field of second-language acquisition, "it seems premature to argue for the 'truth' of one theory over another" (p. 6). Larsen-Freeman and Long (1991) agree, suggesting that it would be counterproductive for SLA researchers to espouse one single dominant theory of language acquisition, particularly as this might discourage competing points of view:

> We must guard against overzealousness on the part of theorists or their devotees who feel that they have a monopoly on the truth. While SLA research and language teaching will benefit from the advantages of theoretically motivated research . . . , it would be dangerous at this stage for one theory to become omnipotent (p. 290).

Practitioners who have been buffeted across the years by pressures to adopt different approaches to teaching, due to the changing winds of theory, may tend to agree with this resistance to theoretical "bandwagons" (Grittner 1990).

Why do language teachers need to know about theory, especially if it seems unlikely that we can reach agreement about how language learning and acquisition take place? One reason might be that most language teaching methodologies have grown out of a particular theoretical framework of second-language acquisition, and it would be helpful for teachers to understand some of the premises underlying those approaches in order to evaluate them. A second reason for understanding a range of theoretical viewpoints is that it may help teachers develop and/or clarify their own set of principles for language teaching. Ellis (1985) maintains that every teacher already has a theory of language learning, but that many teachers may have never articulated what that theory is. The fact, however, that we choose to do certain activities in the classroom and decide not to do others shows that we are working on some underlying assumptions about what is useful in promoting the development of language proficiency. Therefore, before examining some of the theories that have been influential in the field of language teaching over the years, it might be constructive to make a preliminary assessment of some of the assumptions that may underlie our own beliefs about language learning.

Illustration 2.1 presents a set of questions that can serve as a guide for discussion or as an instrument for self-assessment to help teachers clarify and articulate their current beliefs about the way adults develop competence in a second language. The reader may want to consider these questions before going on to the next section.

Exploring Theories of Language Learning

Recent reviews of language acquisition theory (McLaughlin 1978, 1984, 1987; Ellis 1985, 1990; Brown 1987, 1994; Larsen-Freeman 1991) have attempted to group various theoretical perspectives along a kind of continuum, ranging from *empiricist* views on one end to *rationalist* or *mentalist* positions on the other, with theories that blend these two perspectives placed somewhere in between. This opposition

Illustration 2.1
Discussion Guide: Beliefs
about Second-Language
Learning

This set of questions is designed to help teachers explore their assumptions and beliefs about second-language learning and teaching. The questions relate to some of the issues that underlie various theories of language acquisition in this chapter.

1. Do adults learn foreign languages in a manner similar to the way children acquire their native language, or are the processes involved in child and adult language learning different?

2. Are humans born with a special capacity for language that is specific to our species? Or is language learning like other kinds of learning, governed by general cognitive processes not specific to language? If we are born with a specialized capacity for acquiring a native language as children, does it work the same way with adults who are learning a foreign or second language?

3. How does our knowledge of our native language affect our learning of a new language? Does some of the knowledge we have transfer to the new language? If so, is this helpful, or can it be a hindrance?

4. What is the optimum type of "input" for adults who are beginning their study of a foreign language? Do they profit best from listening to native speakers for some initial period of time before being asked to speak? Should the input they receive be ordered or sequenced carefully to correspond to what they already know? Or is it sufficient that the input be relatively comprehensible, even if some structures have not yet been studied?

5. What role does interaction with native speakers, teachers, or other learners have in language acquisition? What kinds of information about the target language can we obtain through such interaction? What kinds of information can we obtain about our own developing language proficiency when we interact with others?

6. What is the role of explicit grammar instruction in adult foreign language learning? Can adults become proficient in a second language without having conscious knowledge of the rules of that language? Or do adults profit in some way from grammar explanations and examples of how specific features are used?

7. Do language learners acquire grammatical features in a predictable order when language learning occurs in natural-use situations? Does instruction in formal classrooms need to follow a "natural order" to be effective?

8. What is the role of practice in adult language learning? Is language learning like the learning of other "skills," such as learning to play a musical instrument, where a great deal of focused practice is necessary to become proficient? Or is language learning fundamentally different from other forms of human learning?

9. Do students need to have an opportunity to practice new forms and structures in "controlled" activities before being asked to communicate their own meaning using those features? Or should students be encouraged to engage in conversation activities where communication is the main focus from the beginning of language instruction? When learners are engaged in meaningful and creative communication, do they tend to make more errors than when they are doing controlled or form-focused activities?

10. What is the role of feedback in language learning? How important is it to give learners information about whether they are making errors as they use the new language? Is it better to correct most or all of the errors students make, or should error correction be minimal in the language classroom? What are optimal ways to provide feedback to adult foreign language learners?

of viewpoints is not new; Chomsky had made the rationalist/empiricist distinction in discussing linguistic theory in 1965, and Diller (1978) spoke of the existence of a longstanding "language teaching controversy" between the *rationalists* and the *empiricists* "whose roots can be traced to the beginnings of modern thought" (p. vii). The basic difference between the two positions seems to lie in the presumed locus of control of the process of language acquisition. The rationalist position includes theories that assume that humans have an innate capacity for the development of language, and that we are genetically programmed to develop our linguistic systems in certain ways (Chomsky 1965). Larsen-Freeman (1991) refers to this point of view as a "nativist" or "innateness" position, which is in strong opposition to the "behaviorist" or "environmentalist" perspective. This latter position is characteristic of the empiricists, who maintain that it is the learner's experience that is largely responsible for language learning and is more important than any specific innate capacity (Larsen-Freeman 1991, p. 323). McLaughlin (1978, 1984) characterizes the empiricist viewpoint as one that is skeptical of any explanation of language learning that cannot be observed. Learning is seen as the result of external forces acting on the organism rather than the programmed unfolding of language through internal biological mechanisms. Empiricists, therefore, assume that there is no special species-specific language ability, but that language learning is just one aspect of general learning ability or capacity.

The next section provides a sampling of theories representing these different categories or classifications, chosen to reflect some of those perspectives that have had the most influence or potential influence on classroom practice. Because there is such a profusion of competing theoretical viewpoints in the professional literature, this discussion will not be comprehensive. The interested reader would do well to consult additional sources such as Ellis (1985, 1990), Brown (1987, 1994), McLaughlin (1987), Spolsky (1989), Larsen-Freeman and Long (1991), Gass and Selinker (1994), Towell and Hawkins (1994), Cook (1996), and Mitchell and Myles (1998) for more detailed treatments of a wide spectrum of theoretical viewpoints.

From Empiricism To Rationalism: A Theoretical Sampler

The various theories of language learning to be discussed in this section have been placed along the continuum in Illustration 2.2, which depicts in graphic form the range of viewpoints referred to in the preceding pages. The placement on the continuum is not meant to be exact or precise, but rather locates theories in a general way in terms of their compatibility with empiricist or rationalist points of view. The characteristics and underlying assumptions of each of these theories will be briefly summarized below. For a more thorough treatment of a particular theory, consult the primary sources in the references.

An Empiricist Perspective: Behaviorism

Since ancient times philosophers have believed that human learning and animal learning might be similar (Chastain 1976). Chastain points out that it was the publication of Darwin's *Origin of the Species* in 1859 that made this belief more

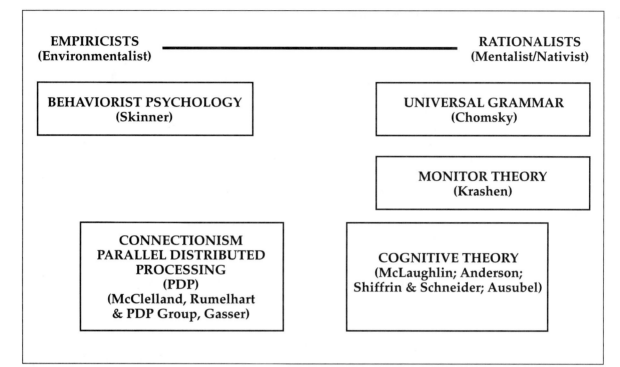

Illustration 2.2 The Rationalist-Empiricist Continuum

credible, since Darwin's theory implied that there was indeed a continuity between the human species and the lower animals, and by implication between the
human mind and the animal mind. In the late nineteenth and early twentieth
centuries, a growing interest in animal behavior led to the growth of experimental psychology and the school of behaviorism.

According to S-R (stimulus-response) psychology, all behavior is viewed as a response to stimuli, whether the behavior is overt (explicit) or covert (implicit). According to the theory, behavior happens in associative chains; all learning is thus
characterized as associative learning, or habit formation, brought about by the repeated association of a stimulus with a response (Hilgard 1962). This process of
habit formation, or *conditioning,* was thought to be of three basic types: (1) classical conditioning, (2) operant conditioning, and (3) multiple response learning
(pp. 253–274).

In *classical conditioning* (best known through experiments done by Pavlov), an
association between a conditioned stimulus and a response was repeatedly
strengthened through the presentation of that stimulus with another, unconditioned one. In Pavlov's experiments with dogs, the unconditioned stimulus was
meat powder and the response was salivation. When Pavlov repeatedly presented
the meat powder with the simultaneous ringing of a bell, the dog learned to sali-

vate to the sound of the bell (the conditioned stimulus), even in the absence of the meat.

In *operant conditioning* (also known as *instrumental conditioning*), the response to a stimulus is learned although it is not normally a natural response to that stimulus. A rat pressing a bar in its cage may at first do so randomly. But if the rat discovers that pressing the bar releases a food pellet, it learns to push the bar again for the same reward. The *operant* (the random bar-pushing behavior) becomes conditioned (purposeful behavior) because it produces an effect that is rewarding.

In *multiple-response learning,* the animal learns a whole chain of behaviors and performs them in succession, always in the same order. A rat that runs a maze learns a fixed series of turns through conditioning, rewarded by a food pellet or two for his trouble.

What has all of this to do with language learning? As Chastain (1976) points out, behaviorism took a strong foothold in the thinking of psychologists by the middle of the twentieth century, influencing, in turn, the views of the education community:

> *Soon behaviorists concluded that all learning consisted of some form of conditioning. The organism was conditioned to respond in a specific way to a selected stimulus. Complex activities were nothing more than a complex collection of conditioned responses. Since all learning is conditioned and since human learning is similar to learning in animals, the next step was to conclude that human learning could be, and is, conditioned in the same way. The belief was that humans are reinforced by their environment in much the same way as the rat in a maze (p. 105).*

B. F. Skinner (1957), perhaps the best known proponent of S-R psychology, used the term *operant conditioning* to describe verbal learning. In his view, language is characterized as a "sophisticated response system" that humans acquire through automatic conditioning processes (Wardhaugh 1976, p. 142). Some patterns of language are reinforced (rewarded) and others are not. Only those patterns reinforced by the community of language users will persist. In Skinnerian psychology, the human being is likened to a machine with multiple working parts. The mind is thought to be "a *tabula rasa* upon which are stamped associations" between various stimuli in the environment and responses chosen from outside the organism for reinforcement (Chastain 1976, p. 133).

Skinner's theory of verbal learning was consistent with the prevailing beliefs of many applied linguists of the 1940s and 1950s who maintained that second languages should be learned through extensive drill and practice without recourse to rationalistic explanation. In his *Outline Guide for the Practical Study of Foreign Languages* (1942), Bloomfield had argued for an essentially behavioristic approach:

> *The command of a language is not a matter of knowledge: the speakers are quite unable to describe the habits which make up their language. The command of a language is a matter of practice. . . . Language learning is overlearning: anything else is of no use (Bloomfield 1942, p. 12, cited in Chastain 1976, pp. 107–08).*

Illustration 2.3
Summary: Behaviorist
Theory (Based on Skinner
1957; Hilgard 1962;
Chastain 1976;
Wardhaugh 1976)

Summary: Behaviorist Theory
1. Human learning and animal learning are similar.
2. The child's mind is a *tabula rasa*. There is no innate pre-programming specifically for language learning at birth.
3. Psychological data should be limited to that which is observable.
4. All behavior is viewed as a response to stimuli. Behavior happens in associative chains; in fact, all learning is associative in nature.
5. Conditioning involves the strengthening of associations between a stimulus and a response through reinforcement.
6. Human language is a "sophisticated response system" acquired through operant conditioning.

Illustration 2.3 summarizes the main points of the behaviorist view of language learning. Behaviorist theory, in conjunction with the structuralist views of language that prevailed in the 1940s and 1950s, laid the theoretical foundations for audiolingual language teaching methodology, discussed in more detail in Chapter 3.

CRITIQUE:

We have seen that behavioristic theories of language learning were based on the assumption that language learning was like any other kind of learning, and, therefore, one could extrapolate heavily from general learning theory and even from animal learning. This viewpoint was seriously challenged by Chomsky (1959) in a very critical review of Skinner's work. Chomsky maintained that language behavior was far more complex than the establishment of S-R connections, and that Skinner's theory could not possibly explain the creativity of children in generating language.

According to McLaughlin (1978, 1984), Skinner's 1957 treatise, *Verbal Behavior*, was not supported by research with human subjects. There was, in fact, no substantial research base ever generated by behaviorists to look at child language use, let alone second-language learning. He adds that evidence gleaned from subsequent studies of child language behavior shows that a simple behavioristic perspective does not provide a satisfactory explanation of what has been found: It seems that imitation and reinforcement have a much smaller role to play in child language than Skinner and his colleagues imagined. For example, children often produce forms that they never heard their parents or other adults say ("I goed" or "two foots"). Thus, imitation of adult speech cannot completely account for the way children produce language: "The child's language is simply too strange" (McLaughlin 1984, p. 15). Furthermore, parents rarely correct their children's grammatical errors but respond instead to the message content (Brown and Hanlon 1970; Brown 1973). If ungrammatical forms are thus positively rewarded (or at least ignored), how then do children eventually eliminate them? A behaviorist view of language, which would predict the need for both imitation and negative feedback in the form of overt corrections, does not seem to explain the way in which children learn.

With Chomsky's review of Skinner's theory there came a paradigm shift toward the other end of the theoretical continuum. If language development was highly creative, then language learning theories needed to account for the creative processing that was taking place in the human mind. By the mid-1960s, the pendulum was swinging in the direction of the rationalist point of view.

▨ Three Rationalist Perspectives of Language Learning

1. Universal Grammar

Various reviews of theories of language learning (Chastain 1976; Wardhaugh 1976; McLaughlin 1978, 1984, 1987; Ellis 1985, 1990; Brown 1987, 1994; Larsen-Freeman 1991) group a variety of perspectives within the "rationalist" camp. Other terms used in association with this perspective are "nativist," "mentalist," and "cognitive." A highly influential nativist viewpoint grew out of Chomsky's work, starting with the publication in 1957 of his book *Syntactic Structures,* and his critique of Skinner in 1959. As we saw earlier, Chomsky had rejected the behaviorist perspective and adopted instead a mentalist viewpoint that was closely related to the basic principles and beliefs of cognitive psychology (Chastain 1976). Other theorists, such as Eric Lennenberg (1967) and David McNeill (1966) believed that language was a species-specific, genetically determined capacity and that language learning was therefore governed by biological mechanisms. In 1965, Chomsky had concluded that children were born with some kind of special language processing ability and had proposed the existence of a "language acquisition device" (LAD). A year later, McNeill (1966) characterized this LAD as having various innate linguistic properties. Brown (1994) summarized them to include: (1) the ability to distinguish speech sounds from other sounds; (2) the ability to organize language into a system of structures; (3) the knowledge of what was possible and what was not possible in any linguistic system; and (4) the ability to construct the simplest possible system based on the linguistic data to which one was exposed.

Chomsky argued further that it must be the case that children were innately programmed to acquire language since they do it so quickly (in just a few years) and with such limited (and less than ideal) input. He also believed that they could not help but construct a certain kind of linguistic system—a particular transformational or generative grammar—any more than they could help the way their visual system perceived solid objects or lines and angles (Chomsky 1965). Although a child's experience with language input could have an effect on language learning, the "ultimate form will be a function of those language universals that exist in the human mind" (McLaughlin 1984, p. 16).

Universal Grammar theory posits the existence of a set of basic grammatical elements or "fixed abstract principles" that are common to all natural human languages and that predispose children to organize the input in certain ways. The principles themselves are thought to be innate, a product of the "LAD." They include *substantive* universals, which consist of fixed features of languages like phonemes or syntactic categories like nouns and verbs, as well as *formal* universals, which are more abstract, and which place limits or constraints on the possible rule systems or on the options children have for constructing a grammar (Chomsky 1965, pp. 27–30; Ellis 1985, pp. 192–93).

Illustration 2.4
Summary: Universal
Grammar Theory (Based
on Chomsky 1965; Ellis
1985; McLaughlin 1987;
Larsen-Freeman 1991)

Summary: Universal Grammar Theory
1. Language is a species-specific, genetically determined capacity.
2. Language learning is governed by biological mechanisms.
3. The ultimate form of any human language is a function of language universals, a set of fixed abstract principles that are innate.
4. Each language has its own "parameters" whose "settings" are learned on the basis of linguistic data.
5. There is a "core grammar," congruent with universal principles, and a "peripheral grammar," consisting of features that are not part of universal grammar.
6. Core grammar rules are thought to be relatively easier to acquire, in general, than peripheral rules.

Ellis (1985) provides the following example of a formal universal: One might formulate certain principles that place limits on how languages can use word order transformations in order to form questions. All languages must operate within those limited options, yet each language has its own particular "parameter settings" for question formation. The child's task is to discover which of the various options applies in his or her language. This is where environmental input is crucial: The child needs to hear the language spoken in order to select the appropriate options and thus set the parameters correctly.

According to Chomsky, the universal principles that children discover constitute their "core grammar," which is congruent with general principles operating across all languages. The "peripheral grammar" consists of rules or features that are not determined by universal grammar, but that might be derived from an older form of the language, borrowed from another language, or that might have arisen accidentally (Cook 1985, cited in Ellis 1985). Rules of the core grammar might be easier to acquire than the rules of the peripheral grammar, since the latter "are thought to be outside of the child's preprogrammed instructions" (McLaughlin 1987, p. 96). Wesche (1994) suggests that language learners probably acquire peripheral rules through the use of "general cognitive abilities" (p. 239).

Chomsky's Universal Grammar theory and associated derivative approaches to the study of linguistic universals are quite complex. Most discussions of the research in this area require some specialized knowledge of theoretical linguistics in order to fully understand the findings. (However, see Pinker [1994] for a very readable discussion of some of the important aspects of this theoretical approach to language acquisition.) As was mentioned earlier, the discussion of theories in this chapter is meant to be introductory in nature; readers interested in a more detailed treatment should consult the sources cited in this section. For a summary of some of the main premises of Universal Grammar theory that have been presented here, see Illustration 2.4.

CRITIQUE:

Although Chomsky's generative grammar theory has had a wide-ranging influence on the field of linguistics and on theories of how children acquire a native language, Universal Grammar theory has not won universal acclaim. Beedham

(1995) reviews the work of a number of scholars who have been critical of generative models (such as Gross 1979; Hall 1987; Moore and Carling 1982, among others) and criticizes the basic methodology of the generative approach to language acquisition. He maintains that all models of "generative grammar" have at least two basic flaws: (1) confusion of "mathematical notation" with linguistic form and (2) circularity of argumentation:

> *The principles and criteria of Principles and Parameters theory are merely assumptions, with nothing to back them up except the circular argument that without them language would be unexplained . . . (Beedham 1995, p. 209).*

Beedham also strongly criticizes generative grammar theory because of what he claims to be its "complete lack of applicability." Although he recognizes that theoretical subjects are different from applied subjects, he maintains that at some point, a theory needs to be empirically tested in some type of application:

> *This is yet to happen to generative grammar. Certainly it is now universally recognized that generative grammar cannot be applied to language teaching (p. 214).*

However, the question of how Universal Grammar might play a role in adult language learning is still a subject of much debate in the field of second-language acquisition. McLaughlin (1987) states that "Universal Grammar theory does not concern itself with second-language acquisition" (p. 91), but that a number of second-language researchers have applied principles of Universal Grammar to this domain in an effort to find sufficiently sophisticated explanations of the very complex characteristics of interlanguages. Wesche (1994) maintains that although Universal Grammar theory is widely accepted in first language acquisition, second-language acquisition specialists disagree about whether Universal Grammar continues to operate in adult learners or play any significant role. She adds that even if it does play a role in second-language acquisition, it is limited to the core grammar and does not help explain how learners acquire such important features of language as the elements of peripheral grammar, vocabulary, discourse competence, or other performance features. It also does not help explain "the dramatic individual differences found in the rate and ultimate mastery of the second language" (p. 239).

Some theorists operate on the assumption that the same universals that children use to construct their native language are available to adults; others believe that they are no longer available, and that different cognitive processes must be involved in adult second/foreign language learning (see Larsen-Freeman 1991). Gass and Selinker (1994), for example, discuss the "Fundamental Difference Hypothesis," proposed by scholars such as Schachter (1988) and Bley-Vroman (1989), who argue that adults no longer have direct access to UG principles. Instead, they maintain that child language acquisition, especially of a first language, and adult language acquisition of a second language are quite different in several important ways. First, adults rarely achieve native levels of proficiency or full competence in a second language, whereas children normally do achieve this in their native language. Children can learn any of the world's languages equally well; adults experience differing levels of difficulty, depending on how closely the foreign language is related to their native language. (We saw this, for example, in the difficulty hierarchies outlined by the Foreign Service Institute in Chapter 1.) Gass and Selinker further point out that adults and children have differing levels of knowledge about how languages work, given that adults already have full competence in their native language when they begin to learn a foreign language. One additional difference is the role that motivation and attitude toward the target language can play in adult language acquisition. Differences in motivation do not seem to have any appreciable impact on the child's learning his or her native language; however, motivation and attitude are important factors for adults learning a foreign language (pp. 124–25).

Nevertheless, many scholars in the field of second-language acquisition still feel that Universal Grammar can play a role, and Gass and Selinker (1994) maintain that much of second-language acquisition research "is driven by the notion that first and second language acquisition involve the same processes" (p. 124). The rationalist theories that are discussed in the next two sections represent two different perspectives on how first- and second-language acquisition are related.

2. Krashen's Monitor Theory: First- and Second-Language Acquisition Are Similar

One of the most influential and widely discussed models of language learning/acquisition in recent years is Stephen Krashen's "Monitor Model." The most complete description of the theory (1982) describes five central hypotheses:

1. *The acquisition-learning distinction,* which "states that adults have two distinct and independent ways of developing competence in a second language": *acquisition,* which is a subconscious process "similar, if not identical, to the way children develop ability in their first language"; and *learning,* which refers to conscious knowledge of the rules of grammar of a second language and their application in production (p. 10).
2. *The natural order hypothesis,* which maintains that acquisition of grammatical structures (primarily morphemes) follows a predictable order when that acquisition is natural (i.e., not via formal learning).
3. *The monitor hypothesis,* which states that acquisition is the sole initiator of all second-language utterances and is responsible for fluency, while learning (conscious knowledge of rules) can function only as an "editor" or "monitor" for the output. This monitor operates only when there is sufficient time, the focus is on form, and the language user knows the rule being applied.
4. *The input hypothesis,* which maintains that we acquire more language only when we are exposed to "comprehensible input"—language that contains structures that are "a little beyond" our current level of competence ($i + 1$), but which is comprehensible through our use of context, our knowledge of the world, and other extralinguistic cues directed to us. According to this hypothesis, acquirers "go for meaning" first, and, as a result, acquire structure as well. A third part of this hypothesis states that input need not be deliberately planned to contain appropriate structures ($i + 1$): If

communication is successful and there is enough of it, $i + 1$ is provided automatically. A final part of the input hypothesis maintains that speaking fluency cannot be taught directly, but rather "emerges" naturally over time. Krashen maintains that although early speech is not grammatically accurate, accuracy will develop over time as the acquirer hears and understands more input.

5. *The affective filter hypothesis* states that comprehensible input can have its effect on acquisition only when affective conditions are optimal: (1) the acquirer is motivated; (2) he has self-confidence and a good self-image; and (3) his level of anxiety is low. When learners are "put on the defensive" (see Stevick 1976), the affective filter is high, and comprehensible input can not "get in." (For a fuller account of these five hypotheses, see Krashen 1982, pp. 9–32.)

Krashen suggests that there are certain implications for classroom practice if language instruction is to be consistent with his theory. Among these are:

1. The main function of the classroom may be to provide comprehensible input in an environment conducive to a low affective filter (i.e., high motivation, low anxiety).

2. The classroom is most useful for beginners, who cannot easily utilize the informal environment for input. That is, it is useful for foreign language students who do not have input sources outside of class or for those whose competence is so low that they are unable to understand the language of the outside world (pp. 33–37).

3. The requirements for optimal input are that it be (a) comprehensible, (b) interesting and relevant, (c) *not* grammatically sequenced, (d) provided in sufficient quantity to supply $i + 1$, and (e) delivered in an environment where students are "off the defensive" (p. 127).

4. Error correction should be minimal in the classroom; it is of *some* limited use when the goal is learning, but of *no* use when the goal is acquisition. Error correction raises the affective filter and should, therefore, not be used in free conversation or when acquisition is likely to take place (pp. 116–117).

5. Students should never be required to produce speech in the second language unless they are ready to do so. Speaking fluency cannot be taught, but "emerges" naturally in time with enough comprehensible input.

Illustration 2.5 summarizes the main premises of Monitor Theory. A more completely developed model of language teaching using Krashen's theory as a basis is given by Terrell (1977, 1982). His "Natural Approach" is discussed in detail in Chapter 3.

CRITIQUE: A number of the hypotheses and assertions in Krashen's theory of second-language acquisition have been challenged in recent years. In an early review of the Monitor Model, Munsell and Carr (1981) questioned the distinction between

Illustration 2.5
Summary of Monitor
Theory (Based on Krashen
1982)

Summary: Monitor Theory

1. Adults have two distinct ways to develop competence in a second language: *acquisition,* which is a subconscious process, and *learning,* which is conscious.
2. *Acquisition* is similar to the process by which children acquire their native language. *Learning* involves conscious knowledge of rules.
3. When *acquisition* is natural, the order in which certain grammatical features of the language are acquired is predictable.
4. *Learning* can function only as an "editor" of what is produced, since *acquisition* is the sole initiator of all second-language utterances. Learning can serve as a "monitor" of performance only under certain conditions.
5. We acquire new structures only when we are exposed to "comprehensible input" ($i + 1$). Input does not need to be deliberately structured or planned for the acquirer. If communication is successful, $i + 1$ will happen automatically.
6. For acquisition to take place, the learner must be motivated, have a good self-image, and be free from anxiety.
7. Error correction should be minimized in the classroom, where the main purpose of instruction should be to provide comprehensible input.

"learning" and "acquisition" and the notion of "conscious" and "unconscious" rules. The reviewers also seem to object to the underlying nativist assumptions of the model and the implications that language learning is distinct from other kinds of learning. In their view, language skill is much like other kinds of skilled performance:

> *Krashen may not wish to extend Monitor Theory to chess, yet the measured characteristics of the knowledge of skilled chess players bear some striking similarities to the characteristics of linguistic knowledge. . . . Similarly, such disparate areas of skill as sports and mathematics seem to benefit from early emphasis on conscious and systematic learning despite the fact that expert performances in these areas also display a number of characteristics that formally resemble expert performance in language. We cannot imagine trying to learn basketball, monopoly, bridge, or quantum mechanics simply by watching people do them, trying them, and creatively constructing the rules. It is much easier to start with some conscious exposition of the rules and build one's skill upon that foundation (pp. 498–99).*

Munsell and Carr imply that Krashen should incorporate language learning theory into a wider context where the nature of human skilled performance in general is explored. This point of view is congruent with the commentary on Monitor Theory made by McLaughlin (1987) who leans toward a more *cognitive* perspective.

McLaughlin's objections to Monitor Theory are summarized in the following five points:

1. "The acquisition-learning distinction is not clearly defined." Therefore, the central claim that Krashen makes that "learning" cannot become "acquisition" cannot be tested (p. 56).
2. Various studies have shown that the Monitor does not work the way Krashen originally thought it would, and he has had to place more and more restrictions on the conditions under which it would be used effectively. McLaughlin believes that these restrictions make Krashen's conceptualization of "learning" of limited usefulness in explaining a learner's conscious knowledge of grammar.
3. The case for the Natural Order Hypothesis is quite weak due to methodological problems. "If the Natural Order Hypothesis is to be accepted, it must be in a weak form, which postulates that some things are learned before others, but not always" (p. 56).
4. Since no clear definition of "comprehensible input" is given, McLaughlin believes the Input Hypothesis is also untestable.
5. The Affective Filter Hypothesis is also questionable, not only because Krashen has not explained how this filter develops, but also because it does not take individual differences among learners into account. McLaughlin states that this hypothesis is incapable of predicting the course of linguistic development with any precision.

Although Krashen's theory has been criticized on a variety of points by a number of scholars, it has also had a strong influence on thinking in the field over the past twenty years. Virtually everyone who talks about language learning in recent years seems compelled to consider whether it is "learning" or "acquisition" that is the focus of attention in one's remarks. Many people feel that the distinction has at least an intuitive appeal and that it represents some psychological reality. In the same way, many practitioners recognize the need to provide learners with "comprehensible input" and find Krashen's recommendation that affective considerations be primary in the classroom very appealing. In many ways, Krashen has articulated in his Monitor Theory hypotheses about language learning that have touched a responsive chord for many practitioners. This is not to say, however, that the criticisms reviewed above should not be considered seriously as one evaluates the merits of Monitor Theory.

As mentioned earlier, some theorists prefer a view of language learning that recognizes essential differences between the way children and adults process information. Although there may be some similarities between child and adult language learning, Cognitive theory predicts that adult second-language learning will differ in some important ways from the way in which children acquire their native tongue.

3. Cognitive Theory: First- and Second-Language Learning Differ

Larsen-Freeman and Long (1991) categorize various cognitive approaches to language acquisition as "interactionist" views, where both external and internal factors are considered in accounting for language acquisition (p. 266). Although this characterization may be valid, the emphasis on environmental factors seems rather limited when compared to the role assigned to internal or mental processes in descriptions of Cognitive theory given by Ausubel (1968), Ausubel, Novak, and Hanesian (1978), Ellis (1985, 1990), and McLaughlin (1987, 1990). For this reason, the theory has been placed toward the rationalist end of the continuum in Illustration 2.2.

We have seen that Universal Grammar theory considers the role of innate linguistic universals in language acquisition and claims that there is a specific *linguistic* capacity that is unique to the human species. Cognitive theory, by contrast, derives from the field of cognitive psychology and focuses on the role of more *general* cognitive processes involved in language acquisition, such as transfer, simplification, generalization, and restructuring (McLaughlin 1987). Like Universal Grammar, Cognitive theory is in direct opposition to Behaviorist theory because, from a cognitive perspective, learning is believed to result from internal mental activity rather than from something imposed from outside the learner (Ellis 1990). McLaughlin (1990) characterizes the cognitive approach to second-language acquisition as follows:

1. Cognitive psychology emphasizes *knowing* rather than *responding* and is concerned with studying mental processes involved in the acquisition and use of knowledge. "The focus is not stimulus-response bonds, but mental events" (p. 113).
2. The cognitive approach emphasizes *mental structure* or *organization.* Cognitive psychology assumes human knowledge is organized and that anything new that is learned is integrated into this structure.
3. Cognitive theory, as opposed to Behaviorist theory, views the learner as one who acts, constructs, and plans rather than simply receives stimuli from the environment. Therefore, a complete understanding of human cognition would require an analysis of strategies used for thinking, understanding, remembering, and producing language.

According to Cognitive theory, second-language learning is seen as "the acquisition of a complex cognitive skill" (McLaughlin 1987, p. 133). For a language learner to become proficient, subskills of this complex task must be practiced, automatized, integrated, and organized into internal representations, or rule systems, that are constantly restructured as proficiency develops.

Automatization refers to the process of making a skill routine through practice. McLaughlin (1987) explains the way this is thought to occur using an information processing model developed by Shiffrin and Schneider (1977). In this model, memory is thought to consist of a large number of "nodes" that become associated with one another and activated in sequence through learning. In *automatic processing,* certain nodes are activated almost every time a certain input is presented. This activation pattern has been built up through consistent practice so that it becomes a learned response over time. Once such an automatic response is learned, it occurs quite quickly and is difficult to suppress or change (Shiffrin and Schneider 1977, pp. 155–56).

In *controlled processing,* memory nodes are activated in a given sequence on a temporary basis—that is, the response has not yet been "learned" or automatized. For the response to happen, the learner has to give the process his full attention. It is difficult, therefore, to do "controlled" tasks if there is any distraction or interference.

Shiffrin and Schneider speculate that for the development of "complex information-processing skills," such as learning to read, learners would use controlled processing first, laying down "stepping stones of automatic processing" as they move from lower to higher levels of learning:

> *In short, the staged development of skilled automatic performance can be interpreted as a sequence of transitions from controlled to automatic processing (p. 170).*

Schmidt (1992) points out that although "automatic" and "controlled" processing were originally thought of in terms of a dichotomy, more recent discussions of these concepts suggest that they really should be viewed as ends of a continuum. He emphasizes the role of *practice* in moving new material along this continuum, affirming the earlier speculations of Shiffrin and Schneider, cited above:

> *The development of skilled behavior involves a shift with practice from controlled to automatic processing. Novices of all kinds, including beginning L2 learners, must pay careful attention to every step of the procedure, whereas experts do not (Schmidt 1992, p. 360).*

In discussing the development of speaking fluency, he suggests that various levels of processing may actually be used simultaneously, a point that Shiffrin and Schneider (1977) also make when referring to complex processing such as reading (see p. 161). Schmidt argues that, rather than thinking of the processing of speech as sequential in nature, it should be seen as a type of "parallel" processing. He cites Levelt's (1989) assertion that if it did not involve parallel processing, "speaking would be more like playing chess: an overt move now and then, but mostly silent processing" (Levelt 1989, p. 27, cited in Schmidt, p. 376). Schmidt adds that for novice speakers, it is indeed the case that "speaking sometimes does seem to require as much thought and effort as planning a chess move" (p. 376). Those of us who have taught beginning language learners can testify to the truth of this observation; it should also lead us to consider the possibility of giving learners more time to plan their discourse when asking them to express their own meaning in the foreign language in beginning and intermediate classes.

The distinction between controlled and automatic processing can be useful as one considers the various tasks involved in second-language learning. Tarone (1982, 1983) describes a whole range of language "styles" that learners produce when engaged in various kinds of tasks. The *vernacular style,* represented by informal use of the language with little attention to form, is produced when language is being processed automatically. The *careful style,* on the other hand, is elicited when learners engage in heavy monitoring and/or attention to the form of their production. This monitoring represents a more controlled processing of the language needed to accomplish the task. Tasks that demand such monitoring include grammaticality judgments or form-focused production activities of various kinds. Tarone (1982) explains that the learners' interlanguage system should be thought of as a *continuum,* ranging from the vernacular to the careful style, and does not, as Krashen (1982) has claimed, consist of two discrete systems differentiated on the basis of whether attention to form is conscious or subconscious.

The "variability" of learner language is evident when students at different proficiency levels engage in tasks of different types. Teachers may have noticed this phenomenon of variability when their students perform differently while doing a discrete-point grammar task on a test or for an assignment than they do when using the language more naturally or informally in conversation or in free composition. Tarone (1987) adds that other factors, such as the identity or the role of the learner's conversational partner, the topic of conversation, the mode of discourse (i.e., the functions that are being performed, such as giving directions, description, narration, argumentation, and the like), and other task or situational variables can have an effect on the accuracy of the language produced. Rather than feeling frustrated and confused by this phenomenon, teachers and students might be encouraged by a view of language learning such as this that accounts for such differences in performance.

While Shiffrin and Schneider contrast controlled and automatic processing, Ellis (1990) adds Anderson's (1980, 1995) distinction between *declarative* and *procedural* knowledge as another way to look at how information is processed and stored. *Declarative knowledge* is explicit and conscious, and can be articulated by the learner. It involves "knowing that" (e.g., definitions of words, facts, rules). *Procedural knowledge,* on the other ha̲ how" (e.g., how to produce language as one performs linguistica
less implicit or explicit, conscious
tively automatic in nature (see A
two types of knowledge). Anders
stages: (1) the cognitive stage, v
edge; (2) the associative stage, w
and (3) the autonomous stage,
matic and errors disappear (And
tempt to explain the processe
eventually "automatic," but eac
ferent ways.

Cognitive theory further ma
skill than automatizing the sub
The learner also has to impos
tion that is constantly being a
the organization of the existi
structured," to accommodate
structuring are key concepts in this view of langu

The idea of the development of internal "structures" or organized cognitive systems and networks is central to views of learning that derive from Cognitive theory. Cognitive psychologists have tried to explain, from a psycholinguistic viewpoint, how such internal representations of the foreign language develop within the learner's mind. Other cognitive theorists, working from an educational perspective, have sought to describe ways in which teachers can organize instruction so that learning is enhanced. One early proponent of applying general principles of cognitive psychology to educational contexts was David Ausubel (1968), who emphasized the importance of active mental participation by the learner in meaningful learning tasks. Central to his understanding of learning was the concept of "cognitive structure," which he defined as "the total content and organization of a given individual's ideas; or, in the context of subject-matter learning, the content and organization of his or her ideas in a particular area of knowledge" (Ausubel, Novak, and Hanesian 1978, p. 625). Cognitive structure, in Ausubel's view, is organized hierarchically. In meaningful learning, new knowledge is related to existing cognitive structure via subordinate or superordinate relationships, or by "combinations of previously learned ideas" (p. 59). Thus the addition of new information implies a reorganization or "restructuring" of the system: "In meaningful learning the very process of acquiring information results in a modification of both the newly acquired information and the specifically relevant aspect of cognitive structure to which the new information is linked" (Ausubel et al. 1978, p. 57).

In discussing types of learning that occur in classrooms, Ausubel makes an important distinction between "rote" and "meaningful" learning. Rote learning is arbitrary and verbatim; that is, the material to be learned is not integrated or "subsumed" into one's "cognitive structure" but is learned as an isolated or discrete piece of information. In this way, the cognitive system is not restructured because the new information does not become integrated. For example, learning lists of paired words—a task that is commonly used in verbal learning experiments—would constitute rote learning since the words are not related to one another meaningfully. Ausubel et al. (1978) note that some classroom learning, such as foreign language vocabulary learning, "does somewhat approach the rote level" (p. 28), but it might best be thought of as "a primitive form of meaningful learning" (p. 28) since the association between the new word and a meaningful concept does exist. However, it is possible to learn "potentially meaningful" material rotely—that is, in a verbatim form without trying to relate it meaningfully to what one already knows. Vocabulary words or dialogue lines that are memorized rotely but that are not integrated into existing cognitive structure might easily be lost later. Conversely, some rotely learned material might be available for years, but such material can only be reproduced verbatim if it is not integrated into the cognitive network in some way. Rotely learned information cannot be changed or paraphrased unless it is processed meaningfully.

Meaningful learning, on the other hand, is relatable to what one already knows and thus can be easily integrated into one's existing cognitive structure. One might illustrate this integration of knowledge with a foreign language learning example: If one knows that in French, descriptive adjectives agree in gender and number with the noun they modify, the new information that possessive adjectives also agree in this way can easily be mastered and retained. In this instance, the concept of adjective agreement might be thought of as the "subsumer," or "anchoring idea" (p. 170), and the possessive adjective agreement rule would be subsumed under it in cognitive structure. Perhaps the same student will study Spanish the following year. The rule that Spanish descriptive adjectives agree with the nouns they modify can then be subsumed via correlation with the French agreement rule.

Ausubel also stresses that in order for learning to be meaningful, the learner has to have an intention to learn—that is, a willingness to approach the learning task with the intention of relating the new material meaningfully to what is already known. A potentially meaningful bit of information might be learned rotely if the learner approaches it as a rote (i.e., verbatim) task and does not relate it to other information he/she already has. In Ausubel's view, learning must be meaningful to be effective and permanent.

How can teachers enhance the meaningfulness of new material for students and increase the chances that it will be anchored to what is already known? Ausubel suggests that the material be organized so that it is more easily relatable to previously learned material. New material should also be sequenced appropriately so that it can be integrated into previous knowledge. He recommends the use of advance organizers, which are introductory materials at a high level of generality presented in advance of the new material to be learned. Such organizers will facilitate the learning process by providing a kind of general anchoring idea to which the new knowledge can be attached—to *bridge the gap* between what the learner *already knows* and what he *needs to know* before he can meaningfully learn the task at hand" (Ausubel et al. 1978, pp. 171–172). Ideas such as these underlie "cognitive approaches" to methodology, treated in Chapter 3.

Illustration 2.6 summarizes some of the assumptions underlying Cognitive theory, as represented by the various perspectives described in this section.

CRITIQUE: How does Cognitive theory hold up under critical scrutiny among the competing theories discussed thus far? McLaughlin's (1987) critique includes several cautionary statements. First, conceiving of language learning as a "complex cognitive skill" is not comprehensive enough. Language learning also involves acquiring a "complex linguistic skill" (p. 150). By itself, Cognitive theory is not capable of explaining some of the constraints on the development of language that may result from linguistic universals, for example. McLaughlin believes that Cognitive theory needs to be linked to linguistic theories of second-language acquisition. If both viewpoints are explored together, a cognitive perspective of language learning might become more powerful. For example, the understanding of "restructuring" in second-language acquisition would be more comprehensive and enriched by research into the linguistic details of the restructuring process. Cognitive theory also does not predict explicitly when certain features of a first language will be transferred to a second language or explain why certain features do not transfer. Linguistic theory may make more specific predictions, thus adding information about language learning that Cognitive theory alone cannot provide.

Illustration 2.6
Summary: Cognitive
Theory

Summary: Cognitive Theory

1. Learning results from internal mental activity. Language learning is a type of general human learning and involves the acquisition of a complex cognitive skill.
2. Subskills involved in the complex task of language learning must be practiced, automatized, and integrated into organized internal representations, or rule systems, in cognitive structure.
3. Internal representations of language are constantly restructured as proficiency develops.
4. Skills are automatized (learned) only after they have first been under "controlled processing." Controlled processing, which requires attention to the task, leads to automatic processing, where attention is not needed to perform the skill (Schneider and Shiffrin 1977; Shiffrin and Schneider 1977; McLaughlin 1987).
5. Some researchers (Tarone 1982, 1983; Ellis 1985) maintain that learners' production is variable, depending on the degree of attention they pay to language form as they carry out various tasks. Informal tasks that demand little active attention elicit the "vernacular style," while tasks that require active attention and monitoring elicit the "careful style."
6. Some cognitive theorists (Anderson 1980, 1995; Ellis 1985) distinguish between *declarative* knowledge, which involves "knowing that," and *procedural* knowledge, which involves "knowing how."
7. Ausubel (1968, 1978) emphasizes that *meaningful learning,* which is learning that is relatable to what we already know, is preferable to *rote learning,* which is arbitrary and verbatim. Only *meaningful* material can be integrated into existing cognitive structure.

Ellis (1990) adds that although Cognitive theory is much more convincing than Behaviorism, it is not able to account satisfactorily for the fact that there are quite a number of regularities in the way in which second-language knowledge is acquired in classroom learning. Although it is important and appropriate to extrapolate from general Cognitive theory when looking at classroom language learning, Ellis feels that second-language learning might be different from other kinds of learning (such as learning history or science) in some important ways. This view is congruent, at least in part, with what Universal Grammar theory is saying about language learning being a specialized kind of competence and not just a subset of general human learning. As with most other theories discussed in this chapter, applications from Cognitive theory must be explored and tested more thoroughly in the years ahead to determine its value in understanding how people become proficient in a second language.

▨ Connectionism: A New Challenge to Rationalist Models of Cognition

The rationalist models described in the last section share a common belief that language is rule-governed behavior and that language learners, therefore, develop complex, internalized rule systems that can be represented symbolically (Gasser 1990). In the past few years, there has been increased interest shown in *connectionist* models of the mind which challenge "traditional symbolic models of cognition" (Gasser, p. 179). Connectionist theorists have attempted to base their models on what is known about the function of the human brain. According to McClelland (1989), the term "connectionist models" was introduced by Feldman (1981) to refer to those models of the mind that describe mental processing by means of connections among very simple processing units. McClelland and other scholars have been interested in determining what kind of processing mechanism the mind really is. Does the human brain process information one step at a time, in a serial or sequential manner, like a conventional computer? Or does it engage in processing information throughout a network of simple processing units that "fire off" simultaneously? Neuroscience indicates that the human brain consists of "some tens of billions of neurons" (McClelland 1989, p. 8) which are available for processing human thought and perception. Neurons are thought to be "relatively sluggish, noisy processing devices, compared to today's computers" (p. 8), yet the mind is capable of recognizing objects or perceiving a complex visual scene in an instant. How are these two facts about mental processing reconciled? McClelland and his colleagues argue that interconnected processing units would have to work in a parallel rather than in a serial manner to achieve such rapid results. Therefore, the mind must be a parallel, rather than a sequential, processor of information.

Theoretical models of mental processing that are based on a parallel view are known as parallel distributed processing (PDP) models, neural models, or connectionist models (McClelland 1989). Connections between simple processing units are thought to have different strengths or "weights." In connectionist models, *learning* consists of adjusting the strengths of connections so that a given "teaching input" eventually results in a desired "output" (Pinker and Prince 1989). That is, connections are either strengthened or weakened in response to regularities in patterns of input that are presented to the system (Gasser 1990). Thus the network of connections is "trained" to make certain associations between inputs and outputs. As Rumelhart and McClelland (1986a) explain, "*knowledge is in the connections* rather than in the units themselves" (p. 132).

Thus connectionist models of the mind do not posit discrete symbols or rules as conceptual or "higher-order" units or sets of units surrounded by a clear boundary; rather, knowledge consists of "fluid patterns of activation across portions of a network" (Gasser 1990, p. 180). Where rationalist models of cognition describe a kind of "central executive" that oversees the general flow of processing, choosing rules or principles to be applied and executing them, connectionist models consider the control of information processing to be distributed among the many parts of the network (Rumelhart and McClelland 1986a, p. 134). As Gasser (1990) explains, "there are no rules to be executed" (p. 181). Larsen-Freeman and Long (1991) add that "the networks control what looks like rule-governed behaviour, but which is simply a reflection of the connections formed on the basis of the relative strengths of various patterns in the input" (p. 250). This perspective of cognition is thus quite different from that of rationalist theories such as Universal Grammar, Monitor theory, or Cognitive theory.

An early example of how a connectionist model might work in language acquisition is described by Rumelhart and McClelland (1986b) and summarized as follows by Pinker and Prince (1989). Rumelhart and McClelland demonstrated that their computerized network model, which had not been programmed with any grammatical rules and had no representations of words, verb stems, suffixes, or conjugation patterns within it, could "learn" to use regular and irregular English past tense verb forms correctly simply by comparing its own version of the past tense forms with the correct versions provided by the "teacher" over an extensive number of trials. The network simply adjusted the strengths of the connections between processing units until the difference between inputs and outputs was sufficiently reduced. The PDP system thus demonstrated rule-like behavior without having any rules. Furthermore, the system exhibited some of the same types of behavior that young children exhibit when learning the verb system of English: First, children use past tense forms (both regular and irregular) correctly; then, as they overgeneralize the *-ed* ending from regular to irregular verbs, they produce incorrect forms like "goed" or "broked"; finally, they work out the rule system and begin to produce both regular and irregular verb forms correctly. The Rumelhart and McClelland demonstration seems to suggest that associationist theories of language acquisition, such as those the behaviorists espoused in the 1950s, might have some merit (Pinker and Prince 1989, p. 183). However, Pinker and Prince take exception to the Rumelhart-McClelland model and point out some empirical flaws, which, in their view, weaken the case of a connectionist account of language behavior. Some of their arguments are summarized in the *Critique* section, below.

Because connectionist models are so new, it is difficult to characterize a connectionist perspective on linguistics or second-language learning at this point other than in very general and tentative terms. One observation that might be made is that in all of the demonstrations of learning with computerized networks discussed earlier and in the next section, the form of the input provided to the computer is very controlled and limited to selected words or short sentences repeated over many trials. Some simulations have used artificial languages for input. Ellis and Schmidt (1997) note that their own use of an artificial language in a connectionist demonstration is "indeed a travesty of natural language," since natural language is far more chaotic in its presentation of data to learners (p. 158). Even when a natural language (such as English or French) is used, its presentation to the network is still far more controlled than in normal language use situations. Thus it is difficult to know how much one might be able to extrapolate from these learning simulations to the real world of second-language learning, even in the controlled environment of the classroom.

A second observation is that many connectionist models have a built-in "back-propagation" capability (Ellis and Schmidt 1997, p. 155) which provides feedback to the network after each learning trial about how close its own output comes to the target output. It is this feedback that is used in adjusting the weights of the connections that result in learning. As Altmann (1997) describes such networks, they cannot learn anything without the equivalent of a teacher and corrective feedback, or "negative evidence." However, as we saw earlier, some studies conducted on the type of feedback available to children learning a first language suggest that negative evidence is not always provided to them when they make grammatical errors. Therefore, many artificial learning networks, dependent as they are on both "positive evidence" (or input) and "negative evidence" (or corrections of error) in order to be successful language learners, do not appear to learn languages the way that children do. (It is still a matter of some debate in the second-language research community whether negative evidence is necessary or useful in second-language acquisition.) More recent connectionist networks have been designed without back-propagation as part of their "architecture"; however, studies using these newer types of networks have led to differing conclusions about how such networks learn (see Marcus 1998, commenting on research using the Elman connectionist model, described in Elman et al. 1996). For a discussion of various types of connectionist models, see Altmann (1997).

Illustration 2.7 summarizes some of the points made in this discussion. For a more thorough treatment of this theory, see the sources cited in this and the following section.

CRITIQUE:

Because input and learning through association plays so crucial a role in the development of knowledge in connectionist models, various scholars have placed this theoretical perspective in the empiricist camp (see, for example, Pinker and Prince 1989; Gasser 1990; Larsen-Freeman and Long 1991). Gasser (1990) points out that some scholars have seen it as a new form of behaviorism. Interestingly, Rumelhart and McClelland (1986a) maintain that PDP models are "quite agnostic about issues of nativism versus empiricism" (p. 139). They suggest that connectionist systems can be viewed from either a nativist or an empiricist world view. The extreme nativist view would suggest that all the interconnections were genetically predetermined, or "wired in," at birth; the extreme empiricist view would hold that there are no predetermined limits on the way the system's network of interconnections might be constituted. A third possibility would be an interactionist perspective, where the nature of the system might be genetically determined but where all the connections could be modified as the person interacted with the environment. Rumelhart and McClelland seem to favor this third perspective and suggest that "there is probably a good deal of genetic specification of neural connection, and there is a good deal of plasticity in the pattern of connectives after birth" (p. 140, note 6). Because many scholars seem to categorize connectionist theory as environmentalist, it has been placed on the left-hand side of the continuum in Illustration 2.2.

As mentioned earlier, various researchers have identified some problems with

Illustration 2.7
Summary: Connectionism
and Parallel Distributed
Processing (Based on
Rumelhart and
McClelland 1986a;
McClelland 1989;
Gasser 1990; Larsen-
Freeman 1991)

Summary: Connectionism and Parallel Distributed Processing

1. Connectionist theory assumes no innate endowment or mechanism specifically pre-programmed for language learning.
2. Learning consists of the strengthening of connections between and among simple processing units in complex neural networks.
3. Cognitive processing is assumed to occur in a parallel and distributed fashion throughout the network rather than in a sequential or serial fashion.
4. Knowledge is in the connections rather than in the processing units themselves.
5. The strength of connections is determined by the relative frequency of patterns in the input.
6. There are no "rules" in connectionist systems, although they exhibit regular or "rule-like" behavior.

PDP models (see, for example, Fodor and Pylyshyn 1988; Lachter and Bever 1988; Pinker and Prince 1989; Marcus 1998). Pinker and Prince argue that "the fact that a computer model behaves intelligently without rules does not show that humans lack rules, any more than a wind-up mouse shows that real mice lack motor programs" (p. 184). In their view, PDP models of language and cognition are incorrect for several reasons. They claim, for example, that the Rumelhart-McClelland model has nothing corresponding to various formal linguistic notions such as *segment* or *string* (relating to phonemes) or to *stem, affix,* or *root* (relating to word formation), making it difficult for the model to distinguish among similar-sounding words. There is also nothing in the model corresponding to constructs such as *regular rule* or *irregular exception*. The authors claim that the model makes wrong predictions about the kinds of rules that would be easy to learn versus those that would be difficult, adding that the computerized model seems to learn bizarre, non-existent rules for forming the past tense as easily as it learns simple, very common rules. Thus it does not seem sensitive to psychologically significant differences between regular and irregular verbs. (See Marcus 1998 for further comments on this problem.)

An additional problem identified by Pinker and Prince relates to the way in which the computerized model begins to make overgeneralization errors in producing past-tense forms. Whereas overgeneralization in the model is triggered by a large influx of regular verb forms into the teaching presentation in stage two, the onset of overgeneralization in children is not associated with changes in the ratio of irregular to regular verb forms in the input. Rather, overgeneralization errors seem to be triggered by some internal changes in the child's language mechanisms. Pinker and Prince believe that "the Rumelhart-McClelland model is an extremely important contribution to our understanding of human language mechanisms" (p. 192) and that the flaws they see in the model provide further insights into how language acquisition occurs.

While some scholars consider PDP models problematic, others see them as representing an interesting alternative view of cognition that is worthy of further exploration (see, for example, Gasser 1990, who has proposed a connectionist framework for second-language acquisition research). Some recent research and scholarly discussions of connectionism include the work of Sokolik (1990) and Sokolik and Smith (1992), who trained a connectionist network to distinguish the gender of French nouns; Ellis and Schmidt (1997), who argue that the acquisition of morphology and syntax in a second language is compatible with the associative learning described by connectionist theory; and Ellis (1998), who maintains that very complex language representations can "emerge" from the interaction of simple learning mechanisms when exposed to complex language data.

Whatever the merits and problems of connectionist accounts of learning might be, this new perspective on cognition presents an interesting challenge to the symbolic/rationalist perspectives that have been dominating our field since the 1960s.

The Role of Individual Learner Factors in Second-Language Learning

Most scholars and practitioners in the field today agree that both the rate and the degree of success of second-language learning is affected by individual learner differences (Ellis 1985). Many also believe that learner factors such as age, aptitude, attitude, motivation, personality, cognitive style, and preferred learning strategies need to be considered in any comprehensive theory of second-language acquisition. Ellis (1985) remarks that SLA researchers may acknowledge the importance of such factors in the eventual attainment of advanced levels of proficiency or in approaches to specific tasks, but research on acquisition orders (or the *route* of SLA) has tended to ignore individual differences or minimize their importance (p. 99). The conventional wisdom, it seems, has been that second-language acquisition theories should attempt to explain how "the learner" develops competence, as though learners were a relatively homogeneous lot. This assumption, however, is being challenged as more and more scholars recognize that differences among people might matter a great deal more than we had once thought.

In recent years, various publications have dealt with the importance of individual learner factors in language learning (see, for example, McLaughlin 1983, 1987; Birckbichler 1984; Ellis 1985, 1990; Brown 1987; Wenden and Rubin 1987; O'Malley and Chamot 1989; Stevick 1989; Tarone and Yule 1989; Galloway and Labarca 1990; and Oxford 1990). Studies of learner characteristics have looked at how various kinds of factors might affect "success" with language learning, as well as learners' approaches to different language learning tasks and students' attitudes toward specific learning environments and situations.

In some of the earlier research on learner characteristics (Naiman, Frohlich, and Stern 1975; Rubin 1975; Stern 1975), investigators were interested in identifying what "good" language learners did or what types of characteristics they had. The intention was to see if some of these characteristics and strategies could be taught to learners who were not so successful. But as Stevick (1989) points out, the search for one definitive set of characteristics that would identify "good" learners from "poor" ones may have begun with a faulty premise. Stevick conducted interviews with a number of language learners who had achieved superior levels of proficiency in a variety of languages. He had hoped to identify how they were alike so that we might "teach their secrets to our students" (p. xi). As he began to analyze his interview data, however, he found that successful learners were even more different from one another than he had expected. It seems that even "good learners" are a rather heterogeneous lot!

Though perhaps disappointing from the point of view of the researcher interested in identifying a formula for "success," Stevick's findings are also quite positive, in that "many of the things [successful learners] were describing fitted well with one or another abstract, theoretical concept in the field" (Stevick 1989, p. xi). Although no one theoretical model of second-language acquisition was unambiguously supported, each model was confirmed in some ways by the interview data he collected.

Galloway and Labarca (1990) have provided an excellent review of recent literature about the host of learner factors that should be considered in any theoretical or practical discussion of second-language learning. In their introduction, the authors note that educators often feel challenged, if not irritated, by differences, irregularities, or change. Dealing with individual differences in the classroom might seem a daunting problem for many teachers, who face multiple classes (with multiple preparations) every day with 20 or 30 students in each class. Yet most everyone agrees, at least in principle, that students must be treated as individual *persons* who have differing needs, styles, and preferences.

What are some of the specific ways in which learners differ? Galloway and Labarca (1990) discuss learner differences in several categories. First, they contend that people sense things differently, responding to the physical environment around them (time of day, degree of comfort, degree of physical activity, amount of light, etc.) in diverse ways. People also tend to learn best through one or a combination of sensory modalities (through the ears, through the eyes, through touch, through movement). It follows that methodological decisions that limit use of a preferred modality will be ill-suited to a significant subset of learners.

For example, if the method prescribes that input to the learners will be primarily auditory in the beginning phases of instruction, learners who depend on visual information may be disadvantaged. Teachers need to consider such modality preferences and use a multi-sensory approach, appealing to all types of learner preferences. "What is called for is not a teaching method, but a teaching repertoire" (Galloway and Labarca 1990, p. 115).

A second way in which learners differ is in their social preferences. Some people prefer learning with others, interacting in small groups or engaging in competitive activities. Others may prefer learning alone and are energized by opportunities to read or do individual projects.

A third variable is the way in which learners tend to process information mentally. Various cognitive style differences have been explored in the literature. Some learning style dimensions include *field independence* (or the degree to which one perceives things globally or analytically), *impulsiveness/reflectiveness* (relating to the speed with which one makes decisions), *systematicness/intuitiveness* (or the preference for following a sequential plan vs. developing one's ideas freely and holistically), *tolerance of ambiguity* (relating to the comfort or lack of comfort one feels in the face of uncertainty), and *flexibility/inflexibility* (relating to the ability to think of many alternative solutions vs. the tendency to focus on one "right" answer). For a review of these and other cognitive style dimensions, see Abraham (1978), Claxton and Ralston (1978), and Birckbichler (1984).

Galloway and Labarca (1990) and Oxford (1990), as well as other researchers studying learner factors, also point out that people adopt different learning strategies as they approach particular tasks. "Learner strategies are task-specific tactics or techniques, observable or nonobservable, that an individual uses to comprehend, store, retrieve, and use information or to plan, regulate, or assess learning" (Galloway and Labarca 1990, p. 141). Many learners are not aware of the strategies that they use to approach a task and would profit, perhaps, from making them explicit. Hosenfeld (1979) did a fascinating study with a high school learner named Cindy who became aware, through strategy training, of her own approach to reading in French as well as to the approach of another student she was studying as a model of a successful reader. After eight sessions with the researcher, thinking aloud while she read and talking about her strategy use, Cindy exhibited some new and effective reading strategies that she had not used previously. Readers interested in learning more about the types of strategies learners typically use should consult such sources as Oxford and Ehrman (1989), O'Malley and Chamot (1990), Oxford (1990), and the other sources mentioned above.

The professional literature of the last three decades is replete with information about learner styles, strategies, and personality differences. Yet how does one accommodate these differences in the second-language classroom? For many practitioners, the very idea of individualizing one's instruction "evokes the defeating image of one-on-one instruction guided by 150 variations on a lesson plan" (Galloway and Labarca 1990, p. 129). Rather than start by trying to identify and meet the needs of all learners in the classroom simultaneously, Galloway and Labarca suggest that we begin by attending to *some* of the needs of *all* of our learners. They advocate "learner-friendly" environments where the teacher makes a concerted effort to arrange instruction so that it is meaningful for learners and fosters their independence. By helping students to become aware of their own strategies and learning preferences, as well as guiding them expertly to become effective and autonomous learners as they approach various learning tasks, teachers can go a long way toward accommodating individual learner needs more effectively.

Relating Theory to Practice: Some Considerations

This chapter has presented a range of theoretical viewpoints about how adults learn second languages. The sample of theories is not meant to be exhaustive, but rather represents differing viewpoints along the rationalist-empiricist continuum. In reviewing various theories of language learning such as these, teachers can become familiar with some of the premises underlying various approaches to language teaching methodology that have been proposed across the years. In addition, Ellis (1997) suggests that SLA theory and research can be a useful resource for teachers as they articulate their own personal theories of language teaching.

One way to relate theory to practice is to consider some of the elements of language teaching that are common to a variety of methods and examine them in the light of different theoretical perspectives. One might then begin to see that the same teaching technique or instructional element can be motivated by different underlying theoretical premises. Take, for example, the role of *practice* in language learning. For the behaviorist, practice is essential because learners need to form new habits (stimulus-response associations) in the second language; this is achieved through massive repetition so that "overlearning" of the new material will occur. For the cognitive theorist, practice is essential for a somewhat different reason: It is needed in order to move from "controlled" to "automatic" processing. Schmidt (1992), for example, discusses the development of language fluency in terms of this controlled/automatic continuum:

> *Practice seems to be the necessary condition for fluency in an L2, and this is given a theoretical justification in models of automatization (p. 362).*

This view of the necessity of practice contrasts with Krashen's (1982) beliefs about the need for practice in speaking:

> *The Input Hypothesis makes a claim that may seem quite remarkable to some people—we acquire spoken fluency* not *by practicing talking but by understanding input, by listening and reading. It is, in fact, theoretically possible to acquire language without ever talking (Krashen 1982, p. 60).*

It is important to add, however, that Krashen does allow for a role for speaking (or "output") in that learners' participation in conversations with native speakers can help students obtain more comprehensible input. He also sees a role for output in language *learning,* "although even here it is not necessary" (p. 61). Thus in three different theoretical frameworks, the same essential element of language teaching is cast in a somewhat different light, and a different rationale for the use of that element is given.

Another element of language teaching that has been open to much debate is the role of *corrective feedback* (or "negative evidence") in language acquisition. From a behaviorist perspective, negative evidence is essential for learning so that the wrong language habits are not formed. For those who believe that Universal Grammar has an important role to play in second-language acquisition, "positive evidence" (or input) is far more important in language learning, while negative evidence may be of little use, at least where "core grammar" is concerned. For Krashen, error correction is useful only for "learning" but is of little or no use for "acquisition" (Krashen 1982, p. 117). Cognitive theory might see an important role for feedback, in that learners' hypotheses need to be shaped by both positive and negative evidence in order for "restructuring" to occur. As we have seen in the discussion of connectionist models of language learning, many of the computer models provide a "feedback" mechanism that compares the output that the network produces to the previously stored "correct" output so that the connection strengths can be properly adjusted for learning. Again, a common element in language teaching may be considered necessary or unnecessary, depending on one's theoretical viewpoint.

As we saw in the last part of the chapter, the theoretical models and empirical studies that teachers evaluate need to be considered as well in the light of the important consideration of learner differences. Some models of SLA have traditionally minimized the role of individual differences. According to Gass and Selinker (1994), "[t]he immediate negative reaction linguists have toward differences in language abilities in a native language has presumably also affected second language scholars trained in linguistics" (p. 234). They contend that behaviorists and psycholinguists have not wanted to consider such factors as motivation or affect either, and many researchers in SLA and related fields have been skeptical about instruments used in measuring such characteristics as aptitude, motivation, attitude, field independence, ambiguity tolerance, personality differences, and the like. Nevertheless, many teachers and specialists in the field of foreign and second-language teaching believe that individual differences have an important role to play in language learning. This may be an area where SLA researchers and language teachers have a different perspective on teaching practice. While experimental research often does not build individual difference factors into study designs, but treats them as part of "error variance," teachers in classrooms must deal with individual differences on a daily basis.

Ellis (1997) discusses how the relationship between SLA research and language pedagogy has been somewhat problematic since the field of SLA began to develop a number of years ago. He points out that researchers in second-language acquisition have often been reluctant to apply their research results directly to language pedagogy, particularly as the field of SLA is still in its infancy and "there are still few certainties" (p. 70). This caution makes sense particularly when research studies are conducted under specific conditions that do not have much congruence with those in one's own classroom, or when study designs are limited in a variety of ways or results are not replicated.

Ellis also discusses the fact that SLA researchers and language teaching practitioners often have different issues that concern them and different types of discourse for discussing those issues. He argues that "what has been missing in SLA is an educational perspective" (p. 71), where issues that are addressed by research have more specific relevance to what is of concern to teachers and arise from issues that teachers themselves consider important. Although there has been an increasing interest in classroom-based research in SLA, Ellis points out that much of it is not actually conducted in classrooms or is not always reflective of problems that teachers themselves find interesting or important. He adds that it is up to teachers to appraise the value of SLA research based on their own experience. Thus, instead of accepting theoretical frameworks or empirical findings as authoritarian or prescriptive in nature, practitioners and applied linguists can "draw on SLA research and theory to initiate, tentatively or confidently, various pedagogic proposals" (p. 76). They can also evaluate their own teaching in light of what they know about language learning from research, or examine particular pedagogical practices in terms of how they are or are not congruent with particular theories of language acquisition with which they are familiar.

Summary: On Learning a Language

In this chapter, various models of second-language acquisition have been selected for discussion from among the many theoretical viewpoints that have been advanced in the field in recent years. The highlights of five theoretical perspectives, chosen to represent different points along the rationalist-empiricist continuum, were reviewed and summarized. Earlier in the chapter, the issue of individual learner factors and their role in language learning and instruction was briefly discussed. As we consider the question: "How do adults become proficient in a second language?", the only certainty is that the question is tremendously complex. Yet the strides that we are making as a profession to answer that question have been encouraging, as research into SLA is flourishing, and the insights we have gained into the nature of the learning process bring promise for the continued improvement of our teaching.

In the next chapter, a set of hypothesized principles of instruction that are derived from concepts in Chapters 1 and 2 will be presented and discussed. We will then consider various approaches to teaching that have been prevalent in the professional literature over the years with a view to understanding their underlying assumptions and essential characteristics. It is hoped that this review of principles, premises, and priorities will enable second-language teachers to articulate more clearly their own convictions about language learning and teaching, and evaluate the many options that are available to them as they plan instruction that is responsive to the needs of their students.

NOTE: I would like to thank my colleague Peter Golato for sharing some of his thoughts on SLA theory and helping me identify useful bibliographic sources as I prepared the revision of this chapter. His comments on the draft have been very much appreciated. I would also like to thank Robert Terry who provided feedback on this and other chapter drafts for this edition. Any errors and shortcomings are, of course, my own responsibility.

Activities for Review and Discussion

1. Go back to Illustration 2.1 and answer the questions in the Discussion Guide to assess some of your own beliefs about second-language learning theory. Then, in small groups, compare and discuss your answers.
2. For each of your answers in the Discussion Guide in Illustration 2.1, identify

the theoretical approach in this chapter with which your viewpoint is compatible. (Some views may be compatible with more than one theory.) Then analyze your own answers to the questionnaire to see if you currently favor one theoretical viewpoint over others. Do you lean toward the empiricist or the rationalist end of the continuum shown in Illustration 2.2?

3. Choose three theoretical approaches described in this chapter and review the main premises associated with each one. (You may want to consult the summary tables at the end of each description.) Then, for each of the three theoretical points of view, make a list of teaching practices that you think would be compatible with that approach. Compare your three lists. Are there practices that would be compatible with all three theories? Are there practices that would be compatible with only one? Explain your answer briefly.

4. Think about the way you approached the learning of a second language, either on your own or in a formal classroom setting. What theoretical approach described in this chapter best characterizes your learning experience? Were there aspects of that learning experience you would like to change if you were to begin the study of a new language? Explain your answer briefly.

5. Many second-language educators believe that learner characteristics play an important role in language learning. How might you deal with individual differences in your classroom? What are some practical ways in which you might accommodate learner differences in preferred learning style, personality, or strategy use?

References: Chapter 2

Abraham, Roberta. "The Nature of Cognitive Style and Its Importance to the Foreign Language Teacher." (1978) [ED 168 358].

Altmann, Gerry T. M. *The Ascent of Babel: An Exploration of Language, Mind, and Understanding.* Oxford: Oxford University Press, 1997.

Anderson, J. *Cognitive Psychology and its Implications.* San Francisco: Freeman, 1980.

———. *Cognitive Psychology and its Implications.* 4th ed. New York: Freeman, 1995.

Ausubel, David. *Educational Psychology: A Cognitive View.* New York: Holt, Rinehart, and Winston, 1968.

Ausubel, David P., Joseph D. Novak, and Helen Hanesian. *Educational Psychology: A Cognitive View,* 2nd edition. New York: Holt, Rinehart, and Winston, 1978.

Beedham, Christopher. *German Linguistics: An Introduction.* Munich: Iudicium, 1995.

Birckbichler, Diane W. "The Challenge of Proficiency: Student Characteristics." Pp. 47–78 in G. A. Jarvis, ed., *The Challenge for Excellence in Foreign Language Education.* Reports of the Northeast Conference on the Teaching of Foreign Languages. Middlebury, VT: Northeast Conference, 1984.

———., ed. *New Perspectives and New Directions in Foreign Language Education.* The ACTFL Foreign Language Education Series. Lincolnwood, IL: National Textbook Company, 1990.

Bley-Vroman, Robert. "What Is the Logical Problem of Foreign Language Learning?" Chapter 2 (pp. 41–68) in Susan Gass and Jacquelyn Schachter, eds., *Linguistic Perspectives on Second Language Acquisition.* Cambridge: Cambridge University Press, 1989.

Bloomfield, Leonard. *Outline Guide for the Practical Study of Foreign Languages.* Baltimore: Linguistic Society of America, 1942.

Born, Warren C., ed. *The Foreign Language Teacher in Today's Classroom Environment.* Reports of the Northeast Conference on the Teaching of Foreign Languages. Middlebury, VT: Northeast Conference, 1979.

Brown, H. Douglas. *Principles of Language Learning and Teaching,* 2nd ed. Englewood Cliffs, NJ: Prentice Hall, 1987. 3rd edition, 1994.

Brown, Roger. *A First Language: The Early Stages.* Cambridge, MA: Harvard University Press, 1973.

Brown, Roger and C. Hanlon. "Derivational Complexity and Order of Acquisition in Child Speech," in J. Hayes, ed., *Cognition and the Development of Language.* New York: John Wiley and Sons, 1970.

Chastain, Kenneth. *Developing Second Language Skills: Theory to Practice,* 2nd ed. Chicago: Rand McNally, 1976.

Chomsky, Noam. *Syntactic Structures.* The Hague, The Netherlands: Mouton and Company, 1957.

———. "A Review of B. F. Skinner's *Verbal Behavior.*" *Language* 35 (1959): 26–58.

———. *Aspects of the Theory of Syntax.* Cambridge, MA: M. I. T. Press, 1965.

Claxton, Charles S. and Y. Ralston. *Learning Styles: Their Impact on Teaching and Administration.* AAHE-ERIC/Higher Education Research Report No. 10 (1978). [ED 167 065].

Cook, Vivian. *Second Language Learning and Language Teaching,* 2nd ed. London: Arnold, 1996.

Diller, Karl Conrad. *The Language Teaching Controversy.* Rowley, MA: Newbury House, 1978.

Ellis, Nick C. "Emergentism, Connectionism and Language Learning." *Language Learning* 48, iv (1998): 631–64.

Ellis, Nick C. and Richard Schmidt. "Morphology and Longer Distance Dependencies: Laboratory Research Illuminating the A in SLA." *Studies in Second Language Acquisition* 19 (1997): 145–71.

Ellis, Rod. *Understanding Second Language Acquisition.* Oxford: Oxford University Press, 1985.

———. *Second Language Acquisition in Context.* Englewood Cliffs, NJ: Prentice Hall, 1987.

———. *Instructed Second Language Acquisition.* Oxford: Basil Blackwell, 1990.

———. "SLA and Language Pedagogy: An Educational Perspective." *Studies in Second Language Acquisition* 19, i (1997): 69–92.

Feldman, J. A. "A Connectionist Model of Visual Memory," in G. E. Hinton and J. A. Anderson, eds., *Parallel Models of Associative Memory.* Hillsdale, NJ: Lawrence Erlbaum Associates, 1981.

Fodor, J. A. and Z. W. Pylyshyn. "Connectionism and Cognitive Architecture: A Critical Analysis." *Cognition* 28 (1988): 3–71.

Galloway, Vicki and Angela Labarca. "From Student to Learner: Style, Process, and Strategy." Chapter 4 in D. Birckbichler, ed., *New Perspectives and New Directions in Foreign Language Education.* The ACTFL Foreign Language Education Series. Lincolnwood, IL: National Textbook Company, 1990.

Gass, Susan M. and Larry Selinker. *Second Language Acquisition: An Introductory Course.* Hillsdale, NJ: Lawrence Erlbaum Associates, 1994.

Gasser, Michael. "Connectionism and Universals of Second Language Acquisition." *Studies in Second Language Acquisition* 12 (1990): 179–99.

Grittner, Frank M. "Bandwagons Revisited: A Perspective on Movements in Foreign Language Education." Chapter 1 (pp. 9–43) in D. Birckbichler, ed., *New Perspectives and New Directions in Foreign Language Education.* The ACTFL Foreign Language Education Series. Lincolnwood, IL: National Textbook Company, 1990.

Hilgard, Ernest R. *Introduction to Psychology,* 3rd ed. New York: Harcourt, Brace and World, Inc., 1962.

Hinton, G. E. and J. A. Anderson, eds. *Parallel Models of Associative Memory.* Hillsdale, NJ: Lawrence Erlbaum Associates, 1981.

Hosenfeld, Carol. "Cindy: A Learner in Today's Foreign Language Classroom." In W. Born, ed., *The Foreign Language Teacher in Today's Classroom Environment.* Reports of the Northeast Conference on the Teaching of Foreign Languages. Middlebury, VT: Northeast Conference, 1979.

Jarvis, G. A., ed. *The Challenge for Excellence in Foreign Language Education.* Reports of the Northeast Conference on the Teaching of Foreign Languages. Middlebury, VT: Northeast Conference, 1984.

Krashen, Stephen. *Principles and Practice in Second Language Acquisition.* New York: Pergamon Press, 1982.

Lachter, J. and T. Bever. "The Relationship Between Linguistic Structure and Associative Theories of Language Learning: A Constructive Critique of Some Connectionist Learning Models." *Cognition* 28 (1988): 195–247.

Larsen-Freeman, Diane. "Second Language Acquisition Research: Staking Out the Territory." *TESOL Quarterly* 25, ii (Summer 1991):315–50.

Larsen-Freeman, Diane and Michael H. Long. *An Introduction to Second Language Acquisition Research.* White Plains, NY: Longman, 1991.

Lennenberg, Eric. *Biological Foundations of Language.* New York: John Wiley, 1967.

Marcus, Gary F. "Can Connectionism Save Constructivism?" *Cognition* 66 (1998): 153–82.

McClelland, James L. "Parallel Distributed Processing: Implications for Cognition and Development." Chapter 2 (pp. 8–45) in R. G. M. Morris, ed., *Parallel Distributed Processing: Implications for Psychology and Neurobiology.* Oxford: Clarendon Press, 1989.

McClelland, James L., D. E. Rumelhart, and the PDP Group, eds. *Parallel Distributed Processing: Explorations in the Microstructure of Cognition. Volume 2: Psychological and Biological Models.* Cambridge, MA: M. I. T. Press, 1986.

McLaughlin, Barry. *Second-Language Acquisition in Childhood. Volume I: Preschool Children.* Hillsdale, NY: Lawrence Erlbaum Associates, 1984.

————. *Theories of Second-Language Learning.* London: Edward Arnold, 1987.

————. "Restructuring." *Applied Linguistics* 11, ii (1990): 113–28.

McLaughlin, Barry., T. Rossman, and B. McLeod. "Second-Language Learning: An Information-Processing Perspective." *Language Learning* 33 (1983): 135–58.

McNeill, David. *Developmental Psycholinguistics.* In F. Smith and G. Miller, eds., *The Genesis of Language: A Psycholinguistic Approach.* Cambridge, MA: M. I. T. Press, 1966.

Mitchell, Rosamund and Florence Myles. *Second Language Learning Theories.* London: Arnold, 1998.

Morris, R. G. M., ed. *Parallel Distributed Processing: Implications for Psychology and Neurobiology.* Oxford: Clarendon Press, 1989.

Munsell, Paul and Thomas Carr. "Monitoring the Monitor: A Review of *Second-Language Acquisition and Second Language Learning." Language Learning* 31 (1981):493–502.

Naiman, N., Maria Frohlich, and H. H. Stern. *The Good Language Learner.* Toronto: Ontario Institute for Studies in Education, 1975.

O'Malley, J. Michael and Anna Uhl Chamot. *Learning Strategies in Second-Language Acquisition.* Cambridge: Cambridge University Press, 1990.

Oxford, Rebecca L. *Language Learning Strategies: What Every Teacher Should Know.* Rowley, MA: Newbury House, 1990.

Oxford, Rebecca and Madeleine Ehrman. "Psychological Type and Adult Language Learning Strategies: A Pilot Study." *Journal of Psychological Type* 16 (1989): 22–32.

Pinker, Steven. *The Language Instinct: How the Mind Creates Language.* New York: William Morrow, 1994.

Pinker, S. and A. Prince. "Rules and Connections in Human Language." Chapter 9 (pp. 182–99) in R. G. M. Morris, ed., *Parallel Distributed Processing: Implications for Psychology and Neurobiology.* Oxford: Clarendon Press, 1989.

Rubin, Joan. "What the 'Good Language Learner' Can Teach Us." *TESOL Quarterly* 9 (1975): 41–51.

Rumelhart, D. E. and J. L. McClelland. "PDP Models and General Issues in Cognitive Science." Chapter 4 (pp. 110–149) in D. E. Rumelhart, J. L. McClelland, and the PDP Research Group, eds., *Parallel Distributed Processing: Explorations in the Microstructure of Cognition. Volume I: Foundations.* Cambridge, MA: The M. I. T. Press, 1986a.

————. "On Learning the Past Tenses of English Verbs." Chapter 18 (pp. 216–71) in J. L. McClelland, D. E. Rumelhart, and the PDP Group, eds., *Parallel Distributed Processing: Explorations in the Microstructure of Cognition. Volume 2: Psychological and Biological Models.* Cambridge, MA: M. I. T. Press, 1986b.

Schmidt, Richard. "Psychological Mechanisms Underlying Second Language Fluency." *Studies in Second Language Acquisition* 14 (1992): 357–85.

Schneider, W. and R. M. Shiffrin. "Controlled and Automatic Processing. I: Detection, Search, and Attention." *Psychological Review* 84 (1977): 1–64.

Shiffrin, R. M. and W. Schneider. "Controlled and Automatic Human Information Processing. II: Perceptual Learning, Automatic Attending, and a General Theory." *Psychological Review* 84 (1977): 127–90.

Skinner, B. F. *Verbal Behavior.* New York: Appleton-Century-Crofts, 1957.

Smith, Frank and George Miller, eds. *The Genesis of Language: A Psycholinguistic Approach.* Cambridge, MA: M. I. T. Press, 1966.

Sokolik, M. E. "Learning Without Rules: PDP and a Resolution of the Adult Language Learning Paradox." *TESOL Quarterly* 24, iv (1990): 685–96.

Sokolik, M. E. and Michael E. Smith. "Assignment of Gender to French Nouns in Primary and Secondary Language: A Connectionist Model." *Second Language Research* 8, i (1992): 39–58.

Spolsky, Bernard. *Conditions for Second Language Learning.* Oxford: Oxford University Press, 1989.

Stern, H. H. "What Can We Learn from the Good Language Learner?" *The Canadian Modern Language Review* 31 (1975): 304–18.

Stevick, Earl. *Memory, Meaning, and Method: Some Psychological Perspectives on Language Learning.* Rowley, MA: Newbury House, 1976.

———. *Success With Foreign Languages: Seven Who Achieved it and What Worked for Them.* Englewood Cliffs, NJ: Prentice Hall, 1989.

Tarone, Elaine. "Systematicity and Attention in Interlanguage." *Language Learning* 32 (1982): 69–84.

———. "On the Variability of Interlanguage Systems." *Applied Linguistics* 4 (1983): 142–63.

———. "Methodologies for Studying Variability in Second Language Acquisition." Pp. 35–46 in R. Ellis, ed., *Second Language Acquisition in Context.* Englewood Cliffs, NJ: Prentice Hall, 1987.

Tarone, Elaine and George Yule. *Focus on the Language Learner.* Oxford: Oxford University Press, 1989.

Terrell, Tracy D. "A Natural Approach to Second Language Acquisition and Learning." *Modern Language Journal* 61 (1977): 325–37.

———. "The Natural Approach to Language Teaching: An Update." *Modern Language Journal* 66 (1982): 121–32.

Towell, Richard and Roger Hawkins. *Approaches to Second Language Acquisition.* Clevedon: Multilingual Matters, 1994.

Wardhaugh, Ronald. *The Contexts of Language.* Rowley, MA: Newbury House, 1976.

Wenden, Anita and Joan Rubin. *Learner Strategies in Language Learning.* Englewood Cliffs, NJ: Prentice Hall, 1987.

Wesche, Marjorie Bingham. "Input and Interaction in Second Language Acquisition." Chapter 10 (pp. 219–249) in C. Galloway and B. Richards, eds., *Input and Interaction in Language Acquisition.* Cambridge: Cambridge University Press, 1994.

3 THREE
On Teaching a Language: Principles and Priorities in Methodology

Once, in the throes of the audiolingual revolution, we "knew the truth." Today, I am working with only a set of working hypotheses for myself as a foreign language teacher (Strasheim 1976, p. 42).

For many years, it seemed that the language teaching profession was engaged in a series of "revolutions," most of which had their origins in an attempt to reach some consensus about the best way—"the one true way" (Strasheim 1976)—to teach a foreign language. Yet despite a few short-lived rallies around a common flag, our professional history has been marked more often by controversy than by consensus. It is true that some of the major shifts in perspective over the years have led to positive and long-lasting change. Yet Grittner (1990) voices concern about the unfortunate recurrence throughout our history of "evangelistic movements that suddenly emerge, capture the attention of many teachers, cause an upheaval in methods and materials, and then—just as suddenly—fade from view" (p. 9). He speaks of these revolutionary movements as "bandwagons" that demand a fervent commitment from their followers to a single theory of teaching and that reject all other methods or approaches as ineffectual and outmoded (p. 10). The common premise behind the search for a unitary approach to learning and teaching seems to be that there exists an ideal method which, once discovered, will unlock the door to language proficiency for all learners and will make the learning process swift and effortless.

Traditionally, language practitioners in search of the "one true way" have grouped themselves along the same empiricist/rationalist continuum that was reviewed in the last chapter, aligning themselves more or less with their counterparts in theoretical linguistics (Chomsky 1965; Diller 1978). For methodologists, the basic distinction between the two ends of the continuum has been one of philosophy. Empiricists believed that language was an oral phenomenon consisting of concrete "signs" that could be described (Diller 1978). Empiricist methodologies treated language learning as habit formation through mimicry, memorization, and drilling. Rationalists saw language not as structure, but as rule-governed

creativity (Chomsky 1965). Rationalist methodologies emphasized meaningfulness and understanding of psychologically real rules of grammar (Diller 1978).

Swaffar, Arens, and Morgan (1982), following Diller, characterize the *rational-
ist/process* approach as one in which high priority is placed on identifying form as
meaningful, using problem-solving strategies. The *empiricist/skills* approach, by
contrast, places highest priority on reproduction of correct forms.

This controversy over methodological approaches is not just a phenomenon of
the twentieth century. Kelly (1976) has described a gradual evolution of language
teaching over 25 centuries that is characterized by frequent shifts in focus, purpose, and practice. Interestingly enough, some of the quarrels of the past have a
familiar ring. Kibbee (1987, 1989) cites evidence, for example, of a heated debate
dating from the sixteenth century about the way in which oral skills ought to be
taught. Claude de Sainliens, in his work entitled *The Frenche Littelton. A most Easie,
Perfect, and Absolute way to learne the frenche tongue,* published in 1576, stated that
one should not entangle students in rules, but allow them to practice first through
dialogue memorization:

> *If the Reader meaneth to learne our tongue within a short space, he must not
> entangle himselfe at the firste brunte with the rules of the pronunciation set (for a
> purpose) at the latter ende of this booke, but take in hande these Dialogues: and
> as the occasion requireth, he shall examine the rules, applying their use unto his
> purpose . . . (de Sainliens 1576, cited in Kibbee 1987, 1989).*

Jacques Bellot attacks this point of view in his *French Method* of 1588:

> *There bee some holding this opinion, that the most expedient, & certaine way to
> attaine to the knowledge of tongues is to learne them without any observation of
> rules: But cleane the contrary I doe thinke that he which is instructed in any
> tongue what so ever by the onely roate, is like unto the Byrd in a cage, which
> speaketh nothing but that which is taught unto him, and (which is much worse)
> not understanding that which he sayth, because he is voyde of all foundation of
> good and certaine doctrine . . . (Bellot 1588, pp. 2–3, cited in Kibbee 1987,
> 1989).*

Four hundred years later, the essential argument has not greatly changed. By
the last decades of the twentieth century, theorists and practitioners had trans-
posed the debate to the modern context, where methodologists steeped in cognitive psychology or transformational grammar argued with those espousing
behaviorism in a vain effort to convince one another that they were right about
language teaching. One of the more recent versions of the age-old debate has
erupted in the controversy surrounding the overt teaching of grammar and the
use of error correction in language instruction. In this instance, "natural" approaches to language learning, where the teaching of grammatical rules and the
use of error correction techniques are largely discouraged in the classroom, are opposed to more "cognitive" orientations toward methodology, which maintain
that students must understand the basic rule system underlying the new language
and receive corrective feedback in order to improve. Many language educators
who have witnessed these various versions of the same arguments over the years

have become somewhat weary of the debate, and are cautious in their enthusiasm for any new trends that seem like old "bandwagons" in disguise. Some have shunned "revolutions" altogether and have decided instead to adopt an "eclectic" approach (Warriner 1980; Brown 1984). And with eclecticism comes a new kind of diversity within the profession, at least on the issue of methodology.

It is not surprising that in the 1980s, many practitioners and foreign language educators still felt the need to reach some sort of consensus about language teaching, but were unsure about how this could be accomplished. The effort to establish uniform goals and standards for language proficiency following the Carter Presidential Commission on Language and International Studies in 1979 was a manifestation of this need for consensus. As was pointed out in Chapter 1, one result of this effort—the development of the *ACTFL Proficiency Guidelines*—sparked a great deal of interest within the language teaching community. But rather than search for consensus about teaching methodology, this project attempted to reach consensus about describing and measuring language abilities, building on the work done previously in language testing by the government language schools. This shift from methodology to measurement questions marked a significant change in direction for the profession. The most recent effort at consensus building has been the development of the *Standards for Foreign Language Learning,* described in Chapter 1, which outline five major content goal areas for language study in grades K–16. Just as in the case of the *ACTFL Proficiency Guidelines,* there are no methodological prescriptions in the *Standards* and no implications that one particular methodology is best for all learners. Instead of searching for one definitive approach to teaching, we have begun looking for some "organizing principle" (Higgs 1984) that can facilitate communication about the nature of language proficiency, and thus about the development of goals and objectives for language teaching.

In the first two editions of this book, I chose the concept of *proficiency,* as defined in the *ACTFL Proficiency Guidelines,* as the organizing principle for discussing issues related to language teaching. This general concept continues to provide a framework for the third edition, broadened somewhat by consideration of the goals outlined in the *Standards* and the potential contributions of new technologies to language teaching. As was emphasized in Chapter 1, neither the *Guidelines* nor the *Standards* constitute a curricular model or a methodological prescription in and of themselves. However, it is certainly possible to derive various implications from them for instruction (Galloway 1987). Because the *Guidelines* describe language abilities in a hierarchical fashion, they can provide insights for organizing instruction. First, practitioners can use the broad level definitions to evaluate the suitability of their current curricular goals and course objectives for learners in their classrooms. Thus a teacher whose students are currently at the Novice level in a given skill area will choose objectives, activities, and materials that differ substantially from those they might choose for students at the Advanced level. Secondly, by understanding what *general* kinds of abilities lie at each level of proficiency, teachers can plan to shift the emphasis of instruction as students progress to allow for the development of requisite skills. In this way, the *Guidelines* can serve as an overall frame of reference within which pedagogical choices can be made.

The newly developed *Standards for Foreign Language Learning* (1996, 1999) can also be helpful as a frame of reference for teachers. As we saw in Chapter 1, the *Standards* articulate general goals for language study that emphasize the potential benefits of learning another language, not just as an end in itself, but as a gateway to understanding other cultures and accessing information in other disciplines. The ability to use language skills for these purposes will develop over time, and judgments about the appropriateness of curricular objectives, classroom activities, and materials will need to be made on the basis of students' overall linguistic and communicative proficiency in both comprehension and productive skills. Thus a general understanding of how language proficiency develops will be essential in creating a workable *Standards*-based curriculum.

There is no doubt that new technologies will also play an important role in language teaching in the twenty-first century. Indeed, the use of technology in foreign language learning has constituted another important revolutionary movement in our discipline in the last half of the twentieth century. Although it has clearly not been a methodological revolution, technological innovation has played an important role in the recent history of language teaching and is bound to have a profound effect on the way that languages are taught in the future. Beginning with the introduction of filmstrips, audiotapes, and language laboratories in "direct method" and "audiolingual" classrooms over forty years ago, technological innovation has moved from the increased use of cassette tapes, videotapes, and overhead projectors and cameras in the past several decades to the introduction of CD-ROMs and the Internet in the 1990s. The possibilities for computer-enhanced language teaching have most recently been explored in distance education programs as well as in the use of local area networks, computer-assisted reading programs, and Web-based classroom activities (see, for example, Nielsen and Hoffman 1996; Bush 1997; Muyskens 1997; Lyman-Hagger and Burnett 1999). Though the use of technology is nothing new in foreign language teaching, its exact role in the curriculum is still being assessed and questioned, particularly in light of the rapidly changing nature of technological aids to instruction. Rather than seeing technology as just another ancillary to be added to our already overladen arsenal of teaching devices, we need to evaluate its potential for enhancing classroom learning as well as for facilitating student-centered, independent learning outside the classroom. In using technological aids and computer-mediated materials in instruction, we also need to bear in mind the level of proficiency of our students and their ability to benefit from the materials that can be made available to them. The use of authentic materials, including those accessible via the Internet, is discussed in more detail in a later section of this chapter and in subsequent chapters.

Orienting Instruction toward Proficiency

If the proficiency level definitions do indeed describe a global developmental progression in language skills, what kinds of implications for instruction might one derive from examining them? The statements below represent my own attempt to identify some guiding principles for organizing and planning instruction in a second language. These principles apply to instruction at all levels of proficiency, from Novice to Superior, and are meant to be flexible enough to relate to varying needs and purposes for study. For example, if students are attempting to learn the language well enough to use it in traveling, exposure to a variety of situations likely to be encountered in the target culture will be necessary. Students will need practice in accomplishing everyday tasks associated with travel and will benefit from understanding some basic facts about life in the target culture. The ability to get their meaning across will be primary, but students will also profit from some practice with language forms to enhance their comprehensibility, as well as their ability to comprehend others. When the students' ultimate, long-range goal is to develop proficiency at the higher levels on the scale, the same principles will hold, but specific objectives and/or criteria for meeting those objectives might change. In order to be rated "Advanced" in oral proficiency, for example, students will need to be able to use the language in a variety of contexts with considerable flexibility and creativity. They will need to communicate with a reasonable degree of precision and coherence. In order to accomplish diverse tasks related to living and working in the culture, they will have to be able to handle a wide range of situations with confidence, showing sensitivity to cultural norms and customs.

The five principles given below outline general characteristics of a classroom environment that I believe would be conducive to the achievement of all of these goals. The principles are stated in the form of hypotheses, in keeping with Strasheim's (1976) observation cited at the beginning of this chapter that none of us can be certain that we "know the truth" about how languages should be taught; however, each of us needs to develop our own set of guiding principles— "working hypotheses"—for teaching based on our own experience with language learners and our best understanding of the knowledge that has been generated in our field. This is what I offer here, using the concept of "proficiency" as a point of departure. Each person's perspectives on teaching will undoubtedly be based on his or her own set of principles. Whatever principles we choose to guide our teaching, they need to be somewhat flexible, particularly since our knowledge base is constantly growing, necessitating revisions and adjustments to accommodate new ideas. Indeed, a few of the hypotheses offered here have been revised somewhat since they first appeared (Omaggio 1983) in an effort to clarify them and incorporate some of the insights generated recently in the field of language teaching.

HYPOTHESIS 1. *Opportunities must be provided for students to practice using language in a range of contexts likely to be encountered in the target culture.*

    COROLLARY 1. *Students should be encouraged to express their own meaning as early as possible after productive skills have been introduced in the course of instruction.*

COROLLARY 2. *Opportunities must be provided for active communicative interaction among students.*

COROLLARY 3. *Creative language practice (as opposed to exclusively manipulative or convergent practice) must be encouraged in the proficiency-oriented classroom.*

COROLLARY 4. *Authentic language should be used in instruction wherever possible.*

HYPOTHESIS 2. *Opportunities should be provided for students to practice carrying out a range of functions (tasks) likely to be necessary in dealing with others in the target culture.*

HYPOTHESIS 3. *The development of accuracy should be encouraged in proficiency-oriented instruction. As learners produce language, various forms of instruction and evaluative feedback can be useful in facilitating the progression of their skills toward more precise and coherent language use.*

HYPOTHESIS 4. *Instruction should be responsive to the affective as well as the cognitive needs of students, and their different personalities, preferences, and learning styles should be taken into account.*

HYPOTHESIS 5. *Cultural understanding must be promoted in various ways so that students are sensitive to other cultures and are prepared to live more harmoniously in the target-language community.*

Each of these principles is explored in more detail in the next section. They are then related to the discussion of specific teaching methodologies. Indeed, most of the methods described in this chapter draw upon principles such as these to varying extents. But before examining the hypotheses in more detail and discussing the way they relate to particular methods, it would be useful to try to clarify the concept of *methodology* itself.

▓ Methodology and Proficiency

Definitions

Richards and Rodgers (1986) maintain that there is a fundamental difference between a philosophy of language teaching at the level of theory and principles and a set of procedures derived from them (p. 15). They cite the work of Edward Anthony (1963), who described three hierarchical levels of conceptualization: (1) *approach,* which was defined by a set of theoretical principles; (2) *method,* which was a procedural plan for presenting and teaching the language; and (3) *technique,* which involved strategies for implementing the methodological plan. Westphal

(1979) uses a similar conceptualization in defining the terms *syllabus, approach,* and *strategy* as follows:

> The syllabus *refers to the subject matter content of a given course or series of courses and the order in which it is presented; the* approach *is, ideally, the theoretical basis or bases which determine the ways in which the syllabus is treated; a* strategy *or technique is an individual instructional activity as it occurs in the classroom (p. 120).*

Westphal goes on to explain that instructors select combinations of these three factors, although some combinations are more congruent with course goals than others. For example, it would be rather difficult to expect students to become proficient enough in speaking to function easily in a foreign setting if their teacher used a literary syllabus, a grammar-translation approach, and strategies for learning activities based primarily on translation. However, Westphal believes that "it is quite possible to meet highly 'academic' objectives using a communicative approach to the grammatical syllabus and incorporating many humanistic strategies" (p. 120). The former combination of factors is not congruent with the goal of functional proficiency, at least not in beginning and intermediate sequences of instruction. The latter combination seems more eclectic, in that the instructor "borrows" from communicative approaches the basic theoretical and philosophical perspectives, uses a grammatical syllabus (instead of a functional or task-based one, which some communicative approaches would suggest), and treats the subject matter using humanistic techniques that have been suggested in yet another type of approach. These three factors, coupled with the actual text and course materials selected and the teacher's own individual style, could be said to constitute a method.

In a somewhat different definition, Swaffar, Arens, and Morgan (1982) conceive of methodology as a "task hierarchy." They maintain that the differences among major methodologies are to be found in the *priorities* assigned to various tasks rather than to the collection of tasks themselves.

> All major methodologies, whether skill- or process-oriented, aspire to the same result: a student who can read, write, speak, understand, translate, and recognize applications of the grammar of a foreign language. Methodological labels assigned to teaching activities are, in themselves, not informative, because they refer to a pool of classroom practices which are universally used (p. 31).

Therefore, it is not *what* activities are used so much as *when* and *how* they are used that distinguishes methods from one another.

Stevick (1976b) also maintains that methods are best differentiated from one another in terms of factors such as "the place of memorization, or the role of visual aids, or the importance of controlling and sequencing structure and vocabulary, or how the teacher should respond when a student makes a mistake, or the number of times a student should hear a correct model, or whether to give the explanation before or after practice or not at all, and so forth" (p. 105). The factors that he mentions go beyond the selection of learning tasks to include philosophical and theoretical principles about ways of proceeding. But whether we adopt these points of view or some other, it makes sense to differentiate methods in terms of priorities rather than make binary oppositions between and among them. In assessing the relative value of various factors in any teaching approach, we can begin to assess the degree to which that approach corresponds to the concept of proficiency. The working hypotheses presented earlier will now be explored in more detail.

Methodology and Proficiency: Five Working Hypotheses

HYPOTHESIS 1. *Opportunities must be provided for students to practice using language in a range of contexts likely to be encountered in the target culture.*

A proficiency orientation will give students, from the beginning of instruction, ample opportunities to (1) learn language in context and (2) apply their knowledge to coping with real-life situations.

The importance of context in language learning has been emphasized by many teacher educators, scholars, and researchers; thus this first hypothesis is not particularly controversial. Frommer (1998) asserts that ". . . it is difficult to overemphasize the importance of context in foreign language learning, and in learning, in general" (p. 203). She goes on to analyze the term "context," as it relates to classroom learning of foreign languages, on six levels:

1) *the lexical-semantic context in which words are presented;*
2) *the context of discourse;*
3) *the cultural context of an utterance or a text, with regard to the target culture;*
4) *each student's personal context—personality and background—which determines his or her reactions and relationship to the material and the classroom situation;*
5) *the expectations that both students and teachers have for the learning context;* and
6) *the classroom atmosphere (Frommer 1998, pp. 203–204).*

For the purposes of this discussion, "context" is used primarily in the sense of Frommer's first three levels; that is, the thrust of this hypothesis is that students need to be able to practice using language in meaningful discourse that flows logically, rather than learning language through disconnected word lists or isolated sentences. New vocabulary and expressions need to be presented and practiced in meaningful, thematically unified lessons, and students should be encouraged to express their own meaning in personalized and communicative activities. In addition, students should be taught the cultural connotation of words and expressions so that they begin to understand how their meaning is embedded in the life experiences of the people who speak the language they are learning. Some of the contexts likely to be included at the Novice and Intermediate levels in general-purpose courses are basic travel and survival needs (food, clothing, hotel accommodations, transportation, and the like), handling daily social encounters appropriately, and coping with school- or work-related situations. Students can also be taught to handle simple question-and-answer situations and discuss or write about concrete topics, such as their own background, family, and interests.

One way to enhance students' appreciation of the cultural significance of what they are learning in their language classes is to arrange for them to communicate with students in classrooms in the target culture. Through the Internet and e-mail, students can have immediate access to authentic language partners in other parts of the world. For example, Haas and Reardon (1997) describe a project connecting students in a 7th grade Spanish classroom in Sleepy Hollow, New York with students from a small town in Chile via e-mail exchanges. The two teachers set up the exchanges to include three rounds: In the first exchange, students described themselves, their families, and their preferences; in the second round, they described their schools, school subjects, and interests; and in the final round, they described their respective towns. By structuring the e-mail exchanges to allow students to write to one another within their current level of linguistic competence, the teachers were able to assure that students could have successful experiences communicating with native speakers in their own age group. Students in New York learned various types of greetings and informal expressions that expanded their sociolinguistic competence beyond the use of expressions in their textbooks and became aware of the reality of some of the cultural information they had been learning in their language lessons. "They discovered that the Chileans *do* often use their mother's and their father's names, that numbers *do* go after street names, and that the day goes before the month" (Haas and Reardon 1997, p. 222). The Chilean students' use of the metric system in sharing personal descriptions (such as height), as well as their sharing of information about such things as school hours and school uniforms, highlighted the kinds of cultural contrasts that were of immediate relevance to the students' lives.

Kern (1998) describes the use of e-mail exchanges between his second-semester French students at Berkeley and a group of high school students (*lycéens*) in Fresnes, France to promote intercultural discussion about family histories, immigration, and acculturation. The students in France had published a prize-winning book entitled *L'Histoire, mon histoire* (1996, cited in Kern 1998, p. 66) recounting how their own families' lives had been "touched by history." Kern and the French teacher, Mme Contrepois, set up the e-mail exchange to allow the French and American students to explore their personal stories together. Teachers interested in setting up exchanges such as this one should consult this source for ideas and information about how the teachers planned the e-mail project to assure its success and avoid some of the problems that can occur, such as technical difficulties. Kern discusses as well some of the problems in finding a "partner class" and provides suggestions and resources for setting up e-mail exchanges and projects.

Whether students communicate with international partners or with other students in their own classrooms, it is important to keep their level of proficiency in mind when designing classroom activities. At the lower levels of proficiency, students will probably be most comfortable with very predictable situations that allow them to use some memorized or learned material or to concentrate on autobiographical information or personal experiences and interests. At the higher levels of proficiency, the range of topics and contexts will expand beyond the "here-and-now" and the very familiar to include more abstract or specialized content.

The first hypothesis has several corollaries that relate to designing and choosing a proficiency-oriented methodology.

COROLLARY 1. *Students should be encouraged to express their own meaning as early as possible after productive skills have been introduced in the course of instruction.*

Therefore, methods that emphasize memorization or that severely limit personal expression in the early stages of instruction are not as easily adaptable to proficiency goals as those that encourage more creative language use. Only at the Novice level do learners work almost exclusively with memorized material. To reach the Intermediate range of proficiency, learners need to be able to create with the language.

COROLLARY 2. *Opportunities must be provided for active communicative interaction among students.*

The use of small-group and paired communicative activities that allow students to practice language in context for some simulated or real communicative purpose should lead more readily to the development of oral proficiency than instructional formats that are primarily teacher-centered or that focus mainly on language forms and convergent answers.

Although this hypothesis may make intuitive sense to many teachers, there has been very little research to date that looks at the effects of small-group or paired communicative practice on language proficiency development, especially in the productive skills. There have been some suggestions in the SLA research community that conversational interaction and negotiation of meaning, particularly between native speakers and nonnative speakers, have a positive effect on language development, especially for comprehension (see, for example, Long 1983b; Lightbown and Spada 1993, 1999; Gass and Selinker 1994). Research by Pica and Doughty (1985) provides some tentative support for small-group work over exclusively teacher-fronted instructional formats in terms of the opportunities it provides for learners to actively practice using the language. They also address the question of whether student production of the target language is less grammatical in small-group practice than it is when students are speaking in teacher-fronted activities, a fear that many teachers voice when discussing the merits and pitfalls of using small-group activities. Using three groups of students from "low-intermediate level ESL classes," the researchers contrasted teacher-fronted and group decision-making activities in terms of the grammaticality of the language produced, the amount of monitoring the learners engaged in, the number of turns each learner took in the interactions, and the overall quantity of language produced by individual students. The researchers found that the input to learners was most grammatical in teacher-fronted activities; it is important to note, however, that it was the teacher who provided most of the grammatically correct input in these situations! Pica and Doughty did *not* find support for their hypothesis that *student talk* would be more grammatical in the teacher-fronted classroom activities; in most cases, student talk was not significantly different in terms of its grammaticality in the teacher-fronted activities from what it was in the group activities: In both situations, "students' production appears to be equally ungrammatical—or grammatical—whether speaking in groups or in the presence of their teacher" (p. 132). However, the authors did find that "individual students appeared to have more opportunities to use the target language in group than in teacher-fronted activities, through either taking more turns or producing more samples of their interlanguage. Such opportunities may have had a positive effect on students' development of linguistic and strategic competence in giving them practice in hypothesizing about interlanguage structures which were still at variable levels of accuracy, or in enhancing their development of second language fluency" (p. 131). Pica and Doughty also suggest that group work does allow students to have a chance to hear some grammatical input and to get feedback on how effectively they are communicating (p. 132).

In spite of the benefits provided by the small-group activities, Pica and Doughty do not recommend an abandonment of whole-class instruction. They caution that a "steady diet of group activities" might "restrict the amount of grammatical input available" to the learner and lead to a "stabilized nontarget variety" of the language (p. 132).

This concern for developing accuracy while maintaining a communicative environment for learning is central to any approach that is oriented toward proficiency goals. Communicative language practice need not be totally unstructured, especially in the early stages of language skills development. Learners will need opportunities to make their own output more comprehensible (see Hypothesis 3 below.) This goal of comprehensibility and greater precision is totally compatible, it seems, with greater involvement by students in the creation of the discourse in the classroom. Gass and Varonis (1985) maintain that active involvement of learners is a necessary aspect of language acquisition, "since it is through involvement that the input becomes 'charged' and 'penetrates' deeply" (p. 150).

Swain (1998) argues that activities that encourage students to produce language ("output" activities) might help them focus on what they cannot yet say in the language, thereby leading them to try to solve these problems by experimenting with new language forms or structures, talking about the language with a conversational partner ("metatalk"), and reflecting consciously about their language use. Some preliminary research that she has done indicates that learners can solve some of their linguistic problems collaboratively. Learners do differ in how much "metatalk" they generate when working on language production activities, and Swain cautions that "not just any task will elicit metatalk" (p. 79). She adds that not all learners react the same way to the same task. She and her colleagues have also found that if students work collaboratively to solve a language problem and come up with a wrong solution, they tend to remember the incorrect solution: "They learned, but they learned the wrong thing. Teachers' availability during collaborative activities and their attention to the accuracy of the 'final' product subsequent to the completion of collaborative activities are potentially critical aspects of student learning" (p. 80). Thus it seems advisable, when asking students to work on tasks in pairs or small groups, that teachers circulate among the groups, offer assistance, make note of problems, and provide feedback to learners either during the activity or in a whole-class, teacher-fronted follow-up activity. Further research on collaborative production tasks and their effectiveness in building proficiency is needed to test the hypotheses presented here. This is especially important in that many teachers, scholars, and teacher educators view collaborative learning as a significant aspect of communicative language instruction.

Most scholars agree that communicative practice is optimal when it involves exchanges of information in situations where some *information gap* (Brumfit and Johnson 1979; Johnson 1982) exists, and that language practice that involves totally predictable (and therefore noncommunicative) exchanges is less useful in building proficiency. A judicious balance of activities that work on communicative skills with those that focus on the development of accuracy seems most sensible. (To illustrate how this might be accomplished, sample activities ranging from structured to unstructured practice are provided in Chapters 5, 6, and 7.)

COROLLARY 3. *Creative language practice (as opposed to exclusively manipulative or convergent practice) must be encouraged in the proficiency-oriented classroom.*

Students who hope to advance in their skills beyond the Novice range must learn to create with the language. They must be encouraged to paraphrase, think divergently (i.e., think of many possible answers), and let their imagination and creative ability function as fully as possible within the limits of their level of linguistic competence. For a very useful set of suggestions for developing creative language practice activities, see Birckbichler (1982).

COROLLARY 4. *Authentic language should be used in instruction wherever possible.*

The contexts for language practice should be devised, as much as possible, from culturally authentic sources. The use of real or simulated travel documents, hotel registration forms, biographical data sheets, train and plane schedules, authentic restaurant menus, labels, signs, newspapers, and magazines will acquaint students more directly with real language than will any set of contrived classroom materials used alone. Videotapes of authentic or simulated exchanges between native speakers, radio and television broadcasts, films, songs, and the like have long been advocated by foreign language educators as stimulating pedagogical aids. The proficiency-oriented classroom will incorporate such material frequently and effectively into instruction at all levels.

One of the newest sources of authentic materials for classroom instruction is the World Wide Web. Target-language sites accessed through the Internet offer both teachers and students a wealth of authentic materials—materials that are current, at least from the day they were downloaded, and far more timely than any material found in teachers' files, textbooks, and ancillaries. The currency of these documents can be easily maintained with periodic visits to those Web sites. It is important to remember, however, that the documents found on the Web, like all authentic materials, have generally been created by and for native speakers of the language and thus are not written with the language learner in mind. For learners at the lower levels of proficiency, some documents may be difficult to read without appropriate support material, and teachers will need to evaluate texts from authentic sources to assess their general readability for learners in their classes. For those materials that seem accessible to Novice and Intermediate readers, worksheets can be created that provide useful vocabulary and extralinguistic cues that will make the authentic material easier to read; in addition, teachers can create tasks that are geared to the proficiency level of their students—tasks that do not require the students to read or understand all of the material in the document. As Terry (1998) points out, "the difficulty of the text is determined only by the task(s) that we ask the learner to carry out based on that material and *not* on the material itself" (p. 281). More will be said about criteria for choosing texts and designing tasks in Chapter 5.

The use of authentic texts does not imply that we should abandon the use of materials created for instructional purposes. Rather, a blend of the two seems more appropriate. Another factor to consider is that students' proficiency levels in listening and reading may be well in advance of their proficiency levels in speaking and writing. Students who could not handle certain materials well in the productive skills may be quite capable of comprehending them.

It is also important to remember that natural language includes the comprehensible input provided by teachers in everyday exchanges in the instructional setting that are communicative in nature, from giving directions to recounting personal anecdotes in the target language. Teachers can also provide input to learners as they communicate with them via e-mail or in chat rooms on local area networks designed for their classes.

HYPOTHESIS 2. *Opportunities should be provided for students to practice carrying out a range of functions (tasks) likely to be necessary in dealing with others in the target culture.*

Traditional classroom instructional settings tend to limit the role of the student to that of responder; that is, students are most often asked to answer questions. In teacher-centered approaches, students are very seldom asked to make inquiries, act out simulated survival situations, narrate or describe events, hypothesize, argue, persuade, provide opinion, or carry out many other language functions that are necessary in everyday encounters with others in the target language. In many cases, functional practice of this sort is reserved for advanced conversation courses, many of which the majority of students never take. Proficiency-oriented methodologies should introduce students to a variety of functional tasks that have been carefully sequenced to help them cope with the real-world communication demands they will face. When possible, e-mail exchanges, such as those described in Haas and Reardon (1997) and Kern (1998), discussed earlier under Hypothesis 1, can expand the range of realistic tasks that learners are asked to carry out. (Some suggestions for activities that afford practice in using language functions are presented in Chapter 6.)

HYPOTHESIS 3. *The development of accuracy should be encouraged in proficiency-oriented instruction. As learners produce language, various forms of instruction and evaluative feedback can be useful in facilitating the progression of their skills toward more precise and coherent language use.*

The role of formal instruction and feedback in language acquisition has been the subject of debate in recent years, with some scholars arguing that "grammar instruction" and "error correction" do very little to encourage lasting positive change in learners' production, either in speech or in writing (see, for example, Newmark and Reibel 1968; Terrell 1977, 1982; Krashen 1982; Savignon 1988; Schwartz 1993; Truscott 1999). Other scholars, however, argue that both instruction and feedback can have a positive impact on second language acquisition (see, for example, Long 1983a; Swain 1985; Ellis 1985, 1990; Herron and Tomasello 1988; Lightbown 1990; Lightbown and Spada 1990; Stern 1990; Gass and Magnan 1993; MacWhinney 1997; Doughty and Williams 1998a; Leow 2000). It seems that some of the debate regarding "error correction" centers on an understanding of the meaning of the term. Ellis (1990) suggests that we adopt Long's (1977) distinction between the terms "feedback" and "correction," where "feedback" refers to the process of giving students information so that they can tell if their production or comprehension of the language is correct, and "correction" refers to the result of feedback, or its effect on learning (Long 1977; Ellis 1990, p. 71).

It might also be useful to distinguish among various forms of corrective feedback, ranging from very direct and immediate correction of errors to more indirect and/or delayed feedback strategies. It seems that those who have argued that no error correction should take place in the classroom are, in actuality, advocating indirect feedback via more comprehensible input or negotiation of meaning among interlocutors. A clearer understanding of the terms being used by various scholars might reveal more consensus on this issue than has been evident from the literature.

The thrust of this hypothesis is that there is a role for form-focused instruction in a proficiency-oriented approach, used in a judicious blend with communicative language teaching practices. It also implies that a whole continuum of feedback strategies may be useful at different times in second-language instruction. If interlanguage consists of variable styles, as Tarone (1983) and Ellis (1985) have suggested, there is a place for "careful style" activities, where attention is given to formal aspects of language, as well as for "vernacular style" activities, where communication of one's meaning is the primary focus. Lightbown (1990), in reviewing some of the recent literature relating to language learning in classrooms, concludes that "we all seem to feel the need to restore form-based instruction and error correction as part of the language teaching/learning context" (p. 90), although she cautions that more research needs to be done to determine the precise benefits of such activities. Lightbown and Spada (1990) point to the benefits of a combination of communicative language teaching and form-focused instruction—a kind of "hybrid" approach that recognizes the contributions of both kinds of teaching to the learning process.

In the last ten years, there has been an increased level of research activity in classroom second-language acquisition investigating the role of "focus on form" within a communicative language teaching approach (see Lightbown and Spada 1993, 1999; Schmidt 1995; Doughty and Williams 1998a; and Lee and Valdman 2000 for a sample of books and edited volumes dealing with research on this issue; see also Spada 1997 for a very useful review of research on form-focused instruction). Results from these studies have been mixed, although numerous studies have shown some beneficial effects of form-focused instruction; some have indicated differential effects, depending on the forms chosen (e.g., Lightbown and Spada 1993, 1999; Doughty and Williams 1998b; Williams and Evans 1998), while others indicate that individual differences play a role (e.g., DeKeyser 1993; Aljaafreh and Lantolf 1994; Swain 1998). Some of the findings relate to the effects of "input enhancement" (Sharwood Smith 1993). According to Sharwood Smith, "positive input enhancement" involves making certain forms in the input more salient or noticeable to learners through such devices as boldfacing, color coding, or other typographical enhancement of the features to be learned; a more "elaborate" form of enhancement of such forms would be the use of grammar explanations and examples. (Many foreign language textbooks have incorporated these types of features for years, but it is only recently that SLA research has begun to explore their effects on language acquisition.) "Negative input enhancement," as Sharwood Smith defines it, "would flag given forms as incorrect, thus signaling to the learner that they have violated the target norms" (p. 177). Thus research on "negative input enhancement" is generally concerned with the effects of certain kinds of feedback on language production.

In addition to work on input enhancement, recent research has looked at the role of instruction in second-language learning. MacWhinney (1997) reviews and comments on some of the research that has been done on "implicit" and "explicit" learning and teaching. He feels that the issue of the role of explicit instruction needs to be broken down into two topics: "First, we need to know whether explicit teaching leads to explicit rule formulation in students. Second, we need to know whether explicit rule formulation in the student leads to higher levels of achievement" (p. 278). In reviewing some of the research that has been done on this topic, MacWhinney comments that any research results showing that learners benefit from explicit instruction, though not surprising to psychologists, still tend to be considered controversial by SLA researchers:

> *Psychologists have shown repeatedly that concept learning with advance organizers and clues is always better than learning without cues. Students who receive explicit instruction, as well as implicit exposure to forms, would seem to have the best of both worlds. . . . From the viewpoint of psycholinguistic theory, providing learners with explicit instruction along with standard implicit exposure would seem to be a no-lose proposition (p. 278).*

He adds that "it is difficult to think of any study that has shown a linguistic pattern for which students do worse when given additional explicit instruction. If such an effect could be achieved, it would need to involve providing instruction that was either hopelessly confusing or actually wrong" (p. 278). MacWhinney tempers his remarks with the observation that explicit instruction may be most effective when rules and/or structures are simple and clear, as "instruction in hopelessly complex rules can be counterproductive" (p. 278). (For discussions about whether it is best to teach "easy" or "hard" rules, see also Hulstijn 1995; Spada 1997; Doughty and Williams 1998b; and Sanz 2000.) MacWhinney concludes that both implicit and explicit processes contribute to language learning, a position that is congruent with the underlying premises of the hypothesis being discussed in this section.

Higgs and Clifford (1982) have suggested that we might be able to help students produce more accurate speech if we adopt an "output hypothesis" similar to Krashen's input hypothesis. That is, students might best acquire productive skills when they are encouraged to engage in tasks that are just beyond their current level of competence. To translate this idea into classroom practice, instructors might (1) provide comprehensible input in addition to formal instruction, (2) encourage students to express their own meaning within, or even slightly beyond, the limits of their current level of competence, and (3) consistently provide appropriate feedback (direct or indirect, immediate or delayed, depending on the activity and its purpose). Swain (1985) has proposed a similar hypothesis, in which students are encouraged to produce "comprehensible" or "pushed" output. In studying productive skills of immersion students in Canada, she found that their grammaticality had fallen far short of native performance (p. 245). This caused her to question Krashen's hypothesis that comprehensible input was the only causal variable in second-language acquisition, since the immersion students she was studying had been receiving comprehensible input for seven years. She concluded that input was not enough to promote grammatical development in a second language, and that something in the immersion setting was still lacking: "What, then, is missing? I would like to suggest that what is missing is output" (p. 248).

Swain argued that one-to-one conversational exchanges certainly provided an excellent opportunity for acquisition to occur, but that the best kinds of exchanges were those in which there had been a communication breakdown—"where the learner has received some negative input—and the learner is pushed to use alternate means to get across his or her message" (p. 248). Although one can succeed in getting across a message using deviant grammatical forms and sociolinguistically inappropriate language, Swain felt that "negotiating meaning needs to incorporate the notion of being pushed toward the delivery of a message that is not only conveyed, but that is conveyed precisely, coherently and appropriately" (pp. 248–249). She saw this idea of being "pushed" in one's output as parallel to Krashen's "$i + 1$" description of comprehensible input, and thus called her idea "the comprehensible output hypothesis." In subsequent discussions of this hypothesis, Swain (1995, 1998) has elaborated on the potential role of output in promoting language acquisition. First, she states that producing the foreign language will enhance fluency through the practice it provides (Swain 1995, p. 125). However, she hypothesizes that output can also enhance accuracy in several ways: (1) by helping learners "notice a gap between what they *want* to say and what they *can* say, leading them to recognize what they do not know, or know only partially" (pp. 125–126); (2) by affording learners an opportunity to test their hypotheses about how the language works and possibly receive feedback that can lead to modification of these hypotheses; and (3) by encouraging conscious reflection on their own use of the forms of the target language, "allowing learners to control and internalize it" (p. 132). The output activities that Swain envisions are those in which students are engaged in expressing meaning in contextualized, communicative activities. In this way, students can make important linkages between the meaning they are trying to express and the forms that they use to communicate their ideas more clearly and precisely. More will be said about this hypothesis, as well as the general role of feedback and instruction in language acquisition, in Chapters 6 and 7.

HYPOTHESIS 4. *Instruction should be responsive to the affective as well as the cognitive needs of students, and their different personalities, preferences, and learning styles should be taken into account.*

As we saw in Chapter 2, learners differ from one another in many ways. In order to teach responsively to the individuals in our classes, we need to be aware that there will be important differences in cognitive style, personality, motivation, aptitude, and modality preference among our learners. This hypothesis speaks to the need to vary classroom activities in a way that will address the needs and preferences of as many students as possible, thus contributing to a more comfortable and flexible learning environment. As Galloway and Labarca (1990) state, "what is called for is not a teaching method, but a teaching repertoire" (p. 115). Any "method" that requires strict adherence to a limited number of techniques or strategies will undoubtedly be very poorly suited to at least a subset of learners in the classroom. Instruction that fosters the growth of language proficiency for all learners will need to be flexible, and will be characterized by a kind of principled or "informed eclecticism" (Richards and Rodgers 1986, p. 158) that takes students' preferences and feelings into account.

One of the hallmarks of several recent methodological developments is the greater emphasis on the affective aspects of learning and acquisition (see, for example, the discussions of the Counseling-Learning Approach, the Natural Approach, and Suggestopedia presented later in this chapter). Scovel (1991) refers to affective factors as "those that deal with the emotional reactions and motivations of the learner" (p. 16), which constitute a subset of factors among the many other learner variables that need to be considered in instruction.

Horwitz and Young (1991) compiled a series of papers examining the role of anxiety in language learning. In the introductory chapter, Daly (1991) links the more general construct of "communication apprehension" to problems encountered with oral communication in second-language classrooms. "Communication apprehension is the fear or anxiety an individual feels about orally communicating" (p. 3). Daly points out that there are other related constructs, such as writing apprehension and receiver apprehension (associated with listening), which may also be relevant to the problems foreign language learners can experience, but that anxiety about oral communication seems to be most directly related to "language anxiety."

Horwitz, Horwitz, and Cope (1991) point out that, in addition to "communication apprehension," test anxiety and fear of negative evaluation can play a role in the development of foreign language anxiety among classroom learners. In addition, they suggest that foreign language anxiety can arise because of the difficulty of engaging in genuine or authentic communication when one's linguistic skills are limited. "The importance of the disparity between the 'true' self as known to the learner and the more limited self as can be presented at any given moment in the foreign language would seem to distinguish foreign language anxiety from other academic anxieties, such as those associated with mathematics or science" (p. 31).

Brown (1984) maintains that lowered anxiety and inhibition may increase comprehensible input and, therefore, affect acquisition, but he cautions that evidence about the precise role of anxiety in language learning is still quite scanty. He hypothesizes that although too much anxiety may have harmful effects on learning, *too little* anxiety may also cause failure. If a student's affective filter is too low, there may be little motivation to learn. "We do well to note that anxiety can be debilitative but it can also be *facilitative*. . . . As teachers we should allow some of the anxiety and tension to remain in our classes lest our students become so 'laid back' that they fail to perceive the input when it comes!" (p. 278).

Scovel (1991) presents various research studies that indicate mixed results about the relationship of anxiety to foreign language learning, with some studies showing that it inhibits performance and other studies showing some anxiety to be facilitative, as Brown (1984) suggests. Clearly, more research is needed to determine the role of emotions such as anxiety in second-language learning.

Daly (1991) suggests that anxiety, or "communication apprehension," may be only one of many possible reasons why students are reluctant to talk in classrooms. Other reasons for reticence might be a lack of preparation or motivation, a lack of confidence, or an unwillingness to disclose one's feelings or thoughts (p. 6). This last consideration is especially important for teachers to remember when planning activities that are personalized in nature. We need to be sensitive to the feelings of students, allowing them the flexibility to participate in discussions in ways that do not require sharing of personal information if they prefer not to do so.

An interesting research question that has been recently explored with the increased use of computer-assisted instruction is the effect that electronic communication has on students' attitudes and general willingness to participate in the discourse among class members. Are students who may be reluctant to talk in class in front of others equally unwilling to engage in electronic "conversations"? According to Beauvois (1997), data from studies on the use of computer-mediated communication (CMC) indicate that students communicate better with the regular use of local area network (LAN) communication "if *better* means using longer, more complete utterances, expressing less superficial ideas, and communicating generally more openly about any given subject" (p. 180). In addition, she states that "affective measures in both synchronous [e.g., chat rooms] and asynchronous [e.g., e-mail] electronic communication have shown positive student and teacher response in this area of CMC" (p. 180).

Meunier (1998) conducted a study using a questionnaire to investigate a number of motivational and affective factors associated with synchronous on-line discussions in French and German college writing classes. She reports that the majority of students (87%) experienced a low level of anxiety while engaging in the on-line discussions, particularly because the computer-mediated communication offered them greater flexibility. Meunier also reports on the relationship of such factors as personality type and gender to student attitudes toward communicating electronically; for example, she found that males tended to feel more overwhelmed by the flow of messages on the screen than did female students, and certain personality types experienced greater or lesser degrees of anxiety when working in a computer-mediated communication environment. She cautions that teachers need to be sensitive to the feelings of different learners toward computer-mediated foreign language communication (CMFLC): "One may be tempted to consider technology a panacea for pedagogical problems, especially when statistics overwhelmingly show that most students are motivated by CMFLC. Yet, relying on general trends may blind us to some underlying problems . . ." (p. 177). Recognizing the very real individual differences among students is crucial, then, in interpreting overall results. Nevertheless, Meunier concludes that synchronous on-line communication was generally a very positive learning experience for students in this study. "In general terms, the results of the survey support the premise that synchronous CMFLC triggers a high level of situational and task motivation as well as a positive attitude among FL students regardless of initial motivations (integrative or instrumental) and computer background" (p. 177). She adds that CMFLC seems to minimize "communication apprehension," as described by Horwitz and Young (1991). Among her many useful pedagogical recommendations is the suggestion that students who do not want to share personal opinions or feelings during electronic discussions be given the option to synthesize what others in the class are saying. This relates to the point made earlier that students should not be pressured to share personal information if they are uncomfortable doing so.

Whether or not we agree with the need to include certain types of affective activities in the classroom, most language educators today recognize that students will probably attain a given degree of proficiency more rapidly and will be more motivated to continue in their studies in an environment that is accepting, relaxed, and supportive.

HYPOTHESIS 5. *Cultural understanding must be promoted in various ways so that students are sensitive to other cultures and are prepared to live more harmoniously in the target-language community.*

For many years, foreign language educators have been emphasizing the need to incorporate a cultural syllabus into the curriculum and to promote global awareness and cross-cultural understanding. (See, for example, Stern 1981.) When language acquisition activities are based on authentic cultural material or embedded in a cultural context, we can begin to attain this important goal. The *Standards for Foreign Language Learning* (1996), described in Chapter 1, articulate goals for cultural learning, as it is integrated with language study, across all levels of the curriculum. Many of the learning scenarios created for this project illustrate how the teaching of culture can be achieved while students engage in communicative tasks. Both the 1996 version of the *Standards* and the 1999 language-specific *Standards for Foreign Language Learning for the 21ˢᵗ Century* are invaluable resources of teaching ideas incorporating cultural learning. Sample activities blending the study of language and culture can also be found in this book in Chapters 5 through 9. Specific strategies for teaching cultural understanding and for incorporating cultural content into language lessons are given in Chapter 8.

The Proficiency Orientation of Existing Methodologies: A Preliminary Appraisal

In order to make a preliminary appraisal of the extent to which various existing teaching approaches and methodologies are oriented toward proficiency, it would be useful to determine how many of the hypothesized elements discussed in the previous section are assigned a relatively high priority in a given approach.

There are several problems, however, in any formal comparison of methods in this way. As stated earlier, it is often difficult to clearly define a method to the satisfaction of everyone familiar with it, since there are currently many individual variations and interpretations of each method being used. If, as Westphal (1979) suggests, we consider method as a combination of a given *syllabus,* a philosophical or theoretical *approach,* and a choice of teaching *strategies,* all of which are then "seasoned" with a teacher's personal style, we may find it relatively difficult to characterize any methodology in the abstract. Before the demise of the purest form of audiolingualism in the late 1960s, such a methodological comparison would not have been as difficult, since teachers using the audiolingual method were expected to follow a particular syllabus, use accepted materials and teaching strategies, and subscribe to the underlying theoretical basis on which the methodology was founded. (However, not all teachers followed the method as rigidly as they had been trained to do, even though it was prescriptive down to the smallest detail.) Since the early 1970s many foreign language practitioners have been electing to use selected techniques from a variety of methods in their classrooms or adapting a given method or approach to suit the abilities, needs, and interests of their students. Therefore, each method or approach presented in the following pages may be interpreted or understood somewhat differently by different people.

A second problem associated with a methodological comparison of this kind is that it will almost certainly be subjective to some extent. Those who favor a given method or approach may attribute to it characteristics that others may not associate with it at all. One way to achieve some objectivity in comparing and contrasting methodologies and approaches would be to refer to a commonly accepted set of descriptions such as those provided by Benseler and Schulz (1980) to the President's Commission, or those found in methods texts published in the past twenty-five years. (See, for example, Rivers 1975, 1981; Chastain 1976, 1988; Allen and Valette 1977; Stevick 1976b, 1980, 1996; Richards and Rodgers 1986.) Using such descriptions as a guide, one could then make a preliminary appraisal of each method or approach in terms of its proficiency orientation, keeping in mind that variations of any given methodology might alter the appraisal considerably.

The pages that follow describe a variety of methods and approaches that have been used and discussed by second-language educators in this century. Because not every method that has been proposed can be treated in detail here, emphasis is placed on those that (1) have had a profound influence on second-language teaching in this country or (2) have received significant attention in the recent literature on language teaching. The description of each method is comprised of four parts: (1) the theoretical and/or philosophical premise upon which the method is based, (2) a list of the method's major characteristics, (3) a preliminary assessment of the proficiency orientation implicit in the method as described, and (4) a discussion of the method's possible drawbacks or commonly perceived shortcomings, particularly in terms of proficiency goals.

Three "Traditional" Methods

The three methods described in this section constitute the most common ways of approaching foreign language teaching before the 1970s, when rapid developments in second-language acquisition research ushered in a profusion of new approaches. These descriptions are based for the most part on characterizations provided by Chastain (1976), Benseler and Schulz (1980), and Rivers (1981), as well as my own experience with grammar-translation and audiolingual methodology as a student of Latin, French, Spanish, and German over the years.

■ The Grammar-Translation Method: "Mental Discipline"

Background   The grammar-translation approach to language teaching was congruent with the view of faculty psychologists that mental discipline was essential for strengthening the powers of the mind. Originally used to teach Latin and Greek, this method was applied to the teaching of modern languages in the late nineteenth and early twentieth centuries. Its primary purpose was to enable students to access and appreciate great literature, while helping them understand their native language better through extensive analysis of the grammar of the target language and translation.

Major Characteristics

The grammar-translation method, in its purest form, had the following characteristics (summary based on Chastain 1976, pp. 103–04):

1. Students first learned the rules of grammar and bilingual lists of vocabulary pertaining to the reading or readings of the lesson. Grammar was learned deductively by means of long and elaborate explanations. All rules were learned with their exceptions and irregularities explained in grammatical terms.
2. Once rules and vocabulary were learned, prescriptions for translating the exercises that followed the grammar explanations were given.
3. Comprehension of the rules and readings was tested via translation (target language to native language and vice versa). Students had learned the language if they could translate the passages well.
4. The native and target languages were constantly compared. The goal of instruction was to convert L1 into L2 and vice versa, using a dictionary if necessary.
5. There were very few opportunities for listening and speaking practice (with the exception of reading passages and sentences aloud), since the method concentrated on reading and translation exercises. Much of the class time was devoted to talking *about* the language; virtually no time was spent talking *in* the language.

For a description of a sample lesson using the grammar-translation method, see Rivers 1991, pp. 1–2.

Proficiency Orientation

Very few, if any of the elements hypothesized to contribute to the development of proficiency are present in the grammar-translation method. Certainly, in terms of oral proficiency, this method has little to offer. There is virtually no sign of spoken language, and the little oral practice that is in evidence consists of reading aloud. There is no personalization or contextualization of the lesson to relate to students' experience, no pair or group interaction for communicative practice, no concern for the teaching of cultural awareness, at least on an everyday level. Affective concerns seem to be nonexistent, as students are clearly in a defensive learning environment where right answers are expected. The only thing that can be said is that there *is* a concern for accuracy, but this concern is so prevalent as to prevent students from creating with the language or venturing to express their own thoughts. It is only while *creating with the language* that students have an opportunity to build toward higher levels of proficiency. In addition, it is during creative language practice that the most informative error-correction feedback can be given, since this type of practice allows students to try out their hypotheses about the target language in a natural way. As Higgs and Clifford (1982) point out, the particular kind of concern for accuracy that characterizes grammar-translation methodology is *not* necessarily conducive to building toward proficiency and may, in fact, be quite counterproductive.

**Potential
Drawbacks**

The lack of orientation toward proficiency goals is the most obvious drawback of this method, at least as it is traditionally described. The meticulous detail of the grammar explanations, the long written exercises, the lengthy vocabulary lists, and the academic forms of language presented in the readings render language learning both strenuous and boring. Perhaps a modified form of grammar-translation methodology would be useful at the higher levels of proficiency, where the purpose of instruction is to fine-tune students' control of the target language, especially in terms of learning to use specialized vocabulary or developing competence in written stylistics. The method does not seem appropriate, however, for students at the Novice through Advanced levels, even though that is where it is typically used.

Strasheim (1976) summed up her appraisal of the shortcomings of the grammar-translation approach with the following personal anecdote:

> It was one day while my third-year class was parsing one of Cicero's lengthier Latin accusations of Catiline that the mental discipline objective proved its real efficacy, for I fell asleep in a class I was teaching. All I can say in my own defense is that the mass of the class had preceded me into the Land of Nod by at least a clause—or two (p. 40).

▓ The Direct Method: A Rationalist Perspective on Language Learning

Background

The direct method movement, as advocated by educators such as Berlitz, originated in the nineteenth century. Advocates of this "active" method believed that students learn to understand a language by listening to it in large quantities. They learn to speak by speaking, especially if the speech is associated simultaneously with appropriate action. The methodology was based essentially on the way children learn their native language: Language is learned through the "*direct* association of words and phrases with objects and actions, without the use of the native language" as the intervening variable (Rivers 1981, p. 32, emphasis added). Various oral and "natural" methods have evolved since the nineteenth-century version to be described next. (See, for example, Terrell's Natural Approach. This variation is treated in a separate section.)

**Major
Characteristics**

The methodology advocated by Berlitz, among others, had the following characteristics (summary based on Rivers 1981, pp. 31–35):

1. Language learning should start with the here-and-now, utilizing classroom objects and simple actions. Eventually, when students have learned enough language, lessons move on to include common situations and settings.
2. The direct method lesson often develops around specially constructed pictures depicting life in the country where the target language is spoken. These pictures enable the teacher to *avoid the use of translation*, which is strictly forbidden in the classroom. Definitions of new vocabulary are given via *paraphrases* in the target language or by miming the action or manipulating objects to get the meaning across.

3. From the beginning of instruction, students hear complete and meaningful sentences in simple discourse, which often takes the form of question-answer exchanges.

4. Correct pronunciation is an important consideration in this approach, and emphasis is placed upon the development of accurate pronunciation from the beginning of instruction. Phonetic notation is often used to achieve this goal.

5. Grammar rules are not explicitly taught; rather, they are assumed to be learned through practice. Students are encouraged to form their own generalizations about grammar through *inductive* methods. When grammar is explicitly taught, it is taught in the target language.

6. Reading goals are also reached via the "direct" understanding of text without the use of dictionaries or translations.

For a detailed description of a direct method class, see Rivers (1981, p. 3).

Proficiency Orientation

Various elements of the direct method are congruent with the hypotheses presented earlier in this chapter. Students are certainly engaged in oral language use that is contextualized and, to some extent, personalized. There is often some description and narration in the direct method lesson, although the bulk of the class is spent in responding to teacher questions. The use of culturally oriented pictures makes students aware of some of the everyday situations they might encounter in the target community, and vocabulary is useful for coping in survival situations. The use of paraphrase to explain vocabulary encourages students to learn that skill, which is important in developing proficiency beyond the Novice level. The affective needs of the student are addressed in group activities that allow for individual contributions without hypercorrection. Yet this lack of correction, which characterized the earliest versions of the direct method, often led to early fossilization, a problem discussed below.

Potential Drawbacks

Rivers (1981) makes the following comments about the direct method:

> *At its best, the direct method provides an exciting and interesting way of learning a language through activity. . . . If care is not taken by the teacher, however, students who are plunged too soon into expressing themselves freely in the new language in a relatively unstructured situation can develop a glib but inaccurate fluency, clothing native-language structures in foreign-language vocabulary. This "school pidgin" is often difficult to eradicate later . . . because it has been accepted and encouraged for so long (p. 33).*

Rivers (1981) argues that, in the purest form of the direct method, insufficient provision was made for systematic practice of structures in a coherent sequence. However, she points out that some modern adaptations of this methodology do use structured practice, grammatical sequences that proceed one step at a time, and grammar explanations, sometimes given in the native language. "To counteract the tendency toward inaccuracy and vagueness" (p. 35), translation is even permitted in some modern versions of the method.

◼ Audiolingual Methodology: An Empiricist Perspective on Language Learning

Background

In Chapter 2, we saw that the theory underlying audiolingual methodology was rooted in two parallel schools of thought in psychology and linguistics. In psychology, the behaviorist and neobehaviorist schools were extremely influential in the 1940s and 1950s. At the same time, the structural, or descriptive, school of linguistics dominated thinking in that field. Chastain (1976) explains that, up until this time, the emphasis had been on historical linguistics, which sought to explain linguistic data through the examination of manuscripts and the documentation of changes in vocabulary and form over time. But as linguists began to concentrate on the study of Indian languages, many of which had no writing systems, the oral form of language became the only data source. From these field studies of Indian languages evolved the school of *structural,* or *descriptive,* linguistics.

The combination of structural linguistics and behaviorist psychology resulted in a new theory of language learning which described the learning process in terms of conditioning. This theory was translated into practice in the 1940s in the Army Specialized Training Program intensive language courses, first taught at the Defense Language Institute. Later, this same essential methodology was to dominate academic programs in the country in the 1950s and 1960s, thanks mainly to summer institutes, funded by the National Defense Education Act (NDEA), which trained and retrained large numbers of pre- and in-service teachers in the audiolingual method (ALM).

Major Characteristics

The audiolingual method, also known as the Aural-Oral, Functional Skills, New Key, or American Method of language teaching (Benseler and Schulz 1980), was considered a "scientific" approach to language teaching. Lado (1964), in a book entitled *Language Teaching: A Scientific Approach,* proposed the following "empirical laws of learning" as the basis for audiolingual methodology:

1. *The fundamental law of contiguity* states that "when two experiences have occurred together, the return of one will recall or reinstate the other."
2. *The law of exercise* maintains that "the more frequently a response is practiced, the better it is learned and the longer it is remembered."
3. *The law of intensity* states that "the more intensely a response is practiced, the better it is learned and the longer it will be remembered."
4. *The law of assimilation* states that "each new stimulating condition tends to elicit the [same] response which has been connected with similar stimulating conditions in the past."
5. *The law of effect* maintains that "when a response is accompanied or followed by a satisfying state of affairs, that response is reinforced. When a response is accompanied by an annoying state of affairs, it is avoided" (Lado 1964, p. 37).

These behaviorist laws underlie the five basic tenets of the audiolingual method, listed in Chastain (1976) and summarized below:

1. The goal of second language teaching is "to develop in students the same types of abilities that native speakers have." Students should, therefore, eventually handle the language at an *unconscious* level (p. 111).
2. The native language should be banned from the classroom; a "cultural island" should be maintained. Teach L2 without reference to L1.
3. Students learn languages through stimulus-response (S-R) techniques. Students should learn to speak without attention to *how* the language is put together. They should not be given time to think about their answers. Dialogue memorization and pattern drills are the means by which conditioned responses are achieved.
4. Pattern drills are to be taught initially without explanation. Thorough practice should precede any explanation given, and the discussion of grammar should be kept very brief.
5. In developing the "four skills," the natural sequence followed in learning the native language should be maintained (based on pp. 111–112).

Rivers (1981) further clarifies the major characteristics of the audiolingual method by listing Moulton's (1961) "five slogans" of the method:

1. *Language is speech, not writing.*
2. *A language is a set of habits.*
3. *Teach the language and not about the language.*
4. *A language is what native speakers say, not what someone thinks they ought to say.*
5. *Languages are different (Rivers 1981, pp. 41–43).*

The last statement relates to the fact that structural linguists rejected the notion of a universal grammar underlying all languages (Rivers 1981, p. 43). Instead, they used contrastive analysis to select those features of the target language that would be especially troublesome for the learner.

An examination of an audiolingual textbook will yield further insights into the way the method was translated into practice (see Chastain 1976, pp. 113–124 for a detailed description of a typical textbook). Every ALM textbook chapter consisted of three basic parts: (1) the dialogue, (2) pattern drills, and (3) application activities. There were very few grammar explanations within the pages of the text: Some books had none at all. If grammar was included, it was always presented after the drills. Types of pattern drills included:

1. *Repetition drills,* in which no change was made. Students simply repeated after the teacher's model.
2. *Transformation drills,* in which the students were required to make some minimal change, reinforced afterward by the teacher or the tape recorder. The various types of transformation drills included *person-number substitutions, patterned response drills, singular-plural transformations, tense transformations, directed dialogue, cued response,* and *translation drills.*

Application activities included such things as dialogue adaptations, open-ended response drills, recombined narratives in which the material presented in the dialogues was transformed slightly, guided oral presentations in which students had a chance to use the memorized material for personal expression, and conversation stimulus activities, which resembled semicontrolled role-plays. In all of these activities, students worked mainly with memorized material, repeating it, manipulating it, or transforming it to meet minimal communicative needs.

For a description of a typical ALM class, see Rivers (1981, pp. 4–6).

Proficiency Orientation

The ALM approach, when adhered to strictly, tends to force students to perform continuously at the Novice level since they are never asked to say anything they haven't seen before or haven't committed to memory. The methodology does not encourage creation on the part of the learner except in very minimal ways. Not until well into the second year of the course syllabus are students asked to do very much in the way of free expression. However, the method does have some positive aspects that should be mentioned. The use of colloquial, sociolinguistically appropriate language in the dialogues and recombination narratives is a feature that was missing in older methods such as grammar-translation. The focus on oral skills led to good pronunciation and accurate speech, at least when students were asked to give structured responses with which they were familiar. Audiolingual methods have also stressed the teaching of culture and prepare students to deal in some measure with everyday situations in the target language community.

Potential Drawbacks

The enthusiasm with which second-language teachers had originally received this revolutionary methodology was dampened within a relatively short time (Chastain 1976; Strasheim 1976). First, the methodology had not delivered what it had promised: bilingual speakers at the end of instruction. Secondly, the method did not take into account the variety of learning styles and preferences of students, favoring those who learned best "by ear" rather than visual learners and ignoring the needs of learners who wanted to understand the rules of the new language and its grammatical system. As a member of one of the early groups of students experiencing ALM methodology in 1962, I studied French with this method for three years in high school. Having studied Latin the year before with a grammar-translation approach (and enjoying it enough to continue taking language for three more years!), I was nonetheless intrigued and delighted when in the first few days and weeks of French class I was able to reproduce whole dialogues with what seemed like a fair amount of fluency. (Nearly forty years later, I can still recite several sizeable portions of those first dialogues I learned, though they are stored in a verbatim form, much like verses of a song.) It was difficult at first to remember what I was learning, as we were not given written versions of the dialogues until several weeks after we had been instructed to memorize them. By that time, as a visual learner, I had already tried to write down the words as I thought they would be spelled, only to discover that I would have to start learning the correct forms of the dialogue lines all over again when the "prereading" period was over. I also remember being quite frustrated when encountering in the dialogues new forms that I couldn't identify (such as the irregular subjunctive that was used in the second dialogue we were taught) and having the teacher tell me that we would learn about that "later." For students like me who were not terribly tolerant of ambiguity, who wanted clear explanations, and who needed to see things written down, the method was sometimes exasperating. (Nevertheless, I must say that I enjoyed French enough to continue it through high school, college, and graduate school, so there were aspects of this approach to learning that must have appealed to me.) Many students and teachers, however, expressed dissatisfaction with the general approach to language learning that ALM represented, and its popularity began to fade by the end of the 1960s. Strasheim (1976) sums up general dissatisfaction with the purest form of audiolingualism as follows:

> *Every student, probably dating from Cain and Abel, has recognized this awful dichotomy between "classroom thinking" and "real-life thinking"; the successful student, for generations, has been the one who could keep them separate. In the late sixties, however, students were not content to keep the two discretely apart . . . Our "one true way" had had a life of under 10 years (p. 41).*

By 1970, many language practitioners were looking for alternatives to ALM, or at least for ways to adapt the approach to suit their students' and their own needs. Today, many teachers continue to use selected audiolingual techniques within an eclectic framework.

Reactions to Audiolingualism: Two Mentalist Perspectives

Background   When second-language acquisition theorists of the late 1960s and early 1970s began to reject behaviorist views of language learning in favor of rationalist and mentalist perspectives, applied linguists began to look for approaches to the classroom that were more congruent with the prevailing theories of the times. Ellis (1990) describes two mentalist perspectives on teaching that contrasted quite strongly with one another. One view was based on principles of first-language acquisition and was characterized by an attempt to simulate "natural" learning processes in the classroom. He characterizes this view, described in a series of articles by Newmark (1966) and Newmark and Reibel (1968), as the *cognitive anti-method*. Contrasting strongly with this perspective was the view that grew out of Chomsky's competence-performance distinction and that held that learners must understand and analyze the rules of the language to build their competence. This view, described most thoroughly by Chastain (1976), was called the *cognitive-code method*. Because these two perspectives have had a strong influence on the development of American language teaching methodologies in subsequent years, they will be described briefly below.

▨ The Cognitive Anti-Method

Major Characteristics   Ellis (1990) describes the following major theoretical assumptions underlying the Cognitive Anti-Method, articulated by Newmark (1966) and Newmark and Reibel (1968):

1. *"Second-language learning is controlled by the learner rather than the teacher"* (Ellis 1990, p. 35). The learner is engaged in problem solving, using the input as the data from which the system of language is discovered.
2. Learners have an innate ability to learn languages. Their language acquisition capacity is qualitatively like that of a child.
3. One need not pay attention to form in order to acquire a language. Linguistic analysis is not necessary for language learning, and grammatical rules and explanations are not useful in the classroom.
4. Learners do not acquire linguistic features one by one but acquire language globally. There is, therefore, no need to sequence instruction through selection and grading of the input.
5. Errors are inevitable and should be tolerated. Learners will eventually discover and correct their own errors and, therefore, do not have to receive error correction from the teacher.
6. L1 interference will disappear with more exposure to the target language. Contrastive analysis and the overt comparison of L1 with L2 is therefore of little use (based on Ellis 1990, pp. 35–37).

Ellis remarks that the *cognitive anti-method* did not have many adherents, partly because it was before its time and partly because it was "too radical" (p. 40). Another problem was that the pedagogical ideas that Newmark and Reibel (1968) proposed were rather fragmentary in nature. Although the authors maintained that the teacher should not interfere with the natural learning process, some of the pedagogical techniques that were used as illustrations in their 1968 article seemed to have behavioristic overtones. For example, Newmark and Reibel suggested that adults would learn a second language most easily and effectively by memorizing dialogues and practicing situational variants of those conversations, "substituting new items from previously learned dialogues corresponding to slight changes [students] wish to introduce into the situation" (p. 153). One of their central concerns was finding ways to "increase the likelihood that the student will imitate the language behavior of his teacher" (p. 153). The use of such terms as "memorization," "substitution," and "imitation" seem somewhat incongruent in an ideological approach that, according to Ellis (1990), was firmly based in Chomsky's "cognitivism" (p. 35).

The most controversial aspect of the cognitive anti-method was the proposal that structural features should not be taught overtly and that language materials need not be ordered grammatically. Many practitioners, as well as scholars, thought this view was too extreme. Diller (1978), for example, considered the idea that grammatical instruction should be abandoned as a rationalist "heresy," and argued instead for a combination of meaningful learning with conscious attention to form using materials graded for difficulty (pp. 90–92).

Some of the ideas advanced by Newmark and Reibel, however, continued to have an appeal for those who believed that classroom language learning was too far removed from real language use. When Krashen introduced his Monitor Theory in the late 1970s, he incorporated some of the same notions that had been proposed in the cognitive anti-method, arguing their merits on somewhat different theoretical grounds. Many practitioners who were looking for more communicative approaches to teaching began to show interest in the *Natural Approach,* which translated Krashen's theory into practice. An evaluation of this approach will be given later in the chapter.

The Cognitive-Code Method

**Major
Characteristics**

A basic assumption underlying cognitive methodology was that meaningful learning was essential to language acquisition, and that conscious knowledge of grammar was important. This viewpoint contrasted strongly with both audiolingualism and the cognitive anti-method described above.

Chastain (1976) has characterized the basic tenets of the cognitive approach, paraphrased below:

1. The goal of cognitive teaching is to develop in students the same types of abilities that native speakers have. This is done by helping students attain a minimal control over the rules of the target language so that they can generate their own language to meet a previously unencountered situation in an adequate fashion.
2. In teaching the language, the instructor must move from the *known* to the *unknown;* that is, the student's present knowledge base (cognitive structure) must be determined so that the necessary prerequisites for understanding the new material can be provided. This knowledge base includes not only the students' present understanding of the new language, but also their understanding of how their native language works, as well as their general "knowledge of the world." Students must be familiar with the rules of the new language before being asked to apply them to the generation of language. The foundation, or *competence,* must come first. *Performance* will follow once the foundation is laid.
3. Text materials and the teacher must introduce students to situations that will promote the *creative use of the language.* The primary concern is that students have practice going from their underlying understanding of the way the language works to using the language in actual communication of ideas.
4. Because language behavior is constantly innovative and varied, students must be taught to understand the rule system rather than be required to memorize surface strings in rote fashion. Therefore, grammar should be overtly explained and discussed in a cognitive classroom.
5. Learning should always be *meaningful;* that is, "students should understand at all times what they are being asked to do" (p. 147). New material should always be organized so that it is relatable to students' existing cognitive structure. Since not all students learn in the same way, the teacher should appeal to all senses and learning styles (based on pp. 146–147).

Proficiency Orientation	The proficiency orientation of a cognitive approach to learning will depend on how that approach is interpreted by textbook and materials writers and by classroom teachers. Many contemporary foreign language textbooks seem to offer a blend of communicative and cognitive teaching approaches, in that some of the key elements of a cognitive orientation (such as grammatical explanations and examples, structured practice activities leading to more open-ended practice, and a focus on meaningful processing of language) are still widely used. Such texts tend to emphasize meaning and communication through the use of thematically organized chapters, the integration of cultural material, and the contextualization of the presentation and practice of new language forms. When teachers provide students with ample opportunities to create with the language, use language in context, and focus on form in meaningful activities and exercises, the approach can be quite congruent with a proficiency orientation.
Potential Drawbacks	Care should be taken when using an essentially cognitive approach to avoid spending too much time on the explanation of grammar, especially in the native language. Many teachers are tempted to devote a large portion of the class hour to explanations, operating on the premise that a cognitive orientation to methodology implies that students need a thorough understanding of the grammatical system of the new language. While this may be an ultimate goal for some students, it is not necessary to devote an inordinate amount of time to explanation per se or to expect a thorough understanding of the details of the grammatical system all at once. Rather, a proficiency-oriented approach will promote this basic understanding through the use of contextualized practice activities in which students constantly use the new structures in a personalized way. Also, structures can be taught in a *cyclical* fashion in which they are constantly reentered in new contexts as instruction progresses over time.

A Functional Approach: Communicative Language Teaching

Background	Richards and Rodgers (1986) describe Communicative Language Teaching (CLT) as an *approach* rather than a method, since it is defined in rather broad terms and represents a philosophy of teaching that is based on communicative language use. CLT has developed from the writings of British applied linguists such as Wilkins, Widdowson, Brumfit, Candlin, and others, as well as American educators such as Savignon (1983), all of whom emphasize notional-functional concepts and communicative competence, rather than grammatical structures, as central to language teaching (Richards and Rodgers 1986, p. 65). Although the movement first began with a reconceptualization of the teaching syllabus in notional-functional terms, CLT has broadened to encompass a wide range of principles for developing communicative competence. Richards and Rodgers (1986), citing Finocchiaro and Brumfit (1983), outline 22 major distinctive features of this approach. Some of these principles are summarized below.
Major Characteristics	1. Meaning is of primary importance in CLT, and contextualization is a basic principle.

2. Attempts by learners to communicate with the language are encouraged from the beginning of instruction. The new language system will be learned best by struggling to communicate one's own meaning and by negotiation of meaning through interaction with others.
3. Sequencing of materials is determined by the content, function, and/or meaning that will maintain students' interest.
4. Judicious use of the native language is acceptable where feasible, and translation may be used when students find it beneficial or necessary.
5. Activities and strategies for learning are varied according to learner preferences and needs.
6. Communicative competence, with an emphasis on fluency and acceptable language use, is the goal of instruction. "Accuracy is judged not in the abstract, but in context" (p. 92) (summary based on Finocchiaro and Brumfit 1983, pp. 91–93, cited in Richards and Rodgers 1986, pp. 67–68).

Richards and Rodgers state that although CLT does not claim a particular theory of language learning as its basis, there are several theoretical premises that can be deduced from a consideration of the approach:

1. *The communication principle:* Activities that involve communication promote language learning.
2. *The task principle:* Activities that involve the completion of real-world tasks promote learning.
3. *The meaningfulness principle:* Learners must be engaged in meaningful and authentic language use for learning to take place (Richards and Rodgers 1986, p. 72).

Sample Classroom Activities

The kinds of classroom activities that would be representative of CLT include interactive language games, information sharing activities, task-based activities, social interaction, and functional communication practice (Richards and Rodgers 1986). Savignon (1983, 1997) suggests designing the curriculum to include language arts (or language analysis activities), language-for-a-purpose (content-based and immersion) activities, personalized language use, theater arts (including simulations, role-plays, and social interaction games), and language use "beyond the classroom" (including inviting L2 speakers into the classroom and planning activities that take learners outside the classroom to engage in real-world encounters). (See Savignon 1997, pp. 170–201 for a thorough description of these curricular components.) She gives many examples of communicative language teaching ideas that can be used to generate a classroom atmosphere conducive to the development of communicative competence in all skill areas. For a more complete treatment of communicative language teaching, consult the sources cited above, as well as Brumfit and Johnson (1979), Littlewood (1981), Finocchiaro and Brumfit (1983), and Yalden (1987).

Proficiency Orientation

Clearly, many of the tenets of CLT are congruent with the principles outlined at the beginning of this chapter. Communicative language teaching, like any instruction oriented toward proficiency goals, is not bound to a particular methodology or curricular design, but represents a flexible approach to teaching that is responsive to learner needs and preferences. In many ways, CLT represents a repertoire of teaching ideas rather than a fixed set of methodological procedures, and as such is not easily defined or evaluated. The congruence of any particular version of CLT with proficiency goals will depend on the choices made by the program designers and instructors.

Modern Adaptations of the Direct Method

Although the two approaches to be described next are in some ways quite different from one another, each has evolved to some extent from direct methodology.

■ Total Physical Response

Background

This approach is based on the belief that listening comprehension should be developed fully, as it is with children learning their native language, before any active oral participation from students is expected. Further, it is based on the belief that skills can be more rapidly assimilated if the teacher appeals to the students' kinesthetic-sensory system. The approach, developed by James J. Asher, utilizes oral commands that students carry out to show their understanding. As with the direct method, the target language is the exclusive language of instruction. Students are exposed to language that is based in the here-and-now and that is easily understood through mime and example.

Major Characteristics

Asher (1972) and Asher, Kusudo, and de la Torre (1974) outline several key ideas that underlie the Total Physical Response approach:

1. Understanding of the spoken language must be developed in advance of speaking.
2. Understanding and retention is best achieved through *movement of the students' bodies* in response to commands. The imperative form of the language is a powerful tool because it can be used to manipulate students' behavior and guide them toward understanding through action. Asher et al. state that their research indicates that most of the grammatical structures of the target language and hundreds of vocabulary items can be learned through the skillful use of the imperative by the instructor.
3. Adult language learning can be modeled after the way children learn their native language.

Sample Classroom Activities

A few examples of commands students respond to in relatively early training will serve to illustrate this methodology. The activities described are presented in Asher, Kusudo, and de la Torre (1974). The reader may want to read this or other source material for a more complete understanding of the way the method works. (See also Asher 1982.)

Listening Training. Students sit in a semicircle around the instructor. The instructor asks them to be silent, listen to commands in Spanish, and then do exactly what she does. The students are encouraged "to respond rapidly without hesitation and to make a distinct, robust response with their bodies" (p. 27). For example, when the teacher commands students to run by saying *¡Corran!,* students are to run with gusto. Commands such as "Stand up! Walk! Stop! Turn! Walk! Stop! Turn! Sit down!" are then executed in succession in Spanish. The instructor simultaneously executes the commands as they are given, accompanied by the two students seated beside her. This routine is repeated several times until individual students indicate that they are willing to try it alone without the instructor acting as a model. Each variation of the routine is different to avoid the memorization of a fixed sequence of behaviors.

Next, commands are expanded to full sentences, such as "Walk to the door! Walk to the window! Walk to the table! Touch the table!" As students learn more vocabulary in this way, "surprises and novelty" are introduced, and the instructor begins to use playful, bizarre, and "zany" directives to keep students' interest high.

Production. Asher et al. state that after about ten hours of training in listening, students are "invited but not pressured" to reverse roles with the instructor and give their own commands in Spanish. The instructor then performs in response to the students' commands. After this is successfully done, about 20 percent of all class time will be spent in role reversal of this type. Later, skits are prepared and performed by students, and still later, problem-solving situations are used. In this latter activity, students are presented with an unexpected difficulty in a typical survival situation or other setting in a Latin country and are expected to talk their way through the situation to a solution.

Reading and Writing. Although there is no formal training in reading and writing in the approach as described by Asher et al., they do state that the instructor spent a few minutes at the end of each class session writing structures or vocabulary on the blackboard for students requesting explanation. Students generally copied the expressions into their notebooks. No English equivalents were given. Most expressions were those already heard during the class session.

Proficiency Orientation

TPR methodology, as described by Asher et al. (1974), is affectively appealing to many students: The atmosphere in the class is warm and accepting, allowing students to try out their skills in creative ways. The focus on listening skills in the early phases of instruction allows students to experience the new language in a low-anxiety environment, and the use of techniques to act out what is understood ensures that comprehension of the language is taking place. It seems that TPR is not really designed to be a comprehensive "method" in and of itself, but represents instead a useful set of teaching ideas and techniques that can be integrated into other methodologies for certain instructional purposes. TPR techniques have been used effectively by many practitioners, and methodologies such as the Natural Approach, described next, include them among their instructional strategies.

Potential Drawbacks	If TPR is the only strategy used for language teaching, there may be some substantial limitations on what can be effectively accomplished in terms of proficiency goals. Although "with imagination, almost any aspect of the linguistic code for the target language could be communicated using commands" (Asher et al. 1974, p. 26), the functional use of language as described in the proficiency guidelines and the contexts normally used in the target culture do not seem to be a natural outcome of this methodology. There is also very little emphasis on the development of accuracy in Asher's description of the method.

The Natural Approach

Background	Terrell (1977, 1982) based his methodology on Krashen's theory of second-language acquisition, discussed in detail in Chapter 2. Terrell's main premise is that "it is possible for students in a classroom situation to learn to communicate in a second language" (1977, p. 325). His definition of communicative competence is interesting in that it resembles the description of Level 1/1+ (Intermediate) proficiency:

> *I use this term to mean that a student can understand the essential points of what a native speaker says to him in a real communicative situation and can respond in such a way that the native speaker interprets the response with little or no effort and without errors that are* so distracting that they interfere drastically with communication. *I suggest that the level of competence needed for* minimal communication *acceptable to native speakers is much lower than that supposed by most teachers. Specifically, I suggest that if we are to raise our expectations for oral competency in communication we must lower our expectations for structural accuracy (1977, p. 326, emphasis added).*

From this statement, it seems that the goal of the Natural Approach is set at an Intermediate (survival) proficiency in the second language, at least in oral/aural skills. This will have important implications for classroom practice. According to Higgs and Clifford (1982), "if the goal is to produce students with Level 1 survival skills, then the optimum curriculum mix would be . . . a primary emphasis on the teaching and practice of vocabulary" (p. 73), with little emphasis on structural accuracy. This principle holds true in some respects in the Natural Approach, as we shall see below.

Major Characteristics	Terrell (1977) provided the following guidelines for classroom practice in the "Natural Approach":

1. *Distribution of learning and acquisition activities.* If communication is more important than form in beginning and intermediate levels of instruction, then most, if not all, classroom activities should be designed to evoke communication. Terrell suggested that the entire class period be devoted to communication activities. Explanation and practice with linguistic forms should be done outside of class for the most part. "This outside work must be carefully planned and highly structured" (p. 330); explanations must be clear

enough to be understood by students so that classroom time is not wasted in grammatical lectures or manipulative exercises. Terrell suggested that teachers make specific assignments, collect student work, and provide some type of systematic feedback on that written work. However, "the student should realize that the primary responsibility is his for improvement in the quality of his output" (p. 330).

2. *Error correction.* According to Terrell, there is "no evidence" to show that "the correction of speech errors is necessary or even helpful in language acquisition." In fact, such correction is "negative in terms of motivation, attitude, embarrassment," and the like, "even when done in the best of situations" (p. 330).

3. *Responses in both L1 and L2.* Terrell suggested that initial classroom instruction involve listening comprehension activities almost exclusively, with responses from students permitted in the native language. "If the student is permitted to concentrate entirely on comprehension by permitting response in L1, he can rapidly expand his listening comprehension abilities to a wide variety of topics and still be comfortable in the communication process" (p. 331). Listening comprehension will, of course, take the form of "comprehensible input," as Krashen has explained that term. At first, simplified speech or "foreigner talk" is used. This type of speech has the following characteristics:

   a. a slower rate, with clear articulation, diminished contractions, longer pauses, and extra volume
   b. the use of explanations, paraphrases, gestures, and pictures to define new words or concepts
   c. simplification of syntax and the use of redundancy
   d. the use of yes/no questions, tag questions, forced choice (either/or) questions, and questions with a sample answer provided (summary based on Terrell 1982, p. 123).

Terrell (1977) suggested four main principles to guide language teaching:

1. Beginning language instruction should focus on the attainment of immediate communicative competence rather than on grammatical perfection.
2. Instruction needs to be aimed at modification and improvement of the student's developing grammar rather than at building that grammar up one rule at a time.
3. Teachers should afford students the opportunity to *acquire* language rather than force them to *learn* it.
4. Affective rather than cognitive factors are primary in language learning (based on p. 329).

For Terrell, the key to comprehension and oral production is the acquisition of vocabulary. "With a large enough vocabulary, the student can comprehend and speak a great deal of L2 *even if his knowledge of structure is for all practical purposes nonexistent*" (p. 333, emphasis added).

Sample Classroom Activities

Three types of activities dominate the classroom lesson in the Natural Approach. All of these activities are highly contextualized and personalized. Terrell (1982) maintained that "a low anxiety situation can be created by involving the students *personally* in class activities. . . . The goal is that the members of the group become genuinely interested in each other's opinions, feelings, and interests, and feel comfortable expressing themselves on the topics of discussion in class" (p. 124).

The three types of acquisition activities are:

1. *Comprehension (preproduction) activities,* which consist of listening comprehension practice, with no requirement for students to speak in the target language. Comprehension is achieved by contextual guessing, TPR techniques, the use of gestures and visual aids, and data gleaned from personalized student input. One technique that Terrell used in beginning classes is description of students in the class in terms of hair color, clothing, height, and other physical attributes. Students are asked to stand up when described, or questions are asked so that students being described are identified by the others in the class.

The preproduction (comprehension) phase of instruction lasts, according to Terrell, about four to five class hours for university students, but could last several months for younger students.

2. *Early speech production* will occur once students have a recognition vocabulary of about 500 words. Production activities begin with questions requiring only single-word answers or with either/or questions in which the alternatives are provided. This type of production parallels that of young children who first begin to speak in holophrastic (single-word) utterances. Another type of production activity is the sentence-completion response, in which a personalized question is asked and the answer is provided except for one word, which students supply.
3. *Speech emergence* occurs after the early speech production phase and is encouraged through the use of games, humanistic-affective activities, and information and problem-solving activities. During all of these activities, the teacher is careful not to correct errors, as this is potentially harmful to the students' speech development.

As can be seen from this description, the Natural Approach classroom is one in which communication activities, contextualized acquisition opportunities, and humanistic learning techniques dominate.

Proficiency Orientation

There are quite a few elements of the proficiency-oriented classroom in the description just given if one bears in mind that the ultimate goal of instruction is survival-level communication. The students learn language *in context* in personalized activities. There is a very warm, affective atmosphere in class, and opportunities for group communicative practice abound. Students are encouraged to *create with the language* at all times. The obvious missing element, however, is the complete lack of corrective feedback during classroom practice. It is also not clear from Terrell's description how important a role cultural authenticity and cultural learning play in classroom activities; no doubt most opportunities to teach students how to cope in the target culture are exploited in this approach.

Potential Drawbacks

One aspect of Natural Approach methodology that may not be congruent with proficiency goals is the lack of form-focused instruction or corrective feedback in classroom instruction. This issue has been a source of controversy in recent years, with some scholars claiming that explicit instruction in grammar is not helpful in the classroom and that errors should never be corrected during oral activities. It is important to remember, however, that Terrell did suggest that there was a role for corrective feedback in written work, although he maintained that the study of grammatical principles and the correction of errors should be the student's responsibility. In his last writings, however, Terrell (1991) seemed to be amending his point of view on the issue of form-focused instruction. He suggested that explicit instruction in grammar might have some benefits for learners acquiring the language in the classroom, including its use as an advance organizer and as a means of establishing form-meaning relationships in communicative activities. In addition, he hypothesized that learners who are able to monitor their speech may produce more grammatical utterances that they will then "acquire." This acknowledgement of a potentially positive role for explicit grammar instruction marks an important modification in the Natural Approach, as described by Terrell in his earlier work.

Humanistic Approaches to Language Teaching

Since the early 1970s, various approaches to language teaching employing humanistic strategies have been advanced, with names such as *confluent, personal, affective, facilitative, psychological, futuristic,* and *humanistic education.* All of these varieties are based on movements in psychotherapy, such as values clarification and sensitivity training, in which the affective development of the individual is the first concern. Galyean (1976) gives a detailed description of many of these approaches, and the reader may want to read this source for a thorough understanding of the humanistic movement in education. One humanistically oriented methodology that has received some attention in recent years is described in the following section.

Community Language Learning

This approach, alternatively called Community Language Learning (CLL) and Counseling-Learning, stresses the role of the affective domain in promoting cognitive learning. Developed by Charles Curran (1976), it is founded on techniques borrowed from psychological counseling. The basic theoretical premise is that the human individual needs to be understood and aided in the process of fulfilling personal values and goals. This is best done in community with others striving to attain the same goals.

Major Characteristics

The first principle of CLL is that the teacher serves as the "knower/counselor" whose role is essentially passive. He or she is there to provide the language necessary for students to express themselves freely and to say whatever it is they want to say. The class is comprised of six to twelve learners seated in a close circle, with one or more teachers who stand outside the circle, ready to help. The techniques used are designed to reduce anxiety in the group to a minimum and to promote the free expression of ideas and feelings. The method provides for five learning stages (summary based on Stevick 1976a):

Stage 1. Students make statements aloud in their native language, based on whatever they desire to communicate to the others in the group. The teacher, placing his or her hands on the student's shoulders, translates the utterance softly into the student's ear. The student then repeats the utterance after the teacher's model, recording it on tape. Another student, desiring to make a response, will signal this desire to the teacher, who then comes around the circle and provides a target-language equivalent for this student in the same way. Again, the response is recorded on tape, so that at the end of the conversation the whole dialogue is recorded. This tape-recorded script is used later in the class session as a source of input for the analysis and practice of the language.

Stage 2. This second stage, known as the "self-assertive stage," differs from the first in that the students try to say what they want to without constant intervention and help from the teacher.

Stage 3. In this "birth stage," students increase their independence from the teacher and speak in the new language without translation, unless another student requests it.

Stage 4. The "adolescent" or "reversal" stage is one in which the learner has become secure enough to welcome corrective feedback from the teacher or other group members.

Stage 5. This "independent" stage is marked by free interaction between students and teacher(s): Everyone offers corrections and stylistic improvements in a community spirit. By this time, the trust level is high, and no individual is threatened by this type of feedback from others in the group. At all times, the atmosphere is one of warmth, acceptance, and understanding (based on Stevick 1973, reprinted and revised in Curran 1976, pp. 87–100).

Proficiency Orientation

Many elements hypothesized to contribute to the building of proficiency are present in this approach: There is contextualized and personalized learning, students are creating with the language, and there is attention to accuracy without sacrificing affective concerns. In fact, one of the major strengths of the method seems to be the warm, community atmosphere that is created by the procedure and the provision of corrective feedback in this humanizing context. The teacher takes care to help students induce the grammatical system from their own input and isolates important and useful vocabulary that they need to review for active control. (See Samimy and Rardin 1994 for a discussion of results of a qualitative study on the affective reactions of adult learners to CLL methodology.)

Potential Drawbacks

One area that may need attention in using CLL methodology is that of course content or context. As described, the procedure does not ensure that a variety of contexts necessary for coping in the target culture is included. Since the content is determined by the participants in the group, who may not necessarily know what to expect in encounters in the target culture, some survival skills may be neglected. This problem may be easily remedied, however, if the teacher is willing to encourage or enable students to include such content in the lesson on occasion. For example, the conversation could center around authentic material that students had read or viewed (Stevick 1992).

Another potential drawback is that some students may feel uncomfortable with the apparent lack of structure or sequence in the introduction of grammatical and lexical items (see, for example, Samimy and Rardin 1994). This problem could also be dealt with if the teacher is willing to introduce some control in this regard.

■ The Silent Way: Learning through Self-Reliance

Background

Introduced by Gattegno (1976), this method can be classified as cognitivist in orientation. In Gattegno's view, the mind is an active agent capable of constructing its own inner criteria for learning. The three key words of the philosophy behind this approach are *independence, autonomy,* and *responsibility.* Every learner must work with his or her own inner resources (i.e., existing cognitive structures, experiences, emotions, knowledge of the world) to absorb learning from the environment. The Silent Way assumes that learners work with these resources and *nothing else,* as they are solely responsible for what they learn. The teacher's role is to guide students in the hypothesis-testing process in which they are constantly engaged. (For a thorough discussion of the theories behind Gattegno's approach, see Gattegno 1976; Stevick 1976b, 1980; and Richards and Rodgers 1986.)

Major Characteristics

Stevick (1976b) outlines five basic principles underlying the Silent Way:

1. *Teaching should be subordinated to learning.*
2. *Learning is not primarily imitation or drill.*
3. *In learning, . . . the mind "equips itself by its own working, trial and error, deliberate experimentation, by suspending judgment, and revising conclusions."*
4. *As it works, the mind draws on everything it has already acquired, particularly . . . its experience in learning the native language.*
5. *If the teacher's activity is to be subordinate to that of the learner, . . . then the teacher must stop interfering with and sidetracking that activity (p. 137).*

The method is perhaps best known for its use of colored rods, called Cuisenaire rods, for teaching the basic structures of the language. A set of color-coded phonetic and word charts is also essential to the Silent Way classroom. As in the direct method, the target language is the exclusive language of instruction. (See Gattegno 1976 for a complete description of this method.)

Sample Classroom Activities

Perhaps one of the best sources of sample lesson material is Stevick (1980), who provides a wealth of examples with insightful commentary on the way the lessons work. For purposes of illustration, Stevick gives workshop audiences an "experience" with the method and is careful to point out that it is not a "demonstration." In this experience, six people are invited to sit around a table in the front of the room, in view of the rest of the audience. The instructor first opens a bag of rods (colored sticks of different lengths) and deposits them on the table. The instructor next picks up various rods, examines them, and then finally selects a long one. Motioning to everyone to be silent and listen, he or she pronounces the word *çubuk,* the Turkish word for "rod."

After a few seconds of silence, the instructor motions the six participants to say the word in chorus. After a few choral repetitions, the individuals are asked one by one to pronounce the word as the instructor picks up the same rod. If any one learner's pronunciation is off, making it difficult for a native speaker to understand, the instructor has the student try again by motioning silently. If this second attempt fails, the instructor motions to someone who has said the word correctly to produce it again. Soon everyone can say "rod" appropriately in Turkish.

Then the instructor pushes all of the rods toward one learner and motions for him or her to pick up one, saying *çubuk* in the process. When this student has successfully produced the word, the rods are placed in front of someone else. This process continues until the students deduce that *çubuk* means "rod," and not a particular length of rod.

After teaching *çubuk,* the instructor then introduces the concept of the numbers 1, 2, and 3 by setting out six rods, one single one, a group of two, and a group of three. The instructor then makes a show of counting them, to get across the idea that the new words to be introduced are numbers. Motioning again for silence and attention, the instructor pronounces each numeral in the same way that the word for "rod" was introduced. Beginning with the word for "two" (*iki*), students soon learn to say *iki çubuk* when the group of two is indicated. Again, students have multiple opportunities to say the words, picking up or pointing at the rods as they do so to confirm what they are saying.

The lesson continues on this principle of "teach, then test, then get out of the way" (Stevick 1980, p. 56). Students use the new words they have learned to manipulate the rods, either through the silent directions given by the instructor or on their own initiative.

Proficiency Orientation

It is difficult to make an assessment of the proficiency orientation or potential drawbacks of this method without first having extensive experience using it. However, from my own limited experience in observing Silent Way demonstration classes, it does seem that this method is oriented in several ways toward proficiency goals. Because students are responsible for their own learning, they must pay close attention and actively interact with others in the class. Students use the language meaningfully and creatively, within the limitations imposed by the vocabulary and structures of the lesson, as they are invited to construct their own messages early in the learning sequence. The students' attention is constantly being directed to accuracy as they attempt to produce the language, and the students themselves, in cooperation with the teacher, serve as monitors of their own output in a low-anxiety, cooperative atmosphere.

Potential Drawbacks

One of the drawbacks of this method is that learners do not work with authentic, culturally based materials or hear authentic native speech, at least in the early phases of instruction. If students are to develop a functional proficiency in the language, it would seem that they need ample opportunities to hear native speakers using the language in authentic exchanges and to practice using the language to cope with everyday situations they might encounter in the target culture. The place of culture and culture-based language instruction is not clear from the literature about the Silent Way. Richards and Rodgers (1986) explain that manuals for teachers are generally not available and that the Silent Way teacher is responsible for designing and sequencing instruction (p. 107).

Suggestopedia: Tapping Subconscious Resources

Background

This method, also known as *Suggestive-Accelerative Learning and Teaching* (SALT), and the *Lozanov Method,* originated in Bulgaria. It was introduced by Georgi Lozanov (1978), a psychotherapist and physician, who believes that relaxation techniques and concentration will help learners tap their subconscious resources and retain greater amounts of vocabulary and structures than they ever thought possible.

Hallmarks of the method include the "suggestive" atmosphere in which it takes place, with soft lights, baroque music, cheerful room decorations, comfortable seating, and dramatic techniques used by the teacher in the presentation of material. All of these features are aimed at totally relaxing students, allowing them to open their minds to learning the language in an unencumbered fashion.

Chastain (1988) describes Suggestopedia as a wholistic method that tries to direct learning to both the left and right hemispheres of the brain. Learning should involve both analysis and synthesis at the same time, using both the conscious and the unconscious mind. Because Lozanov sees anxiety as a hindrance that severely limits learning potential, two teaching principles are proposed to break down the sociopsychological constraints of traditional learning environments. The first principle is that of *infantilization,* which is designed to help students recapture the kind of learning capacities they had as children. The second is that of *pseudopassivity,* which refers to a relaxed physical state of heightened mental activity and concentration (Chastain 1988, p. 104).

Major Characteristics and Sample Classroom Activities

A four-hour instructional cycle in the original Lozanov method, as described by Bancroft (1978), consists of three parts:

1. First, there is a review of previously learned material, mainly through the use of conversations, games, and skits. Mechanistic practice is avoided. As

students begin the course, they are given new names (often containing repeated phonemes, such as French nasal sounds) and a foreign role to play. Bancroft provides the example of a student receiving the name "Léon Dupont" and being told "he lives at 11 (*onze*), rue Napoléon, that he works as a *maçon*, and so on" (p. 170).

2. The second part of the lesson is presented in a somewhat traditional fashion using both grammar and translation techniques, although classes are conducted in the foreign language as much as possible. New material is given in the form of lengthy dialogues representing typical language-use situations. The dialogues are constructed to have continuity in plot and context and represent events and activities so that they will be more easily acted out and remembered.

3. The third part of the class, or "séance," is meant to reinforce learning of the new material at an unconscious level through memorization. The séance has both an active and a passive ("concert") phase. Relaxation techniques and rhythmic breathing are used to help students internalize the material. In the active part of the session, students listen as the teacher reads the dialogue lines, varying his or her presentation by changing the volume of the voice and using different intonations. "The loudness or softness of the voice and the quality of the suggestion (declarative, subtle, authoritative) are used for variety and contrast and probably also to prevent the rhythmically-breathing students from falling asleep in class" (p. 171)! Students look at the text as they hear the foreign language phrase and mentally repeat the material to themselves. The active session lasts for about 20 to 25 minutes.

    During the passive, or "concert," phase, students listen to slow-moving, soft baroque music and meditate on the text with their eyes closed as the teacher acts out the dialogue "with an emotional or artistic intonation" (p. 171). After some 20 to 25 minutes of this concert phase, students are brought out of their relaxed state with a selection of fast, cheerful baroque music.

Some American adaptations of Suggestopedia include shorter class periods, larger class sizes, and shortened forms of the active séances (see, for example, Bancroft 1978, 1982). They also emphasize the use of various relaxation procedures (Bancroft 1978). Readers interested in more detailed discussion of this method should consult Lozanov 1978; Stevick 1980; Bancroft 1978, 1982; and Richards and Rodgers 1986.

Proficiency Orientation

This method seems to have a variety of features that are helpful in the development of language proficiency. The language is initially presented in context through dialogues that are culturally based. Such texts based on everyday life give students models that can be used to develop functional proficiency through role-plays and other interactive language-practice activities. The method also addresses the affective needs of students by providing a relaxed and nonthreatening atmosphere for learning. There also seems to be an interest in the development of accuracy, as explanations are provided for grammatical structures learned and the material is practiced and reviewed in Phases 1 and 3 of the instructional cycle.

Potential Drawbacks

One possible drawback with a dialogue-based approach is that the input material seems to be almost exclusively pedagogically prepared. The use of authentic input material, both for reading comprehension and for listening, seems somewhat limited, at least from descriptions of the method in the literature. Perhaps the dialogue material is supplemented at some point with unedited, authentic presentation texts; if not, this might be one way in which the Lozanov method could be adjusted to correspond more closely to proficiency goals.

Chastain (1988) maintains that adapting Suggestopedia to the typical classroom situation "presents huge problems because Lozanov recommends implementation only in its original and complete format, which does not fit the typical classroom schedule" (p. 103). The adaptations mentioned earlier (see Bancroft 1978, 1982) have attempted to address this difficulty.

Summary: On Teaching a Language

In this chapter we have seen how principles and priorities in language teaching have shifted and changed over the years, often in response to paradigm shifts in linguistic and learning theory. Historically, methods that adhere to empiricist viewpoints have contrasted sharply with those that derive from a rationalist perspective of human learning. The various methodologies and approaches that have been reviewed in this chapter have experienced differential success and popularity among practitioners. Today, many teachers are adopting an eclectic approach to language learning and teaching, believing that the age-old search for the "one true way" can be futile and frustrating. As we realize that learning is an extremely complex process and that learners are individuals with different personalities, styles, and preferences, we have begun to look for a multiplicity of ways to respond to the challenge of teaching. Eclecticism, however, needs to be principled if instruction is to be effective, and techniques and activities need to be chosen intelligently to relate to specific program objectives (Richards and Rodgers 1986).

This chapter has proposed some general principles that might orient our teaching toward proficiency goals. The hypothesized principles focus on providing instruction that is meaningful, interactive, and responsive to learner needs. In the next chapter, we explore the important role that context plays in fostering this type of learning environment.

Activities for Review and Discussion

1. Give a brief definition for each of the following terms:

    a. Methodology
    b. Syllabus
    c. Approach
    d. Strategy
    e. Eclecticism
    f. Proficiency-oriented instruction

2. What are the five working hypotheses outlined in this chapter? How does each relate to the idea of teaching language in context?

3. In which methods or approaches described in this chapter would the following classroom activities or teaching practices be prevalent or receive a high priority? Explain briefly why these practices are considered beneficial to language study by advocates of the approach you identify.

    a. Frequent use of manipulative pattern drills
    b. Learning of grammar rules with exceptions and irregularities noted
    c. Tape-recorded group conversations, with the teacher acting as a counselor/informant
    d. Musical accompaniment to language-learning activities
    e. Frequent use of commands
    f. Translation of reading passages from native to target language and from target to native language
    g. Exclusive use of the target language in all phases of instruction
    h. Absence of error correction during class sessions
    i. Heavy emphasis on correct pronunciation
    j. Observance of the "natural order" of listening, speaking, reading, and writing in language teaching activities
    k. Use of colored word charts and Cuisenaire rods in instruction

4. Of the five working hypotheses outlined in this chapter, are there any hypotheses that you don't agree with? Are there any hypotheses that you might want to add to the ones discussed in this chapter?

5. Consider, in light of the five working hypotheses, the teaching approach you currently use, or one that you are familiar with through observation or personal experience. What characteristics of this approach would you consider conducive to the development of proficiency? What characteristics might need modification to make the approach more proficiency-oriented?

References: Chapter 3

Aljaafreh, Ali and James P. Lantolf. "Negative Feedback as Regulation and Second Language Learning in the Zone of Proximal Development." *The Modern Language Journal* 78, iv (1994): 465–83.

Allen, Edward D., and Rebecca M. Valette. *Classroom Techniques: Foreign Languages and English as a Second Language.* New York: Harcourt Brace Jovanovich, 1977.

Anthony, E. M. "Approach, Method, and Technique." *English Language Teaching* 17 (1963): 63–67.

Asher, James. "Children's First Language as a Model for Second Language Learning." *The Modern Language Journal* 56, iii (1972): 133–39.

———. *Learning Another Language through Actions: The Complete Teacher's Guide.* Los Gatos, CA: Sky Oak Productions, 1982.

Asher, James, JoAnne Kusudo, and Rita de la Torre. "Learning a Second Language through Commands: The Second Field Test." *The Modern Language Journal* 58 (1974): 24–32.

Bancroft, W. Jane. "The Lozanov Method and Its American Adaptations." *The Modern Language Journal* 62 (1978): 167–75.

———. "Suggestopedia, Sophrology, and the Traditional Foreign Language Class." *Foreign Language Annals* 15 (1982): 373–79.

Beauvois, Margaret Healy. "Computer-Mediated Communication (CMC): *Technology for Improving Speaking and Writing.*" Pp. 165–184 in M. D. Bush, ed., *Technology-Enhanced Language Learning.* The ACTFL Foreign Language Education Series. Lincolnwood, IL: National Textbook Company, 1997.

Bellot, James. *The French Method, Wherein is Contained a Perfite Order of Grammar for the French Tongue.* London: Robert Robinson, 1588. Reprinted: Scolar 1970. (Cited in Kibbee 1987.)

Benseler, David P. and Renate A. Schulz. "Methodological Trends in College Foreign Language Instruction." *The Modern Language Journal* 64 (1980): 88–96.

Birckbichler, Diane W. *Creative Activities for the Second Language Classroom.* Language in Education: Theory and Practice Series, no. 48. Washington, DC: Center for Applied Linguistics, 1982.

———, ed. *New Perspectives and New Directions in Foreign Language Education.* The ACTFL Foreign Language Education Series. Lincolnwood, IL: National Textbook Company, 1990.

Bragger, Jeanette. Personal communication, 1991.

Brown, H. Douglas. "The Consensus: Another View." *Foreign Language Annals* 17 (1984): 277–80.

Brumfit, C. J. and K. Johnson, eds. *The Communicative Approach to Language Teaching.* Oxford: Oxford University Press, 1979.

Buck, Kathryn, Heidi Byrnes, and Irene Thompson, eds. *The ACTFL Oral Proficiency Interview Tester Training Manual.* Yonkers, NY: ACTFL, 1989.

Bush, Michael D., ed. *Technology-Enhanced Language Learning.* The ACTFL Foreign Language Education Series. Lincolnwood, IL: National Textbook Company, 1997.

Byrnes, H. and M. Canale, eds. *Defining and Developing Proficiency: Guidelines, Implementations and Concepts.* The ACTFL Foreign Language Education Series. Lincolnwood, IL: National Textbook Company, 1987.

Chastain, Kenneth. *Developing Second Language Skills: Theory to Practice,* 2nd ed. Chicago: Rand McNally, 1976.

———. *Developing Second Language Skills: Theory and Practice,* 3rd ed. New York: Harcourt Brace Jovanovich, 1988.

Chomsky, Noam. *Aspects of the Theory of Syntax.* Cambridge, MA: M.I.T. Press, 1965.

Cook, G. and B. Seidlhofer, eds. *Principle and Practice in Applied Linguistics: Studies in Honour of H. G. Widdowson.* Oxford: Oxford University Press, 1995.

Curran, Charles. *Counseling-Learning in Second Languages.* Apple River, IL: Apple River Press, 1976.

Daly, John. "Understanding Communication Apprehension: An Introduction for Language Educators." Chapter 1 (pp. 3–13) in E. Horwitz and D. Young, eds., *Language Anxiety: From Theory and Research to Classroom Implications.* Englewood Cliffs, NJ: Prentice Hall, 1991.

DeKeyser, Robert. "The Effect of Error Correction on L2 Grammar Knowledge and Oral Proficiency." *The Modern Language Journal* 77, iv (1993): 501–14.

de Sainliens, Claude. *The Frenche Littelton. A most Easie, Perfect, and Absolute way to learne the frenche tongue.* London: Thomas Vautroullier, 1576. (Cited in Kibbee 1987.)

Diller, Karl Conrad. *The Language Teaching Controversy.* Rowley, MA: Newbury House, 1978.

Doughty, Catherine and Jessica Williams, eds. *Focus on Form in Classroom Second Language Acquisition.* Cambridge, England: Cambridge University Press, 1998a.

———. "Pedagogical Choices in Focus on Form." Chapter 10 (pp. 197–261) in C. Doughty and J. Williams, eds., *Focus on Form in Classroom Second Language Acquisition.* Cambridge, England: Cambridge University Press, 1998b.

Ellis, Rod. *Understanding Second Language Acquisition.* Oxford: Oxford University Press, 1985.

———. *Instructed Second Language Acquisition.* Oxford: Basil Blackwell, Ltd., 1990.

Finocchiaro, M. and C. Brumfit. *The Functional-Notional Approach: From Theory to Practice.* New York: Oxford University Press, 1983.

Frommer, Judith G. "Cognition, Context, and Computers: Factors in Effective Foreign Language Learning." Pp. 199–223 in J. A. Muyskens, ed., *New Ways of Learning and Teaching: Focus on Technology and Foreign Language Education.* AAUSC Issues in Language Program Direction. Boston, MA: Heinle & Heinle, 1998.

Galloway, Vicki. "From Defining to Developing Proficiency: A Look at the Decisions." Chapter 2 (pp. 25–73) in H. Byrnes and M. Canale, eds., *Defining and Developing Proficiency: Guidelines, Implementations and Concepts.* The ACTFL Foreign Language Education Series. Lincolnwood, IL: National Textbook Company, 1987.

Galloway, Vicki and Angela Labarca. "From Student to Learner: Style, Process, and Strategy." Chapter 4 (pp. 111–58) in D. Birckbichler, ed., *New Perspectives and New Directions in Foreign Language Education.* The ACTFL Foreign Language Education Series. Lincolnwood, IL: National Textbook Company, 1990.

Galyean, Beverly. "Humanistic Education: A Mosaic Just Begun." Chapter 7 (pp. 201–44) in G. Jarvis, ed., *An Integrative Approach to Foreign Language Education: The Challenge of Communication.* The ACTFL Foreign Language Education Series, vol. 8. Lincolnwood, IL: National Textbook Company, 1976.

Gass, Susan M. and Carolyn G. Madden. *Input in Second Language Acquisition.* Rowley, MA: Newbury House, 1985.

Gass, Susan M. and Sally Sieloff Magnan. "Second-Language Production: SLA Research in Speaking and Writing." Chapter 7 (pp. 156–97) in A. O. Hadley, ed., *Research in Language Learning: Principles, Processes, and Prospects.* The ACTFL Foreign Language Education Series. Lincolnwood, IL: National Textbook Company, 1993.

Gass, Susan M. and Larry Selinker. *Second Language Acquisition: An Introductory Course.* Hillsdale, NJ: Lawrence Erlbaum Associates, 1994.

Gass, Susan M. and E. M. Varonis. "Task Variation and Nonnative/Nonnative Negotiation of Meaning." Chapter 9 (pp. 149–161) in S. Gass and C. Madden, eds., *Input in Second Language Acquisition.* Rowley, MA: Newbury House, 1985.

Gattegno, Caleb. *The Common Sense of Foreign Language Teaching.* New York: Educational Solutions, 1976.

Grittner, Frank M. "Bandwagons Revisited: A Perspective on Movements in Foreign Language Education. Chapter 1 (pp. 9–43) in D. Birckbichler, ed., *New Perspectives and New Directions in Foreign Language Education.* The ACTFL Foreign Language Education Series. Lincolnwood, IL: National Textbook Company, 1990.

Haas, Mari and Margaret Reardon. "Communities of Learners: From New York to Chile." Pp. 213–41 in J. K. Phillips, ed., *Collaborations: Meeting New Goals, New Realities.* Northeast Conference on the Teaching of Foreign Languages. Lincolnwood, IL: National Textbook Company, 1997.

Hadley, Alice Omaggio, ed. *Research in Language Learning: Principles, Processes, and Prospects.* The ACTFL Foreign Language Education Series. Lincolnwood, IL: National Textbook Company, 1993.

Harley, B., P. Allen, J. Cummins, and M. Swain, eds. *The Development of Second Language Proficiency.* Cambridge: Cambridge University Press, 1990.

Harper, J., M. Lively, and M. Williams, eds. *The Coming of Age of the Profession.* Boston, MA: Heinle & Heinle, 1998.

Herron, Carol and Michael Tomasello. "Learning Grammatical Structures in a Foreign Language: Modelling versus Feedback." *The French Review* 61, vi (May 1988): 910–22.

Higgs, Theodore V. "Language Teaching and the Quest for the Holy Grail." Introduction (pp. 1–10) in T. V. Higgs, ed., *Teaching For Proficiency, the Organizing Principle.* The ACTFL Foreign Language Education Series. Lincolnwood, IL: National Textbook Company, 1984.

Higgs, Theodore V. and Ray Clifford. "The Push Toward Communication." In T. V. Higgs, ed., *Curriculum, Competence and the Foreign Language Teacher.* The ACTFL Foreign Language Education Series, vol. 13. Lincolnwood, IL: National Textbook Company, 1982.

Horwitz, Elaine K., Michael B. Horwitz, and Jo Ann Cope. "Foreign Language Anxiety." Chapter 3 (pp. 27–36) in E. K. Horwitz and D. J. Young, eds.,

Language Anxiety: From Theory and Research to Classroom Implications. Englewood Cliffs, NJ: Prentice Hall, 1991.

Horwitz, Elaine K. and Dolly J. Young, eds. *Language Anxiety: From Theory and Research to Classroom Implications.* Englewood Cliffs, NJ: Prentice Hall, 1991.

Hulstijn, Jan H. "Not All Grammar Rules are Equal: Giving Grammar Instruction its Proper Place in Foreign Language Teaching." Pp. 359–86 in R. Schmidt, ed., *Attention and Awareness in Foreign Language Learning.* Technical Report #9. Honolulu, HI: University of Hawaii, Second Language Teaching and Curriculum Center, 1995.

Jarvis, Gilbert A., ed. *An Integrative Approach to Foreign Language Education: The Challenge of Communication.* The ACTFL Foreign Language Education Series, vol. 8. Lincolnwood, IL: National Textbook Company, 1976.

Johnson, Keith. *Communicative Syllabus Design and Methodology.* Oxford: Pergamon Press, 1982.

Karambelas, James. "Teaching Foreign Languages 'The Silent Way.' " *ADFL Bulletin* 3 (1971): 41.

Kelly, L. G. *Twenty-Five Centuries of Language Teaching: 500 BC–1969.* Rowley, MA: Newbury House, 1976.

Kern, Richard G. "Technology, Social Interaction, and FL Literacy." Pp. 57–92 in J. A. Muyskens, ed., *New Ways of Learning and Teaching: Focus on Technology and Foreign Language Education.* AAUSC Issues in Language Program Direction. Boston, MA: Heinle & Heinle, 1998.

Kibbee, Douglas. "Plus ça change . . . 600 Years of French Dialogues." Paper presented at the Annual Meeting of the American Association of Teachers of French. San Francisco, CA, 1987.

———. "L'Enseignement du français en Angleterre au XVIe siècle." Pp. 54–77 in P. Swiggers and W. Van Hoecke, eds., *La Langue française au XVIe siècle: Usage, enseignement, et approches descriptives.* Paris: Leuven University Press, 1989.

Krashen, Stephen. *Principles and Practice in Second Language Acquisition.* New York: Pergamon Press, 1982.

Lado, Robert. *Language Teaching.* New York: McGraw-Hill, 1964.

Lafayette, Robert C., ed. *National Standards: A Catalyst for Reform.* Lincolnwood, IL: National Textbook Company, 1996.

Lee, James F. and Albert Valdman, eds. *Form and Meaning: Multiple Perspectives.* AAUSC Issues in Language Program Direction. Boston, MA: Heinle & Heinle, 2000.

Leow, Ronald P. "Attention, Awareness, and *Focus on Form* Research: A Critical Overview." Pp. 69–96 in J. F. Lee and A. Valdman, eds., *Form and Meaning: Multiple Perspectives.* AAUSC Issues in Language Program Direction. Boston, MA: Heinle & Heinle, 2000.

Lightbown, Patsy M. "Process-Product Research on Second Language Learning in Classrooms." Chapter 6 (pp. 82–92) in B. Harley, P. Allen, J. Cummins, and M. Swain, eds., *The Development of Second Language Proficiency.* Cambridge: Cambridge University Press, 1990.

Lightbown, Patsy and Nina Spada. "Focus-on-Form and Corrective Feedback in Communicative Language Teaching: Effects on Second Language Learning." *Studies in Second Language Acquisition* 12, iv (1990): 429–48.

————. *How Languages Are Learned.* Oxford: Oxford University Press, 1993. 2nd edition, 1999.

Littlewood, W. *Communicative Language Teaching.* Cambridge: Cambridge University Press, 1981.

Long, Michael. "Teacher Feedback on Learner Error: Mapping Cognitions." In H. Brown, C. Yorio, and R. Crymes, eds., *On TESOL '77.* Washington, DC: TESOL, 1977: 278–94.

————. "Does Second Language Instruction Make a Difference? A Review of the Research." *TESOL Quarterly* 17 (1983a): 359–82.

————. "Linguistic and Conversational Adjustments to Non-Native Speakers." *Studies in Second Language Acquisition* 5 (1983b): 177–93.

Lozanov, Georgi. *Suggestology and Outlines of Suggestopedy.* New York: Gordon and Breach, 1978.

Lyman-Hager, Mary Ann and Joanne Burnett. "Meeting the Needs of All Learners: Case Studies in Computer-Based Foreign Language Reading." Chapter 6 (pp. 219–52) in J. K. Phillips and R. M. Terry, eds., *Foreign Language Standards: Linking Research, Theories, and Practices.* The ACTFL Foreign Language Education Series. Lincolnwood, IL: National Textbook Company, 1999.

MacWhinney, Brian. "Implicit and Explicit Processes." *Studies in Second Language Acquisition* 19 (1997): 277–81.

Meunier, Lydie. "Personality and Motivational Factors in Computer-Mediated Foreign Language Communication (CMFLC)." Pp. 145–97 in J. Muyskens, ed., *New Ways of Learning and Teaching: Focus on Technology and Foreign Language Education.* AAUSC Issues in Language Program Direction. Boston, MA: Heinle & Heinle, 1998.

Moulton, W. G. "Linguistics and Language Teaching in the United States: 1940–1960." Pp. 82–109 in C. Mohrmann, A. Sommerfelt, and J. Whatmough, eds., *Trends in European and American Linguistics, 1930–1960.* Utrecht: Spectrum, 1961. [Cited in Rivers 1981.]

Muyskens, Judith A., ed. *New Ways of Learning and Teaching: Focus on Technology and Foreign Language Education.* AAUSC Issues in Language Program Direction. Boston, MA: Heinle & Heinle, 1998.

Newmark, L. "How Not to Interfere in Language Learning." In E. Najam, ed. *Language Learning: The Individual and the Process. International Journal of American Linguistics* 32 (1966) Part 2: 77–83. (Reprinted in Brumfit and Johnson, 1979.)

Newmark, L. and D. Reibel. "Necessity and Sufficiency in Language Learning." *International Review of Applied Linguistics in Language Teaching* 6 (1968): 145–64.

Nielsen, Mel and Elizabeth Hoffman. "Technology, Reform, and Foreign Language Standards: A Vision for Change." Pp. 119–37 in Robert C. Lafayette, ed., *National Standards: A Catalyst for Reform.* Lincolnwood, IL: National Textbook Company, 1996.

Omaggio, Alice C. "Methodology in Transition: The New Focus on Proficiency." *The Modern Language Journal* 67, iv (1983): 330–341.

Phillips, June K., ed. *Building on Experience: Building for Success.* The ACTFL Foreign Language Education Series, vol. 10. Lincolnwood, IL: National Textbook Company, 1979.

————, ed. *Collaborations: Meeting New Goals, New Realities.* Northeast
    Conference on the Teaching of Foreign Languages. Lincolnwood, IL:
    National Textbook Company, 1997.
Phillips, June K. and Robert M. Terry, eds. *Foreign Language Standards: Linking
    Research, Theories, and Practices.* The ACTFL Foreign Language Education
    Series. Lincolnwood, IL: National Textbook Company, 1999.
Pica, Teresa and Catherine Doughty. "Input and Interaction in the
    Communicative Language Classroom: A Comparison of Teacher-Fronted
    and Group Activities." Chapter 7 (pp. 115–32) in S. Gass and C. Madden,
    eds., *Input in Second Language Acquisition.* Rowley, MA: Newbury House,
    1985.
Richards, Jack C. and Theodore S. Rodgers. *Approaches and Methods in Language
    Teaching: A Description and Analysis.* Cambridge: Cambridge University Press,
    1986.
Rivers, Wilga M. *A Practical Guide to the Teaching of French.* New York: Oxford
    University Press, 1975.
————. *Teaching Foreign Language Skills,* 2nd ed. Chicago: University of Chicago
    Press, 1981.
Samimy, Keiko K. and Jennybelle P. Rardin. "Adult Language Learners' Affective
    Reactions to Community Language Learning: A Descriptive Study." *Foreign
    Language Annals* 27, iii (Fall 1994): 379–90.
Sanz, Cristina. "What Form to Focus On? Linguistics, Language Awareness, and
    the Education of L2 Teachers." Pp. 3–23 in J. F. Lee and A. Valdman, eds.,
    Form and Meaning: Multiple Perspectives. AAUSC Issues in Language Program
    Direction. Boston, MA: Heinle & Heinle, 2000.
Savignon, Sandra J. *Communicative Competence: Theory and Classroom Practice.*
    Reading, MA: Addison-Wesley, 1983.
————. "In Second Language Acquisition/Foreign Language Learning,
    Nothing is More Practical than a Good Theory." *IDEAL* 3 (1988):
    83–98.
————. *Communicative Competence: Theory and Classroom Practice.* 2nd ed. New
    York: McGraw-Hill, 1997.
Schmidt, Richard, ed. *Attention and Awareness in Foreign Language Learning.*
    Technical Report #9. Honolulu, HI: University of Hawaii, Second Language
    Teaching and Curriculum Center, 1995.
Schwartz, Bonnie D. "On Explicit and Negative Data Effecting and Affecting
    Competence and *Linguistic Behavior.*" *Studies in Second Language Acquisition* 15
    (1993): 147–63.
Scovel, Thomas. "The Effect of Affect on Foreign Language Learning: A Review of
    the Anxiety Research." Chapter 2 (pp. 15–23) in E. Horwitz and D. Young,
    eds. *Language Anxiety: From Theory and Research to Classroom Implications.*
    Englewood Cliffs, NJ: Prentice Hall, 1991.
Sharwood Smith, Michael. "Input Enhancement in Instructed SLA." *Studies in
    Second Language Acquisition* 15 (1993): 165–79.
Spada, Nina. "Form-Focussed Instruction and Second Language Acquisition: A
    Review of Classroom and Laboratory Research." *Language Teaching* 30
    (1997): 73–87.
Standards for Foreign Language Learning in the 21st Century. National Standards in
    Foreign Language Education Project, 1999.

Standards for Foreign Language Learning: Preparing for the 21st Century. National Standards in Foreign Language Education Project, 1996.

Stern, H. H. "Directions in Foreign Language Curriculum Development." In *Proceedings of the National Conference on Professional Priorities.* Hastings-on-Hudson, NY: ACTFL, 1981.

———. "Analysis and Experience as Variables in Second Language Pedagogy." Chapter 7 (pp. 93–109) in B. Harley, P. Allen, J. Cummins, and M. Swain, eds., *The Development of Second Language Proficiency.* Cambridge: Cambridge University Press, 1990.

Stevick, Earl W. "Review Article: Counseling-Learning: A Whole-Person Model for Education." Pp. 87–100 in Charles Curran, *Counseling-Learning in Second Languages.* Apple River, IL: Apple River Press, 1976a. (Reprinted with modifications from *Language Learning* 23, ii [1973]: 259–71.)

———. *Memory, Meaning and Method: Some Psychological Perspectives on Language Learning.* Rowley, MA: Newbury House, 1976b.

———. *Teaching Languages: A Way and Ways.* Rowley, MA: Newbury House, 1980.

———. *Humanism in Language Teaching.* Oxford: Oxford University Press, 1990.

———. Personal communication, 1992.

———. *Memory, Meaning, & Method: A View of Language Teaching.* 2nd edition. Newbury House Teacher Development. Boston: Heinle & Heinle, 1996.

Strasheim, Lorraine. "What is a Foreign Language Teacher Today?" *Canadian Modern Language Review* 33 (1976): 39–48.

Swaffar, Janet K., Katherine Arens, and Martha Morgan. "Teacher Classroom Practices: Redefining Method as Task Hierarchy." *The Modern Language Journal* 66 (1982): 24–33.

Swain, Merrill. "Communicative Competence: Some Roles of Comprehensible Input and Comprehensible Output in Its Development." Chapter 14 (pp. 235–53) in S. Gass and C. Madden, eds., *Input in Second Language Acquisition.* Rowley, MA: Newbury House, 1985.

———. "Three Functions of Output in Second Language Learning." Chapter 8 (pp. 125–44) in G. Cook and B. Seidlhofer, eds., *Principle and Practice in Applied Linguistics: Studies in Honour of H. G. Widdowson.* Oxford: Oxford University Press, 1995.

———. "Focus on Form through Conscious Reflection." Chapter 4 (pp. 64–81) in C. Doughty and J. Williams, eds., *Focus on Form in Classroom Second Language Acquisition.* Cambridge, England: Cambridge University Press, 1998.

Tarone, Elaine. "On the Variability of Interlanguage Systems." *Applied Linguistics* 4 (1983): 142–63.

Terrell, Tracy D. "A Natural Approach to Second Language Acquisition and Learning." *The Modern Language Journal* 61 (1977): 325–37.

———. "The Natural Approach to Language Teaching: An Update." *The Modern Language Journal* 66 (1982): 121–32.

———. "The Role of Grammar Instruction in a Communicative Approach." *The Modern Language Journal* 75 (1991): 52–63.

Terry, Robert M. "Authentic Tasks and Materials for Testing in the Foreign Language Classroom." Pp. 277–90 in J. Harper, M. Lively, and M. Williams, eds., *The Coming of Age of the Profession.* Boston, MA: Heinle & Heinle, 1998.

Truscott, John. "What's Wrong with Oral Grammar Correction?" *The Canadian Modern Language Review* 55, iv (June 1999): 437–56.

Warriner, Helen. "Foreign Language Teaching in the Schools–1979: Focus on Methodology." *The Modern Language Journal* 64 (1980): 81–87.

Westphal, Patricia. "Teaching and Learning: A Key to Success." Pp. 119–56 in J. K. Phillips, ed., *Building on Experience: Building for Success*. The ACTFL Foreign Language Education Series, vol. 10. Lincolnwood, IL: National Textbook Company, 1979.

Williams, Jessica and Jacqueline Evans. "What Kind of Focus on Which Forms?" Chapter 7 (pp. 139–55) in C. Doughty and J. Williams, eds., *Focus on Form in Classroom Second Language Acquisition*. Cambridge, England: Cambridge University Press, 1998.

Yalden, Janice. *The Communicative Syllabus: Evolution, Design, and Implementation*. Englewood Cliffs, NJ: Prentice Hall, 1987.

4 FOUR The Role of Context in Comprehension and Learning

HYPOTHESIS 1. *Opportunities must be provided for students to practice using language in a range of contexts likely to be encountered in the target culture.*

Chapters 1 and 3 presented a rationale for orienting instruction toward proficiency goals, using the interrelated concepts of content/context, function, and accuracy as organizing threads. This chapter explores the first of these ideas, beginning with the hypothesis that second-language programs should provide students with ample opportunities to (1) learn language in context and (2) apply their knowledge to coping with authentic language-use situations.

As mentioned in Chapter 3, this first principle is not particularly controversial in nature. Most educators agree today that students must eventually know how to use the language forms they have learned in authentic communication situations. Some would agree that this goal can best be achieved if the forms of language are presented and practiced in communicative contexts, where focus on meaning and content is primary. The idea that language learning should be contextualized is certainly not new in language teaching, at least from a theoretical point of view. Indeed, nearly one hundred years ago, Jespersen (1904) had urged in his text *How to Teach a Foreign Language* that "we ought to learn a language through sensible communications" (p. 11). He saw that "sensible communication" involved a certain connection in the thoughts communicated, implying that language lessons built around random lists of disconnected sentences were unjustifiable. Yet theory is often many years ahead of practice, and language lessons in many classrooms throughout the twentieth century were dominated by exercises presenting language for practice in non sequiturs. Seventy-five years after Jespersen's admonition, scholars such as Widdowson (1978) and Slager (1978) were still emphasizing the need for context and longer, more natural discourse as a basis of language teaching, as many language classrooms at the time were dominated by the monotonous drills, non sequiturs, and endless repetitions characteristic of audiolingual methodology. The communicative language teaching movement of the last quarter of the twentieth century, the call for proficiency-based teaching, and the *Standards* initiative have all continued to emphasize this need for contextualization and authenticity, with the result that contemporary textbooks are conceived differently than their predecessors. For example, many texts now come packaged with a wide variety of ancillary/supplementary materials, including a CD-ROM, a dedicated Web page that includes world-wide links, and online activities that include sound and videoclips. While many textbooks are still produced with workbooks and lab manuals, more and more are appearing with the workbook on a CD-ROM packaged with the text. Some textbook packages offer additional CD-ROMs that contain the full audio tape program or that have imaginative and interesting exercises, videoclips, and supplementary cultural information. Audio CDs are also being offered in addition to audiocassette tapes.

The ready availability of authentic materials from the Internet, satellite downlinks, and videotapes, DVDs, and computer software provide today's students with truly contextualized and up-to-date information. However, although such materials are in the target language, there is no assurance that the language use is always normative or that the materials are fully comprehensible to language learners. As was mentioned in Chapter 3, authentic materials in the purest sense of the term are those that were intended for use by native speakers of the language and are thus not tailored to a particular language-learning curriculum. Instructors will need to evaluate such materials and prepare activities and tasks based on them that are appropriate to the level of proficiency of their students. Chapter 5 presents ideas for using this type of material and provides a number of guidelines and references that teachers can use to evaluate software and Internet resources.

With the advent of communicative approaches, proficiency-based instruction, and the *Standards for Foreign Language Learning*—all advocating the use of authentic materials and open-ended, interactive communication—some educators may question the value of including analytic exercises that focus on language forms in contemporary textbooks. Yet there are a number of scholars who believe that a program that fosters the development of proficiency should incorporate both analytic and experiential approaches to language learning (see, for example, Allen, Swain, Harley, and Cummins 1990; Stern 1990). Stern explains that an analytic approach is one in which the language is the object of study, and an experiential approach is one in which language is learned through communication, such as in immersion and content-based classrooms. Allen et al. feel that these two types of teaching may be complementary and "provide essential support for one another in the L2 classroom" (p. 77). Stern assumes that an analytic strategy "of necessity decontextualizes linguistic features" in order to allow for isolation of the forms for analysis (p. 99). He hastens to add, however, that the forms under study should then be recontextualized. Allen et al. express the belief that learners may benefit most if form and function are instructionally linked. "There is no doubt that students need to be given greater opportunities to use the target language. But opportunities alone are not sufficient. Students need to be motivated to use language accurately, appropriately, and coherently" (p. 77). They discuss the need for some focused practice activities, involving not only grammar, but also functional, organizational, and sociolinguistic aspects of the target language. In these kinds of activities, they posit a role for feedback and correction, and state that more research needs to be done to determine how this can be maximally effective.

The thesis of this chapter is that language use in the classroom, whether for analytic or experiential purposes, ought to be contextualized. Even analytic activities and form-focused practice exercises will be improved if they consist of sentences that are connected to one another in a logical sequence or relationship.

The following sample exercises illustrate two ways in which analytic practice (where the focus is on a particular feature of language) can be devised. The first sample is decontextualized and is typical of some of the exercises still used in some language classrooms. The linguistic feature to be practiced is the use of the subjunctive mood after certain verbs of volition in French.

Sample 1
Modèle: Le prof/vouloir/les étudiants/regarder/son/livres
Le prof veut que les étudiants regardent leurs livres.

1. Je/préférer/mon/camarade/choisir/film/ce soir
2. Nous/vouloir/examens/être/plus/facile
3. Tu/exiger/ton/amie/venir/restaurant, etc. . . .

Model: *The teacher/to want/the students/to look at/his/books*
The teacher wants the students to look at their books.

1. *I/to prefer/my/friend/to choose/film/tonight*
2. *We/to want/tests/to be/easier*
3. *You/to insist/your/friend/to come/restaurant,* etc. . . .

The second sample illustrates how the same kind of analytic practice activity can be contextualized to conform to the theme of a particular unit of study, such as looking for an apartment in a unit on lodging or student housing.

Sample 2
A la recherche d'un appartement. Jean-Philippe et son camarade de chambre, Paul, veulent trouver un nouvel appartement dans le quartier universitaire. Créez leur conversation, en utilisant les éléments donnés. Suivez le modèle:

Modèle: Jean-Philippe: Je/vouloir/l'appartement/être/près/université
Je veux que l'appartement soit près de l'université.
Jean-Philippe: Je/préférer/l'appartement/avoir/beaucoup/lumière naturelle
Paul: Et/nous/vouloir/chambres/être/suffisament/grand
Jean-Philippe: Tu/aller/exiger/ils/repeindre/murs? etc. . . .

Looking for an apartment. Jean-Philippe and his roommate, Paul, want to find a new apartment near the university. Create their conversation, using the elements given. Follow the model:

Model: *Jean-Philippe: I/to want/the apartment/to be/near/university*
                           I want the apartment to be near the university.
Jean-Philippe: I/to prefer/the apartment/to have/a lot/natural light
                           Paul: And/we/to want/rooms/to be/sufficiently/large
Jean-Philippe: You/to be going to/insist/they/to repaint/walls? etc. . . .

Samples 1 and 2 are roughly equivalent in difficulty and structure. But while the sentences in the first example would hardly be said in sequence in a real-world situation, the sentences in the second could conceivably be said in a conversation about apartment hunting. The use of the subjunctive to express volition, preference, and other emotions is also bound to occur naturally in this context. For these reasons, the second activity is more natural than the first, although it is still highly structured and focused on a particular grammatical point. Note that it is also possible to do both sample activities without processing the sentences meaningfully. Meaningful processing can be assured for Sample 2 by adding a follow-up task in which students are asked to use the models given to create their own statements about finding lodging or a new apartment. For example, students in small groups could complete sentences such as the following:

> *Nous voulons que l'appartement. . . .*
> *Nous exigeons que la cuisine. . . .*
> *etc.*
> *[We want the apartment. . . .*
> *We insist that the kitchen. . . .*
> *etc.]*

Students might also rank order their own concerns about housing, using the exercise in Sample 2 as a point of departure.

Sample activities 1 and 2 could be thought of as "precommunicative" in nature (Littlewood 1981). That is, they focus primarily on forms and are structured to prepare students to use those forms in communicating their own meanings in subsequent language-practice activities. The fundamental difference between noncontextualized and contextualized practice of this type is that the latter links form with meanings that language learners might genuinely want to convey in natural communicative situations. In designing structured, precommunicative practice, thematically coherent exercises are clearly preferable for this reason.

We have seen that the use of analytic or structured practice, focusing on particular formal features of the language, is recommended by scholars such as Stern (1990) and Allen et al. (1990), in conjunction with experiential language learning. In immersion settings, the focused practice is designed to enable students to refine and shape their communicative output to conform to target language norms. The purposes of precommunicative practice activities are somewhat different, since they are designed to be used *before* students engage in more communicative and open-ended exchanges. Their use is consistent with the positions on language acquisition in adults described by various researchers who affirm that focused practice can be beneficial as students' skills are developing. (See, for example, McLaughlin 1978, 1983, 1987; Slager 1978; Seliger 1979; Higgs and Clifford 1982; Long 1983; Swain 1985, 1995; Ellis 1990; Lightbown and Spada 1993, 1999; Schmidt 1995; Doughty and Williams 1998; Lee and Valdman 2000.) Higgs and Clifford (1982) concluded that if accuracy is one of the goals of instruction, students need to pass through a period of meaningful, yet structured or "monitored" practice, in order to move toward more open-ended communication. For this reason, they argue against approaches that push too soon for unconstrained communication.

Littlewood (1980) suggests that classroom activities be designed to follow a sequence in which meaning gradually plays a greater role. He characterizes linguistic activities along a continuum that progresses through the following types: (1) primary focus on form, (2) focus on form (plus meaning), (3) focus on meaning (plus form), and (4) primary focus on meaning. Type 1 activities should be kept to an absolute minimum in proficiency-oriented instruction. Contextualized and meaningful exercises (Type 2 activities) constitute "precommunicative" practice, and are also only one small subset of the types of contextualized activities that can be useful in a communicative language-learning environment. Open-ended creative and personalized practice, as well as interactive activities, "information-gap" activities (Brumfit and Johnson 1979), role-plays, games, debates, discussions, and other communicative formats (Littlewood's Types 3 and 4) should also be encouraged for the development of oral proficiency. (See the first three corollaries to Hypothesis 1, pp. 90–91.) The use of satellite television, Internet resources, and other technological aids to instruction can increase opportunities for meaningful comprehension and production activities as well. For example, one might use video or Internet-based materials first for comprehension activities. Students might then be asked to look at a sample text to identify important lexical or grammatical features they have been studying, and move from there to production activities that are based on these texts and designed to progress from focus on form to focus on meaning, as Littlewood suggests. In this way, analytic and experiential aspects of language learning can be combined. Content-based instruction and immersion experiences are "experiential" in nature and offer full contextualization of instruction by definition. More will be said about the benefits of this type of learning environment later in this chapter.

Thus far, we have been concentrating on types of activities that would be useful in developing productive skills in the foreign language. Chapters 6 and 7 will provide samples of such activities in various languages for learners at the Novice through Advanced levels in speaking and writing. In the next section of this chapter, some of the research about the role of context and background knowledge in the comprehension process is reviewed. The discussion will be supplemented by practical guidelines for designing listening and reading instruction in Chapter 5.

The Importance of Context and Background Knowledge in the Comprehension Process: Some Theoretical Considerations

The reasons that have been offered thus far for using contextualized language-practice materials have been based largely on the intuitive appeal of such an approach. Most second-language educators would agree, at least in theory, with the idea that learning and practicing language in meaningful contexts is more appealing to both students and teachers than learning isolated bits of language through extensive memorization and drilling. Yet the rationale for contextualizing and personalizing classroom activities should not rest solely upon intuition. When one examines various theories of language comprehension and learning, it becomes clear that additional support can be found for the use of authentic or simulated authentic input in listening and reading, as well as meaningful and contextualized materials for encouraging language production.

■ The Role of Background Knowledge in Understanding and Interpreting Texts

Many language students have experienced at one time or another the difficulties and frustrations that can arise when attempting to understand a spoken or written text in the foreign language, especially when one is in the earliest stages of language study. What are some of the causes of difficulties in comprehension? Why are some texts more difficult to understand than others? How might language students approach listening or reading tasks differently to enhance comprehension? How can teachers prepare students so that listening and reading materials become more comprehensible to them? Answers to these and other questions can be found as we look at various comprehension theories that have been proposed over the years and examine available research about the comprehension process.

As we saw in Chapter 2, a common thread running through various perspectives on language acquisition is the view that the meaningfulness and familiarity of second-language materials play a crucial role as learners begin to develop their second-language skills. Beginning in the 1960s, the role of meaningfulness and organization of background knowledge was particularly emphasized by cognitive psychologists. Educators such as Ausubel (1968, 1978) believed that learning must be meaningful to be effective and permanent. For material to be meaningful, it must be clearly relatable to existing knowledge that the learner already possesses. Furthermore, this existing knowledge base must be organized in such a way that the new information is easily assimilated, or "attached," to the learner's cognitive structure. Ausubel stressed that teachers need to provide "advance organizers"—pedagogical devices that activate relevant background knowledge—to facilitate the learning and retention of new material. Hanley, Herron, and Cole (1995) point out that, although Ausubel was referring to textual organizers, many researchers and practitioners have used the term "advance organizer" in recent years to refer to an array of pedagogical aids, including pictures, titles, topic summaries, preposed questions, and the like. Research about whether such devices are effective will be discussed in the next sections of this chapter.

How does what learners know impact specifically on second-language acquisition? It might first be helpful to think about the kinds of knowledge learners can bring to comprehension tasks. In the second-language comprehension process, at least three types of background knowledge are potentially activated: (1) *linguistic information,* or one's knowledge of the target-language code; (2) *knowledge of the world,* including one's store of concepts and expectations based on prior experience; and (3) *knowledge of discourse structure,* or the understanding of how various kinds or types of discourse (such as conversations, radio broadcasts, literary texts, political speeches, newspaper and magazine stories, and the like) are generally organized. When language practice is limited to the manipulation or processing of linguistic form, only the first type of background knowledge is involved. By contrast, language learning activities that provide relevant context should be helpful in activating students' knowledge of the world and of familiar discourse structure. One might hypothesize that the need for activating knowledge beyond that of the linguistic code is greatest for learners at lower levels of proficiency, whose imperfect control of the language can be a serious hindrance to comprehension.

This hypothesis is supported by research done by Yorio (1971), who isolates the following factors in the reading process:

1. knowledge of the language (the code),
2. ability to predict or guess in order to make correct choices,
3. ability to remember the previous cues, and
4. ability to make the necessary association between the different cues selected.

Yorio suggests that second-language readers and listeners are at a disadvantage for several reasons: (1) Rather than recalling cues with which they are familiar, they are forced to recall cues that they either do not know at all or know imperfectly. Because of this, readers and listeners will forget those cues much faster than they would cues in their native language. (2) They must simultaneously predict future cues and make associations with past cues, a slow and painful process in the second language for many inexperienced learners. In response to a questionnaire administered by Yorio, 30 students at the English Language Institute reported that they felt they understood what they were reading while in the process of reading it, but easily "lost the thread," forgetting what went on before as they processed the subsequent sentence. Yorio attributes this difficulty to the need to concentrate on a triple process: storage of past cues, prediction of future cues, and associations between the two. "If they try to predict what is coming, they forget the past cues; if they try to concentrate on the past cues, prediction is impaired" (p. 111).

The problems encountered by Yorio's students are familiar to many language teachers, especially those whose students are at the Novice or Intermediate levels of proficiency. Students at these levels often try to process language in a "word-for-word" fashion, drawing only on one kind of background knowledge—their imperfect knowledge of the target-language code. If such students can be encouraged to use other cues to meaning, such as their knowledge of the world and of discourse structure, the process of understanding should be facilitated. Teachers can help students in this process by providing supplementary cues to meaning, drawing on all three types of background knowledge discussed earlier.

The view that individuals utilize various types of background knowledge when attempting to comprehend written and oral texts was proposed by reading theorists writing in the 1970s, such as Smith (1971) and Goodman (1972). Both researchers addressed first-language reading comprehension primarily, although they have had a strong influence on the development of second-language theories about the nature of the listening and reading process (Barnett 1989). Smith (1971) maintained that efficient readers process selected elements of the text rather than use all the visual cues available on the printed page. He described the process of comprehension as the "reduction of uncertainty" (p. 12). Goodman (1972) suggested that reading is a "psycholinguistic guessing game," involving the interaction between thought and language. He argued that "the ability to anticipate that which has not been seen . . . is vital in reading, just as the ability to anticipate what has not yet been heard is vital in listening" (p. 16). Both Smith and Goodman described "top-down" models of reading comprehension, where the reader is thought to begin with higher-order concepts (such as one's general knowledge of a topic or situation) and work down to the actual features of the text (such as words, phrases, morphology, syntax, and rhetorical structure) (Barnett 1989). In their view, readers sample the textual cues, make use of redundancies, and formulate their hypotheses about what the text is going to say, actively using background knowledge to make appropriate predictions about the ongoing discourse. The sampling process also serves to help readers confirm or reject their hypotheses as they process the information in the text.

Kolers (1973) also claimed that skilled readers do not process words as such, but work on the semantic or logical relations of the material, "even to the point of disregarding, in a certain sense, the actual printed text" (p. 46). In his view, readers sample the visual cues to formulate concepts that are relatable to what they already know. Anderson, Reynolds, Schallert, and Goetz (1977) suggested that what one brings *to* a text is actually more important than what is *in* the text (p. 369).

As we will see later in this chapter and also in Chapter 5, strictly "top-down" theories of comprehension have been replaced in popularity by more "interactive" models of reading, which suggest that comprehension involves an interactive process between the reader and the text that moves in a cyclical, rather than a linear, fashion between the reader's own mental activities and the textual features. In such models, "text sampling and higher-level decoding and recoding operate simultaneously" (Barnett 1989, p. 13). In these more recent models, the important role of background knowledge is retained, but is tempered by a recognition of the complexity of factors involved and the nonlinear nature of the comprehension process. One such theoretical perspective, which has had a great deal of influence on second-language theory and research, is described in the next section.

▣ Schema Theory: Using Background Knowledge to Enhance the Language-Comprehension Process

The role played by background knowledge in language comprehension is explained and formalized in a theoretical model known as Schema Theory (Carrell and Eisterhold 1983). One of the basic tenets of this theory is that any given text does not carry meaning in and of itself. Rather, it provides *direction* for listeners or readers so that they can construct meaning from their own cognitive structure (previously acquired or background knowledge). The previously acquired knowledge structures accessed in the comprehension process are called *schemata* (the plural of *schema*). The term "schema" was introduced by Bartlett (1932) in his very influential book, *Remembering: A Study in Experimental and Social Psychology,* in which he demonstrated the role that one's previous experience and knowledge has on perception and memory. Other closely related terms that are similar, but not quite synonymous, are *scripts, plans, goals, frames, expectations,* and *event chains* (Carrell and Eisterhold 1983, p. 556; see also Schank and Abelson 1977; Rumelhart 1980; Minsky 1982).

Rumelhart (1977) defines a schema as "an abstract representation of a generic concept for an object, event, or situation" (p. 266). For example, each of us has an abstract representation for the concept *house,* which may be altered considerably depending upon whether one adds adjectives such as *elegant* or *enormous,* as opposed to *ramshackle* or *squalid.* Cultural differences may also alter the abstract representation for a given concept: *house* may have many of the same attributes as *maison,* yet there will undoubtedly be different mental images associated with the two terms because of cultural factors. According to Rumelhart, "misunderstanding" happens when we have found the wrong schema for a given concept or event.

When a schema represents a whole situation (such as going to a movie, repairing a car, going on a picnic, buying groceries, doing laundry, etc.) a chain of stereotypic events or features is called up in an individual's mind in association with the situation. Schank and Abelson (1977) explain this phenomenon using the term *script,* defined as a structure that describes in a predetermined, stereotypic fashion appropriate sequences of events in a particular context. For example, a generic script for the situation "going to a restaurant" might be as follows: One may call for a reservation, depending on the restaurant, get in the car, arrive at the restaurant, sit at a table, order from the menu, eat the meal in a stereotypic sequence, ask for the check, pay the cashier, and leave. Very different "tracks" of the restaurant script might be activated, however, for the situation "going to a three-star restaurant" versus "going to a fast-food restaurant." In the three-star restaurant situation, the stereotypic sequence of actions would include making a reservation, getting dressed up, going to the restaurant, being seated, having a drink, ordering from the menu, having coffee and an elegant dessert, and the like. If one were going instead to a fast-food establishment, an entirely different sequence of events would be activated. (For a discussion of various tracks of restaurant scripts, see Schank and Abelson 1977, pp. 40–50.)

Hudson (1982) refers to the selection of a particular form of a schema as *instantiation,* a term used by Anderson et al. (1976). In the case of the "restaurant schema" mentioned above, one instantiation might involve a quick trip to a drive-up window for a hamburger, while another might involve an elegant evening of fine dining at a restaurant downtown. Comprehending someone's story about going to a restaurant depends, in part, on the schema that is instantiated as one listens. The listener would need to construct a correspondence between the schema he or she had activated and the actual information in the message itself. When both sources of information match sufficiently, the message is said to be understood. Comprehension, therefore, is not a matter of simply processing the words of the message, but involves fitting the meaning of the message to the schema that one has in mind (Hudson 1982; see also Anderson, Prichert, Goetz, Schallert, Stevens, and Trollip 1976; Rumelhart 1980).

Any one individual's interpretation of a message will be heavily influenced by his or her personal history, interests, preconceived ideas, and cultural background. For second-language learners, distortions in comprehension may be due not only to misunderstandings of the linguistic aspects of the message, but also to misreadings of the script or schema due to cultural differences (Bartlett 1932; Carrell 1981a; Johnson 1982; Carrell and Eisterhold 1983).

As mentioned earlier, schema theorists describe an interactive model of comprehension. They posit two separate but interrelated modes of information processing: *bottom-up processing* and *top-down processing* (Rumelhart 1980). Carrell and Eisterhold (1983) explain the difference between these two operations in terms of the type of information that is used in comprehending the message and the way in which that information enters the system. When a message is interpreted principally by paying attention to the specific details (including the decoding of individual words or other linguistic cues) and the listener or reader attempts to instantiate the best fitting lower-level schema for the incoming data, bottom-up processing is taking place. This type of processing is considered *data-driven,* moving from the parts to the whole concept (Rumelhart 1980). If, on the other hand, the listener/reader begins with a more general higher-order schema, makes predictions based on background knowledge, and then searches the input for information to fit into the "slots," top-down processing is occuring. This latter type of processing is considered to be *conceptually driven,* moving from the whole to the parts (Rumelhart 1980; Carrell and Eisterhold 1983, p. 557).

Schema theorists point out that bottom-up processing and top-down processing occur at the same time. Details are attended to in order to instantiate the appropriate schema while conceptual understanding of a more general nature allows the listener or reader to anticipate and predict. "Bottom-up processing ensures that the listeners/readers will be sensitive to information that is novel or that does not fit their ongoing hypotheses about the content or structure of the text; top-down processing helps the listeners/readers to resolve ambiguities or to select between alternative possible interpretations of the incoming data" (Carrell and Eisterhold 1983, p. 557).

Carrell (1988) maintains that skilled readers constantly shift from one processing mode to the other as they accommodate to the demands of the task, while lower-proficiency readers tend to rely too much on one or the other mode of processing, resulting in problems with comprehension (pp. 101–102). Lower-proficiency readers may be too text-bound—relying too heavily on bottom-up decoding of the words and morpho-syntactic features—or conversely too dependent upon their background knowledge, making unwarranted assumptions and missing relevant features of the input. She attributes this unidirectional processing to five possible causes: (1) lack of relevant background knowledge to help readers use top-down processing; (2) failure to activate available schemata; (3) linguistic or reading skill deficiencies; (4) misconceptions about reading, especially in a foreign language; and (5) individual differences in cognitive style (p. 103). The problems alluded to in (4) may include those induced by inefficient approaches to the teaching of reading, where teachers have students read a text in order to answer questions on numerous details that may have little to do with the overall meaning. Test questions that place heavy emphasis on details and fail to encourage inferencing or global processing may promote decoding and one-way (bottom-up) processing, which in turn may result in lack of comprehension of the main ideas. Teachers need to be careful, therefore, to devise questions and activities that encourage the bidirectional processing that skilled readers use.

Carrell and Eisterhold (1983) explain that there are two basic kinds of schemata used in understanding messages: (1) *content schemata* (relating to one's background knowledge and expectations about objects, events and situations) and (2) *formal schemata* (relating to one's knowledge of the rhetorical or discourse structures of different types of texts). Both types of schemata are important to the comprehension process, as we will see in the next section.

Research on the Role of Context in Comprehension

In recent years, a significant amount of research evidence has been gathered to support the theoretical models of comprehension discussed thus far in this chapter. In this section, a variety of such studies are summarized. Virtually all of them can be said to lend support to Schema Theory in that they deal with the role of advance organizers (Ausubel 1968; Ausubel, Novak, and Hanesian 1978), scripts, and other types of contextual support in language comprehension. The sample of studies is not meant to be comprehensive, but shows the breadth of evidence for a schema-based approach to reading and listening.

Some of the practical questions that second-language teachers have asked about the teaching of reading and listening comprehension are addressed in the studies reviewed below. The studies have been grouped to correspond to the following questions:

1. Can pictures, drawings, or other visual organizers actually enhance students' comprehension of texts in the second language? If so, what types of help do they provide? What kinds of pictures might be best to use? Are lots of pictures

needed or does one visual aid suffice? Do students at all levels of proficiency benefit in the same way or to the same degree from the use of pictorial aids? How does the presentation of pictures compare to other kinds of prereading activities?

2. What are the effects of non-pictorial prereading or prelistening activities on comprehension of target-language materials? Does going over key vocabulary with students prior to having them read or listen to a passage enhance their comprehension of the text? What is the effect of giving the students a brief outline, summary, or title of the passage on comprehension? How useful are prequestioning techniques in facilitating comprehension?

3. How important is it for students to have some knowledge of the subject and/or cultural connotations in a passage prior to attempting to read or understand the text? Does a student's cultural background play a role in comprehension?

4. Does the type of text influence the facility with which students comprehend a passage in a foreign language? Are some rhetorical structures easier to understand than others? Does it help students to have a description or preview of the organization of a passage before attempting to read it?

The Role of Visual Organizers

Since the early 1970s, there have been a number of experiments looking at the role that visual and other kinds of organizers might play in both listening and reading comprehension. Some of the earliest work included four studies conducted by Bransford and Johnson (1972). Their research showed clearly that when prose passages are ambiguous or do not present clear cues to the topic, relevant contextual information (or background knowledge) is needed to comprehend them, even though the texts are written in the native language (in this case, English).

A number of subsequent studies that looked at listening or reading comprehension in a foreign language have shown that visual materials, be they still pictures, video, or graphic organizers, also generally enhance comprehension of a target-language text, particularly when learners are at a fairly low level of proficiency. Results such as these make intuitive sense, since second-language learners are often faced with input (both in listening and reading tasks) that is by nature unfamiliar, difficult, and therefore unpredictable because of the learner's lack of familiarity with the linguistic code. The provision of additional contextual information in the form of a visual should make the comprehension task easier by providing an organizational schema for the passage as a whole. However, in studies that compared low-proficiency to higher-level learners or native speakers, pictorial materials did not enhance comprehension to any significant degree for the readers/listeners who were more proficient (Omaggio 1977, 1979; Mueller 1980). This may be because the texts were relatively easy for more advanced learners to comprehend without enhancement. Another finding in research on pictorial organizers is that not all pictures are equally effective at enhancing comprehension, and that several pictures used together are not necessarily better than using just one (Omaggio 1977, 1979). Differential effects have also been found when still pictures versus video have been compared (Chung 1994; Hanley, Herron, and Cole 1995). Table 4.1 summarizes some of the research results on the use of visual organizers in listening and reading comprehension in both the native and foreign languages. A number of studies that have been done comparing or combining visual organizers with other kinds of prereading/prelistening activities are treated in the next section.

Visual Organizers Compared to Other Prereading and Prelistening Activities

In the previous section, we saw that certain kinds of visual materials presented to language learners in advance of a listening or reading task can enhance their comprehension and memory for the new material, especially if learners are at lower levels of proficiency. Table 4.2 summarizes research studies that compare the effects of visual organizers with the effects of other kinds of prereading and prelistening treatments. In general, these studies indicate that nonpictorial prereading/prelistening activities such as studying vocabulary or answering or coming up with questions can have significantly positive effects on comprehension. Several studies indicate that pictorial organizers are particularly helpful to students at the lower levels of proficiency and may enhance comprehension most for beginning and intermediate learners, whereas nonpictorial aids can be as or more effective for learners at higher levels.

**Titles, &
Topic Cues**

The studies summarized in Table 4.3 have investigated the effects of providing subjects with a title or topic for a passage before reading or listening. In the first two studies with native speakers, the passages are somewhat ambiguous; in the third study with students studying French, a key word in the passage has been replaced with a nonsense word. In all three cases, a very familiar event sequence, or "script," is used to construct a passage describing a common activity, such as washing clothes, playing tennis, or doing grocery shopping. The researcher looks at whether the provision of the topic in a brief sentence or two before reading or listening may "activate a script" (Schank and Abelson 1977) and thus enhance comprehension of the passage.

**Summaries,
Questions, and
Captions**

In addition to looking at the effects of giving a topic or title to activate background knowledge, second-language researchers have investigated the effects of summaries of the main ideas of a passage, prequestioning techniques, and the use of captions with videotaped materials. In a series of experiments, Herron (1994), Herron, Cole, York, and Linden (1998), and Herron, Corrie, Cole, and Henderson (1999) looked at the use of summaries and questions as advance organizers to examine their effects on college students' comprehension of video materials in French. The results of these three studies, as summarized in Table 4.4 (p. 157), indicate that both declarative and interrogative forms of advance organizers that

Table 4.1. Summary of Research Results on Visual Organizers

Study/Date	Subjects/Language	Treatments	Findings
Bransford and Johnson (1972)	Adult native English speakers	Subjects listened to an ambiguous passage in native language under one of five conditions: (1) no context provided; (2) visual context before listening; (3) visual context after listening; (4) partial visual context before listening; and (5) no context, but passage was heard twice.	Context-before group (2) had a significant advantage over the other groups in comprehending or recalling the listening passage. (Measured by ratings of comprehensibility and recall of facts from passage.)
Omaggio (1977, 1979)	Second-semester (college) English-speaking students of French reading a story in French; native speakers of English reading the same story in English	Subjects either read a story in L2 (French) or in L1 (English) or had no story to read under six pictorial context conditions: (1) no visual organizer; (2) picture of object depicting story title; (3) contextual picture from beginning of story; (4) contextual picture from middle of story; (5) contextual picture from end of story; (6) all three contextual visuals.	No significant differences on either recall protocol, multiple choice/true-false test, or error scores for subjects reading text in L1. Significant effects for the composite mean of groups having a picture while reading in French (L2); best picture (the one responsible for most of the composite effects and significantly better on its own) was one depicting action from the beginning of the story. No significant difference among subjects having only visuals and no text.
Mueller (1980)	Beginning college English-speaking students of German, one group (Experiment 1) with little or no prior study of German and a second group (Experiment 2) with 4–6 semesters of high school German	Subjects in both experiments listened to a taped interview in German under one of three conditions: (1) a line drawing provided showing the general situation before listening; (2) the same line drawing shown after listening; (3) no visual.	For Experiment 1, students at lower levels of proficiency having the visual before listening performed significantly better on an English-language recall task than students having the visual after or having no visual. Both the "visual before" and the "visual after" groups performed better than those with no visual. In Experiment 2, where students had a higher level of proficiency, the visual variable did not produce a significant difference.
Chung (1994)	University English-speaking students of French (intermediate/advanced)	Students heard four naturalistic dialogues in four presentation conditions: (1) audio only; (2) single still image; (3) multiple still images; (4) motion video.	Listening to dialogue with some kind of visual support significantly enhanced comprehension, with video condition being the most effective.
Hanley, Herron, and Cole (1995)	Fifth grade English-speaking students of French (FLES)	Students read texts after either (1) seeing a related video segment in French prior to reading; or	Students having the video advance organizer had a significant advantage over those having the teacher-read text and four still

		(2) listening to the teacher read the text of the video segment accompanied by four still pictures prior to reading.	pictures on short-answer tests of comprehension.
Tang (1992)	Seventh-grade ESL students	Students read academic texts either (1) with the aid of graphic classification trees reflecting the text's organization during prereading instruction and while reading; or (2) without graphic organizer.	Students having the graphic organizer performed significantly better on recall protocol than those without the graphic organizer.

briefly outline the main events of a video can enhance comprehension, and that using a set of questions relating to the main events in advance of viewing can foster deeper processing of the material (Herron et al. 1999).

Though many studies have shown that various kinds of advance organizers are effective, not all studies demonstrate a comprehension advantage when an advance organizer is used. A study by Chung (1999) with Taiwanese college-level EFL students suggests that the textual advance organizer students received before viewing a video did not give the listeners an advantage, whereas the use of captions while viewing had a significant effect on comprehension. These results differ from those of Herron (1994), in which an organizer consisting of a brief summary of the main scenes of a video was helpful to students listening in French. It would be interesting to know whether the difference in results might be due to the difference in language studied, the level of the students, or some other factor. Chung hypothesized that the students in his study may not have needed the organizer (most had studied English for about six years); he also speculates that the results may have been different had the organizers been provided in written form rather than orally.

In a study with advanced university-level ESL students, Markham (1999) found that the provision of captions (in English) for educational television video materials significantly enhanced the students' ability to recognize new vocabulary they had encountered in the videotape on post-viewing listening comprehension tests, where the orally presented multiple-choice items contained that vocabulary. He suggests that the positive benefits of combining listening material with target-language captions will eventually transfer to listening-only tasks. Markham's 1999 study provided further support for his finding in previous research (Markham 1993, cited in the 1999 study) that captions "dramatically improved the general comprehension of university-level ESL students particularly when the pictorial component of the video did not correlate with the audio portion of the episode" (Markham 1999, p. 322).

Table 4.4 presents a summary of the studies discussed above. In general, the research reviewed here indicates that advance organizers such as brief summaries and prequestions can have very positive effects on learners' comprehension of listening materials; however, as in the previous studies reviewed in this chapter, the

Table 4.2. Summary of Research Results on Visual Organizers Compared to Other Prereading/Prelistening Activities

Study/Date	Subjects/Language	Treatments	Findings
Hudson (1982)	Beginning, intermediate, and advanced adult ESL students	Subjects' reading comprehension was assessed on three passages under each of three treatment conditions: (1) subjects saw pictures related to passage, received focus questions, and wrote down predictions before reading; (2) subjects received vocabulary list and discussed definitions before reading; (3) subjects read passage/took test/reread passage/took test again.	At lower levels of proficiency, the pictorial + questions/predictions condition was more effective, but at more advanced levels, the vocabulary and read/test/reread/retest treatments were as or more effective than the pictorial + questions/ predictions treatment. Hudson concluded induced schemata via picture cues can overcome deficits of lower-proficiency readers; more advanced readers are able to bring more nonvisual information to the process of reading comprehension.
Taglieber, Johnson, and Yarbrough (1988)	Sixth-semester college EFL students in Brazil	Subjects each given four genres of reading material, each passage under one of four conditions: (1) pictorial context (visual condition) where subjects saw three pictures from passage, described them, guessed how they might be related to passage; (2) vocabulary preteaching, where eight words from passage were presented in noncontextualized but meaningful sentences; (3) prequestioning, where students formulated questions based on one-sentence summary of passage topic; and (4) control (no treatment).	Subjects' reading comprehension scores were significantly better in all three preteaching conditions than in control condition, but the vocabulary condition was less effective than the other two treatments. Researchers concluded that visual and prequestioning treatments seemed to produce deeper, more active involvement of students before reading.
Lee (1986)	Third-year English-speaking college students of Spanish	Subjects read both a "familiar" passage (for which they had prior knowledge) and a "novel" passage (depicting an unusual situation for which they had no prior knowledge) under one of four treatment conditions: (1) "context-transparent" (a title and picture page as well as specific concrete vocabulary relevant to content was provided in text); (2) "context-opaque" (title and picture page were provided, but specific concrete vocabulary was not provided in text); (3) "no-context-transparent" (no picture or title was provided but specific concrete vocabulary was in text); (4) "no-context-opaque" (neither picture/title page nor specific	Significant interactions showed all three components of background knowledge affected recall differently across the other components; components affected recall in combination. Subjects' performance on recall protocols written in the native language (English) showed significantly better comprehension with contextual cues (picture + title) on familiar topic only, particularly when vocabulary was transparent in text. The novel topic was best comprehended without the title and picture. Author concludes that even advanced learners needed to rely on context, familiarity, and transparency

		concrete vocabulary provided in text).	to comprehend passages.
Herron, Hanley, and Cole (1995)	Second-semester college students of French	Students viewed videos under one of two conditions: (1) "Description only," where short sentences summarizing major scenes were given before viewing; and (2) "Description + Pictures," where a contextual picture was added to (1).	Students had significantly better comprehension scores when they had both the picture and the summary sentences than when they had the summary alone. Follows up on Herron (1994) where just having a summary of scenes in French before viewing video yielded significantly better comprehension/retention than with no advance organizer.

effects of these various kinds of organizers may be different for learners depending on their proficiency level, with lower-proficiency learners generally benefitting the most from these sorts of comprehension supports. The research also indicates that the use of captions while viewing video material can be beneficial to learners even at advanced levels of language study.

Reader's Background Knowledge and Topic Interest

In the studies reviewed in this section, the researchers were interested in how the background knowledge or level of interest subjects brought to the task of listening or reading affected their ability to comprehend various kinds of material. In general, the studies indicate that students comprehend texts more successfully when the topic is familiar to them than when it is unfamiliar.

However, when students' own schemata do not correspond on given points with the passage content, some problems may occur. For example, Long (1990) reports on an exploratory study that looked at the effects of background knowledge on listening comprehension in Spanish (see Table 4.5, pp.158–159, for a brief summary of this and the other studies in this section). She noted some "dysfunctional effects" of the schemata used by a subgroup of students who overextended their rather limited knowledge about the California gold rush of 1898 while listening to a text about a modern-day gold rush in Ecuador. "For example, many of these subjects wrote that the forty-niners built temporary housing of plastic and cardboard. Some mentioned the high price of gasoline and Coca-Cola in the California mining camps. Others mixed temporal details like the existence of plastics factories and movies with exploits of the Spanish conquistadores" (p. 72).

This phenomenon of overextension and distortion of schemata was pointed out by Bartlett in his 1932 research on "remembering." Bartlett reports at great length on his experiments with British subjects trying to remember the details of folk tales from other cultures, including the North American Indian folk story, "The War of the Ghosts." He mentions that some omissions and distortions of the story may be due to individual differences, but some seem to be attributable to cultural influences. Some more recent research illustrating the role of cultural schemata on comprehension will be treated in the next section.

Table 4.3. Summary of Research Results on Titles and Topic Cues

Study/Date	Subjects/Language	Treatments	Findings
Bransford and Johnson (1972)	Adult native English speakers	In three experiments, subjects listened to ambiguous passage in their native language with or without title or topic. Some had no title/topic; some were given topic before; some were given topic after.	Those receiving topic/title before hearing passage rated it more comprehensible and had significantly better recall than topic-after or no-topic condition.
Schallert (1976)	Adult native English speakers	Subjects reading an ambiguous text in native language with or without title. Groups given one of three tasks while reading: (1) counting surface features; (2) rate text for ambiguity; (3) study text to learn it.	Meaningful processing is influenced by provision of context in title, but effects influenced by type of task students asked to do when reading. Effect of context greater with "deeper processing" (conditions 2 and 3).
Adams (1982)	Adult native English speakers learning French	Students read passages about familiar routines of daily life where key words deleted and replaced with nonsense words. Subjects in experimental condition received a script activator—oral provision of topic before reading.	Subjects having script activator scored significantly higher on vocabulary measure than did those without the script activator. Advance organizer most beneficial to subjects with lower proficiency.

A study done by Carrell and Wise (1998) suggests that although prior knowledge has often been shown to affect reading comprehension in both L1 and L2, it does not always do so. They suggest that readers do not always activate the knowledge they have, and that the significance of factors such as prior knowledge and interest in the topic can differ with different populations and different proficiency levels. They recommend, on the basis of their study, that teachers should avoid low-interest, low prior knowledge topics for readings, or allow students to self-select readings when possible.

Another interesting result reported in Chen and Donin's (1997) study (see Table 4.5) relates to the effects of the language used when writing recall protocols to show comprehension. In their study with Chinese-speaking graduate students, writing recall protocols in the native language (Mandarin Chinese) vs. writing them in the L2 (English) did not make a significant difference or give students a significant advantage. These results contradict those found by Lee (cited in Lee 1986) that students had superior recall of a passage when they wrote their recalls in their native language. Chen and Donin noted that the lack of any advantage

Table 4.4. Summary of Research Results on Summaries, Questions, and Captions

Study/Date	Subjects/Language	Treatments	Findings
Herron (1994)	Second-semester English-speaking students of French	Subjects saw videos under two conditions: (1) advance organizer (sentences outlining main scenes on board in French) given in advance of video viewing; (2) no previewing/preteaching treatment.	Significant comprehension advantage for students having advance organizer before viewing.
Herron, Cole, York, and Linden (1998)	Second-semester English-speaking students of French	Groups saw videos under three conditions: (1) advance organizer (as in Herron 1994) given orally in declarative form; (2) advance organizer given orally in interrogative form with three possible answers; (3) no advance organizer.	Both declarative and interrogative organizers significantly aided comprehension of video, as measured by short-answer questions; no difference between two types of organizers.
Herron, Corrie, Cole, and Henderson (1999)	Second-semester English-speaking students of French	Groups saw video under one of two conditions: (1) declarative organizer (as in Herron 1994) given both orally and written on overhead transparency; (2) interrogative organizer with three choices of possible answers embedded in the questions.	Interrogative form of the advance organizer superior to declarative form in enhancing scores on postviewing tests (multiple-choice, short-answer, and open-ended questions).
Chung (1999)	Taiwanese college students (4th year) studying English (EFL)	High and low groups (based on course grade) viewed video twice under four treatment conditions: (1) textual advance organizer outlining main scenes of video before viewing; (2) captions while viewing; (3) combination of treatments 1 and 2; (4) neither treatment (control)	Significant main effects for both treatment and level. Treatment 3, combining advance organizer and captions, better than other groups but not significantly better than captions alone; captions alone better than advance organizer alone; no differences between advance organizer group and control group. No interaction of treatment by level.
Markham (1999)	Advanced university-level ESL students	Groups viewed educational television segments with or without captions.	On post-treatment multiple-choice tests of vocabulary administered orally, students recognized significantly more words when captions were available than when they had no captions.

Table 4.5. Summary of Research Results on Reader's Background Knowledge and Topic Interest

Study/Date	Subjects/Language	Treatments	Findings
Anderson, Reynolds, Schallert, and Goetz (1977)	Adult native English speakers	Two groups of subjects (physical education majors and music students) read two ambiguous passages that could be interpreted two ways, one congruent with their interests and one not related to their interests.	Interpretation of passages strongly related to subjects' background and interests.
Long (1990)	Third-quarter English-speaking students of Spanish	Students listened to two passages, one less familiar (about a gold rush in Ecuador) and one more familiar (about a popular rock music group). Prior to listening, students completed a questionnaire probing their general background knowledge about gold rushes and rock groups.	Comprehension, as measured on recall and recognition tasks, was significantly greater for more familiar passage than for less familiar passage. Significant, moderate correlations between course grade from previous course and number of ideas recalled.
Bartlett (1932)	Adult British subjects reading in native language	For "War of the Ghosts" story using the *Method of Repeated Reproduction* (Bartlett 1932, p. 63 ff), subjects were asked to retell stories (in written recalls) at several time intervals after having read the story twice at the beginning of experiment. First reproduction 15 minutes after reading; subsequent retellings at differing intervals for individual subjects (a week, several weeks, months, in some cases years).	Recalls showed subjects had become confused about the role of the ghosts and many dropped out supernatural element. Subjects tended to simplify stories, omitting details they felt were irrelevant, changing unfamiliar elements to more familiar ones congruent with own culture.
Chen and Donin (1997)	Chinese graduate students reading in L1 and L2	Subjects with high background vs. low background knowledge in biology read biology texts in L1 and L2.	Results showed that reading in L2 (where proficiency is lower) affected lower-level processing (vocabulary/syntax level), making reading speed slower, particularly for low background knowledge group; however, having high level of background knowledge had strong positive effect on retention of semantic information in both L1 and L2, as measured by a recall protocol.
Carrell and Wise (1998)	University ESL students	Students at four proficiency levels read four expository passages, each under one of four conditions related to background knowledge and topic interest: (1) high interest/high prior knowledge; (2) high interest/low prior knowledge; (3) low interest/high	Only significant main effect was found for proficiency level. Significant interaction between prior knowledge and topic interest: if both were low, mean comprehension score lower.

		prior knowledge; (4) low interest/low prior knowledge.	
Barry and Lazarte (1995)	High school English-speaking students studying Spanish	Two groups of students (one with high prior knowledge of Incas and one with low prior knowledge) read passages at three levels of syntactic complexity.	Recall scores for students with high prior knowledge significantly better than for students with low prior knowledge at levels 1 and 2 of syntactic complexity; for passages with most complex syntax, no significant advantage for high prior knowledge group.

for writing recalls in Chinese may be due to the fact that there is a greater distance between Chinese and English than between English and other Western European languages, and that shifting back and forth between the two languages may be more demanding than writing the recalls in the same language as the text itself. They suggest that researchers should be cautious about applying study results from Indo-European languages to languages in other more distant language families. However, as Chen and Donin point out, their subjects were graduate students and might have had higher levels of proficiency than students in other studies where advantages for native-language recall have been found.

One additional factor that has been researched in this area of inquiry is the effect of syntactic complexity of readings when prior knowledge is also taken into account. A study by Barry and Lazarte (1995) with high school students studying Spanish showed that students with high prior knowledge about the Incas recalled significantly more essential information about passages on this topic when levels of syntactic complexity were low. However, the advantage of prior knowledge seemed to be cancelled out at a higher level of syntactic complexity. Barry and Lazarte point out that expository passages written by native-language Spanish writers tend to consist of long sentences with fairly complex syntax that contain embedded clauses and digressions. Students in this study had had 3–4 years of high school Spanish, but the researchers state that they can assume, based on their results, that "most students still have not acquired sensitivity to the schematic grid or propositional schema necessary to process complex Spanish sentences efficiently" (p. 502). They add that content-based instruction, particularly on historical or cultural topics, may require careful adaptation of texts, reading strategy instruction for processing more complex syntactic cues, or both.

These suggestions are important for teachers and materials writers to consider when developing content-based courses in a second language. They are also important to consider when instructors teaching beginning and intermediate language courses attempt to implement the "Connections" goals of the standards framework through the use of authentic texts in various academic subject areas. The effects of cultural background cues and rhetorical schemata may play an important role with such texts. Research about these topics is reviewed in the next two sections.

Cultural Background Cues

The results of two ESL studies relating to the effects of cultural background knowledge on passage comprehension are summarized in Table 4.6. Findings suggest not only that background knowledge of this type can enhance comprehension, but also that attitudes and emotional reactions may have a role in the activation of schemata and ultimately in the comprehension process.

Rhetorical Structure and Comprehension

Research on the effects of *rhetorical* (as opposed to *content*) schemata shows that comprehension also suffers when the *structure* of a story violates the expected norm. For example, most stories involve a problem-solving episode of some type in which (1) something happens to the protagonist, (2) this event sets up a goal to be accomplished, and (3) the remainder of the story is a description of the problem-solving behavior used to accomplish the goal (Rumelhart 1977). Most simple stories, such as fables, tales, and short narratives, use this generic problem-solving motif as their essential rhetorical structure. Violations of this stereotypic structure might cause the reader to fail to comprehend.

Second-language research (Carrell 1984b; Lee and Riley 1990) has also shown the effects of rhetorical structure on the comprehension of expository texts. For second-language readers, highly organized types of expository narrative struc-

Table 4.6. Summary of Research Results on Cultural Background Cues

Study/Date	Subjects/Language	Treatments	Findings
Johnson (1982)	ESL students reading in English	Students read passages in which some information was familiar and some unfamiliar under one of four conditions: (1) no vocabulary list given; (2) opportunity to study definitions of unfamiliar vocabulary before reading; (3) read passage with words glossed; (4) condition #2 + definitions of words glossed in text.	On comprehension measures after reading (written recall in English and true/false questions on passage) + recall of vocabulary on cloze task two weeks later, students remembered familiar material better than unfamiliar material. Students in group 2 recalled more than group 4. Background knowledge enhanced comprehension more than knowledge of vocabulary did.
Markham and Latham (1987)	ESL students listening to passages in English	Christian, Moslem, and "neutral" subjects listened to two passages about Christian and Moslem prayer practices.	Christian students outperformed others in comprehending passage on Christian prayer; Moslem students outperformed others for passage on Islamic prayer. Students with some type of religious preference had higher mean recollection scores on both passages than "neutral" group.

tures, such as in texts that discuss a problem and suggest a solution, are easier to comprehend than are more loosely organized texts, such as those that consist of a collection of descriptions. Research has also shown that second-language readers can benefit from instruction about the rhetorical structure of such texts before reading. Table 4.7 summarizes research results on narrative structure and its effects on readers' comprehension.

Conclusion: Contextualization and Schema-Based Understanding

It seems clear from many of the studies reported in this chapter that comprehension is an active process where students *interact* with the text, using background knowledge that they bring to the comprehension process as well as the linguistic and rhetorical features of the text itself (Carrell and Eisterhold 1983). When the input provided to language learners is organized and easily relatable to what they already know, the burden of comprehension and learning is eased considerably. Research into schema-based understanding supports the view that learning language in context (i.e., larger discourse frameworks) may be easier than processing language in "bits and pieces" or in isolated sentence frames. "By dealing with related units of information rather than isolated bits, more efficient processing becomes possible" (McLaughlin et al. 1983, p. 138).

This brings us back to the point at which this chapter began: Students need to learn language in logical contexts, either through authentic discourse-length input or through language learning materials that simulate authentic input using sentences that follow in logical sequence. Their reading and listening input, as well as productive practice activities, need to extend beyond the borders of the single sentence to encompass the widest possible contexts in which language is used for communicative purposes. While linguistic science (and pedagogical materials, by analogy) have traditionally centered on the sentence for the purpose of analysis, the field of discourse analysis has increasingly emphasized the importance of *intersentential* relationships in understanding and producing language (Brown 1980, 1987, 1994).

Second-language learners must be made aware of the conventions and constraints of discourse in the target language if they are to fully understand and communicate with the speakers of that language. The role of sociocultural factors, such as appropriate style or register of speech to be used in a given situation, needs to be taught overtly at various points along the course of the curriculum. Students also need to learn expressions and structures that will help them speak and write cohesively and coherently so that their discourse competence, an important component of communicative competence, can be developed. Obviously, if second-language students are never given an opportunity to use language beyond the sentence level in classroom practice activities, the development of these and other important discourse skills will be neglected.

Table 4.7. Summary of Research Results on Rhetorical Structure and Comprehension

Study/Date	Subjects/Language	Treatments	Findings
Carrell (1984a)	Intermediate-level ESL students	Subjects read stories under one of two conditions: (1) story structured in stereotypic fashion; (2) story structure violated.	Second-language reading comprehension suffered when story structure violated.
Riley (1993)	Three levels of English-speaking university students of French	Subjects at each of three levels (2nd semester, 4th semester, 2–4 courses beyond 4th semester) read medieval tale under one of three conditions: (1) ideal structure; (2) flashback; (3) scrambled.	Significant main effects found for English-language recalls for both story organization and language level. Story 1 recalled significantly more accurately than Stories 2 or 3, and Level 3 students outperformed Level 2 students, who outperformed Level 1 students. Level 2 students most affected by story structure violations.
Lee and Riley (1990)	Third-semester English-speaking university students of French	Students read two types of texts (collection of descriptions and problem/solution organization) under one of three advance organizer conditions: (1) no rhetorical framework provided before reading; (2) minimal framework provided; (3) expanded framework provided.	Problem/solution passage significantly easier to comprehend. Students with expanded framework as advance organizer remembered significantly more than those with minimal or no framework.
Raymond (1993)	High-intermediate English-speaking students of French (5 semesters university coursework)	Subjects read two texts of problem/solution type in one of two treatment conditions: (1) experimental subjects trained in five discourse structures and "signal words"; (2) control subjects had no rhetorical training but answered questions on texts.	Experimental group benefitted from rhetorical structure training, having higher comprehension scores for one of the texts that subjects found more difficult. For both groups, significant loss from pretest to posttest for text that was more familiar, but experimental group had significant gain on the difficult, unfamiliar text.
Hague and Scott (1994)	Survey of Spanish high school and college texts	Fifteen textbooks examined to see whether type of expository texts used matched the type of texts lower-proficiency learners found easier to process (more organized structures, such as comparison, causation, problem/solution).	70% of sample texts were of the more loosely organized "description" and "collection" type, making them difficult to process, especially when material is unfamiliar.

The Role of Computers in Providing Richer Contexts for Language Learning

One of the newest resources for language teachers in providing an enriched context for learning is the computer. Frommer (1998) points out that computers, when used appropriately, can provide meaningful contexts as well as background information that students need to understand the cultural framework in which the target language is used, and thus help students learn language in its "full cultural meaning" (p. 211). Frommer lists at least three dimensions that computers, along with new technologies such as interactive videodiscs, CD-ROMs, the Internet, and the World Wide Web, add to the learning environment for foreign language learners: "(1) exposing students to larger quantities of text, images, and authentic materials; (2) increasing time on task in an efficient way; and (3) allowing students to assume responsibility for their own learning" (p. 211). Whether used in the tutorial (directed) mode or in the exploratory (browsing) mode, computers offer many features that provide context and aid memory and cognition. Specifically, Frommer points out a number of advantages to using this new technology:

- "The computer is *multisensory*," providing materials in more than one modality, thereby providing students with "richer mental images to support language learning" (p. 212).
- "The computer can be programmed to allow users to *control* both the conditions of viewing and what is viewed" (p. 212), so that information and tasks can be tailored to suit the learners' own level and address their individual interests (pp. 212–213).
- "The computer is *multidimensional* and extensible" (p. 213). That is, hypertext, which allows the computer to provide links between pieces of data, is not physically limited in space and can take the form of visuals, motion video, sound, or words.
- When students use computers to connect to the Internet and the World Wide Web, they can gain access to a multitude of authentic texts created by and for native speakers, engage in e-mail exchanges, and learn about various aspects of culture as well. "By familiarizing themselves with this authentic material, learners can gradually construct their own contexts" (p. 214).
- "The computer . . . offers students an *interactive* learning experience" (p. 214). Frommer points out that good computer programs require students to make choices and act in order for the program to continue, thus demanding the student's active attention. Furthermore, computer interactivity offers reactions to what the student does and thus provides informative feedback and evaluation.

Although it is easy to see that computers can offer a great deal of potential advantages for learning and teaching language, we need to evaluate carefully how best to use this resource to maximize its benefits for our students. Cubillos (1998) addresses the issue of the validity of the computer as a pedagogical tool in the communciative classroom. He rightly points out that teachers, not administrators, are the ones who need to make the decisions about which materials and equipment are most suited to the needs of their learners—decisions that should be informed by research evidence of the effectiveness of these types of pedagogical tools as well as appropriate training in their use. Cubillos maintains that, "in the case of Computer Assisted Instruction (CAI) a healthy dose of skepticism on the part of faculty is warranted and even desirable" (p. 39). He proposes that language teachers "gain ownership over these technologies so that they can be incorporated into our curricula in ways that are consistent with our current understanding of Second Language Acquisition (SLA) processes" (p. 39).

Although Cubillos acknowledges that research about the effectiveness of new technologies is still somewhat limited, he outlines a number of insights that research studies have contributed to our understanding of the role that technology can play in language acquisition. In his research review, he presents evidence that technology can (1) facilitate vocabulary learning; (2) increase students' awareness of language structure through more sophisticated error-feedback programs; (3) support reading and writing development; (4) help teachers keep track of students' processing of language; (5) facilitate students' exploration of the target culture; (6) enhance motivation; and (7) enhance teaching resources through such tools as grading programs, presentation software, and e-mail communication with students as well as other professionals. He also points out that some technological materials are not as good as others, and that evaluation of software and computer programs is necessary in order to make optimal choices for use in instruction. Interested readers should consult this source for more detailed information concerning the research evidence reviewed and for additional pedagogical advice about incorporating technology in instruction.

Integrating Language and Content: Immersion and Content-Based Instruction

One way to ensure that language learning occurs in a meaningful context and that language processing goes beyond the level of the isolated sentence is to develop instructional models where language and content are closely intertwined. In recent years, numerous scholars have discussed the merits of *content-based instruction* for the teaching of foreign languages in the United States. (See, for example, De Lorenzo and Gladstein 1984; Genesee 1985; Brinton, Snow, and Wesche 1989; Swain and Lapkin 1989; Snow, Met, and Genesee 1989; Met 1991, 1999; Stryker and Leaver 1997; Bragger and Rice 1998; Shrum and Glisan 2000.) Many of the principles of content-based instruction are derived from those used in the design of *immersion* programs, begun in Canada in 1965 and widely used in the teaching of French to Anglophone children in Canadian schools. Adaptations of the immersion model for schools in the United States have served various purposes: (1) as educational, cultural, and linguistic enrichment programs in the elementary grades; (2) as magnet schools to bring about an ethnic and/or racial balance within a school district; and (3) as a means of achieving a kind of two-way bilingualism in communities with large minority populations (Genesee 1985, p. 544). Although the initial purposes for the development of immersion and content-based instruction differed in Canada and the United States, a common goal of such programs is the development of significant levels of language proficiency through experiential learning in subject-matter areas.

Content-based and immersion programs in this country have been most prevalent in the early grades, at least in the teaching of foreign languages to English-speaking children (Genesee 1985). Programs at the secondary school level and at the university level have been developed for the most part to accommodate the needs of limited English proficiency (LEP) learners or to help non-native speakers of English integrate successfully into English-language instructional contexts (see, for example, Mohan 1986; Cantoni-Harvey 1987; Crandall 1987; Snow and Brinton 1988; Snow, Met, and Genesee 1989). Met (1991) defines content-based foreign language learning as "instruction [that] uses learning objectives and activities drawn from the elementary school curriculum as a vehicle for teaching foreign language skills" (p. 281). She adds that the foreign language can be the sole language of instruction, or it can be used to augment and supplement instruction in the native language. Included under the rubric of "content-based instruction" are partial and total immersion models as well as programs for language-minority children in the United States, where instruction in their native language is supplemented by content-based instruction in English.

Because current models of content-based foreign language instruction in the United States are derived in large part from Canadian programs, it would be useful to understand what the term "immersion" means in that context. Genesee (1985) defines Canadian immersion programs as those in which the target language is used for teaching regular school subjects. He describes three immersion models that have been used successfully in Canadian schools. The first is called *early immersion,* where the first two, three, or even four grades of schooling are done completely in French, followed by a gradual incorporation of English-language instruction up until sixth grade, when instruction in the two languages is evenly divided. The second model is *delayed immersion,* where students in the fourth and fifth grades receive instruction in French, followed by a reintegration into the regular English-language curriculum in subsequent grades. The third model is *late immersion,* beginning with all-French instruction in seventh or eighth grade, usually following one year of "core French," which consists of a daily period of language instruction in an otherwise English-language curriculum (Swain and Lapkin 1989). Programs can be characterized as either *total immersion* or *partial immersion* models, the latter involving approximately 50 percent of the school day in French and the other half in English. Swain and Lapkin (1989) add that at the secondary level, early immersion students can choose to take several subjects in French if they so desire, as can students completing the delayed or late immersion programs after one or more years of French-language instruction in all subjects.

Extensive research has been done on the effects and benefits of immersion programs in Canada (see, for example, Pawley 1985, who lists over 30 research reports). Studies generally show that students develop a relatively high level of functional proficiency in the second language (Swain and Lapkin 1989). While it is true that early immersion learners sometimes show a slight advantage in listening and speaking skills, these differences are not always significant, and early immersion students do not surpass late-immersion students in literacy skills. Swain and Lapkin characterize adolescent and adult learners as being more efficient, especially in the areas of reading and writing. They posit several possible reasons for this greater efficiency among the older learners: (1) they already know how to read and write in their native language when they begin the immersion experience, and thus can transfer these skills to the new language; and (2) they are cognitively more mature than the younger learners, and are thus "better able to abstract, to generalize, and to classify from the beginning of their second language learning experience" and to attend consciously to what they are learning (p. 152). Swain and Lapkin conclude that teachers of adults in second-language learning situations should therefore not be discouraged: "Your learners have many cognitive and language learning strategies to draw on, and your task is, in part, to help them to make use of these strategies" (p. 153).

This is not to say that early immersion programs should be abandoned. On the contrary, the success of enrichment programs such as the ones in Culver City, California and Montgomery County, Maryland, as well as magnet school programs such as those in Cincinnati, Milwaukee, and San Diego is well documented, and such American innovations are extremely promising (Genesee 1985). It seems clear that more children should have the opportunity to benefit from early content-based instruction in American schools. But even when such opportunities are not available, the Canadian data suggest that it is possible for older learners to benefit from content-based instruction as well. In some ways, older learners may have some advantages over younger learners.

A recent publication edited by Stryker and Leaver (1997) addresses content-based instruction for adult learners and provides a number of case studies in a variety of settings (universities, a graduate professional institute, and government schools). Articles in this collection include one by Vines (1997), who describes a Language for Specific Purposes approach in French for journalism and telecommunications majors. A growing number of universities are offering Language for Specific Purposes courses in foreign languages in a variety of disciplines, particularly in business. Many of these courses are offered after the first- and second-year courses in a foreign language are complete, although some content-based courses are also offered in the lower division. Ballman (1997), for example, discusses how beginning language courses can be enhanced through "content-enriched instruction," in which "vocabulary, grammar, and content are integrated to reflect a specific theme or converge to represent a specific topic" (p. 173). In her 1997 review of several first-year textbooks in Spanish, Ballman points out that cultural content, though included, often was in the form of author-written readings or realia that were not exploited adequately. Although many newer textbooks are offering more content-enriched instruction through the inclusion of well-conceived authentic materials, Web-based activities, and other ancillaries, Ballman's suggestions for ways of improving first-year courses can be helpful to teachers as well as to textbook writers and publishers. For example, by including more target-language activities based on these new materials that focus on learning both the language and the content, students can be held accountable for the cultural information that is part of the unit of study. Readers interested in more details about this approach should consult this source, which outlines an integrated six-day plan for a unit on the family in Hispanic cultures as an example of how content can be integrated into early language instruction for adults.

Bragger and Rice (1998) also outline ways to address the "connections" goal of the standards in "theme-based" content courses, characterized by the use of authentic texts to explore various themes or topics as students develop competence in a second language. They emphasize that when implementing the "connections" standards, one should not give too much emphasis to "content" so that it becomes the main purpose of instruction, nor minimize the content of the course so that it has no real substance and thus becomes "diluted." They maintain that "content-based instruction" is *not* a "shift from teaching/learning language to teaching/learning content" (p. 194), since such courses are still primarily focused on teaching language within a meaningful context. However, the content is not used merely to teach language forms and vocabulary items, but rather presents learners with issues that are interesting and valuable to learn about in their own right. Bragger and Rice give the example of using paintings in a content-based course: One can use them to teach a variety of vocabulary and functions (such as description of places and people), but unless the paintings are also treated in their historical context and discussed in terms of their artistic characteristics or cultural significance, the goal of interdisciplinarity has not really been fulfilled by the inclusion of this type of content in the curriculum (p. 195). In terms of the language difficulties associated with discussing more complex content in beginning levels, Bragger and Rice suggest that content might be most appropriately dealt with in early levels by having students comprehend texts, but discuss them in the native language. As learners' skills progress in the foreign language, the content can be dealt with in both comprehension and production tasks.

Met (1999) describes a continuum of programmatic possibilities for integrating language and content learning, ranging from the most *content-driven* language programs on one end of the continuum to those that are primarily *language-driven* on the other. This seems to be a very useful and flexible description of the range of possibilities for integrating language and content instruction, as it distinguishes the more content-driven "immersion programs, in which the school curriculum is taught through the medium of another language" (p. 144) from programs where language mastery is most important. In between these two extremes, Met arranges partial immersion programs, sheltered courses (where a subject is taught in the target language), adjunct courses (where both the subject matter and language instruction are taught together), and theme-based courses (where language instruction is arranged around thematic modules or units), all of which are described and illustrated in Brinton, Snow, and Wesche (1989). Met adds that "in all likelihood the vast majority of foreign language teachers will be operating from the perspective of a language-driven program. That is, foreign language teachers will be seeking ways in which content can promote language learning and facilitate student acquisition of course outcomes" (p. 146). In Met's view, the implementation of content-based instruction, as advocated in the "connections" goal of the standards, does not mean that current program models need to be completely abandoned or restructured. Instead, teachers need only reconsider how content can serve to integrate language learning and other disciplines.

While the goal of integrating language and content instruction is being discussed more and more frequently in the professional literature, particularly in light of the standards and the new technologies that enable us to have easier access to authentic material, it is also important to point out that the issue of how language structures are learned in such an approach must be addressed. As early as the 1980s, discussions about the need to "focus on form" within content-based instructional approaches had already begun, particularly in the context of Canadian and ESL language programs.

Swain and Lapkin (1989) point out that the immersion model is not without its problems. The spoken and written French of both early- and late-immersion students have fallen short of native-like proficiency, even after 5,000 or more hours of instruction. They attribute this problem to the fact that content has been emphasized at the expense of language skills in most immersion classes:

> . . . we have learned that grammar should not be taught in isolation from content. But then, neither should content be taught without regard to the language involved. A carefully planned integration of language and content, however, holds considerable promise (p. 153).

Snow, Met, and Genesee (1989) and Met (1991) agree that it is unlikely that desired levels of proficiency in the second language will emerge simply through content-based teaching, and argue for a careful planning of language learning objectives that will be integrated and coordinated with content instruction.

In discussing the effectiveness of a content-based instructional program at the college level for ESL students, Snow and Brinton (1988) come to many of the same conclusions about the need to integrate language and content in a coherent fashion. In the "adjunct model" for ESL students at the University of California at Los Angeles, minority-language students take part in a Freshman Summer Program designed to help them adjust to university life and prepare for academic coursework in English. In this program, students enroll concurrently in two linked courses: a language course, such as intermediate-level ESL for academic purposes, and a content course, such as Introduction to Psychology. Key features of this model include the integration of native and non-native English-speaking students in the content course with a "sheltering" of the ESL students in the language course. The assignments in the ESL course are designed to complement and support the learning in the content course. "The focus in the ESL class is on essential modes of academic writing, academic reading, study skills development, and the treatment of persistent structural errors" (p. 557). Instructors from both the content and ESL language courses meet regularly to plan assignments so that the ESL courses can best serve the students' linguistic and academic needs. The authors give an example of a typical written assignment, where students use the content course lecture notes to write definitions of concepts, and from there build paragraphs or write a more extensive definition paper. "In all such assignments, emphasis is placed on both the accuracy of content and on the accuracy and sophistication of the language used to communicate this content" (p. 559).

In all of these content-based instructional settings, then, the collective wisdom seems to be that simply teaching language through content or content through language is not enough. Rather, an integration of form-focused activities and content-based assignments is needed to achieve the best results, regardless of the age or level of proficiency of the students.

Summary: The Role of Context in Comprehension and Learning

In this chapter, the role of context in comprehension and learning has been explored. We have seen both the intuitive appeal of such an approach and the theoretical and research base that exists to support it. While our linguistic and pedagogical traditions have concentrated on the sentence for the purpose of analysis and instruction, it seems clear that language teaching in the years to come must concentrate on the wider contexts of authentic language use and actively teach discourse skills in the classroom.

In the next three chapters, practical suggestions for selecting reading and listening input, as well as for teaching reading, listening, speaking, and writing *in context* are presented within the framework of a proficiency-oriented approach. The ideas offered should help students make rapid progress in the comprehension skills as well as expand and enrich their competence in using language beyond the sentence level, an important step in developing functional proficiency in a second language.

Activities for Review and Discussion

1. Define and give several examples of each of the following concepts:

   a. Background knowledge
   b. Advance organizer
   c. Schema

2. Look at the list of practical questions on pp. 149–150. After having read the review of studies in this chapter, what tentative answers might you give to each of these questions? What do we still need to know in order to clarify the issues and find more definitive answers? Discuss with others in your group how teachers might be involved in seeking information that will add to our current knowledge about the role of context in comprehension and learning.

3. Examine your current language textbook and evaluate it in light of the principles discussed in the chapter. Do the textbook's chapters explore themes that are relevant for learners and based on authentic cultural contexts? To what degree are language exercises contextualized and/or personalized? To what extent are students encouraged to use language in discourse-length rather than sentence-length frames? Are readings drawn from authentic sources? To what extent are advance organizers provided? Make a list of the strengths and weaknesses of the textbook. What suggestions would you make to the publisher if you were asked to provide input for a revision of the text?

References: Chapter 4

Adams, Shirley J. "Scripts and Recognition of Unfamiliar Vocabulary: Enhancing Second Language Reading Skills." *The Modern Language Journal* 66 (1982): 155–59.

Allen, Patrick, Merrill Swain, Birgit Harley, and Jim Cummins. "Aspects of Classroom Treatment: Toward a More Comprehensive View of Second Language Education." Chapter 5 (pp. 57–81) in B. Harley, P. Allen, J. Cummins, and M. Swain, eds., *The Development of Second Language Proficiency.* Cambridge: Cambridge University Press, 1990.

Anderson, R. C., J. W. Prichert, E. T. Goetz, D. L. Schallert, K. V. Stevens, and S. R. Trollip. "Instantiation in General Terms." *Journal of Verbal Learning and Verbal Behavior* 15 (1976): 667–79.

Anderson, R. C., R. E. Reynolds, D. L. Schallert, and T. E. Goetz. "Frameworks for Comprehending Discourse." *American Educational Research Journal* 14 (1977): 367–81.

Ausubel, David. *Educational Psychology: A Cognitive View.* New York: Holt, Rinehart, and Winston, 1968.

Ausubel, David, Joseph D. Novak, and Helen Hanesian. *Educational Psychology: A Cognitive View, 2nd ed.* New York: Holt, Rinehart, and Winston, 1978. (Reprinted by Werbel and Peck, 1986.)

Ballman, Terry L. "Enhancing Beginning Language Courses Through Content-Enriched Instruction." *Foreign Language Annals,* vol. 30, ii (1997): 173–86.

Barnett, Marva. *More than Meets the Eye: Foreign Language Reading.* Language in Education: Theory and Practice, no. 73. CAL/ERIC Series on Language and Linguistics. Englewood Cliffs, NJ: Prentice Hall, 1989.

Barry, Sue and Alejandro Lazarte. "Embedded Clause Effects on Recall: Does High Prior Knowledge of Content Domain Overcome Syntactic Complexity in Students of Spanish?" *The Modern Language Journal* 79, iv (1995): 491–504.

Bartlett, Frederick C. *Remembering: A Study in Experimental and Social Psychology.* Cambridge: Cambridge University Press, 1932. (Reprinted 1950.)

Bragger, Jeannette D. and Donald B. Rice. "Connections: The National Standards and a New Paradigm for Content-Oriented Materials and Instruction." Pp. 191–217 in J. Harper, M. Lively, and M. Williams, eds., *The Coming of Age of the Profession: Issues and Emerging Ideas for the Teaching of Foreign Languages.* Boston, MA: Heinle & Heinle, 1998.

Bransford, John D. and Marcia K. Johnson. "Contextual Prerequisites for Understanding: Some Investigations of Comprehension and Recall." *Journal of Verbal Learning and Verbal Behavior* 11 (1972): 717–26.

Brinton, Donna M., Marguerite Ann Snow, and Marjorie Bingham Wesche. *Content-Based Second Language Instruction.* Boston, MA: Heinle & Heinle, 1989.

Brown, H. Douglas. *Principles of Language Learning and Teaching.* Englewood Cliffs, NJ: Prentice Hall, 1980. 2nd ed., 1987, 3rd ed., 1994.

Brumfit, C. J. and K. Johnson. *The Communicative Approach to Language Teaching.* Oxford: Oxford University Press, 1979.

Cantoni-Harvey, Gina. *Content-Area Language Instruction.* Reading, MA: Addison-Wesley Publishing Company, 1987.

Carrell, P. L. "Culture-Specific Schemata in Second-Language Comprehension." In R. Orem and J. Haskell, eds., *Selected Papers from the Ninth Illinois TESOL/BE Annual Convention, the First Midwest TESOL Conference.* Chicago, IL: TESOL/BE, 1981a: 123–32.

———. "The Role of Schemata in L2 Comprehension." Paper presented at the 15th Annual TESOL Convention. Detroit, MI, March, 1981b. (Cited in Carrell and Eisterhold 1983.)

———. "Evidence of a Formal Schema in Second Language Comprehension." *Language Learning* 34, ii (1984a): 87–112.

———. "The Effects of Rhetorical Organization on ESL Readers." *TESOL Quarterly* 18 (1984b): 441–69.

———. "Facilitating ESL Reading by Teaching Text Structure." *TESOL Quarterly* 19 (1985): 727–52.

———. "Some Causes of Text-Boundedness and Schema Interference in ESL Reading." Chapter 7 (pp. 101–113) in P. Carrell, J. Devine, and D. Eskey, eds., *Interactive Approaches to Second Language Reading.* Cambridge: Cambridge University Press, 1988.

Carrell, P. L., J. Devine, and D. Eskey, eds. *Interactive Approaches to Second Language Reading.* Cambridge: Cambridge University Press, 1988.

Carrell, P. L. and J. Eisterhold. "Schema Theory and ESL Reading Pedagogy." *TESOL Quarterly* 17 (1983): 553–73.

Carrell, Patricia and Teresa Wise. "The Relationship Between Prior Knowledge and Topic Interest in Second Language Reading." *Studies in Second Language Acquisition* 20 (1998): 285–309.

Chen, Qin and Janet Donin. "Discourse Processing of First and Second Language Biology Texts: Effects of Language Proficiency and Domain-Specific Knowledge." *The Modern Language Journal* 81, ii (1997): 209–27.

Chung, Jing-mei. "The Effects of Using Video Texts Supported with Advance Organizers and Captions on Chinese College Students' Listening Comprehension: An Empirical Study." *Foreign Language Annals* 32, iii (1999): 295–305.

Chung, Ulric K. "The Effect of Audio, A Single Picture, Multiple Pictures, or Video on Second-Language Listening Comprehension." Ph.D. Dissertation, The University of Illinois at Urbana-Champaign, 1994.

Coady, James. "A Psycholinguistic Model of the ESL Reader." In R. Mackay, B. Barkman, and R. R. Jordan, eds., *Reading in a Second Language.* Rowley, MA: Newbury House, 1979.

Cook, G. and B. Seidlhofer, eds. *Principle and Practice in Applied Linguistics: Studies in Honour of H. G. Widdowson.* Oxford: Oxford University Press, 1995.

Crandall, JoAnn, ed. *ESL Through Content-Area Instruction.* CAL/ERIC Language in Education: Theory and Practice, no. 67. Englewood Cliffs, NJ: Prentice Hall, 1987.

Cubillos, Jorge H. "Technology: A Step Forward in the Teaching of Foreign Languages?" Pp. 37–52 in J. Harper, M. Lively, and M. Williams, eds., *The Coming of Age of the Profession: Issues and Emerging Ideas for the Teaching of Foreign Languages.* Boston, MA: Heinle & Heinle, 1998.

De Lorenzo, William D., and Lois A. Gladstein. "Immersion Education à l'Américaine: A Descriptive Study of U.S. Immersion Programs." *Foreign Language Annals* 17, i (1984): 35–40.

Doughty, Catherine and Jessica Williams, eds. *Focus on Form in Classroom Second Language Acquisition.* Cambridge: Cambridge University Press, 1998.

Ellis, Rod. *Instructed Second Language Acquisition.* Oxford: Basil Blackwell, 1990.

Frommer, Judith G. "Cognition, Context, and Computers: Factors in Effective Foreign Language Learning." Pp. 199–223 in Judith A. Muyskens, ed., *New Ways of Learning and Teaching: Focus on Technology and Foreign Language Education.* AAUSC Issues in Language Program Direction. Boston, MA: Heinle & Heinle, 1998.

Genesee, Fred. "Second Language Learning Through Immersion: A Review of U.S. Programs." *Review of Educational Research* 55 (Winter 1985): 541–61.

Goodman, Kenneth S. "Reading: A Psycholinguistic Guessing Game." In L. Harris and C. Smith, eds., *Individualizing Reading Instruction: A Reader.* New York: Holt, Rinehart, and Winston, 1972.

Hague, Sally and Renee Scott. "Awareness of Text Structure: Is There a Match Between Readers and Authors of Second Language Texts?" *Foreign Language Annals* 27, iii (1994): 343–63.

Hanley, Julia, Carol Herron, and Steven Cole. "Using Video as an Advance Organizer to a Written Passage in the FLES Classroom." *The Modern Language Journal* 79, i (1995): 57–66.

Harley, B., P. Allen, J. Cummins, and M. Swain, eds. *The Development of Second Language Proficiency.* Cambridge: Cambridge University Press, 1990.

Harper, J., M. Lively, and M. Williams, eds. *The Coming of Age of the Profession: Issues and Emerging Ideas for the Teaching of Foreign Languages.* Boston, MA: Heinle & Heinle, 1998.

Haugeland, John, ed. *Mind Design.* Cambridge, MA: M.I.T. Press, 1982.

Herron, Carol. "An Investigation of the Effectiveness of Using an Advance Organizer to Introduce Video in the Foreign Language Classroom." *The Modern Language Journal* 78, ii (1994): 190–98.

Herron, Carol, Steven Cole, Holly York, and Paul Linden. "A Comparison Study of Student Retention of Foreign Language Video: Declarative versus Interrogative Advance Organizer." *The Modern Language Journal* 82, ii (1998): 237–47.

Herron, Carol, Cathleen Corrie, Steven Cole, and Pablo Henderson. "Do Prequestioning Techniques Facilitate Comprehension of French Video?" *The French Review* 72, iv (1999): 1076–90.

Herron, Carol, Julia Hanley, and Steven Cole. "A Comparison Study of Two Advance Organizers for Introducing Beginning Foreign Language Students to Video." *The Modern Language Journal* 79, iii (1995): 387–95.

Higgs, Theodore V. and Ray Clifford. "The Push toward Communication." In T. Higgs, ed., *Curriculum, Competence, and the Foreign Language Teacher.* The ACTFL Foreign Language Education Series, vol. 13. Lincolnwood, IL: National Textbook Company, 1982.

Hudson, Thom. "The Effects of Induced Schemata on the 'Short Circuit' in L2 Reading: Non Decoding Factors in L2 Reading Performance." *Language Learning* 32 (1982): 1–31.

Jespersen, Otto. *How to Teach a Foreign Language.* London: George Allen and Unwin, Ltd., 1904.

Johnson, Patricia. "Effects on Reading Comprehension of Building Background Knowledge." *TESOL Quarterly* 16 (1982): 503–16.

Kolers, Paul A. "Three Stages of Reading." In F. Smith, ed., *Psycholinguistics and Reading.* New York: Holt, Rinehart, and Winston, 1973.

Laberge, D. and S. I. Samuels, eds. *Basic Processes in Reading: Perception and Comprehension.* Hillsdale, NJ: Lawrence Erlbaum Associates, 1977.

Lee, James F. "Background Knowledge and L2 Reading." *The Modern Language Journal* 70, iv (1986): 350–54.

Lee, James F. and Gail Riley. "The Effect of Prereading, Rhetorically-Oriented Frameworks on the Recall of Two Structurally Different Expository Texts." *Studies in Second Language Acquisition* 12, i (1990): 25–41.

Lee, James F. and Albert Valdman, eds. *Form and Meaning: Multiple Perspectives.* AAUSC Issues in Language Program Direction. Boston, MA: Heinle & Heinle, 2000.

Lightbown, Patsy M. and Nina Spada. *How Languages Are Learned.* Oxford: Oxford University Press, 1993. 2nd edition 1999.

Littlewood, William T. "Form and Meaning in Language Teaching Methodology." *The Modern Language Journal* 64 (1980): 441–45.

———. *Communicative Language Teaching: An Introduction.* Cambridge University Press, 1981.

Long, Donna Reseigh. "What You Don't Know Can't Help You." *Studies in Second Language Acquisition* 12 (1990): 65–80.

Long, Michael. "Does Second Language Instruction Make a Difference? A Review of the Research." *TESOL Quarterly* 17 (1983): 359–82.

Mackay, R., B. Barkman, and R. R. Jordan, eds. *Reading in a Second Language.* Rowley, MA: Newbury House, 1979.

Markham, Paul. "Captioned Videotapes and Second-Language Listening Word Recognition." *Foreign Language Annals* 32, iii (1999): 321–28.

Markham, Paul and Michael Latham. "The Influence of Religion-Specific Background Knowledge on the Listening Comprehension of Adult Second-Language Students." *Language Learning* 37, ii (1987): 157–70.

McLaughlin, Barry. "The Monitor Model: Some Methodological Considerations." *Language Learning* 28 (1978): 309–32.

———. *Theories of Second Language Learning.* London: Edward Arnold, 1987.

McLaughlin, Barry, T. Rossman, and B. McLeod. "Second Language Learning: an Information-Processing Perspective." *Language Learning* 33 (1983): 135–58.

Met, Myriam. "Learning Language through Content: Learning Content through Language." *Foreign Language Annals* 24 (1991): 281–95.

———. "Making Connections." Pp. 137–64 in J. K. Phillips and R. M. Terry, eds., *Foreign Language Standards: Linking Research, Theories, and Practices*. The ACTFL Foreign Language Education Series. Lincolnwood, IL: National Textbook Company, 1999.

Minsky, Marvin. "A Framework for Representing Knowledge." In J. Haugeland, ed., *Mind Design*. Cambridge, MA: M.I.T. Press, 1982.

Mohan, Bernard A. *Language and Content*. Reading, MA: Addison-Wesley Publishing Company, 1986.

Mueller, Gunter A. "Visual Contextual Cues and Listening Comprehension: An Experiment." *The Modern Language Journal* 64 (1980): 335–40.

Muyskens, J., ed. *New Ways of Learning and Teaching: Focus on Technology and Foreign Language Education*. AAUSC Issues in Language Program Direction. Boston, MA: Heinle & Heinle, 1998.

Omaggio, Alice C. "The Effects of Selected Pictorial Contexts on Measures of Reading Comprehension in Beginning College French." Ph.D. Dissertation, The Ohio State University, 1977.

———. "Pictures and Second Language Comprehension: Do They Help?" *Foreign Language Annals* 12 (1979): 107–16.

Pawley, Catherine. "How Bilingual are French Immersion Students?" *The Canadian Modern Language Review* 41, v (1985): 865–76.

Phillips, June K. and R. M. Terry, eds. *Foreign Language Standards: Linking Research, Theories, and Practices*. The ACTFL Foreign Language Education Series. Lincolnwood, IL: National Textbook Company, 1999.

Raymond, Patricia. "The Effects of Structure Strategy Training on the Recall of Expository Prose for University Students Reading French as a Second Language." *The Modern Language Journal* 77, iv (1993): 445–58.

Riley, Gail. "A Story Structure Approach to Narrative Text Comprehension." *The Modern Language Journal* 77, iv (1993): 417–32.

Rumelhart, David. "Understanding and Summarizing Brief Stories." In D. Laberge and S. Samuels, eds., *Basic Processes in Reading: Perception and Comprehension*. Hillsdale, NJ: Lawrence Erlbaum Associates, 1977.

———. "Schemata: The Building Blocks of Cognition." Chapter 2 (pp. 33–58) in R. Spiro, B. Bruce, and W. Brewer, eds., *Theoretical Issues in Reading Comprehension*. Hillsdale, NJ: Lawrence Erlbaum Associates, 1980.

Schallert, D. C. "Improving Memory for Prose: The Relationship between Depth of Processing and Context." *Journal of Verbal Learning and Verbal Behavior* 15 (1976): 621–32.

Schank, Roger and Robert Abelson. *Scripts, Plans, Goals, and Understanding: An Inquiry into Human Knowledge Structures*. Hillsdale, NJ: Lawrence Erlbaum Associates, 1977.

Schmidt, Richard, ed. *Attention and Awareness in Foreign Language Learning*. Technical Report #9. Honolulu, HI: University of Hawaii, Second Language Teaching and Curriculum Center, 1995.

Seliger, Herbert W. "On the Nature and Function of Language Rules in Language Teaching." *TESOL Quarterly* 13, (1979): 359–69.

Shrum, Judith L. and Eileen W. Glisan. *Teacher's Handbook: Contextualized Language Instruction, 2nd ed.* Boston, MA: Heinle & Heinle, 2000.

Slager, William R. "Creating Contexts for Language Practice." In E. Joiner and P. Westphal, eds., *Developing Communication Skills*. Rowley, MA: Newbury House, 1978.

Smith, Frank. *Understanding Reading*. New York: Holt, Rinehart, and Winston, 1971.

Snow, Marguerite Ann and Donna M. Brinton. "Content-Based Language Instruction: Investigating the Effectiveness of the Adjunct Model." *TESOL Quarterly* 22, iv (1988): 553–74.

Snow, Marguerite Ann, Myriam Met, and Fred Genesee. "A Conceptual Framework for the Integration of Language and Content in Second/Foreign Language Instruction." *TESOL Quarterly* 23, ii (1989): 201–17.

Standards for Foreign Language Learning: Preparing for the 21st Century. National Standards in Foreign Language Education Project, 1996.

Stern, H. H. "Analysis and Experience as Variables in Second Language Pedagogy." Chapter 7 (pp. 93–109) in B. Harley, P. Allen, J. Cummins, and M. Swain, eds., *The Development of Second Language Proficiency*. Cambridge: Cambridge University Press, 1990.

Stryker, Stephen B. and Betty Lou Leaver. "Content-Based Instruction: From Theory to Practice." Chapter 1 (pp. 3–28) in S. B. Stryker and B. L. Leaver, eds., *Content-Based Instruction in Foreign Language Education: Models and Methods*. Washington, D.C.: Georgetown University Press, 1997.

———. eds. *Content-Based Instruction in Foreign Language Education: Models and Methods*. Washington, D.C.: Georgetown University Press, 1997.

Swain, Merrill. "Communicative Competence: Some Roles of Comprehensible Input and Comprehensible Output in its Development." Chapter 14 in S. Gass and C. Madden, eds., *Input in Second Language Acquisition*. Cambridge, MA: Newbury House, 1985.

———. "Three Functions of Output in Second Language Learning." Chapter 8 (pp. 125–44) in G. Cook and B. Seidlhofer, eds., *Principle and Practice in Applied Linguistics: Studies in Honour of H. G. Widdowson*. Oxford: Oxford University Press, 1995.

Swain, Merrill and Sharon Lapkin. "Canadian Immersion and Adult Second Language Teaching: What's the Connection?" *The Modern Language Journal* 73, ii (1989): 150–59.

Taglieber, Loni K., Linda L. Johnson, and Donald B. Yarbrough. "Effects of Prereading Activities on EFL Reading by Brazilian College Students." *TESOL Quarterly* 22, iii (1988): 455–71.

Tang, Gloria. "The Effect of Graphic Representation of Knowledge Structures on ESL Reading Comprehension." *Studies in Second Language Acquisition* 14 (1992): 177–95.

Vines, Lois. "Content-Based Instruction in French for Journalism Students at Ohio University." Chapter 6 (pp. 119–40) in Stephen B. Stryker and Betty Lou Leaver, eds., *Content-Based Instruction in Foreign Language Education: Models and Methods*. Washington, D.C.: Georgetown University Press, 1997.

Widdowson, H. G. *Teaching Language as Communication*. Oxford: Oxford University Press, 1978.

Yorio, Carlos A. "Some Sources of Reading Problems for Foreign Language Learners." *Language Learning* 21 (1971): 107–15.

5 FIVE A Proficiency-Oriented Approach to Listening and Reading

In the last chapter we saw that comprehension, both in listening and in reading, is an active process involving at least three interrelated factors: (1) the individual's knowledge of the linguistic code, (2) cognitive skills of various types, and (3) the individual's knowledge of the world. We saw how relevant contextual information can play an important role in comprehension, especially at lower levels of proficiency, where extra-linguistic cues and advance organizers can activate appropriate schemata to close the gaps in comprehension caused by an imperfect knowledge of the code.

This chapter explores practical issues relating to the teaching of listening and reading. The questions addressed are the following: Why should these skills be actively taught? How are listening and reading skills similar? How are they different? How can authentic materials be used in teaching comprehension skills in the lower proficiency ranges? What specific strategies can be used for teaching listening and reading, particularly at the Novice, Intermediate, and Advanced proficiency ranges?

A Rationale for Teaching Listening and Reading

When audiolingual methodologies became popular in the early 1960s, many second-language programs and materials began to place primary emphasis on the development of oral proficiency, a reversal of the trend in the grammar-translation era that emphasized reading as the primary goal of language study. In the years that followed, oral communication continued to receive high priority in many second-language classrooms. Yet an increasing number of educators today are recognizing the need to achieve a balance in program goals through the reintroduction of comprehension-based activities and materials into the curriculum.

Attitudes about the importance of comprehension skills in language acquisition have been influenced, in large part, by developments in second-language acquisition theory. Certainly Krashen's (1982) views about the need for comprehensible input in language acquisition have sparked interest in comprehension-based methodologies and materials. As we saw in Chapter 2, most recent language acquisition theories recognize the important role that input plays in the development of proficiency in all skill modalities, and an increasing number of scholars and practitioners believe that comprehension processes and strategies need to be taught actively in second-language classrooms.

Barnett (1989) maintains that reading has always held an important place in foreign- and second-language programs, with the possible exception of the period when audiolingual methodology dominated in American classrooms. But she adds that reading is now seen in a different light, namely "as communication, as a mental process, as the reader's active participation in the creation of meaning, as a manipulation of strategies, as a *receptive* rather than as a *passive skill*" (p. 2). She cites Byrnes (1985), who refers to both reading and listening as receptive skills in which readers and listeners actively "*produc[e] understanding*" (Byrnes 1985, p. 78; Barnett 1989, p. 2). As a source of "comprehensible input," reading becomes valued in the communicative classroom, especially when authentic materials can serve the dual purpose of developing reading skills and of fostering cultural insights and understanding. Barnett goes on to list other reasons for including reading skill development as a vital part of the second-language curriculum: (1) Reading is still essential in the teaching of literature, which remains an important goal in many programs; (2) it is a skill that can be maintained after students complete formal language study; (3) it fosters the development and refinement of literacy skills. Indeed, second-language reading research may have a significant impact on our understanding of this larger issue of literacy, which is of national concern.

Although most of the research studies involving the development of foreign language receptive skills have been devoted to understanding the reading process (Lund 1991), there is a very strong interest in the language teaching community today to increase students' listening comprehension skills as well. James (1986) advocates the direct teaching of listening skills for motivational reasons. He cites research by Lowe (1985), who found that, in terms of the ILR Proficiency scale, English-speaking learners performed better in listening comprehension tasks than in speaking activities 47 percent of the time in French and 76 percent of the time in Spanish, as averaged over all levels of proficiency (p. 37). In Spanish, the listening comprehension advantage tended to be strongest at ILR levels 2 through 4+. At levels 1+ and lower, the listening and speaking scores tended to be equal (p. 37). In French, the offset in listening and speaking began sooner, and the comprehension advantage was measurable at the 0+/1 border (p. 40). However, Lowe cautions that a greater facility in listening than in speaking may not hold across different languages, and there may in fact be a negative offset for some languages (i.e., where listening proves more difficult than speaking). James' (1986) point, in reviewing Lowe's data, is that if there is indeed a comprehension advantage, then introducing more listening activities early into the learning process will be motivating to learners and allow them to experience success.

Long (1986) argues that teaching oral skills is teaching only half of the process of communication and adds that students gain a sense of confidence with the language when their listening abilities are well developed. Feyton (1991) further comments that the field of language teaching has moved from a "response-oriented paradigm to one of input, or stimulus-oriented learning" (p. 175) and adds that listening should not be thought of as an "activity," but taught directly as a skill in its own right.

Joiner (1986, 1997) cites four trends that have brought more attention to the development of listening skills in recent years: (1) *comprehension-based approaches,* which advocate a prespeaking or "silent period" and which maintain that listening is the foundation skill for all language development; (2) *emphasis on the receptive skills* in general, which has been growing since the early 1980s; (3) the prevalence of *functional-notional approaches* and concepts, with their emphasis on oral communication; and (4) *the development of the ACTFL Proficiency Guidelines,* fostering an interest in the use of authentic materials for listening and reading and emphasizing communicative skill development.

Swaffar, Arens, and Byrnes (1991) argue forcefully for the inclusion of more reading, listening, and writing activities in a communicative curriculum to allow students to use their higher-order cognitive skills. Authentic reading and listening materials, as well as writing activities that involve analysis and interaction with texts, give adult learners more of an opportunity to engage in challenging tasks appropriate to their level of cognitive maturity.

Rivers (1975) has pointed out another important reason for developing both listening and reading skills, citing research early in the 20th century that showed that adults spend 45 percent of their time listening and 11 to 16 percent of their time reading (Rankin, cited in Rivers 1975, p. 58). Joiner (1997) also refers to Rankin's research, and adds that in the era in which his study was done (1926), listening took place most often in either face-to-face conversational encounters or in the presence of the speaker (as when listening to a lecture, public debate, or theatrical performance); written communication was the primary means of sharing information at a distance. When one considers the enormous changes relating to the way information is received today, particularly with the advent of new and more interactive technologies, the amount of time spent in listening and/or reading may be even higher:

> In the present era, referred to variously as the "information age" and the "postliterate age," the role of electronic media in communication is increasing almost daily. The telephone call has all but replaced the personal letter; tape pals, and even cyberpals, coexist with pen pals; newspapers are struggling to remain competitive with radio and television; classroom walls have been expanded via distance learning; commuters listen to audiobooks as they drive to work; live theater shares the entertainment stage with film and video; and the dusty roads traveled by Pony Express riders have been replaced by an information superhighway, capable of transmitting not only text but real-time audio and video as well (Joiner 1997, p. 77).

If more than three-fifths of all communicative interaction involves comprehension skills, the importance of focusing on effective strategies for enhancing those skills becomes even more apparent.

In the past several decades, there has been a growing interest in designing materials to teach comprehension more actively, especially through the use of culturally authentic texts, videotaped materials, and computer-assisted instruction that allows for greater interaction between the learner and the text. Teachers need more access to listening and reading materials based on natural disourse along with appropriate comprehension activities that teach the process of comprehension so that skills are transferable to other situations and texts. Publishers of foreign- and second-language instructional materials are recognizing this need, and there is an increasing number of high-quality texts and ancillaries designed especially for this purpose. The ready availability of CD-ROMs that are now packaged with student textbooks affords much better sound quality (digital vs. analog) and greater accessibility to listening materials both inside and outside of the classroom. As audiocassette tapes are gradually being transferred to CD-ROMs, an additional benefit—the control of pausing and relistening—is added; "in this way, the *immediacy* skill of listening can be made to resemble the *recursive* skill of reading" (Joiner 1997, p. 82).

In addition to new and better materials, teachers need ideas for structuring and sequencing instruction so that a classroom plan for teaching listening and reading comprehension can be devised. Effective ways to integrate comprehension and productive skills with the teaching of culture are also needed. Some specific ideas for planning instruction of this type are provided in this and subsequent chapters. First, however, it would be useful to look at some of the similarities and differences in listening and reading tasks, many of which derive from the relationship between speech and writing.

Similarities in Listening and Reading

We have already seen that listening and reading comprehension are both highly complex processes that draw on knowledge of the linguistic code, cognitive processing skills, schema-based understanding, and contextual cues both within and outside the text. Both skills can be characterized as problem-solving activities involving the formation of hypotheses, the drawing of inferences, and the resolution of ambiguities and uncertainties in the input in order to assign meaning.

Bernhardt and James (1987) use the metaphor of the jigsaw puzzle to describe the comprehension process. The reader/listener begins constructing the puzzle by selecting pieces, very slowly at first, until a hypothesis about the whole picture can be formed. Once this initial hypothesis is made, the image of the whole can guide further selection and interpretation of the parts. Of course, if the initial hypothesis is wrong, problems in comprehension will arise, and the process of building the puzzle can break down or become frustrating, "especially when the puzzle constructor is convinced that some of the pieces are either *missing* or were even cut wrong" (p. 66).

Although the goals and some of the global processes in listening and reading comprehension are often similar, the nature of the input (speech or writing) and the way in which that input is processed are quite different.

Differences between Spoken and Written Discourse

Richards (1983) has outlined several ways in which speech differs from writing. For example, written discourse—particularly in texts produced for a wide and essentially anonymous audience—is normally organized in well-formed grammatical sentences arranged in coherent paragraphs. Ideas are planned and produced by one person, allowing the discourse to flow logically as the topic is developed. In contrast, spoken discourse—particularly in conversational exchanges—can often include ungrammatical or reduced forms, dropped words, and sentences without subjects, verbs, auxiliaries, or other parts of speech. Conversations are often marked by pauses, hesitations, false starts, and fillers, and topics can shift as the conversation is co-constructed with others. A number of things may be left unsaid because both parties assume some common knowledge. In many types of written discourse, however, meaning cannot be negotiated directly with the reader and common knowledge cannot always be assumed.

Stevick (1984) points out that the way in which the communication is organized for delivery also differs in speech and in writing. Whereas spoken language moves along a time axis, written language is visually presented, and its overall duration and organization can be seen at a glance. He hypothesizes that for this reason aural comprehension may be more difficult than reading. Lund (1991) found this to be the case in a study involving beginning and intermediate students of German, where their reading comprehension was superior to their comprehension in listening. This reading advantage appeared to diminish somewhat by the time students reached the third semester, however. Lund concluded that although there may be an initial advantage for listening in the case of children who are learning to read in their native language, the opposite appears to be true for adults engaged in second-language learning. "There may be in many situations an initial advantage to readers for unfamiliar and authentic texts, but this conclusion may not hold for noncognate languages or where diverse writing systems are involved" (p. 201).

Lund (1991) also found that having a text presented twice, either in reading or listening, significantly benefited students at all levels in the study. However, the study clearly indicated that for beginning students, reading and rereading resulted in superior comprehension to listening and relistening. This may be due, in part, to the fact that listeners cannot control the pace of presentation of the text and often appear to be "grasping at words" (p. 201). This relates to what Stevick (1984) calls the "accessibility" of the text, which differs in the two modalities. In reading, one can look back at what was read before and also look ahead to get an idea of what is coming. The listener, however, cannot do this, and any inattention to what is being said at the moment may easily cause him or her to lose an important part of the message, or even all of it.

Joiner (1997) maintains that one of the most obvious advantages of computer-assisted multimedia applications is virtual instantaneous random-access to any segment on the sound source and the ability to easily and effectively replay and relisten to difficult passages. Although this particular feature in itself is quite help-ful to listeners, multimedia applications can also add text and other online assis-tance that helps in the comprehension process. This additional assistance and textual reinforcement is similar to the "visual safety net" that video offers and that contributes visual and kinesthetic clues to meaning (pp. 82, 88).

The contrasts between oral and written language become more complex when one considers the range and variety of text types that can be encountered. In dis-cussing the nature of oral language, Byrnes (1984), following Beile (1980), identi-fies four basic modes of speech:

1. *Spontaneous free speech,* characterized by the interactiveness and production constraints reviewed above;
2. *Deliberate free speech,* such as that which is characteristic of interviews and discussions;
3. *Oral presentation of a written text,* as in newscasts, more formal commentaries, and lectures; and
4. *Oral presentation of a fixed script,* such as that produced on stage or in a film (p. 319).

Written discourse also has a variety of text types. Grellet (1981) identifies some of the kinds of texts readers might encounter in the target language. A summary of her comprehensive list, regrouped into categories, is given below:

1. **Literary texts,** such as novels, short stories, plays, poems, essays, and the like;
2. **Specialized or technical texts,** such as reports, reviews, textbooks, handbooks, statistical data, diagrams, flow charts, etc.;
3. **Correspondence,** such as personal or business letters, postcards, notes, or telegrams;
4. **Journalistic literature,** such as articles from newspapers and magazines, editorials, headlines, classified ads, weather reports, television listings;
5. **Informational texts,** such as dictionaries, guidebooks, phrase books, telephone books, timetables, maps, signs, price lists, etc.;
6. **Miscellaneous realia** of various kinds, such as tickets, menus, recipes, advertisements, etc. (Based on Grellet 1981, pp. 3-4.)

To this list, of course, can be added newer types of texts that are characteristic of the information age, from e-mail correspondence to the texts found in a variety of formats on Internet sites, as well as in multimedia course materials. These types of resources often present learners with information that requires the integration of listening and reading skills and can easily involve productive skills such as writ-ing as well. In addition, texts such as these are often rich in cultural information and can help learners make connections to other disciplines, all of which serves to develop the abilities that have been outlined in the *Standards for Foreign Language Learning* (1996), as we shall see in the next section.

Integrating Listening, Reading, and the Productive Skills:
The Vision of the *Standards for Foreign Language Learning*

When we consider the varieties of text types that can be encountered when listening to or reading the foreign language, as well as the many contexts of communication in which listening and reading skills are used, it becomes clear that teaching "listening" or "reading" is no simple matter. Some scholars have suggested that the idea of teaching "the four skills" is somewhat limiting and even outmoded, as authentic communication requires the integrated use of the various modalities. The view taken in this chapter is that both a "skills" perspective and an integrative, more "communicative" view of authentic language use can be helpful in designing foreign language curricula. For example, targeted instruction in particular skill areas can be beneficial in beginning foreign language classes, where strategies for comprehending and producing the new language can be taught and practiced. Specific skills-based instruction may be useful as well in more advanced classes, such as those devoted to teaching academic listening or professional or technical writing. (For a recent discussion of teaching the listening skill, with particular attention to strategy instruction, see Mendelsohn 1998.) However, one must also work at all levels of instruction toward the integration of skills for the purposes of communication, not only with others in the language classroom but also beyond the classroom and across cultures. This integration of skills is essential for attaining higher levels of proficiency as well as for addressing the goals of language study that have been articulated in the *Standards for Foreign Language Learning* (1996).

In 1995, Brecht and Walton applied a new interpretation to cultural discourse, dividing it into three communicative modes: *interpersonal/negotiated, interpretative,* and *presentative* (p. 116). These three modes appear in the 1996 national standards as *interpersonal, interpretive,* and *presentational* (see Illustration 5.1). As can be seen in the examination of the three modes of communication, all four skills are involved, with listening and reading listed most prominently in the *interpersonal* and *interpretive* paths to communication. It is in the *interpersonal* mode where the receptive skills are linked most directly to the productive skills of speaking and writing. This framework can be useful as one designs different types of communication tasks for the classroom and can help teachers assess the value of various listening and reading activities for practicing the requisite component skills for these different modes of communication.

When one considers the variety of text types and modes of speech, it becomes clear that "successful comprehension" will depend on the purposes for which the individual is listening or reading. "Understanding a written [or oral] text means extracting the required information from it as efficiently as possible" (Grellet 1981, p. 3). "Extracting the required information" may mean in one instance that the listener or reader simply scans the input to find some detail of interest, such as listening to a series of sports scores or scanning a television log to find an interesting program. In another situation, certain main ideas and a few supporting details

Illustration 5.1 **Framework of Communicative Modes**

	INTERPERSONAL	INTERPRETIVE	PRESENTATIONAL
D E F I N I T I O N S	Direct oral communication (e.g., face-to-face or telephonic) between individuals who are in personal contact Direct written communication between individuals who come into personal contact	Receptive communication of oral or written messages Mediated communication via print and non-print materials Listener, viewer, reader works with visual or recorded materials whose creator is absent	Productive communication using oral or written language Spoken or written communication for people (an audience) with whom there is no immediate personal contact or which takes place in a one-to-many mode Author or creator of visual or recorded material not known personally to listener
P A T H S	Productive abilities: speaking, writing Receptive abilities: listening, reading	Primarily receptive abilities: listening, reading, viewing	Primarily productive abilities: speaking, writing, showing
C U L T U R A L K N O W L E D G E	Knowledge of cultural perspectives governing interactions between individuals of different ages, statuses, backgrounds Ability to recognize that languages use different practices to communicate Ability to recognize that cultures use different patterns of interaction	Knowledge of how cultural perspectives are embedded in products (literary and artistic) Knowledge of how meaning is encoded in products Ability to analyze content, compare it to information available in own language and assess linguistic and cultural differences Ability to analyze and compare content in one culture to interpret U.S. culture	Knowledge of cultural perspectives governing interactions between a speaker and his/her audience and a writer and his/her reader Ability to present crosscultural information based on background of the audience Ability to recognize that cultures use different patterns of interaction

KNOWLEDGE OF THE LINGUISTIC SYSTEM

The use of grammatical, lexical, phonological, semantic, pragmatic, and discourse features necessary for participation in the Communicative Modes.

Source: Standards for Foreign Language Learning, 1996, p. 33. Reprinted by permission of the National Standards in Foreign Language Education Project.

may be required to ensure successful comprehension (such as listening to directions to get to someone's house). In still another situation, the listener or reader might need to get all of the finer details of the message in order to understand it well enough to carry out some specific purpose or function (such as reading a set of directions to build or make something). The design of appropriate comprehension tasks for oral or written discourse, then, becomes a function of text type, the purpose for which the comprehender is listening and reading, and the information and skills the listener/reader brings to the text. Bernhardt and James (1987) add that "the road to effective instruction must lie in acknowledging individual differences in readers *and* texts" (p. 71). The importance of these considerations will become apparent in the next sections, where suggestions for listening and reading activities for various proficiency levels are given.

Teaching Listening Comprehension

▓ Some Processes and Skills Involved in Listening Comprehension

type
↓
scripts
↓
inference of goal
↓
meaning
↓
remembering & acting

Although there have been a small number of studies in recent years investigating factors affecting second-language listening comprehension (see Chapter 4, as well as Rubin 1994 and Lynch 1998 for a review), research in this aspect of L2 development is still in its infancy. However, some insights about the processes involved in listening can be gleaned from native language research. Richards (1983) proposes a tentative model of the listening process that involves the following steps: (1) determining the type of interaction or speech event (such as a conversation, lecture, discussion, or debate) in which the listener is involved; (2) recalling scripts (or schemata) relevant to the situation; (3) making inferences about the goals of the speaker; (4) determining the propositional meaning of the utterance; (5) assigning an illocutionary (functional) meaning to the message; and (6) remembering and acting upon the information, while deleting the original form of the message.

In addition to outlining this general model of the listening process, Richards provides a list of 33 microskills that are needed in listening to conversational discourse, and adds 18 more that are used in academic listening (pp. 228–29). These skills range from very discrete tasks, such as discriminating among individual sounds, recognizing syntactic patterns, and identifying key words, to more global tasks, such as extracting main ideas and understanding the relationships among the parts of the discourse. Different listening activities can be devised to help learners develop these various microskills at each level of proficiency, and the choice of skills for a given task can be tailored to the nature of the specific objectives for listening.

▓ Planning Instruction for the Development of Listening Proficiency

low proficiency:
predictable
interesting.

How can teachers determine which types of materials and tasks to use for listening instruction for their students? There are some indications in the recent literature on comprehension that may help. Most scholars agree that at the lowest proficiency levels, listening materials that present very familiar and/or predictable content and that are relevant to students' interests will be best, given that students will be able to use their knowledge of the world to aid them in comprehension when their linguistic skills are deficient. For example, videotaped materials can be especially useful at the lower ranges of proficiency because of the visual contextual support they provide, as long as students know that they are not expected to understand every word.

As teachers design the tasks to be accomplished with various listening materials, they should keep in mind the normal or natural purposes for which someone might listen to a given text. The tasks need to be geared to such purposes but also to the overall level of competence of the students. One can expect, in general, that students will be able to understand the gist and/or a few main ideas in familiar passages at the lower levels of proficiency and eventually extract more and more precise information of a detailed nature from a given listening text as their proficiency develops. Beginning and intermediate students will need prelistening activities to help them anticipate and predict the relevant content in the passage. Preliminary research indicates that multiple opportunities to listen for a variety of different purposes will also be helpful in increasing students' understanding (Lund 1991).

Lund (1990) describes a plan for designing listening instruction, based partly on Richards (1983) and partly on the *ACTFL Proficiency Guidelines* for listening. He constructs a taxonomic framework for listening comprised of two basic elements: (1) *listener function,* which relates to what the learner attempts to process from the message and (2) *listening response,* which corresponds to the way in which the listener shows comprehension of the message. Illustration 5.2 presents Lund's taxonomy for teaching second-language listening. He suggests that this matrix be used to design instruction so that the full range of competencies in listening is practiced. The sample tasks given for purposes of illustration all relate to listening to an authentic text type: radio advertisements.

The six functions, listed across the top of the taxonomic framework, refer to what the listener is trying to attend to in the message. Each function thus represents a potential goal of listening comprehension. Listener function, in Lund's view, is perhaps the most important consideration in designing instruction in listening, since it provides listeners with a purpose for listening, and thus defines how they need to approach the task. The six functions are described briefly below (Lund 1990, pp. 107–109):

1. *identification:* recognition or discrimination of aspects of the message rather than attention to the overall message content. This category might include identification of words, word categories, phonemic distinctions, morphological distinctions, or semantic cues to meaning.
2. *orientation:* identification of important facts about the text, such as the participants, the situation, the general topic, the tone, the text type, and the like. "Orientation is essentially 'tuning in' to or preparing to process the information" (p. 108). Lund considers this function to be especially important for Novice listeners, who need advance organizers and/or script activators to enhance comprehension.
3. *main idea comprehension:* understanding of the higher-order ideas in the

Function / Response	Identification	Orientation	Main Idea Comprehension	Detail Comprehension	Full Comprehension	Replication
Doing			Pantomime the product			
Choosing			Match ads and pictures		Select best ad	
Transferring	List adjectives		Write magazine ad	List the selling points		
Answering		What kind of text?	What goods are advertized?			
Condensing			Write close-caption text			
Extending			Second ad in campaign			
Duplicating			– – – – – – –			Transcribe the text
Modeling			Create own ad			
Conversing			"Talk back" to the ad			

Illustration 5.2
Lund's Function-
Response Matrix for
Listening (Advertisement
Example)

Source: Lund, Randall J. "A Taxonomy for Teaching Second Language Listening." *Foreign Language Annals* 23, ii (1990), p. 111. Reprinted by permission.

listening passage. An example drawn from advertisements is understanding what product is being promoted. Lund, following the *ACTFL Guidelines* descriptions, states that this function "typically distinguishes the intermediate listener from the novice" (p. 108). His 1991 study of Novice and Intermediate German students indicates that listeners seem to rely more on top-down (schema-based) understanding than they do when they are reading an equivalent text. Listeners seemed to report more main ideas, but also made more erroneous assumptions that were based on the wrong choice of schema (Lund 1991, p. 200).

4. *detail comprehension:* understanding of more specific information. "The amount of detail one can understand typically distinguishes the advanced listener from the intermediate" (p. 108). In his study with first-, second-, and

third-semester German students, Lund (1991) found corroboration for this assertion for both listening and reading. Memory for details in both modalities improved as course level increased. Understanding of detail was also improved with a second listening of the text.

5. *full comprehension:* understanding of both the main ideas and supportive detail. Lund maintains that this level of comprehension is the goal of instruction in listening proficiency. Although one does not need or want to listen to every message with full comprehension, the ability to do so when desired marks a superior level of listening proficiency.

6. *replication:* ability to reproduce the message in either the same modality (through repetition of the content) or in a different modality (such as transcription or dictation). Lund explains that replication does not imply a higher level of proficiency than full comprehension, but represents a different purpose and thus a different way of attending to the message.

These six listener functions are combined with the nine listening responses (listed vertically on the taxonomy) and a particular text to define listening tasks. The nine responses are derived in part from a list of common task types provided by Richards (1983): *matching or distinguishing, transferring, transcribing, scanning, extending, condensing, answering,* and *predicting* (p. 235). Lund's list of tasks is described briefly as follows:

1. *doing,* which implies a physical response of some sort, such as in TPR methodology;
2. *choosing,* which involves activities such as putting pictures in order or matching a product to an advertisement;
3. *transferring,* which might involve drawing, tracing a route, filling in a graph, or other kinds of transferring of information from one modality to another;
4. *answering,* such as completing a set of questions asking for specific information in the text;
5. *condensing,* involving such activities as preparing an outline, taking notes, or preparing captions for pictures based on the listening passage;
6. *extending,* which implies going beyond the text to create an ending, complete a partial transcript, change the text, or embellish it in some way;
7. *duplicating,* which provides evidence that the function of replication has been accomplished;
8. *modeling,* which involves imitation of features of the text or of the text as a whole; and
9. *conversing,* implying some kind of interaction with the text, either in a face-to-face conversation or in using interactive video programs.

Lund maintains that growth in listening proficiency can be understood in terms of progressing through these listening functions, learning to do new functions with familiar texts or performing lower-level functions with more difficult texts. This suggests that texts should be used recurrently. "Learners can be led to orient themselves to a text, then to process main ideas, then to fill in details. . . . Texts can also be reused over greater time spans or in different levels of instruction" (p. 112).

Like the proficiency guidelines descriptions, Lund's taxonomy is not meant to suggest a linear progression, but a cyclical one. "The proficiency guidelines appear as a linear scale only because they identify the *highest* function that can be performed on the wide and unselected range of texts that can be expected in the target culture" (Lund 1990, p. 112). Lund adds that many of the microskills that Richards (1983) lists can be integrated into the various cells of his taxonomy.

Some scholars discussing the incorporation of listening tasks into the curricular sequence suggest that it is not the *text* that should be graded, but rather the *task* itself (see for example Byrnes 1985; Joiner 1986; Bacon 1989; Lund 1990). Various techniques that may be appropriate for learners at different levels of proficiency are suggested in Illustration 5.3. Several of the techniques included at the lower two levels (Novice/Intermediate) include extralinguistic support, such as pictures, graphic materials, or physical activity to help students whose listening skills are relatively weak. At the higher levels of proficiency, tasks require the fuller comprehension of the text, including more detail and an understanding of nuances. The subdivision of tasks in Illustration 5.3 should not be viewed, however, as a rigid hierarchy; indeed, many tasks can be appropriate at *any* level of proficiency, provided appropriate adjustments in the task demands are made to coincide with learners' listening abilities. Several tasks, such as "recursive listening," "inferential listening," and "paraphrase" are listed for both major subdivisions, and tasks such as "comprehension checks" and "reaction/analysis activities" can be used at any proficiency level as long as they are tailored to the students' current level of competence.

Many of these task types are illustrated in the next sections. Before discussing specific techniques, however, we need to consider the type of materials that might be used in the classroom for building listening skills.

Using Authentic Materials for Listening and Reading Instruction

In Chapter 3, it was recommended that authentic materials be used in instruction whenever possible (see, for example, the discussion relating to Corollary 4, p. 97). As Geddes and White (1978) have noted, this move toward authenticity in language instruction reflects the increased interest in recent years in the communicative functions of language. Yet they caution that using *only* unedited, nonpedagogical materials in the classroom would seem to create more problems than it would solve, since materials are often difficult to select, obtain, or sequence for learners at lower proficiency levels. Unmodified authentic discourse is often random in respect to vocabulary, structure, functions, content, situation, and length, making some of it impractical for classroom teachers to integrate successfully into the curriculum on a frequent basis (p. 137). Some scholars have suggested that authentic listening materials may be very frustrating for beginners (Ur 1984; Dunkel 1986) and listening to material that is beyond the learner's compre-

Illustration 5.3
Listening Tasks

Suggested Tasks for Building Listening Proficiency

Novice/Intermediate
Prelistening activities
Listening for the gist
Listening with visuals
Graphic fill-ins
Matching descriptions to pictures
Dictation and variations (familiar content, simple structures)
Clue searching (listening for cues to meaning, such as key words, syntactic
     features, actor/action/object, etc.)
Distinguishing registers (formal/informal style)
Kinesics/physical response
Recursive listening (multiple sequenced tasks)
Inferential listening (drawing inferences not presented overtly in the text)
Paraphrase in native language
Completion of native language summary
Comprehension checks (various formats)
Remembering responses of others

Advanced/Superior
Dictation and variations (may include unfamiliar content, more complex structures)
Completing target language summary
Paraphrasing (target language)
Note taking/outlining
Summarizing (native language/target language)
Recursive listening (multiple tasks)
Inferential listening (drawing inferences, conclusions not presented overtly in the text)
Identifying sociolinguistic factors
Style shifting
Reaction/analysis activities
Creative elaboration activities

hension can be anxiety-producing (Meyer 1984; Byrnes 1984; Joiner 1986). Other scholars have advocated the use of authentic materials early in instruction, provided that texts that can be related to the learners' experience are chosen; the text length is not too great; and advance organizers, orientation activities, and schema-based prelistening techniques are used (James 1986; Long 1986; Bacon 1989; Lund 1990, among many others). Appropriate listening strategies also need to be actively taught, especially to low-proficiency learners. In arguing for the use of authentic texts in listening, Bacon (1989) states that while we are "protecting our students from the frustration of extended speech, . . . we may also be denying them the satisfaction of being exposed to and understanding real speech." She adds that real language must be "intelligible, informative, truthful, relevant, and sociolinguistically appropriate" (p. 545).

The term "authentic material" can have a variety of meanings in the literature on listening and reading comprehension. Rogers and Medley (1988) refer to authentic materials as "language samples—both oral and written—that reflect a naturalness of form and an appropriateness of cultural and situational context that would be found in the language as used by native speakers" (p. 468). They group materials into video, audio, and print media resources and provide a very useful list of resources in French and Spanish that teachers of these languages would do well to consult. Geddes and White (1978) distinguish between two types of authentic discourse: (1) *unmodified authentic discourse,* which refers to language that occurred originally as a genuine act of communication, and (2) *simulated authentic discourse,* which refers to language produced for pedagogical purposes but which exhibits features that have a high probability of occurence in genuine acts of communication (p. 137).

As Geddes and White (1978) have pointed out, the difficulties students face when encountering unmodified authentic speech are well known to most teachers: Often students tend to panic when they hear native speakers in conversations, radio broadcasts, films, or other natural contexts. Learners typically try to focus their attention equally on every part of the discourse. Because they cannot possibly attend successfully to everything heard with equal intensity, students often give up, even when it would have been possible for them to get the gist or understand a few of the important details. Teachers can help students overcome these problems by using controlled and guided activities for listening such as those illustrated in the next few pages.

"Teacher talk," or "caretaker speech," is another type of listening material that contributes to the acquisition of the language. According to Krashen, Terrell, Ehrman, and Herzog (1984), it tends to consist of a simplified code, characterized by slower, more careful articulation, the more frequent use of known vocabulary items, and attempts to ensure comprehension via restatements, parapharases, and nonverbal aids to understanding. Yet "teacher talk" can sound quite authentic since it is generally not planned or scripted. Rather, it flows naturally as the teacher develops a given theme or topic and often involves interactive exchanges with students. These exchanges, when not contrived or overly structured, have the flavor of a real conversation.

"Teacher talk" might also include the recounting of personal anecdotes relating to the instructor's own experiences in the target culture. (Some sample reading activities based on teacher anecdotes are given later in this chapter.) Native-speaker visitors can also provide comprehensible input, especially if they are aware of the level of listening ability of the students and gear their comments to that level. Students might be asked to prepare questions in advance of the visit and thereby have some control over the conversational topics.

A good way to incorporate simulated authentic discourse into the classroom is through the use of semiscripts (Geddes and White 1978). A semiscript is a set of notes or a simple outline that is provided to native speakers for the purpose of generating a monologue or conversation that sounds authentic. The notes might include specific vocabulary or structures that should be incorporated in the speech sample, or simply indicate the general ideas to be mentioned or discussed. The discourse that is created from the semiscript can be recorded on audio or videotape for use in the classroom.

3.   Another way to integrate authentic listening and reading into instruction is through the use of multimedia software. Noblitt defines multimedia as "a technique that combines images, sounds, and text with interactive control by the learner" (Noblitt 1990, cited in Joiner 1997, p. 88). Joiner (1997) notes that one criterion for evaluating the effectiveness of audio, video, or multimedia resources is the extent to which the medium can be compared to "face-to-face communication" (p. 79). She outlines five characteristics of face-to-face communication that can benefit listeners: (1) it is immediate; (2) it is interactive in nature; (3) it is multisensory, involving both linguistic and extralinguistic cues; (4) if it is unsuccessful, speakers/listeners can get help by various means; and (5) it can be controlled by speakers and listeners through the use of simple strategies (p. 80). Joiner points out that multimedia applications can bring to listening activities many of the benefits of face-to-face communication as well as the recursive capabilities of reading. However, she cautions that such programs may not always be the best choice in every situation and that "a key factor in the decision to purchase multimedia programs for the development of listening-comprehension skills is faculty attitude toward computers in general and toward the use of computers as teaching devices in particular" (p. 91). She adds that "the most effective medium for teaching listening is the medium that will be used the most frequently by students and instructors" (p. 91).

In addition to multimedia software packages, authentic materials for listening and reading can be found on the Internet, especially through Web links on the sites of language-specific professional organizations, college and university foreign language departments, and individual faculty members. There are additional materials that are available through satellite downlinks from target-language-speaking countries (SCOLA, TV5, and Deutsche Welle, for example). Many foreign language videos offer subtitling, and DVDs now provide multiple language tracks and the capability of viewing with or without subtitles. There is an increasing number of software programs that offer language practice, instruction, and/or entertainment. Most of the listening activities mentioned in this chapter, as well as activities for other skill areas, can be carried out using resources from the Internet or other multimedia sources.

As multimedia software and resources become more plentiful, their various features will need to be evaluated as teachers consider whether to use them to supplement classroom instruction. Readers may want to consult recent professional volumes dealing with technology in language instruction, such as those edited by Bush (1997) and Muyskens (1998) for general guidelines and samples of specific programs. There are several sources that offer print and Web-based guidelines for evaluating Internet and software materials. For example, Thompson, Hiple, and Schmidt of the University of Hawaii National Foreign Language Resource Center (NFLRC) have developed, with a team of experts in different fields, a very useful and comprehensive "Taxonomy of Features for Evaluating Foreign Language Multimedia Software" ("Taxonomy . . ." 1999). The foreign language multimedia evaluation criteria were developed at an invitational symposium funded by the United States Department of Education and held at the National Foreign Language Resource Center of the University of Hawaii on February 26–28, 1998. In addition to outlining general criteria, with guidelines for evaluating the description of a given program, its operation, and its special features, the taxonomy also contains pedagogical criteria by skill. These skill-based criteria include the specification of input, activities, strategy instruction, tools, and interface for speaking, reading, listening, writing, script (or writing system), vocabulary, and pronunciation. The full set of materials can be accessed on the Web at *http://nts.lll.hawaii.edu/flmedia.* (An adapted version of the general criteria and of the criteria for listening and reading are given in Appendix B.)

In the sections that follow, various sample classroom activities that can be used for listening and reading practice are explored. These activities include those that are designed to focus on either the listening or reading skill alone or on integrated skills at various levels of proficiency. Activities range from simple listening and reading tasks that can be designed by the teacher using simulated authentic discourse to those that utilize resources available on the World Wide Web.

Sample Formats for Listening Comprehension

Listening for the Gist

SAMPLE (NOVICE)

Objective: Students identify products that are being advertised by matching pictures of the products to the passages heard. (See Lund's Taxonomy p. 186.)

Text: Various radio commercials are recorded from a target-language station.

Student Task: Drawings of the products (or pictures, if available) are marked with a letter (A, B, C, etc.) and placed in the front of the classroom. Students listen to the recorded advertisements one at a time. As they listen, they try to identify which product is being described by writing down the appropriate letter of the visual that matches the description.

Recursive Listening

In recursive listening activities, students listen to the same text several times, each time with a different listening purpose. In the following samples, prelistening activities and organizers are illustrated as well as the specific listening tasks themselves.

SAMPLE 1 (NOVICE/INTERMEDIATE)

Objective: Students listen to a passage that includes announcements on board an airplane interspersed with conversation between two passengers. On the first listening, students attempt to distinguish between the formal register of the announcements and the informal register of conversation. On the second listening they will fill out a form with some pertinent flight information.

Prelistening Activities: The teacher orients the students to the passage by telling them that it takes place on an international flight. She explains that the passage includes both formal and informal speech and asks the students to listen the first time for differences in tone of voice, speech overlap (indicated in italics in the passages below), and delivery. They are instructed to raise their hands each time they hear the register shift.

Passage:

VIASA ¡Donde el tiempo pasa volando!

Capitán: Señores pasajeros, a nombre del comandante, quien les habla, Pedro Lange Churión, y de la tripulación de VIASA, Venezolana Internacional de Aviación, donde el tiempo pasa volando quisiéramos darles la bienvenida al vuelo 804 con destino a Nueva York. Vamos a volar a una altura de 20.000 pies y a una velocidad de 900 KM por hora. Aterrizaremos en el aeropuerto Kennedy a la una de la tarde, hora de Nueva York. Los dejo en manos de la tripulación que estará encantada de atenderles en este viaje.

Azafata: Buenos días. ¿Qué desea tomar?

Viajera: Buenos días. Bueno, este, . . . e . . . ¿Qué tiene?

Azafata: De todo . . . depende . . . bebidas, vino, tragos . . .

Viajera: *¿Qué bebidas* tiene?

Azafata: Usted tiene . . . Coca Cola . . . limón . . . jugo de naranja . . .

Viajera: *Ah, bueno,* deme un jugo de naranja, sin hielo.

Azafata: ¿Sin hielo? Está bien. Y para comer . . . ¿Qué prefiere, pollo o . . . o . . . pescado?

Viajera: Este . . . pollo, por favor.

Azafata: Muy bien. ¿Algo más?

Viajera: Eh . . . ¿Qué periódicos tiene?

Azafata: Tenemos *El . . . Tiempo,* eh . . . el *New York Times . . . El Nacional . . .*

Viajera: *El Tiempo, El Tiempo.*

Azafata: *¡El Tiempo!* Bueno. Muy bien. Ahora mismo se lo traigo, señorita. [bip . . . bip]

Capitán: Señores pasajeros, en este momento estamos a punto de aterizar. Favor de abrocharse los cinturones de seguridad y de poner el respaldo . . . el respaldo de su asiento en posición vertical.

Azafata: Por favor, suba la mesita, abroche su cinturón. Gracias.

Second Listening: Students fill out the form below as they listen to the passage a second time, this time attending to some important details.

COMPREHENSION EXERCISE

"VIASA ¡Donde el tiempo pasa volando!"

You are about to embark on an adventure in flying. Supply the missing information.

Nombre del piloto: _____Lange-Churión

Nacionalidad de la aerolínea: _____

Número del vuelo:_____

Destino: _____

Altura: _____ pies; Velocidad: _____ KM/hora

Aeropuerto: _____ ; Hora de llegada: _____

Una bebida que se ofrece: _____

Una comida que se ofrece: _____

Un periódico que se ofrece: _____

Source: Bacon 1989. Passage and exercise reprinted by permission from "Listening for Real in the Foreign Language Classroom," *Foreign Language Annals,* vol. 22, no. 6, 1989, p. 548.

SAMPLE 2 (INTERMEDIATE)

Objective: Students listen to a brief news report about an official order given to inspect aircraft that transport military personnel. They listen first to extract pertinent vocabulary in order to focus on the topic. The second cycle asks students to listen for the basic story line in the news report. A third and fourth hearing focus on supporting details.

Passage: *La secretaria de transporte de los Estados Unidos, E.D., ordenó una intensa inspección de las compañías de aviación con vuelos de alquiler especialmente esas empresas que rentan sus aviones para vuelos militares. Esta es la cuarta inspección ordenada después del accidente de AeroAir en que murieron doscientos cuarenta y ocho soldados.*

First Listening: The instructor tells students that the news report they will hear deals with flying and asks them to write down some words they hear that deal with this topic.

Second Listening: The instructor probes the students' knowledge of the world to see if they can anticipate the general theme of the article. Students are asked to think of a recent airline disaster and see if the news story talks about it.

Third Listening: Students listen for reactions to the events and write down words associated with these reactions.

Fourth Listening: More detail is now elicited so that full comprehension of the news report is achieved.

Source: Weissenrieder, Maureen. "Listening to the News in Spanish." *The Modern Language Journal* 71, i (1987), p. 24. Reprinted by permission.

Listening with Visuals

In this kind of activity, students listen to material that corresponds to a visual aid of some kind and either identify a picture being described, identify objects within the picture, follow a map or diagram, or draw a simple sketch.

SAMPLE 1 (NOVICE)

Objective: Students listen to a passage to identify and draw common objects in a room and show comprehension of expressions of location.

Prelistening Activity: Students activate relevant background knowledge by thinking of vocabulary for objects in their rooms or by identifying common objects in a picture or drawing of a student room.

Illustration 5.4
Drawing of Living Room
for Novice-Level Listening
Activity with Visuals
(Sample 1)

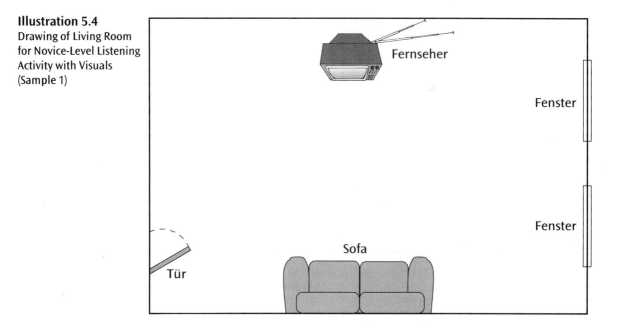

Passage: A native-speaking exchange student provides a simple sketch of his/her living room with most of the furniture missing, but with a few items designated in the sketch and labeled. The student either describes the room on tape or comes to the class as a visitor and provides the description orally.

Student Task: See Illustration 5.4 for a sample sketch (in German). Students complete the sketch as they listen. They may ask the visitor questions for clarification.

SAMPLE 2 (NOVICE/INTERMEDIATE)

Objective: Students listen to a series of conversations about choosing food from a restaurant menu provided in their textbook. They attempt to understand various aspects of these conversations, including the attitudes of the speakers toward the choice of food, the selections they make, and the prices they pay.

Prelistening: Before listening to the audiotaped conversations, students study the menu in their textbook in small groups and answer various questions about the foods. The textbook includes a chart with food groups, and students are asked to place the menu items under the appropriate category.

Listening Tasks: Students listen to a series of mini-conversations on audiotape.

1. Students listen to a conversation between two customers discussing the menu. They then answer questions about one of the customer's impressions of the fare.

Textarbeit

1. Szene 1: Wer bekommt was? Kreuzen Sie die passende Spalte an.

	Mann	Frau	Kind
Exportbier			
Wein			
Cola			
Suppe			
Rindsbraten			
Entenviertel			
Hähnchen			

2. Szene 2: Was bestellt der Mann, was bestellt die Frau? Füllen Sie die Tabelle aus.

	Hauptgericht	Beilage	Getränk
Frau			
Mann			

Text work   (*English Translation*)

1. Scene 1: Who gets what? Mark the appropriate column.

	Man	Woman	Child
Export Beer			
Wine			
Cola			
Soup			
Roast Beef			
Duck			
Chicken			

2. Scene 2: What does the man order, what does the woman order? Fill out the chart.

	Main dish	Side dish	Drink
Woman			
Man			

Illustration 5.5
Forms Used in German
Listening Activity with
Visuals (Sample 2)

Source: Arendt et al. *Kreise: Erstes Jahr Deutsch im Kontext.* Boston: Heinle & Heinle, 1992, p. 98.

2. Students listen to two exchanges between a waitress and her customers. They fill out forms, such as the ones in Illustration 5.5, as they listen.

3. Students hear two more conversations between a waitress and her customers to determine what they ate, drank, and paid for the meal. They enter this information onto a form provided in the text.

Source: J. Arendt, C. Baumann, G. Peters, and R. Wakefield. *Kreise: Erstes Jahr Deutsch im Kontext.* Boston: Heinle & Heinle, 1992, pp. 97–99.

Other ways in which visuals or pictures can be used for Novice and Intermediate level listening comprehension include:

1. *Map Activities.* Students are provided with a simple map of a fictitious city, campus, or street with boxes denoting houses, stores, etc. After a prelistening activity in which appropriate vocabulary for place names and prepositions of place have been reviewed, students are given a set of directions. As they listen, they follow the directions by (a) filling in names of places on the map or (b) drawing a pathway on the map according to the directions given.

2. *Ordering or Sequencing Pictures.* Students look at a series of pictures or drawings that are in scrambled sequence. As they listen to a simple set of descriptions of the actions, objects, or people depicted, they indicate the order of the pictures by placing a number next to each one (i.e., 1 next to the picture in

the first simple description, 2 next to the second description, and so on). It is best to use descriptions that form continuous discourse. When the pictures, sequenced appropriately, form a simple narrative or dialogue, students hear language in contexts beyond the sentence level and have a better opportunity to develop comprehension skills that will be transferrable to natural settings.

3. *Choosing the Correct Picture from a Description.* In this activity, students are given a set of similar pictures with one or two details differing in each one. For example, the same person can be depicted wearing slightly different clothing in a series of three or four visuals. As students listen to a passage in which clothing is described, they choose the most appropriate visual to match the information provided.

4. *Drawing Sketches from a Description.* A simple description of objects, people, or actions can be read several times while students attempt to draw what is being described. For the Novice level, the descriptions should involve vocabulary that is very familiar and sentence structure should be quite simple. This same technique can be used in more complex descriptions for the Intermediate or Advanced level, and may also be combined with a production task by having students provide the descriptions from a drawing themselves.

Graphic Fill-Ins

Graphic fill-ins consist of incomplete forms, diagrams, or other graphic material that can be completed as students listen to a passage, either with native-language words or with words or short phrases in the target language. Items might also be circled or underlined to complete the printed form. (See Illustration 5.5 as well as the sample that follows.)

SAMPLE (NOVICE/INTERMEDIATE)

Objective: Students in ESL listen to travel plans for María Sanchez for the month of November. They note down on a calendar the nature of the activity as well as the time, if given, and any other details.

Directions: Instruct students to listen to the travel plans read by the teacher or recorded on tape. They will hear the passage twice, with pauses after each sentence so that they can write down the needed information on their calendars.

Passage: *Here are the activities for the month of November for María Sanchez. Listen as she tells you what she is going to do this month. In the spaces on the calendar, write in her activities.*

1. *On Tuesday, November the thirteenth, I am going to Caracas for three days.*
2. *I'll return to Buenos Aires on Thursday, November the fifteenth at 7:30 P.M.*
3. *Then, on Wednesday of the next week, I'm having lunch with Señora Gonzalez at the Hotel de la Playa at noon.*
4. *On Friday the twenty-third, I leave for Asunción, where I will stay for two days.*
5. *I leave Asunción on the twenty-fifth and go to Bogotá. I'll be there overnight and leave the next morning for La Paz and then on to Quito.*

6. *When I leave Quito on the night of the twenty-sixth, I head to New York. My plane leaves at 11:45 P.M. It's American Airlines, flight 245.*
7. *I'll return from New York on the thirtieth. Well . . . I actually leave New York on the twenty-ninth on American, flight 136, at 9:30 P.M. I arrive back in Buenos Aires the next day at 10:10 A.M.*

Student Task: See Illustration 5.6.

Listen to the travel plans for the month of November for María Sanchez. As you listen, fill in the calendar with her activities. Indicate times and other details.

You will hear the passage twice.

Source: Terry 2000 (personal communication).

Illustration 5.6
Calendar Activity

NOVEMBER

SUN	MON	TUE	WED	THU	FRI	SAT
				1	2	3
4	5	6	7	8	9	10
11	12	13	14	15	16	17
18	19	20	21	22	23	24
25	26	27	28	29	30	

Comprehension Checks

Teachers often use comprehension questions of various sorts to test students' understanding of a listening passage. Such questions have often required students to extract somewhat detailed factual information from the passage, regardless of its relative value in enabling the listener to accomplish some communicative purpose. When using comprehension checks such as those described below, teachers should consider (1) the purpose of the listening activity and (2) the type of information that would be needed to accomplish that purpose in an authentic situation. These considerations can then help teachers decide on the quantity and specificity of information required as they design the comprehension task.

A variety of comprehension checks are typically used with listening material, including open-ended questions on the content, true/false questions, multiple-choice alternatives, completions, and summaries. When using comprehension checks, two considerations should be kept in mind to ensure more effective listening strategies on the part of the learners:

1. Consider providing the questions, completions, or other types of comprehension checks *before* students hear the passage. This gives students an idea of the passage content, thus serving as an advance organizer and providing a "schema" for comprehension.
2. Have students try to do some of the comprehension exercises *while listening* to the passage rather than after it has been read or played. This helps students focus on relevant features of the discourse as they are being heard rather than requiring them to retrieve a set of facts from memory.

Listening/Writing Formats

A combination of listening and writing tasks that resembles the real-world skill of note-taking can be used to build comprehension skills at all levels of proficiency. Integrative formats such as dictations, variations on dictation, and other kinds of gap-filling exercises are especially useful.

One advantage of dictation as an exercise in listening and writing is that it can combine many discrete points of structure and vocabulary in natural language contexts. Teachers may construct their own dictations (for Novice through Advanced levels) or use authentic discourse as the source of the dictated material (Advanced and Superior levels).

Among the listening/writing formats that may be used from the Novice through Superior levels are:

1. *Dictation of Questions in the Target Language.* Students first write down the questions dictated by the teacher. They then write answers to those questions in the target language. Questions should either follow one another in logical sequence or relate to a given theme.
2. *Partial, or Spot, Dictations.* Students fill in gaps on their written copy of a passage.
3. *Dictation of Sentences in Random Order.* All sentences, when rearranged, form a logical paragraph or conversation. Students first write the dictated material and then rearrange it.
4. *Dictation of Directions for Arriving at a Destination.* Students first write a set of directions dictated by the teacher. They then follow the directions on an accompanying map.

5. *Dictation of a Description.* Students write the dictated material and then, from a set of alternatives, choose the picture that matches the description they have written down.

6. *Full Dictation of a Passage.* Students might be asked to answer comprehension questions on a passage after they have written it down. They might also be asked to circle items of a certain lexical or grammatical category (such as all the verbs in the future tense) to draw their attention to a topic that is being emphasized in a particular lesson.

SAMPLE 1 (NOVICE)

Objective: Students listen to directions for buying various food items and write down the items they hear in French on a graphic "notepad."

Prelistening Activity: Students review vocabulary for various food items in French using pictures with captions provided by the textbook, the teacher, or in a small-group activity where captions for pictures are created by the students using the text as a resource.

Text: The instructor reads the following text or prepares with another instructor a taped recording of a simulated phone conversation between an exchange student and the mother of his or her host family:

> Janine: Mme Rivière? Ici Janine. Je vais avec une amie en ville et je peux aller au supermarché si vous voulez avant de rentrer. . . .
>
> Mme Rivière: Ah, oui? Ce serait génial! Voyons . . . alors, tu peux acheter peut-être du lait, du pain—une baguette—et un peu de fromage, si tu veux. Tu as assez d'argent? Je vais te rembourser, bien sûr!
>
> Janine: Pas de problème. C'est tout? Nous avons besoin de fruits, n'est-ce pas?
>
> Mme Rivière: Ah oui, c'est vrai. Tu peux acheter des bananes aussi. Et deux ou trois tomates. Je crois que c'est tout . . .
>
> Janine: D'accord. Je rentre dans une heure.
>
> Mme Rivière: Bien, . . . alors, merci beaucoup, Janine! A plus tard!

Student Task: Au supermarché. Listen to the following conversation where Janine, an exchange student in France, calls her host-family mother to offer to pick up some things at the store. Write down in French the items she mentions on the note pad provided below.

Follow-up Task: Students can be asked to plan a dinner in small groups, creating a menu that includes appetizers, drinks, main dishes, side dishes, and desserts. For inspiration, teachers might want to supply students with a set of pictures depicting foods, either from magazines, store circulars, or photographs, such as those depicted in Illustration 5.7 on page 202. Groups can share their dinner plans, and the class can vote on which dinner sounds the most appetizing.

A note-taking activity that has potential for developing cultural awareness is given below. This activity combines listening, speaking, reading, and writing in an integrative fashion as the students engage in the process of completing its various steps.

SAMPLE 2 (ADVANCED)

Objective: Students sharpen their listening skills through a note-taking exercise with a series of associated production tasks in writing and speaking.

Prelistening Activity: Students are told they will be listening to an interview recorded with an exchange student from the target country. They are asked to fill out a form with the information they hear in the recorded interview, writing in the target language. They are also told that not all of the information requested on the form will be given in the interview. They will therefore have to design appropriate questions to elicit the needed information after they have heard the passage twice.

Text: The instructor records an interview with an exchange student from the target culture, eliciting information about his or her interests, family life, etc. The instructor then prepares a short form such as the one below. The example is given in English for purposes of illustration, but the form can be in the target language to include writing practice:

Student: Fill in the information requested on this form as you listen to the interview. You will hear the passage twice. There are some items on your form for which no information is given. After you have filled in all the facts you hear, design appropriate questions to get the rest of the information you need.

Interviewee's name _____

Occupation _____

Home country _____

Town where born _____

Reason for visiting the United States _____

_____

Preferred leisure activities _____

Impressions of this university _____

_____

Illustration 5.7
Photos Taken in
France

(1) Pastries in a
Shop Window

(2) Cheeses

(3) Open-Air
Market in
Annecy

Similarities noticed between United States and native country_____

_____

_____

Cultural differences noticed_____

_____

_____

Future plans_____

_____

Etc.

Follow-up: If possible, the teacher invites the exchange student to visit the class the next class period, and students use their questions to continue the interview.

The suggestions in this chapter for teaching listening comprehension skills, though certainly not exhaustive, represent some of the techniques that are available to teachers who are dealing mostly with students at the Novice, Intermediate, and Advanced levels. It has been stressed that listening comprehension should not be assumed to developed "naturally," without any guidance from the teacher: The processes involved in language comprehension need to be actively taught if students are going to attain optimal levels of proficiency. The same can be said about reading comprehension, discussed next.

Teaching Reading Comprehension

Some Processes and Skills Involved in Reading Comprehension

As we saw in Chapter 4 in the general discussion of comprehension processes, both visual and nonvisual information is involved in comprehension. The reader's preexisting knowledge about the linguistic code, as well as his or her knowledge of the world, can be as important as the actual words of the text. In fact, it seems that the more nonvisual information the reader possesses, the less visual information is needed (Phillips 1984).

Various models of reading comprehension have been developed in association with first-language reading research, and a few of these were referred to in Chapter 4. A very comprehensive and helpful review of many reading models in both first- and second-language reading can be found in Barnett (1989). She categorizes these models into three basic types. The first type is comprised of *bottom-up models,* which are essentially "text-driven": The reader begins essentially by trying to decode letters, words, phrases, and sentences and "builds up" comprehension in a somewhat linear fashion from this incoming data. The second type includes *top-down models,* which can be thought of as "reader-driven," where schemata that the reader brings to the text drive comprehension. Models in the third group are considered *interactive* in nature. Such models posit an interaction between reader and text: High-level decoding and sampling from the textual features happen simultaneously and in a cyclical fashion. A variation on this third type of model in native-language reading is Pearson and Tierney's (1984) "composing model" of reading, which "views comprehension as the act of composing a new version of the text for an inner reader" (Barnett 1989, p. 31). Barnett classifies this type of conceptualization as a *reading/writing model,* since it takes into consideration similarities in the reading and writing processes. In many of the native-language reading models described in Barnett's review, it is the reader rather than the text that is primary in the comprehension process.

Swaffar, Arens, and Byrnes (1991) have developed a "procedural model for integrative reading" (pp. 73–91) that synthesizes text and reader-based features. Their model is "procedural" in that it is meant to guide reading behavior rather than predict reader processing. It assumes that there are two parallel sets of interactive top-down and bottom-up processes, with one set relating to the reader and the other relating to the text (p. 74). Thus the message of the text interacts with the perceptions, knowledge background, and skills of the reader. The Swaffar et al. model is designed to deal with the practical issues surrounding second-language reading, although it is derived in part from theoretical perspectives in first-language reading.

It is clear that native-language reading models cannot be applied directly to second-language reading, especially for adult learners who are already literate in their native language. However, many of the insights from native-language reading research can and have been used to gain an understanding of L2 reading processes. For second-language readers, especially in beginning levels, the reading task often becomes a laborious "bottom-up" decoding process, mainly because readers lack knowledge of the code, as well as knowledge of the cultural context of the reading material. Bernhardt (1986) reviews research in second-language reading in which bottom-up (text-dependent) models have been applied. She concludes that, in general, second-language readers become more efficient at gathering information from the text as their proficiency develops (p. 97). This is consistent with Lund's (1991) research on reading in German, reported earlier (see p. 185 ff).

Second-language reading research within the framework of top-down or schema-based models was reviewed to some extent in Chapter 4. Bernhardt, in summarizing some of the L2 research done within this framework, suggests that comprehension of discourse seems to be influenced more by conceptual factors than by linguistic factors. In a study she conducted with German students reading literary texts, for example, she found that the reader's ability to visualize the passage content and relate to it personally was more important in predicting comprehension than was his or her linguistic competence and conversational proficiency (p. 99). Yet no one model or type of model is sufficient in itself to explain what happens when language learners try to comprehend written texts. Bernhardt argues for an approach that reconciles the strengths of all the different types of models and acknowledges their different insights. "It is clear from all the models that the comprehender is an active participant in the comprehension process who *perceives and selects features of text and features of the world at large for processing and for synthesizing*" (p. 99).

The importance of considering our students as individuals who approach a text with differing background knowledge, interests, motivations, skills, and strategies becomes clear when one considers the interactive nature of reading. In order to help students become more efficient and successful readers, teachers need to keep such individual factors in mind. They also need to think about both the purposes for which students might be reading and the reading skills, strategies, and processes involved in achieving these purposes.

According to Phillips (1984), reading purposes have often been dichotomized into *reading for information* or *reading for pleasure.* She cautions that the lines between these types of reading are not really rigid, and in fact both objectives can be facets of a single reading assignment. The determination of the purpose(s) for reading a given passage should have implications for the way in which the reading task is designed and comprehension is assessed. For example, when a student is reading for specific information, it makes sense to consider the accuracy with which details are understood as well as the amount of detail reported relating to that information. When students are reading something for pleasure, evidence of comprehension might be assessed differently. In a similar manner, the stages or sequenced steps a reader will go through when approaching a passage will also be a function of the reader's own purposes or objectives. An individual might skim the table of contents of a target-language magazine to get a global view of the type of topics covered and then read an article of particular interest more intensively.

Phillips (1984) reviews work by Munby (1979) and Grellet (1981) who have analyzed various reader purposes and processes in second-language reading.

Munby's (1979) model of reading instruction divides types of reading into two categories according to purpose: He characterizes reading as being either *intensive* or *extensive.* In *intensive reading,* often for information, students need to understand linguistic as well as semantic detail and pay close attention to the text. In *extensive reading,* often for pleasure, students need not necessarily comprehend all the details of the text. Rather, speed and skill in getting the gist are the most important criteria for training in this type of reading task. Understanding in a general way the author's intent, getting the main ideas, and reacting to the material personally are also reading goals when reading extensively (Phillips 1984).

Grellet (1981) discusses four main ways that one can read a given text: (1) *skimming,* or quickly running one's eyes over the text to get the gist; (2) *scanning,* or quickly searching for some particular piece of information in the text; (3) *extensive reading;* and (4) *intensive reading.* She points out that these different ways to approach reading are not mutually exclusive, but may in fact be done in succession when approaching a given text.

In teaching reading comprehension, we need to design tasks that correspond to all of these purposes and processes in reading. Grellet (1981) proposes that activities designed to check comprehension relate to both the content of the passage and its discourse structure, or organization. Questions or tasks can be designed to clarify the passage's function, its general argumentative organization, its rhetorical structure, the use of cohesive devices, and the understanding of intersentential relationships. To help students understand the *content* of the passage, tasks can relate to understanding the plain facts, the implications, the suppositions, and evaluation of the text (Munby 1979; Grellet 1981; Phillips 1984).

Using Authentic Materials

The same rationale for the use of authentic materials relates to reading as well as listening comprehension practice. Reading specialists point out that simplifying texts reduces their natural redundancy, which might actually make them more difficult to read. Authentic written materials should also be presented, if possible, in their original form to allow students to use nonlinguistic cues to interpret meaning (Grellet 1981). Although for the lowest levels of proficiency one needs to select texts that deal with familiar, interesting topics or present cultural information (including realia) in a fairly straightforward fashion, a wide variety of text types can be used, as long as the tasks are geared to the students' capabilities in reading. Some tasks that might be appropriate for different levels of reading proficiency are presented in Illustration 5.8. As in the case of the listening task types presented earlier in the chapter, the difficulty of the task will vary depending on the nature of the text, its level of familiarity and interest, the precision of detail that is necessary in carrying out the task, and the knowledge and competence that the student brings to the reading material. Thus the lists in Illustration 5.8 should be interpreted as a set of suggestions and not as rigid prescriptions for developing learning activities.

Illustration 5.8
Reading Tasks

Suggested Tasks for Building Reading Proficiency

Novice/Intermediate	Advanced/Superior
Anticipation/Prediction activities	Skimming/Scanning
Prereading activities (various)	Comprehension checks (various)
Skimming	Contextual guessing
Gisting	Making inferences
Detecting functions of texts	Extracting specific detail
Scanning	Paraphrasing (target language)
Extracting specific information	Resumé (native or target language)
Contextual guessing	Note taking/Outlining
Simple cloze (multiple choice)	Identifying sociolinguistic features
Filling out forms	Understanding idioms
Comprehension checks (various)	Understanding discourse structure
Clue searching	Understanding intentions
Making inferences	Analysis and evaluative activities
Scrambled stories	Creative elaboration
Resumé (native language)	
Passage completion	
Identifying sociolinguistic features	
Identifying discourse structure	
Identifying link words/referents	

As mentioned earlier in this chapter, both Internet sites and multimedia software programs offer teachers and students an ever increasing source of authentic materials for the classroom. The set of guidelines for evaluating multimedia software programs that has been developed by the University of Hawaii's National Foreign Language Resource Center ("Taxonomy . . ." 1999) includes criteria for evaluating these kinds of reading materials (see Appendix B). Questions in the evaluation criteria include those related to the authenticity of the appearance of the reading material, its content, the quality of any reading activities provided with the material, the availability of reading tools (such as links to a spoken version of the passage, glosses, cultural information, and online dictionaries or grammars), and the nature of the navigation among the passages offered and the tools for assisting readers in comprehending them. There is also a strong emphasis in this set of criteria on reading strategy instruction. Teachers who are considering multimedia programs and Internet texts may want to consult the NFLRC's Web site for this material (http://nts.lll.hawaii.edu/flmedia).

Techniques for Teaching Reading Skills

This section illustrates how various reading comprehension formats can be used with Novice, Intermediate, Advanced, and Superior level learners. Some activity types are more appropriate to one level of proficiency; many of them, however, can be used at various levels. To adapt a given sample activity format to a particular level of proficiency, a teacher can simply choose an appropriate topic, create task demands that are congruent with reading purposes at that level, and adjust his or her expectations for accuracy in comprehension accordingly.

Any of the activities listed here can be used in isolation, but Phillips (1984) points out that a whole range of practice activities might be used in concert to integrate individual skills so that higher levels of proficiency might be achieved. She has developed a five-stage plan for reading instruction that can be used in the classroom, in individualized instructional settings, or in computer-adaptive instruction. The five stages she identifies are:

1. *Preteaching/Preparation Stage.* This important first step helps develop skills in anticipation and prediction for the reading of graphic material. Phillips points out that students need to build expectancies for the material that they are about to read. This assertion is supported by the research reviewed in Chapter 4, where we saw how important advance organizers and contextual cues are in helping readers build and/or retrieve from memory appropriate schemata to help them comprehend. Some activities Phillips recommends for this first stage of reading include:

   a. Brainstorming to generate ideas that have a high probability of occurrence in the text;
   b. Looking at visuals, headlines, titles, charts, or other contextual aids that are provided with the text;

    c. Predicting or hypothesizing on the basis of the title or first line of a text what significance it might have or what might come next (pp. 289–90).

2. *Skimming/Scanning Stages.* Both of these steps are distinct processes involving, as we saw earlier, getting the gist (skimming) and locating specific information (scanning). Phillips points out that skilled readers do some scanning while attempting to skim a text; however, she feels that practice is needed in each skill for second-language students. Some of the practice activities needed for this stage include:

    a. Getting the gist of short readings, paragraphs, or other graphic material;

    b. Identifying topic sentences and main ideas;

    c. Selecting the best paraphrase from multiple-choice options of the main idea of a text or of the conclusion;

    d. Matching subtitles with paragraphs;

    e. Filling in charts or forms with key concepts;

    f. Creating titles or headlines for passages;

    g. Making global judgments or reacting in some global fashion to a reading passage (p. 290).

Swaffar (1983) proposes that teachers have students move directly from skimming to scanning with any reading task. First students skim the passage to determine what general category fits the content of the passage (i.e., is it about a problem, people or organizations, events, or ideas?). Then students scan the text more carefully to locate a few of the main ideas relating to this global category.

3. *Decoding/Intensive Reading Stage.* Phillips maintains that this stage is most necessary when students are "learning to read" rather than "reading to learn." Decoding involves guessing from context the meaning of unknown words or phrases and may be needed at the word, intrasentential, intersentential, or discourse level. The extent of decoding that will go on in this stage will depend on the purpose for reading a given passage. As Phillips states, "in the final analysis, conscious, detailed decoding is not a common goal of reading" (p. 293). Rather, fluency and rapid understanding are the most common objectives in reading, and it is only when comprehension is impeded by unknown words, complex structures, or very unfamiliar concepts that skilled readers resort to decoding.

4. *Comprehension Stage.* In this step, comprehension checks of various sorts are made to determine if students have achieved their reading purpose(s).

5. *Transferable/Integrating Skills.* In this final stage of teaching reading, Phillips maintains that exercises should be used that help students go beyond the confines of the specific passage to enhance reading skills and effective reading strategies per se. Exercises that encourage contextual guessing, selective reading for main ideas, appropriate dictionary usage, and effective rereading strategies to confirm hypotheses are among those identified as especially helpful in this stage (pp. 294–95).

Finding and Selecting Sources for Reading Activities

The sample activities given in the next section of the chapter are drawn from a number of types of sources:

Textbook readings and realia. A few of the activities illustrated in this section use realia that are provided in the student's textbook but exploit that realia in ways that go beyond the exercises accompanying the material. Because of space limitations, textbook authors can often provide only one or two comprehension activities to accompany a reading drawn from an authentic source; in some cases, realia that have a great deal of potential for reading comprehension practice are found on the pages of the text, but few reading activities are given to accompany these materials. Teachers may want to look at the authentic material in their own course texts to see how new and interesting activities can be designed to take full advantage of these often colorful and varied resources.

Realia drawn from brochures, newspapers, magazines, and other sources. Teachers may have access to a variety of printed authentic materials that they or colleagues have gathered on various trips to the target culture. This may include maps, circulars, tickets, travel brochures, and the like, many of which can be used to design classroom activities. A few of the activities in this section are based on this kind of material.

Photographs. Teachers who have taken photographs on their own trips abroad can use these creatively in designing classroom activities of various sorts. For example, students can be asked to listen to a description of various activities that the teacher describes orally and select the appropriate photograph that accompanies the description from a set of four or five photos displayed on an overhead camera or in the front of the room. Alternatively, students can be given a set of photos taken by the teacher and asked to put them in chronological order as they read a short narrative that is instructor-written. Pictures can also be used to stimulate students' own written or oral production in the language, which can be shared with others in the class.

Web-based materials. When planning to use Web sites as a source of authentic materials for classroom exercises and activities, it is very beneficial to know how to locate specific information. Today an increasing number of course textbooks have accompanying Web sites that provide a variety of links to Internet sources keyed to topics in the chapters of the text. These materials can be an excellent starting point, and some textbook sites provide suggested activities to use as well. Teachers need not be limited, of course, to the links accompanying their course text's Web site. Using any Web browser, such as Netscape or Internet Explorer, the user simply needs to type the name of one of several very powerful search engines to locate information, often in the target language. Some of the most well-known search engines are Excite, Lycos, Yahoo!, and Altavista. All of these search engines offer sites in a variety of languages. The list of target-language sites is normally found near the bottom of the opening page of the search engine site. You can begin your search by typing in English the major category in which you are looking for materials and/or information. Since the sites in other languages are very similar to the English site, by analogy you will have an idea of where—under which heading—to look. If you are looking for examples of housing (hotels, private homes, rentals, inns, etc., including photos and e-mail or Web addresses), begin by scanning the search engine site for logical headings—Tourism or Business and Economy. Then it is nothing more than a simple click-and-search procedure to find a particular site that offers what you need.

In *Untangling the Web,* Blyth (1998) offers a basic set of guidelines for the foreign language learner and teacher who want to know more about the Internet and how to access culturally authentic documents in the foreign language. The book includes a chapter on "Searching the Foreign Language Web," in which the author gives several tutorials that guide the user through both simple and complex searches. An additional resource, *Open Sesame: Your Guide to Exploring Foreign Language Resources on the World Wide Web* (Santore and Schane 2000), provides specific guidelines for searching the Web for foreign language resources, and includes a list of search engines by languages and countries. Teachers can also find a number of articles in professional journals that include Web resources (see, for example, Walz 1998, who provides Web-based activities keyed to the Standards), and professional newsletters often include a list of interesting Web sites for teachers.

Before you plan to use a Web site you have identified or have your students access it, you should verify that the site is still active by checking out the link(s) that you plan to use. Since so many Web sites are apparently temporary or transitory, the Web-based activities at the end of this section are either based on a site that seems more permanent or are constructed from a simulated example of the type that might be found on a Web site of a certain kind. Even when planning to use sites that you consider fairly permanent (such as the French train system, SNCF, used for the sample activity on pp. 218–219), it is still advisable to verify the URL (Uniform Resource Locator, or address). The sample activities provided later in this chapter should therefore be considered as illustrative of the *type* of activities that can be created by teachers using the most current resources available to them rather than as actual materials to be copied and used in class.

Sample Formats for Reading Comprehension

Anticipation/ Prediction

SAMPLE (NOVICE/INTERMEDIATE)

Objective: Students anticipate the content of personal ads drawn from a magazine or newspaper in Spanish and then scan the ads to find information about the various people who wrote them.

Prereading Activity: Students are presented with the list below consisting of types of personal information. They mark the items they would expect to find in personal ads:

a. age	**c.** annual income
b. race	**d.** occupation

    e. religion   **h.** astrological sign
    f. number of credit cards   **i.** telephone number
    g. physical description   **j.** marital status

After marking their choices, students look over the text of the ads and try to determine the format of a typical ad in Spanish. They then list the types of information they find and match that list to the items they marked above. They then discuss whether their expectations were met and what aspects of the ads they did not anticipate.

Text: See Illustration 5.9.

Scanning: Students scan the ads in Illustration 5.9 (p. 212) to see if they can find the individuals described below. They place the name of the individual in the blank next to the description that matches.

    a. She likes rock music and wants to meet young men with the same
       interest. _____
    b. A young avant-garde blond man who is a little bit punk wants to meet and
       make friends. _____
    c. An intelligent thin young man with blue eyes seeks a pen pal. _____
    d. A happy young woman who likes peace, classical music, and nature is
       looking for her soul mate. _____
    e. A tall dark-haired woman would like to have friends from any part of
       South America. _____

Skimming/ Getting the Gist

SAMPLE 1 (NOVICE)

Objective: Students match English-language synopses to descriptions of excursions in French to show comprehension of the gist of the text.

SAMPLE 2 (INTERMEDIATE)

For Intermediate readers, the synopses are in French and students name the excursion, describe and give details about departure/return times, price, day of the week, etc.

Text: See Illustration 5.10, page 213.

Student Task: The Novice-level task is given below:

EXCURSIONS EN PROVENCE. Several American students studying in Provence are writing postcards and letters home telling of sights they have seen in the south of France. Match the excerpts from their correspondence to the descriptions in the travel brochure to discover which of the six excursions they took. Place the number next to each excursion in the blank next to the excerpt that matches it.

1. _____ *" . . . We spent the whole day touring the ancient cities of the region. It seems so hard to believe that I saw a real Roman arena. . . ."*

Illustration 5.9
Personal Ads in
Spanish

Para él	Para ella

Soy una chica alta y morena y me gustaría tener amigos de cualquier parte de Sud América.

> Raquel. Residencia Miramar,
> 18. Puerto Real. Cádiz, España.

Si quieres tener una amiga joven, educada y bonita, yo soy la persona más indicada.

> Patricia. Avenida La Habana,
> 45. Motril. Granada, España.

Soy una muchacha alegre y hogareña. Me gusta la paz, la música clásica y la naturaleza. Si eres mi alma gemela, escríbeme.

> María Elena. Urbanización Guadalmar,
> R. Oliva, 14. Málaga, España.

Soy una chiflada por la música *rock* y me gustaría conocer a muchachos con el mismo interés.

> Eva. Jesús Gaviota, 48.
> Puerto de Santa María. Cádiz, España.

Si quieres tener un buen amigo, inteligente, delgado y de ojos azules, escríbeme pronto.

> Ramón. 214 W 7th St.
> Los Ángeles, CA. U.S.A.

Soy un joven peruano, moreno, simpático y de buenos sentimientos. Deseo conocer muchacha soltera y hogareña.

> Apartado postal 38. Lima, Perú.

Si de verdad te gustan los rubios de vanguardia y un poco *punk,* deseo conocerte y ser tu amigo.

> Xavier
> Apartado 4444. Barcelona.

Soltero 21 años de físico y carácter agradable desea hacer amistad con chica de iguales características.

> Apartado 2351.
> Toledo, España.

Source: Illustration 5.9 is from Gilman and Bijuesca, *Horizontes,* 3rd ed., Heinle & Heinle, 1997, p. 31. Prereading activities adapted from Laura Martin, *Entre Líneas,* 2nd ed., Heinle & Heinle, 1991, p. 66.

2. _____ *" . . . You'll never believe this, Mom, but I had the best dinner last night—a kind of fish soup that was really delicious!"*
3. _____ *" . . . and last Thursday we went on this beautiful tour around a nearby mountain, with about six stops along the way to see the sights. . . ."*
4. _____ *" . . . I saw the neatest castle last weekend—built on some cliffs that were kind of a golden color. We saw this rustic little village too. . . ."*

**Skimming/
Scanning/
Getting the
Main Idea**

SAMPLE 1 (INTERMEDIATE)

Objective: Students skim and scan descriptions of short stays in the country in France and match them to French-language descriptions of types of trips students want to make.

Text: See Illustration 5.11.

Student Task: SEJOURS A LA CAMPAGNE. Trouvez le séjour qui correspond le mieux aux besoins suivants:

Illustration 5.10   Travel Brochure (Sample 2)

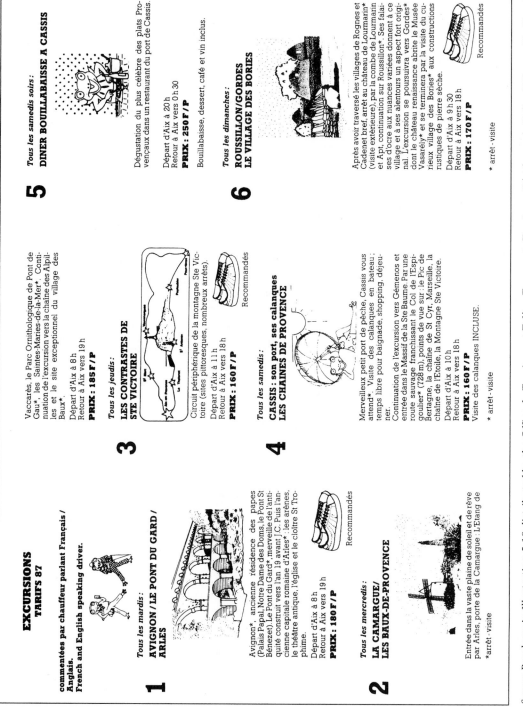

EXCURSIONS
TARIFS 87

commentées par chauffeur parlant Français /
Anglais.
French and English speaking driver.

1

Tous les mardis :
AVIGNON / LE PONT DU GARD / ARLES

Avignon*, ancienne résidence des papes (Palais Papal, Notre Dame des Doms, le Pont St Bénezet) Le Pont du Gard*, merveille de l'antiquité construit vers l'an 19 avant J.C. Puis l'ancienne capitale romaine d'Arles* : les arènes, le théâtre antique, l'église et le cloître St Trophime.

Départ d'Aix à 8h
Retour à Aix vers 19h
PRIX : 180 F / P

Recommandés

2

Tous les mercredis :
LA CAMARGUE / LES BAUX-DE-PROVENCE

Entrée dans la vaste plaine de soleil et de rêve par Arles, porte de la Camargue : L'Etang de

*arrêt - visite

Vaccarés, le Parc Ornithologique de Pont de Gau*, les Saintes-Maries-de-la-Mer*. Continuation de l'excursion vers la chaîne des Alpilles et le site exceptionnel du village des Baux*.

Départ d'Aix à 8h
Retour à Aix vers 19h
PRIX : 185 F / P

3

Tous les jeudis :
LES CONTRASTES DE STE VICTOIRE

Circuit périphérique de la montagne Ste Victoire (sites pittoresques, nombreux arrêts).

Départ d'Aix à 11h
Retour à Aix vers 18h
PRIX : 160 F / P

Recommandés

4

Tous les samedis :
CASSIS : son port, ses calanques LES CHAÎNES DE PROVENCE

Merveilleux petit port de pêche, Cassis vous attend*. Visite des calanques en bateau ; temps libre pour baignade, shopping, déjeuner.
Continuation de l'excursion vers Gémenos et entrée dans le Massif de la Ste Baume. Par une route sauvage franchissant le Col de l'Espigoulier* (728 m), points de vue sur : le Pic de Bertagne, la chaîne de St Cyr, Marseille, la chaîne de l'Etoile, la Montagne Ste Victoire.

Départ d'Aix à 10h
Retour à Aix vers 18h
PRIX : 160 F / P
Visite des calanques INCLUSE.

* arrêt - visite

5

Tous les samedis soirs :
DÎNER BOUILLABAISSE À CASSIS

Dégustation du plus célèbre des plats Provençaux dans un restaurant du port de Cassis.

Départ d'Aix à 20h
Retour à Aix vers 0 h 30
PRIX : 250 F / P

Bouillabaisse, dessert, café et vin inclus.

6

Tous les dimanches :
ROUSSILLON/GORDES LE VILLAGE DES BORIES

Après avoir traversé les villages de Rognes et Cadenet bref, arrêt au château de Lourmarin* (visite extérieure), par la combe de Lourmarin et Apt, continuation sur Roussillon*. Ses falaises d'ocre aux nuances variées donnent à ce village et à ses alentours un aspect fort original. L'excursion se poursuivra vers Gordes* dont le château renaissance abrite le Musée Vasarély* et se terminera par la visite du curieux village des Bories* aux constructions rustiques de pierre sèche.

Départ d'Aix à 9 h 30
Retour à Aix vers 18h
PRIX : 170 F / P

Recommandés

* arrêt - visite

Source: Brochure in Illustration 5.10 distributed by the Office du Tourisme et Tylène Transports Tourisme, Résidence de Galice D Square Dr. Henri Bianchi 13090 Aix-en-Provence. Illustration by Michel Palmi. Reprinted by permission.

Illustration 5.11   Vacations in the Country (Sample 1)

SÉJOUR PÉDESTRE

BELLEGARDE-EN-MARCHE, carte K4.
Séjour pédestre 1 semaine en Haute Marche et Combraille.
Du 7 juillet au 1er septembre, sauf semaine du 15 août.
Randonnées en étoile, à la découverte du pays. Un accompagnateur, M. Guy Couturier, de Bellegarde, vous fera découvrir des chemins presque oubliés dont d'anciennes voies gallo-romaines; accès par train direct Paris-Auzances.
Hébergement : rustique, dans une vieille maison; feu de cheminée, veillées...
Prix, par personne, en pension complète :
Du samedi 11 h 30 au samedi 16 h. 800 F
Informations et réservation :
M. Guy Couturier,
23190 Bellegarde-en-Marche,
tél. (55) 67.68.79.

BERSAC-SUR-RIVALIER, carte F3.
Week-end pédestre.
Petites vacances scolaires et week-ends.
Randonnées accompagnées par un jeune berger.
Hébergement : en maison familiale de vacances.
Prix, par personne, en pension complète :
Du vendredi 18 h au dimanche 18 h : 110 F
Journée supplémentaire .... 55 F
Informations et réservation :
Vacances en Limousin,
Bersac-sur-Rivalier,
87370 Saint-Sulpice-Laurière,
tél. (55) 71.43.69.

CUSSAC, carte C5.
Week-end ou 1 semaine à pied au pays des Feuillardiers.
Ouvert toute l'année.
Séjour dans un petit village caractéristique de ce terroir limousin : Fayollas, situé à 2 km du bourg de Cussac. Le propriétaire du gîte se propose de vous guider par les chemins du pays des feuillardiers pour vous en faire découvrir la vie et les traditions.
Hébergement : gîte pour 4 personnes; séjour avec coin cuisine et cheminée; 2 chambres, 1 lit 2 places, 2 lits simples, avec draps et couverture; salle d'eau; wc, chauffage.
Prix, forfait-gîte pour 4 personnes, repas non compris.
1 semaine,
Du samedi 16 h au samedi 10 h : 500 F
Week-end sauf juillet et août,
Du vendredi 18 h au dimanche 18 h : 167 F
Informations et réservation :

SR 23–87. Service de réservation Loisirs-Accueil Creuse, Haute-Vienne en Limousin, n° 87-7904. C.C.I., 16, place Jourdan, 87000 Limoges, tél. (55) 34.70.11.

SAINT-GENIEZ-Ô-MERLE, carte J9.
Week-end « découverte de la Xaintrie ».
Toute l'année sauf juillet et août.
Accueil de groupes de 12 à 32 personnes, avec accompagnement.
A travers la Xaintrie, pays fait de croupes vallonnées, inséré entre les gorges profondes de la Maronne et de la Dordogne, 35 km de sentiers vous feront apprécier cette région si paisible, pleine de charme et de nuances, découvrir ses précieux vestiges d'un passé riche d'histoire, le mur vitrifié de Sermus, l'église du Vieux Bourg, la Croix Percée de Rouzeyrol et les prestigieuses tours et ruines de Merle.
Hébergement : capacité totale 32 personnes; bungalows au lieu-dit « Moulin de Lacombe », gîte d'étape ; repas et petits déjeuners en auberge rurale, un repas gastronomique composé exclusivement de spécialités régionales.
Prix, par personne en pension complète :
Week-end du samedi 8 h au dimanche 20 h .... 230 F
Journée supplémentaire .... 80 F
Informations et réservation :
Mairie de Saint-Geniez-Ô-Merle,
service du tourisme,
19220 Saint-Privat, tél. (55) 28.21.86.

SÉJOUR BICYCLETTE

COMPREIGNAC, carte E4.
1 semaine le Haut-Limousin à vélo.
Toute l'année.
Circuit du lac de Saint-Pardoux à la Basse-Marche par les étangs, et les monts de Blond; itinéraire au profil vallonné mais sans difficulté majeure, alternant une journée de transfert d'hébergement et une journée de libre randonnée autour du gîte. Sans accompagnement, bicyclettes et documentation fournies au départ.
Hébergement : en gîtes-chambres d'hôte à la ferme ou au village ; déjeuner libre.
Prix, par personne en demi-pension :
1 semaine, du samedi 18 h au samedi 10 h :
Vélo compris .... 560 F
Sans location de vélo .... 500 F
Informations et réservation :
SR 23-87   Service de réservation.
Loisirs Accueil, Creuse, Haute-Vienne
en Limousin, n° 87-3901,
C.C.I., 16, place Jourdan, 87000 Limoges, tél. (55) 34.70.11.

CAMPS, carte I10.
Séjour cyclo 1 semaine.
Toute l'année.
Entre les vallées de la Cère et de la Dordogne, à proximité des ruines de Merle : itinéraires et circuits établis suivant les possibilités de chacun; bicyclettes fournies.
Hébergement : en hôtel-restaurant, 5 chambres ou en camping à quelques pas du plan d'eau.
Prix, en pension complète :
1 semaine, du samedi ou dimanche 18 h, au samedi ou dimanche 18 h :
Hôtel, 2 personnes,
Chambre double .... 750 F
Hôtel, 1 personne......................................1050 F
Camping, 1 personne .... 550 F
Informations et réservation :
M. et Mme Solignac,
le bourg de Camps, 19430 Mercœur,
tél. (55) 28.51.83.

DUN-LE-PALESTEL, carte H2.
Week-end ou 1 semaine, séjour vélo et carriole
Ouvert toute l'année sauf 3e semaine d'octobre.
Séjours composant des promenades autour de Dun-le-Palestel, en vélo et en carriole et la possibilité de pratiquer le tennis et la pêche. Mise à disposition du vélo pendant toute la semaine.
Hébergement : en hôtel 1 étoile, dans le bourg, chambres individuelles ou doubles dans cette maison rustique.
Prix, en pension complète :
1 semaine, du lundi 18 h au dimanche 18 h :
1 personne .... 999 F
2 personnes ....1665 F
Week-end, du vendredi 18 h au dimanche 18 h :
1 personne .... 333 F
2 personnes .... 555 F
Informations et réservation :
SR 23-87   Service de réservation
Loisirs-Accueil, Creuse, Hte-Vienne
en Limousin, n° LF 23-8,
C.C.I., 16, place Jourdan, 87000 Limoges,
tél. (55) 34.70.11.

1. _____ Vous voulez rester dans un petit village du terroir limousin et faire des randonnées guidées.
2. _____ Vous voulez voyager à bicyclette dans une région où il y a de beaux paysages, des lacs et des vallons, mais vous n'êtes pas préparé(e) pour des chemins montagneux ou difficiles.
3. _____ Votre rêve c'est de faire un séjour dans une vieille maison rustique, et de faire des promenades romantiques à l'étoile. . . .
4. _____ Vous n'avez qu'un weekend libre, mais vous avez l'occasion de le passer dans une maison de vacances et de faire des promenades guidées avec un berger! etc.

VISITS TO THE COUNTRY. Find the visit that corresponds best to the following requirements:

1. _____ *You want to stay in a little village in the Limousin area and take guided hikes.*
2. _____ *You want to go biking in a region where there are beautiful vistas, lakes, and valleys, but you aren't ready to take on mountainous or difficult paths.*
3. _____ *Your dream is to take a short vacation and stay in an old rustic house, with romantic walks under the stars. . . .*
4. _____ *You only have one free weekend, but you have the chance to stay in a vacation home and take guided walks with a shepherd! etc.*

Follow-up: Students indicate which excursion appeals to them the most and say why. They may also discuss the various options in small groups and then come to a group consensus about which excursion they will take together.

Source: Brochure in Illustration 5.11 is distributed by the Comité Régional de Tourisme du Limousin, Centre Impression: Limoges, France 1980. Reprinted by permission.

SAMPLE 2 (NOVICE/INTERMEDIATE)

Objective: Students skim/scan a description of a hotel in order to get the main ideas.

Text: See Illustration 5.12.

Student Task: Students complete the following activity that asks them to match the paragraph in the text to the amenities that a friend wants in a hotel. The example is given in English, but the task can also be done in Spanish since the ideas are paraphrased.

> *Imagine that your friend, who does not read Spanish, has been given information found in an advertisement about a hotel in Yabucoa (see Illustration 5.12). Help him or her decide if the hotel is a good choice by looking for the amenities he or she mentions. Indicate which paragraph in the ad gives the appropriate information. Then decide if this hotel meets your friend's needs.*
>
> *Paragraph #_____ I can't decide whether I'd rather spend my vacation by the ocean or in the mountains. Where is this place located?*

Paragraph #_____ I'd like to be able to go swimming, and it would be nice if there were a place to get some other exercise too!

Paragraph #_____ I'd like a room with a private bath and a great view.

Paragraph #_____ I don't want to have to go out every night to find a restaurant—I'd prefer to eat sometimes right in the hotel.

Paragraph #_____ I hope I can use my credit card. I've got Visa.

Paragraph #_____ I hope the place is air-conditioned . . . I can't stand sleeping in a hot room!

Paragraph #_____ I wonder if they have TV there—I'd really like to be able to watch some television in the evenings.

Illustration 5.12
Hotel Ad (Sample 2)

1. Nuestras instalaciones están ubicadas frente al Balneario de Playa Lucía en Yabucoa. Aquí podrá disfrutar del hermoso mar y el verdor de las montañas al mismo tiempo.
2. Contamos con 19 cómodas habitaciones dobles, todas con aire acondicionado, televisor a colores con TV cable, baños privados y balcones con vista a la piscina y al mar.
3. Nuestro restaurante cuenta con un menú de exquisitos platos con especialidad en mariscos.
4. Para su entretenimiento, contamos además, con piscina, cancha de baloncesto y, naturalmente, la playa.
5. Para actividades de negocios o sociales, contamos con un amplio Salón de Actividades con aire acondicionado y capacidad para 150 personas.
6. Estacionamiento disponible. Aceptamos las principales tarjetas de crédito: Visa, MasterCard y American Express.

Source: Illustration 5.12 is from Jorge Cubillos, *Temas: Spanish for the Global Community.* Heinle & Heinle, 2000, pp. 175–76.

Scanning/ Extracting Specific Information

SAMPLE 1 (INTERMEDIATE)

Objective: Students read a text about French meal customs and scan for information that will help them complete the table given below. The table can be completed in either French or English, depending on whether the instructor wants to mix skills or use the activity as a test of reading comprehension only.

Text: See Illustration 5.13.

Student Task: Complete the table below, using the information given in the reading about meals in France.

Follow-up: Students can discuss their answers in small groups or compare answers in a whole-class discussion.

SAMPLE 2 (NOVICE/INTERMEDIATE)

Objective: Students search the Web site of the French train system in order to get information they would need to plan a trip from Paris to Barcelona, Spain.

Illustration 5.13   Meals in France (Sample 1)

consider

Les repas en France

Pendant le repas, gardez les mains sur la table de chaque côté de votre assiette. Vous mettrez le pain directement sur la table. Sauf pendant le petit déjeuner, mangez-le sans beurre en petits morceaux que vous détachez discrètement. Les tartines du petit déjeuner se mangent entières et avec du beurre et de la confiture.

En France, on fait souvent resservir les invités et il est poli de reprendre un peu de l'un des plats (même en petite quantité). Il est aussi poli de refuser en disant que c'est très bon mais qu'on n'a plus faim. Les repas français sont plus longs que les repas américains parce qu'en général, les Français ne mangent pas entre les repas.

Les enfants, cependant, prennent un goûter en rentrant de l'école, et de plus en plus de jeunes grignotent (*snack*) au lieu de déjeuner.

Après le repas, restez pour bavarder avec vos hôtes. Si vous fumez, offrez des cigarettes aux autres. En partant, complimentez l'hôte/l'hôtesse pour son repas.

En quoi les habitudes américaines sont-elles différentes?

Habits/customs	U.S. or your home culture (if other than U.S.)	France
Where do you place your hands while at the table?		
Where do you place your bread?		
What do you typically put on your bread at dinner?		
Is it polite to ask for or accept a second helping?		
Is it polite to refuse another serving if offered?		
Do most people eat between meals?		
How long should you stay after the meal is finished?		
Is it OK to smoke after dinner? What customs should you observe?		

Source: Cultural reading from Muyskens, Harlow, Vialet, and Brière, *Bravo! 3rd ed.* Heinle & Heinle, 1998, p. 62.

Student Task: *Allons à Barcelone. (Let's go to Barcelona!)*

Imaginez que vous et un copain/une copine participez à un programme d'études étrangères à Paris. Vous avez maintenant une semaine de libre pour voyager . . . et vous décidez d'aller à Barcelone. Allez au site de la SNCF (*http://www.sncf.fr*) et organisez votre voyage. Puis, complétez le formulaire suivant avec les renseignements que vous y trouvez.

(Imagine that you and a friend are on a study abroad program in Paris. You have a free weekend for travel . . . and you decide you would like to visit Barcelona. Go to the Web site for the French train system, the SNCF (http://www.sncf.fr), and plan your trip. Then fill out the following form, giving the information that you find.)

(See Illustration 5.14 for the form that students fill out.)
Source: Terry 2000.

SAMPLE 3 (NOVICE/INTERMEDIATE)

Objective: Students extract specific information from a print brochure or a Web site depicting hotels, motels, or small houses for rent in order to select a place to stay while on vacation.

Student Task: Students read a number of advertisements, such as the one in Illustration 5.15, and complete the following activities. (For those teachers wishing to have a "pure" reading comprehension task, students could be asked to read the ads in French and write their responses to the questions in English. For an integrated skills activity, students can be asked to write their answers in French, as directed below.)

Activity 1: You would like to take a vacation in the province of Quebec. You have located a real estate site on the Web. On this site, you find a list of rental locations, either by week or by month. Scroll down the list of places available for rent and indicate three that particularly interest you. Write a brief paragraph in French for each location you choose explaining your reasons for choosing it.

Activity 2: Several friends have said that they would be interested in vacationing in this area next summer. Choose an advertisement that best fits the criteria they've outlined below and place the number of the ad in the blank. Briefly explain why you think this particular accommodation is best suited to their needs.

_____1. Nous voulons trouver un endroit très calme et tranquille, loin des grandes villes. J'aimerais aller à la pêche ou circuler sur les routes de campagne à bicyclette, et mon mari veut prendre des photos de la nature. Nous avons besoin d'une chambre avec un lit pour deux, et j'aimerais bien avoir une petite cheminée dans le salon. *(We want to find a very calm and peaceful place, far from big cities. I'd like to go fishing or go bike riding on country roads, and my husband wants to take nature photos. We need a room with a double bed, and I'd like to have a little fireplace in the living room.)*

_____2. Nous préférons une petite maison sur le St-Laurent, si possible, avec tous les conforts—une cuisine équipée, au moins deux chambres

Illustration 5.14
Form to be Used to
Search the SNCF Web
Site on French Trains
(Sample 2)

RENSEIGNEMENTS	RÉPONSES
Date du voyage—départ de Paris	
Heure du départ de Paris	
Premier choix d'horaire	
Durée du voyage	
Heure d'arrivée à Barcelone	
Type de train	
Renseignements supplémentaires	
Date du voyage—retour de Barcelone	
Heure du départ de Barcelone	
Premier choix d'horaire	
Heure d'arrivée à Paris	
Type de train	
Renseignements supplémentaires	
Qu'est-ce que c'est que la carte 12–25?	

avec des lits doubles, une télé, une salle de bains très moderne,
l'usage d'un téléphone, bien sûr, et tout et tout. *(We prefer a little
house on the Saint Lawrence River, if possible, with all the comforts—a
full kitchen, at least two bedrooms with double beds, a television set, a
really modern bathroom, a telephone to use, of course, and
everything.)*

Etc.

**Intensive
Reading/Guessing
from Context**

SAMPLE 1 (NOVICE/INTERMEDIATE/ADVANCED)

Objective: Students learn to guess at the meaning of unknown words by using
contextual cues in the passage.

Illustration 5.15
Simulated
Advertisement for
Vacation Rental
(Sample 3)

DOSSIER #3078: RÉGION DE QUÉBEC

Prix par semaine: 500$ can.

Localisation: Québec, 70 km.

La maison: Cette jolie petite maison est située en pleine nature, loin des bruits de la circulation et des lumières des grandes villes. Les grandes fenêtres du salon vous donnent une vue magnifique des collines lointaines et de la forêt autour de la maison. Un grand salon meublé avec cheminée, télé; une chambre avec lit double; une salle de bain spacieuse joliment décorée; cuisine équipée, vaisselle fournie; laveuse. Eau courante et électricité. Pas de téléphone.

Les activités: Petite rivière à 10 km. Idéale pour la pêche et le canoë. Piste cyclable à proximité. Belle région pour prendre des photos!

Les repas: On peut préparer ses propres repas dans la cuisine bien équipée ou prendre des repas à un des restaurants du village voisin (15 km).

Source: Illustration 5.15 is a simulated advertisement similar to those that can be found on Web sites or in printed travel brochures.

Student Task: Students read a short passage and underline any words or expressions they do not know. The whole class then considers each unknown word and tries to see how much they can guess about it. For Novice-level readers, the text can be another student's composition, a pedagogically prepared text with recombined material and a few new words, a set of signs or simple labels, etc. For Intermediate and Advanced readers, texts can be taken from authentic sources, such as journalistic literature or short stories.

Reading Strategies: Teachers can help students become better contextual guessers by teaching them to approach unknown words or expressions with specific strategies, such as:

   a. Figuring out what part of speech the word must be, using the surrounding context or the morphology as cues

    b. Seeing if the word is used elsewhere in the context or if a contrast or analogy that can help derive meaning is implied

    c. Using one's knowledge of the world or of the specific context of the reading to deduce possible meanings for the word

Source: Grellet 1981, p. 42.

SAMPLE 2 (INTERMEDIATE/ADVANCED)

Objective: Students guess the meaning of an unknown word that is repeated several times within a paragraph by using contextual guessing strategies.

Student Task: In the travel brochure excerpt below, guess the meaning of the word "gîte" from its context. Explain your rationale for the guess you make.

SÉJOUR PÉDESTRE

CUSSAC, carte C5.

Week-end ou 1 semaine à pied au pays des Feuillardiers.

Ouvert toute l'année

Séjour dans un petit village caractéristique de ce terroir limousin : Fayollas, situé à 2 km du bourg de Cussac. Le propriétaire du gîte se propose de vous guider par les chemins du pays des feuillardiers pour vous en faire découvrir la vie et les traditions.

Hébergement: gîte pour 4 personnes; séjour avec coin cuisine et cheminée; 2 chambres, 1 lit 2 places, 2 lits simples, avec draps et couverture; salle d'eau; wc, chauffage.

Prix, forfait-gîte pour 4 personnes, repas non compris.

1 semaine,

Du samedi 16 h au samedi 10 h: 500 F

Week-end sauf juillet et août,

Du vendredi 18 h au dimanche 18 h: 167 F

Informations et réservation:

SR 23-87. Service de réservation Loisirs-Accueil Creuse, Haute-Vienne en Limousin, n° 87-7904. C.C.I., 16, place Jourdan, 87000 Limoges, tél.

(03) (55) 34.70.11.

Source: Comité Régional de Tourisme du Limousin, 1980. Technique adapted from Grellet 1981. Text reprinted by permission.

Intensive Reading/ Understanding Link Words and Referents

SAMPLE 1 (INTERMEDIATE)

Objective: Students develop skill in understanding the relationship between pronouns and referents in a text.

Student Task: Students read a short selection in Spanish. They then are given a few sentences extracted from the reading in which pronouns are used. From a set of multiple-choice alternatives, they identify the appropriate referent for the pronouns.

Passage:

La tamalera

Una mujer, envuelta en su rebozo, recorre las plazas, calles y mercados ofreciendo su mercadería.

rojos — ¡Tamales! ¡Tamales verdes y *colorados*! ¡Cómpre**los** calientitos! Nomás *unos*
unos pocos *cuantitos*. ¿Cuántos **le** doy, marchantita?

—Para **mí,** dos de chile. Al niño dé**le** uno de dulce.

—Si **me** compra cuatro, **se los** dejo por menos. ¡Ay marchantita! ¡Qué cara está la vida! Si **nos** han subido el precio de todos los productos: la carne, la masa, la
husk *hoja*. Ya casi no ganamos nada.

Otros clientes se van acercando, atraídos por el olor de los ricos tamales, y la tamalera va sacándo**los** de la olla y poniéndo**los** en los platos, mientras *se*
se prepara *apresta* a repetir su historia.

1. ¿Cuántos **le** doy, marchantita?
"**le**" refers to . . .

    a. you (*la marchantita*)

    b. the *tamal*

    c. the vendor

2. Al niño dé**le** uno de dulce.
"**le**" refers to . . .

    a. the *tamal*

    b. the boy

    c. you (*la marchantita*)

3. Otros clientes se van acercando, atraídos por el olor de los ricos tamales, y la tamalera va sacándo**los** de la olla . . .
"**los**" refers to . . .

    a. the pot

    b. the *tamales*

    c. the clients

Source: Idea adapted from Grellet 1981. Passage and photo are from Gilman and Bijuesca, *Horizontes,* 3rd ed., Heinle & Heinle, 1997, p. 159.

Objective: Students learn to recognize and use connectors in narration by substituting synonyms for italicized words in a brief story.

Student Task: Students read a passage in which there are temporal expressions in italics that indicate the order of events in the narrative. They then find a synonymous expression in the list below and substitute it for each of the italicized words.

Passage: This anecdote has been provided by Gail Guntermann, Arizona State University, and illustrates how a teacher's own story can serve as source material for a personalized and thus "authentic" text.

> . . . *Aquel domingo* mi amiga y yo fuimos en taxi al Panecillo, una colina que queda en el centro de Quito, para desde allí tomar fotos de la ciudad colonial localizada al fondo de dicha colina. *Luego* decidimos bajar a pie, por las escalinatas y sendas de la pendiente. *Después de un rato* nos empezaron a temblar las piernas y nos sentimos un poco débiles. *Mientras* caminábamos por un sitio en construcción, yo no miraba por donde iba, y *de pronto* metí el pie en un agujero, di una vuelta y me caí, oyendo el sonido "¡Crac! ¡Crac! ¡Crac!" *Al principio* pensé que sólo había dislocado el tobillo, pero *mucho más tarde,* en el hospital, me di cuenta de que me había roto tres huesos . . .

> Sinónimos posibles: primero, después, enseguida, antes, cuando, a medida que, poco después, en cuanto, tan pronto como, por último, de repente, aquella mañana, entonces, mucho después.

> . . . *That Sunday my friend and I went in a taxi to the Panecillo, a hill that is in the center of Quito, to take pictures of the colonial city located at the foot of that hill. Then we decided to climb back down on foot, by the stairways and paths of the steep hillside. After a while our legs began to tremble and we felt a little weak. While we were walking through a construction site, I wasn't watching where I was going, and suddenly I stuck my foot in a hole, pivoted around, and fell, hearing the sound of "Crack! Crack! Crack!" At first I thought that I had only dislocated my ankle, but much later, in the hospital, I realized that I had broken three bones. . . .*

> *Possible synonyms: first, then, right away, before, when, while, a little later, as soon as, in the end, suddenly, that morning, then, much later.*

Source: Anecdote by Gail Guntermann. Idea adapted from Grellet 1981.

Transferable Skills: Teaching Reading Strategies

Hosenfeld, Arnold, Kirchofer, Laciura, and Wilson (1981) suggest a sequence of seven steps to help students develop successful reading strategies when approaching any text.

Diagnosis:

1. *Teach students to self-report while reading.* Hosenfeld et al. describe the self-report procedure as one in which students are encouraged to "think aloud" as they try to attach meaning to a second-language text. (For an extensive description of this procedure, see Hosenfeld 1979.) As students report their thinking processes, the teacher has an opportunity to diagnose reading difficulties and identify specific reading strategies.

2. *Identify students' reading strategies.* Using a checklist of successful reading strategies (such as contextual guessing, identification of grammatical categories of words, recognition of cognates, use of cues from illustrations and glosses, and

the like), the teacher records whether a given individual's use of such strategies is satisfactory, unsatisfactory, or nonexistent. This checklist then serves as a diagnostic tool in helping students improve their reading techniques.

Creation of Class Climate:

3. *Help students to understand the concept of strategy and to recognize that some strategies are successful, some unsuccessful, and others only moderately successful.* In this step, Hosenfeld et al. suggest that teachers help students compare and contrast the various problem-solving strategies that they are using and identify those strategies that are most successful. One possibility is to ask several students to think aloud as they read a short paragraph. Class members then discuss the strategies used by these students and their effectiveness in understanding the discourse.

Introduction:

4. *Help students to identify successful strategies used when reading in their native language.* Beginning with a cloze passage in the native language or with a passage containing nonsense words, students talk about ways in which they can identify the missing words or the meaning of the nonwords in the passage. Students' guessing strategies can be listed on the board for further discussion.

5. *Help students identify successful strategies for reading text in the second language.* Using a type of activity similar to that described in Step 4, the teacher helps students identify decoding and word-solving strategies in the second language that parallel those they used in their native language.

6. *Provide instruction and practice for specific reading strategies.* Instruction in contextual guessing and other successful reading strategies can be given with a variety of short texts so that students can see their wide applicability across reading tasks. Students can talk about their problem-solving strategies with several types of practice texts: They might work together on a series of cloze passages, use texts with new vocabulary that has been italicized but not glossed, or simply underline any words, expressions, or sentences in a passage that they do not understand and share those problems with other class members. Students who have resolved those problems can explain how they arrived at their conclusions; several students can share problem-solving strategies that worked so that the group can see the variety of techniques available to achieve comprehension.

7. *Repeat Step 2: Identify students' reading strategies.* In this final step in the reading sequence, Hosenfeld et al. suggest that strategies be recorded again on the checklist and matched against those used before the reading instruction sequence began. However, they caution against using this comparison as a basis for assigning a grade in reading, since the interview procedure and the checklist are meant as diagnostic, rather then evaluative, tools for the improvement of reading strategies.

The exercises and teaching suggestions offered in this section are only a few of the many possible reading comprehension and development activities that can be used in a proficiency-oriented approach. For many more ideas and innovative formats for teaching reading in a second language, see Hosenfeld (1979), Hosenfeld et al. (1981), Grellet (1981), and Phillips (1984).

Summary:
A Proficiency-Oriented Approach to Listening and Reading

In this chapter we have explored various ways to teach more actively the receptive skills of listening and reading. We have seen that both of these skills, though similar in some ways, involve somewhat different processes. In addition, the structures and types of discourse involved in listening and reading are quite different in nature. Comprehension is not a static concept to be assessed in the same fashion at all times; rather, we should think of comprehension in terms of the purpose of the listening or reading activity, the type of text or input that is being processed, and the characteristics of the readers themselves.

The classroom plan for reading instruction provided by Phillips (1984) and summarized in this chapter can be adapted for listening instruction as well (see, for example, Glisan 1988; Shrum and Glisan 2000). Swaffar, Arens, and Byrnes (1991) have also developed a pragmatic approach to reading instruction for students whose skills are somewhat more advanced. Teachers using such plans should find that proficiency goals in listening and reading will be reached more easily and more rapidly by second-language students, and that the valuable skills students learn in their language classes will transfer to other areas of the curriculum. Such skills should also be of value in learning to speak and write more clearly and coherently—skills that are addressed in the next two chapters.

Activities for Review and Discussion

1. As a foreign- or second-language learner, what difficulties did you experience with listening and reading comprehension? What strategies did you use that you think would be helpful for your students? What strategies did you use that you would not recommend?
2. Imagine that you would like to create a monologue or dialogue on a given theme to provide listening practice for students in your class. You want the text to sound as authentic and unrehearsed as possible. You have access to videotaping facilities and have located several native speakers who are willing to play the roles you designate. Design a semiscript that will provide direction for them as they record the scene.
3. Design a listening activity that includes a visual aid or a graphic of some kind.
4. Using Lund's Function-Response Matrix for Listening on p. 186, describe briefly five or more activities you could do with the same listening material. Choose the listening material from an authentic source, your own textbook materials, or create a passage of your own.

5. Review the five stages of reading that Phillips has identified. Then, using a reading passage from your textbook, supplementary reader, or an authentic source, explain how you would design activities that correspond to each of these reading stages.

6. In your view, what considerations are important in choosing "authentic materials" for either listening or reading comprehension? What potential problems might there be in using certain texts (for example, negative stereotypes, images, or language that might be offensive, etc.)? What type of cultural lessons would you incorporate when using the authentic texts you chose in the activities above?

7. Look at the *Standards for Foreign Language Learning* illustrated in Chapter 1. Choose several sample listening and reading activities in this chapter and discuss which of the goals listed in the *Standards* are being addressed in each activity. Then consider how you might modify the activity to enrich its potential for working toward the goals outlined in the *Standards*.

References: Chapter 5

Arendt, J., C. Baumann, G. Peters, and R. Wakefield. *Kreise: Erstes Jahr Deutsch im Kontext.* Boston: Heinle & Heinle, 1992.

Bacon, Susan. "Listening for Real in the Foreign Language Classroom." *Foreign Language Annals* 22, vi (1989): 543–51.

Barnett, Marva A. *More than Meets the Eye: Foreign Language Reading.* Language in Education: Theory and Practice, no. 73. CAL/ERIC Series on Languages and Linguistics. Englewood Cliffs, NJ: Prentice Hall, 1989.

Beile, Werner. "Methodische Überlegungen zur Entwicklung der Hörverstehensfähigkeit." *Zielsprache Deutsch* 2 (1980): 7–15. [Cited in Byrnes, 1984.]

Bernhardt, Elizabeth. "Reading in the Foreign Language." Pp. 93–115 in B. Wing, ed., *Listening, Reading, and Writing: Analysis and Application.* Reports of the Northeast Conference on the Teaching of Foreign Languages. Middlebury, VT: Northeast Conference, 1986.

Bernhardt, Elizabeth and Charles James. "The Teaching and Testing of Comprehension in Foreign Language Learning." Chapter 5 (pp. 65–81) in D. Birckbichler, ed., *Proficiency, Policy and Professionalism in Foreign Language Education.* Report of the Central States Conference on the Teaching of Foreign Languages. Lincolnwood, IL: National Textbook Company, 1987.

Birckbichler, Diane W., ed. *Proficiency, Policy and Professionalism in Foreign Language Education.* Report of the Central States Conference on the Teaching of Foreign Languages. Lincolnwood, IL: National Textbook Company, 1987.

Blyth, Carl. *Untangling the Web.* New York: St. Martin's Press, 1998.

Børn, Warren, ed. *The Foreign Language Learner in Today's Classroom Environment.* Reports of the Northeast Conference on the Teaching of Foreign Languages. Middlebury, VT: Northeast Conference, 1979.

Brecht, Richard D. and A. Ronald Walton. "The Future Shape of Language Learning in the New World of Global Communication: Consequences for Higher Education and Beyond." Pp. 110–152 in Richard Donato and Robert M. Terry, eds., *Foreign Language Learning: The Journey of a Lifetime.* The ACTFL Foreign Language Education Series. Lincolnwood, IL: National Textbook Company, 1995.

Bush, Michael, ed. *Technology-Enhanced Language Learning.* The ACTFL Foreign Language Education Series. Lincolnwood, IL: National Textbook Company, 1997.

Byrnes, Heidi. "The Role of Listening Comprehension: A Theoretical Base." *Foreign Language Annals* 17 (1984): 317–34.

———. "Teaching toward Proficiency: The Receptive Skills." Pp. 77–107 in Alice C. Omaggio, ed., *Proficiency, Curriculum, Articulation: The Ties that Bind.* Reports of the Northeast Conference on the Teaching of Foreign Languages. Middlebury, VT: Northeast Conference, 1985.

Chastain, Kenneth and Gail Guntermann. *¡Imaginaté!,* 2nd ed. Boston, MA: Heinle & Heinle, 1991.

Cubillos, Jorge. *Temas: Spanish for the Global Community.* Boston, MA: Heinle & Heinle, 2000.

Donato, Richard and Robert M. Terry, eds. *Foreign Language Learning: The Journey of a Lifetime.* The ACTFL Foreign Language Education Series. Lincolnwood, IL: National Textbook Company, 1995.

Dunkel, Patricia A. "Developing Listening Fluency in L2: Theoretical Perspectives and Pedagogical Considerations." *The Modern Language Journal* 70, ii (1986): 99–106.

Feyton, Carine M. "The Power of Listening Ability: An Overlooked Dimension in Language Acquisition." *The Modern Language Journal* 75, ii (1991): 173–80.

Geddes, Marion and Ron White. "The Use of Semi-scripted Simulated Authentic Speech in Listening Comprehension." *Audiovisual Language Journal* 16, iii (1978): 137–45.

Gilman, Graciela A. and K. Bijuesca. *Horizontes,* 3rd ed. Heinle & Heinle, 1997.

Glisan, Eileen W. "A Plan for Teaching Listening Comprehension: Adaptation of an Instructional Reading Model." *Foreign Language Annals* 21 (1988): 9–16.

Grellet, Françoise. *Developing Reading Skills.* Cambridge: Cambridge University Press, 1981.

Guntermann, Gail. Personal communication, 1992.

Hosenfeld, Carol. "Cindy: A Learner in Today's Foreign Language Classroom." In W. Born, ed., *The Foreign Language Learner in Today's Classroom Environment.* Reports of the Northeast Conference on the Teaching of Foreign Languages. Middlebury, VT: Northeast Conference, 1979.

Hosenfeld, Carol, V. Arnold, J. Kirchofer, J. Laciura, and L. Wilson. "Second Language Reading: A Curricular Sequence for Teaching Reading Strategies." *Foreign Language Annals* 14 (1981): 415–22.

James, Charles, ed. *Foreign Language Proficiency in the Classroom and Beyond.* The ACTFL Foreign Language Education Series. Lincolnwood, IL: National Textbook Company, 1985.

———. "Listening and Learning: Protocols and Processes." Pp. 38–48 in B. Snyder, ed., *Second Language Acquisition: Preparing for Tomorrow.* Reports of the Central States Conference on the Teaching of Foreign Languages. Lincolnwood, IL: National Textbook Company, 1986.

Joiner, Elizabeth. "Listening in the Foreign Language." Pp. 43–70 in B. Wing, ed., *Listening, Reading, Writing: Analysis and Application.* Reports of the Northeast Conference on the Teaching of Foreign Languages. Middlebury, VT: Northeast Conference, 1986.

———. "Teaching Listening: How Technology Can Help." Pp. 77–120 in Michael D. Bush, ed., *Technology-Enhanced Language Learning.* The ACTFL Foreign

Language Education Series. Lincolnwood, IL: National Textbook Company, 1997.

Krashen, Stephen D. *Principles and Practice in Second Language Acquisition.* Oxford: Pergamon Press, 1982.

Krashen, Stephen, Tracy Terrell, Madeline Ehrman, and Martha Herzog. "A Theoretical Basis for Teaching the Receptive Skills." *Foreign Language Annals* 17, iv (1984): 261–75.

Long, Donna R. "Listening: What's Really Going on in the Classroom?" Chapter 5 (pp. 28–37) in B. Snyder, ed., *Second Language Acquisition: Preparing for Tomorrow.* Lincolnwood, IL: National Textbook Company, 1986.

Lowe, Pardee, Jr. "The ILR Proficiency Scale as a Synthesizing Research Principle: The View from the Mountain." Pp. 9–53 in C. James, ed., *Foreign Language Proficiency in the Classroom and Beyond.* The ACTFL Foreign Language Education Series. Lincolnwood, IL: National Textbook Company, 1985.

Lund, Randall J. "A Taxonomy for Teaching Second Language Listening." *Foreign Language Annals* 23, ii (1990): 105–15.

———. "A Comparison of Second Language Listening and Reading Comprehension." *The Modern Language Journal* 75, ii (1991): 196–204.

Lynch, Tony. "Theoretical Perspectives on Listening." *Annual Review of Applied Linguistics* 18 (1998): 3–19.

Mackay, R., B. Barkman, and R. R. Jordan, eds. *Reading in a Second Language: Hypotheses, Organization, and Practice.* Rowley, MA: Newbury House, 1979.

Martin, Laura. *Entre Líneas: A Strategy for Developing Reading Skills,* 2nd ed. Boston: Heinle & Heinle, 1991.

Mendelsohn, David J. "Teaching Listening." *Annual Review of Applied Linguistics* 18 (1998): 81–101.

Meyer, Renée. "Listen, my children, and you shall hear . . ." *Foreign Language Annals* 17, iv (1984): 343–44.

Morley, Joan. *Listening and Language Learning in ESL: Developing Self-Study Activities for Listening Comprehension.* Language in Education: Theory and Practice. CAL/ERIC Series on Languages and Linguistics. Orlando, FL: Harcourt Brace Jovanovich, Inc., 1984.

Munby, John. *Communicative Syllabus Design.* Cambridge: Cambridge University Press, 1978.

———. "Teaching Intensive Reading Skills." Pp. 142–58 in R. Mackay, B. Barkman, and R. R. Jordan, eds., *Reading in a Second Language: Hypotheses, Organization, and Practice.* Rowley, MA: Newbury House, 1979.

Muyskens, Judith A., ed. *New Ways of Learning and Teaching: Focus on Technology and Foreign Language Education.* AAUSC: Issues in Language Program Direction. Boston, MA: Heinle & Heinle, 1998.

Muyskens, Judith, Linda Harlow, Michèle Vialet, and Jean-François Brière. *Bravo!* 3rd ed. Boston, MA: Heinle & Heinle, 1998.

Omaggio, Alice C., ed. *Proficiency, Curriculum, Articulation: The Ties that Bind.* Reports of the Northeast Conference on the Teaching of Foreign Languages. Middlebury, VT: Northeast Conference, 1985.

Pearson, P. D. and R. Tierney, "On Becoming a Thoughtful Reader: Learning to Read like a Writer." In A. Purves and O. Niles, eds., *Becoming a Reader in a Complex Society.* Chicago: Chicago University Press, 1984.

Phillips, June K. "Practical Implications of Recent Research in Reading." *Foreign Language Annals* 17, iv (1984): 285–96.

Purves, A. and O. Niles, eds. *Becoming a Reader in a Complex Society.* Chicago: Chicago University Press, 1984.

Rankin, P. T. "Listening Ability: Its Importance, Measurement, and Development." *Chicago Schools Journal* 12, pp. 177–79, quoted in D. Spearritt, *Listening Comprehension—A Factorial Analysis* (Melbourne: Australian Council for Educational Research, 1962), p. 2. [Cited in Rivers 1975, p. 58.]

Richards, Jack C. "Listening Comprehension: Approach, Design, Procedure." *TESOL Quarterly* 17 (1983): 219–40.

Rivers, Wilga M. *A Practical Guide to the Teaching of French.* Oxford: Oxford University Press, 1975.

Rogers, Carmen V. and Frank W. Medley, Jr. "Language With a Purpose: Using Authentic Materials in the Foreign Language Classroom." *Foreign Language Annals* 21, v (1988): 467–88.

Rubin, Joan. "A Review of Second Language Listening Comprehension Research." *Modern Language Journal* 78, ii (1994): 199–221.

Santore, Françoise and Sanford Schane. *Open Sesame: Your Guide to Exploring Foreign Language Resources on the World Wide Web.* Boston: Heinle & Heinle, 2000.

Shrum, Judith L. and Eileen W. Glisan. *Teacher's Handbook: Contextualized Language Instructions,* 2nd ed. Boston, MA: Heinle & Heinle, 2000.

Snyder, Barbara, ed. *Second Language Acquisition: Preparing for Tomorrow.* Reports of the Central States Conference on the Teaching of Foreign Languages. Lincolnwood, IL: National Textbook Company, 1986.

Standards for Foreign Language Learning: Preparing for the 21st Century. National Standards in Foreign Language Education Project, 1996.

Stevick, Earl. "Similarities and Differences between Oral and Written Comprehension: An Imagist View." *Foreign Language Annals* 17 (1984): 281–83.

Swaffar, Janet K. *Reading: The Cognitive Process Approach.* Paper presented at the Northeast Regional Conference on Strengthening the Humanities through Foreign Language and Literacy Studies. Philadelphia, PA, 1983. [Cited in Phillips 1984.]

Swaffar, Janet K., Katherine M. Arens, and Heidi Byrnes. *Reading for Meaning: An Integrated Approach to Language Learning.* Englewood Cliffs, NJ: Prentice Hall, 1991.

"Taxonomy of Features for Evaluating Foreign Language Multimedia Software." University of Hawaii National Foreign Language Resource Center (NFLRC), 1999. [http://nts.lll.hawaii.edu/flmedia]

Terry, Robert. Personal communication, 2000.

Ur, Penny. *Teaching Listening Comprehension.* Cambridge: Cambridge University Press, 1984.

Walz, Joel. "Meeting Standards for Foreign Language Learning with World Wide Web Activities." *Foreign Language Annals* 31, i (1998): 103–114.

Weissenrieder, Maureen. "Listening to the News in Spanish." *The Modern Language Journal* 71, i(1987): 18–27.

Wing, Barbara, ed. *Listening, Reading, and Writing: Analysis and Application.* Reports of the Northeast Conference on the Teaching of Foreign Languages. Middlebury VT: Northeast Conference, 1986.

6 SIX Developing Oral Proficiency

In recent years, much of the discussion relating to proficiency-oriented instruction and testing has focused on the development of oral skills. The emphasis on speaking proficiency can be attributed to a variety of factors, many of which are traceable to the widespread popularity of audiolingual methodologies in the 1960s and the communicative competence movement that began in the 1970s. This interest in oral communication continues today, as contemporary communicative language teaching approaches are emphasizing the importance of having learners engage in "tasks" that encourage meaningful interaction (see, for example, Long 1985; Nunan 1989; Gass 1997; McDonough and Mackey 2000). Recent research in second-language acquisition has also considered oral interaction as an important factor in the shaping of the learner's developing language. A number of studies have investigated the role of interaction in second-language development, particularly in conversations between native and nonnative speakers and among nonnative speakers working in pairs or small groups (for a review of some of this research, see Gass 1997). Swain (1985, 1995) has also highlighted the role of output in language learning and describes a variety of communication activities that can help learners develop accuracy as well as fluency through consciously reflecting on their language production.

Yet methodological trends and movements and new developments in theory and research are not the only impetus for a continued interest in oral proficiency. Many language students consider speaking ability one of their primary goals of study (Harlow and Muyskens 1994), either because they would derive some personal satisfaction from being able to speak a second language or because they feel it would be useful in travel or in pursuing other interests or career goals. It is clear that oral proficiency in a second language can be an important asset for anyone seeking employment in business and industry in the twenty-first century.

As we saw in the last chapter, this emphasis on oral proficiency does not and should not mean that other skill areas ought to be neglected in the language curriculum. However, because the ability to function adequately in speaking continues to be an important goal for many second-language learners, it is incumbent upon us as language teachers to identify some effective strategies for teaching oral skills that will maximize opportunities for the development of useful levels of proficiency.

As mentioned in Chapter 1, the goal of oral proficiency is incorporated in the *Standards for Foreign Language Learning* (1996) under the first of the five major goals—"Communication"—which is subdivided into the *interpersonal, interpretive,* and *presentational* modes (see Illustration 5.1, p. 183). Some activities that are appropriate for the "interpretive" mode were discussed in the last chapter, where listening and reading development were the focus, but these receptive skills will also be interwoven into classroom activities designed to develop oral proficiency. Oral communication can be characterized as "interpersonal" when individuals are engaged in conversation and "presentational" when they are presenting their ideas to an audience of listeners. These different modes of communication can be addressed by varying classroom tasks so that students are afforded practice in a range of activities, from paired or small-group conversation to situational role-plays, whole-class presentations, videotaped skits, newscasts, debates, and the like.

In the age of computer-mediated communication, the lines between oral and written language seem somewhat less distinct, especially in the interpersonal mode. Beauvois (1997), in analyzing a pilot study that used computer-mediated communication (CMC) on a local area network (LAN), found that there is a possible transfer of skills from written production to oral expression in the target language (p. 181). In her study with fourth-semester French students, those who had engaged only in (written) electronic discussions of course material performed significantly better on three oral exams than students who had discussed the materials orally in class. These preliminary results suggest that synchronous electronic discussion can be effective in promoting oral skill development. Beauvois suggests that this type of electronic communication is more efficient in terms of time on task than classroom discussion since (1) "more is communicated in less time," and (2) "all students can and usually do participate" due to a low-stress atmosphere, resulting in more use of the target language by all members of the class (p. 181). One of the main benefits of the LAN discussion is that it slows down the communicative process, which is a benefit to students who have limited oral skills and who want to express their ideas. Beauvois (1998) also points out that the use of the LAN connects students affectively and intellectually. By including those students who are sometimes marginalized in the traditional classroom for a variety of reasons, "the pool of scholarship is augmented—the entire discourse community is enhanced by the addition of each student's participation" (p. 109).

Our discussion of strategies for teaching the productive skills, whether orally or in writing, begins with an exploration into the nature of *interlanguage* (Selinker 1972)—also called *language-learner language* (Corder 1978)—and how it is thought to develop. The language produced by our students differs in important ways from both child and adult native language use. The first section of this chapter considers several viewpoints of the nature of interlanguage and its development. The second part of the chapter then presents strategies for teaching oral skills, with sample activities illustrating how students can engage in oral production in meaningful and personalized contexts. In the last section of the chapter, ways in which both native speakers and teachers tend to respond to language-learner language are explored, and a range of feedback strategies is suggested to facilitate students' progress toward more precise and coherent language use.

The Nature of Interlanguage

At any given stage of proficiency, the oral and written language competence of nonnative speakers, though different from that of native speakers, can be characterized as a coherent system governed by some set of internalized rules. These "rules" should not be confused with the pedagogical rules that one finds in textbooks; many times the learners' rules differ from those that they may have been taught. Often learners are unable to explicitly state the rules by which they are operating. (The same can be said of many native speakers, who know how to use their first language expertly but are unable to explicitly state the rules that govern their language use.)

Seliger (1988) reviews various ways in which nonnative rule systems have been described in the literature. Corder (1967) refers to language-learner language as "transitional competence," implying that learner systems are constantly changing. Nemser (1971) refers to the developing grammar as an "approximative system," focusing on the incompleteness of the system as it moves progressively along a kind of continuum between the learner's native language and native competence in the second language. Selinker (1972) characterizes the learner's developing system as "interlanguage," describing it as an intermediate system located somewhere between the learner's native language and the target language, but governed by its own unique and coherent internalized rule system that rarely becomes totally congruent with the system of the second language. Selinker refers to this incongruence between the interlanguage and the target language as "fossilization." He suggests that certain items, rules, or subsystems that are not fully congruent with the target language can become a permanent part of the learner's interlanguage, resistant to further instruction or explanation (Selinker 1974, pp. 118–19).

Corder (1978) and Selinker both think of interlanguage as a continuum, but Corder suggests that there may be various types of continua that can explain how language-learner language develops. One view might conceive of the learner progressively adjusting the native language system so that it gradually approximates the system of the target language. Such a view of interlanguage can be called a *progressive restructuring,* and the continuum implied can be called a *restructuring continuum* (Corder 1978, p. 75). This type of conceptualization seems to account for the fact that interlanguage, particularly in its earliest developmental stages, frequently manifests various characteristics of the learner's native language. However, not all learners show consistent evidence of transfer from the native language and certainly not to the same degree across learners. Corder believes that because this is true and because the interlanguage is typically simpler, overall, than adult native speech in the language being acquired, one could conceptualize a second type of continuum, called a *recreation,* or *developmental continuum.* Like child language, the system becomes more complex as the language is acquired. However, the child begins with no knowledge of the language, whereas the adult second-language learner begins with cognitive structures already intact, in conjunction with comprehensive knowledge of a first-language system (Corder 1978, p. 75).

Corder suggests that both continua might actually work in consort and are not necessarily mutually exclusive. It is possible, for example, that learners might follow a restructuring continuum (i.e., going from the native language to the target language) when acquiring the phonological system, but progress along a developmental continuum (i.e., moving from simple to more complex forms and structures) when learning the syntactic system. A second possibility is that learners in a natural setting follow a developmental continuum, while students in formal classroom settings progress along a restructuring continuum. This point of view is compatible, to some extent, with Krashen's (1982) acquisition/learning distinction (see Chapter 2). A third possibility is that both restructuring and developmental processes are operating together in language learning and that there is a great deal of variability in the way the interlanguages of different individuals develop (Corder 1978, p. 79).

Ellis (1985) emphasizes the notion of variability in his conceptualization of interlanguage and maintains that language learners have a number of competing rules at any given stage of development, with one rule prevailing in one context and another in a different context. In his view, a learner's "competence" is therefore not homogeneous, but heterogenous. Basing his theory partly on Tarone's (1983) work, he suggests that learners have several "styles" from which they select in order to carry out specific tasks (p. 83), and that therefore their performance is quite variable. Illustration 6.1 (p. 234) depicts the sources of variability that can affect linguistic performance, according to Ellis' model of competence.

In Ellis' model of interlanguage competence, variability can be *systematic* or *non-systematic. Systematic* variability, in turn, can be subdivided into *individual* variability (due to learner characteristics) or *contextual* variability (due either to the linguistic context or the situational context in which the language is being used) (p. 75). *Non-systematic* variability, on the other hand, can be further subdivided into *free variability* (where competing forms or rules operate in free variation with one another) or *performance variability* (due to the learner's emotional or physical condition, which can provoke slips or hesitations) (pp. 75–76). Although all language use, including that of native speakers, is thought to be variable, Ellis maintains that language-learner language is even more variable (p. 81).

One source of *contextual variability* is the type of task the learner is engaged in doing. In Chapter 2, we saw that Tarone (1983) suggests that tasks that demand very little active attention, such as "natural" conversation among proficient speakers, elicit the *vernacular style,* while tasks that are heavily monitored, such as making grammaticality judgments or filling in blanks with grammatical forms, elicit a very *careful style* (Tarone 1983, p. 152). This task effect may account for

Illustration 6.1

Types of Variability in
Interlanguage

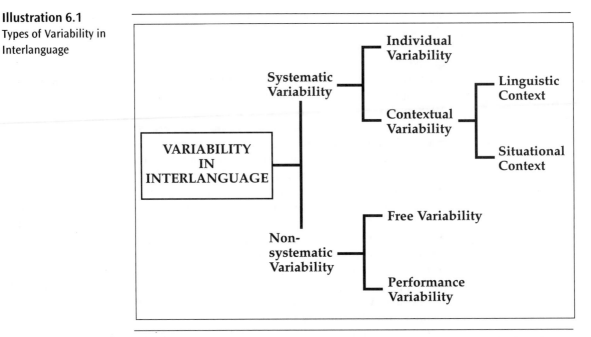

Source: Ellis, Rod. *Understanding Second Language Acquisition.* Oxford: Oxford University Press, 1985, p. 76. Reprinted by permission of Oxford University Press.

the fact that second-language students often perform differently while doing a focused activity than when using the language in conversation or free composition.

A source of variability attributable to *linguistic context* is the level of complexity of the language the learner is attempting to use (Ellis 1985, p. 83). Learners may vary in the forms they use in simple constructions vs. those that they use when sentence structure is more complex. This might, in part, explain why learners' language seems to "break down" when they attempt to communicate more complex ideas in the "probe" phase of oral interviews, or when they attempt to express complex ideas in compositions that require a higher level of proficiency than they currently can control. The type of linguistic features present in language-learner language may be a function of both the nature of the task itself and task difficulty (Ellis 1985). Thus a variable competence view of interlanguage would predict that learners engaged in simple tasks and attending to form would perform most accurately. Indeed, Ellis (1982) found in a study he conducted that second-language learners performed most accurately on tasks that were cognitively simple (involving concrete situations in the present time frame) and attributed this to the fact that there was more opportunity for learners to attend to form in such situations (Ellis 1985, p. 89).

Perhaps one of the most interesting hypotheses that Ellis proposes is the idea

*careful/
vernacular
style*

that "careful style" tasks can have an impact on the development of more accurate usage over time in the "vernacular style." The vernacular style is thought to be the most stable style, since it contains the forms of the interlanguage that the learner has most fully automatized. The careful style, on the other hand, has more interlanguage forms than the vernacular style, since it includes those forms that have not yet become fully automatic and that occur in free variation with more automatic forms. Ellis, following Tarone (1983), suggests that new forms that are initially part of learners' careful style could eventually spread to their vernacular style. "Whereas vernacular forms are instantaneously available, careful forms are not. However, as the careful forms are used, they are practised, with the result that they become more automatic, require less attention, and so are available for use in interlanguage styles nearer the vernacular end of the continuum" (p. 95). As second-language proficiency develops, competing forms in the interlanguage that have been used in free variation are sorted out as the learner figures out what forms are used in what contexts. Any forms that are redundant are eventually eliminated. This "mapping" of forms to functions is a slow process involving a constant reorganization of the interlanguage system (pp. 95–96).

One might hypothesize on the basis of these observations that a variety of tasks should be used in the second-language classroom, ranging from careful style activities where learners practice using language in planned discourse that is cognitively simple to vernacular style activities, where more complex communicative tasks involving less monitoring are undertaken. A balance of practice with tasks drawn from the whole continuum of styles might lead to more proficient performance in terms of accuracy and fluency.

In the next section, ways to plan oral practice activities so that a balance such as that suggested above might be achieved are described and illustrated. The section begins with a brief rationale for planning instruction that is derived from the oral proficiency descriptions provided by the *ACTFL Proficiency Guidelines* (see Appendix A).

Planning Instruction for the Development of Oral Proficiency

*Teslires the
"range"*

Appropriate teaching strategies are likely to vary, depending on students' current level(s) of proficiency and the level envisioned as an instructional goal. In order to provide optimal speaking practice in a given class, we need to determine, at least in some global fashion, what range of levels is likely to be attainable in the course of instruction. The term *range* is used here because it is unrealistic to expect that all students in a given course will be at the same level of oral proficiency at the end of instruction. Determining an expected range of proficiency upon completion of a course might best be accomplished experientially through a preliminary assessment of students' oral proficiency at the beginning and end of the course using the interview procedure described in Chapter 9. After several semesters of testing, an expected range of proficiency should be relatively easy to identify. One can then begin to reorient instruction toward carefully defined goals, derived in part from appropriate level descriptions. Classroom activities can be selected to correspond to current levels of proficiency and to those in the next highest range so that opportunities for progress along the scale can be maximized.

What types of goals are appropriate for students at the Novice, Intermediate, and Advanced levels of speaking proficiency? What kinds of classroom activities are optimal at each of these levels? What emphasis should be placed on activities in each of the communicative modes? A variety of curricular plans for instruction in oral skills could be derived from an examination of the *ACTFL Proficiency Guidelines* for speaking. As was pointed out in earlier chapters, it is important to bear in mind that the guidelines are *not* a set of goal statements in and of themselves but are rather descriptions of typical competencies (as well as patterns of weakness) that language users are expected to have at each of the levels of proficiency. As Heilenman and Kaplan (1985), Higgs (1986), and Galloway (1987) have observed, the guidelines are meant to be evaluative in nature and should not be used directly and verbatim as course objectives.

The proficiency descriptions, used in conjunction with the *Standards for Foreign Language Learning* (1996, 1999), can be useful in the goal-refinement process when planning curricula. Each group of individuals responsible for designing a local curriculum will need to consider what the guidelines and standards imply for their own situation. Although different curricular plans might be roughly similar, no two groups of classroom teachers or curriculum planners are likely to come up with identical goal statements, especially since local conditions and the interests and needs of individual groups of students differ. Nevertheless, if one uses the guidelines as a point of departure for planning instruction, it seems clear that beginning-level students at the Novice level will be most successful and comfortable if speaking activities are initially limited to vocabulary and structure they have learned, such as structured conversations using simple question/answer exchanges; naming or identifying objects, persons, or places; or making lists of activities or preferences. These Novice level activities should be meaningful and contextualized so that students can begin to make the transition to creative language use as soon as possible. As learners' skills develop, students will gradually be able to participate in more open-ended conversations, describe objects or processes in more detail, conduct brief surveys or polls, and engage in more social interaction activities, role-plays, skits, and communicative tasks that involve exchanges of information. Some sample formats for activities such as these at Novice, Intermediate, and Advanced levels of proficiency are given in the next section.

Sample Formats for Oral Practice

The activities described in this chapter are organized according to the first two working hypotheses, presented in Chapter 3, for designing a framework for instruction that is oriented toward proficiency goals:[1]

HYPOTHESIS 1. *Opportunities must be provided for students to practice using language in a range of contexts likely to be encountered in the target culture.*

HYPOTHESIS 2. *Opportunities should be provided for students to practice carrying out a range of functions (tasks) likely to be necessary in dealing with others in the target culture.*

Activities are further classified according to (1) the proficiency level(s) for which the oral practice formats seem best suited, (2) the communicative mode addressed, and (3) the structural and functional goals of the activity being illustrated.

Oral practice can and should be used in an integrated fashion with practice in other skill areas. Many of the samples given in the following pages include suggestions for integrating reading, listening, and writing practice with oral practice, either through prespeaking or follow-up activities. The integration of cultural content is also an important consideration when planning oral practice, and can be done through the choice of content as well as through the choice of communicative modes and formats. For example, students can practice communicating in the presentational mode by preparing cultural presentations or oral reports using library resources or materials on the Web. Interpersonal communication skills can be developed with conversational activities, games, and role-plays. These activity types have the added benefit of fostering cooperative learning and small-group interaction, which can be especially conducive to the development of oral proficiency.

The first group of sample activities in this section illustrates precommunicative practice (Littlewood 1981) that is meaningful and personalized, but that allows students to focus on formal features of the code. These activities are grouped under the discussion of the first corollary to Hypothesis 1. More open-ended and task-based activities are then presented in the discussion associated with Corollaries 2 and 3. Finally, particular attention is given in the discussion associated with Hypothesis 2 to culturally based learning activities that involve a blend of functions or tasks, including a sample learning scenario provided in the *Standards for Foreign Language Learning in the 21st Century* (1999).

COROLLARY 1. *Students should be encouraged to express their own meaning as early as possible after productive skills have been introduced in the course of instruction.*

Most of the activity types in this first section allow students to engage in practicing new features of the language (vocabulary, grammatical forms, pragmatic formulae, etc.) in order to develop some confidence and facility in using them. Formal practice activities have had a place in a variety of approaches to language teaching, although the rationale for their use and the way they were designed has varied considerably. In behavioristic orientations popular in the 1960s, for example, structured "drills" were designed to enable students to form new language "habits." Most of these drills revolved around morphological or syntactic features and were usually not contextualized or meaningful. When cognitive theory became popular in the 1970s, "pattern drills" were replaced with structured but *meaningful* practice activities. These meaningful and communicative exercises represented a way for students to practice subskills involved in the complex process of language learning so that they might become integrated eventually into their internal representations or "cognitive structure." It was thought that through extensive practice, subskills would eventually become "automatized."

Gatbonton and Segalowitz (1988), arguing from an information-processing perspective of language acquisition, suggest that fluency in oral skills can be promoted by means of "creative automatization." Following Shiffrin and Schneider (1977), they also maintain that the development of automaticity requires "a great deal of practice" (p. 474). Language use becomes automatic when the speaker does not need to focus attention on producing forms and thus divert his or her attention away from the meaningful communication task at hand. Gatbonton and Segalowitz suggest that students practice a basic repertoire of expressions or phrases that are commonly needed in many communicative situations, and that such practice be incorporated within communicative activities where repetition of such phrases would occur naturally.

One other aspect of focused practice that should be considered when planning instruction at the Novice or Intermediate level is its affective value. Some students are most comfortable with structured learning environments because of either personality variables or cognitive style preferences. Formal practice activities may be most suitable for students who have a low tolerance of ambiguity or who are reluctant to take risks, especially when they are just beginning language study. The linguistic support of "precommunicative" practice allows such students to practice oral skills within a controlled framework and thus build confidence.

The activities described in the next few pages are designed using formats that are common to many first-year language textbooks and that have been used by language teachers for many years. They include sentence builders, contextualized grammar practice activities, personalized either-or questions, word association activities, logical conclusions, and personalized completions.

Sentence Builder

SAMPLE 1 (NOVICE)

Context: Discussing clothing choices

Function: Expressing preferences

Grammatical Features: *-er* verbs in French, *faire* expressions, *aller, jouer à*

Communicative Mode: Interpersonal Communication

Student Task: Students discuss in pairs what they and people they know like to wear when doing certain activities, using the sentence-builder frame below.

Follow-up: Students can be asked to write out some of their sentences to share orally with the class in a report-back activity.

Student Task: Qu'est-ce que vous portez? Using elements from each of the columns below, make up five sentences that express what you and your friends and family like to wear when doing various activities. The question mark (?) invites you to add other people, clothing items, or activities if you would prefer to do so.

Modèle: Je porte un jean et un tee-shirt quand je fais de la bicyclette.

Sujets	Verbe	Vêtements		Activités
Je		une robe		faire du jardinage
Ma mère		un tee-shirt		aller au cinéma
Mon père	. . . porter . . .	un costume	. . . quand. . .	faire de la bicyclette
Mes amis		un jean		dîner dans un restaurant élégant
Ma soeur		un chapeau		aller à la plage
Mes amis et moi		un short		jouer au basketball
Mon frère		un maillot de bain		aller au bureau
?		?		?

Contextualized Grammar Practice

SAMPLE 2 (INTERMEDIATE)

Context: Social conventions and rules of behavior

Function: Giving advice

Grammatical Features: Affirmative and negative imperative

Communicative Mode: Interpersonal Communication

Student Task: Students in pairs give one another advice about how to be a perfect host/hostess using the directions below.

Follow-up: (Listening/Writing/Reading/Culture) Students in small groups make their own lists of things to do and not to do in various contexts: getting together for an informal party, meeting with a professor for an appointment after class, going for the first time to dinner at the home of a new acquaintance, etc. The teacher has previously solicited similar lists from native speakers (colleagues, friends, exchange students) for the same contexts in the target culture. Students compare their own lists to those prepared by native speakers and note any similarities and differences.

Student Task: L'hôte (l'hôtesse) parfait(e)! Voici une liste de choses à faire ou à éviter si vous invitez quelqu'un à passer le week-end chez vous. Quels sont vos conseils pour l'hôte ou l'hôtesse parfait(e)? Présentez vos idées à l'impératif, affirmatif ou négatif, selon votre opinion.
1. oublier de faire le lit
2. mettre votre chien de garde dans la salle de bains
3. faire cuire les plats préférés de vos invités
4. acheter de jolies fleurs pour la chambre de vos ami(e)s
5. parler du bon vieux temps
6. être de mauvaise humeur
   etc.

The Perfect Host (Hostess)! Here is a list of things to do or to avoid doing if you invite someone to your house for the weekend. What is your advice for the perfect host or

hostess? Put your ideas in the affirmative or negative imperative form, according to your opinion.

1. *to forget to make the bed*
2. *to put your guard dog in the bathroom*
3. *to make your guests' favorite foods*
4. *to buy pretty flowers for the guests' rooms*
5. *to talk about the good old days*
6. *to be in a bad mood*
etc.

Word Associations

SAMPLE 3 (NOVICE)

Context: Campus life

Function: Descriptions

Communicative Mode: Interpersonal Communication

Student Task: Students think about associations they have with various locations on their campus. They think of as many words as they can for the following places:
1. the library
2. their favorite campus bar or restaurant
3. the classroom
4. the sports arena, etc.

Follow-up: (Cultural enrichment) The teacher obtains word associations from a native speaker or several native speakers for these same concepts. Students compare their own lists of words with those of the native speaker(s) and discuss similarities and differences. (See also Kramsch 1983 and Seelye 1984 for ideas for teaching the connotation of words and concepts.)

Either/Or Questions

SAMPLE 4 (NOVICE)

Context: Leisure-time activities

Function: Discussing preferences, pastimes

Communicative Mode: Interpersonal Communication

Student Task: A set of either/or questions relating to preferences in leisure-time activities is asked, either in a whole-class instructional format or in smaller groups. If students are placed in groups of two or three, one student may be asked to formulate the questions from cues or to read them from cards while the others answer.
1. Preferisce guardare la televisione o leggere?
2. Preferisce passare le serate con gli amici o in famiglia?
3. Preferisce stare zitto o parlare quando ci sono molte persone? etc.

1. *Do you prefer to watch television or read?*
2. *Do you prefer to spend the evening with your friends or with your family?*
3. *Do you prefer to keep quiet or talk when there are a lot of people? etc.*

Logical Sequence

Context: Weekend activities

Function: Describing daily activities

Grammatical/Lexical Focus: Expressions with *faire*

Communicative Mode: Interpersonal Communication

Student Task: Students react to the sentences by (a) deciding whether or not they form a logical sequence and (b) creating a new sequence if necessary.
1. Je n'ai plus de vêtements dans l'armoire! Je dois faire la vaisselle!
2. Nos placards sont vides et il n'y a rien dans le frigo. Nous devons faire le marché!
3. J'ai besoin d'exercice. Allons faire le linge.
   etc.

1. *I don't have any more clothes in the closet. I need to do the dishes!*
2. *Our cupboards are bare and there's nothing in the refrigerator. We need to go shopping!*
3. *I need some exercise. Let's go do the laundry.*
   etc.

Like the either/or activity explained earlier, this format permits students who are not quite ready for more open-ended exercises to use the structure provided in the model sentences, enabling them to practice making sequences of statements rather than one-sentence utterances. The format allows for some creativity on the part of the student, yet limits the need for such creativity to structures and vocabulary that the Novice can handle.

Personalized Completions

Context: Making personal decisions, discussing imaginary situations

Function: Speculating about events, hypothesizing

Grammar Topic: Conditional Sentences/Subjunctive

Communicative Mode: Interpersonal Communication

Student Task: The class is divided into groups of three or four. Each group receives one or several cards depicted below. Students describe what they would do in the situation(s) described on their card(s). They are given a time limit of 2–3 minutes to come up with several ideas. Each group presents its ideas and the teacher asks the other students what they would do in the same situation. The class can then vote on which ideas are the most creative.
Source: Golato (2000).

Sample Card

> Stellen Sie sich vor, . . .
>   . . . Sie wandern im Himalaja Gebirge. Plötzlich treffen Sie den Yeti. Was würden Sie tun?
>   . . . ein UFO landet in Ihrem Garten. Was würden Sie tun?
>   . . . Sie fliegen mit einem kleinen Flugzeug über den Urwald im Amazonas.
>   Plötzlich stürzt Ihr Flugzeug ab, aber Sie überleben. Was würden Sie tun?
>   . . . Sie werden zum Präsidenten der USA gewählt. Was würden Sie tun?
>   . . . Sie werden plötzlich Lehrer(in) Ihres Deutschkurses. Was würden Sie tun?

> Imagine . . .
>   . . . you are hiking in the Himalayas. Suddenly you encounter Big Foot. What would you do?
>   . . . a UFO has landed in your backyard. What would you do?
>   . . . you are flying a small plane across the jungle in the Amazon region. Suddenly
>   your plane crashes but you survive. What would you do?
>   . . . you are elected President of the United States. What would you do?
>   . . . you are suddenly the teacher of your German class. What would you do?

Conversation Cards

SAMPLE 7 (NOVICE/INTERMEDIATE)

Paired interviews and conversation activities are commonly provided in many contemporary beginning and intermediate textbooks to help students learn vocabulary and structures that have been recently presented in class. Such activities can be beneficial in helping students develop their interpersonal communication skills. More than 25 years ago, Bonin and Birckbichler (1975) developed an interview format called a *conversation card* that prompts students to formulate meaningful questions with some attention to accuracy of form. This activity may constitute a type of "pushed output" (Swain 1985, 1995), where students are encouraged to make their language use more precise through the negotiation of both meaning and form as they work in pairs. In the variation given below, students work in groups of three. Two students have question prompts (which can be in either the native or the target language), and the third student serves as a group "monitor," who is responsible for helping the others formulate their questions accurately. Students answer their partner's questions, and the third student can be asked to think of follow-up questions to keep the conversation going. As students work on this type of activity (as well as in other small-group and paired activities discussed in this section), teachers should circulate to help and give feedback so that students can derive the full benefits of working on their language skills within this communicative framework.

Context: Planning vacations and travel

Functions: Asking questions, discussing future plans and goals

Communicative Mode: Interpersonal Communication

Student Task: The questions below are in English, requiring students who are native speakers of English to formulate the questions in their own words in the target language, which is German.

Follow-up: Group monitors can report the discussion back to the rest of the class.

Card 1

Ask your partner . . .

- where he/she plans to go this summer
- how long he/she will stay
- whether he/she will travel by car, by plane, or by train
- who he/she will travel with

Card 2

Ask your partner . . .

- whether he/she plans to travel to a German-speaking country one day
- what country or countries he/she prefers to visit
- what cities he/she would like to see

Card 3

Help your classmates ask their interview questions by using the cues below. Be careful to correct your partners when necessary, but be flexible and accept any correct form of the questions. Take notes on the answer you hear so you can report the discussion back to the rest of the class. You should also think of additional questions to ask each person once he/she finishes the set.

Student 1:

1. Wohin möchtest du diesen Sommer reisen?
2. Wie lange bleibst du dort?
3. Reist du mit dem Auto, dem Flugzeug oder dem Zug?
4. Mit wem reist du?

Student 2:

1. Reist du eines Tages in ein deutschsprachiges Land?
2. Welches Land oder welche Länder möchtest du lieber besuchen?
3. Welche Städte möchtest du sehen?
4. Wie lange möchtest du in Deutschland bleiben?

In using activities such as those described here and in the following sections, it is important to remember that sequencing activities for practice is almost as important as designing contextualized practice in the first place. It is best to integrate the whole sequence of lesson materials into a single theme, context, or general situation, at least in designing one class day's work or unit of study, instead of jumping from one content or topic to another. The latter practice is the norm in many language classes in which course materials are not contextually or thematically organized.

COROLLARY 2. *Opportunities must be provided for active communicative interaction among students.*

COROLLARY 3. *Creative language practice (as opposed to exclusively manipulative or convergent practice) must be encouraged in the proficiency-oriented classroom.*

Both of these corollaries relate to the need to move students beyond the "pre-communicative" stage of language use to a stage where they use the language creatively to communicate their own meaning. In the activities that follow, a number of small-group and social-interaction activities are suggested that encourage students to paraphrase ideas, ask questions, and pool information in order to solve a problem, make a decision, or complete an activity sheet of some kind.

Group Puzzles

SAMPLE 1 (NOVICE/INTERMEDIATE)

Context: Description of home and furnishings

Function: Describing, paraphrasing

Grammatical Features: Various

Communicative Mode: Interpersonal Communication

Student Task: Students in groups of three to five receive a card or cards with a word in the target language that they must describe without using the word itself. As they paraphrase their words successfully so that the others in the group can guess them, they write them down. When all words have been guessed, they take the first letter of each word (bold-faced on the card) to make a group word, which solves the puzzle. (Letters will need to be unscrambled and put in order to make the group's secret puzzle word.)

Follow-up: Teachers should have one or two more sets of words than there are groups of students in the class so that when one group is finished with a puzzle, a new puzzle can be given to the group to work on as the other groups finish.

Students can be invited to create puzzles of their own, and these can be collected and redistributed to other groups.

Source: Adapted from Omaggio (1976). For an example in French, see also Omaggio (1982).

Before beginning this activity, especially with lower-level students, teachers should go over various ways to give a definition or paraphrase of a word. For example, expressions such as "This is something you use to . . . ," "This word is the same as (the opposite of) . . . ," "This is a [*category,* such as piece of furniture, a room in the house]," or "This is something [*adjective,* such as a color word, size, etc.]" can help learners give definitions more successfully.

Teachers and students can create puzzles by using the vocabulary lists at the end of chapters they have studied. First choose a word with five or more letters. This will be the "secret" puzzle word. Then for each letter of the secret word, find words in the vocabulary list to put on 3 x 5 cards. This set of cards constitutes the puzzle. The teacher can keep the "secret" words aside until the puzzle is solved. (See the following for a sample puzzle in Spanish.)

Puzzle "secret" word: lámpara

Student cards:

> los①ibros
> el ⓐtico
> la ⓜesa de noche
> la ⓟlanta baja
> el ⓐrmario
> el ⓡefrigerador
> el ⓐlfombra

SAMPLE 2 (NOVICE/INTERMEDIATE)

Context: Description of home and furnishings, people

Function: Giving definitions, paraphrasing

Grammatical Features: Various

Communicative Mode: Interpersonal Communication

Student Task: Each student in a group of four receives a card and a blank cross-word puzzle grid. The card has three to four words on it and an indication of their number and direction in the puzzle. (See Illustration 6.2, p. 246) As students describe their puzzle words through definitions and paraphrasing (and without using the word itself), students in the group fill in the crossword grid.

Follow-up: Students can be invited to construct their own puzzles and exchange them with other groups in the class.

Source: For an example of this puzzle idea in French, see Omaggio (1982).

Calendar Activity

SAMPLE 3 (NOVICE/INTERMEDIATE)

Objective: To discuss activities during a given month and find a date open for everyone in order to plan a party

Context: Everyday activities

Functions: Discussing dates, extending invitations, accepting and refusing invitations

Communicative Mode: Interpersonal Communication

Student Task: Each student in a group of three has a calendar in French in which the days of a given month are displayed, as in Illustration 6.3 (p. 247). For nine specific dates on each of the three calendars, activities of various sorts are noted. Each calendar has different activities, and all the dates for the activities are different so that only three dates are "free" for everyone.

Illustration 6.2
Spanish Crossword Puzzle
(Sample 2)

¹S	O	³T	A	N	O	⁶	F	⁸	¹⁰C

TARJETA 1		TARJETA 2	
Horizontal	**Vertical**	**Horizontal**	**Vertical**
1. sótano	48. cama	33. hacer	1. sillones
53. ser			10. cocina
			35. corto

TARJETA 3		TARJETA 4	
Horizontal	**Vertical**	**Horizontal**	**Vertical**
16. nieto	8. feo	71. sitio	3. techos
41. ojo		77. baño	6. once

Students consult their calendars and try to find a date when everyone is free to plan a party. Exchanges among the students take the following form:

Student 1: Tu es libre vendredi le 15 septembre?
Student 2: Oui, je suis libre ce jour-là.
Student 3: Ah non, dommage! J'ai quelque chose à faire. Je vais manger chez un ami à 8 heures ce soir-là. Mais je n'ai rien à faire vendredi le 22 septembre. Et toi? etc.

Student 1: Are you free on Friday, September 15?
Student 2: Yes, I'm free that day.
Student 3: Oh no, too bad! I'm busy. I'm having dinner at a friend's house at 8 P.M. that night. But I'm not busy on Friday the 22nd. What about you? etc.

Illustration 6.3   Calendar Activity, Student 1

			SEPTEMBRE			
L	**M**	**M**	**J**	**V**	**S**	**D**
				1 *dîner chez maman 8h*	2 *travailler au MacDo*	3
4 *étudier avec michel 7h30*	5 *à la bibliothèque*	6 *travailler 6h30-10h30*	7	8	9	10
11	12	13 *travailler 6h30-10h30*	14	15	16	17
18	19 *examen de chimie demain!*	20	21	22	23 *anniversaire de Pierre soirée chez Natalie*	24
25	26	27	28	29 *à Lyon pour le week-end*	30	

Follow-up: When students have found a free date, they plan a party, making a list of guests, plan foods, etc. If students immediately discover a free date, the teacher may ask them to continue searching for an alternate date so that they may get additional practice using the expressions involved in the dialogue.

Variation: Ur (1988) suggests a similar activity for ESL in which pairs of students compare a week's schedule of activities and try to find a time to meet. Schedules are in the form of a 7-day diary, with 2-hour slots to be filled in, from 7 A.M. to 11 P.M., Monday through Sunday. This activity is especially useful for practicing telling time of day and using the future expression "going to." Consult this source for sample diaries, full directions, and suggestions for further variations.

Family Tree

SAMPLE 4 (NOVICE/INTERMEDIATE)

Context: Discussing family relationships

Functions: Identifying people and relationships, sharing biographical information, making inquiries about family members, describing people's physical attributes, giving dates

Grammatical Features: Various

Communicative Mode: Interpersonal Communication

Student Task: Each student in a group of six receives a drawing of a family tree with slots for information to be filled in (see Illustration 6.4). Each student also receives a biographical information card that describes him- or herself as well as other family members. Students must share the information on their cards to complete the family tree.

Follow-up: Students compare their completed tree diagrams with a key provided by the teacher. An additional activity in which students draw their own family tree and describe it to others in a small group can be done the same class period or the following day.
Source: Adapted from Omaggio (1982).

Preteaching Activity: Teachers provide students with a set of questions that can be useful in describing people and asking for biographical and other descriptive information when playing this interactive game. Some possible questions in French include the following:

Questions possibles:
- Comment vous appelez-vous? *(What is your name?)*
- Quel âge avez-vous? *(How old are you?)*
- Quel est votre passe-temps préféré? *(What is your favorite leisure activity?)*
- Donnez votre description physique. *(Describe yourself.)*
- Quelle est la date de votre anniversaire? *(When is your birthday?)*
- Décrivez votre famille. Avez-vous un frère? une soeur? un fils? une fille? Comment s'appelle-t-il(elle)? *(Describe your family. Do you have a brother? a sister? a son? a daughter? What is his/her name?)*

Illustration 6.4 Family Tree Activity (Student Copy)

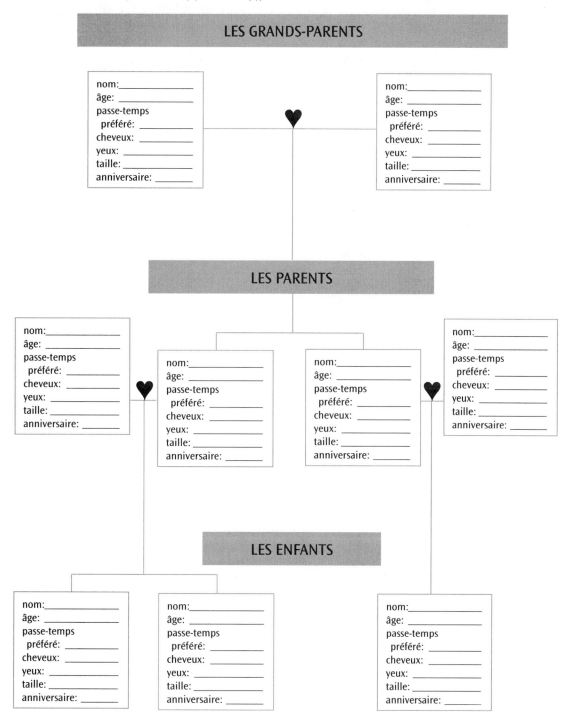

Biographical Data Cards. These cards can be given to students in the target language or in English, depending on their level of proficiency. For Novice learners, it might be best to give them the cards in French so that they have less to recall. For Intermediate learners, cards can be given in English so that they are required to remember the vocabulary and formulate the questions and answers needed to complete the puzzle.

CARD 1

Name: Pierre LeClerc
Age: 39
Leisure Activity: playing tennis
Hair: blond
Eyes: blue
Height: tall
Birthdate: February 23
Wife: Fifi LeClerc
　　Age: 35
　　Hair: blond
　　Eyes: brown
　　Height: medium
　　Birthday: Nov. 15
Sister: Lisette Dulac
Brother-in-law: Jean Dulac
We have two children.

CARD 2

Name: Henri LeClerc
Age: 69
Leisure Activity: listening to classical
　　　　　　　　music
Hair: gray
Eyes: brown
Height: average
Birthdate: August 25
Wife: Henriette LeClerc
　　Age: 67
　　Hair: white
　　Eyes: blue
　　Height: short
　　Birthday: July 14
　　Leisure Activity: watching
　　　　　　romantic movies
Our children are Pierre and Lisette.

CARD 3

Name: Fifi LeClerc
Husband: Pierre
Daughter: Alice
　　Age: 11
　　Favorite Activity: playing
　　　　　with dolls
　　Hair: blond
　　Eyes: brown
　　Height: petite
　　Birthday: September 30
Son: Jacques
　　Age: 9
Niece: Marie
　　Age: 7
　　Favorite Activity: playing with
　　　　her cousins

CARD 4

Name: Lisette Dulac
Age: 32
Favorite Activity: playing piano
Birthdate: March 16
Brother: Pierre LeClerc
Husband: Jean Dulac
　　Age: 36
　　Favorite Activity: watching
　　　　football on TV
　　Birthday: December 4
Daughter: Marie
　　Age: 7
　　Hair: black
　　Eyes: brown
　　Height: very petite
　　Birthday: May 13

CARD 5

Name: Alice LeClerc
Age: 11
Brother: Jacques
　　Favorite Activity: playing
　　　　baseball
　　Hair: blond
　　Height: short
　　Birthday: September 21
Cousin: Marie Dulac
Aunt: Lisette
　　Hair: black
　　Eyes: brown
　　Height: medium
Uncle: Jean

CARD 6

Name: Marie Dulac
Age: 7
Father: Jean Dulac
　　Hair: black
　　Eyes: green
　　Height: very tall
No brothers or sisters
Cousins: Jacques and Alice
Aunt: Fifi
　　Favorite Activity: garden work
Uncle: Pierre
Cousin Jacques has blue eyes.

Group Decision Making

Group Picture Story

Objective: To create an original story by synthesizing the contributions of all group members

Functions: Telling and listening to stories, recounting events, hypothesizing

Grammatical Features: Interrogative words and expressions, descriptive adjectives, past tenses

Student Task: The teacher chooses from magazines several pictures that depict people in odd situations or show several people in some type of conversation. The more "interesting" the situation (or the more ambiguous), the better. The teacher mounts the pictures on construction paper and affixes a sheet of lined paper to the back.

The teacher then distributes the pictures to groups of three to five students, one picture to a group. The students look at the picture and brainstorm for a few minutes to create as many possible questions as the picture can provoke. A group leader may be chosen to write down the questions on the lined sheet, or the picture and writing task can be passed from student to student as each thinks of a question to ask.

Once the groups have had a chance to generate their set of questions, the teacher collects them (as well as the pictures to which they are attached) and redistributes them, each one to a different group. Group members then read the questions associated with their new picture and agree on a story that will answer all of the questions asked. They must recount their story in the past, making sure that the narrative is coherent and complete enough to answer all the questions. A group leader can be responsible for writing the story down as it unfolds, sharing it later with the rest of the class.

Source: Omaggio (1982).

Social Interaction

Objective: To use the foreign language to locate persons with certain hobbies, ideal for a warm-up activity to get students to interact with each other, to review vocabulary

Context: Spare-time activities, hobbies

Functions: Inquiring about personal preferences, asking and answering questions

Grammatical Features: Question formation

Communicative Mode: Interpersonal Communication

Student Task: Students receive a sheet such as the one below on which are listed various activities students like to do. Students must circulate, asking each other questions to find a person or several persons who like to do the activities listed on the sheet. Once they find someone who likes a particular activity, they write down the student's name. In more advanced classes, students can be instructed to ask one follow-up question (for example: How often do you play tennis? Do you play it well?, etc.). Each student can pose only one question from the card to another student—this way you ensure that they talk to a number of different people.

Follow-up: The teacher can tally the responses on the board or on an overhead to find out which are the favorite activities in the class. This game can be tailored to the interests of the class and can also be used with different vocabulary items (i.e., countries one has been to, favorite pets, things someone ate over the weekend, etc.).

Source: Golato (2000).

STUDENT ACTIVITY SHEET

Schatzsuche: Suchen Sie eine Person für jedes Hobby

Beispiel: Student A: Spielst du Basketball?
Student B: Ja, jeden Tag./Manchmal./Nein, nie.

Golf spielen _____   Wandern_____

Joggen _____   Gewichte heben_____

Stricken_____   Bücher lesen_____

Treasure Hunt: Find a person for each hobby

Example: Student A: Do you like playing basketball?
Student B: Yes, I play it every day. /Sometimes./ No, never.

playing golf_____   hiking _____

jogging _____   lifting weights_____

knitting_____   reading books_____

Situational Role-Plays

Role-plays have been long suggested as a technique that can be enjoyable and entertaining while encouraging creative use of the language. In role-plays, a situation is presented to a small group of students who may prepare their parts, if necessary, and then act them out for the rest of the class or record them on videotape for playback later. To include a cultural dimension, teachers may have students role-play scenes from short stories, plays, films, or textbook video programs filmed in the target culture, giving them an opportunity to practice their "presentational communication" skills. Some excellent ideas for role-plays of all kinds can be found in sources such as Zelson (1978), Kramsch (1981), Bragger (1985), Hahn and Michaelas (1986), and numerous recent language textbooks.

Role-plays can be used effectively at virtually any proficiency level. For students at the Novice level, highly structured role-play cards can be designed, with vocabulary hints or partial dialogues supplied, based either on material already presented in class or on the simplest of survival or courtesy situations, such as those found in the ACTFL OPI Tester Training materials. Intermediate level learners can practice role-plays designed around common situations one might encounter in traveling or living in a foreign country. At higher levels of oral proficiency, the role-play can introduce a conflict situation in which someone must persuade someone else to act in a certain way, talk his or her way out of trouble, or lodge a complaint. Role-plays can be derived from lesson themes and structured around a few communicative functions and/or structural features, or they can be more open-ended. To succeed in helping students build proficiency, teachers should be careful to present role-play situations that are at an appropriate level of difficulty for students.

SAMPLE ROLE-PLAY (NOVICE)

Students who have just been studying foods in their text and learning how to read restaurant menus role-play a scene in a restaurant. Several students play the customers and one student plays the server. Students can be supplied with authentic menus, or they can search restaurant sites on the Web and find menus that they can use or adapt. Alternatively, menus can be created by the teacher or by other students in the class. (For a writing activity in which students create their own menus, see Chapter 7, Illustration 7.3, p. 286.) Forms can be created for waiters to fill out as they take orders, and the waiter can present the "check" to the customers at the end of the meal. Teachers may want to supply students with role-play cards on which are written common pragmatic expressions for ordering foods (for the customers) and for taking orders (for the servers).

VARIATION (INTERMEDIATE)

After studying pragmatic expressions relating to complaining, offering apologies, and other similar functional expressions, students role-play a scene in a restaurant where they imagine that they have just gotten food that is unacceptable in some way (e.g., food that is too cold or too salty, soup with a foreign object in it, meat that is too tough). The customer(s) complain about the food, and the server responds with an apology, an offer to bring something else, or the offer of a free dessert.

Creative Language Practice: Additional Suggestions

One of the hallmarks of language users in the Intermediate range and beyond is that they can create with the language. In order to develop this ability, students must have opportunities to learn to paraphrase, think divergently, and let their imaginations and creativity function as fully as possible. Birckbichler (1982) has compiled an extremely valuable set of suggestions for creative language practice.

Basing her definition of creativity on Guilford's (1959) Structure-of-Intellect Model, she proposes four types of divergent-production factors that relate to the development of creativity in language use. These factors are (1) *fluency,* or the ability to produce a large number of ideas relatively quickly, (2) *flexibility,* or the ability to produce a diversity of ideas belonging to different classes, (3) *elaboration,* or the ability to add to or embellish a given idea or set of ideas, and (4) *originality,* or the ability to produce uncommon, unconventional, or clever ideas. Drawing on sources from various fields of research on creativity, Birckbichler presents 64 classroom-activity formats related to these four factors. Some ideas that are suitable for several proficiency ranges are presented below.

Fluency

SAMPLE (INTERMEDIATE)

Brainstorming Activities

One way to help students develop greater fluency of ideas is to provide them with opportunities for "brainstorming" activities. For example, Birckbichler (1982) suggests that students can be asked to work in small groups to generate as many questions as possible to use in an interview for a native-speaker visit the next day. They might be given one or two stimulus questions to get them started and then be asked to think of several follow-up questions for each of the stimulus questions.

Another possibility is to give students in small groups a list of four or five adjectives (depicting colors, sizes, feelings, or other attributes) and have groups compete to think of as many objects as they can fitting each of the adjectives in a given time period. Groups can share their responses at the end of the competition to see who has the longest or most original list.

Flexibility

SAMPLE (ADVANCED)

Change the Story

Students listen to or read a short story in the target language and are asked to create a new story by changing the original story in some way. They may tell the story from the point of view of one of the characters, change the time frame to that of another era, imagine a different ending, etc. In doing this, students have an opportunity to be creative with the language while practicing the Advanced level function of narration in the past.

Elaboration

SAMPLE (ADVANCED)

Cue Insertion

This activity, based on the first draft of a composition written by students, can be done orally or in writing. If the activity is done in writing, students can be asked to present their new compositions to the class orally during the next class period. The activity requires that students expand each sentence of their original composition by adding more information whenever they see an asterisk.

The following example in English illustrates this technique. The teacher asks a student to use relative clauses to elaborate on a fictitious story he wrote about his vacation. She encourages him to use his imagination, adding details that are serious, funny, mysterious, or sinister, according to his own wishes. The student reworks the composition at home and presents it to the class orally during the next period.

Teacher's comment on student's first draft:

Make the story you wrote more interesting by adding a relative clause each time you see an asterisk. For example, you wrote: "I spent my vacation in a hotel." Embellish this by adding a clause, such as the following: "I spent my vacation in a hotel that was really mysterious! (. . . whose inhabitants were old; . . . where famous people had stayed; . . . that my brother had recommended; . . . where ghosts had been seen!)"

Student's first draft with cues inserted:

I spent my vacation in a hotel*. The hotel is located on a little street*. The concierge* was really quiet. He only talked to his wife*. Their garden* was very tranquil and looked out on the street. I often sat on a bench* and looked at the people*. . . . (etc.)

Source: Adapted from Omaggio (1981), p. 56

Originality

SAMPLE (INTERMEDIATE/ADVANCED)

Inventing Machines

Using a sentence-builder format, students develop creative and unusual questions, which others then answer or use as a basis for creating a group story. In the sample activity that Birckbichler (1982) cites from Debyser and Laitenberger (1976), various people, objects, and places appear in numbered lists in three columns. People in Column 1 include such character types as a general, a dancer, or a plumber; the list of objects in Column 2 comprises such items as a sack of sugar, a hammer, or a hard-boiled egg; places included in Column 3 range from a refrigerator or a toolbox to a violin case. The questions created are in the form: "Why did the . . . put a/an . . . in his/her/the . . . ?"

Students can either create their own questions by combining elements from the three columns or draw three numbers to determine their question. For example, a given number combination would generate the question: "Why did the president put a kilo of sugar in the tool box?" Students working in pairs or small groups can create a reasonable explanation or short narrative to answer this unusual query. Birckbichler warns that teachers must use such "verbal play" activities with some caution, and only on occasion: ". . . some students may find playing with language to be an interesting and challenging aspect to second language learning, whereas others who tend to view language solely as an expression of reality will be frustrated by verbal play activities" (p. 74).

Many creative writing and guided description activities can be used to encourage autonomous expression in the target language. Students can be asked to generate a context from a list of words, from a picture or series of pictures that may or may not be related to one another, or from a group of random objects. In an activity called "Geschichten aus dem Sack" (*Stories out of a Bag*), Schmidt (1977) suggests that a paper bag be filled with unrelated objects, which students select one at a time for the purpose of generating a group story, incorporating each of the objects drawn out of the bag into the plot as the story unfolds. Rivers et al. (1976) suggest an activity called "Gossip," in which students are given a sheet of paper containing a series of questions with space after each for writing answers. Each student answers one question. He or she then hides the answer by folding the paper back and passes the sheet on to the next student. After the last question has been answered, the story, which is often quite amusing, is read to the class. These and other similar formats have been used by classroom teachers to help students create with the language in a structured, yet open-ended way and are excellent for developing oral skills beyond the Novice level.

HYPOTHESIS 2. *Opportunities should be provided for students to practice carrying out a range of functions (tasks) likely to be necessary in dealing with others in the target culture.*

As we saw in Chapter 3, students need to be able to carry out a variety of language functions or tasks in order to develop proficiency beyond the Novice level. The term *function,* as it has been used in the proficiency descriptions, refers to a set of generic, global tasks that language users must be able to perform at a given level of proficiency, such as obtaining information or expressing one's point of view. In addition to these basic tasks, one can list many more specific language functions that students might learn to carry out in the target language. *"Functions,"* in this sense, "refer to the hundreds of purposes for which people communicate, either orally or in writing" (Guntermann and Phillips 1982, p. 5). In order to help teachers identify functions for active practice, Guntermann and Phillips list some common purposes of language use in all four skill modalities. In speaking and listening, for example, they list such functions as *socializing, establishing and maintaining relationships, influencing others' actions, talking one's way out of trouble,* and the like. For each of these main functions, they provide an inventory of related sub-functions. Similar functional inventories can be found elsewhere in the literature (see, specifically, Van Ek 1975; Wilkins 1976; and Kramsch 1981, who outlines applications of discourse analysis to the second-language classroom).

An example of an activity that is focused primarily on functional language practice is given below. It is taken from a text that is centered around language functions and conversational strategies, presented in audiotaped native-speaker interchanges. In this particular Spanish text, students listen to native-speaker conversations and learn various communication strategies, which they then practice in small-group activities, such as the one below:

SAMPLE (INTERMEDIATE)

Context: Health care, a visit to the doctor

Functions: Giving advice, responding to advice, giving one's opinion

Communicative Mode: Interpersonal Communication

Student Task: After hearing a conversation in Spanish between a doctor and a patient, students study various expressions given in the text for giving and receiving medical advice. They then engage in the role-play activity depicted in Illustration 6.5.

As seen in Illustration 6.5, students are directed to play the roles of a doctor and a patient. To prepare for playing the doctor's role, students begin by imagining what the doctor is like and how he/she would act, preparing a list of possible questions to ask the patient. To prepare for playing the patient's role, students are asked to think of what the patient is like, whether he/she will be willing to follow the doctor's directions, and what the nature of the imaginary illness is.

Illustration 6.5
Functional Practice
Activity in Spanish

Expresiones útiles para responder a los consejos

Está bien, pero será difícil.	*That's O.K., but it will be difficult.*
¿Crees que . . . ?	*Do you think . . . ?*
¿De veras?	*Really?*
¿De verdad?	*Really?*
Ah, no puedo.	*Oh, I can't.*
Ah, no quiero . . .	*Oh, I don't want . . .*
Porque no me gusta . . .	*Because I don't like to . . .*
Estoy preocupado(a).	*I'm worried.*
No había pensado en eso.	*I had not thought about that.*
Te agradezco los consejos.	*I appreciate your advice.*
(No) Lo haré.	*I will (not) do it.*

El (La) paciente y el (la) médico(a). Con un(a) compañero(a) de clase, hagan el papel de un(a) paciente y el de un(a) médico(a).

1. El papel del (de la) médico(a)

    a.   ¿Cómo es el (la) médico(a)? ¿simpático(a)? ¿antipático(a)? ¿paciente? ¿impaciente?
    b.   ¿Cómo saluda a los pacientes?
    c.   ¿Cómo los trata?
    ch. Prepara una lista de preguntas para averiguar qué problema(s) tiene el (la) paciente.
    d.   Prepara una lista de recomendaciones.

2. El papel del (de la) paciente

    a.   ¿Cómo eres tú? ¿Qué tipo de persona eres?
    b.   ¿Estás dispuesto(a) a seguir las recomendaciones del (de la) médico(a)?

3. Prepara una descripción de tu problema o enfermedad.

4. Piensa en las preguntas más comunes que un(a) médico(a) le hace a un(a) paciente. También, piensa en una enfermedad (imaginaria, claro) y en algunas expresiones para describirla. Leugo, en grupos de dos, hagan el papel de médico(a) y de paciente. Los dos deben alternarse en los dos papeles. Fíjense en las recomendaciones del (de la) médico(a) y en la actitud del (de la) paciente al oírlas.

5. Haz el papel de médico(a) y explica a los otros estudiantes

    a.   el problema del (de la) paciente
    b.   tus recomendaciones para su mejoría.

Source: Chastain and Guntermann 1991, p. 139.

Once these preparations have been made, students take turns playing the roles of doctor and patient in groups of two. As a follow-up activity, individual students are asked to play the role of the doctor and explain to others in the class what the patient's problem is and how it will be treated.

Source: K. Chastain and G. Guntermann, *¡Imagínate!,* 2nd ed. Heinle & Heinle, 1991.

Students can practice *writing* by imagining that they are (1) the patient, writing in his/her journal about the "ordeal" at the doctor's office that day or (2) the doctor, writing in his/her notebook some comments about the patient, his/her illness, attitude, cure, etc.

Functional practice activities such as the one in this sample not only help students learn to carry out various real-world tasks, but also provide them with conversational strategies that are appropriate to the culture of the language they are studying. Such activities contribute to the development of discourse competence, sociolinguistic competence, and strategic competence, all of which are important factors to include in a well-designed program for teaching oral communication skills.

A rich source of task-based activities that involve a blend of language functions, modes of communication, and cultural exploration can be found in the *Standards for Foreign Language Learning in the 21st Century* (1999). In addition to the generic standards, language-specific standards for Chinese, Classical Languages, French, German, Italian, Japanese, Portuguese, Russian, and Spanish are provided. After the presentation of the standards for each particular language, including sample progress indicators for grades 4, 8, 12, and 16, learning scenarios are illustrated that demonstrate how a variety of standards can be reflected in classroom activities. These scenarios have been developed by classroom teachers and many have been tested at schools involved as pilot sites during the standards-setting process (p. 71). At the end of each scenario is a section entitled "Reflection," which highlights the "weave" of curricular elements, such as the language system, communication strategies, culture, learning strategies, other subject matter areas, critical thinking skills, and technology (p. 305). Teachers should consult the learning scenarios not only for the language they teach, but also for the other languages, for valuable ideas and activities. Although most scenarios are targeted for a particular level, they can be adapted for students of diverse ability levels. A sample scenario for Italian is given in Illustration 6.6.

Responding to the Learner

When learners engage in language production activities such as those illustrated in this chapter, they are bound to produce errors of various kinds as they struggle to get their meaning across. This is especially true in communicative and open-ended activities, where activity formats are not heavily structured and monitoring of formal features is not as likely to be central to the task. There is no question that a great many of the errors committed by second-language learners are sys-

Illustration 6.6
Learning Scenario
for Italian

ITALY BY TRAIN

In this scenario a third-year Italian class in Spring
Valley, NY plans an itinerary for train travel in
Italy. They research train schedules, travel
distances, and time of travel between cities,
converting kilometers to miles. Students

Targeted Standards
1.1 Interpersonal Communication
1.2 Interpretive Communication
1.3 Presentational Communication
2.1 Practices of Culture
3.1 Making Connections
4.2 Cultural Comparisons

create travel brochures with information gathered from various sources and present them to the class.

Reflection

1.1 Students provide and exchange travel information.

1.2 Students read Italian train schedules, maps, and travel brochures.

1.3 Students design and discuss the tours they have developed, and write letters requesting
     accommodations in Italian hotels.

2.1 Students research Italian travel practices via the Internet.

3.1 Students use math to calculate distances and convert kilometers into miles.
     They further calculate times of travel between cities by various means of transportation.

4.2 Students demonstrate knowledge of preferences in national transportation modes in Italy
     and the United States.

Source: Standards for Foreign Language Learning in the 21st Century (1999),
pp. 313-314. Reprinted by permission.

tematic. But where do such errors come from? What processes in language learning might be potential sources for production errors in speaking or in writing?
What kinds of strategies do learners use in producing language when the ideas
they want to communicate require proficiency beyond their current level of competence? How do native speakers react to language-learner language? How can
teachers respond to help students develop more precise and coherent language
use? These questions form the basis for the discussion in the last part of this chapter. Various answers that have been proposed in the literature in recent years are
presented and illustrated in the next sections.

Some Sources of Error in Interlanguage

Selinker (1974) identifies five processes that he believes to be central to second-
language learning and acquisition, each of which can force non-native items,
rules, and subsystems to appear and possibly remain indefinitely in the interlanguage systems of language learners. These five processes are: *language transfer,* or
interference from the mother tongue, *transfer-of-training,* or errors due to the nature of the language-learning materials and approaches themselves, *strategies of
second language learning,* or errors due to the learner's own approach to the mate-

rial to be learned, *strategies of second language communication,* or errors due to the way in which the learner attempts to communicate with native speakers in natural language-use situations, and *overgeneralization of target language rules,* or errors due to the way in which the learner restructures and reorganizes linguistic material.

Language Transfer. Gass and Selinker (1994) note that in the mid- to late 1970s, the notions of "language transfer" and "interference" were broadened and reconceptualized as new theories of language learning replaced behavioristic explanations that relied in large part on these concepts to explain second-language acquisition. They cite the work of Kellerman and Sharwood Smith (1986), who suggest that the term "cross-linguistic influence" might be a useful way to characterize the phenomenon of transfer, as well as avoidance, language loss, and rate of learning (Gass and Selinker 1994, p. 89). Errors that can be attributed to cross-linguistic influence can be found at the level of pronunciation, morphology, syntax, vocabulary, or meaning (Richards 1974). Transfer errors in vocabulary and the encoding of meaning can occur when learners use strategies such as literal translation or language switch (the use of a native-language term without translation) to solve their communication problems (Tarone 1978). An example of an interference error often committed by English-speaking students of French is the use of the expression *"avoir un bon temps"* to mean "to have a good time." The use of a word-for-word literal translation strategy in this case results in an awkward phrase that not only is incorrect, but may also be incomprehensible to native speakers.

Transfer-of-Training. Selinker (1974) maintains that some errors may be due to the nature of the learning materials or procedures used in formal second-language learning. He cites the example of Serbo-Croatian speakers who learned English from a textbook in which the third-person singular was almost always presented in the masculine form. The interesting fact is that Serbo-Croatian has the same gender distinction as English. Yet, because the learners practiced only the *he* form in textbook drills and exercises, they never really learned to include *she* in their interlanguage repertoire.

Overgeneralization of Target Language Material. Errors derived from overgeneralization result when a previously available strategy or rule is used in new situations where that rule does not apply. For example, students of French often use the auxiliary verb *avoir* exclusively when forming the *passé composé* instead of conjugating certain verbs with the auxiliary *être*. Many ESL students do not add an *-s* to the third-person singular verb form in the present tense, overgeneralizing the use of the form without *-s* in the remaining persons. Overgeneralization is one of the strategies used in reorganizing linguistic material and is sometimes a valuable acquisition tool, but when rules are misapplied and never later refined, this strategy can be an important source of persistent error in interlanguage.

Strategies of Second Language Learning. Language-learning strategies are attempts to develop competence in the language and may include such procedures as the use of formal rules, rote memorization, deliberate rehearsal, contextual guessing, looking for recurring patterns, imitating formulaic routines, seeking opportunities to obtain comprehensible input, appealing for assistance from native speakers or teachers, and the like. Tarone (1980) distinguishes language-learning strategies from language-use strategies, such as communication and production strategies. Production strategies represent attempts to use one's interlanguage system efficiently and clearly, with a minimum of effort, and might include such things as simplification and discourse planning. Communication strategies are quite different from learning strategies and parallel to some extent Selinker's next category, strategies of communication.

Strategies of Second Language Communication. When learners attempt to negotiate meanings with native speakers in authentic language-use situations, they may frequently find themselves at a loss for words due to their imperfect knowledge of the target language. Errors can result from heavy communication demands made on their interlanguage, demands that force them to use strategies like approximation, word coinage, circumlocution, translation, language switch, appeals for assistance, and mime, or else to abandon their message altogether or choose to avoid the topic (Tarone 1978; 1980, p. 429).

It is important to recognize that many of these communication strategies can be extremely valuable in the language acquisition process and can contribute to the development of the learner's strategic competence, discussed in Chapter 1. The use of paraphrasing strategies, such as approximation and circumlocution, as well as mime or appeals for assistance, can often provide learners with new expressions, structures, and vocabulary that they then successfully add to their linguistic repertoire. Teachers need to help learners develop their strategic competence through classroom activities that focus on using circumlocution, definitions, and other paraphrasing techniques that lead to successful communication of meaning. Expressions in the target language such as "I don't understand," "Could you please repeat that?" or "Could you speak more slowly?" can also be taught overtly so that students can appeal for assistance when it is needed. Problems may arise, however, when learners are consistently faced with communication situations that far outstrip their current level of proficiency, leading to over-reliance on compensatory strategies and the use of incomprehensible forms in an attempt to get their message across.

Selinker (1974) uses the term *fossilization* to refer to the permanent retention of non-native interlanguage forms in the learners' developing linguistic system. Selinker and Lamendella (1979) make a distinction between *fossilization* and *stabilization;* in the latter case, non-native items, structures, or subsystems in the interlanguage grammar are not permanent, but may eventually "destabilize" or change toward the target-language norm. If, however, such items remain in the interlanguage, even when the learner's motivation, persistence, ability, and opportunity to learn are optimal, then fossilization may have indeed occurred. Selinker and Lamendella suggest that fossilization is more likely to occur if learners see no reason to improve their interim grammar and decide that it is adequate to serve their needs. Swain's (1985) "pushed output" hypothesis, which was discussed in Chapter 3, is consistent with this viewpoint. She suggests that learners sometimes need to receive negative feedback when they use language imprecisely or incoherently and be encouraged to find more appropriate ways to express their meaning. Classroom activities that challenge learners to move just beyond their current level of competence and that give them feedback about the degree of precision and coherence in their target-language use can provide an optimal balance among proficiency goals as students' skills develop.

How should teachers respond to language-learner language in order to provide helpful feedback without stifling creativity? Which errors should be selected for correction and/or feedback? We may gain some insight into these questions by considering first the way native speakers react to learners' errors, both orally and in writing. The next section presents a summary of results of some studies that have been conducted on this question in a variety of language communities.

Attitudes Toward Interlanguage: Native-Speaker Reaction Studies

There has been a good deal of interest among scholars interested in interlanguage in documenting the reactions of native speakers to the language use of non-natives in an effort to understand what constitutes successful and unsuccessful communication. Although linguistic considerations have been central to many of the studies, affective reactions to learners themselves have also been subject to inquiry.

One important variable to be considered in assessing the results of a given research effort is the nature of the interlanguage sample used to elicit reactions. The speech samples and/or writing samples provided to native-speaker judges essentially define interlanguage operationally for that study. In the studies examined here, the samples have ranged from artificially created sentence pairs, presented out of context, to audiovisual tapes of connected discourse, obtained in naturalistic interview situations. Given that the samples vary considerably, the studies are not directly comparable (Ludwig 1982), and results cannot be as clearly interpreted, therefore, as one might like.

The studies reviewed in this chapter are a sampling of the research that has been done to assess native-speaker reactions to learner language in the past 25 years. Ludwig (1982) provides a useful review and synthesis of 12 such studies, some of which are summarized briefly in Table 6.1 (p. 264). A number of more recent studies are also included in the present overview. Readers should consult Ludwig (1982), as well as the original reports of the studies cited here, for additional information and analysis of the data.

In general, much of the research on native-speaker reactions indicates that many of the grammatical errors made by non-native speakers do not seriously interfere with the comprehensibility of their speech, although there are some types of errors (such as some vocabulary problems, verb forms, and tense usage) that can confuse native speakers and lead to a communication breakdown. It may also be the case that there are cultural differences in error tolerance (see, for example, Ngame 1992, comparing native speaker reactions in French and Swahili), as well as differences in reaction to error between teachers of language and native speakers who are not teachers (Ervin 1977, cited in Ludwig 1982; Galloway 1980;

Schairer 1992). The studies summarized here suggest that some attention should be paid to errors, particularly with regard to those that interfere with comprehensibility, but that choices will undoubtedly need to be made about which types of errors to correct, and when and how to treat them. This topic is the subject of the last section of this chapter.

Error Correction Strategies for the Classroom

In Chapter 3, a rationale for providing students with corrective feedback was presented in the discussion associated with Hypothesis 3, reproduced below:

HYPOTHESIS 3. *The development of accuracy should be encouraged in proficiency-oriented instruction. As learners produce language, various forms of instruction and evaluative feedback can be useful in facilitating the progression of their skills toward more precise and coherent language use.*

Throughout this chapter, as well as in Chapters 5 and 7, a whole range of instructional formats and strategies that can be used to help learners develop their language skills has been illustrated. The formats that are presented range along a kind of continuum from those that focus on formal features of the target language to those that invite students to use the language in task-based, more creative ways. This section examines the types of evaluative feedback that can be useful in responding to learner language as students engage in speaking activities of various types. (Feedback strategies useful in responding to student writing are presented and discussed in Chapter 7.)

Many scholars and practitioners agree that the type of feedback one provides to students should vary according to the purposes of the activity in which they are engaged. When learners are focused on mastery of particular features of the language, they will probably profit most from fairly direct and immediate feedback on the correctness of their responses. If, on the other hand, they are attempting to communicate ideas in an open-ended or creative task, the most beneficial feedback may be a positive response to the message that is being conveyed and further input from the teacher or their classmates that is meaningful and communicative in nature. Any corrective feedback that is needed can be reserved for a later time or provided indirectly in substantive responses. Teachers need to develop a whole range of feedback mechanisms and determine when and how to use them to foster optimal growth in proficiency.

How can one determine what feedback strategies are most useful for students involved in particular kinds of practice activities? The answers are certainly not simple. As was pointed out in Chapter 2, learners differ widely in terms of their personality characteristics, learning styles, and learning preferences. What works for one student may not work well for another. Furthermore, students at a relatively low level of oral proficiency may need different kinds of feedback than students whose proficiency is higher. A few examples from studies on the effects of feedback on student attitudes illustrate the complex nature of the issues involved

Table 6.1. Summary of Studies on Native-Speaker Reactions to Nonnative Speech

Study/Date	Subjects/Language	Research Design	Results
Guntermann (1978)	Corpus of language samples taken from oral interviews in Spanish of 30 Peace Corps volunteers in El Salvador (all tapes rated 1+ on FSI scale). Judges of comprehensibility were 30 native speakers of Spanish. Judges of acceptability were 78 adult NSs of Spanish studying English.	Three phases: (1) determine kinds of errors most frequently made in oral interviews; (2) determine which frequent errors interfered most with communication through eliciting NS restatements of recorded sentences; (3) ask native speakers to react to sentence pairs constructed with common errors in FSI oral interviews and indicate most acceptable sentence.	• Most frequent errors: agreement errors (noun-modifier and subject-verb) and substitutions of *ser/estar/haber* for one another. • Only 22% of sentences misunderstood; multiple errors of same type (e.g., tense or mode) made sentences most incomprehensible; of single errors, substitutions of *ser/estar/haber* and of tense more likely to be misinterpreted. • Article agreement errors much less acceptable than article omissions; verb errors in person generally less acceptable than errors in tense. • Author concluded most grammatical errors do not interfere significantly with communication, but comprehensibility may not be the only criterion in determining error tolerance.
Politzer (1978)	German teenagers (n=146) served as native-speaker judges of test sentence pairs.	60 pairs of German sentences were constructed to correspond to typical errors made by Americans. Subjects listened to sentence pairs and judged which of each pair was the more serious error in German.	• Most serious errors (i.e., those judged least acceptable) were those in vocabulary, followed by grammatical errors (verb morphology, word order, and gender confusion). • Errors in phonology and case endings were judged less serious.
Albrechtsen, Henriksen, and Faerch (1980)	Native speakers of English reacting to interviews of Danish-speaking learners of English.	NSs reacted to speech samples using 14 bipolar adjective scales. Four criteria were evaluated: personality, content, language accuracy, and comprehensibility. Results compared with objective analysis of texts.	• Highly significant correlations between language factor on the bipolar scales and most of performance features analyzed. • Only use of communication strategies correlated significantly with comprehension. • Learners who made extensive use of communication strategies were judged more harshly. Most positive judgments were of samples with few lexical or syntactic errors and fewer communication strategies. • Authors conclude that "all errors are equally irritating" (p. 394), and it is fruitless to search for hierarchy of error gravity on error type alone.

Chastain (1980)	Spanish native speakers (n=48) judging constructed sentences with common errors.	Sentences constructed from list of most frequent errors judged as serious by TAs in Spanish. (Sentences were not contextualized.) NSs of Spanish evaluated sentences for comprehensibility and acceptability.	• 90% or more of NSs comprehended most of the sentences. • 23 of 48 errors were considered comprehensible but unacceptable by 50% or more of evaluators. Most dealt with verb forms. • About half of the errors considered serious/stigmatizing to teachers were considered acceptable by native-speaker judges, showing relatively high degree of tolerance by non-teaching NSs.
Galloway (1980)	Four groups of respondants (non-native teachers of high school Spanish, native-speaking teachers, non-teaching native speakers of Spanish with fair to good English; non-teaching NSs in Spain with no or poor command of English) reacting to speech of 2nd-semester university students of Spanish.	Videos of 10 students' unrehearsed answers to Spanish questions evaluated by respondants in the 4 groups on a set of criteria, including quantity of communication, effort to communicate, comprehensibility, overall impression, and effects of paralanguage, as well as judgmental reactions.	• Native speakers who were *not* teachers were most accepting and sympathetic to students experiencing difficulty speaking who made effort to communicate. • Overall, native speakers seemed to focus on message, whereas nonnative teachers focused more on grammatical accuracy. • Most errors did not interfere with communication, though confusion of tenses was more serious for native-speaker judges. • Author concludes teachers should focus on communicative language use and focus in correction most on forms that can disrupt communication.
Ensz (1982)	250 French native speakers reacted to taped speech samples of Americans speaking French.	3 passages created, each with 5 versions: (1) pronunciation good, vocabulary and grammar weak; (2) pronunciation and grammar good, vocabulary weak; (3) good grammar, but weak pronunciation and vocabulary; (4) good grammar and vocabulary, weak pronunciation; (5) most native-like, with some weaknesses in pronunciation only. NSs rated speakers in each version on set of personality characteristics.	• Grammatical errors least tolerable of three error types emphasized in study. • Most preferred version was #5 (most native-like), followed by versions #2 and #4. • Lowest rating given to #1, the only sample with grammar errors. • Author concludes that ". . . American speakers of French should be most concerned that they speak with the greatest possible grammatical accuracy" (pp. 137-38).
Ludwig (1982)	Reviewed studies in French, German, Spanish, EFL, Russian of NS reactions to oral and written language.	Surveyed 12 studies in native-speaker reactions, exploring themes of *comprehensibility, irritation,* and *acceptability.*	• Author concluded students must be encouraged to communicate. • Teachers should correct errors selectively, focusing on elements native speakers find most irritating or distracting (verb errors, vocabulary, and global errors that interfere with comprehension) and not try to correct every error.

Table 6.1. Summary of Studies on Native-Speaker Reactions to Nonnative Speech *continued*

Study/Date	Subjects/Language	Research Design	Results
Gynan (1984)	NSs of Spanish from variety of backgrounds evaluating five samples of Spanish: a typical standard Mexican variety, a Northern Mexican variety, a fluent nonnative Spanish speaker, an intermediate learner of Spanish, and a beginning learner.	Questionnaire solicited NSs reaction to speech samples in terms of form, their attitude toward the speech, and attitude toward the speaker.	• Attitudes toward *speech* measurably different from attitudes toward *person speaking*. • Mean affect scores higher than mean language scores. • Students' non-native speech judged negatively for work potential, showing they were not at threshold of communicative proficiency needed to satisfy practical demands when living off the economy.
Ngame (1992)	NSs of French reacting to non-native speech in French and NSs of Swahili reacting to non-native speech in Swahili.	NSs of French and Swahili evaluated 10 intermediate language samples in their language drawn from OPI interviews on comprehensibility, acceptability, grammatical accuracy, fluency, vocabulary, and pronunciation. Second sample of 50 single sentences drawn from interviews but not contextualized also rated.	• Two native-speaker groups rated intermediate samples in parallel fashion, but Swahili speakers rated more leniently than French speakers. • Comprehensiblity rated higher than acceptability and the four linguistic measures. • Fluency and pronunciation rated lowest. • No difference in ratings for contextualized vs. decontextualized samples. • Author concluded that linguistic and cultural backgrounds have important impact on perceptions of non-native speech.
Schairer (1992)	Native-speaking teachers and non-teaching native speakers of Spanish.	18 taped speech samples selected to provide sample of pronunciation ranging from elementary to native proficiency were rated for comprehensibility, agreeableness of voice, nativeness of accent. Researcher also did phonetic analysis of samples.	• Teachers generally more strict in ratings of comprehensibility of samples than non-teachers. • NSs who do not speak English more tolerant than those who do. • Both groups responded similarly to phonetic features analyzed for the study. • Author suggests that non-native speaker comprehensibility may be improved by first concentrating on native-like pronunciation of vowels, then on linking of word-final consonants and vowels, and finally on production of consonants.

in responding to learner needs and preferences. In the context of oral work, Cathcart and Olsen (1976) found that students felt the need to be corrected and preferred consistent corrective feedback. Courchêne (1980) reports similar results in a study with ESL students. On the other hand, Walker (1973) reports that students believe frequent correction destroys their confidence and prefer to be allowed to communicate freely without constant intervention from the teacher. In a more recent survey of student and teacher attitudes toward grammar instruction and feedback, Schulz (1996) found that 80% of the students surveyed in eight languages at various levels of instruction felt that grammar instruction was essential, and 90% of students stated that they would like to have their spoken errors corrected (p. 363). An even larger percentage—97%—said that they wanted their written errors corrected (p. 364). When Schulz posed similar questions to the teachers in the survey, she found that their attitudes toward explicit grammar study and corrective feedback differed from those of their students. For example, a smaller percentage of teachers (64%) agreed that the study of grammar was essential to mastery of the language, and only 30% of the teachers agreed that spoken errors should be corrected. (It is interesting to note, however, that 92% of the teachers thought that written errors should be corrected.) Schulz concludes her study with the recommendation that teachers should try to ascertain the beliefs of their students about these and other language learning issues and "establish a fit between their own and their students' expectations" (p. 343).

In a wide-ranging survey of the attitudes of first- and fourth-semester learners of French, Spanish, German, and Italian, Conrad (1997, 1999) found that subjects in his study wanted an approach to language learning that emphasized both communicative language use and attention paid to structure, form, and accuracy. For example, the percentage of students responding to the survey who agreed that understanding grammar was important for their learning ranged from 85.7% to 95.9%, while 69.3% to 87.9% of the students agreed with the statement that they wanted teachers to correct any and all oral errors they might make. (The range of agreement among the students about wanting their written errors corrected was 91% to 100%.)

Though the majority of these studies indicate that students want to receive feedback on their errors, the exact nature of "feedback" that learners receive or the conditions under which they are corrected may differ considerably from study to study and from class to class. The assumption that all learners receive corrective feedback in the same way and with the same degree of enthusiasm is also problematic. As we examine various feedback strategies below, we need to keep in mind that they may work differently with different learners (see, for example, DeKeyser 1993) and should therefore not be used in a rigid or prescriptive fashion.

Walz (1982) has provided a useful review of issues related to error correction and gives practical suggestions for responding to students' errors. He presents various opinions that had been voiced in the literature of the 1970s and early 1980s about which errors should be corrected and which could be safely ignored. Some of the conclusions reached by scholars such as Burt and Kiparsky (1974), Allwright (1975), Cohen (1975), Hendrickson (1979), Ervin (1981), and Walz (1982) were that errors that interfere with comprehension of meaning as well as those that are (1) of high frequency, (2) stigmatizing, or (3) the subject of pedagogical focus should receive the most attention. Walz adds that teachers should be sensitive to the needs and individual concerns of their students and their preferences for feedback.

More recent scholarship investigating the role of feedback in the development of oral skills continues to look at the questions of which errors should receive feedback, when feedback should be given, and what types of feedback are most useful. Several studies have investigated a number of correction strategies, many suggested by Walz and other scholars mentioned above. Strategies range from overt and explicit correction of student errors to more implicit types of feedback. For example, Lyster and Ranta (1997) identified six types of feedback teachers gave students in their study of primary school French immersion classes in Canada. *Explicit correction* involved giving the correct form to learners and telling them that what they said was incorrect. *Recasts* were more implicit, as teachers rephrased students' utterances to eliminate the errors. *Clarification requests*, also a fairly implicit type of correction, were responses where teachers indicated they didn't understand what the student said by saying something like "Pardon?" *Metalinguistic feedback* involved commenting on or asking questions about the form of the students' utterance without explicitly correcting it. *Elicitation* techniques were used to try to get the student to produce the correct form, either by completing the teacher's own restatement, asking the student questions about how something should be said, or asking students to repeat the utterance in a reformulated version. *Repetition* of the incorrect utterance was sometimes used, often with rising intonation or emphasis so that students knew which part was in need of repair (pp. 46–48). Lyster and Ranta found that teachers in the classes they observed overwhelmingly chose recasts as a response to student errors. They also report that this type of corrective response was relatively ineffective as a means of getting students to make a repair in their own speech, and add that students may find recasts somewhat ambiguous, since they may not know if the teacher is responding to the content or the form of what they said. They note that elicitation, metalinguistic feedback, clarification requests, and teacher repetition of errors led to more student self-correction than did recasts or explicit correction by the teacher and that this type of "negotiation of form" (p. 58) can help learners be more actively involved in their own learning.

Because recasting students' errors seems to be a fairly popular form of feedback in content-based and communicative classrooms, there have been a number of other recent studies that have examined its effectiveness as a feedback technique. Long, Inagaki, and Ortega (1998) found some support for the use of recasts over models in helping students of Spanish learn adverb placement, but for a more difficult structure (object topicalization) neither modeling of the correct structure nor recasting was helpful. Results in a group of learners of Japanese were also mixed: There was no significant difference between groups having recasts vs.

models nor any advantage over a control group in learning two Japanese structures (adjective ordering and locative expressions), though both the groups receiving a model and those receiving a recast of a specific morphological feature involved in adjective ordering did perform significantly better than a control group on that feature.

Doughty and Varela (1998) found that recasts were effective in helping learners in a content-based middle-school ESL science class learn to use past tense forms more correctly in science reports. In their study, two intact classes did six science experiments and wrote reports over a period of several weeks of instruction. One group received "focus-on-form" instruction and the other group had no attention to form in their science lessons. The form-focused group received several kinds of feedback that incorporated recasts: (1) small groups working on their reports together were given corrective recasts by the teacher as she circulated among them; (2) recasts were given whenever students produced past and conditional errors in speaking or writing during the experimental period, with some kind of additional drawing of attention to the error; (3) teachers sometimes recasted student responses to questions and then had the whole class repeat the recast; (4) videos were made of student reports and the class looked at them to make improvements, with the teacher pausing the tape when an error of the target type was made and having students repeat the recast; and (5) teachers circled errors of past-time reference in written reports and wrote recasts next to the errors, in addition to providing content-based feedback. The experimental group made significant gains on the two post-tests used in the study, one of which was delayed until two months after the treatment, whereas the control group made no significant progress on the same tests. The authors concluded that "the implementation of the focus on form into the communicative science curriculum was more effective than leaving students to their own devices to develop targetlike ability in past time reference" (p. 135).

A study by Mackey and Philp (1998) also found that intensive recasts were beneficial for more advanced level ESL learners engaged in conversational exchanges and that receiving these recasts was better than just engaging in the interactions alone. The authors looked at the production of questions by students in the experimental and control conditions and found that students whose questions were recast for them received more targeted input, which may have led to the production of more higher-level questions, at least for learners at higher stages of readiness. They also suggest that even though many of the recasts were not repeated by students in their study, they still might have long-term effects, as students who were at more advanced stages of development did significantly improve their use of higher-level questions as a result of the treatment.

Carroll and Swain (1993) compared explicit and implicit types of feedback in a study with adult Spanish-speaking, low-intermediate ESL students. They gave groups of students training in a difficult feature of English (dative alternation) under five different feedback conditions: Group A received explicit metalinguistic information about the feature to be learned when they made an error; Group B students simply were told they were wrong; Group C students were given a model of the correct response with implicit negative feedback about their own response; Group D students were asked if they were sure about their response when they made a mistake; and Group E students received no feedback. Results showed that the students receiving explicit metalinguistic feedback (Group A) did best on the two test sessions following training (with the exception that Group C performed about as well on the first test as Group A). However, all feedback treatment groups (implicit and explicit) performed better than the control group on both tests. Although the researchers suggest that the results should be interpreted with caution due to the limitations of the study, they do conclude that their results indicate that feedback can be helpful in learning linguistic generalizations and applying rules correctly.

Although a number of recent studies have concluded that the provision of feedback in one form or another can be helpful to learners, there are some scholars who would argue that oral feedback in the form of "negative evidence" is either of limited use (e.g., Schwartz 1993) or that it is of no use at all (e.g., Truscott 1999). Truscott further cautions that error correction could have harmful side effects if the teacher's feedback is inconsistent or confusing or if there are negative affective reactions, such as embarrassment or feelings of inferiority. Lyster, Lightbown, and Spada (1999), in responding to Truscott, argue that although knowing when and how to provide effective response to error can be difficult, there is "a growing body of classroom research [that] provides evidence that corrective feedback is pragmatically feasible, potentially effective, and in some cases, necessary" (p. 457). Perhaps the most we can conclude at present from the information reviewed here is that many researchers, teachers, and students feel that some kind of focus on form and response to learner errors ought to be integrated into language instruction, but that more needs to be known about the range of variables that can influence the effectiveness of feedback for different learners and in different instructional situations.

Correction and feedback strategies may differ not only in terms of the learner's capabilities or level of performance, the task at hand, and the focus of the activity, but also in terms of the modality in which the task is accomplished (i.e., oral vs. written production). Written errors may reflect different processing strategies than oral errors and thus require different treatment. In addition, feedback given on written work is usually more private than that given during oral activities and thus might be more extensive. For these and other reasons already mentioned, error-correction policies need to be flexible. However, a certain consistency in the teacher's response to student work is also desirable if students are to derive maximum benefit from the feedback they receive. Swain and Lapkin (1989) point out that inconsistent feedback that has been noted in some Canadian immersion classrooms can lead to confusion and contradictory messages. The dilemma in content-based and communicative language approaches, in their view, is that correcting every error will break the communication flow, while ignoring errors may well hamper progress in learning the language. They suggest that error correction be provided in a "regularized place" in classroom activities, and that rather than have students just repeat a corrected version of their utterances provided by the teacher, they be given opportunities to correct their own work through peer and self-correction.

Thus far in this discussion, we have been considering ways in which teachers can provide feedback or can elicit self-correction from students through such techniques as asking for clarification, pinpointing the error for the student, giving them cues about what might be wrong with what they said, or simply recasting their responses for them so that they might notice the error. Swain and Lapkin's suggestions for small-group work, where individual students work together to improve their own language production efforts, add some interesting possibilities to the repertoire of techniques for responding to error. Earlier in this chapter it was suggested that students might play the role of "monitors" in activities such as the "conversation cards" described earlier, where one student has a card that provides cues to the correct form of questions for structured conversational activities. Swain and Lapkin (1989) propose that students might be asked to listen to or read a sample of their own spontaneous production (either spoken or in writing) and, through discussion with peers and the teacher, using various resources such as dictionaries and textbooks, prepare an "error-free version" (p. 155). They also suggest that it might be helpful for students to have a recording of their own speech or conversations in small groups on occasion, following this with a group correction activity where closer attention can be paid to form and/or content.

Most of the research that has been reviewed in this section relates to integrating a focus on form within a primarily communicative and meaningful approach to language teaching. The challenge for us as teachers is to find ways to provide students with the feedback they need without sacrificing the communicative goals that underlie the majority of language programs today.

Summary: Developing Oral Proficiency

In this chapter, we have considered the nature of language-learner language and explored ways to help students develop their proficiency in speaking. As we have seen throughout this chapter, a proficiency-based approach to oral skill development should provide not only a wide variety of instructional techniques and activity formats, but also a balanced approach to feedback and correction strategies geared to the purposes of the activities chosen for practice. Communicative activities should be encouraged from the beginning of instruction, but there is reason to believe that such activities should be carefully planned so that they are within the range of the students' competence. Activities that require students to communicate their own meaning, yet are easy enough to avoid over-reliance on communication strategies, seem to hold the most promise in a proficiency-oriented approach. Attention to accuracy does not imply a classroom environment where grammar rules reign supreme and correction is rigidly imposed. Rather, the proficiency-oriented classroom is one in which students have ample opportunities to use language creatively and to obtain appropriate feedback with which they can progressively build and refine their interlanguage to approximate the target-language norm. This feedback is provided in an atmosphere characterized by acceptance of error as a necessary condition for linguistic growth, an atmosphere in which the teacher is seen as a valuable resource in the language-learning process.

The ideas presented in this chapter represent only a small sampling of those that have been suggested in the professional literature in recent years. The reader is encouraged to explore some of the sources in the references at the end of the chapter for more ideas for activities and creative practice formats.

Note:

1. Portions of the discussion of the hypotheses and corollaries in Chapter 3 as well as sections in this chapter are revised and expanded from earlier work (Omaggio 1983, 1984). For additional suggestions for classroom practice based on these hypotheses, see "The Proficiency-Oriented Classroom" (Omaggio 1984), listed in the references.

Activities for Review and Discussion

1. Define briefly each of the following terms:

   a. Interlanguage
   b. Fossilization
   c. Variability
   d. Overgeneralization
   e. Interference
   f. Performance error
   g. Communication strategies
   h. Feedback

2. Discuss briefly the five processes central to language acquisition identified by Selinker. Give one or two concrete examples of each of these processes, drawing from your own language-acquisition experience or that of your students, if applicable. If possible, get a sample (oral or written) of language-learner language and identify the possible source(s) of error in that sample.

3. The following terms refer to categories of activities or exercises that can be used to practice oral skills. For each term, give a brief definition and an appropriate sample exercise or activity format.

   a. Precommunicative practice
   b. Either/or questions

    c. Logical conclusions

    d. Personalized completions

    e. Sentence-builders

    f. Conversation cards

    g. Situational role-plays

4. List some of the advantages of using small-group or paired activities for building oral skills. Then list some potential problems or disadvantages in using this type of instructional format. How can such problems be handled or avoided? What are some important considerations to bear in mind when planning small-group work?

5. Examine various language textbooks and evaluate them in terms of their potential for fostering the development of oral skills. Begin your evaluation by listing various criteria that you would consider important in proficiency-oriented textbook materials. Then compare several texts on the basis of your list of criteria.

6. Review the group puzzles, group decision-making activities, and social interaction games that accompany the discussion of Corollaries 2 and 3 (pp. 244–253). Using these activities as a guide, design a simple communication game that could be used with beginning or intermediate students. Be sure to state your objective(s), the context used, the function(s) practiced, and any grammatical features or lexical items highlighted in the activity.

7. What conclusion have you drawn about the effect of errors on native speakers' reactions to interlanguage? List at least five statements summarizing your conclusions, based on your reading of this chapter.

8. Should students' oral errors be corrected in the language-learning process? If not, why not? If so, what criteria would you use for giving feedback on error? Discuss whether your criteria would vary, depending on the type of language activity in which students are involved (e.g., communicative versus manipulative practice, etc.).

References: Chapter 6

Albrechtsen, D., B. Henriksen, and C. Faerch. "Native Speaker Reactions to Learners' Spoken Interlanguage." *Language Learning* 30 (1980): 365–96.

Allwright, R. L. "Problems in the Study of the Language Teacher's Treatment of Learner Error." In M. K. Burt and H. C. Dulay, eds., *On TESOL '75: New Directions in Second Language Learning, Teaching, and Bilingual Education.* Washington, DC. TESOL, 1975.

Beauvois, Margaret Healy. "Computer-Mediated Communication (CMC): *Technology for Improving Speaking and Writing.*" Pp. 165–84 in Michael D. Bush, ed., *Technology-Enhanced Language Learning.* The ACTFL Foreign Language Education Series. Lincolnwood, IL: National Textbook Company, 1997.

————. "Write to Speak: The Effects of Electronic Communication on the Oral Achievement of Fourth Semester French Students." Pp. 93–115 in Judith A. Muyskens, ed., *New Ways of Learning and Teaching: Focus on Technology and Foreign Language Education.* AAUSC Issues in Language Program Direction. Boston: Heinle & Heinle, 1998.

Birckbichler, Diane W. *Creative Activities for the Second Language Classroom.* Language in Education: Theory and Practice Series, no. 48. Washington, DC: Center for Applied Linguistics, 1982.

Bonin, Thérèse and D. Birckbichler. "Real Communication through Conversation Cards." *The Modern Language Journal* 59 (1975): 22–25.

Bragger, Jeannette D. "The Development of Oral Proficiency." In A. Omaggio, ed., *Proficiency, Curriculum, Articulation: The Ties That Bind.* Middlebury, VT: Northeast Conference, 1985.

Burt, Marina and C. Kiparsky. "Global and Local Mistakes." In J. Schumann and N. Stenson, eds., *New Frontiers in Second Language Learning.* Rowley, MA: Newbury House, 1974.

Carroll, Susanne and Merrill Swain. "Explicit and Implicit Negative Feedback: An Empirical Study of the Learning of Linguistic Generalizations." *Studies in Second Language Acquisition* 15 (1993): 357–86.

Cathcart, Ruth L. and Judy E. W. Olsen. "Teachers' and Students' Preferences for Correction of Classroom Conversation Errors." In J. F. Fanselow and R. H. Crymes, eds., *On TESOL '76.* Washington, DC: TESOL (1976): 41–53.

Chastain, Kenneth. "Native Speaker Reaction to Instructor-Identified Student Second Language Errors." *The Modern Language Journal* 64 (1980): 210–15.

Chastain, Kenneth and Gail Guntermann. *¡Imagínate! Managing Conversations in Spanish,* 2nd ed. Boston: Heinle & Heinle, 1991.

Cohen, Andrew. "Error Correction and the Training of Language Teachers." *The Modern Language Journal* 59 (1975): 414–21.

Conrad, Dennis G. "Self-Reported Opinions and Perceptions of First- and Fourth-Semester Foreign Language Learners toward their Language Learning Experience: A Cross-Sectional, Cross-Linguistic Survey." Ph.D. Thesis, University of Illinois at Urbana-Champaign, 1997.

————. "The Student View on Effective Practices in the College Elementary and Intermediate Foreign Language Classroom." *Foreign Language Annals* 32, iv (1999): 494–512.

Corder, S. P. "The Significance of Learners' Errors." *International Review of Applied Linguistics* 5, iv (1967): 161–70.

————. "Language-Learner Language." In J. C. Richards, ed., *Understanding Second and Foreign Language Learning: Issues and Approaches.* Rowley, MA: Newbury House, 1978.

Courchêne, Robert. "The Error Analysis Hypothesis, the Contrastive Analysis Hypothesis, and the Correction of Error in the Second Language Classroom." *TESL Talk* 11 (1980).

Debyser, Francis and H. Laitenberger. "Le Crocodile et le moulin à vent." *Le Français dans le monde* 123 (1976): 14–19.

DeKeyser, Robert M. "The Effect of Error Correction on L2 Grammar Knowledge and Oral Proficiency." *The Modern Language Journal* 77, iv (1993): 501–14.

Doughty, Catherine and Elizabeth Varela. "Communicative Focus on Form." Chapter 6 (pp. 114–38) in C. Doughty and J. Williams, eds., *Focus on Form in Classroom Second Language Acquisition.* Cambridge, England: Cambridge University Press, 1998.

Doughty, Catherine and Jessica Williams, eds. *Focus on Form in Classroom Second Language Acquisition.* Cambridge, England: Cambridge University Press, 1998.

Ellis, Rod. "Discourse Processes in Classroom Second Language Development." Ph.D. Thesis, University of London, 1982. [Cited in Ellis, 1985.]

————. *Understanding Second Language Acquisition.* Oxford: Oxford University Press, 1985.

Ensz, Kathleen. "French Attitudes toward Speech Errors." *The Modern Language Journal* 66 (1982): 133–39.

Ervin, G. "A Study of the Use and Acceptability of Target-Language Communication Strategies Employed by American Students of Russian." Ph.D. Dissertation, The Ohio State University, 1977. [Cited in Ludwig, 1982.]

————. Preconference Workshop for College Teachers of Foreign Languages, Wisconsin Association of Foreign Language Teachers' Conference, Madison, WI, October 1981. [Cited in Magnan, 1982.]

Galloway, Vicki. "Perceptions of the Communicative Efforts of American Students of Spanish." *The Modern Language Journal* 64 (1980): 428–33.

————. "From Defining to Developing Proficiency: A Look at the Decisions." Chapter 2 (pp. 25–73) in H. Byrnes and M. Canale, eds., *Defining and Developing Proficiency: Guidelines, Implementations and Concepts.* ACTFL Foreign Language Education Series. Lincolnwood, IL: National Textbook Company, 1987.

Gass, Susan M. *Input, Interaction, and the Second Language Learner.* Mahwah, NJ: Lawrence Erlbaum Associates, 1997.

Gass, Susan M. and Larry Selinker. *Second Language Acquisition: An Introductory Course.* Hillsdale, NJ: Lawrence Erlbaum Associates, 1994.

Gatbonton, Elizabeth and Norman Segalowitz. "Creative Automatization: Principles for Promoting Fluency Within a Communicative Framework." *TESOL Quarterly* 22, iii (1988): 473–92.

Golato, Andrea. Personal communication, 2000.

Guilford, J. P. "Three Faces of Intellect." *American Psychologist* 14 (1959): 469–79.

Guntermann, Gail. "A Study of the Frequency and Communicative Effects of Errors in Spanish." *The Modern Language Journal* 62 (1978): 249–53.

Guntermann, Gail and J. K. Phillips. *Functional-Notional Concepts: Adapting the Foreign Language Textbook.* Language in Education: Theory and Practice Series, no. 44. Washington, DC: Center for Applied Linguistics, 1982.

Gynan, Shaw N. "Attitudes toward Interlanguage: What is the Object of Study?" *The Modern Language Journal* 68 (1984): 315–21.

Hahn, Sidney and Joyce Michaelis. "Classroom Activities: Oral Proficiency in Action." Chapter 7 (pp. 68–81) in Barbara Snyder, ed., *Second Language*

Aquisition: Preparing for Tomorrow. Report of the Central States Conference on the Teaching of Foreign Languages. Lincolnwood, IL: National Textbook Company, 1986.

Harlow, Linda L. and Judith A. Muyskens. "Priorities for Intermediate-Level Language Instruction." *The Modern Language Journal* 78, ii (1994): 141–54.

Heilenman, Laura K. and Isabelle Kaplan. "Proficiency in Practice: The Foreign Language Curriculum." In Charles James, ed., *Foreign Language Proficiency in the Classroom and Beyond.* ACTFL Foreign Language Education Series, vol. 16. Lincolnwood, IL: National Textbook Company, 1985.

Hendrickson, James M. "Evaluating Spontaneous Communication Through Systematic Error Analysis." *Foreign Language Annals* 12 (1979): 357–64.

Higgs, Theodore V. "Proficiency Assessment and the Humanities." *ADFL Bulletin* 18, i (1986): 6–8.

Kramsch, Claire J. *Discourse Analysis and Second Language Teaching.* Language in Education: Theory and Practice Series, no. 37. Washington, DC: Center for Applied Linguistics, 1981.

———. "Culture and Constructs: Communicating Attitudes and Values in the Foreign Language Classroom." *Foreign Language Annals* 16, vi (1983): 437–48.

Krashen, Stephen. *Principles and Practice in Second Language Acquisition.* New York: Pergamon Press, 1982.

Littlewood, William. *Communicative Language Teaching: An Introduction.* Cambridge: Cambridge University Press, 1981.

Long, Michael. "A Role for Instruction in Second Language Acquisition: Task-Based Language Training." Pp. 77–99 in K. Hyltenstam and M. Pienemann, eds., *Modelling and Assessing Second Language Development.* Clevedon: Multilingual Matters, 1985.

Long, Michael, Shunji Inagaki, and Lourdes Ortega. "The Role of Implicit Negative Feedback in SLA: Models and Recasts in Japanese and Spanish." *The Modern Language Journal* 82, iii (1998): 357–71.

Ludwig, Jeannette. "Native Speaker Judgments of Second Language Learners' Efforts at Communication: A Review." *The Modern Language Journal* 66 (1982): 274–83.

Lyster, Roy, Patsy M. Lightbown, and Nina Spada. "A Response to Truscott's 'What's Wrong with Oral Grammar Correction.' " *The Canadian Modern Language Review* 55, iv (June 1999): 457–67.

Lyster, Roy and Leila Ranta. "Corrective Feedback and Learner Uptake: Negotiation of Form in Communicative Classrooms." *Studies in Second Language Acquisition* 19 (1997): 37–66.

Mackey, Alison and Jenefer Philp. "Conversational Interaction and Second Language Development: Recasts, Response, and Red Herrings?" *The Modern Language Journal* 82, iii (1998): 338–56.

Magnan, Sally S. "Native Speaker Reaction as a Criterion for Error Correction." In A. Garfinkle, ed., *ESL and the Foreign Language Teacher.* Report of the Central States Conference on the Teaching of Foreign Languages. Lincolnwood, IL: National Textbook Company, 1982.

McDonough, Kim and Alison Mackey. "Communicative Tasks, Conversational Interaction and Linguistic Form: An Empirical Study of Thai." *Foreign Language Annals* 33, i (2000): 82–91.

Nemser, W. "Approximative Systems of Foreign Language Learners." *International Review of Applied Linguistics* 9, ii (1971): 115–23.

Ngame, Matuku. "A Comparison of French and Kiswahili Native-Speaker Reactions to Nonnative Speech." Ph.D. Dissertation, University of Illinois at Urbana-Champaign, 1992.

Nunan, David. *Designing Tasks for the Communicative Classroom.* Cambridge, England: Cambridge University Press, 1989.

Omaggio, Alice C. "Real Communication: Speaking a Living Language." *Foreign Language Annals* 9, ii (1976): 131–33.

———. *Helping Learners Succeed: Activities for the Foreign Language Classroom.* Language in Education: Theory and Practice Series, no. 36. Washington, DC: Center for Applied Linguistics, 1981.

———. "Using Games and Simulations for the Development of Functional Proficiency in a Second Language." *Canadian Modern Language Review* 38 (1982): 517–46.

———. "Methodology in Transition: The New Focus on Proficiency." *The Modern Language Journal* 67, iv (1983): 330–41.

———. "The Proficiency-Oriented Classroom." In T. V. Higgs, ed., *Teaching for Proficiency, the Organizing Principle.* ACTFL Foreign Language Education Series, vol. 15. Lincolnwood, IL: National Textbook Company, 1984.

Politzer, R. L. "Errors of English Speakers of German as Perceived and Evaluated by German Natives." *The Modern Language Journal* 62 (1978): 253–61.

Richards, Jack C. "Error Analysis and Second Language Strategies." Pp. 32–53 in J. H. Schumann and N. Stenson, eds., *New Frontiers in Second Language Learning.* Rowley, MA: Newbury House, 1974.

Rivers, Wilga M., M. M. Azevedo, W. H. Heflin, Jr. and R. Hyman-Opler. *A Practical Guide to the Teaching of Spanish.* New York: Oxford University Press, 1976.

Schairer, Karen E. "Native Speaker Reaction to Non-Native Speech." *The Modern Language Journal* 76, iii (1992): 309–19.

Schmidt, Elizabeth. *Let's Play Games in German.* Lincolnwood, IL: National Textbook Company, 1977.

Schulz, Renate A. "Focus on Form in the Foreign Language Classroom: Students' and Teachers' Views on Error Correction and the Role of Grammar." *Foreign Language Annals* 29, iii (1996): 343–64.

Schumann, John H. and Nancy Stenson, eds. *New Frontiers in Second Language Learning.* Rowley, MA: Newbury House, 1974.

Schwartz, Bonnie D. "On Explicit and Negative Data Effecting and Affecting *Competence* and *Linguistic Behavior.*" *Studies in Second Language Acquisition* 15 (1993): 147–63.

Seelye, H. Ned. *Teaching Culture: Strategies for Intercultural Communication.* Lincolnwood, IL: National Textbook Company, 1984. 3rd edition, 1993.

Seliger, Herbert. "Psycholinguistic Issues in Second Language Acquisition."

Chapter 1 (pp. 15–40) in Leslie M. Beebe, ed., *Issues in Second Language Acquisition: Multiple Perspectives*. Rowley, MA: Newbury House, 1988.

Selinker, Larry. "Interlanguage." *International Review of Applied Linguistics* 10, iii (1972): 209–31.

———. "Interlanguage." In J. Schumann and N. Stenson, eds., *New Frontiers in Second Language Learning*. Rowley, MA: Newbury House, 1974.

Selinker, Larry and John T. Lamendella. "The Role of Extrinsic Feedback in Interlanguage Fossilization." *Language Learning* 29 (1979): 363–75.

Shiffrin, R. and W. Schneider. "Controlled and Automatic Human Information Processing: II. Perceptual Learning, Automatic Attending and a General Theory." *Psychological Review* 84 (1977): 127–90.

Standards for Foreign Language Learning: Preparing for the 21st Century. National Standards in Foreign Language Education Project, 1996.

Standards for Foreign Language Learning in the 21st Century. National Standards in Foreign Language Education Project, 1999.

Swain, Merrill. "Communicative Competence: Some Roles of Comprehensible Input and Comprehensible Output in Its Development." Chapter 14 (pp. 235–53) in Susan M. Gass and Carolyn S. Madden, eds. *Input in Second Language Acquisition*. Rowley, MA: Newbury House, 1985.

———. "Three Functions of Output in Second Language Learning." Chapter 8 (pp. 125–44) in G. Cook and B. Seidlhofer, eds., *Principle and Practice in Applied Linguistics: Studies in Honour of H. G. Widdowson*. Oxford, England: Oxford University Press, 1995.

Swain, Merrill and Sharon Lapkin. "Canadian Immersion and Adult Second Language Teaching: What's the Connection?" *The Modern Language Journal* 73, ii (1989): 150–59.

Tarone, Elaine. "Conscious Communication Strategies in Interlanguage: A Progress Report." In H. Brown, C. Yorio, and R. Crymes, eds., *On TESOL '77: Teaching and Learning ESL*. Washington, DC: TESOL, 1978.

———. "Communicative Strategies, Foreigner Talk, and Repair in Interlanguage." *Language Learning* 30 (1980): 417–31.

———. "On the Variability of Interlanguage Systems." *Applied Linguistics* 4 (1983): 143–63.

Truscott, John. "What's Wrong with Oral Grammar Correction." *The Canadian Modern Language Review* 55, iv (June 1999): 437–56.

Ur, Penny. *Grammar Practice Activities: A Practical Guide for Teachers*. Cambridge: Cambridge University Press, 1988.

Van Ek, J. A. *The Threshold Level in a European Unit/Credit System for Modern Language Learning for Adults*. Strasbourg: Council of Europe, 1975. (Republished in 1980 by Pergamon Press as *Threshold Level English*.)

Walker, John L. "Opinions of University Students About Language Teaching." *Foreign Language Annals* 7 (1973): 102–5.

Walz, Joel C. *Error Correction Techniques for the Foreign Language Classroom*. Language in Education: Theory and Practice Series, no. 50. Washington, DC: Center for Applied Linguistics, 1982.

Wilkins, D. A. *Notional Syllabuses*. Oxford: Oxford University Press, 1976.

Zelson, Sidney. "Skill-Using, Self-Expression and Communication Exercises in Three Dimensions." In E. Joiner and P. Westphal, eds., *Developing Communication Skills*. Rowley, MA: Newbury House, 1978.

7 SEVEN
Becoming Proficient in Writing

If learning to write in a second language were simply a matter of knowing how to "write things down" in the new code, then teaching writing would be a relatively easy task. A few minutes in each class period could be devoted to dictation, transcription, or manipulative written exercises, and a few guided compositions could be assigned for homework during the course of the semester, after which we could all rest easy because we had cleverly managed to work the fourth skill into our crowded curriculum with a minimum of effort.

Unfortunately, learning to write—even in one's native language—is not simply a matter of "writing things down." The fact that it took 45 minutes to compose the preceding paragraph, and that it is taking even longer to write this one, attests to the truth of the statement that writing is more than the mere transcription of speech. Most people who have attempted to put pen to paper to communicate ideas would agree that expressing oneself clearly in writing can be a slow and painful process. Rivers (1975) makes this point in her discussion of the differences between speech and writing:

> Many who know how to "write things down" in their native language avoid expressing themselves in writing almost completely, even in personal letters. To write so that one is really communicating a message, isolated in place and time, is an art which requires consciously directed effort and deliberate choice of language. The old saying, "If you can say it, you can write it," is simplistic in its concept of the communicative aspect of writing (p. 237).

In order to capture the complexity of the writing process, various scholars have suggested the use of more precise terminology to clarify the distinction between the mechanical aspects of writing and the more sophisticated processes involved in written communication. For example, Bizzell (1986) distinguishes between *composing,* which refers to all the processes that lead to the writing of something— reflection about the topic, gathering of information, taking of notes, working on a series of drafts, revising—and *writing,* which refers specifically to the transcription of the material itself. In her view, then, *writing* is subsumed under *composing.*

Dvorak (1986), on the other hand, subsumes both *transcription* (focusing on form) and *composition* (focusing on effective development and communication of ideas) under the more generic term *writing,* which she uses to refer to "all of the various activities that involve transferring thought to paper" (p. 145).

Perhaps *writing* might best be viewed as a continuum of activities that range from the more mechanical or formal aspects of "writing down" on the one end to the more complex act of composing on the other. This seems most sensible in the context of second and foreign language learning, where beginning language students must first struggle with the transcription of speech before they can engage in more complex forms of written expression. This is particularly true in languages where the writing system itself poses a difficult challenge, such as in Japanese, Chinese, Arabic, Russian, or Hebrew, for English-speaking learners. But even when the same basic alphabet is used in the new language, "writing down" can be a difficult task for the Novice or Intermediate student.

Magnan (1985) suggests that in secondary schools and in lower-level college classrooms, we might expect students at first to write down or transcribe in the second language something they might say. In that way, writing might be considered primarily as a support skill for speaking. Gradually, however, we can help students shape their written production in the direction of the conventions of proficient writers, teaching the cognitive processes of organization, elaboration, comparison and contrast, explanation, generalization, and the like.

The distinction between writing as a support skill and writing as a communicative art parallels, to some extent, Rivers's (1975) distinction between skill-getting and skill-using activities. In Rivers's schema, skill-getting emphasizes the understanding of the way the language operates, while skill-using emphasizes the use of the code for expressive writing and purposeful communication. Written practice in the skill-getting phase includes two categories of activities: (1) *writing down,* or exercises involving copying or reproduction of learned material, concentrating on the conventions of spelling, punctuation, grammatical agreements, and the like, and (2) *writing in the language,* in which students engage in a variety of grammar-practice activities of a controlled nature in order to reinforce their growing knowledge of the linguistic system. Because these two categories of activities focus on writing as a support skill and do not constitute creative or expressive writing, Rivers describes a second set of activities under skill-using that take students beyond linguistic manipulation. Such activities are designed to develop flexibility and creative language use and include (1) *flexibility measures,* in which students begin writing within a framework (including transformation exercises, sentence-combining practice, expansions, embellishments, idea frames, and similar activities), and (2) *expressive writing,* which includes guided and free compositions that fulfill the normal purposes for which we write in the real world. These "normal purposes" include such things as practical concerns (note taking for study purposes, letter writing, getting and giving information) and creative writing for entertainment and self-expression.

Rivers points out that the most difficult task for the teacher is to know how to effectively bridge the gap between skill-getting and skill-using activities. Perhaps one solution is to minimize the use of writing practice activities that are manipulative or impersonal in nature and choose instead activities that are contextualized, meaningful, and personalized, even when students are focusing primarily on form. Another possibility is to include various kinds of creative writing activities, such as journal writing or *cinquain* poetry (see pp. 288–289), in beginning courses to encourage students to express their own meaning within the limits of their developing competence. As was suggested in the last chapter, a blend of diverse tasks that elicit performance ranging from the "careful style" to the "vernacular style" (Tarone 1983) may be most beneficial for the development of spoken or written proficiency at all levels.

Most of the activities described in this chapter attempt to combine writing purposes to some extent: Writing is directed in some fashion in the lower ranges of proficiency to support that which is learned in class (i.e., grammatical structures, vocabulary, discourse features), yet assignments and exercises present language in the context of full discourse so that students learn how to write for communicative purposes. As students' competence increases, writing assignments become less structured, less teacher-directed, and more creative in nature. Students are encouraged to use the language independently to inform, narrate, describe, question, persuade, express feelings and attitudes, discuss ideas, and support points of view. Writing instruction can be designed to help students understand writing as discourse with specific rhetorical strategies and qualities that can vary according to the writer's purpose, and even according to the writer's cultural background (Kaplan 1966, 1988). Various conventions of written language that distinguishes it in style and tone from spoken discourse can be learned and practiced. Second language writing instruction that is carefully planned can help students learn more about the composing process itself, a recursive, problem-solving activity that has the potential to affect students' writing and thinking skills in their native language, thus extending the benefits of language study well beyond the limits of the second-language classroom.

As we explore various activities for teaching writing in the foreign language classroom, it is important to consider the many options that are now available to students and teachers, from the traditional tools of worksheets, workbooks, compositions, and journals to the use of CD-ROMs, e-mail, computer conferencing, word processors, and writing assistant programs. Kern (1998) presents a well-rounded discussion of the role that technology can play in fostering social interaction and foreign language literacy through written communication, pointing out that "technological advances have always created new possibilities as well as challenges . . ." (p. 57). Several ideas for incorporating technology in the writing curriculum from the Novice to the Advanced levels are given throughout the next portions of this chapter, with a more extensive discussion of the use of technology in the teaching of writing on pages 301–310.

The remainder of this chapter is divided into two main sections. The first section presents activities that are most appropriate for students at the Novice and Intermediate levels of writing proficiency. It includes a blend of guided and open-ended writing practice formats, beginning with strategies for teaching writing as a *support skill,* where the focus is primarily on the mastery of formal features of the written language. Activities designed to bridge the gap to free expression are also included in this section, followed by a discussion of technology and its potential for enhancing students' writing. The second section of the chapter discusses approaches to writing primarily for expressive communication. Research about the composing process from both first-language and second-language perspectives is reviewed, and various approaches to teaching writing are described. Following this review of the literature, creative writing activities for both the Intermediate and Advanced levels are illustrated, and practical suggestions for responding to student writing are given.

Approaches to Teaching Writing at the Lower Levels of Proficiency

Let us turn now to an examination of several writing activities, beginning with those most appropriate to the Novice level.

Techniques for Teaching Writing as a Support Skill

In almost all of the following activities, writing is not practiced in isolation; rather, skills are practiced in an interdependent fashion. For example, a transcribing activity, such as dictation or note taking, will involve listening and/or reading comprehension. An activity in which students fill out a form or schedule will involve the ability to read the document to be completed. Obviously, simultaneous use of several skills is common in natural and authentic communication, and it makes sense to practice various skills in concert in the second-language classroom to approximate this type of authenticity.

Second, although the activity samples in this section are chosen to illustrate how writing can be used to *support* the learning of formal aspects of the new language, there is some concern as well for structuring these tasks so that students can begin to write in discourse-length frames for communicative purposes. Thus there is a planned overlap in these early writing activities between form and function so that the gap between skill-getting and skill-using can be bridged more effectively as students' writing skills progress.

Novice-Level Activities

Simple Description with Visuals

Content: Objects in a room

Functions: Identifying and listing, simple description

Student Task: Students who have just learned vocabulary for the rooms of the house and some of the furnishings describe a simple picture or pictures in their text, such as the one in Illustration 7.1. Students could be given prompts to start the description, such as the following:

En el dormitorio de Alicia, hay . . .

pero Alicia no tiene . . .

In Alice's dorm room, there is/there are. . . ,

but Alice doesn't have . . .

Source: The picture in Illustration 7.1 is taken from Hendrickson and Borrás Alvarez (1999), p. 43. A similar idea for a Novice-level description is given in Magnan (1985), p. 125. See this source for a variety of suggestions for Novice-level descriptions with pictures.

Illustration 7.1
Student
Dormitory Room

Source: Hendrickson and Borrás Alvarez, *Intercambios*, 3rd ed. Boston, MA: Heinle & Heinle, 1999, p. 43.

Variations: (1) Teachers can supply pictures of places in which they have stayed in the target culture, and students can work on writing simple descriptions of a picture of their choice. (Alternatively, teachers might supply students with brochures of hotels, bed-and-breakfast guidebooks, or the like, with pictures of rooms to be described.) (2) Students can be asked to go to a target-language Web site for hotels or other types of lodging where pictures of rooms are available. Students can then select a room of their choice to describe.

Follow-up: For situations where a particular picture has been selected for students to describe, the teacher might provide his or her own description to students after the task has been completed so that they can compare their descriptions with the model.

Guided Description with Student-Generated Visual

Content: Personality traits/physical description

Functions: Describing a person, talking about likes/dislikes

Grammatical Feature: The use of *c'est* vs. *il/elle est* in French

Student Task: Students are asked to draw a picture of someone they know—their roommate, a family member, a friend—or of a famous person of their choice (a political figure, a rock star, etc.). They then write one sentence telling whether they like or dislike this person, followed by a number of sentences using the target grammatical feature to describe the person, as in the example in Illustration 7.2. *Source:* Terry (2000).

Illustration 7.2
Describing a Friend or Family Member

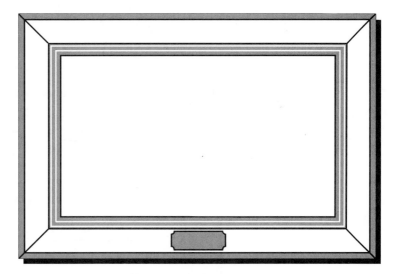

J'aime . . . Je déteste

In the box below, draw a picture of your roommate (or brother or sister). Identify the "victim." Then, write one sentence telling if you like or dislike this person. Then write *three* sentences using **ce** as the subject and *three* using **il/elle** in which you tell me something about this person.

Voici un «portrait» de _____ .

1. _____

2. _____

3. _____

4. _____

5. _____

6. _____

Dictation and Variations

Many of the ideas for dictation presented in Chapter 5 (see pp. 199–200) are usable with students at the Novice level. Though the dictation activity can be based on familiar material, it is best to use some recombination or novel approach to that material so that students are stimulated to use both their listening and writing skills. Dictated passages of at least a paragraph in length are best, since this presents language in a discourse-length context. Partial dictations or variations on dictation should also be contextualized. (For an excellent source of ideas on using dictation at various levels of proficiency, see Davis and Rinvolucri 1988.)

Filling in Forms

SAMPLE 1

A Restaurant Menu

Content: Foods

Functions: Naming and listing

Student Task: Students are provided with the incomplete menu in Illustration 7.3. They are told that they have just opened a restaurant and that it is up to them to decide what dishes they would like to offer. Categories of foods (appetizers, fish, meat, dessert, and drinks) are given, but no specific foods are named. Students are also asked to make up a name for their restaurant.

Illustration 7.3
Form for Use in Completing a Restaurant Menu

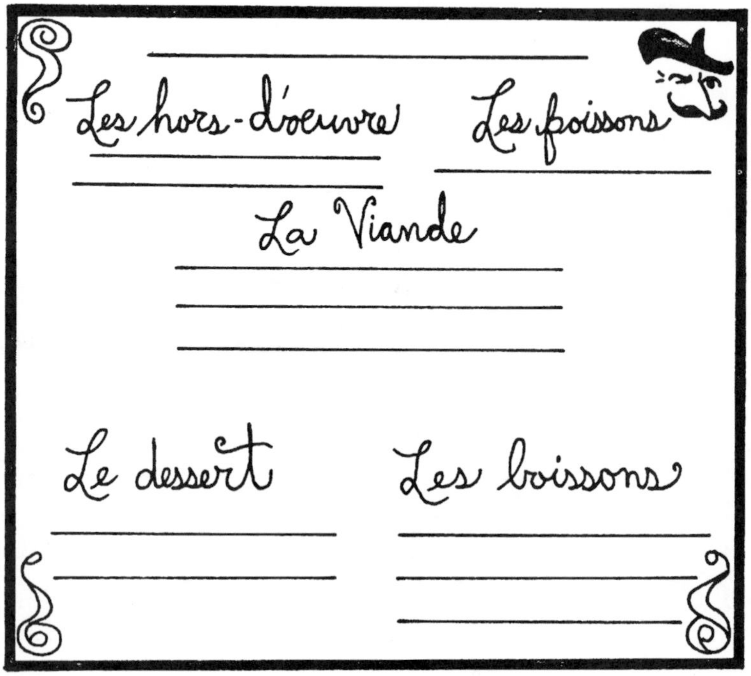

Source: Adapted from Terry (1985).

Personal Information and Preferences

Content: Autobiographical information, likes and dislikes

Functions: Listing, simple description

Student Task: Students are given the computer-dating form pictured in Illustration 7.4. They are told to fill out the form, giving as true a picture of themselves as possible.

Illustration 7.4
Computer-Dating
Form

Ordena-Par
Calle Velázquez, N°40
piso 2
Madrid 28016
España

Adjuntar
una foto
reciente
aquí

Apellido _____ Nombre _____

Dirección _____

Teléfono _____ Profesión _____ Nacimiento_____

Busco _____

_____

_____

Soy _____

_____

_____

Me gusta(n) _____

_____

_____

No me gusta(n) _____

_____

_____

Información adicional _____

_____

_____

_____

(firmado)

Source: Terry (2000).

Sending an Electronic Postcard

There are a number of Internet sites in various languages that offer free electronic greeting cards or postcards that students can send. Such sites are easily found by accessing a search engine in the target language and typing the foreign language equivalent for "postcard" in the search box. The sample that follows in Spanish represents in generic form some of the types of information that such sites typically ask for. These sites also offer a number of colorful picture choices for the front of the "card," often in categories such as flowers, animals, travel scenes, signs of the zodiac, and the like. Cards can be chosen to commemorate birthdays and other occasions, and some sites offer musical selections that can be "played" along with the greeting.

Content: A short message of several sentences based on familiar themes/topics

Functions: Writing a postcard, using connected discourse

Student Task: Students are asked to write a brief message to their instructor using a target-language site that offers free electronic greeting cards or postcards.

Sample: See Illustration 7.5.

Source: Generic sample of postcard information in Illustration 7.5 is provided by Terry (2000).

Cinquain Poetry

Content: Varied

Functions: Creating poetry within a simple framework

Student Task: Students, either individually, in small groups, or as a whole class, create simple poems within a very structured framework, using vocabulary they have learned and any supplied by the teacher, as requested. A *cinquain* poem consists of five lines, constructed according to the following scheme:

Line 1: States a subject in one word (usually a noun).

Line 2: Describes the subject in two words (often a noun and an adjective or two adjectives).

Line 3: Describes an action about the subject in three words (often three infinitives or a three-word sentence).

Line 4: Expresses an emotion about the subject in four words.

Line 5: Restates the subject in another single word that reflects what has already been said (usually a noun).

Sample Poems in English, French, and Spanish

Tree

Green branches

Growing, living, reaching

Your shade protects me

Peace

Hachikof.

I'll Try to work.

Chien
Optimiste perpetuel
Attend son maître
Il entend des pas . . .
Joie!

SIU
big, small
International, home Uni...
go Salukis go dawg
Salukis

Casa
Hogar sencillo
Necesita pintura, reparos
Llena de tantos recuerdos
Refugio

Source: The format for *cinquain* poetry is from Allen and Valette (1977), pp. 321–322.

Illustration 7.5
Sample Electronic Postcard

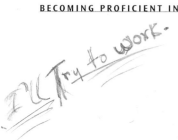

Example:

Para: [nombre del destinatario]
¡Eres un gran amigo!
[Mensaje opcional]
De: [su nombre aquí]
roberto@xxxx.com

Personalice su postal gratis rellenando en formulario que aparace a continuación

Nombre del destinatario:	
Correo-e del destinatario:	
Tu nombre:	
Tu correo-e:	
Tu mensaje: (Máx. 4.000 caracteres)	
Mensaje opcional (Máx. 4.000 caracteres)	
Elegir la fecha de envío:	HOY ▼

■ Intermediate-Level Activities: Preparing for Advanced-Level Writing

The activity types suggested in this section can serve as a kind of "bridge" between the structured writing activities of the previous section and those that are designed for writing on a more advanced level, to be described in the second half of this chapter. Students in the Intermediate range in writing are generally able to create with the language in very familiar contexts, using simple vocabulary, limited narration and description in present time, and very basic grammatical structures. As students' skills develop, a wider range of tasks, structures, and vocabulary can be included in designing composition topics. Some newer first-year textbooks include guidelines for developing composing skills and step-by-step instructions to help students create texts that coincide with their present level of proficiency. (For an example in French, see Muyskens and Omaggio Hadley 1998.) In addition to textbook guidelines, writing assistant computer programs are available that can give students in the Novice and Intermediate range guidance in task-oriented writing. (For specific examples of computer-assisted writing tasks using such programs, see the section entitled "Writing and the Computer" later in this chapter.) Teachers can also prepare their own writing activities, either to teach requisite skills (such as writing a simple narration in the past, combining sentences to produce fuller discourse, or generating paragraphs from notes) or to engage students in a multidraft composing process. Suggestions for teacher-created activities such as these are included in the following pages.

The first few activities in this section emphasize focused written practice. In order to move toward the Advanced level, students will need practice in using both past and future time in more extended narration and description. Therefore, activities that are designed to encourage the use of past and future tenses in both structured practice and guided composition are appropriate for students presently at the Intermediate level.

There are also suggestions in this section for guided writing activities that proceed in stages, with each task adding something new to the written text as students learn to refine and elaborate upon their previous drafts. The use of the computer and sample activities from a computer-assisted instructional program for writing in French are also illustrated.

Slash Sentences

SAMPLE (INTERMEDIATE)

Context: Summer leisure activities

Function: Simple narration in the present

Student Task: This activity directs students to write a short narrative from the sentence cues given. The story is about the LeBlanc's summer activities.

> *Un été à la campagne.* Faites des phrases complètes selon le modèle.
>
> Modèle: Les LeBlanc/passer/l'été/à la campagne
>   Les LeBlanc passent l'été à la campagne.
>
> 1. le matin/tout/famille/se réveiller/vers/8 heures
> 2. M. LeBlanc/descendre/la cuisine/préparer/café

3. Son/femme/faire/petit déjeuner/puis/sortir/dans/le jardin

4. M. LeBlanc/et/son/fils/aller/à la pêche

5. Natalie/se promener/dans/collines/près de/maison . . . etc.

A Summer in the Country. Make complete sentences according to the model.

Model: The LeBlancs/to spend/summer in the country
The LeBlancs spend the summer in the country.

1. *In the morning/all/family/to get up/around/8 o'clock*

2. *Mr. LeBlanc/to go downstairs/the kitchen/to prepare/coffee*

3. *His/wife/to make/breakfast/then/to go outside/in/the garden*

4. *Mr. LeBlanc/and/his/son/to go/fishing*

5. *Natalie/to take a walk/in/hills/near/house . . . etc.*

Follow-up Task: (Preparing for Advanced level)
Students are now directed to write the paragraph in the past, talking about the way this family used to spend summer vacations. They are asked to embellish the story, adding details about the surroundings, the weather, and specific activities. In French, this story would be written in the imperfect tense. The exercise thus focuses on practicing past-tense narration and adding some elaborative detail, preparing students for writing at the Advanced level.

Variation: Students write a narration about their own family's summer activities, using this exercise as a prewriting stimulus activity.

Telegraphic Sentences

SAMPLE (INTERMEDIATE; PREPARING FOR ADVANCED LEVEL)

Context: Current events

Function: Reporting facts of a story

Purpose: Like slash sentences, telegraphic sentences provide the essential elements to be incorporated into a story, but the format of the stimulus material looks more like a set of notes than a grammatical exercise, thus more closely simulating an authentic task. Students are encouraged to embellish the story as they like. As an Intermediate-level task, students are asked to describe the events using the present tense, as if they were eyewitnesses reporting the action as it happens. As a preparation for Advanced-level writing, students narrate the events as a reporter would, using appropriate past tenses as they tell the story presented in the telegraphic cues.

Student Task: You are a journalist who has just interviewed a witness to a UFO incident. The notes you made during the interview are given below. Write out your report in as much detail as you can, recounting the events in the past. (Notes can be in the target language or in English, depending on how much structure and vocabulary the teacher wishes to provide to guide the writing task.)

Notes: Henry Stewart, in field, working, about 10 A.M., June 13. Hears strange noise, looks up. Sees blinding light. Distinguishes three objects. Gets frightened. Drops everything and runs for farmhouse. Calls wife to come see. Objects disappear as quickly as they came. Wife doesn't believe story.

Partial Translation

SAMPLE (INTERMEDIATE)

Context: A visit to Spain as an exchange student

Function: Writing a thank-you letter

Purpose: This activity encourages students to use recently learned vocabulary and grammatical structures in a context that is appropriate to the Intermediate level—writing a letter to family and friends. The activity is structured to focus on discrete points of grammar, but the end product of the writing task can serve as a model for letter writing in a subsequent activity.

Student Task: Patrick has just returned from studying abroad in Granada, Spain, and is writing a thank-you letter to the family with whom he stayed. Complete the letter in Spanish, using the translation that follows it as a guide to the missing words.

Santa Fe, 10 de julio de 2000

Queridos Sr. y Sra. Álvarez,
_____ que salé de Granada y los extraño. Mi estancia en su casa _____ y les agradezco con todo el corazón su hospitalidad. _____ mucho en España y _____ mis estudios de español en mi escuela y _____ en la universidad. _____ a mis amigos de mi escuela de Granada y de mi familia española.
   Mil gracias y _____ que Uds. puedan visitar la ciudad de Santa Fe _____ . Mis padres quisieran conocerlos.

Un abrazo,
Patrick

Dear Mr. and Mrs. Álvarez,
   I left Granada two weeks ago, and I miss you. My stay in your house was unforgettable, and I thank you with all my heart for your hospitality. I learned a lot in Spain, and I'm going to continue my studies in Spanish in my school and afterwards at the university. I'm going to talk to my friends at school about my school in Granada and my Spanish family.
   Many thanks, and I hope that you can visit the city of Santa Fe some day. My parents would like to meet you.

Hugs,
Patrick

Source: Text adapted from Gutiérrez and Rosser (1992), p. 164.

Sentence Combining

SAMPLE (PREPARING FOR ADVANCED LEVEL)

Context: Story in a film

Function: Narrating a story

Purpose: To help students link simple propositions into more complex sentences. In sentence-combining activities, a set of simple sentences or propositions are consolidated through the embedding of words, phrases, and clauses so that the meaning of the whole set is conveyed in one sentence. For example, the following set of simple propositions is combined below:

1. The man is tall.
2. The man has dark hair.
3. The man is standing by the counter.
4. The man looks suspicious.

Combination: The tall, dark-haired man standing by the counter looks suspicious.

Exercises in sentence combining can be used at the sentence, paragraph, or composition level. Students can be asked to produce a story several paragraphs in length. For example, a description of a film or other narrative could be broken down into simple propositions. Students then try to combine those propositions into more complex sentences and compare their combinations to the original. This technique can be used to teach principles of sentence and paragraph construction and to help students recognize the importance of connectors, qualifiers, and other discourse features.

For extensive examples of sentence-combining activities, see Cooper 1980; Cooper, Morain, and Kalivoda 1980; Johnson 1982; and Trivelli 1983.

Paragraph Completion

SAMPLE (INTERMEDIATE)

Context: Personal appearance

Function: Description

Purpose: This task is designed to aid writers at the Intermediate level in improving their ability to describe someone in detail.

Student Task: Students writing in French use their imagination to complete the description of the person in the photograph given in Illustration 7.6.

Paragraph

M. Duval était un ___ homme ___ aux cheveux ___ et ___. Il avait les yeux ___ et portait une barbe ___ et ___. C'était un homme très ___ qui pensait beaucoup (à) ___. Ce matin-là, il avait l'air ___ parce qu'il ___. . . .

Mr. Duval was a ___, ___ man with ___, ___ hair. He had ___ eyes and wore a ___, ___ beard. He was a very ___ man who thought a lot about ___. That morning, he seemed ___ because he ___. . . .

Source: Idea for activity format from Raimes (1978). Activity original.

■ Guided Compositions: A Bridge to Free Expression

The activity suggestions that follow have some of the characteristics of an approach to writing instruction that Hillocks (1986) calls "the environmental mode" (p. 122) and that Applebee (1986) refers to as "a structured process" orien-

Illustration 7.6
Photograph for Use in
Writing a Personal
Description

tation to composition (p. 105). In this approach, specific tasks are organized by the teacher to help students engage in the composing process and practice certain aspects of writing that are important to the task at hand. Other aspects of this approach might include the use of model texts and small-group interaction as students work to improve their compositions, using evaluative checklists or other tools provided by the teacher (Hillocks 1986). The suggestions given here show how composition tasks can be guided through the use of prewriting and semi-structured writing activities for Intermediate-level writers who are preparing to engage more fully in the composing process.

Multiple Tasks Based on a Picture

Scanlan (1980) suggests that compositions might be based on the analysis of a photograph, where students practice extensive description and narration and react personally to the elements in the picture. He recommends that pictures be set in the target culture, incorporating clear elements that characterize it, and that they be easy for students to identify with personally. To exploit the picture for writing practice, Scanlan advises that students be asked not only to describe the picture in detail but also to imagine what might have happened before or after it was taken or visualize themselves in the scene interacting in some way with the people depicted. Raimes (1983) also suggests developing a sequence of writing tasks around a culturally authentic picture, such as a wedding photo, with each task selected to move students to a slightly higher level of difficulty as they add vocabulary, structural sophistication, and/or organizational skills. In the series of tasks given below, a number of these ideas are put into practice, using the picture in Illustration 7.6 as a point of departure and a stimulus for creativity.

Task 1: *Prewriting* (Intermediate)
Students in small groups look at the picture and write as many words and expressions that come to mind as they can. They may be asked to think of vocabulary that will be useful in describing the person or objects in the picture, and also to write down words associated with those items to form semantic networks. In addition, students can write down words and expressions depicting feelings that the picture evokes. Groups might then be asked to share their lists with others in the class, or the teacher might make a master list on the board.

Task 2: *Prewriting* (Intermediate)
An alternate task (or one done subsequent to Task 1, above) involves small groups writing down questions that the picture evokes in their minds. Each group then shares its list of questions with the rest of the class to provide a further stimulus for writing.

Task 3: *Description* (Intermediate)
Using the vocabulary generated from Task 1, above, students write a brief composition describing the photograph in as much detail as they can. Students then share their descriptions with one or two other students in the class. The group members can be asked to pool their descriptions to write a second, more complete draft describing the photograph.

Task 4: *Narration* (Intermediate)
Using the question sets generated from Task 2, individuals or small groups of students write a narration about the man in the picture, answering the questions given to them by another group in the class. Stories can then be read aloud and compared or shared by exchanging them with stories written by classmates.

Task 5: *Narration in the Past* (Preparing for Advanced level)
Students are asked to imagine that the man in the photograph is thinking about the first time he visited Paris as a young man. In small groups, they develop a list of possible events, places visited, and persons he might have met in his travels.

After discussing various possibilities, students create a story, individually or in small groups, and recount the events in the past, with as much imaginative detail as possible.

Elaboration

Context: A trip to Paris

Functions: Narration and description

Purpose: Students learn to write fuller descriptions and narrations through the use of cues supplied by the teacher on their first draft. For example, the teacher might take a student's composition and insert an asterisk at every point in the narration where an elaboration could be made. Elaborations might include the addition of adjectives, adverbs, relative clauses, or whole sentences. A more complex cuing system consists of a series of notes, such as those in the example below.

Student Task: The student has written an imaginary description of the trip to Paris described in Task 5, above. The teacher asks the student to rewrite the opening paragraph in the second draft as follows:

Using the cues in the paragraph below, write a new paragraph that is more detailed and interesting than the original.

Mon premier voyage à Paris était très intéressant[a]. Je suis allé avec mon camarade de chambre[b]. Nous avons loué une voiture[c], mais il était très difficile de conduire à Paris[d]. . . .

My first trip to Paris was very interesting[a]. I went with my roommate[b]. We rented a car[c], but it was very difficult to drive in Paris[d]. . . .

Notes: (These can be in French or English. English is used here for purposes of illustration.)

a. Add a few details about when you took this trip. Also, try to find another word to substitute for the adjective you used here—"interesting" doesn't give us much information.
b. Describe your roommate in a sentence or two. Why did you want to go with him?
c. Add some adjectives to your description of the car.
d. Instead of telling the reader that it was difficult to drive in Paris, try describing the traffic, the parking, or other situations that made driving so hard, and let the reader *conclude* that it was difficult from your description.

Note how the teacher's cues in the sample relate primarily to the content and style of the student's story rather than to mechanics or grammar. By providing substantive comments of this type, the teacher encourages students to revise in a way that will enhance their creative expression.

Guided Composition Based on Oral Interview

Context: Varied topics relating to personal life and preferences

Functions: Narration and description in past, present, and future time

Purpose: To encourage students to practice skills needed at the Advanced level, both orally and in writing.

Student Task: Students are asked to interview a partner by choosing one topic from each of several categories, such as those listed below. They are told to take notes on what their partners say. As a follow-up to the oral interview, they are asked to write a unified composition of at least three paragraphs, telling either (1) what they learned about the person they interviewed, or (2) what they would say about themselves on these topics. In the first instance, the composition would consist of a description narrated in the third person; in the second, the composition would be autobiographical. Students are reminded that they should include narration in past, present, and future time.

Topics:

Present

- Talk about yourself and your family (i.e., where you're from, where your family lives, who the people in your family are, etc.).
- Talk about why you are at this university and why you are taking this course.
- Talk about what you like and dislike about life at this university.
- Talk about things that bore you (interest you, make you happy/angry) and why.

Past

- Describe a recent Christmas (summer/spring) vacation.
- Describe what your life was like last year.
- Talk about a memorable event in your life.

Future

- Describe your career goals and plans.
- Talk about what you'd like to do with the French (Spanish, German, Italian, other language) you know now.
- Talk about your plans for the end of the semester.
- Describe your plans for the coming weekend.

Guided and Free Composition: Writing Letters and Notes

From writers at the Intermediate level, teachers might expect short essays of two or three paragraphs on themes with which they are familiar. Most appropriate for these students are topics that elicit personal information and simple statements about preferences, concrete experiences, and the like, such as the following:

1. Imagine you are on vacation at your favorite resort. Write a postcard or short letter explaining what you are doing, what you like about the place, who you are meeting, and similar details. (See Illustration 7.7.)
2. You are writing a letter home to your parents about college life. Give them a description of your typical day at school. Include a short paragraph about your roommate (your favorite teacher/your least favorite class/your dorm room/the food at school), and tell what you like/dislike about that person (situation).
3. Write a description of (a) a good friend, (b) a member of your family, (c) a teacher you like/dislike, or (d) your roommate. Give as many details about the person's appearance, personality, and habits as you can. (Note: This expands the guided description task in Illustration 7.2 to create a task at a somewhat higher level.)
4. Your best friend at another school has a new roommate who comes from France (Spain, Germany, Italy, country where target language is spoken). Write a letter to your friend, including a list of questions you would like him or her to ask this exchange student about life in his or her country.

Here are a few topics that indicate the type of composition that might be assigned when learners are in the Intermediate range but need to develop skills to progress to the Advanced level:

1. Write a Christmas card to your teacher telling him or her what you plan to do during vacation. (See Illustration 7.8, p. 300, an exercise suggested by Terry 1985.)
2. Write a page in your personal diary describing your activities during the last semester. (See Illustration 7.9, p. 300, another exercise suggested by Terry 1985.)
3. You are planning on getting married (getting a new job, moving to another town) and anticipate some major changes in your life. Describe what will be different after you get married (get the new job, move) and how you think you will feel about these changes.
4. You just had a very eventful (fabulous/horrible/exciting/unusual) weekend, and you can't wait to write to your penpal in France (Spain, Germany, Italy, country where target language is spoken) to tell him

or her all about it. Recount the events of your weekend in as much detail as possible.

For more ideas on teaching and evaluating writing at this level, see Terry (1989).

Dialogue Journals (Novice through Advanced levels)

One form of free composition that seems particularly appropriate for beginning and intermediate students is the *dialogue journal* (Staton 1983; Peyton and Reed 1990). These journals provide a way for students and teachers to carry on a writ-

Illustration 7.7
Writing a Postcard
about a Vacation

UNA TARJETA POSTAL

You have recently arrived in Mexico for a two-week stay. You want to send a postcard to your Spanish teacher back in the United States, telling him/her about your trip. You arrived in Cancún three days ago. Write a message to your teacher on the postcard below.

La playa de Cancún

Source: Terry (2000).

Illustration 7.8
Composition Topic
for Intermediate-
Level Students
Preparing for the
Advanced Level
(Topic 1)

Una tarjeta de Navidad. In order to impress me with the wealth of knowledge you have gained in 101, shortly before you leave campus you send me a Christmas card—written entirely in Spanish. You include a note of at least *five* sentences telling me what you, your family, and your friends *are going to do* during vacation.

Source: Terry (1985).

Illustration 7.9
Composition Topic
for Intermediate-
Level Students
Preparing for the
Advanced Level
(Topic 2)

Cher Journal Intime (Dear Diary). In your personal diary (which you keep under lock and key in your sock drawer), you make your last entry for 200_. Write *eight* sentences telling *what you did* (i.e., in the *passé composé*) during this last semester. Be sure to include several memorable occasions and activities.

mardi, le 31 décembre	200__

Source: Terry (1985).

ten conversation with one another and can continue for any length of time during the course of a semester or year. Students obtain a bound composition book or notebook and write on a daily or weekly basis about topics of interest to them, using the full range of functions (questions, promises, apologies, complaints) that might be used in a face-to-face conversation. The teacher then reads the journal entries and responds substantively and personally to them. Because writing at the Novice and Intermediate levels often consists of writing down what students would say orally, this type of journal might be appealing as an alternative or adjunct to structured compositions assigned by the teacher on a periodic basis.

Peyton and Reed (1990) have written an informative handbook incorporating many examples of dialogue journals and the techniques that instructors can use to supplement other types of writing instruction. The authors present some caveats, however, that need to be taken into consideration when using a journal-writing approach. One concern that some teachers and/or students have voiced is that the journals are not corrected for structural errors. Research evidence on the effectiveness of error correction in second-language writing is conflicting, as is research on the attitudes of students toward correction of their work. However, studies by Cathcart and Olsen (1976), Leki (1986, 1990, 1991), Jones (1988), and Fathman and Whalley (1990) have revealed that many ESL students want their errors corrected on both written and oral work, a result corroborated in studies by Schulz (1996) and Conrad (1997, 1999) involving foreign language students. Jones (1988) researched this issue specifically in reference to dialogue journals and found that almost all of the adult ESL students in his study at the beginning level and almost half of the more advanced students wanted correction in their journals. Peyton and Reed (1990) recognize the importance of responding to this concern and suggest that teachers talk to students about the purposes of the journal as opposed to the purposes of other writing tasks where corrective feedback is given more systematically. As an activity that falls on the "vernacular style" end of the continuum of writing tasks, dialogue journals can provide students with an opportunity to develop fluency without constantly worrying about form. Nevertheless, teachers might want to go over journals with students who express a desire to be corrected, scheduling conferences with them or negotiating with them that certain kinds of errors will be corrected during a given time period. Leki (1991) adds that ". . . we do well at least to become aware of students' perceptions of their needs and their sense of what helps them progress" (p. 210). Perhaps the best solution is to offer students options and teach them different perspectives or strategies for approaching a writing task, but ultimately respect their right to choose the kind of feedback they believe will enhance their learning most effectively and try to provide it for them.

Writing and the Computer

In the past decade, there has been a significant increase in the number of conference presentations and publications advocating the use of the computer to support the teaching of various language skills, from Novice to Advanced levels. Publishers of foreign language materials have expanded their offerings in this regard, and the newest generation of first- and second-year foreign language textbooks offer ancillaries such as CD-ROMs with creative activities in all four skills and electronic workbooks that offer additional, more focused practice. A number of language texts also have associated Web pages that offer students links to Internet sources that can be explored in connection with chapter themes. Many of these computerized materials can support the goal of learning to write in the target language.

As we saw in the last chapter, the lines between speaking and informal writing have become somewhat less distinct with the advent of new technologies, such as e-mail and computer-mediated communication (Beauvois 1997; Kern 1998; Meunier 1998). Thus in the earlier stages of writing in the foreign language, where students essentially try to write down what they might say (Magnan 1985; Beauvois 1997, 1998), the use of these technologies can be particularly helpful, not only as a way to practice writing, but also as a support skill for speaking. With the advent of local area networks (LANs), students can more comfortably interact and discuss various issues among themselves and with their instructor. This interaction can be through synchronous conferencing using a computer, or asynchronous e-mail using the Internet. Kern (1998) points out the different features of more traditional forms of written communication on the one hand and synchronous conferencing on the other (see Illustration 7.10). His comments about synchronous conferencing could easily be applied to communication via e-mail as well.

Both types of writing (i.e., using pen and paper or the computer) fall under two of the three communicative modes outlined in the *Standards for Foreign Language Learning* (1996)—interpersonal and presentational. Synchronous conferencing is

Illustration 7.10
Features of Written Communication Highlighted in the Use of the Two Technologies of Writing (Kern 1998, p. 65)

Pen and paper writing	Synchronous conferencing
• Formal accuracy • Global coherence • Reinforcement of canonical written discourse conventions • Uninterrupted exploration of one's own personal voice	• Fluency of self-expression • Interactive responsiveness • Blend of "orate" and "literate" forms of communication • Juxtaposition of multiple voices, perspectives

the written equivalent of interpersonal communication in which the interlocutors can negotiate meaning since they are in personal contact, although not face-to-face. As with e-mail technology, computer-mediated communication is often fairly spontaneous, and there can be a tendency for students to pay less attention to grammatical accuracy and spelling and to focus more on communication of the message, just as they often do in more spontaneous spoken communication. Beauvois (1997), commenting on the transcripts of a second-year ESL literature class engaged in synchronous computer-mediated communication, points out that "[a]lthough the students' errors may seem striking because written, they are not more numerous than mistakes in students' spoken target language" (p. 173). She adds that, because teachers do not generally interrupt the flow of communication to attend to errors in form, some practitioners may be concerned that students will remember these errors. However, she contends that "studies to date have not shown this to be true" (p. 173). Beauvois suggests that teachers can respond to students' errors within the context of the ongoing communication by rephrasing the sentence to provide a correct version (i.e., a recast), or they can examine the transcripts to focus on certain common problems in a follow-up session. Another possibility is to have students work on portions of their own transcripts in small groups in a follow-up session, using dictionaries, books, and consultation with the teacher to prepare an "error-free version," an idea suggested by Swain and Lapkin for working with student-generated output (1989, p. 155). In this way, students first focus on communicating their meaning and then use their own output to focus on form, which may lead to further language learning. Swain (1998) suggests that "it may be that the modified, or reprocessed, output can be considered to represent the leading edge of a learner's interlanguage" (p. 68). Because computer-mediated communication constitutes fairly spontaneous language use, it may be particularly fruitful to use this type of output as a basis for reprocessing activities.

Smith (1990) describes an experiment in which fourth-semester Spanish students were given opportunities to use two types of computer-based writing tools for the writing component of the course: (1) a computer-conferencing system and (2) a word-processing program. The computer-conferencing system enabled students to engage in discussions and collaborative writing activities with others in the course. Each new message that was added to a particular discussion became automatically available to all participants, who could consider it and comment upon it as they wished. Smith reports that students using this system engaged in lively debates and creative self-expression, devoting an average of three hours per week for computer-mediated conversational writing. These students paid more attention to meaning than to accuracy, since the computer-conferencing format was not used for editing or revision in this study. The second group of students, who used a word-processing program (WordPerfect) as a composition tool, worked primarily on composing and rewriting compositions with a view to producing more accurate writing samples. Students in this group averaged 90 minutes per week on computer-assisted composition work, with some students working in pairs, brainstorming, or peer editing one another's work. A third group of students in the study had no computer-assisted writing opportunities but did write compositions at home.

Smith compared the groups' achievement on a variety of measures at the end of the semester and found that the computer users improved significantly in their ability to read and express oral and written ideas (pp. 80–81). The students in the control condition improved in their general accuracy in written composition, as did those who were using the word-processing tool for composition. However, the control group did not develop the same level of expressive skills in writing as did those who had worked with the computer. Smith concludes that a combination of activities stressing *both* creative conversational writing (as in the computer-conferencing condition) and attention to form (as in the word-processing condition) are necessary to promote the development of writing proficiency.

Kern (1998) also recommends that synchronous conferencing be used as one of a number of tools in the teaching of writing, but cautions that it should not be considered as a substitute for normal classroom discussion or a means for improving one's more formal writing ability (see Illustration 7.10):

> *From the standpoint of foreign language literacy development, it is important to note that synchronous conferencing and traditional pen and paper writing tend to emphasize different aspects of written communication. Questions of "effectiveness" therefore need to be framed in terms of specific goals. . . . grammatical accuracy, stylistic development, coherence, and continuity of thought are more likely to be fostered by pen and paper writing. Synchronous conferencing, on the other hand, tends to encourage fluency (in terms of both speed and quantity of language production), lively responsiveness of expression, a blending of "oral" and "written" language forms and communicative devices, and the voicing of multiple perspectives on issues (p. 65).*

Kern also compares pen and paper writing with writing via e-mail, as outlined in Illustration 7.11. He points out that using e-mail can have a number of advantages, among which are (1) its relative simplicity in bringing a language learner into contact with native speakers; (2) its dialogic structure that helps learners pre-

Illustration 7.11
Comparison of Features of Written Communication via Pen and Paper and E-Mail Technologies in Foreign Language Classrooms (Kern 1998, pp. 74–75)

Pen and paper writing	Electronic mail
• Normally limited audience (teacher) • Often limited communicative purpose (display of competence) • Tends to be perceived as relatively permanent and "on record" • Intensive, recursive process that fosters elaboration and development of ideas • Adherence to formal norms (language, genre, style) generally plays more important role	• Contact with real people outside the classroom • Wide range of communicative purposes (informing, persuading, etc.) • Tends to be perceived as relatively ephemeral and disposable • Emphasis on speed and succinctness of expression • Adherence to formal norms tends to be relaxed (e.g., mixing of oral/written genres, grammar/spelling mistakes)

dict meaning through the normal give-and-take of statements, questions, and responses; (3) its contribution to the learners' metacognitive awareness since, when there are misunderstandings, the participants have recourse to a written record that can help locate the source of misunderstanding; and (4) its direct support of cultural learning by providing new and alternative perspectives (Kern 1998, p. 75). However, he also mentions three major challenges associated with the use of e-mail in foreign language instruction: (1) finding a partner class that has Internet access; (2) meeting technical requirements for those languages using non-roman scripts or that use accents and diacritical marks; and (3) recognizing that e-mail can obscure important sociocultural differences, such as the emphasis in each culture on social distance, perceptions of the appropriateness of topics and registers, and the like (pp. 73–74).

Lafford and Lafford (1997) summarize several research studies on the effectiveness of the use of e-mail in foreign language instruction and learning. They report on a study by Barson, Frommer, and Schwartz (1993), which looked at the use of collaborative e-mail among three universities by students of French in intermediate-level classes. Students reported more confidence in their use of the target language and a positive attitude toward the use of e-mail as an instructional tool. In addition, negotiation of meaning was successfully carried out between instructors and students in their e-mail exchanges through students' clarification requests. In another study conducted by Oliva and Pollastrini (1995) at the University of Utah, students in various advanced-level Italian classes communicated with native speakers daily through e-mail, newsgroups, and Internet Relay Chat (IRC) in addition to their work in more traditional instructional activities. Students assessed their progress at the end of the course through an evaluation questionnaire. Results revealed that 57.8% of the students perceived writing to be the most improved among the four skills, and many of the students judged e-mail to be the most helpful technology they had used in the experiment. Students noted that there were some difficulties experienced in using the Internet resources for the course, particularly for those requiring higher levels of computer skills (such as the newsgroups and Internet Relay Chat); some students also expressed a desire to have more speaking activities in class in addition to the computer-based written communication. However, many students felt that the skills gained during the course would be usable in future careers and appreciated the wide range of learning possibilities provided by communicating on the Internet.

Lafford and Lafford (1997) point out that instructors who plan to integrate various types of online activities into their course curricula need to allow sufficient time for training students in the use of those technologies. In addition, there should be clearly written, readily accessible instructions on the use of the technologies available for students.

▓ Teaching Writing with Word Processors and Writing Assistants

The use of word-processing programs in teaching composition can provide a number of benefits to both students and teachers. For example, Greenia (1992) describes intermediate and advanced Spanish composition classes in which students work almost exclusively on the computer, using a standard word-processing program such as WordPerfect or Microsoft Word. He estimates that students using computer-based instruction can produce three to seven times more writing in a semester than can those working without the aid of a computer, multiplying their opportunities to improve through daily assignments of various types. Greenia provides useful and comprehensive guidelines for setting up a writing course of this type. The teacher responds to student work turned in on a diskette, which holds a variety of files including course information and syllabus, a working space for ongoing assignments, a storage space for completed work, a file containing models of writing, another file for practical exercises, a file for a private dialogue journal, and a directory for an open class bulletin board. In this computer-assisted instructional setting, students and teacher work together as a writing community, with students responding to one another's work in a cooperative learning environment.

Writers at the Novice and Intermediate levels can also profit from using word-processing programs, particularly if they are asked to prepare multiple drafts of their work. In addition, writing assistant programs such as *système-D* (Noblitt, Pet, and Solá 1999), *Atajo* (Domínguez, Noblitt, and Pet 1999), and *Quelle* (Kossuth, Noblitt, and Pet 1999) are designed to facilitate the writing process in another language (French, Spanish, and German, respectively) so that students and teachers "can interact with a written text in new and useful ways" (Scott and Terry 1992, p. 1). These programs offer (1) a bilingual dictionary that includes reference notes, examples, and a verb conjugator, and (2) three references—a vocabulary index that contains topical vocabulary lists, a grammar index that contains fundamental explanations of grammar points, and a phrase index that is essentially a listing with examples of language functions. According to Scott and Terry (1992), writing assistant programs are unique writing tools that lend themselves to a systematic developmental writing program. First, they provide resources for students at all levels of language study, although they are most useful for writers at the Novice and Intermediate levels. Second, they help students develop critical thinking skills through reading, analyzing, and choosing appropriate items from information screens, seeing word associations, and understanding the link between language functions and linguistic structures. Third, they build a bridge between skill-getting and skill-using when students request information and then use it in their writing task (pp. 1–2).

Scott (1992) and Scott and Terry (1992) advocate using task-oriented writing, especially for students in beginning- and intermediate-level language courses. In this type of writing activity, students are given (1) a general situation or context that describes the function and the purpose of the writing exercise; (2) several specific tasks that describe explicitly the steps the students must take to achieve the purpose of the assignment; and (3) a specific directive for each task asking students to find the functional, lexical, and grammatical information necessary to carry out the task (Scott 1992, p. 5). These guidelines provide an organizational framework that allows the students to communicate a comprehensible message without being distracted by trying to express their more sophisticated ideas with limited ability in the target language. Scott maintains that when students are given writing tasks in their native language, they typically begin with an idea of what they want to say and that idea, in turn, generates the language structures and vocabulary they need. When they are given writing tasks in another language, students may try to use this same process and simply translate from one language into the other, a phenomenon that most often leads to incomprehensible writing. Given the limited vocabulary that beginning and intermediate students typically have in their repertoire in the L2, computerized writing assistants may help students overcome these difficulties to some extent through organized, systematic guidance and the provision of functional vocabulary, expressions, and structures geared specifically to the writing tasks.

Two samples of task-oriented writing activities are given in Illustrations 7.12 and 7.13. In the first example (Illustration 7.12, taken from Muyskens, Harlow, Vialet, and Brière 1998), students in a second-year program follow a four-stage process throughout the course of a chapter in their textbook to produce three drafts of a composition with the aid of the writing assistant, *système-D*.

Illustration 7.12 Four-Part Composing Process (Muyskens, Harlow, Vialet, and Brière 1998)

VOCABULARY:
Sports; traveling; family members (NOTE: these are only suggestions for the above topics. Browse the vocabulary index to find help for other topics.)

GRAMMAR:
Compound past tense

Préparation (p.137)

In this chapter, you will practice writing a personal narrative in which you will tell or narrate something that happened to you or someone you know.

1. First of all, choose two or three important events in your life (for example, receiving an award, meeting the person of your dreams, a sporting event, your wedding or a wedding you were in, a memorable vacation, the worst/best day of your life, getting arrested, a funny/embarrassing moment, a sad or touching event).

2. After you have listed these events, next to each item, write some interesting details that you remember about the event.

3. Free write on one or more of these topics to see how much you have to say. Describe what happened and try to organize your notes in a time-ordered sequence.

4. In pairs or small groups, share your notes to get ideas from classmates.

PHRASES: Writing an essay; describing people, objects, weather; sequencing events

VOCABULARY:
Clothing; women's clothing; colors; hair colors

GRAMMAR:
Compound past tense; past imperfect

Premier brouillon (p. 150)

1. After you have chosen your topic in Lesson 1, organize the notes you have written by thinking about these important elements of a narrative: *Characters:* for example, how old were the characters at the time of the incident? What did they look like? How were they dressed? *Setting:* if it is important to your narrative, give descriptive details about the time and place. *Plot:* because you are telling about something that really happened, you know the basic plot. Will there be a conflict? What final words will you use to close your narrative?

2. Begin writing your introductory paragraph by focusing on the topic sentence that describes the incident for the reader. Use your opening paragraph to get your reader's attention.

3. Write two or three paragraphs in which you use details to describe the events. Since this is a narrative about a past event, you will have to make decisions about your use of the **imparfait** and **passé composé.**

4. Write a concluding paragraph in which you end your story with a description of the last event.

PHRASES: Writing an essay; sequencing events

GRAMMAR: Pluperfect; prepositions with times and dates; time expressions

Deuxième brouillon (p. 159)

1. Write a second draft of the paper that you wrote in Lesson 2, focusing particularly on the order in which the events happened. Try to add details on pertinent events that happened before the events described in the narrative (i.e., using the **plus-que-parfait**).

2. To strengthen the time order used for the events that occurred, try to incorporate some of the following expressions that deal with chronological order:

EXPRESSIONS UTILES: à ce moment-là . . . , pendant (+ nom)/pendant que (+ verbe conjugué) . . . , en même temps . . . , hier . . . , avant-hier . . . , la semaine dernière . . . , après-demain . . . , la semaine prochaine . . . , la veille *(the night before),* l'avant-veille . . . , l'année précédente . . . , le lendemain . . . , cinq jours après . . .

PHRASES: Writing an essay; sequencing events

GRAMMAR: Compound past tense; past imperfect; pluperfect; participle agreement

Révision finale (p. 160)

1. Reread your composition and focus on the unity of the paragraphs. All of the sentences within the paragraph must be on the same topic. If a sentence is not directly related to the topic, it does not belong in the paragraph.

2. Bring your draft to class and ask two classmates to peer edit your composition using the symbols on page 415.* They should pay particular attention to whether the narrative contains a well-developed beginning, middle, and conclusion, and uses chronological order effectively.

3. Examine your composition one last time. Check for correct spelling, grammar, and punctuation. Pay special attention to your use of the **passé composé, imparfait,** and **plus-que-parfait** tenses, and agreement with past participles.

4. Prepare your final version.

Source: Muyskens, Harlow, Vialet, and Brière (1998), pp. 137, 150, 159, and 160.

* For the set of symbols, or codes, referred to here, see Appendix C.

An additional example in French is given in Illustration 7.13. This sample, provided by Scott and Terry (1992), shows how teachers can create their own task-based writing assignments using a writing assistant program.

Illustration 7.13
A Task-Oriented
Writing Activity for
French, Using
système-D.

SAMPLE (STAGE 2—INTERMEDIATE)

Context: You are writing to your French pen pal with whom you have been corresponding regularly.

Tasks:

1. Use the appropriate letter format.
    Phrases: Writing a letter (informal)
2. Talk about and describe your best friend.
    Phrases: Describing people
    Grammar: Nouns after *c'est, il est;* Possessive adjectives (6 groups)
3. Tell what you did during your last vacation.
    Grammar: **Passé composé;** Verbs with auxiliary **avoir** or **être;** Agreement of past participle; Prepositions with geographical places.
    Vocabulary: Traveling; Means of transportation
4. Tell what the weather was like during your vacation.
    Phrases: Describing weather
    Grammar: **Imparfait**
5. Ask five questions.
    Grammar: Interrogative adjective **quel;** Interrogative adverbs; Interrogative pronouns **que, quoi;** Interrogative pronoun **qui**
6. End your letter with the appropriate closing.

Source: Scott and Terry (1992), p. 31.

In this example, as well as in the other writing tasks suggested by Scott and Terry, students receive a good deal of structure and direction for their assignments. Some students or teachers might find this specificity somewhat limiting. Scott and Terry acknowledge this possibility in their instructor's guide. "While most students are grateful for the explicit directions provided in the task-oriented exercises, it is important to note that some students feel that the tasks limit their creativity. The best response to this legitimate criticism is to allow time for free creative expression either with or without *système-D,* but only after they have had sufficient practice with task-oriented exercises" (p. 42). The authors clearly believe that designing tasks that are explicitly structured in this way is helpful to students whose writing proficiency in the language is at a relatively early stage, and that some guided practice is therefore necessary before encouraging students to engage in free writing. This approach seems congruent with the "comprehensible output hypothesis" described in Chapter 3, in which it was suggested that tasks should be designed to help students practice language at their current level of competence or just a little beyond it to encourage greater accuracy of expression (Higgs and Clifford 1982). Swain's (1985) version of this hypothesis would encourage students to achieve greater precision of expression through "pushed output," where students' written or oral production would be reworked until it approached native-like form. With writing assistant programs such as those described in this section, there seems to be a concern for helping students develop accuracy of expression as well as communicative facility through the provision of grammar and vocabulary resources of various sorts. However, the authors caution that students' compositions will not be error-free when they use these programs, and that students will need to engage in self-monitoring and receive additional help with improving their written work as they would with a more conventional writing program. Some of the possible ways to respond to students' written work are treated later in this chapter.

Expressive Writing at the Intermediate and Advanced Levels: Approaches to Teaching the Composing Process

This section begins with a brief review of research about native-language and second-language writing at the Intermediate to Advanced level, followed by a summary of the kinds of approaches to the teaching of writing as creative communication that have been suggested by various scholars in recent years. Some examples of Advanced-level writing activities are then given, followed by suggestions for responding to student writing through various feedback and evaluation strategies.

What Do We Know about Writing? Insights from First-Language Research

Because the preponderance of writing research to date has been done with students writing in their native language, second- and foreign-language teachers have had to rely primarily on insights from first-language studies. Although there may be many commonalities between first- and second-language writing, the differences should also be recognized. Kroll (1990) suggests that writing in a second language is more complex, given that the problems native speakers have with composing are compounded in the foreign language context by difficulties with the new code. She also points out that direct transfer of literacy skills from the native to the foreign language cannot be assumed. "In fact, while a background in first language writing may help inform the explorations of second language writing teachers and researchers, it should not be presumed that the act of writing in one's first language is the same as the act of writing in one's second language. For example, first and second language learners may not approach a writing task in the same way nor attend to feedback in the same way" (p. 2). As we have seen in the first part of this chapter, it is possible that, even *within* the context of second-language writing, Novice and Intermediate writers may approach tasks and use feedback far differently than Advanced writers, with whom most of the research in second-language writing has been done. Therefore, it makes sense to be cautious in our interpretation of this research when applying the results to our second-language classrooms, especially at the lower levels.

An additional consideration is that most of the research on second-language writing has been done, to date, on writing in English as a second or foreign language rather than on writing by English-speaking learners in a foreign language (Hedgcock and Lefkowitz 1994; Reichelt 1999). For example, Reichelt examined the 81 articles published in the *Journal of Second Language Writing,* which first appeared in 1992, and found only 3 articles dealing with writing in a language other than English. Her review of research and theoretical literature in second-language writing revealed the same imbalance between English and foreign language writing, although she does point out that there has been an increase in articles on writing in foreign languages other than English since the early 1990s. Her review article provides a summary of the range of foreign language research studies as well as the literature on writing pedagogy, with a comprehensive bibliography of works dating from 1969 to 1999 that is an excellent resource for foreign language teachers and researchers alike. Reichelt notes that the foreign language specialists in her review drew on a broad base of knowledge generated in both the L1 and L2 (ESL) writing literature as well as on other research in foreign language writing, SLA research, linguistic theory, and educational research. She adds that many ESL articles tend to draw less on foreign language writing research than on research about English, and that "most ESL writing literature does not deal with writing instruction at the beginning level of English study, as does a good portion of the FL writing literature . . ." (pp. 186–187). This is an important distinction between research and pedagogical practice in ESL and FL writing. As was pointed out at the beginning of this chapter, beginning- and intermediate-level writing instruction may have a number of purposes, ranging on a continuum from writing as a support skill for language development to writing for creative expression. Reichelt (1999) emphasizes as well that the purposes of writing instruction typically differ in ESL and FL writing contexts, with ESL courses designed to prepare students for academic writing in university courses and FL courses generally designed with other writing purposes in mind. (One might add, however, that more advanced-level writing courses in foreign languages are often designed to help learners write about academic subjects, such as literature, business, and commerce.) Nevertheless, Reichelt's point is well taken when she maintains that differences between ESL and FL writing instruction are understandable and appropriate, given these different purposes and levels of instruction:

> *While FL writing may do well to borrow some concepts and practices from English-language writing instruction, it is important for FL writing to forge its own identity by delineating its own research agenda and pedagogical practices (Reichelt 1999, p. 193).*

Thus our discussion of studies in L1 and L2 (ESL) writing in the next sections of the chapter, while potentially informative, need to be viewed within the context of the differences in writing levels and purposes in English L1 and L2 writing instruction and instruction in FL writing. Further research about foreign language writing needs to be done to help us determine what aspects of the L1 and ESL literature may transfer to foreign language writing and what differences exist that might lead us in different directions.

With these caveats in mind, what can we learn from studies conducted with native language writers? Let us begin with a description of what good writers do as they engage in the composing process.

Characteristics of Good Writers

Most scholars would agree with Rivers (1975) that good writing in any language involves knowledge of the conventions of written discourse in that culture as well as the abilities to choose from near synonyms the precise word that conveys one's meaning, select from a variety of syntactic structures those that transmit one's message most precisely, and adopt a style that will have the most positive rhetorical effect. Obviously, such expertise will not develop merely from practice exercises in grammar and vocabulary at the sentence level (p. 238). For many years, instruction in rhetoric had emphasized writing at the paragraph level and beyond, and instruction in composition typically provided students with exercises in the development of outlines and plans, the creation of paragraphs with topic sentences, the inclusion of supporting detail, techniques in comparison and contrast, and strategies for smooth transitions. According to Emig (1971), many of the composition texts used before 1970 basically described the writing process as linear in nature, proceeding from the development of an outline to the writing of a first draft, followed by a revision and a final draft. In most of these manuals, writing was seen as "a tidy, accretive affair that proceeds by elaborating a fully preconceived and formulated plan" (p. 22). Yet in interviews she had conducted in the 1960s with established writers, Emig found evidence that contradicted many of the precepts of the composition texts. For one thing, experienced writers reported that they proceeded differently in different genres or types of writing. No one ever seemed to outline before writing poetry, and the novelists and short story writers in her sample seldom made outlines, or at least not elaborate ones. They also said that they did not engage in a linear process of planning, writing, and revision, but rather in a more recursive and integrated process that was not sequenced or fixed. For these expert writers, the "stages" of writing of the composition manuals were not a reality, at least not in a chronological sense.

In a landmark study of the composing process of high school students, Emig (1971) found that the twelve seniors she interviewed, most of whom had been identified as "good" writers by their teachers, did not typically follow the process that the composition manuals were suggesting. Most of them did have a kind of plan for the writing in mind before beginning to write, although it usually wasn't down on paper. The prewriting, planning, and reformulation processes among the students in her sample also varied depending on whether the composition was a "school-sponsored" topic or a topic of their own choosing. Emig's study further revealed that student writing was evaluated most often on criteria that emphasized "the accidents rather than the essences of discourse—that is, spelling, punctuation, penmanship, the length rather than thematic development, rhetorical and syntactic sophistication, and fulfillment of intent" (p. 93). Emig concluded that "much of the teaching of composition in American high schools is essentially a neurotic activity" (p. 99), and certainly not modeled on what good writers typically do.

Krashen (1984) reviewed research on the composing process in the native language and concluded that good writers differ from poor writers in at least three ways:

1. *Planning.* Good writers seem to plan more than poor writers do. This does not necessarily mean that they use an outline in the prewriting stage, but they do show some evidence of planning or organizing before they sit down to write the first draft. They also tend to take more time before beginning to write and tend to have flexible plans.
2. *Rescanning.* Good writers stop rather frequently to reread what they have already written before continuing to compose. Krashen maintains that rescanning helps good writers maintain a sense of the whole composition and that by rereading, planning what to write next, and then rescanning to see if the plan fits, writers invariably end up with better products.
3. *Revising.* Good writers tend to revise more than poor writers do, and they revise somewhat differently. Whereas poor writers tend to pay attention more often to surface form in their revisions, good writers make more changes in content and try to ascertain the logic of their argument in the finished draft in order to see if revisions are necessary (pp. 12–15).

Krashen adds that highly proficient writers often write *recursively*—that is, many use a nonlinear approach to the composing process. While writing a draft, for example, proficient writers may interrupt their writing because they have made some discovery that sends them back to reformulate their original idea. Less experienced writers, on the other hand, often feel that they are *not allowed* to do this and try to follow some fixed set of rules they learned in composition class instead. While the good writer understands that composition is a "messy process that leads to clarity" (Shaughnessy 1977, p. 79, cited in Krashen 1984, p. 18), the poor writer often does not have a clear idea of the value of revision.

One additional characteristic of proficient writers is their awareness of their audience and their concern for the reader's point of view. Whereas poor writers are "tied to the topic" and writer-centered (Flower and Hayes 1980, cited in Krashen 1984, p. 19), proficient writers are reader-centered and avoid the use of ambiguous referents, words with special meanings of which the reader may be unaware, and the disorganized exposition of ideas that characterize the work of poor writers. Krashen believes that a high degree of writing competence can be achieved through extensive reading, although he bases this hypothesis on evidence that is drawn exclusively from research on native language writers.

Scott (1996) defines a competent writer as "someone who has achieved a given level of ability and is able to communicate effectively and convincingly" (p. 2). According to Scott, there are general descriptions of "good writing" on which most writers agree. These descriptions include features such as "clarity, explicitness, conciseness, clear paragraph structure, and overall organization . . . Ultimately, however, the quality of a text is based on the judgment of the reader, and the reader's own criteria become the essential measure of quality" (Scott 1996, p. 3).

Hillocks (1986) reviewed nearly 2,000 articles on the teaching of writing and compared results of over 500 empirical studies of native language writing practices. His description of the characteristics of better writers vs. weak writers coincides in many ways with the summary provided by Krashen. Yet Hillocks cautions us not to jump to premature conclusions about how writing should be taught. "The obvious question is one of cause and effect. Are good writers good because they plan more and are more concerned with content, organization, and even audience? Or do good writers devote more attention and energy to planning and content because they have mastered mechanics and need not be preoccupied by such matters?" (p. 28). Hillocks suggests that the hypothesis that instruction should concentrate on planning, organization, or content and abandon attention to mechanics has not been tested thoroughly to date, and that extrapolations from research on good writers to designs for writing instruction may thus be premature.

Applebee (1986) agrees that prescriptions for teaching writing drawn from descriptions of what experts do can lead to inadequate solutions for novice writers. In his view, these kinds of easy, direct applications lie at the heart of process-oriented approaches. He warns that such approaches can become trivialized or reduced to a new formula of lockstep procedures if they are thought of in a generic fashion. Applebee suggests reconceptualizing process instruction so as to link process with product and with a particular writing purpose. In this way, different strategies that writers use to achieve a given purpose can be taught at different times: Some writing tasks would require only "the routine production of a first and final draft" (p. 106), while others would require more complex problem-solving strategies. Progress in writing would thus involve the gradual development of a wider repertoire of writing strategies for an ever-broadening range of situations.

Research on the Composing Process: First Language Studies

In reviewing a wide variety of studies done on the composing process of native language writers, Hillocks (1986) identified various findings that are of potential interest to teachers. Some of his conclusions are summarized below:

1. **Teaching Grammar in Isolation.** None of the studies reviewed supported the notion that teaching grammatical concepts in isolation had any positive effect on writing among native speakers. Hillocks speculates that this might be so because grammatical instruction in sentence-level frames only touches the surface of discourse and does not address the other aspects of the composing process that are measured in empirical studies.
2. **Sentence-Combining Practice.** Research shows positive results for sentence-combining practice, although the effects of this practice might slowly disappear if the practice is not reinforced. Monroe (1975) and Cooper (1977, 1981) also found that sentence combining yielded positive results in foreign language writing instruction. (For a sample of sentence-combining practice in English, see pp. 292–293.)
3. **Using Models of Good Writing.** Research on the use of models of good writing in writing instruction yields mixed results, with some studies showing benefits and others showing no significant differences between groups. However, Hillocks maintains that the use of models, especially "to illustrate a

single characteristic of effective writing, such as the use of concrete detail" can be beneficial at all grade levels (p. 155).

4. **Using Criteria/Checklists for Peer Evaluation.** Strong positive effects have been found in studies where students used a set of criteria or a checklist of questions supplied by their teachers when engaging in peer editing and review of compositions. "As a group, these studies indicate rather clearly that engaging young writers actively in the use of criteria, applied to their own or to others' writing, results not only in more effective revisions, but in superior first drafts" (p. 160).

5. **Free Writing Practice.** The research reviewed, much of which was done with young children, showed very few positive effects for the use of free writing activities as the main focus of instruction, although these activities might be useful in generating ideas for subsequent writing in a different mode (p. 231).

6. **Teacher Comments.** Most of the studies reviewed showed no significant effects of teacher comments of any kind on the quality of writing, although positive feedback seemed to be preferred in some studies to negative feedback or no feedback. These results seem more conclusive than results in second-language studies, which tend to be more contradictory. (Second-language studies on feedback effects will be reviewed in the next section.)

Hillocks concludes from these results that some combination of treatments (studying examples of writing, using checklists in peer evaluation and correction, and engaging in revision) seems to be indicated if we hope to improve writing instruction in the native language. However, it is difficult to know exactly what combinations will work with what students until more research is done. In addition, Hillocks makes it clear that much of the research he reviewed was faulty in its design, and more than 80% of the 500 studies he examined could not be considered in his meta-analysis because of lack of control of important variables (p. 110). It is thus wise for teachers to exercise caution in extrapolating from research studies on writing and keep their limitations in mind. This is especially true when extrapolating from native-language research studies in designing foreign- and second-language instructional programs.

▓ Research on Writing in the Second Language

The amount of research done in second-language contexts on writing processes is limited at this time, and much of it relates to the composing processes of advanced learners of ESL. Writing research involving foreign language classroom learners is generally focused on feedback strategies, although some studies have looked at other issues. This section briefly summarizes some of the findings in foreign- and second-language writing.

Research on the Composing Process: Second-Language Studies

Krapels (1990) reviewed process research studies in second languages, and reports that there were several commonalities in their designs: (1) studies were either strongly guided by or based on studies in the native language; (2) studies typically involved very small numbers of subjects (typically 4–6 learners); (3) subjects were typically female, advanced in their proficiency, undergraduate ESL learners whose native language was either Spanish or Chinese; and (4) students were seldom chosen randomly, and sometimes were in the researcher's own classes.

Krapels reports contradictory and inconclusive findings with regard to the applicability of native-language research results to the second- or foreign-language context. Some studies indicated that L1 and L2 processes were similar, while others suggested that they were different. The use of the native language in composing in the foreign language varied across studies. Several researchers found that the use of the L1 varied according to the topic, with topics that are rooted in the native language culture engaging more L1 use than topics that focused on the target culture (see, for example, Friedlander 1990). Krapels cites Silva (1988), who reviewed college-level writing process research between 1982 and 1987 and maintains that one of the greatest problems in second-language writing research lies in the interpretation of findings by the researchers or by those who consult their studies. He points out that while some researchers have been modest and tentative in their conclusions, others have made rather bold assertions based on too little evidence, generalizing unjustifiably from very small samples to the larger population of learners, suggesting premature implications, or making "sweeping claims that go way beyond findings in support of a particular popular approach or orientation to writing instruction" (Silva 1988, p. 6, cited in Krapels 1990, p. 50). Krapels agrees with Silva that second- and foreign-language researchers should begin to look for some of the *differences* between L1 and L2 writing rather than concentrating on the similarities (p. 52).

In the foreign language context, far fewer studies on the composing process *per se* have been done. A pilot study by Bland, Noblitt, Armington, and Gay (1990) used the computer software *système-D* with 10 volunteer subjects in first- and second-year college French and tracked their use of resources on the system as they wrote various composition assignments. The researchers found in the query logs of these students three kinds of requests for help: (1) *token matching,* where the students try to find a direct translation of a morphologically complex word or a phrase from English to French, without making any adjustments to the word or phrase; (2) *type matching,* where the students ask for the base forms of words they are looking for in the dictionary (such as infinitives or singular nouns) or ask for a grammatical concept (such as "negation" or "adjective"); and (3) *relexicalization,* which represents an attempt to construct meaning through synonyms, paraphrases, or structurally different expressions. The authors maintain that this third strategy shows a willingness on the part of students to depart from the native language and begin to construct meaning in the new language. They suggest that their findings "confirm the value of assessing facility in circumlocution to distinguish between elementary and intermediate level students" (p. 447). Follow-up interviews suggested that most of the students did not yet understand the value of paraphrasing as a strategy in helping them express their own thoughts in the second language, and the authors recommend that such strategies be actively taught as a part of writing instruction. This study illustrates clearly that learners typically will resort to the use of their native language when composing in the foreign language, especially at the lower levels of proficiency.

Scott (1996) reports on subsequent studies using *système-D*'s tracking capabilities (Scott and New 1994; New 1994). In the Scott and New study, several findings related to dictionary usage among intermediate students using the writing assistant as they composed in French: (1) the English-French dictionary was frequently consulted, indicating a translation strategy beginning with the native language; (2) students whose compositions were judged as better, both in terms of stylistics and grammaticality, used the English-French dictionary less; (3) some of the good writers in the study used the French-English dictionary creatively to test their hypotheses about words they had encountered. An additional finding was that all but one of the students wrote in a linear fashion from beginning to end, with little editing or recursive writing. New's (1994) study showed that students engaged in writing using *système-D* focused their revisions almost entirely on formal and mechanical features of their writing, rarely changing clauses or sentences. "Moreover, they revised their texts more when writing than they did when asked to revise a composition that they had written during a previous writing session. New concluded that students perceived a finished text as 'fixed' and less easily adaptable to later revisions" (Scott 1996, p. 44).

Friedlander (1990) investigated the effects of advanced writers using their native language on the quality of their writing in English as a second language. He cites studies by Chelala (1981), Lay (1982), and Johnson (1985) that corroborate his own findings that students can profit from using their native language while composing on topics in a foreign language in certain instances. The use of the native language can help students retrieve more information on certain kinds of topics and thus enhance the quality of their final compositions. Friedlander's 28 Chinese subjects profited differentially, however, from using Chinese, depending on the topic of the composition: They wrote more on topics related to Chinese experiences when they used their native language to plan their writing, but profited more from using English to plan compositions relating to experiences rooted in English-speaking culture. Friedlander argues against forcing students who are at an advanced level in the second language to plan compositions or engage in parts of the composing process in the target language when this might add to the burden and constraints they are under already. However, he suggests that ESL students at lower levels should be encouraged to do everything in English, since they need as much practice as possible, and their use of their native language would perhaps not be best for them. If developing *linguistic* skills is not the main point of the writing, but refining skills already developed is the goal, then use of the native language in certain aspects of the composing process may be advantageous.

Research on Evaluation and Feedback: Second-Language Studies

Opinions about how and when to evaluate student written work vary widely. For example, some researchers, scholars, and practitioners recommend that we respond primarily to content and not to form. Others suggest that we respond to both form and content, with some scholars recommending that response to form be reserved to the final draft and others preferring to respond to formal features throughout the process. There seems to be a general consensus that involving students in their own correction is helpful (Lalande 1982; Hedgcock and Lefkowitz

1992; Aljaafreh and Lantolf 1994), and that a combination of teacher-, peer-, and self-evaluation might yield the most successful results.

Empirical studies on the effects of feedback and evaluation in second- and foreign-language writing have yielded contradictory results. Studies that seem to indicate that corrective feedback on form was not helpful include those by Semke (1984), Zamel (1985), Cohen (1987), and Kepner (1991). In Semke's study, German students writing journals who were given no corrective feedback on form and were graded solely on amount of communication responded more favorably to that type of treatment and wrote significantly more words on a free-writing posttest than did students who were graded on accuracy alone and had obtained some kind of corrective feedback from the teacher. However, it is possible that the effects of grading and feedback strategy were confounded in this study, since the group of students who received no corrective feedback were rewarded for quantity only and the others who received corrective feedback were rewarded only for accuracy. Students in the no-feedback condition were also directed to write twice as much for an A as students in the other groups. Thus the effects of feedback *per se,* divorced from the other variables present in the study, are not entirely clear.

Zamel's (1985) study revealed that teachers' feedback on advanced ESL compositions was often inconsistent and contradictory, and that that might render error correction ineffective. Cohen (1987) studied various students' responses to feedback on their compositions and found that teachers' comments were often confusing, vague, and inconsistent, and that most comments focused exclusively on form. In addition, most of the students in his study were never asked to write a second draft after receiving the teachers' input. He recommends that teachers focus more on process in their comments and use multi-draft assignments. Students also should be taught how to use feedback to enhance their writing skills. Kepner (1991) explored types of feedback given to students on eight journal writing assignments in intermediate college Spanish. She compared the effectiveness of a treatment using message-related comments, in which no errors were identified or corrected, to a surface-error treatment, in which students' errors were directly corrected by the teacher and supplemented with brief notes or rules explaining the corrections. An analysis of the sixth journal entry revealed that there was no significant difference between groups in terms of surface-level accuracy, but that students in the message-related condition wrote journal entries with significantly greater numbers of higher-level propositions. Kepner concluded that error correction feedback was not helpful in either eliminating surface errors or encouraging higher-level writing performance. However, as Ferris (1999) points out, Kepner's subjects were writing journal entries rather than papers that were later revised, and results might differ when feedback on accuracy is followed by revision.

In an essay by Truscott (1996) reviewing both L1 and L2 studies on written feedback, the author argues that correcting students' errors in writing is ineffective and should be abandoned. Ferris (1999) responds that, although some of Truscott's points may be valid and should be considered by teachers and researchers, an overall conclusion that error correction is never helpful to students is not warranted, particularly in light of the relatively limited number of studies to date. She adds that the research on second- and foreign-language feedback needs to be assessed carefully before generalizations can be made, particularly because studies vary greatly on such key design features as duration of the treatments, the way feedback is given, the subjects involved, and instructional methods. Additional factors that vary in research designs include the language being studied, the level of proficiency of the students, and the instrumentation used for measuring the effectiveness of treatments. Although the studies reviewed thus far in this section suggest that error correction is not particularly effective, the research presented next demonstrates a more positive role for error feedback on student writing.

Studies by Lalande (1982), Fathman and Whalley (1985,1990), Rieken (1991), Frantzen (1995), and Ferris (1997) have shown beneficial results from teachers' corrective feedback on compositions of second- and foreign-language learners. Lalande (1982) compared the effects of self-correction versus teacher-correction on compositions in fourth-quarter college German classes. The students in the control group were corrected by their teachers and asked to rewrite their compositions. Students in the experimental group received error codes and charts indicating where they had committed errors and were asked to self-correct using these aids. Self-correction in this second condition was done in class, with students engaged in problem solving using the codes, their texts, and teacher or peer assistance if necessary. The self-correcting group had statistically fewer errors at the end of the experimental period than did the control group, who received teacher corrections and rewrote their work. Lalande concludes that the combination of awareness of one's errors and rewriting with problem-solving techniques was significantly beneficial for developing writing skills in German.

A study in English as a Foreign Language conducted by Robb, Ross, and Shortreed (1986) compared four types of feedback on Japanese students' surface errors in an effort to see if the salience of the feedback had an effect on students' writing over time. The researchers compared the effects of having teachers correct all lexical, syntactic, and stylistic errors directly to three other treatments: (a) giving students codes to indicate the nature of their errors; (b) marking errors with a yellow text-marking pen, without an indication of the nature of the errors; and (c) tallying the number of errors per line in the margin of the composition and asking students to search the line to identify and correct their own errors. Over the course of the academic year, students wrote five narratives that were then analyzed on a range of measures, clustered into factors depicting accuracy, fluency, and complexity. Results indicated no significant difference between the treatment groups on accuracy, but there was a gradual improvement over time regardless of the method of feedback given. The authors suggest that overt corrections and comprehensive treatment of surface errors may not be worth the time taken to provide them, and that "less time-consuming methods of directing student attention to surface error may suffice" (p. 91). These results are somewhat different from those in the Lalande (1982) study, where the use of codes was helpful. However, the two studies are not directly comparable, as students in Lalande's study who received error codes were given opportunities to work on revisions with teacher guidance, input from peers, and consultation of other resources in a problem-solving situation. Lalande's students also kept track of their error types over time, which may have helped them prioritize their attention to particular errors that were problematic for them.

Fathman and Whalley (1990) found that when teachers underlined grammatical errors in their students' texts, students made fewer grammatical errors in rewriting their compositions than when no such feedback was provided. Their study also indicated that grammatical and content feedback can beneficially be provided at the same time without overburdening the students. The 72 ESL students in their study rewrote their compositions in class in response to four feedback conditions: (1) no feedback, (2) grammatical feedback (where errors were underlined), (3) content feedback, and (4) both grammar and content feedback. While the majority of students receiving no feedback increased their scores just by rewriting, students made more improvement when they received feedback. There was a significant reduction in grammatical errors for students receiving grammatical feedback (conditions 2 and 4). Most of the students who received only content feedback improved their content scores, but 35% of them made more grammar errors in their revisions. When students received *both* grammar and content feedback, they all improved on grammar significantly, and 77% also improved on content. The authors concluded that grammar and content feedback, whether given alone or in concert, positively affect rewriting, and that grammatical feedback had more effect on correction of errors than content feedback had on the improvement of the content of the students' second draft.

Rieken's (1991) study investigated the possibility that there might be an interaction between feedback type and cognitive style. She looked at the effects of three different levels of feedback on the writing of high school students of French who differed in the cognitive-style dimension of field independence. She examined the effects of (1) no corrective feedback, (2) indirect correction through substantive comments in which corrections were embedded, and (3) direct correction of errors on frequency and accuracy of students' use of the *passé composé*. All students received positive evaluative comments on their compositions and were directed to rewrite them. She found that students who had explicit corrections were significantly more accurate in their use of the *passé composé* when accuracy was calculated on the number of different verbs used, but that there were no significant differences among groups on frequency of use of the past tense. There was also no difference among groups when accuracy was calculated on the *total* number of verbs used, including those that were repeated within the composition. (That is, significant differences appeared on the accuracy criterion only when the percentage of error across the range of different verbs was considered.) Rieken found no differences among groups on a post-treatment cloze test except among students with low field independence (FI). Low FI students who had had direct correction performed more accurately on the cloze test than low FI students in the other feedback conditions. The results suggest that various correction strategies may be differentially effective, depending on the student's cognitive style.

Rieken also found a significant teacher effect, a dimension that is ignored in many empirical studies. It may be that the teacher's attitude toward correction, the way in which correction is offered to students, and students' own feelings about the teacher in general are significant factors in the effectiveness of correction strategies.

Another factor that may affect writing performance is whether the work is evaluated for a grade. Chastain (1990) examined the effects of grading compositions on the quality of student writing. His study examined the compositions of 14 advanced undergraduate Spanish students, most of whom were majors in their third or fourth year and who were characterized by the researcher as having "good" language skills and high motivation. The course emphasized process over product, and students were expected to write second drafts before turning in compositions for a grade. Compositions in this experiment were written in clusters of three, the first two of which were ungraded and the third one graded. Near the end of the semester, Chastain examined one ungraded and one graded composition for each of the 14 students in the class. He found that students wrote significantly more for the graded composition than for the ungraded one and used significantly longer and more complex sentences. However, he found no significant differences in the two compositions in terms of errors, content, or organizational grades. Chastain notes that the percentage of error to total words was very low (less than 5% for the whole class) and that students "did study some of the grammar that confounds advanced as well as beginning students" (p. 11). He adds that most of the students were products of grammar-based classes. It is possible that these learners may have been well prepared for a class that emphasized process writing through early concentration on more structured or focused tasks. However, it is difficult to conclude from the study itself what might have led to the relatively low level of error among these motivated students.

In a study with intermediate Spanish students in a content-based course, Frantzen (1995) looked at the effects of supplementing the content-based instruction with a grammar component on students' performance on both a discrete-point test and an open-ended essay. In the grammar-supplement sections, students had a 10–15 minute review of a grammar topic and received direct corrections of their errors on their compositions, supplemented with a marginal note in Spanish to explain corrections that were judged to be potentially unclear. In the nongrammar group, there was no grammatical instruction in class, but errors on compositions were indicated by circling or underlining the word containing the error, without direct correction. Frantzen found that both groups of students improved on grammar and on other measures for several of the essay variables over time (from pretest to posttest essays written on the same topic), but that the grammar-supplement group improved significantly more than the nongrammar group on the discrete-point measure. Frantzen concluded that grammatical accuracy on written essays "can be significantly improved by simply interacting in the language in a meaningful context," and that grammar supplementation can be beneficial in a content course when performance on discrete-point tests is important (pp. 329, 339). However, it is important to note that both groups in this study received feedback on error, though the degree of directness of that feedback differed.

In a study with ESL students, Ferris (1997) analyzed over 1600 marginal and end notes made by teachers on 220 advanced-level student compositions (110 pairs of first and second drafts). She then looked at the revised versions of these essays to see how such comments were used. Teacher comments included questions, statements about the students' writing, suggestions to elaborate or clarify, positive comments, and suggestions for correcting surface errors. Most comments were focused on the ideas rather than on grammatical problems, although summary notes at the end sometimes dealt with particular surface errors underlined in the text. Ferris found that students generally made fairly substantive changes in response to teacher questions on content, and that comments on grammar resulted in positive change, especially when they were paired with underlinings in the text. She adds that "simultaneous attention to content and form (a false dichotomy in any case) does not short-circuit students' ability to revise their ideas but may . . . improve their end products, because they receive more accuracy oriented feedback throughout the writing process" (p. 333).

Thus far we have been looking at the effects of teachers' response to student writing. Several studies have also looked at peer and self-correction, as well as expert help in a collaborative editing of student work. In a study by Hedgcock and Lefkowitz (1992) with college students in an accelerated first-year French course, small groups in the experimental condition revised two multidraft compositions collaboratively. Each student in a group of three read his or her composition aloud, with group members responding orally according to a written protocol supplied by the teacher. The control group received only written instructor feedback on the drafts of their essays. Results showed that there were no significant differences between groups when the two essay results were pooled, but that there were some quantitative differences between Essays 1 and 2. These differences seemed to indicate more attention to accuracy on Essay 2 for students receiving the instructor feedback and more attention to content and organization for those in the collaborative peer response condition. The authors point out that there are limitations in the study, in that the two essays were not counterbalanced and that performance differences cannot therefore be attributed only to feedback type. They conclude that collaborative peer response is an effective means of providing feedback to learners that does not sacrifice accuracy, and that this means of responding to student work "can free the teacher from time-consuming, painstaking correction which frequently leads to little or no change in learners' long-range writing competence" (p. 264). They add that they do not claim that peer response is superior to instructor feedback, but that it can be used to help learners participate more actively in the composing process.

A study by Aljaafreh and Lantolf (1994) investigated the collaboration between "expert" and "novice" writers to see how individual students react to and utilize various kinds of expert feedback to revise their work. The authors maintain that feedback needs to be individualized through collaborative negotiation "on-line with the learner" (p. 466). In this study, three students in a level-two ESL reading and writing class volunteered to work with the researcher on a one-to-one basis once a week in a tutorial to collaborate on revising their essays. Before they began the collaborative session, students were asked to read their essays, underlining errors and trying to correct them. The tutor then worked with each individual in a dialogic exchange, providing help as indicated by the learner's individual needs. The authors identified five levels of development, from not noticing an error or not being able to correct it, even with expert help, to eventually noticing and correcting errors and subsequently using the structures correctly independently. The authors also found that different learners require different levels of help from the tutor, as they may be at different levels of development for any given structure. On the basis of their qualitative research, the authors conclude that "the types of error correction (i.e., implicit or explicit) that promote learning cannot be determined independently of individual learners interacting with other individuals" (p. 480), and that effective feedback will have a "dynamic character" as learners move toward self-reliance and require less help from others as their skills develop.

The points made by Aljaafreh and Lantolf may help us understand why, at least in part, the results of studies on feedback may be variable. Other reasons for conflicting results may include the differences in study designs, the levels and languages of the participants, and the range of contexts under which the studies were conducted. The effectiveness of feedback may depend, in part, on the level of motivation of students, their current level of proficiency, their cognitive style, the clarity of the feedback given, the way feedback is used, and the attitudes of students toward their teacher and the class. The studies reviewed do seem to indicate that teacher feedback is sometimes confusing, inconsistent, and contradictory, and that feedback that is exclusively focused on form is discouraging to many students. These findings can be useful to teachers as they consider their own feedback strategies and evaluate various ways to respond to student work.

Approaches to Teaching Writing as Creative Communication

Kroll (1990) notes that among many scholars in native language writing instruction there seems to have been a paradigm shift away from a focus on writing as *product* toward a focus on *process*. This same shift has been called for by scholars in foreign language instruction as well. (See, for example, Dvorak 1986; Barnett 1989; and Scott 1996.) Some researchers (for example, Raimes 1983; Kaplan 1988; and Silva 1990) urge a balanced approach that takes both process and product into account. This section briefly summarizes some of the possible approaches to writing instruction that have been advocated by scholars in both native- and second-language contexts.

Hillocks (1986) identifies four "modes" of writing instruction in native language composition:

1. *The Presentational Mode,* with clear and specific objectives, teacher-centered discussions of writing principles, and assignments involving imitation and analysis of models of writing;

2. *The Natural Process Mode,* which encourages free writing, including the use of daily journals, emphasizes positive feedback from peers and the teacher, fosters cooperative learning with a low level of structure in assignments, and is nondirectional about the qualities of writing to be developed;

3. *The Environmental Mode,* emphasizing clear and specific objectives and group work on particular processes important to some aspect of composing (such as increasing the use of detail in a description). In this approach, principles are taught by the teacher through concrete examples and models. Students work together on specific problems, provide one another with peer evaluation, and use teacher-provided checklists, structured questions, or other specific criteria to respond to their own and others' work. This approach is similar to what Applebee (1986) has called a "structured process mode."

4. *The Individualized Mode,* where students are instructed through tutorials or programmed materials, and the instruction is geared specifically to student needs (Hillocks 1986, pp. 116–126).

For ESL classes, Raimes (1983) recommends an eclectic approach to writing and asserts that there is no one answer to the question of how writing should be taught. Rather, "there are as many answers as there are teachers and teaching styles, or learners and learning styles" (p. 5). She reviews six different writing approaches, which are described briefly below. Some of these approaches have also been prevalent in foreign language classes:

1. *The Controlled-to-Free Approach,* which stresses accuracy over fluency or originality and is essentially based in ALM teaching practice. In this approach, students write variations first on sentences, then on paragraphs, then on very controlled compositions, and finally work on free composition when their skills are at an advanced level;

2. *The Free-Writing Approach,* which encourages vast amounts of fluency-based writing with little correction;

3. *The Paragraph-Pattern Approach,* which stresses organization over fluency or accuracy and provides model paragraphs for students to copy, analyze, or imitate;

4. *The Grammar-Syntax-Organization Approach,* which works simultaneously on various formal features as students write to carry out specific writing functions;

5. *The Communicative Approach,* stressing purpose and audience and encouraging interaction among students and the teacher, with less emphasis on form and correctness; and

6. *The Process Approach,* emphasizing the writing process over product, with adequate time provided to develop a piece of writing, a recognition of the recursiveness of the process, and the encouragement of exploration of topics through writing (pp. 7–10).

Raimes points out that there is a degree of overlap in all of these approaches and advocates an eclecticism that is responsive to learner needs as their skills develop.

Silva (1990) describes what he considers the four most influential approaches in ESL writing from the period 1945 to 1990 as follows:

1. *Controlled Composition,* similar to the "Controlled-to-Free" approach described by Raimes (1983), above;
2. *Current-Traditional Rhetoric,* which is product-oriented, focusing on proper mechanics and usage as well as rhetorical organization and style. This approach tends to focus on paragraph construction (topic sentences, the use of supportive detail, cause-effect or comparison/contrast patterns) and on essay development (writing introduction, body, and conclusion). It also explores various kinds of expository writing styles. Silva says that although this approach has been "under attack" for a number of years, it is still quite dominant in ESL classrooms (p. 15).
3. *The Process Approach,* reacting against prescriptive techniques and characterized by prewriting activities, multiple drafts, and peer-editing, with final editing for form reserved for the final draft; and
4. *English for Academic Purposes,* where students are taught to write for an academic audience (Silva 1990, pp. 12–17).

Scott (1996) suggests that, although "it would be clearly unwise to propose a single prescriptive approach to teaching FL writing" (p. 45), research about the composing process in L1, L2, and FL writing leads to various classroom implications. For example, she recommends that teachers talk to students about the composing process, both in the native and foreign language, so that students become more aware of the processes and strategies they use when writing. She also emphasizes teaching writing as "discovery," suggesting that students begin with foreign language words and expressions as a means of generating ideas for composition, rather than beginning with ideas in the native language and trying (often unsuccessfully) to translate these ideas into the target language. Another suggestion is that teachers help students link grammar and writing by emphasizing the role of grammar in the writing process. "Students can be taught to shift their focus from thinking of writing as a linguistic exercise in which quality is measured by the degree of accuracy, to thinking of writing as an activity in which linguistic information can help them shape their ideas" (p. 48). Rather than focusing on writing as a grammatical exercise, students can be helped to see writing as a way to create personal meaning. Scott suggests that teachers use a "task-oriented approach" to writing assignments, such as the one shown in Illustration 7.13, p. 309 (an activity drawn from Scott and Terry 1992). Such tasks consist of giving students a situation or context and a set of specific directives for meeting the requirements of the assignment. Directives typically include having students consult the phrases, vocabulary, and grammar helps in the writing assistant program *système-D*. In this way, a link is made in the writing task between form and meaning, "thereby avoiding an exclusive focus on accuracy" (p. 49). Finally, Scott suggests that students need to be explicitly taught strategies for revising their work, and recommends that teachers include writing conferences with students as part of their instructional approach.

Many of these suggestions apply to teaching writing as "composing" rather than as a support skill for learning the language code. Again, it is important to emphasize that purposes for writing, particularly at lower levels of proficiency, can vary, and the methodological approach and task characteristics should fit the writing purpose. It seems that the choice of method will be determined in part by the level of the students, the situation in which they are learning (native language, second language, or foreign language contexts), the goals of instruction, and the needs and preferences of the students. What kinds of skills do students currently have, and what skills do they need to develop? If students are at a relatively low level of writing proficiency, they may need to have the support of a structured approach, such as "controlled composition," a "paragraph-pattern approach," a "structured-process mode," or a "task-oriented approach" that emphasizes defined objectives and provides clear feedback and evaluative criteria. An eclectic approach, integrating assignments where self-expression through journaling or free writing is encouraged with tasks that are more structured might also be a good option for students in the Intermediate ranges of proficiency. For students who are relatively advanced and who want to improve their expressive or rhetorical skills, a "communicative" approach, stressing such factors as purpose and audience, or an "academic purpose" course, emphasizing writing for a particular kind of audience, might be a good choice. In the final analysis, it is the teacher working with particular students who will need to determine which approach is best. As in any discussion of methodological trends, we are limited in our perspective if we search for just "one true way." Silva (1990) urges teachers to avoid methodological bandwagons and make a professional and reasoned evaluation of the various approaches, preserving the insights that are useful from all of them. This represents both the privilege and the challenge of the classroom teacher of the twenty-first century, who is left with more questions than answers, given the present state of our knowledge in this domain.

Advanced-Level Activities: Preparing for Superior-Level Writing

Students who are currently writing at the Advanced level in the second language are generally able to write reasonably accurate, coherent discourse dealing with both concrete and abstract topics. They can narrate events in past, present, and future time and, at the Advanced-High level, are often able to support a point of view relatively coherently. Obviously, students whose writing is at this level will still need to work on improving their grammatical accuracy, their choice of vocabulary, and their rhetorical skills and can profit from a variety of structured practice activities that refine their control of the language in these domains.

However, in addition to developing expertise in the use of advanced features of the language through structured or semistructured language-practice activities, students at this level of competence need to learn more about the composing process itself. The activities suggested in this section are, for the most part, semiguided and free composition tasks that involve rather extensive work on the improvement of discourse skills as well as practice in the composing process. According to Jacobs, Zingraf, Wormuth, Hartfiel, and Hughey (1981), the overall aim of composition practice at the Advanced level should be the development of authentic discourse processing skills. The primary focus of such writing practice "should not be the word, the phrase, or the sentence, but the larger elements and processes that must be integrated and synthesized for effective written communication" (p. v). The authors suggest various criteria that should be used in designing composition tasks and tests at this level, and provide the evaluative checklist given in Illustration 7.14.

When designing writing practice at the Advanced level, it is important to include various aspects of the composing process in the instructional sequence. Cooper (1975) identifies the following subprocesses that may be involved in composing:

> *Composing involves prewriting gestation (varying from minutes to months or years); planning the particular piece (with or without notes or outlines); getting started; making continuous decisions about diction, syntax and rhetoric in relation to the intended meaning and to the meaning taking shape; reviewing what has accumulated and anticipating and rehearsing what comes next; tinkering and reformulating; stopping; contemplating the finished piece; and perhaps, finally, revising (p. 113).*

The various steps of the composing process need to be taught, discussed, and practiced more overtly than has typically been the case in many foreign language programs, especially when students are at the Intermediate or Advanced level of writing proficiency. In response to this need, a number of process-oriented writing texts have appeared in recent years that are designed for language learners at the second-year college level and beyond. (For an excellent example of a writing text for French at the advanced undergraduate level, see *A vous d'écrire: Atelier de français* by Loriot-Raymer, Vialet, and Muyskens 1996.) Such texts lead students through various steps or stages as they engage in creative and expressive writing, providing them with target-language models in various rhetorical styles. Guidance is given on organization, style, and the development of greater precision of grammar and vocabulary as students work through the writing process. Students are also encouraged to revise their writing, using guidelines provided in the text, and to share their drafts with peers in small groups to obtain feedback on all aspects of their work. The Loriot-Raymer et al. (1996) text also integrates grammar review, providing a grammar section at the end of the book with marginal notes within the body of the text to signal important grammar topics that are relevant to the task at hand. Teachers who use process-writing texts without integrated grammar reviews or who would like a comprehensive review as part of the course may want to include a reference grammar, selecting grammatical topics to support each of the writing tasks assigned in the course.

Prose Style Analysis and Pastiche

A procedure suggested by Gaudiani (1981) encourages students to study various styles of writing and make analyses of stylistic elements used by a variety of authors in the target language. She asks students to write style analyses in English, after which they write a composition on a theme of their choice, imitating the style of the author under study.

Illustration 7.14
Checklist for Preparing
the Writing Task

Does the task:

[ ] require writers to *compose* a piece of connected discourse?

[ ] establish a clear purpose for communicating, especially by indicating the intended reader and a context for the task?

[ ] motivate writers to communicate their knowledge and perception of the topic?

[ ] reflect the kind of writing students will normally be expected to do in their academic programs or the real world?

[ ] provide a subject that will interest students of this age, sex, educational level, field of study, and cultural background?

[ ] present a topic about which these students will have knowledge?

[ ] appear to be the right level of difficulty for students of this proficiency range?

[ ] provide a topic that is free of hidden elements of bias?

[ ] present a clearly defined task that cannot easily be misinterpreted?

[ ] provide a topic that is broad enough for every writer to approach from some angle?

[ ] use as few words as possible, and definitions if necessary?

[ ] give clear and concise instructions that indicate also the time allowed for writing and the approximate number of words or length of composition expected?

[ ] present a writable and readable topic, pretested with students similar to the test group?

[ ] include as many modes of discourse as are appropriate to the purpose of the test and to the actual writing needs of the students?

[ ] provide at least two writing occasions, in order to produce an adequate sample of a student's ability?

[ ] require all students to write on the same topic, unless skill at choosing a topic is a part of the abilities being tested?

[ ] allow enough writing time for a reasonable performance?

[ ] provide ruled paper for writing?

[ ] use a coding system for identifying writers so that authorship will be anonymous during the evaluation?

[ ] Is the writing task appropriate to the specific purpose(s) of this test?

Source: Jacobs et al. (1981), p. 22. Reprinted by permission.

When students are ready to begin the prose style analysis phase of their training in composition, Gaudiani has them read the excerpt that will be used for the pastiche. They discuss style and organization and notice grammatical and lexical features that the author has chosen to create certain effects. Then working in small groups, students try to write a sample of prose in a fashion that resembles the model. Later students do a second prose style analysis on a new text and write a pastiche individually as their next composition assignment.

The following example in French is designed to help intermediate to advanced composition students to analyze literary prose and incorporate some of the strategies the author uses in their own writing. In this case, students work with a short passage from *L'Etranger* by Albert Camus in which he describes the scene at a nursing home where the leading character's mother has just died. The description of the residents is both impersonal and yet photographic in its detail. Camus uses sound, light, and movement to capture the mood of the residents, and the use of adjectives is especially artful in this particular description.

Before reading the passage, students can be asked to engage in various activities that elicit their own ideas and images around the theme of the text to be studied. For example, students in small groups can discuss their experiences with the elderly and/or with nursing home environments, generating a list of descriptive words and images that come to mind. They might also list words or phrases that express their feelings about these experiences or about the living conditions of many elderly people in their own culture. Anticipation activities can also be designed to help students predict how the author might deal with the scene in the passage to be read.

After reading the passage, students engage in a series of activities that help them analyze the style of the author. The sample "Analyse du texte" provided below asks students to react to the author's perspective as he surveys the scene at the nursing home and notice the stylistic use of images. Students extract words and expressions from the text that relate to sounds, light, and movement both in the physical surroundings and in the descriptions of the people themselves (see table, p. 330). Students then find examples of the impersonality of the description and react to the lack of compassion on the part of the principal character in the novel.

SAMPLE PROSE ANALYSIS ACTIVITY OF AN EXTRACT FROM CAMUS' *L'ETRANGER*

Analyse du texte

1. Après avoir lu ce passage, quelle est l'impression principale que vous avez de l'asile et de ses résidents? *[After having read the passage, what is the principal impression that you have of the nursing home and of its residents?]*

   a. C'est un endroit bien triste sans espoir. *[It's a very sad, hopeless place.]*

   b. C'est un environnement bizarre et effrayant. *[It's a strange and frightening environment.]*

   c. C'est une communauté où les résidents expriment leur affection les uns pour les autres. *[It's a community where the residents express their affection for one another.]*

   d. _____?

2. Comment Meursault voit-il l'asile et ses résidents? *[How does Meursault (the principal character of the novel) see the nursing home and its residents?]*

   a. comme un observateur très sympathique *[as a very sympathetic observer]*

   b. comme un étranger—aliéné sans compréhension *[as a stranger, alienated and uncomprehending]*

   c. comme un jeune homme qui ne s'intéresse pas vraiment à un groupe de vieillards *[like a young man who is not very interested in a group of old people]*

   d. _____?

3. En faisant son portrait de l'asile, Camus utilise beaucoup d'images frappantes: le jeu de la lumière, les descriptions assez détaillées des vieux, les sons, les mouvements. Analysez ces aspects de la description ci-dessous en mettant des mots ou des expressions du texte dans le schéma: *[In creating his portrait of the nursing home, Camus uses a lot of striking images: the play of the light, rather detailed descriptions of the old people, sounds, and movements. Analyze these aspects of the description below by placing words and expressions from the text in the boxes of the graph.]*

4. Donnez quelques détails qui montrent que Meursault a de la difficulté à voir ou à entendre les vieux dans la salle: *[Give a few details that show that Meursault has problems seeing or hearing the old people in the room.]*

5. Donnez quelques détails qui montrent que Meursault les voit comme des objets plutôt que des êtres humains: *[Give a few details that show that Meursault sees them as objects rather than as people.]*

6. Comment Meursault réagit-il en ce qui concerne ses émotions? Citez des exemples du texte: *[How does Meursault react emotionally? Give some examples from the text.]*

7. Meursault comprend-il les émotions des vieux dans la salle? Expliquez votre réponse: *[Does Meursault understand the emotions of the old people in the room? Explain your response.]*

	LA SALLE *(THE ROOM)*	LES VIEUX *(THE ELDERLY)*
SONS *(SOUNDS)*		
LUMIÈRE *(LIGHT)*		
MOUVEMENTS *(MOVEMENTS)*		

After analyzing the excerpt, students are asked to write a description of a different scene in the same style or to change the description written by Camus to one in which the author takes a different point of view of the same scene (for example, a more compassionate view). This task can be done cooperatively in groups or by individuals working alone. Follow-up activities include peer editing of the work produced, as described in the next section.

Refining the Written Draft

Peer Editing: Gaudiani (1981) has written an excellent monograph in which she proposes various ideas for teaching composition at the Advanced level. One of the procedures she suggests is the "class editing process," in which students help one another improve their drafts through a series of "passes."

Each week in the composition class, a small group of students provides for all the others in the class a mimeographed copy of their first draft of the assigned theme. The compositions are typed triple spaced to enable everyone ample room for written comments. The steps in the class editing procedure, described below in paraphrased form, are:

1. *Comprehension of Meaning.* Students listen as one of the people who has prepared a mimeographed composition reads it aloud. Class members ask for clarification of any words or expressions they do not understand during this first pass.
2. *Correction of Grammar.* The teacher reads each sentence of the composition and asks the author and the others in the class to provide any needed grammatical corrections.
3. *Analysis of Prose Style.* After the composition has been corrected in the second pass, the class reads it once again silently, after which they comment on the style. When problems relating to sentence length, repetition of words, lack of precision in vocabulary or expression, etc. are discovered, the teacher asks for solutions from class members.
4. *Analysis of Organization.* Students read the composition a fourth time, looking now for such things as paragraphing, the use of topic sentences, and summaries. Suggestions are made on the basis of this fourth pass through the draft.
5. *Overview/Synthesis.* Finally, the class offers general comments on the effectiveness of the composition as a whole in communicating a message (summary based on Gaudiani 1981, p. 14).

Birckbichler (1985) has suggested that the class editing process may be most effective if students in a composition class work on anonymous writing samples provided from outside their own group, thus eliminating any reluctance to critique the samples for fear of hurting someone's feelings. She suggests using samples from a similar class in a previous year or from another class offered the same semester. (In either case, it is important to obtain permission from students whose work is being evaluated to use it for peer editing purposes.) In Birckbichler's experience, students said more and got more out of the class editing procedure when working with anonymous compositions than they did when judging the work of their peers within the same class.

Birckbichler also points out that peer editing activities need a clear focus so that students know exactly what they should be concentrating on in any given part of the process. She suggests that specific questions might be designed by the teacher to guide discussion in each of the steps of the class editing procedure.

Terry (2000) reports on the success of using an Internet conferencing program in a fifth-semester composition course. Students were put in peer-editing groups of three or four. A conference was set up for individual groups, each member of which posted his or her rough draft composition written with a word processor. Peer editors then downloaded the composition, made editorial comments and corrections, and reposted the composition. The author could accept or reject the peer editors' comments in preparing the first draft that was submitted to the instructor. In the individual conference groups, students were given the opportunity to have conference chats, i.e., real-time synchronous conversations on the Internet concerning the draft compositions. The first draft of the composition was not corrected, but was edited using a series of editorial codes. A grade was assigned and the composition returned to the author for corrections. When the final draft was submitted, the first draft and comment/correction sheet were attached in order to compare the two drafts. The final draft was again edited and graded, and the final grade on the composition was the average of the grades of both drafts.

Self-Editing Using Teacher-Developed Guidelines

Barnett (1989) outlines a self-editing approach to writing that requires advanced students to write two drafts before turning in their compositions for a grade, followed if necessary by a third draft that is written after they receive substantive feedback on form and content, style, organization, and the like. She suggests collecting students' notes used in the planning of their first draft, as well as the first draft itself when grading the second draft. The guidelines for writing and self-editing that she provides to students are quite comprehensive, including advice about getting started, strategies for taking notes and using them to develop and organize one's ideas, and procedures for writing successive drafts and evaluating one's writing. The approach encourages students to focus on meaning during the writing of their first draft and correct the form later. One of the strengths of this method is that it does not neglect attention to form, but rather makes it one of several concerns involved in the composing process. In Barnett's approach, teacher comments on the multiple drafts incorporate various aspects of feedback. In response to the first draft, most comments relate to the content and include requests for clarification of ideas and suggestions for reorganization. One or two general comments about form are also included, and positive feedback is given to encourage the student by pointing out strengths. In the response to the second draft, the teacher underlines all remaining errors, highlights a few for focused attention and correction, points out a few places where the student still needs to improve organization, and assigns a dual grade based on form (50%) and content (50%). Barnett maintains that this kind of approach to feedback on compositions yields far more satisfying results for both teacher and students than does an approach based on morphological or syntactic repairs alone.

Evaluation and Grading of Student Writing

Teacher response to students' written compositions has typically taken two forms: (1) corrective feedback on the microlevel and (2) an overall evaluation in the form of a grade. Scott (1996) maintains that both correction and evaluation represent essential components of teaching foreign language writing. Each of these aspects of evaluation represents a complex task that should be integrated throughout the entire writing process and not used only for responding to the final draft. We have just seen how various kinds of qualitative feedback can be given to students through teacher commentary, peer editing, and self-editing using guidelines, codes, or checklists. The second type of response—evaluation of the work on a macrolevel—can be given using a variety of scoring schemes and objective techniques. Perkins (1983) has outlined the assumptions, procedures, and consequences of using three principal types of scoring in the evaluation of compositions: (1) holistic scoring, (2) analytical scoring, and (3) primary trait scoring.

1. *Holistic Scoring.* When one is attempting to assess the overall proficiency level of a given written sample, Perkins maintains that holistic scoring has the highest construct validity. In this type of scoring procedure, one or more readers assigns a single grade (or rating) to a text based on an overall impression. The criteria involved in producing this impression might include some of the following:

a. The clarity with which the thesis is stated, developed, and supported;
b. The effectiveness with which an issue has been raised, treated, and resolved;
c. The sufficiency of the support and development of the thesis for the reader;
d. The degree to which the writer has accommodated the needs of the intended audience;
e. The degree of grammatical and lexical cohesion and overall coherence of the piece; and
f. The effective use of rhetorical devices, etc. (Perkins 1983)

Generally, holistic evaluation is done quickly and impressionistically. A guided procedure may be used for sorting a set of papers or ranking them against one another. Papers can be scored holistically for prominence of certain features considered to be important for the type of writing assigned. The evaluation can be in the form of a letter or number grade, or, in the case of proficiency testing, a rating such as those used in the ACTFL Guidelines.

One of the main drawbacks of holistic scoring methods, according to Perkins, is that they can be highly subjective. In addition, fatigue factors, previous acquaintance with the student, and shifting standards from one paper to the next can lead to unreliable scoring. If judges assign different weights to the scoring criteria, it is difficult to obtain reliable scores. Until everyone agrees on what constitutes good writing, consensus among judges might be hard to reach.

One way to avoid the problem of subjectivity is to insist on rater competence and training. If specified criteria are to focus the readers' attention, if some common standard is applied, and if multiple samples of writing are elicited, the chances of success in using a holistic scheme are increased.

2. *Analytical Scoring.* This technique involves the separation of the various features of a composition into components for scoring purposes. One advantage of scoring features separately, especially in classroom instruction, is that more precise diagnostic feedback can be provided to the student. Because the teacher's criteria are more focused, grading tends to be more reliable as well (Perkins 1983). Two different analytic scoring schemes are provided in Illustrations 7.15 and 7.16, representing suggestions by Gaudiani (1981) and Jacobs et al. (1981).

Perkins (1983) points out that analytic scoring techniques may have several disadvantages:

Illustration 7.15
Composition Scoring Scheme and Sample Grades (Gaudiani 1981)

(1) Grammar/vocabulary:
  A = fluent with moments of elegance, few errors
  B = comprehensible, some errors
  C = substantial and significant errors
  D = one or more blocks to communication
  F = unintelligible

(2) Stylistic technique:
  A = skilled use of syntax in terms of content, variation in syntax
  B = clear, appropriate, and sophisticated syntax
  C = errors, but attempts at sophistication and appropriateness
  D = errors and/or inappropriate syntax
  F = garbled syntax

(3) Organization:
  A = well-organized paragraphs, use of clear topic and summary sentences, convincing, easy to follow
  B = good evidence of structuring of paragraphs (perhaps an unwieldy use of patterns of organization)
  C = some attempts at organization, but few topic, development, summary sequences
  D = hard to follow, organization undermines intelligibility
  F = no evidence of planning in structure of paragraphs

(4) Content:
  A = significant, interesting, appropriate, well thought out, appropriate to assignment
  B = generally good work, but facts may be unsupported, or repetitions or clichés may be apparent
  C = careless development of data relevant to content
  D = no effort to make content significant to composition
  F = incoherent or wildly inappropriate content

Illustration 7.15, continued

A well-written but poorly organized composition will be graded, for instance, as follows:

Grammar/Vocabulary	B = 3
Style	A = 4
Organization	C = 2
Content	B = 3

$$12 \div 4 = 3 \text{ or } B$$

Or, a student who writes unsophisticated syntax in perfect Spanish with little thought about organization or content may receive a poor grade despite "perfect" grammar.

Grammar/Vocabulary	A = 4
Style	D = 1
Organization	D = 1
Content	F = 0

$$6 \div 4 = 1.5 \text{ or } D+$$

On the other hand, students who try hard to write sophisticated sentences, use logical connectives, and organize a well thought out content intelligently may make more grammar/vocabulary errors.

Grammar/Vocabulary	C = 2
Style	B = 3
Organization	B = 3
Content	A = 4

$$12 \div 4 = 3 \text{ or } B$$

Source: Gaudiani 1981, pp. 20–21. Reprinted by permission.

---

a. A text is more than the sum of its parts, and analytic scoring may isolate the features of the writing from their overall context.

b. The highest score on any given feature may represent a standard that is too much to expect from writers at a given level of proficiency.

c. Scoring weights ought to be adjusted, to reflect the type of discourse, since scales with equal weights are not sensitive to variations in purpose, writer's role, or conception of the audience.

d. The procedure is relatively time consuming.

Despite these potential problems, this type of scoring for evaluating compositions can be a good choice, particularly if teachers take into account the issues mentioned above by Perkins (1983). For example, it would be important in a first- or second-year program to adjust the weights of the scales and the descriptions of the component scores to be as congruent as possible to the proficiency level of beginning- and intermediate-level students. Because this type of scoring can be relatively easy to use and provides students with focused feedback on various dimensions of their work, component scoring may be preferable for open-ended compositions on classroom tests as well. It is a good idea to devote at least

Illustration 7.16 ESL Composition Profile

			ESL COMPOSITION PROFILE	
STUDENT			DATE TOPIC	
	Score	Level	Criteria	Comments
CONTENT		30–27	EXCELLENT TO VERY GOOD: knowledgeable•substantive•thorough development•relevant to assigned topic	
		26–22	GOOD TO AVERAGE: some knowledge of subject•adequate range•limited development of thesis•mostly relevant to topic, but lacks detail	
		21–17	FAIR TO POOR: limited knowledge of subject•little substance•inadequate development of topic	
		16–13	VERY POOR: does not show knowledge of subject•non-substantive•not pertinent•OR not enough to evaluate	
ORGANIZATION		20–18	EXCELLENT TO VERY GOOD: fluent expression•ideas clearly stated/supported•succinct•well-organized•logical sequencing•cohesive	
		17–14	GOOD TO AVERAGE: somewhat choppy•loosely organized but main ideas stand out•limited support•logical but incomplete sequencing	
		13–10	FAIR TO POOR: non-fluent•ideas confused or disconnected•lacks logical sequencing and development	
		9–7	VERY POOR: does not communicate•no organization•OR not enough to evaluate	
VOCABULARY		20–18	EXCELLENT TO VERY GOOD: sophisticated range•effective word/idiom choice and usage•word form mastery•appropriate register	
		17–14	GOOD TO AVERAGE: adequate range•occasional errors of word/idiom form, choice, usage *but meaning not obscured*	
		13–10	FAIR TO POOR: limited range•frequent errors of word/idiom form, choice, usage•*meaning confused or obscured*	
		9–7	VERY POOR: essentially translation•little knowledge of vocabulary, idioms, word form•OR not enough to evaluate	
LANGUAGE		25–22	EXCELLENT TO VERY GOOD: effective complex constructions•few errors of agreement, tense, number, word order/function, articles, pronouns, prepositions	
		21–18	GOOD TO AVERAGE: effective but simple constructions•minor problems in complex constructions•several errors of agreement, tense, number, word order/function, articles, pronouns, prepositions, *but meaning seldom obscured*	
		17–11	FAIR TO POOR: major problems in simple/complex constructions•frequent errors of negation, agreement, tense, number, word order/function, articles, pronouns, prepositions and/or fragments, run-ons, deletions•*meaning confused or obscured*	
		10–5	VERY POOR: virtually no mastery of sentence construction rules•dominated by errors•does not communicate•OR not enough to evaluate	
MECHANICS		5	EXCELLENT TO VERY GOOD: demonstrates mastery of conventions•few errors of spelling, punctuation, capitalization, paragraphing	
		4	GOOD TO AVERAGE: occasional errors of spelling, punctuation, capitalization, paragraphing *but meaning not obscured*	
		3	FAIR TO POOR: frequent errors of spelling, punctuation, capitalization, paragraphing•poor handwriting•*meaning confused or obscured*	
		2	VERY POOR: no mastery of conventions•dominated by errors of spelling, punctuation, capitalization, paragraphing•handwriting illegible•OR not enough to evaluate	
	TOTAL SCORE		READER COMMENTS	

Source: From *Testing ESL Composition* by Holly Jacobs et al., Copyright 1981, Newbury House Publishers, Inc., Rowley, MA 01960. Reprinted by permission of the publisher.

one class session in a graduate methodology course or a course meeting to evaluating student writing, giving teaching assistants opportunities to rate a sample composition both holistically and with component scores. If individuals first rate a sample text alone and then compare their ratings with those of others, any differences can be discussed so that the components of the scale can be interpreted by each teacher in essentially the same way. Comparing holistic evaluations with component score results is also a helpful exercise, as both methods should yield a similar overall grade if the scales are adjusted properly for the level of the students.

3. *Primary Trait Scoring.* Perkins (1983) explains that in this type of evaluation scheme, scores are assigned holistically based on a certain feature of the writing that is being emphasized, such as the organization or structure of the piece, the vocabulary, or the tone. The teacher needs to decide to what extent the writing sample exhibits certain characteristics (primary traits) that are essential to accomplishing a given writing purpose. For example, if a student's essay was designed to persuade others to adopt his point of view on an issue, the grade might be based on the number of reasons given in the support of his argument, the elaboration of those reasons, the authorities to whom he appealed, and other features of the discourse related to the function of persuasion. An obvious advantage of this type of scoring is that it focuses on the purpose of the writing task directly; a disadvantage is that it ignores other aspects of writing that are important in the composing process. In addition, this type of scoring can be time consuming (Perkins 1983, pp. 658–661).

Perkins's discussion of these three types of scoring procedures is very helpful for classroom teachers who are looking for more objective measures of written performance, and the reader is encouraged to consult this source for a more detailed discussion. In choosing an evaluative tool, classroom teachers will need to weigh the advantages and disadvantages of each to arrive at a procedure that is objective, fair, and efficient, especially if the teaching of composition receives a higher priority in language classrooms in the coming years.

Summary: Becoming Proficient in Writing

In this chapter, a variety of approaches to the teaching of writing in the second-language classroom has been suggested. Ways in which writing can be introduced early in the curriculum as a support skill have been balanced with suggestions for teaching the composing process that leads to effective written communication.

It is important to consider ways to integrate writing with practice in listening, speaking, and reading so that language skills are not artificially separated. An integrative approach provides students with opportunities to use the language they are learning in authentic communication while solidifying control of various aspects of the new language through writing as a support skill. Even when writing activities are used simply as a pedagogical aid, they can be structured in ways that help students learn to produce cohesive and coherent discourse. At every level of proficiency, written practice can also provide diagnostic feedback that will help learners improve their linguistic accuracy. Writing activities can also be used effectively to support and enhance cultural instruction, a topic that is treated in more detail in the next chapter.

Activities for Review and Discussion

1. Compare briefly some of the similarities and differences between speech and writing. Give a rationale for teaching writing as a separate skill in the foreign language classroom. Discuss the difference between writing as a support skill and writing as a creative activity, and the place of each in the foreign language curriculum.
2. If possible, examine samples of student writing in the language you teach (or are planning to teach). Discuss what level of proficiency each of your samples illustrates, giving your rationale.
3. Design at least one original writing activity that would be appropriate for each of the following levels of proficiency: (a) Novice, (b) Intermediate, and (c) Advanced. You may use activity formats suggested in this chapter as models, or create formats of your own.
4. Design at least one activity that will help students write more cohesive and coherent discourse. Include a statement of your objective(s), the context to be used, and the function(s) and/or grammar topics to be emphasized. Give clear directions for the student plus any accompanying stimulus materials (such as visuals, charts, presentation texts, key words, or other organizers).
5. Imagine that you are teaching a class in conversation and composition at the Intermediate level. Using the ideas presented in this chapter as your point of departure, discuss how you would lead your students through the composing process. State (a) how you would determine course goals and objectives for writing, (b) how you would select topics for composition, (c) your methods of providing feedback, (d) the types of feedback you would provide, and (e) your grading procedures.

References: Chapter 7

Aljaafreh, Ali and James P. Lantolf. "Negative Feedback as Regulation and Second Language Learning in the Zone of Proximal Development." *The Modern Language Journal* 78, iv (1994): 465–83.

Allen, Edward and Rebecca Valette. *Modern Language Classroom Techniques,* 2nd ed. New York: Harcourt Brace Jovanovich, 1977.

Applebee, Arthur N. "Problems in Process Approaches: Toward a Reconceptualization of Process Instruction." Chapter 6 (pp. 95–113) in A. Petrosky and D. Bartholomae, eds., *The Teaching of Writing.* Eighty-Fifth

Yearbook of the National Society for the Study of Education, Part II. Chicago: University of Chicago Press, 1986.

Barnett, Marva A. "Writing as Process." *The French Review* 63, i (1989): 31–44.

Beauvois, Margaret Healy. "Computer-Mediated Communication (CMC): *Technology for Improving Speaking and Writing.*" Pp. 165–84 in Michael D. Bush, ed., *Technology-Enhanced Language Learning.* ACTFL Foreign Language Education Series. Lincolnwood, IL: National Textbook Company, 1997.

———. "Write to Speak: The Effects of Electronic Communication on the Oral Achievement of Fourth Semester French Students." Pp. 93–115 in Judith A. Muyskens, ed., *New Ways of Learning and Teaching: Focus on Technology and Foreign Language Education.* AAUSC Issues in Language Program Direction. Boston: Heinle & Heinle, 1998.

Birckbichler, Diane W. Personal communication, 1985.

Bizzell, Patricia. "Composing Processes: An Overview." Chapter 4 (pp. 49–70) in A. Petrosky and D. Bartholomae, eds., *The Teaching of Writing.* Eighty-Fifth Yearbook of the National Society for the Study of Education, Part II. Chicago: University of Chicago Press, 1986.

Bland, Susan K., James Noblitt, Susan Armington, and Geri Gay. "The Naive Lexical Hypothesis: Evidence from Computer-Assisted Language Learning." *The Modern Language Journal* 74, iv (1990): 440–50.

Camus, Albert. *L'Etranger.* Germaine Brée and Carlos Lynes, Jr., eds. New York: Appleton-Century-Crofts, 1955.

Cathcart, Ruth L. and Judy E. W. Olsen. "Teachers' and Students' Preferences for Correction of Classroom Conversation Error." In J. F. Fanselow and R. H. Crymes, eds., *On TESOL '76.* Washington, DC: TESOL, 1976.

Chastain, Kenneth. "Characteristics of Graded and Ungraded Compositions." *The Modern Language Journal* 74, i (1990): 10–14.

Chelala, S. "The Composing Process of Two Spanish-Speakers and the Coherence of Their Texts: A Case Study." Ph.D. Dissertation, New York University, 1981. [Cited in Friedlander, 1990.]

Cohen, Andrew D. "Student Processing of Feedback on Their Compositions." Chapter 5 in A. Wenden and J. Rubin, eds., *Learner Strategies in Language Learning.* Englewood Cliffs, NJ: Prentice Hall, 1987.

Conrad, Dennis G. "Self-Reported Opinions and Perceptions of First- and Fourth-Semester Foreign Language Learners toward their Language Learning Experience: A Cross-Sectional, Cross-Linguistic Survey." Ph.D. Thesis, University of Illinois at Urbana-Champaign, 1997.

———. "The Student View on Effective Practices in the College Elementary and Intermediate Foreign Language Classroom." *Foreign Language Annals* 32, iv (1999): 494–512.

Cooper, C. R. "Measuring Growth in Writing." *English Journal* 64 (1975): 111–20.

Cooper, Thomas. "A Strategy for Teaching Writing." *The Modern Language Journal* 61 (1977): 251–56.

———. "A Study of Sentence-Combining Techniques for Developing Written and Oral Fluency in French." *The French Review* 53 (1980): 411–23.

———. "Sentence Combining: An Experiment in Teaching Writing." *The Modern Language Journal* 65 (1981): 158–65.

Cooper, Thomas, Genelle Morain, and Theodore Kalivoda. *Sentence Combining in*

Second Language Instruction. Language in Education: Theory and Practice Series, no. 31. Washington, DC: Center for Applied Linguistics, 1980.

Davis, Paul and Mario Rinvolucri. *Dictation: New Methods, New Possibilities.* Cambridge: Cambridge University Press, 1988.

Domínguez, Frank, James Noblitt, and Willem Pet. *Atajo: Writing Software for Spanish.* Boston, MA: Heinle & Heinle, 1999.

Dvorak, Trisha. "Writing in the Foreign Language." Pp. 145–67 in B. Wing, ed., *Listening, Reading, Writing: Analysis and Application.* Reports of the Northeast Conference on the Teaching of Foreign Languages. Middlebury, VT: Northeast Conference, 1986.

Emig, Janet. Pilot study and Questionnaire, 1964. [Cited in Emig 1971.]

———. *The Composing Process of Twelfth Graders.* NCTE Research Report No. 13. Urbana, IL: National Council of Teachers of English, 1971.

Fathman, Ann K. and Elizabeth Whalley. "Teacher Treatment of Error and Student Writing Accuracy." Paper presented at the 19th Annual TESOL Convention, New York, March, 1985. [Cited in Fathman and Whalley 1990.]

———. "Teacher Response to Student Writing: Focus on Form versus Content." Chapter 11 (pp. 178–190) in B. Kroll, ed., *Second Language Writing: Research Insights for the Classroom.* Cambridge: Cambridge University Press, 1990.

Ferris, Dana R. "The Influence of Teacher Commentary on Student Revision." *TESOL Quarterly* 31, ii (1997): 315–39.

———. "The Case for Grammar Correction in L2 Writing Classes: A Response to Truscott (1996)." *Journal of Second Language Writing* 8, i (1999): 1–11.

Frantzen, Diana. "The Effects of Grammar Supplementation on Written Accuracy in an Intermediate Spanish Content Course." *The Modern Language Journal* 79, iii (1995): 329–55.

Friedlander, Alexander. "Composing in English: Effects of a First Language in Writing in English as a Second Language." Chapter 7 (pp. 109–25) in B. Kroll, ed., *Second Language Writing: Research Insights for the Classroom.* Cambridge: Cambridge University Press, 1990.

Gaudiani, Claire. *Teaching Composition in the Foreign Language Curriculum.* Language in Education: Theory and Practice Series, no. 43. Washington, DC: Center for Applied Linguistics, 1981.

Greenia, George D. "Computers and Teaching Composition in a Foreign Language." *Foreign Language Annals* 25, i (1992): 33–46.

Gutiérrez, John and Harry Rosser. *¡Ya verás! Segundo nivel.* Boston: Heinle & Heinle, 1992.

Hedgcock, John and Natalie Lefkowitz. "Collaborative Oral/Aural Revision in Foreign Language Writing Instruction." *Journal of Second Language Writing* 1, iii (1992): 255–76.

———. "Feedback on Feedback: Assessing Learner Receptivity to Teacher Response in L2 Composing." *Journal of Second Language Writing* 3, ii (1994): 141–63.

Hendrickson, James M. "The Treatment of Error in Written Work." *The Modern Language Journal* 64 (1980): 216–21.

Hendrickson, James M. and Guiomar Borrás Álvarez. *Intercambios,* 3rd ed. Boston, MA: Heinle & Heinle, 1999.

Higgs, Theodore V. and Ray T. Clifford. "The Push Toward Communication." In T. Higgs, ed., *Curriculum, Competence, and the Foreign Language Teacher.*

ACTFL Foreign Language Education Series, vol. 13. Lincolnwood, IL: National Textbook Company, 1982.

Hillocks, George. *Research on Written Composition: New Directions for Teaching.* Urbana, IL: ERIC Clearinghouse on Reading and Communication Skills and the National Conference on Research in English, 1986.

Jacobs, Holly L., S. Zingraf, D. Wormuth, V. Hartfiel, and J. Hughey. *Testing ESL Composition: A Practical Approach.* Rowley, MA: Newbury House, 1981.

Johnson, C. "The Composing Processes of Six ESL Students." Ph.D. Dissertation, Illinois State University, 1985. [Cited in Friedlander 1990.]

Johnson, P. "Sentence Combining: A Summary and Bibliography." *ERIC/CLL News Bulletin* 5 (March 1982): 3–4.

Jones, P. "Knowing Opportunities: Some Possible Benefits and Limitations of Dialogue Journals in Adult Second Language Instruction." Masters' Thesis, School for International Training, Brattleboro, VT, 1988. [Cited in Peyton and Reed 1990.]

Kaplan, Robert B. "Cultural Thought Patterns in Intercultural Education." *Language Learning,* 16 (1966): 1–20.

———. "Contrastive Rhetoric and Second Language Learning: Notes Toward a Theory of Contrastive Rhetoric." Chapter 11 (pp. 275–304) in A. Purves, ed., *Writing Across Languages and Cultures: Issues in Contrastive Rhetoric.* Written Communication Annual: An International Survey of Research and Theory, vol. 2. Newbury Park, CA: Sage Publications, 1988.

Kepner, Christine Goring. "An Experiment in the Relationship of Types of Written Feedback to the Development of Second-Language Writing Skills." *The Modern Language Journal* 75, iii (1991): 305–13.

Kern, Richard G. "Technology, Social Interaction, and FL Literacy." Pp. 57–92 in J. A. Muyskens, ed., *New Ways of Learning and Teaching: Focus on Technology and Foreign Language Education.* AAUSC Issues in Language Program Direction. Boston, MA: Heinle & Heinle, 1998.

Kossuth, Karen, James Noblitt, and Willem Pet. *Quelle: Writing Assistant for German.* Boston, MA: Heinle & Heinle, 1999.

Krapels, Alexandra R. "An Overview of Second Language Writing Process Research." Chapter 3 (pp. 37–56) in B. Kroll, ed., *Second Language Writing: Research Insights for the Classroom.* Cambridge: Cambridge University Press, 1990.

Krashen, Stephen D. *Writing, Research, Theory and Applications.* Oxford: Pergamon Press, 1984.

Kroll, Barbara, ed. *Second Language Writing: Research Insights for the Classroom.* Cambridge: Cambridge University Press, 1990.

———. "Introduction." Pp. 1–5 in B. Kroll, ed., *Second Language Writing: Research Insights for the Classroom.* Cambridge: Cambridge University Press, 1990.

Lafford, Peter A. and Barbara A. Lafford. "Learning Language and Culture with Internet Technologies." Pp. 215–62 in Michael D. Bush, ed., *Technology-Enhanced Language Learning.* ACTFL Foreign Language Education Series. Lincolnwood, IL: National Textbook Company, 1997.

Lalande, John. "Reducing Composition Errors: An Experiment." *The Modern Language Journal* 66 (1982): 140–49.

Lay, N. "Composing Processes of Adult ESL Learners: A Case Study." *TESOL Quarterly* 16 (1982): 406.

Leki, Ilona. "ESL Student Preferences in Written Error Correction." Paper presented at the Southeast Regional TESOL Conference, Atlanta, GA, October, 1986. [Cited in Leki 1990.]

———. "Coaching from the Margins: Issues in Written Response." Pp. 57–68 in B. Kroll, ed., *Second Language Writing: Research Insights for the Classroom.* Cambridge: Cambridge University Press, 1990.

———. "The Preferences of ESL Students for Error Correction in College-Level Writing Classes." *Foreign Language Annals* 24, iii (1991): 203–18.

Loriot-Raymer, Gisèle, Michèle E. Vialet, and Judith A. Muyskens. *A vous d'écrire: Atelier de français.* New York: McGraw-Hill, 1996.

Magnan, Sally S. "Teaching and Testing Proficiency in Writing: Skills to Transcend the Second-Language Classroom." In A. Omaggio, ed., *Proficiency, Curriculum, Articulation: The Ties that Bind.* Reports of the Northeast Conference on the Teaching of Foreign Languages. Middlebury, VT: Northeast Conference, 1985.

Meunier, Lydie. "Personality and Motivational Factors in Computer-Mediated Foreign Language Communication (CMFLC)." Pp. 145–97 in J. Muyskens, ed., *New Ways of Learning and Teaching: Focus on Technology and Foreign Language Education.* AAUSC Issues in Language Program Direction. Boston, MA: Heinle & Heinle, 1998.

Monroe, James. "Measuring and Enhancing Syntactic Fluency in French." *The French Review* 48, vi (1975): 1023–31.

Muyskens, Judith A., ed. *New Ways of Learning and Teaching: Focus on Technology and Foreign Language Education.* AAUSC Issues in Language Program Direction. Boston, MA: Heinle & Heinle, 1998.

Muyskens, Judith A. and Alice Omaggio Hadley. *Rendez-vous: An Invitation to French,* 5th ed. New York: McGraw-Hill, 1998.

Muyskens, Judith A., Linda L. Harlow, Michèle Vialet, and Jean-François Brière. *Bravo!* 3rd ed. Boston, MA: Heinle & Heinle, 1998.

Noblitt, James S., Willem J. A. Pet, and Donald Solá. *Système-D: Writing Assistant for French.* Boston, MA: Heinle & Heinle, 1999.

Oliva, Maurizio and Yvette Pollastrini. "Internet Resources and Second Language Acquisition: An Evaluation of Virtual Immersion." *Foreign Language Annals* 28, iv (1995): 551–63.

Perkins, Kyle. "On the Use of Composition Scoring Techniques, Objective Measures, and Objective Tests to Evaluate ESL Writing Ability." *TESOL Quarterly* 17 (1983): 651–71.

Peyton, Joy Kreeft and Leslee Reed. *Dialogue Journal Writing with Nonnative English Speakers: A Handbook for Teachers.* Alexandria, VA: TESOL, 1990.

Raimes, Ann. *Focus on Composition.* New York: Oxford University Press, 1978.

———. *Techniques in Teaching Writing.* Oxford: Oxford University Press, 1983.

Reichelt, Melinda. "Toward a More Comprehensive View of L2 Writing: Foreign Language Writing in the U.S." *Journal of Second Language Writing* 8, ii (1999): 181–204.

Rieken, Elizabeth. "The Effect of Feedback on the Frequency and Accuracy of Use of the *Passé Composé* by Field-Independent and Field-Dependent Students of Beginning French." Ph.D. Dissertation, University of Illinois at Urbana-Champaign, 1991.

Rivers, Wilga M. *A Practical Guide to the Teaching of French.* New York: Oxford University Press, 1975.

Robb, Thomas, Steven Ross, and Ian Shortreed. "Salience of Feedback on Error and Its Effect on EFL Writing Quality." *TESOL Quarterly* 20, i (1986): 83–93.

Scanlan, Timothy. "Another Foreign Language Skill: Analyzing Photographs." *Foreign Language Annals* 13, iii (1980): 209–13.

Schulz, Renate A. "Focus on Form in the Foreign Language Classroom: Students' and Teachers' Views on Error Correction and the Role of Grammar." *Foreign Language Annals* 29, iii (1996): 343–64.

Scott, Virginia M. "Write from the Start: A Task-Oriented Developmental Writing Program for Foreign Language Students." Pp. 1–15 in Robert M. Terry, ed., *Dimension: Language '91—Making a World of Difference.* Report of the Southern Conference on Language Teaching. Valdosta, GA: Southern Conference on Language Teaching, 1992.

———. *Rethinking Foreign Language Writing.* Newbury House Teacher Development. Boston, MA: Heinle & Heinle, 1996.

Scott, Virginia M. and Robert M. Terry. *Système-D: Writing Assistant for French. Teacher's Guide.* Boston: Heinle & Heinle, 1992.

Semke, Harriet D. "Effects of the Red Pen." *Foreign Language Annals* 17, iii (1984): 195–202.

Shaughnessy, M. *Errors and Expectations.* New York: Oxford University Press, 1977. [Cited in Krashen 1984.]

Silva, Tony. "Research on the Composing Processes of College-Level ESL Writers: A Critical Review." Paper presented at the 39th Annual CCCC Convention, St. Louis, MO: March, 1988. [Cited in Krapels 1990.]

———. "Second Language Composition Instruction: Developments, Issues, and Directions in ESL." Chapter 1 (pp. 11–23) in B. Kroll, ed., *Second Language Writing: Research Insights for the Classroom.* Cambridge: Cambridge University Press, 1990.

Smith, Karen L. "Collaborative and Interactive Writing for Increasing Communication Skills." *Hispania* 73, i (1990): 77–87.

Standards for Foreign Language Learning: Preparing for the 21st Century. National Standards in Foreign Language Education Project, 1996.

Staton, J. "Dialogue Journals: A New Tool for Teaching Communication." *ERIC/CLL News Bulletin* 6 (March 1983): 1–2, 6.

Swain, Merrill. "Communicative Competence: Some Roles of Comprehensible Input and Comprehensible Output in Its Development." Chapter 14 (pp. 235–53) in S. Gass and C. Madden, eds., *Input in Second Language Acquisition.* Rowley, MA: Newbury House, 1985.

———. "Focus on Form through Conscious Reflection." Chapter 4 (pp. 64–81) in C. Doughty and J. Williams, eds., *Focus on Form in Classroom Second Language Acquisition.* Cambridge: Cambridge University Press, 1998.

Swain, Merrill and Sharon Lapkin. "Canadian Immersion and Adult Second Language Teaching: What's the Connection?" *The Modern Language Journal* 73, ii (1989): 150–59.

Tarone, Elaine. "On the Variability of Interlanguage Systems." *Applied Linguistics* 4 (1983): 142–63.

Terry, Robert M. Personal communication, 1985.

———. "Teaching and Evaluating Writing as a Communicative Skill." *Foreign Language Annals* 22, i (1989): 43–54.

———. Personal communication, 2000.

Trivelli, R. J. "Sentence Combining in Italian." *Canadian Modern Language Review* 39 (1983): 237–42.

Truscott, John. "Review Article: The Case Against Grammar Correction in L2 Writing Classes." *Language Learning* 46, ii (1996): 327–69.

Zamel, Vivian. "Responding to Student Writing." *TESOL Quarterly* 19 (1985): 79–101.

8 **EIGHT** Teaching for Cultural Understanding

Introduction

Paul Simon, in his provocative book *The Tongue-Tied American* (1980), recounts the story of a Georgia school board member who approached Genelle Morain of the University of Georgia with the question: "Why should a student who will never leave Macon, Georgia, study a foreign language?" Her reply was succinct but profound: "That's *why* he should study another language" (p. 76).

The school board member's question echoes the sentiments of many Americans across the years who have considered the study of other languages and cultures inconsequential or superfluous in their children's "basic" education. It is no secret that the American foreign language teacher has had to fight long and hard to maintain a place for languages in the curriculum, if only as an elective subject. Yet the tide may be turning as we begin a new century, particularly with the inclusion of foreign languages among the subject areas that have developed national standards as part of the Goals 2000 strategy for reforming education. Whether or not this initiative can stimulate the expansion of language course offerings or bring about longer sequences of language study is a question that remains to be answered in the years ahead.

The new foreign language standards (*Standards* 1996) emphasize the need to integrate the teaching of culture in the language curriculum, a need that has been accentuated in the professional literature for many years. This focus on the importance of cultural learning is rooted in at least two widely held beliefs among foreign language professionals: (1) that language study is an essential component in the curriculum, in part because it can lead to greater cross-cultural understanding, and (2) that language and culture are inseparably intertwined.

The need for a strong commitment to the development of cultural understanding within the language program is clear, particularly in light of recent developments both nationally and internationally. Reports of "ethnic cleansing" in Eastern Europe, evidence of "hate crimes" against various ethnic and social groups both in this country and abroad, and continued strife among warring factions throughout the world reveal the crying need for understanding and mutual acceptance among the world's people. The valuing of ethnic and cultural diversity must continue to be a high priority in education as our students learn to live in an increasingly interdependent world. There is no question that the successful integration of culture and language teaching can contribute significantly to general humanistic knowledge, that language ability and cultural sensitivity can play a vital role in the security, defense, and economic well-being of this country, and that global understanding ought to be a mandatory component of basic education (Galloway 1985b; Lafayette and Strasheim 1981; Strasheim 1981).

Yet Lange (1999) states that although there has been a strong commitment to including culture in the language curriculum for over 40 years, "culture still remains a superficial aspect of language learning . . ." (p. 58). Walker and Noda (2000) add that "in the study of language, nothing has been discussed more and with less effect than the relationship between language and culture" (p. 187). Lange (1999) suggests several reasons for the difficulty of achieving the important goal of integrating culture into the foreign language curriculum. First, there has been a lack of agreement over the years about what aspects of culture we should teach. Second, there has been little consensus on how the teaching of language and culture should be integrated. However, Lange points out that recent initiatives, such as the National Standards Project (*Standards* 1996) and the American Association of Teachers of French (AATF) National Commission on Cultural Competence (Singerman 1996), have begun to provide us with new leadership in this regard. These projects, discussed later in this chapter, can offer some needed guidance to teachers as they continue to work toward the goal of including cultural instruction in their language classrooms. But before examining the frameworks that these projects offer, it might be helpful to review some additional reasons why the goal of teaching for cultural understanding has been so difficult to achieve.

Problems in the Teaching of Culture

The resources for teaching culture and for accessing authentic materials have been increasing substantially in recent years, particularly with the advent of new technologies. As mentioned in earlier chapters, newer textbooks often come with videotapes filmed in the target culture, CD-ROMs with culturally based activities, and/or Web sites that provide links to Internet resources relevant to chapter themes, making it easier for teachers to integrate these types of materials into their courses. While the cultural content of the curriculum is undoubtedly improving, there are still several reasons why the integration of culture and language teaching remains a challenge. First, the study of culture involves time that many teachers do not feel they can spare in an already overcrowded curriculum (Galloway 1985a). Often teachers content themselves with the thought that students will be exposed to cultural materials *later,* after they have mastered the basic grammar and vocabulary of the language. Unfortunately, "later" never seems to come for most students (Seelye 1984). Furthermore, an approach that envisions the teaching of language and culture in a serial fashion misses the important point that the two are intertwined.

Secondly, many teachers are afraid to teach culture because they fear that they don't know enough about it. Seelye (1984, 1993) maintains that even if teachers' own knowledge is quite limited, their proper role is not to impart facts, but to help students attain the skills that are necessary to make sense out of the facts they themselves discover in their study of the target culture. In his view, the objectives that are to be achieved in cross-cultural understanding involve processes rather than facts. Indeed, a "facts only" approach to culture for which the only goal is to amass bits of information is destined to be ineffective for several reasons:

1. "Facts" are in a constant state of flux, especially when they relate to current life-style. Specific data may not hold true across time, location, and social strata (Jarvis 1977; Galloway 1985a).
2. An "information-only" approach to culture may actually *establish* stereotypes rather than diminish them, since such an approach provides no means of accounting for cultural variation (Crawford-Lange and Lange 1984).
3. Amassing facts leaves students unprepared when they face cultural situations not previously studied. If no problem-solving contextually based approach to culture has been used, the students have acquired no tools for processing new phenomena in a way that will facilitate understanding (Crawford-Lange and Lange 1984).

A third reason that some teachers neglect the teaching of culture is that it involves dealing with student attitudes—"a somewhat threatening, hazy, and unquantifiable area" (Galloway 1985a). Mantle-Bromley (1992) notes that when teaching for cross-cultural understanding in her beginning college Spanish class, she became aware of how little her students understood the notion that their ways of behaving, reacting, thinking, and feeling were bound by their own culture. As Nostrand (1989) expresses it, understanding the variability of cultural concepts "must involve the difficult, relativistic insight that cultures differ in respect to the grid through which reality is perceived" (p. 190). Students often approach target-culture phenomena assuming that the new patterns of behavior can be understood within the framework of their own native culture. When cultural phenomena differ from what they expect, students often react negatively, characterizing the target culture as "strange" or "weird." Mantle-Bromley compares the assumption of equivalence between cultural systems to a similar assumption of equivalence between linguistic systems, an assumption that Bland, Noblitt, Armington, and Gay (1990) have called the "naive lexical hypothesis." According to Bland et al., many beginning language students seem to assume that for every word in the native language there is an exact equivalent in the target language. This notion is similar to what Higgs (1979) had earlier called the "Lexical Analog Hypothesis," which holds that "the foreign language is the same as the native language, except that it uses different words" (p. 338). Students working under such an assumption typically believe that, in order to master the target language, one simply substitutes foreign language words for native language words, using the same syntactic patterns and word orders of the L1. Mantle-Bromley suggest that "teachers . . . not only need to help students revise their *linguistic* patterns, they likewise need to help students revise their *cultural* patterns" (p. 117). She cautions that as this process of acculturation and adjustment occurs, some students may feel that they have to lose their own identity in order to accept and use new behaviors.

Galloway (1992) stresses the importance of recognizing the pervasive influence of culture on one's attitudes, emotions, beliefs, and values, and the concomitant dangers of projecting one's native frame of reference on that of the culture being studied:

> *Cultures are powerful human creations, affording their members a shared identity, a cohesive framework for selecting, constructing, and interpreting perceptions, and for assigning value and meaning in consistent fashion. The complex systems of thought and behavior that people create and perpetuate in and for association are subtle and profound, so elementally forged as to be endowed by their bearers with the attributes of universal truth: Things that fit into this cultural framework are given the labels "human nature," "instinct," "common sense," "logic." Things that don't fit are different, and therefore either illogical, immoral, nonsensical, or the result of a naive and inferior stage of development of "human nature" (p. 88).*

Galloway asserts that to understand another culture, one must construct "a new frame of reference in terms of the people who created it" (p. 89). In order to help students do this, Galloway recommends that they begin with an understanding of their own frame of reference, and then, with teacher guidance, explore the target culture through authentic texts and materials. More will be said about the use of authentic materials for fostering cultural understanding later in this chapter.

As we consider the various difficulties that are inherent in teaching culture, the reluctance that some teachers feel in approaching this aspect of foreign language instruction becomes quite understandable. Even if one is committed to accept the challenges of teaching for cross-cultural understanding, one must still grapple with the problem of deciding what aspects of culture to teach. While it is certainly true that the teaching of culture must go beyond the presentation of facts alone, it is also true that cultural instruction is not fact-free! Many instructors feel the need for some sort of organizing scheme that would help them select appropriate cultural content. Without such a scheme, the teaching of culture can become a kind of trivia game based on isolated bits of information. Galloway (1985b) illustrates the possible results in her characterization of four common approaches to teaching culture:

1. **The Frankenstein Approach:** *A taco from here, a flamenco dancer from there, a gaucho from here, a bullfight from there.*
2. **The 4-F Approach:** *Folk dances, festivals, fairs, and food.*

3. ***The Tour Guide Approach:*** *The identification of monuments, rivers, and cities.*
4. ***The "By-the-Way" Approach:*** *Sporadic lectures or bits of behavior selected indiscriminantly to emphasize sharp differences.*

Crawford-Lange and Lange (1984) propose that teachers may not have been adequately trained in the teaching of culture and, therefore, do not have strategies for integrating culture study with language, or for creating a viable framework for organizing instruction around cultural themes. The development of such a framework depends in part on one's definition of *culture*. Stern (1981) believes that the problem of definition has been the source of much of our difficulty in designing quality instruction:

> *The area of what constitutes culture is poorly defined, and courses offered in universities on culture or civilization generally lack a foundation in theory and research. As long as there is such a lack of adequate research it is very difficult to develop a cultural syllabus of quality. Some improvisation is inevitable, and only gradual improvement, as the data base grows, can be expected (p. 16).*

Stern does acknowledge the substantial work of several individuals in the past three decades who have proposed definitions, models, and inventories for the teaching of culture. These frameworks can serve as useful resources for curriculum planners, materials writers, and classroom teachers as they plan cultural instruction. Some of the proposed models are discussed in the next section.

Definitions, Models, Inventories, and Frameworks: Capturing the Essence of "Culture"

Brooks (1975) has said that "of the several meanings of culture, two are of major importance for us: culture as *everything* in human life and culture as the *best* of everything in human life" (p. 20). Prior to the 1960s, the latter definition took precedence in most classrooms. The primary reason for second-language study was to permit access to the great literary masterpieces of the target culture and thereby to its "civilization" (Allen 1985). Brooks (1971) referred to this relatively elitist conceptualization as "Olympian culture," or "culture MLA," understood to mean the great music, literature, and art of the country.

While learning about a society's contributions to the arts, sciences, and humanities is important, it is only part of what should be included in cultural study. Seelye (1993) defines culture as "a broad concept that embraces all aspects of human life, from folktales to carved whales" (p. 22). He adds that it encompasses everything that people learn to do. This definition includes, therefore, not only "Olympian culture," but also what Brooks (1971) calls "Hearthstone culture," or "culture BBV" (beliefs, behavior, and values) (Brooks 1975, p. 21). This anthropological approach to the study of culture includes the patterns of everyday life, the "do's" and "don'ts" of personal behavior, and all the points of interaction between the individual and the society. Brooks maintains that the first, most basic, and all-pervasive element of hearthstone culture is control of the native language, "a group possession and an individual possession as unique and as deeply attached to the personality as the fingers are to the hand or the arms to the body" (1971, p. 57).

With the advent of ALM in the 1960s, hearthstone culture (also called "little-c" culture) began to be emphasized over formal (or "big-C") culture. In order to capture the concept of this type of culture and relate it to instruction, complex schemes for analyzing culture were developed in the late 1960s and early 1970s. Allen (1985) presents a comprehensive review of several of these theoretical models and inventories, beginning with Brooks' (1968) five-part definition of culture:

Culture 1: Biological growth
Culture 2: Personal refinement
Culture 3: Literature and the fine arts
Culture 4: Patterns for living
Culture 5: The sum total of a way of life (p. 210)

Brooks feels that language teachers should emphasize Culture 4 in their classrooms first. He further defines it as:

> . . . the individual's role in the unending kaleidoscope of life situations of every kind and the rules and models for attitude and conduct in them. By reference to these models, every human being, from infancy onward, . . . associates with those around him, and relates to the social order to which he is attached (Brooks 1968, p. 210, cited in Allen 1985).

Once students have been introduced to Culture 4, some of the aspects relating to Cultures 3 and 5 can be added as the learners' competence increases.

Other frameworks for designing a cultural curriculum have been proposed by Nostrand (1967), Nostrand and Nostrand (1970, 1971), Seelye (1984, 1993), and Lafayette (1988). Nostrand's (1967) Emergent Model presents an inventory for analyzing and describing a culture using the main "themes" of the culture as a way to grasp the system. Nostrand explains that "theme" in this system is not just any "topic" or even a "value." Rather, it is "an emotionally charged concern, which motivates or strongly influences the culture bearer's conduct in a wide variety of situations" (Nostrand 1974, p. 277). (Some examples from the twelve themes that he identifies for French culture are "individualism," "realism," "intellectuality," and "the art of living.") Goals for cultural learning go beyond identifying key aspects of culture to include procedural knowledge that would enable students to observe and analyze cultural elements and patterns. For example, Nostrand and Nostrand (1970, cited in Lafayette and Schulz 1975, p. 106) outlined nine objectives, including, among others, the need for students to be able to react appropriately in various social situations, recognize and explain patterns of behavior, and understand attitudes that are expressed within the cultural framework of a society.

Seelye (1993) has modified the "kinds of understanding" identified by Nostrand and Nostrand (1970, cited in Seelye 1993) to develop a set of six instructional goals, which he offers as "the basic frame for courses in intercultural communication" (p. 30). The goals, paraphrased here, include: (1) developing interest in another culture, as well as empathy toward its people; (2) realizing that the way people speak and behave is affected by social variables relevant to who they are and the role they play in a society; (3) understanding that people think, act, and react in response to culturally conditioned images, and that effective communication requires discovery of what those images are; (4) recognizing that behavior is shaped by both situational variables and the conventions of the culture; (5) realizing that people use the options provided by their society for taking care of their basic needs; and (6) developing the ability to explore the culture, locating information and evidence from a variety of sources, and evaluating generalizations (based on Seelye 1993, p. 31). Seelye sums up the first five goals in a brief sentence: "In other words, we can help the student develop *interest* in *who* in the target culture did *what, where* and *when,* and *why*" (p. 30).

Lafayette (1988) suggests that what is needed in the teaching of culture is a simple, direct approach that exploits existing content and practice. Although Lafayette acknowledges that a focus on "facts" has been criticized by various scholars, he believes that students should be knowledgeable about a "basic repertoire of information necessary for the comprehension of most cultural concepts" (p. 49). He provides a set of 13 goal statements that he groups into five categories, including (1) knowledge of formal or "high" culture, such as major geographical monuments, historical events, institutions, and artistic accomplishments; (2) knowledge of everyday or popular culture; (3) affective objectives, such as valuing different peoples and societies; (4) multicultural objectives, including understanding the culture of target language-related ethnic groups in the United States and non-European peoples speaking the target language around the world; and (5) process objectives, such as evaluating the validity of statements about a culture and developing research and organizational skills (summary based on Lafayette 1988, pp. 49–50).

Seelye's list of goals and Lafayette's incorporation of factual, affective, and process objectives are congruent in many ways with the conceptualization of "culture" that is outlined in the *Standards for Foreign Language Learning* (1996). In the standards document, culture is defined in terms of "the philosophical perspectives, the behavioral practices, and the products—both tangible and intangible—of a society" (p. 43). *Perspectives* are further defined as the "meanings, attitudes, values, and ideas" of a culture, all of which combine to form the cultural group's "world view" (p. 43). *Practices* are defined as "patterns of social interactions" (p. 43), and involve knowing "what to do when and where" (p. 46). The standards emphasize the importance of helping students understand that cultural practices are related to the society's view of the world that underlies them. In the same way, the *products* of a culture, including such things as "books, tools, foods, laws, music, [and] games" (p. 43), are reflective of the perspectives of the society from which they come. The intimate connection between language and culture that is exemplified in the standards derives from the fact that language is one of the primary means used to express one's perspectives of the world and to participate in social interactions (p. 43). Both formal and informal aspects of culture (its literature, history, scientific, and artistic products as well as all aspects of daily life) "are inextricably woven into the language of those who live in the culture" (p. 44).

Because the framers of the standards believe that both formal and informal aspects of the target culture should be represented in the curriculum at all levels, the standards document includes such content as learning about the daily life of the people, their social institutions, their works of art and literature, and their attitudes and priorities (p. 30). Similar categories of knowledge are outlined in the frameworks described above, as well as in the document entitled *Acquiring Cross-Cultural Competence: Four Stages for Students of French* (Singerman 1996), prepared by the American Association of Teachers of French (AATF) National Commission on Cultural Competence. This documents is also offered to the profession as a type of organizer which seeks to reach a consensus on a "core of cultural competence" (p. 1) that students can attain at various stages in their study of French. "The core consists of behavioral skills, cognitive abilities, and the affective capacity for dealing with intercultural differences in a constructive spirit" (p. 5). Elements of cultural competence in this model include developing empathy toward other cultures and learning how to observe and analyze cultural phenomena. Categories of knowledge that are outlined include seven areas: (1) "Communication in Cultural Context"; (2) "the Value System"; (3) "Social Patterns and Conventions"; (4) "Social Institutions"; (5) "Geography and the Environment"; (6) "History"; and (7) "Literature and the Arts" (p. 8). Four stages of competence are delineated for each of these knowledge categories, and the document focuses on five areas of the French-speaking world (France, North America, Sub-Saharan Africa, the Caribbean, and North Africa). Lange (1999) comments that consensus-building efforts such as the national standards initiative and the AATF National Commission on Cultural Competence, as well as those of a large number of states, have resulted in a level of agreement on what constitutes culture and what should be taught that is greater than at any other time in our recent history (p. 61).

In analyzing the two national standards-setting efforts as well as documents containing cultural standards from 33 states, Lange does point out some differences among them in terms of the complexity of cognitive and affective outcomes that are delineated. Using Bloom's (1956) taxonomy of educational objectives in the cognitive domain and a taxonomy of affective objectives by Krathwohl, Bloom, and Masia (1964), Lange (1999) evaluated each of the performance indicators for grades 4, 8, and 12 of Standards 2, 3, 4, and 5 from the *Standards for Foreign Language Learning* (1996) and assigned them to a category of either the cognitive or affective taxonomic structures. In the same manner, he also evaluated the AATF indicators of competence for understanding culture (but did not include the area-specific culture outcomes for francophone countries) and the standards documents for 33 states. The results of his analysis for cultural standards showed that there was a good deal of focus in the national standards document on the areas of knowledge and comprehension (the two least complex levels of Bloom's taxonomy) and on receiving and responding for affective outcomes (again, the two lowest levels in the Krathwohl et al. taxonomy). There was less focus or no focus in the cognitive domain on higher levels, such as application, analysis, synthesis, and evaluation. The same pattern of minor focus or no focus was true of the affective categories of valuing, organization, and characterization. The same basic results were found for the "Connections" and "Communities" standards, as well as for the standards produced by states that followed the national standards fairly directly. By contrast, Lange's results for the AATF standards indicated that they emphasized a wider range of levels of the taxonomies in the cognitive and affective domains and were thus focused on some more complex categories of outcomes. Lange concludes that, for the national standards, there is a gap between the level of performance he found in the performance indicators and the level implied in the standards themselves that needs to be further explored. However, he does find the national standards "credible, flexible, and useful" and maintains that "they project high expectations" (p. 70). Lange expresses concern that the AATF culture standards may be difficult to apply to the classroom or to assess, given their level of complexity. However, the AATF document includes a substantial section devoted to testing cultural competence, with many innovative suggestions for assessing these kinds of outcomes. Guidelines such as these should be helpful to teachers as they attempt to implement the teaching of culture in their classrooms. However, as Lange points out, we will need to wait to see how the various problems and challenges associated with the national and state standards-setting efforts will be resolved in the years ahead.

Achieving Balance and Avoiding Bias: Two Considerations in Developing a Cultural Syllabus

Lalande (1985a) has emphasized the need for a balanced perspective of culture when designing curricula, suggesting that presenting only popular culture to the exclusion of "high" culture can shortchange students intellectually (p. 71). Although he would not recommend trying to achieve an exact equilibrium in terms of time and materials to both "high" and "popular" culture, Lalande does suggest that students should be exposed to various aspects of the target culture's intellectual achievements—both artistic and scientific—even in early phases of instruction. He also recommends that cultural information in textbooks be balanced in terms of gender-related issues, the socio-economic classes depicted, and representations of both rural and urban life styles.

Patrikis (1988) recognizes the dangers of ethnocentrism and bias in the presentation of cultural material, and warns about several "sins of commission" that can occur in discussions of culture. The first of these is *stereotyping,* which consists of exaggerating some aspect or characteristic of a culture or its people. Patrikis affirms that we must "learn to distinguish between *types* (common traits) and *stereotypes* (fixed images), to teach our students to identify types and to recognize the limitations of the types" (p. 18). The second "sin" is that of *triviality,* which consists of "reducing the dizzying variety of cultural elements to the silly, the out-of-date, or the quaint" (p. 18), thus presenting "tokens" of a culture divorced from the meaning of their context. The third "sin" is that of *political bias,* which can result either consciously or unconsciously when we select elements of the culture to feature or include while ignoring others. Patrikis gives the example of portraying the lives of women in a culture exclusively from the viewpoint of committed feminists, or, alternatively, from the point of view of opponents to this perspective. Related to this problem is the fourth "sin" of *"dangerous incompleteness"* (p. 20), which consists of leaving a whole subculture or other crucial part of a culture out of the discussion. A course on the Middle East that focuses only on Islamic culture, for example, leaves out consideration of Jews, Christians, members of the Baha'i faith, and other minorities who are part of that cultural reality (p. 20).

Patrikis recognizes that objectivity is not an easy goal to achieve:

> *For good or for bad, we all have biases. We see things in terms of what we know. Education, however, can turn a bias into a perspective that opens the eyes and allows understanding rather than into a blinder that restricts vision and ensures ignorance. Perhaps it is not possible to be fully and absolutely objective, but awareness of the problem can lead us to a kind of practical objectivity (p. 16).*

Becoming aware of our own biases and helping students to recognize theirs are thus important first steps in teaching for cultural understanding in our classrooms.

We have reviewed thus far in this section a variety of models for organizing specific cultural phenomena that might serve as a basis for developing a cultural syllabus, as well as various caveats about the need for balance and fairness in the selection of topics and materials. Most scholars have emphasized the importance of including process objectives in any instructional plan, recognizing that "the study of culture and the teaching of culture are acts of inquiry" (Patrikis 1988, p. 17).

Exploring Behaviors and Values: Models for Building Cross-Cultural Understanding

Galloway (1984) has proposed the development of a framework for building cultural understanding based primarily on *process* skills, but incorporating within this framework both factual and sociolinguistic content. She suggests organizing instruction around four primary categories of understanding:

1. *Convention*. The goal of this type of instruction is to help students recognize and understand how people in a given culture typically behave in common, everyday situations (see Seelye's Goal 4). Galloway identifies two types of conventions: (1) *context-determined* conventions, which include extralinguistic behaviors that are characteristic in a given situation, and (2) *function-determined* conventions, relating to sociolinguistic formulae or conventional utterances that are used to perform tasks in the context. If one is teaching about the topic of social amenities, for example, a convention cluster could be designed that would consist of both customary behaviors associated with socializing (such as observing appropriate protocol, touching, social distance, concept of time, and the like) and conventional linguistic

expressions that would occur in everyday social contexts (such as greetings and leave-takings, making polite requests, or giving and receiving compliments). In using convention clusters such as these, there is a dual focus on understanding cultural behavior and linguistic considerations in an integrated fashion.

2. *Connotation.* The category of connotation deals with the many culturally significant meanings that are associated with words (see Seelye's Goal 3). As students examine their own networks of associations, they can begin to discover that the underlying meanings of words are determined by their cultural frame of reference.

3. *Conditioning.* A third category of cultural understanding has to do with the fact that people act in a manner consistent with their cultural frame of reference, and that all people respond in culturally conditioned ways to basic human needs (see Seelye's Goals 3 and 5).

4. *Comprehension.* This category of cultural understanding includes such skills as analysis, hypothesis formation, and tolerance of ambiguity (see Seelye's Goal 6). According to Galloway, comprehension goals can best be achieved by paying attention to the source of one's information, examining one's stereotypes, avoiding overgeneralizations, and learning about ways to resolve conflicts through experience-based simulations.

Galloway points out that her four-part treatment of culture is not hierarchically arranged. All four of these skills in cultural understanding need to be developed from the beginning through the more advanced levels of proficiency. She suggests, however, that one might derive insights about levels of cultural understanding from Hanvey's (1979) scheme for measuring cross-cultural awareness. His scheme consists of four stages:

Level I: Information about the culture may consist of superficial or visible traits, such as isolated facts or stereotypes. The individual very likely sees the culture as odd, bizarre, and exotic. Ideas are often expressed in terms of what the culture lacks. Culture bearers may be considered rude, ignorant, or unrefined at this stage of understanding.

Level II: Learners at this stage focus on expanded knowledge about the culture in terms of both significant and subtle traits that contrast with those of their own culture. The learners might find the culture bearer's behavior irrational, frustrating, irritating, or nonsensical.

Level III: At this stage, the individual begins to accept the culture at an intellectual level, and thus the culture becomes believable because it can be explained. The individual can see things in terms of the target culture's frame of reference.

Level IV: This level, the level of empathy, is achieved through living in and through the culture. The individual begins to see the culture from the viewpoint of the insider, and thus is able to know how the culture bearer feels (Hanvey 1979).

Hanvey concludes that achieving Level IV would be an ideal goal, but Level III may be more achievable. In any case, the levels represent stages of understanding or awareness that can fluctuate quite a bit, and the resultant instability of these levels should be kept in mind by anyone wishing to derive a workable sequence of instruction from them.

Ortuño (1991) proposes using a modification of the Kluckhohn model, designed by Kluckhohn and Strodtbeck (1961) to analyze a particular culture's value system, as a framework for analyzing one's own cultural values as well as for making cross-cultural comparisons. She has used an adaptation of this model to teach the cultural component of both elementary language courses and in third- and fourth-semester Spanish literature courses. The Kluckhohn model is predicated on the assumptions that (1) there is a finite number of common problems that humans face in all societies; (2) solutions to these problems vary, though not randomly; and (3) all alternatives to solutions are universally available, but differentially preferred (Kluckhohn and Strodtbeck 1961, cited in Ortuño 1991, p. 450.) Kluckhohn grouped universal human problems into five basic concerns:

1. *What is man's assessment of innate human nature? (Perception of Self and Others)?*
2. *What is man's relation to nature? (World View)?*
3. *What is the temporal focus of life? (Temporal Orientation)?*
4. *What is the group's principal mode of activity? (Forms of Activity)?*
5. *What is the modality of the group's relationships to others? (Social Relations)?* *(Ortuño 1991, p. 450)*

Kluckhohn postulated a range of variations that occur across cultures for each of these value orientations. Consider, for example, the first common concern: man's assessment of human nature. One might consider basic human nature to be evil, neutral, a mixture of good and evil, or basically good. Each of these variations within and across cultures has important consequences in shaping the beliefs and behaviors of the individuals who are part of that cultural orientation. In terms of the second common concern identified by Kluckhohn—man's relation to nature—some cultures view man as subjugated to nature, others see the relationship as one of harmonious coexistence, and still others consider man to be master over nature. The third concern listed—the temporal orientation of cultures—varies from a primary focus on the past and its traditions, to living in the present, to focusing on the future (an orientation toward goals). Cultures also differ in the way one's personal value is determined ("Forms of Activity"). For some societies, one's essential "being" is all-important, while for others, inner development (or "becoming") is stressed. Still another way of viewing one's personal value or worth is by observing what one "does" or "achieves." Kluckhohn's last category looks at group relationships within a society. In some cultures, relationships are defined by means of dominant-subordinate or authoritarian relationships, while in others, the group is seen as a working whole making collective decisions. A third variation views the individual as autonomous and emphasizes egalitarian relationships (Ortuño 1991, pp. 450–51).

Ortuño presents the five value orientations identified by Kluckhohn with their range of variations in a chart form, and illustrates how students can use this framework for understanding their own culture as well as comparing it to that of the target culture. She cautions, however, that teachers need to remind students that although one can make some generalizations about cultural patterning, one must not forget that "a wide range of acceptance of intracultural variants is built into each individual system as well" (p. 457), variants that provide societies with potential sources for change.

Walker and Noda (2000) propose an innovative way to approach the teaching of both language and culture in an interrelated fashion. They conceive of culture as a kind of "performance" or "situated knowledge" (p. 189), suggesting that one doesn't really learn a foreign language, but rather how to do things *in* another language:

> *The flow of social life occurs in a sequence of* performances: *discrete frames of specified times, places, roles, scripts, and audiences. We understand the intentions of specific behaviors of others because our cultures provide possible performances in which to situate that behavior (p. 189).*

They add that expertise in a foreign language builds as one learns to do more and more things in that language. By learning a series of culturally appropriate behaviors and the associated language used while performing various functions in the culture, learners accumulate memories that will help them in future language use situations.

In order to put this type of performance-based teaching into practice, Walker and Noda suggest that teachers might first demonstrate a culturally appropriate "performance" in the second language, such as greeting behavior in Japanese. They might begin by showing a scene from a video or movie, reading a literary excerpt, or presenting a pedagogically constructed dialogue. Teachers would point out the important elements of that performance and then have learners try to enact that same performance by engaging in target-language role-plays, participating in monitored simulations, and creating improvisations in the foreign language that are acceptable to members of the culture. By acting out "specified roles with specified scripts in the specified time and place in front of a specified audience" (p. 208) learners build memories (or "stories") that they can compile over time. By accumulating "stories" into "cases"—"a series of stories about doing something in a culture"—and "sagas"—"a series of stories about a specific set of people or a specific location" (p. 204)—learners can eventually begin to construct a world view that is congruent with that of the target culture. Walker and Noda add that as students go through the compilation process over many hours of instruction, they will develop a memory not only of the cultural phenomena themselves, but also of the process of compiling these memories, "which will stay with learners beyond the classroom" (p. 209).

In this section, we have been looking at various theoretical approaches to engaging in the process of building cross-cultural understanding, with a view to integrating language learning with the learning of culture. In the next section, specific strategies that have been proposed over the years for teaching language through culture and culture through language are presented. Some ideas for doing this have already been presented in Chapters 5, 6, and 7, particularly in activities that use authentic texts (including video and audio materials) as a point of departure for comprehension and production activities. Additional teaching suggestions are presented in the next section.

Strategies for Teaching Culture

Some General Considerations

In designing activities for cultural instruction, it is important to consider the purpose for the activity, as well as its usefulness in teaching language and culture in an integrative fashion. Lafayette (1978, 1988) feels that the most basic issue in cross-cultural education is the degree to which the study of language and culture are integrated. He makes several suggestions for achieving this type of integration:

1. Cultural lessons and activities need to be planned as carefully as language activities and integrated into lesson plans.
2. Present cultural topics in conjunction with related thematic units and closely related grammatical content whenever possible. Use cultural contexts for language-practice activities, including those that focus on particular grammatical forms.
3. Use a variety of techniques for teaching culture that involve speaking, listening, reading, and writing skills. Do not limit cultural instruction to lecture or anecdotal formats.
4. Make good use of textbook illustrations and photos. Use probing questions to help students describe and analyze the cultural significance of photos and realia.
5. Use cultural information when teaching vocabulary. Teach students about the connotative meaning of new words. Group vocabulary into culture-related clusters.
6. Use small-group techniques, such as discussions, brainstorming, and role-plays, for cultural instruction.
7. Avoid a "facts only" approach by including experiential and process learning wherever possible.
8. Use the target language whenever possible to teach cultural content.
9. Test cultural understanding as carefully as language is tested (summary based on Lafayette 1978, 1988).

Crawford-Lange and Lange (1984) suggest a set of questions that teachers might ask themselves in determining the value of a given cultural activity. The questions, listed below, represent minimum criteria for achieving the integration of language and culture study.

Does the process (activity) . . .

1. *Make the learning of culture a requirement?*
2. *Integrate language learning and culture learning?*
3. *Allow for the identification of a spectrum of proficiency levels?*
4. *Address the affective as well as the cognitive domain?*
5. *Consider culture as a changing variable rather than a static entity?*
6. *Provide students with the skill to re-form perceptions of culture?*
7. *Provide students with the ability to interact successfully in novel cultural situations?*
8. *Exemplify that participants in the culture are the authors of the culture?*
9. *Relate to the native culture?*
10. *Relieve the teacher of the burden of being the cultural authority? (p. 146)*

Finding resources for teaching culture and language in an integrated fashion has been a challenge for language teachers over the years. There is no doubt that technology can have a strong impact on language instruction now and in the future, particularly in terms of the exponential increase we are experiencing in the availability of culturally authentic materials in the form of texts, images, and sounds. This wealth of resources can facilitate the integration of language and culture, enabling us to address Lafayette's suggestions as well as the set of questions outlined by Crawford-Lange and Lange, above. The use of the Internet in particular in the creation of activities in culturally authentic contexts does indeed remove a great deal of the burden of being the cultural authority from the teacher. There are important caveats, however, that should be kept in mind. These include the need to determine the reliability and authority of the information given on the Internet—the authenticity, purpose, and permanence of a given site and the credentials of its author(s) or sponsor(s). Teachers using textbooks for which associated Web sites have been chosen may want to explore these resources first, as they have been selected to complement the themes in their textbooks. Another possibility is to examine sites that are developed by target-language government agencies, foreign press services, or other organizations whose authenticity and reliability are well established.

Additional sources that teachers may want to consult include cross-cultural guidebooks that explore a number of themes, comparing American culture with that of another country. An example of this type of resource *is Culture Shock! Germany* (Lord 1996), one of a series of *Culture Shock!* guidebooks published by Graphic Arts Center Publishing Company for over 40 different countries throughout the world. Another source for understanding cultural contrasts between France and the United States is Carroll's (1987) *Evidences invisibles,* available in both a French and an English version. These types of cross-cultural guides can be particularly useful to students who are planning to travel to the country, international business students, or anyone else who would like additional background information on cultural practices in the country whose language they are studying.

The activities illustrated in the next sections represent formats that can be used to teach culture in a purposeful, integrative fashion in the second-language classroom. The instructional goal statements that are given for sample activities correspond to goals outlined in one or more of the frameworks reviewed earlier. Relevant standards from the *Standards for Foreign Language Learning* (1996) are also noted for several of the activities given below.

The Lecture

Perhaps the most common technique that has been used by classroom teachers is the lecture. This strategy can be effective if teachers are careful to (1) keep it brief; (2) enliven it with visuals, realia, and accounts of personal experience; (3) focus on some specific aspect of cultural experience; (4) have students take notes; and (5) use follow-up techniques in which students use the target language actively, either in order to ask questions or to practice the new vocabulary, structures, or situations in the lecture in a cultural context.

SAMPLE: DESCRIPTIONS OF HOUSING IN FRANCE

Level: If the lecture is done in very simple French and/or in English, this activity can be used with students at the Novice level of proficiency. When minilectures are presented exclusively in French, an Intermediate level of comprehension and production ability would be necessary.

Goals: Understanding the cultural connotations of common words *(la maison);* developing awareness of regional styles in housing in the target culture. Standards 1.2 (Interpretive communication), 2.2 (Understanding products and perspectives of another culture), 4.2 (Cultural comparisons).

Procedure: The teacher begins by showing pictures on an overhead projector of common styles of housing in the students' own community, commenting on some of the characteristics of houses in their local region (for example, the types of materials normally used, size, openness to the street, variety of styles and building materials within the same neighborhood, and the like). She then begins to show pictures of houses she has taken in various regions in France during trips abroad. The students' attention is drawn to the various regional styles, and as each type of house is presented, the region where it is located is shown on a map of France. Brief commentary is given about the harmony of style of houses within a given region or community, the types of materials used in building, the presence of walls, fences, and shutters for ensuring privacy, and other common features of housing in the target culture. Some newer houses are also shown, illustrating some changes that are taking place in housing styles in recent years. Students take notes as they listen, using a worksheet prepared by the teacher on which each region discussed is listed.

Follow-up: (1) As a first follow-up activity, students can be asked to match the pictures of houses, shown again, but in a different order, to the regions in which they are located.

(2) A second follow-up activity can be done in which students compare and contrast features of housing in their own home community with those they have seen depicted during the minilecture. Students can be asked to summarize how the words "house" and *"la maison"* have different connotations in the two languages. This can be done by creating a list of features associated with each word.

(3) Students are asked to go to a target-language Web site identified for them by the teacher that depicts houses from various regions of France or another location in the francophone world. A Web site for vacation lodging, such as bed-and-breakfasts or rural rentals, may be ideal for this type of activity. Students note features of the houses they find and write a brief composition describing a house they would like to stay in if they were to travel in the target culture.

Native Informants

Native informants can be valuable resources to the classroom teacher, both as sources of current information about the target culture and as linguistic models for students. Universities with exchange programs often have several teaching assistants from the target culture, many of whom are the same age or a little older than the students studying the language. Native informants might also be identified within the community if exchange students are not available.

Galloway (1981) gives a number of guidelines for ensuring a successful classroom visit by a native speaker informant. She suggests that the class compile a directory of resource persons in the community as a project, an idea that relates to the goal of "Communities" in the national standards. Before native speakers come to the class, the teacher may want to prepare students by having them develop, with the teacher's guidance, a set of questions they would like to ask in the target language. Teachers may also want to provide maps or other information about the country, region, or city from which the native speaker comes for students to study before the visit. Galloway adds that it is best not to expect native speaker informants to give a formal presentation; rather, they can engage in an informal dialogue with students.

SAMPLE: CUSTOMS AND PRACTICES ASSOCIATED WITH VISITING A FRENCH HOME

Level: See sample activity entitled "Descriptions of housing in France" (pp. 360–361).

Goals: Standards 1.2 (Interpretive communication), 2.1 (Understanding the relationship between practices and perspectives of another culture), 4.2 (Cultural comparisons).

Procedure: Students can learn more about customs and practices *within* the French home through activities such as the following:

(1) The teacher invites a native speaker to the class to talk about his or her home, as well as customs associated with inviting others to one's home in France. If possible, the guest might bring photographs of his or her own home and discuss the characteristics of houses in the region where he or she lives.

(2) In preparation for the visit in activity 1, students are asked to read about the French home using a text such as Carroll's (1987) *Evidences invisibles* or other sources where cross-cultural differences relating to customs that surround inviting a guest to one's home are explained. Students can then prepare questions regarding these customs to ask the native speaker during his or her visit. The teacher may also want to share with the guest the cultural reading that students will have read prior to the visit so that he or she is aware of the background information they have on this topic.

Audiotaped Interviews

Information about the target culture, as well as individual insights and perspectives, may be easily obtained by means of an informal interview with a native speaker. Teachers who have contacts with native speakers in the community who are willing to engage in a recorded, informal conversation can pursue a number of topics relevant to the themes in their course materials, using language at a level that will be comprehensible to their students. Before playing the tape in class, teachers may want to develop a set of materials to use for prelistening activities. These may include such things as lists of important vocabulary, anticipation activities, or brief outlines of the main interview questions or themes. While listening to the interview, students can be asked to take notes or to fill in detailed information within the framework of the outline or question set provided to them before listening. Students can also be asked to write a brief summary of the information they gleaned from the interview as a follow-up activity.

Videotaped Interviews/Observational Dialogues

Videotaped interviews and situational role-plays are excellent for providing natural, authentic linguistic exchanges that include paralinguistic information as well. They can be used to demonstrate not only conventional language in a variety of survival situations, but also certain conventional gestures and other cultural features, such as appropriate social distance, eye contact, and the like. They are usually best when prepared without a complete script, although partial scripts might be helpful. When students watch the videotaped materials, they should be asked to note certain behaviors and conventional linguistic expressions on an observation instrument of some type. Preview and follow-up activities should be planned to help students get the most out of the activity.

In institutions where both videotaping facilities and native speakers are available, locally produced materials can provide a rich resource for both listening comprehension and cultural learning. Videotapes that depict "survival situations," such as those typically used in oral interviews, are particularly useful in beginning and intermediate language classes.

Another technique is to exchange videotapes (or audiotapes) with a school in the target culture. Students in both the American and the foreign classrooms make tapes in their respective native languages, talking about issues of common interest. The tapes are then exchanged, and each class has an authentic language sample to listen to and answer—a technologically advanced variation on the pen pal, which, of course, is an excellent way to provide language students with culturally authentic material in written form.

Kinginger, Gourvès-Hayward, and Simpson (1999) describe a French-American intercultural communication course they developed using teleconferencing technology. The authors paired classes in the United States and France and had them collaborate on a set of parallel tasks and texts so that students could see aspects of French and American culture "in telling juxtaposition" (p. 853). The course focused on French-American cultural differences and looked at difficulties in communicating between the two cultures, using selections drawn from Scollon and Scollon's book, *Intercultural Communication: A Discourse Approach* (1995) and Carroll's *Evidences invisibles* (1987). The course content focused on childhood socialization practices in France and in the United States, as seen through children's literature and film. The authors chose French films that had been remade into English, and had both classes watch both versions. The students in the two classes chose children's books that were familiar to them and that they considered either classics or works with some personal significance.

Communication between the classes was achieved using e-mail, Web pages, and two-way group teleconferencing (audio and video). Students were required to post their assignments on their class Web page, and these were then read, after discussion and revision, by the partner class. Students also engaged in two teleconference sessions, which gave them opportunities to exchange views and ask one another questions that could clarify and further explore the intercultural differences that they were learning about as they read the course materials and viewed the films. Kinginger et al. sum up the benefits of their cross-cultural experience as follows:

> In our courses, teleconferencing and other technical tools provide a new dynamism and immediacy to our students' work. In our view, however, the contribution of telecommunications technology is not to organize the classroom, but to support the activities of people who are working toward understanding each other. . . . Through their access to each other and to the parallel texts, our students . . . learned that the adequacy of their generalizations about culture is always relative (pp. 862–863).

Videotaped materials that have been filmed in the target culture are available from a number of publishers. Rosser (1992) has developed a videotaped program presenting six cultural themes illustrated with images and commentary from various countries in the Spanish-speaking world. This particular program is especially exemplary in that much of the commentary and information given is provided by interviews with native speakers themselves, whose viewpoints can be heard from their own frame of reference. For example, one of the scenes in the videotape presents a Mexican classroom where school children are learning about the gradual loss of Mexican territory to the United States. By listening to this lesson in history and geography from a Mexican perspective, unfiltered through a

United States frame of reference, American students can begin to understand how historical events may be differentially interpreted in another culture.

Terry (2000) reports using amateur video footage of a typical American wedding when working with a group of Brazilian EFL teachers in São Paulo, Brazil. A videotape depicting significant events such as this can lead to in-depth discussions of the typical American family, its values and concerns, as well as its traditions. Students can be invited to describe parallel events in their home culture and compare and contrast the traditions and values that underlie the practices in the two countries.

Using Readings and Realia for Cross-Cultural Understanding

As was pointed out earlier in this chapter, students often approach target-cultural phenomena from within their own native-language cultural framework. This is certainly understandable if we adopt a schema-based view of comprehension, whether it be of written or oral texts or of culturally conditioned behavior. Just as students bring their own network of associations and background knowledge to the comprehension of a text, they bring these same elements to the task of understanding another culture. Nostrand (1967, 1974, 1989), Kramsch (1983), Galloway (1984, 1985a, 1985b, 1992), Seelye (1984, 1993), Byrnes (1991), and Mantle-Bromley (1992) are among the long list of scholars who have emphasized the importance of helping students recognize and understand the cultural schemata associated with the phenomena they encounter.

Byrnes (1991) suggests that second-language instruction "inherently is in danger of trivializing the impact of culture, of tending to emphasize universals, of building on a sense of all humans being alike, of playing to the 'global village' syndrome" (p. 207). She finds it difficult to simulate the appropriate second-culture framework in a classroom where students are surrounded by their native culture, as in the teaching of foreign languages in the United States. For this reason, she prefers to use texts as a vehicle for gaining cross-cultural understanding. Since students will undoubtedly try to interpret target-language texts through the use of their native-language cultural schemata, there is a danger that they will miss the way that the materials represent the reality of the foreign cultural context. Byrnes suggests two ways to alleviate this problem. First, teachers should begin with L2 texts about the target culture that are not too far removed from the reality of the native culture or from the learners' own cultural experiences. Secondly, learners might begin by working with foreign language texts that deal with some familiar aspect of their own native culture. In treating a given theme or topic, Byrnes suggests the following progression of activities: (1) reading about an aspect of the student's own culture in the native language; (2) reading about that same phenomenon, but this time in the target language and from the perspective of the target culture; (3) reading about the same theme or topic in the target culture in the student's native language; (4) reading about the target culture in the target language. By reading a variety of texts on the same topic from different cultural perspectives, students can begin to discern how the cultural phenomenon itself may differ in the two contexts, as well as how attitudes about the phenomenon may differ. Such an intensive look at some circumscribed topics contrasts with the kind of "smorgasbord" approach that is used in many classrooms today. But Byrnes suggests that "an exemplary in-depth treatment of a few topics, broadly related to each other, is likely to yield a greater harvest for the development of cross-cultural competence than a wide casting of the nets" (p. 213). This use of discovery procedures, in her view, should be the core of a program in which cross-cultural competence is the goal. Given that this approach requires students to read unedited authentic texts with attention to detail, it is probably most appropriate for students who are at an Advanced level of proficiency in reading.

Moorjani and Field (1988) caution against an approach to the teaching of culture that does not take into account both the native culture of the students and the target culture, as represented in authentic texts. They cite the work of Tedlock (1983), an anthropologist, who maintains that it is futile to try to present another culture strictly on its own terms without reference to one's own culture. "In other words, the study of a second culture can only be a contrastive process, a dialogue between two ways of living and viewing the world" (Moorjani and Field 1988, p. 26). The authors believe that students should not be expected to understand a second culture by inducing its characteristics through authentic materials alone. "In fact, one infrequently discussed liability of authentic materials is that they assume no intercultural dialogue and can only be effective (as far as the teaching of culture is concerned) with the help of an interculturally sophisticated instructor" (p. 26). Although one might argue about the level of "sophistication" needed by teachers using authentic materials in their classes, the point that students need some kind of guidance as they read and interpret authentic materials is well taken.

Galloway (1992) outlines a four-stage approach to a *cultural reading* of authentic materials, an approach that leads students through the process of guided exploration and discovery. In Stage I (*Thinking*), students engage in various prereading tasks that help them make their own C1 frame of reference more explicit, activating background knowledge and discussing their own beliefs about a topic that they will be encountering in the authentic target-language text. Stage II (*Looking*) involves tasks that help learners orient themselves to the authentic text, such as getting the gist or its global meaning, looking at its organization, structure, genre, and/or intentionality or purpose, and attempting to confirm various expectations or predictions that were elicited in Stage I. In Stage III (*Learning*), students examine various cross-cultural contrasts and form or test hypotheses about the target culture, identifying areas that need further research. At this stage, students might also work more intensively with the text, searching for details, discussing word connotations, and finding evidence to support their developing ideas about the culture. The last stage in this recursive reading process (*Integrating*) involves reflection on what was read, with a view to integrating the knowledge gained with other related information from readings on the same or similar topics so that a cohesive framework for understanding the culture can begin to form. Galloway suggests that this is a good opportunity to engage students in writing tasks, encouraging them to react to the material personally and/or reflect on what they have learned. She provides many other specific teaching suggestions for all four stages of this process approach to cultural reading. Teachers who would like to use authentic materials in the classroom would do well to consult this source.

An example is given below of an activity in which students activate native-culture schemata in preparation for making cross-cultural comparisons when reading a target-language text. This reading relates to the ways in which parents raise their children in France and in the United States.

SAMPLE: RAPPORT BETWEEN PARENTS AND CHILDREN

Level: Intermediate

Goals: Exploring behaviors and values; understanding cultural conventions. Standards 1.2 (Interpretive communication), 2.1 (Understanding practices and perspectives of another culture), 4.2 (Cultural comparisons).

Prereading: Students discuss in French aspects of familial relationships in their home culture, particularly with regard to the way small children are raised. They discuss their perspectives on how American parents, in general, deal with issues such as discipline, development of independence, and self-esteem. The teacher asks students to think of families that they know and talk about any variations they have noticed that would provide a counter-example to the cultural "norm" they have described. In this way, the importance of avoiding stereotyping, while still recognizing the existence of cultural patterns in the society, is emphasized.

Reading Activity: Students read the short text shown in Illustration 8.1 about the relationship of parents and children in France and in America. As they read, they fill in the chart in Illustration 8.2, highlighting contrasts between French and American cultural practices.

Postreading Activities:
1. Students discuss the cultural contrasts highlighted in the activity and talk about the differences noted in child-rearing practices.
2. The class researches the issue further by reading about child-parent relationships in France. (A possible choice for further reading on this and other French/American contrasts is Carroll's [1987] *Evidences invisibles: Américains et Français au quotidien.*) Students discuss their findings, as well as the possibility that there is intracultural variation within each cultural system that permits a range of possible child-rearing practices among individual families.
3. Students write an essay in which they reflect on typical patterns of child-raising in the two cultures, giving their own viewpoint about the customs in each system.

Source: The text in Illustration 8.1 is taken from Muyskens, Harlow, Vialet, and Brière (1998), p. 112.

Illustration 8.1
Cultural Reading on
French Child-rearing
Practices

LES RAPPORTS ENTRE PARENTS ET ENFANTS

Si vous habitez en France, vous remarquerez que les rapports entre parents et enfants sont différents de ceux qui existent en Amérique. En France, on exige que l'enfant, même quand il est très petit, sache se tenir comme il le faut . . . debout ou assis à table. L'obéissance est très importante en France: un Français va corriger son enfant même devant des invités ou des étrangers. Les enfants américains, eux, demandent souvent «pourquoi» quand leurs parents leur disent de faire quelque chose, et reçoivent souvent une explication. En France, les parents ont toujours raison.

Quand on devient parents en France, on est censé apprendre à l'enfant à bien se conduire au sein de la société. Les parents ont une responsabilité vis à vis de la société en ce qui concerne l'éducation de leurs enfants. De façon générale, ils doivent s'assurer que leurs enfants deviennent des êtres sociables, honnêtes et responsables. Les parents américains contractent une obligation envers l'enfant plutôt qu'envers la société. On apprend, bien sûr, à l'enfant américain les bonnes manières et les usages de la société mais c'est pour lui donner une chance de plus dans la vie. L'enfance est surtout une période de jeux et d'expérimentation. A l'adolescence, les jeunes Français obtiennent plus de liberté. Par contre, les adolescents américains sont encouragés à prendre des responsabilités financières.

Source: Muyskens, Harlow, Vialet, and Brière (1998), p. 112.

The sample just shown is appropriate for students at the Intermediate level of proficiency in reading and is based on materials found in an intermediate-level text. Teachers can develop similar activities using authentic materials drawn from various sources. Lalande (1979) suggests ways in which students themselves can collect authentic materials through correspondence with various businesses and institutions in the foreign culture. A sample letter to a German Chamber of Commerce appropriate for students in a first-year German program is given in Illustration 8.3 on page 369. Lalande allows students to choose their own letter destination and content, maintaining that freedom of choice is a vital ingredient in generating student enthusiasm and motivation for the letter-writing project. He gives several examples of the types of documents students in his German class solicited and obtained. One student was interested in learning about how to maintain some headphones he had bought that were manufactured in Austria. After asking for information from the company in a letter, the student received a booklet and various instructions for preventive maintenance of his equipment. Another student, who was majoring in journalism, wrote to the editor of a leading German newspaper, inquiring about a variety of topics and policy issues, and in particular asking about freedom of the press in Germany. He received a personal two-page letter from the editor, along with a photocopy of relevant sections of the German constitution relating to guarantees of freedom of the press (p. 18). Lalande reports that students are enthusiastic about the responses they receive and are pleased with their own ability to communicate successfully in a genuine encounter with German-speaking correspondents.

Di Donato suggests a related activity that has students write letters to people chosen at random from German phone directories, asking about German customs

Illustration 8.2
Activity Comparing
Customs of Child-
rearing in the U.S.
and France

LES RAPPORTS ENTRE PARENTS ET ENFANTS

Lisez le passage suivant. Puis, trouvez les coutumes françaises qui font contraste avec les coutumes américaines données ci-dessous, selon le texte.

Aux Etats-Unis . . .	En France . . .
1. L'enfance est une période de jeux et d'experimentation. Pour cette raison, beaucoup de parents ne sont pas très strictes ou exigeants avec leurs enfants quand ils sont très petits.	1.
2. Les enfants américains veulent souvent une explication quand leurs parents leur demandent de faire quelque chose.	2.
3. La première responsabilité des parents américains est de donner à leurs enfants une chance de plus dans la vie. Donc ils éprouvent une obligation envers l'enfant plutôt qu'envers la société.	3.
4. Les adolescents américains doivent commencer à prendre des responsabilités financières.	4.

RELATIONSHIPS BETWEEN PARENTS AND CHILDREN

Read the following passage. Then find the French customs that contrast with the American customs given below, according to the text.

In the United States . . .	In France . . .
1. Childhood is a period of games and experimentation. For this reason, a lot of parents are not very strict or demanding of their small children.	1.
2. American children often want an explanation when their parents tell them to do something.	2.
3. The first responsibility felt by many American parents is to give their children a better chance in life. Therefore they feel a preliminary obligation toward their children rather than toward society.	3.
4. American adolescents have to begin assuming some financial responsibility for themselves.	4.

Illustration 8.3

Example of Letter to
Chamber of
Commerce—
Appropriate for
Students in a First-Year
German Program

Oswego, d.11. Januar 2000

Verkehrsamt Graz
Herrengasse 16
A-8010 Graz
Austria

Sehr geehrte Damen und Herren,

ich lerne Deutsch an der Staatsuniversität New York in Oswego. Meine Freunde und ich
kommen vielleicht im Sommer nach Graz. Was gibt es in Graz zu sehen? Bitte schicken Sie
uns Informationen über Ihre Stadt. Vielen Dank.

Mit freundlichem Gruß

Ihre

Joanne Rosenberger

English translation of above letter:

Dear Madam or Sir:

I'm studying German at the State University of New York at Oswego. My friends and I might
come to Graz this summer. What is there to see in Graz? Please send us some information
about your city. Thank you very much.

Sincerely,

Source: Lalande (2000).

relating to holidays like Christmas and Easter (Di Donato, cited in Lalande 1985b).
These activities have produced many interesting texts for students to read and
enjoy, and have even led to further correspondence in some cases. Needless to say,
the potential for cultural learning inherent in this type of project is substantial.

Lalande (1985b), Scanlan (1986), Berwald (1988), and García (1991) are among
the many scholars and practitioners who have suggested using various forms of
realia to help students learn about aspects of daily life in the target culture. An activity for German students provided by Lalande (2000) has students analyze the
contents of a German newspaper (see Illustration 8.4, p. 370). After examining
the various parts of the paper, students discuss their findings and share their impressions about how this particular newspaper compares to newspapers in the
United States. A follow-up activity involves scanning the entertainment pages
and answering questions about the movies that are depicted (see Illustration 8.5,
pp. 372–373). This activity can be linked to discussions about dating practices or
the influence of foreign films on stereotypes in both German and American culture.

García (1991) has developed a unit for her second-year Spanish course around
"Rituals in Hispanic Culture," using authentic materials drawn from newspapers.
She uses birth, marriage, and death notices from both American and Hispanic
newspaper sources to help students understand the underlying sociocultural con-

Illustration 8.4
Analyzing a German
Newspaper

Search Object	Comments (e.g., is it there? If so, where & what is it like?)
Table of Contents	
Weather Forecast/Map	
Sports	
Editorials	
Classified Ads	
Obituaries	
Movie/Theater Guides	
Radio/TV Guides	
Political Cartoons	
Cartoons	
Letters to the Editor	
Business Section	
Culture Section	
Crossword Puzzle	
Jokes/Humor	
Shape of Paper	
Cost	

Advertisements
—for food and drink
—for jobs
—for anything American
—for anything Japanese
—for anything really unusual

Any English words?

Now sum up: Which things were similar and dissimilar between this paper and a comparable American newspaper? To which American newspaper might this one best be compared?

Source: Lalande (2000).

text of these documents. Students begin by uncovering their own cultural schemata surrounding these events by reading announcements in their native language. As they look at the announcements, they are directed to focus on key words, content, and structures used. García has her students discuss this material in Spanish, answering various questions that have relevance to the focus of the cultural lesson. For a set of birth announcements, for example, students answer questions in Spanish about the English-language material and then fill out a grid with category designations such as the name of the parents, the name of the child, and the place the child was born. They then look at a similar set of announcements drawn from a Spanish-language newspaper and complete a similar grid, as well as a family tree inferred from the information given. One cultural feature that becomes salient in this activity is the system of Spanish surnames. As students encounter difficulty with this, the teacher gives a brief explanation to allow them to proceed with the task.

Once these activities have been completed, students discuss differences and similarities between the two cultures. Students consider the fact, for example, that Spanish birth announcements mention the name of the hospital first, whereas announcements in United States newspapers usually reserve this information for last. Students are invited to speculate on reasons for differences such as these, and complete a post-reading assignment outlining similarities and differences for homework. A second task García suggests involves writing their own Spanish-language birth announcement in the manner appropriate to the culture, using a set of information given by the teacher.

García recommends the use of a variety of grids such as those described here to help students take pertinent notes and analyze what they discover from their reading. (Interested readers should consult this source, which presents a wealth of ideas for creating charts and activity formats.) She points out several advantages to using authentic materials in this way:

1. Students are encouraged to think about their own culture and customs and how those customs reflect the values of the society in which they live.
2. Students begin to see how the values and way of life in other societies are manifested in their customs and behaviors.
3. The act of doing comparisons and contrasts and the accompanying analysis activities help students learn to understand and accept different ways of handling basic human needs and see them as valid.

Understanding Culturally Conditioned Behavior: Some Common Teaching Techniques

A number of time-honored teaching ideas have been grouped under this category to illustrate some specific formats for cultural instruction designed to sensitize students to contrasts and commonalities in conventional behavior in the home and target culture. The majority of these ideas were introduced in the 1960s and 1970s, and many are still popular with classroom teachers today. For a number of sample activities using these formats, see Seelye (1993), as well as the other sources provided below.

Culture Capsules

A culture capsule is a short description, usually one or two paragraphs in length, of one minimal difference between an American and a target-culture custom, accompanied by illustrative photos, slides, or realia (Seelye 1993). The technique was developed by Darrel Taylor, a foreign language teacher, and John Sorensen, an

Illustration 8.5

Analyzing Movie
Listings

Im Kino—In Deutschland

1. Gibt es Filme, die Sie schon gesehen haben? Welche?

2. Am Wochenende wollen Sie mit Ihrem kleinen Bruder oder mit Ihrer kleinen
   Schwester ins Kino. Welche drei Filme kommen vielleicht in Frage?

   a) _____   b) _____

   c) _____

3. Sie sind mit einem Freund nach Deutschland geflogen. Am Flughafen haben Sie von
   Avis ein Auto gemietet. Jetzt wollen Sie mit Ihrem Freund zu einem *drive-in theater.*
   Wie heißt so was auf Deutsch? Schreiben Sie unten den Namen des Filmes (aber nicht
   von einem amerikanischen Film), der dort gezeigt wird.

   drive-in theater = _____

   der Filmtitel = _____

   die englische Übersetzung des Filmes = _____

4. Geben Sie die Namen von drei amerikanischen Filmen, die Sie noch nicht erwähnt
   haben.

   a) _____   b) _____

   c) _____

5. Lesen Sie, was gerade im *Mathäser Filmpalast* läuft (in der Spalte ganz links). Wie
   früh kann man am Samstag oder am Sonntag ins Kino? _____ Wie heißt der
   Film? _____ Welcher Film läuft da schon länger als alle anderen? _____
   Welches ist das Mindestalter für Kinder, die den Film *Ghostbusters* sehen wollen?

   _____

6. Gibt es *film matinees?* _____ Bitte erklären Sie Ihre Antwort.

7. In welcher Stadt Deutschlands sind diese Filme und Kinos wohl zu finden? _____

8. In welchem Kino kann man Bette Midler's *Divine Madness* sehen? _____ Und wo
   ist das Kino? _____ Und wie ist seine Telefonnummer? _____ Um wie viel Uhr
   wird der Film gezeigt? _____ Und in welcher Sprache? _____

9. Was meinen Sie? Wie alt oder neu ist dieses Kinoprogramm? _____ Bitte erklären
   Sie Ihre Antwort.

10. Was halten Sie von der Filmauswahl an diesem Wochenende? Warum?

11. Welchen Film würden Sie mit Ihrem Date gern anschauen? _____ Und nicht
    anschauen? _____ Bitte erklären Sie beide Antworten.

12. Was für Unterschiede und Ähnlichkeiten gibt es beim Kinogehen und in den
    Kinoprogrammen zwischen den USA und Deutschland?

(Andere mögliche Gesprächsthemen: Kosten, Erfrischungen im Kino, *dating,* der Einfluß
ausländischer Filme auf Stereotypen)

Source: Lalande (2000).

At the Movies—In Germany

1. Are there some movies which you have already seen? If so, which ones?

2. Over the weekend you would like to take your younger brother(s) and/or sister(s) to the movies. Find three movies which you could take them to see.

   a) _____   b) _____

   c) _____

3. You've flown with a friend to Germany. At the airport you rent a car from Avis. A week later you want to visit a drive-in theater. What are they called in German? Write below the name of a non-American film being shown at the drive-in.

   drive-in theater = _____

   German film title = _____

   English translation of above film title = _____

4. Give the names of three American-made movies which you have not already used.

   a) _____   b) _____

   c) _____

5. Look at the movie listings for the *Mathäser Filmpalast* (far left column). Which one will be the first or earliest to be shown on Saturday or Sunday? _____ At what time? _____ Which of the films has been running for the longest consecutive period at that theater? _____ What is the youngest recommended age for viewing "Ghostbusters" as indicated in the movie ad? _____

6. Are there any film matinees to go to? _____ Please explain.

7. In which German city are these movie theaters probably located? _____

8. In which theater can you see Bette Midler's "Divine Madness"? _____ Where is the theater located? _____ And its telephone number? _____ (Why do you suppose German movie theaters include their telephone numbers in their ads?) What time will the movie be shown? _____ And in what language? _____

9. How old or recent do you think this movie listing is? _____ Please explain.

10. What do you think of the movie selection/variety on this weekend? Why?

11. Which movie might you like to go to with your date? _____ And which one would you definitely not like to go to with your date? _____ Please explain both of your answers.

12. What are some of the similarities and differences between movie-going in Germany and in the USA? And between newspaper movie guides/listings?

(Possible follow-up activities/discussion on: ticket prices, refreshments, dating, influence of foreign films on cultural stereotypes)

Source: Lalande (2000).

anthropologist (see Taylor and Sorensen 1961). The technique can be used for independent study, in small groups, or with the full class. Culture capsules may be written by students or teachers or purchased commercially (see, for example, Miller and Loiseau 1974).

To construct a culture capsule, Lett (1977) suggests the following steps:

1. Select a topic of cultural contrast, coordinating it with topics being treated in the textbook.
2. List differences and similarities between target-culture and home-culture customs in relation to this point of contrast.
3. Define student learning objectives.
4. Organize and outline specific content.
5. Write the capsule in language that will be comprehensible to the students who will use it (i.e., at an appropriate level of proficiency).
6. Check the accuracy of the content and language of the capsule with a native speaker and/or other colleagues.
7. Rewrite as necessary.
8. Prepare or collect appropriate multimedia aids (visuals, slides, clippings, realia, etc.)

The teacher may wish to record the capsule on tape for students to listen to as a group or independently, or the capsule may be read aloud, either by the teacher or by a student. The students might also read the capsule in class or as a homework assignment, or follow along with a printed script as the capsule is presented orally. Another alternative is to have students form small groups, with each person in the group responsible for reading part of the narrative to the others. Such an activity affords good practice in listening comprehension and speaking skills.

Among the follow-up activities Lett suggests are those below:

1. Students perform role-plays based on the capsule, with situations and/or scripts provided by the teacher.
2. Groups of students write role-plays based on the information in the capsule.
3. Individuals or groups write new capsules on closely related topics, creating a "culture cluster" (discussed in the next section).
4. Individuals or groups research and report on related topics of special interest suggested by the capsule.
5. The content of the capsule is integrated into language-learning activities, such as listening and reading comprehension exercises, communicative oral exercises, and written follow-up activities (dictation, rewriting, short compositions, resumes, and the like).

Culture Clusters

Culture clusters, developed by Meade and Morain (1973), consist of about three illustrated culture capsules that develop related topics plus one 30-minute simulation that integrates the information in the capsules and dramatizes it through a skit or situational role-play (Seelye 1993). The development of the culture cluster might best be approached by selecting a central theme and working backwards to arrive at three or four components that might lend themselves to culture capsules.

Culture Assimilators

According to Seelye (1993), the culture assimilator was first envisioned as a programmed, out-of-class technique that would help individuals adjust to a new culture. Developed by social psychologists (Fiedler, Mitchell, and Triandis 1971), a culture assimilator might consist of as many as 75 to 100 "critical incidents" or episodes that take place between an American and a member of the target culture in which some type of conflict or misinterpretation develops. The source of conflict or puzzlement on the part of the American is the lack of an appropriate cultural framework for understanding the incident.

Lett (1977) describes three basic parts to each episode:

1. A critical incident occurs, illustrating some kind of miscommunication between an American and a member of the target culture. This incident may be presented as a dialogue or in narrative form.
2. Students are then presented with four possible explanations of the source of the conflict in multiple-choice form.
3. As students make a choice of explanation, they are directed to a paragraph that provides them with feedback about whether their choice was correct. Feedback paragraphs may provide additional cultural information to further clarify the cultural point around which the critical incident has been designed. Distractors (incorrect choices) are designed to be attractive to students who are operating under false stereotypic perceptions or ethnocentric interpretations of the situation.

Culture Minidramas

A minidrama can be constructed from three to five episodes in which a cultural conflict or miscommunication occurs, as in the culture assimilator above (Seelye 1993). As each episode is experienced, students attempt to explain what the source of the miscommunication is through class discussion, led by the teacher. After each episode in the series, more cultural information is given, but not enough to identify the precise cause of the problem, which becomes apparent only in the last scene. Seelye explains that the function of this technique is to lead students to experience the vagueness of much cross-cultural communication due to differeing assumptions in the two cultures about the connotation of words or about everyday events and practices. Students see how they might easily jump to false conclusions about the people in the target culture because they are reacting on the basis of their own ethnocentric biases and perceptions (pp. 70–71).

Deriving Cultural Connotations

In the activities that follow, students learn to associate culturally representative images with words and phrases they are learning in the new language. Techniques include the use of visual support materials as well as word-association activities.

SAMPLE 1: WORD ASSOCIATION

Students learn to examine their own connotations for words and see that they are not only idiosyncratic, but also culturally bound to some extent. The teacher gives a stimulus word related to a theme in the textbook and asks students to list as many associated words as possible. For the word *house,* for example, students might associate words like *large, split-level, brick, windows, home, lawn, garage,* and so forth.

Students can work individually to generate the lists and then be put into groups to rank-order the words according to their frequency on group members' lists.

The teacher can demonstrate how these images are culture-bound by obtaining similar data from speakers of the target language prior to this activity and presenting that data to students after they have reported their own results. Discussions about the similarities and differences in word-association chains will reveal how words cannot simply be translated from one language to the other, but must be situated in their own cultural context to be fully comprehended.

A slide presentation of houses in the target culture may be used to lend visual support to this activity.

SAMPLE 2: SEMANTIC MAPPING

Semantic mapping is a technique that was originally developed by Johnson and Pearson (1978) to teach vocabulary to children learning to read in their native language. It consists of creating a graphic arrangement of associated word clusters around a key word, idea, or concept. Hague (1987) proposes various strategies for using this technique in teaching foreign language vocabulary. To create a semantic map, she outlines six steps: (1) write the foreign language word or concept on the blackboard or put it on a transparency; (2) ask class members to think of as many related words as they can; (3) write the words suggested by the class in categorical clusters, arranged around the original word; (4) have students provide category names for the clusters; (5) discuss the words and their relationships on the semantic map that has been created; (6) revise the map, if necessary, after the group has discussed the various meanings and nuances of the vocabulary that has been elicited.

Hague presents a sample semantic map that can be used in a cultural presentation about "La Corrida de Toros" ("The Bullfight") (see Illustration 8.6). Again, it might be useful to ask a group of native Spanish speakers to create a similar map independently, using the same process outlined above. After American students have created and discussed their own maps, they can then study the map created by the native speakers and discuss any differences in the connotations revealed in the two versions. This same process can be used in creating semantic maps associated with any theme, value, institution, abstract concept, cultural event (such as holidays), or culturally conditioned behavior. Teachers who have access to a group of native-speaking colleagues or students might want to plan for this type

Illustration 8.6
Semantic Map Based on
the Concept of the
Bullfight

EXAMPLE OF A SEMANTIC MAP

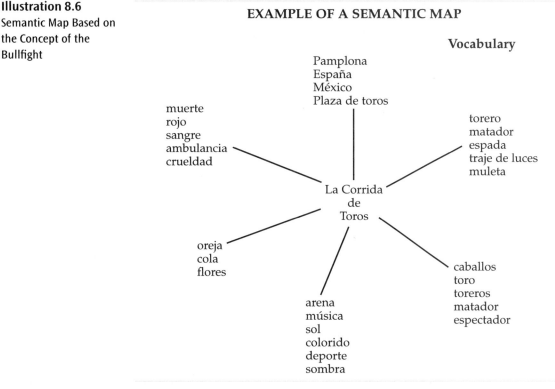

Vocabulary

Source: Hague (1987), p. 222.

of cultural instruction by choosing significant concepts that are related to textbook chapters in courses they are teaching and elicit a series of semantic maps. Maps could be placed in drop files for each cultural unit and collected over a number of semesters. Once enough maps are collected, thematic units associated with new vocabulary can be developed around the cultural connotation of words.

SAMPLE 3: PRACTICING COMMON VOCABULARY IN CULTURAL CONTEXTS: A CROSS-CULTURAL PRESENTATION OF FOODS

Spinelli and Siskin (1992) maintain that many current textbooks have provided useful vocabulary presentations by grouping new words into semantic clusters, but that cross-cultural differences between seemingly equivalent vocabulary items need to be made more obvious. One of the many examples they give is food vocabulary, which is often presented in semantic groupings (such as drinks, meats, vegetables, fruits, etc.) in language textbooks. However, Spinelli and Siskin argue that there is frequently no mention made of the cultural significance of these foods or drinks or the contexts in which they are normally consumed.

Lafayette (1988) agrees, suggesting, for example, that food vocabulary be presented in clusters associated with particular meals.

Some recent textbook presentations do go beyond the simple denotation of vocabulary items to include connotative meanings and depict cultural realities more overtly than in the past. For example, Muyskens and Omaggio Hadley (1998) present food items in their first-year text through drawings depicting foods placed on a table to depict particular meals throughout the day, as well as tables set appropriately according to the conventions of the target culture. There are also several drawings and photos of meals that are culturally representative, and specialty items are featured in a cultural reading that describes certain dishes in the francophone world. Foods in a subsequent chapter are regrouped by depicting them in drawings and photographs of the windows of different specialty stores where they are sold, in open-air markets, and in authentic menus from a variety of restaurants. In this way, students become acquainted with the various cultural connotations of foods while engaging in both focused and open-ended language practice activities in different skill areas.

Spinelli and Siskin (1992) give the example of a food presentation based on an authentic Spanish-language document, instructing people in the art of eating a taco. Using a document such as this allows food vocabulary to be presented within both a functional and cultural framework that is interesting to students. The authors also suggest that teachers use charts and graphs to help students analyze when certain foods and drinks are conventionally consumed in the target culture or complete sentences that show knowledge of various customs associated with foods, gifts, etiquette, and the like. In summarizing their criteria for teaching vocabulary, Spinelli and Siskin recommend that teachers present vocabulary and have students practice it (1) within culturally authentic semantic groupings; (2) in ways that allow students to see differences between the native and target culture; (3) through the use of visuals where native-culture/target-culture referents differ; and (4) in ways that will reinforce appropriate conventional target-culture behavior (p. 313).

SAMPLE 4: COLLAGES

Seelye (1993) suggests that students select a word that intrigues them and compile images of that word from magazine and newspaper clippings or from their own photography. For example, a student selecting the word *mujer* (woman) illustrates through a collection of magazine photos how social class, age, and Indian and African backgrounds affect the appearance of women in Latin America (p. 100). Students exploring the abstract notion of *beauty* might compile two different collages, one representing United States culture and one representing the foreign culture.

Hypothesis Refinement

Jorstad (1981) describes a seven-step process that enables students to refine their initial perceptions of an aspect of the target culture through research skills. The activity can be related to Seelye's Goal 6 (evaluating statements about a society and researching another culture). The following example has been adapted from Jorstad (1981) to illustrate the process:

Step 1: Students perceive an aspect of the culture through learning materials, teacher presentation, or other source.

Example: Based on films and advertisements they have seen, students notice that German teenagers seem to be riding bikes, motorcycles, and other two-wheeled vehicles more often than driving cars.

Step 2: Students make a statement about the culture as a result of this perception.

Example: "German teenagers seem to use bikes, cycles, and motorbikes more than they use cars."

Step 3: Students seek multiple sources of information about the statement, such as newspapers, movies, slides, books, as well as other media, realia, and native speaker informants.

Example: Students see many ads, textbook pictures, magazines, articles, etc. showing young people on two-wheeled vehicles. A news item about the expense of gasoline in Europe states that gas in Germany costs three to four times as much as it does in the United States. Students' pen pals and acquaintances tell them that a family generally has one car, and young people take the bus, ride bikes, or walk to get around.

Step 4: Students question and compare their sources, examining them for potential limitations, such as publication date, intended audience, and purpose. They describe, analyze, and report their findings.

Step 5: Students modify the statement in Step 2 and continue to seek additional information that can refine the statement further.

Step 6: Students examine a related feature of their own culture using the same process.

Step 7: Students compare their refined statements about their own and the target culture, describing similarities and differences they have found.

In doing these activities, students should use the target language as much as possible—in discussions, in searching through target-language sources, and in making the statements, refined hypotheses, and comparisons between the home and target cultures.

Artifact Study

Artifact study is designed to help students discern the cultural significance of certain unfamiliar objects from the target culture (Galloway 1985a). The activity involves giving descriptions and forming hypotheses about the function of the unknown object. If possible, the teacher brings in the article in question or obtains pictures of it. Once the article is displayed for all to see, students form small groups and answer such questions as the following, suggested by Galloway:

1. What are the physical qualities of the object? Give as complete a description as possible.
2. How was it made, by hand or by machine?
3. What is its purpose?
4. Is it supposed to be decorative?
5. What role does it play in the culture? What is its social meaning, if any? (Does it have associations with status, wealth, power, prestige?)
6. What facts can be determined about the culture from this object?
7. If this object were yours, what would you do with it?
   Etc.

Group discussions should take place in the target language whenever possible. After a suitable amount of time for discussion, the groups report their answers to the questions and compare responses. The teacher then gives a brief explanation of the artifact and its use in the society, and students examine how closely their own hypotheses conform to this explanation. Students determine to what extent their own cultural biases played a role in the formation of their hypotheses about the unknown object.

Decreasing Stereotypic Perceptions

Activities of this type help students understand the dangers of making unwarranted generalizations about the people of another culture and help sensitize them to the variability within cultures that such generalizations can never capture. Stereotypes are most harmful if they create barriers to understanding and prevent the development of empathy. They are especially unfair if the behavior of one individual from the target culture is generalized to all of its people, a phenomenon that happens very often in tourist encounters. How many Americans have returned from a whirlwind tour of Paris to say that the city was beautiful, but "the people were rude"? How many Americans have the strong impression that all Spanish-speaking peoples eat tacos and hot foods, go to bullfights, and take abundant naps? These and other stereotypic impressions can be subjected to scrutiny through well-designed classroom activities.

Heusinkveld (1985) proposes that the foreign language classroom can provide an excellent forum for discussing and understanding cultural stereotypes. She outlines a series of practical classroom activities that will sharpen students' awareness of their own cultural background, followed by activities that enable students to compare and contrast their native cultural context to that of the target country.

The first priority in Heusinkveld's approach is to have students realize how much their own priorities, likes, and dislikes are shaped by their culture. Her classroom activities, thus, first concentrate on heightening students' awareness of American cultural patterns. One activity, for example, asks students to design a short course for foreigners on American culture. In deciding what to include in such a course, students begin to see what is important to them. Heusinkveld provides a list of some 80 American cultural phenomena to help students begin categorizing their culture. They select 15 to 20 topics from this list, discussing and comparing their choices in the target language.

After examining such aspects of surface culture, or external manifestations of underlying values, students then try to discover what those underlying values are. For example, in examining the role of fast-food restaurants in American society, students begin to see how much Americans tend to value convenience, efficiency, and cleanliness. By contrast, they may notice from examining the eating habits of Hispanic or French people that they tend to value family unity, family interaction, a leisurely pace at mealtimes, and the enjoyment of a well-prepared meal.

Heusinkveld also suggests that, once values of both the home and target cultures have been discovered, students can begin to argue *against* United States practices and *for* the practices of the other culture. They thus begin to discover how stereotypes originate. For example, they begin to see how foreigners might easily view our culture as a plastic society obsessed with time and cleanliness, unconcerned about the "finer things" in life. Heusinkveld presents other interesting strategies for heightening cultural awareness through classroom visitors, values activities, and the use of photographs, advertisements, and periodicals from the foreign culture to teach students to observe and interpret cultural differences more effectively.

Mantle-Bromley (1992) suggests that teachers use various attitude-readiness lessons to increase students' self-awareness, look at their own culturally conditioned behavior more closely, recognize the pluralism that exists in every culture, and recognize the riskiness of overgeneralization, which easily leads to stereotypic thinking. One activity that she advocates involves putting an object that can be dismantled into its various pieces into a bag and letting students try to guess the whole from the parts. As students try to guess what the object is from handling the smaller pieces, they can begin to understand how difficult it is to understand another culture by approaching it in a piece-meal fashion (p. 123).

In order to understand stereotypic perceptions, Mantle-Bromley suggests that teachers have students collect items that reinforce stereotypes in our own culture, such as advertisements. Students can discuss how well (or how poorly) advertisements represent the people of the culture and thus can begin to understand how stereotypes originate, how they persist, and why they are so difficult to dispel. Another suggestion she makes is to have students read target-language articles that present counter-examples to specific stereotypes, having students note those things that support or don't support a commonly-held view. An activity that can be useful in underlining the problem of stereotyping might best begin with a target-language article about an American phenomenon, since students will probably be most sensitive to stereotypes about their own culture.

Using Proverbs in Teaching Cultural Understanding

Richmond (1987) points out that in many cultures, particularly in Africa, proverbs are a significant part of everyday cultural expression. In sub-Sahara Africa, for example, proverbs are used in court disputes, political discourse, education—literally in every facet of daily life. Because proverbs are so pervasive in these cultures, they can provide significant insights into the way of life of the people. "African proverbs do carry culture-specific messages which must be understood if the language learner is to interact positively with members of the society" (Richmond 1987, p. 214). Richmond points out that in some sub-Saharan cultures, mastery of proverbs is expected among conversational partners, and indeed needs to be considered in judging proficiency levels in these languages. "Here, the concept of proficiency is tied not so much to the structure of the language, but to the appropriate use of the proverb in culturally-specific situations" (p. 215).

Merely collecting proverbs to present to students is not sufficient. According to Richmond, proverbs need to be categorized so that the concepts contained in them can be related accurately to seemingly similar concepts in the students' native language. "It is important to compare the target language proverbs to those found in the native language of the learner, not only to ascertain if similar values are extant across cultures, but also to avoid misinterpretation by the learner, who may see a false resemblance to one found in the native language" (p. 214). Richmond has developed a "Model of Cross-Cultural Proverb Relationships," identifying and analyzing five categories of proverbs. In his category definitions, he gives examples of proverbs from the Mandinka culture of The Gambia, in West Africa:

Category 1—*Target language proverb similar in meaning and expression to native-language proverb.*

> *English: Grass won't grow on a busy street.*
>
> *Mandinka: Grass will never grow on the street.*

Category 2—*Target language proverb similar in meaning to native language proverb, but different in expression.*

> *English: There's no use crying over spilled milk.*
>
> *Mandinka: When water falls on the ground you can't pick it up.*

Category 3—*Target language proverb similar in expression to native language proverb, but different in meaning.*

> *English: Don't lock the barn door after the horse has run away. (alludes to preventative measures)*
>
> *Mandinka: It is no use to beat the snake's tracks after the snake has gone. (alludes to missed opportunities or inappropriate timing)*

Category 4—*Proverb not found in native language, but meaning is comprehensible to outsider of target culture.*

> *English: (No equivalent proverb)*
>
> *Mandinka: An old man can see farther sitting down than a child can see standing up.*

Category 5—*Proverb not found in native language; meaning incomprehensible to outsider of target culture.*

> *English: (No equivalent proverb)*
>
> *Mandinka: The sword will neither stand on its tip nor lie flat. (indicating a refusal of several options relating to a request)*

Source: Richmond 1987, p. 214. Reprinted by permission.

Richmond's model is useful in that it points out the dangers of presenting cultural material, such as proverbs, in a way that implies that the underlying ideas and allusions are necessarily equivalent. This point further emphasizes one of the principles with which this chapter began: significant cross-cultural understanding can begin to happen only when students become aware that their own view of the world is culturally bound, and that the viewpoint of those in another culture cannot be fully understood until one begins to appreciate the different cultural framework through which they perceive the world.

Humor as a Component of Culture: Exploring Cross-Cultural Differences

Various language educators have advocated the use of cartoons and other forms of humor in language teaching (see, for example, Mollica 1976; Brown 1977; Morain 1991). Brooks (1968) includes humor among the ten basic themes around which culture study should be based. But as Morain (1991) suggests, humor is one of the neglected areas in the foreign language curriculum, perhaps in part because a foreign culture's humor is sometimes difficult to understand. "My students know that people in other cultures eat different foods, speak different languages, and get married, harried, and buried in different ways. But one of the hardest things for them to grasp is that people in other cultures laugh in the special ways their cultures have taught them to laugh" (p. 397).

Morain (1991) describes a study in which the reactions of American and international students were sought to American cartoons appearing in *The New Yorker* in 1990. She discovered that there were five general areas of culture with which one must be familiar in order to understand the cartoons that were analyzed: (1) *the social world* (including domestic interactions, popular cultural situations and scenes, social expectations associated with stereotypic character types, and the entertainment world); (2) *the working world* (business, government, the professions, as well as miscellaneous jobs of all kinds); (3) *the language world* (including puns, word plays, slang, folk sayings, body language); (4) *the intellectual world* (history, art, music, science, philosophy, religion, etc.); and (5) *any other world* (including visual gags and fantasy).

Morain discovered that the international students found humor to be hard to understand, and most said they experienced a sense of isolation and even alienation from the target culture group when humor passed by them (p. 407). She makes several suggestions for incorporating the study of humor into the foreign language curriculum. Teachers should try to (1) provide students with authentic examples of cartoons, jokes, puns, and other forms of humor across all levels of the curriculum; (2) enrich the cultural component of the curriculum by including childhood experiences, which can supply missing cultural referents; (3) teach students about the conventions of humor in the target culture; (4) help students explore the scripts/frames of cartoons and jokes so that they are better equipped to analyze humor; and (5) give students opportunities to share humor from the target culture with one another (pp. 407–08). Giving students a chance to experience the humor of the target culture will not only be a motivating factor in their study of language, but will also benefit them in terms of their sense of integration into the social life of the people with whom they are trying to communicate.

Summary: Teaching for Cultural Understanding

The activities for teaching culture presented in this chapter are meant to provide a sampling of ideas for the classroom teacher and are not meant to be exhaustive. They represent some of the most common approaches to the teaching of culture that have been proposed since the early 1970s and that have been tried and tested by classroom teachers. Selection of instructional ideas from among these techniques and activity samples should be guided by the level of cultural awareness and sophistication of the students, as well as by their level of linguistic proficiency, especially in the case of those activities that draw on textual materials. Teachers might want to examine their current course texts carefully to see how various themes and pervasive elements of culture are treated and then design activities that can supplement what has already been provided. The theoretical frameworks and inventories in the first part of the chapter can be useful in doing such a thematic analysis of a textbook, and can certainly be worthwhile for teachers or curriculum committees that are engaged in the process of selecting new materials.

As our understanding of cultural proficiency grows, we will no doubt discover some new ways to infuse cultural goals into a proficiency-oriented curriculum. The problem of how to teach culture in a way that truly integrates this important subject matter with language study is one that should receive high priority in the next decade.

Note: A special debt of gratitude is owed to Dr. Vicki Galloway for sharing many of her ideas on the teaching of culture with me. Her valuable input is greatly appreciated.

Activities for Review and Discussion

1. Imagine that you were asked to speak to your local board of education in defense of a high school language program that is being eliminated due to budgetary constraints. How would you argue for retention of that program? If you include cultural learning as one of the important outcomes of language study, how would you argue that a language course is better than a social studies course in this regard? You may want to draw on some of the points made in the beginning of this chapter as you develop your argument.

2. What are some of the difficulties that language teachers encounter when attempting to teach culture? Do you personally have any reservations about teaching culture? What might language teachers and teacher training candidates do to increase their competence in teaching cultural understanding?

3. Review the various definitions, models, and frameworks for teaching culture that are presented in this chapter. Which one(s) do you prefer? What topics

would you choose to emphasize or elaborate on in conjunction with the textbook you are currently using? Explain the rationale for your choice.

4. Which of the strategies for teaching culture described in this chapter do you consider most useful for the language classroom? Why do you think these particular strategies might work for you?

5. In a small group, compare your answers to questions 3 and 4 above. Using criteria that the group agrees upon, design an instrument for evaluating the cultural content and learning activities of language textbooks. Your evaluation instrument might take the form of a set of questions, a checklist of features, or both. You may want to include some of the following ideas in your evaluation criteria: (a) the significance and/or relevance of the cultural topics presented, (b) the types of cultural learning goals included in the program, (c) the value of the cultural learning activities accompanying the material, and (d) the integration of cultural learning with language learning.

6. Using the evaluation instrument generated in question 5, examine and critique your current language textbook (or textbooks provided by your instructor). If the textbook seems deficient in its presentation of culture, discuss how it could be changed.

7. Using one of the models provided in this chapter, design a cultural activity for a particular chapter in the language textbook you are using or in a textbook provided by your instructor.

References: Chapter 8

Allen, Wendy W. "Toward Cultural Proficiency." In A. Omaggio, ed., *Proficiency, Articulation, Curriculum: The Ties that Bind*. Reports of the Northeast Conference on the Teaching of Foreign Languages. Middlebury, VT: Northeast Conference, 1985.

Berwald, Jean-Pierre. "Mass Media and Authentic Documents: Language in Cultural Context." Pp. 89–102 in A. J. Singerman, ed., *Toward a New Integration of Language and Culture*. Reports of the Northeast Conference on the Teaching of Foreign Languages. Middlebury, VT: Northeast Conference, 1988.

Birckbichler, Diane W. and Robert M. Terry, eds. *Reflecting on the Past to Shape the Future*. The ACTFL Foreign Language Education Series. Lincolnwood, IL: National Textbook Company, 2000.

Bland, Susan K., James S. Noblitt, Susan Armington, and Geri Gay. "The Naive Lexical Hypothesis: Evidence from Computer-Assisted Language Learning." *The Modern Language Journal* 74, iv (1990): 440–50.

Brooks, Nelson. "Teaching Culture in the Foreign Language Classroom." *Foreign Language Annals* 1 (1968): 204–17.

———. "A Guest Editorial: Culture—A New Frontier." *Foreign Language Annals* 5 (1971): 54–61.

———. "The Analysis of Language and Familiar Cultures." In R. C. Lafayette, ed., *The Cultural Revolution*. Reports of the Central States Conference on Foreign Language Education. Lincolnwood, IL: National Textbook Company, 1975.

Brown, James W. "Comics in the Foreign Language Classroom: Pedagogical Perspectives." *Foreign Language Annals* 10 (1977): 18–25.

Byrnes, Heidi. "Reflections on the Development of Cross-Cultural Communicative Competence in the Foreign Language Classroom." Chapter 3 (pp. 205–18) in B. Freed, ed., *Foreign Language Acquisition Research and the Classroom*. Lexington, MA: D.C. Heath and Company, 1991.

Carroll, Raymonde. *Evidences invisibles: Américains et Français au quotidien*. Paris: Editions du Seuil, 1987. Trans. by Carol Volk as *Cultural Misunderstandings: The French-American Experience*. Chicago: University of Chicago Press, 1988.

Crawford-Lange, Linda and Dale Lange. "Doing the Unthinkable in the Second-Language Classroom." In T. Higgs, ed., *Teaching for Proficiency, The Organizing Principle*. ACTFL Foreign Language Education Series, vol. 15. Lincolnwood, IL: National Textbook Company, 1984.

Di Donato, Robert. Personal communication cited in Lalande, 1985b.

Fiedler, Fred E., Terence Mitchell, and Harry C. Triandis. "The Culture Assimilator: An Approach to Cross-Cultural Training." *Journal of Applied Psychology* 55 (1971): 95–102.

Galloway, Vicki B. *Communicating in a Cultural Context: The Global Perspective*. Proceedings of the 1981 Summer Cross-Cultural Workshop for Foreign Language Teachers. Columbia, SC: South Carolina State Department of Education, 1981.

———. "Communicating in a Cultural Context." *ACTFL Master Lecture Series*. Monterey, CA: Defense Language Institute, 1984.

———. "Communicating in a Cultural Context." Workshop given at the Northeast Conference Winter Workshop, Wakefield, MA, 1985a.

———. "A Design for the Improvement of the Teaching of Culture in Foreign Language Classrooms." ACTFL project proposal, 1985b.

———. "Toward a Cultural Reading of Authentic Texts." Pp. 87–121 in H. Byrnes, ed., *Languages for a Multicultural World in Transition*. Reports of the Northeast Conference on the Teaching of Foreign Languages. Lincolnwood, IL: National Textbook Company, 1992.

García, Carmen. "Using Authentic Reading Texts to Discover Underlying Sociocultural Information." *Foreign Language Annals* 24, vi (1991): 515–26.

Hague, Sally A. "Vocabulary Instruction: What L2 can Learn from L1." *Foreign Language Annals* 20, iii (1987): 217–25.

Hall, Edward T. *The Silent Language*. New York: Doubleday, 1959.

Hanvey, Robert. "Cross-Cultural Awareness." In E. C. Smith and L. F. Luce, eds., *Toward Internationalism: Readings in Cross-Cultural Communication*. Rowley, MA: Newbury House, 1979.

Heusinkveld, Paula R. "The Foreign Language Classroom: A Forum for Understanding Cultural Stereotypes." *Foreign Language Annals* 18 (1985): 321–25.

Higgs, Theodore V. "Some Pre-Methodological Considerations in Foreign Language Teaching." *The Modern Language Journal* 63, vii (1979): 335–42.

Jarvis, Donald K. "Making Cross-Cultural Connections." In J. K. Phillips, ed., *The Language Connection: From the Classroom to the World*. ACTFL Foreign

Language Education Series, vol. 9. Lincolnwood, IL: National Textbook Company, 1977.

Johnson, Dale and P. David Pearson. *Teaching Reading Vocabulary.* New York: Holt, Rinehart, and Winston, 1978. [Cited in Hague, 1987]

Jorstad, Helen. "Inservice Teacher Education: Content and Process." In *Proceedings of the National Conference on Professional Priorities.* Hastings-on-Hudson, NY: ACTFL, 1981.

Kinginger, Celeste, Alison Gourvès-Hayward, and Vanessa Simpson. "A Telecollaborative Course on French-American Intercultural Communication." *The French Review* 72, v (1999): 853–66.

Kluckhohn, Florence R. and Fred I. Strodtbeck. *Variations in Value Orientations.* Evanston, IL: Row, Peterson, 1961; rpt. Westport, CT: Greenwood, 1976. [cited in Ortuño, 1991]

Kramsch, Claire J. "Culture and Constructs: Communicating Attitudes and Values in the Foreign Language Classroom." *Foreign Language Annals* 16, vi (1983): 437–48.

Lafayette, Robert. *Teaching Culture: Strategies and Techniques.* Language in Education: Theory and Practice Series, no. 11. Washington, DC: Center for Applied Linguistics, 1978.

———. "Integrating the Teaching of Culture into the Foreign Language Classroom." Pp. 47–62 in A. J. Singerman, ed., *Toward a New Integration of Language and Culture.* Reports of the The Northeast Conference on the Teaching of Foreign Languages. Middlebury, VT: Northeast Conference, 1988.

Lafayette, Robert and Renate Schulz. "Evaluating Cultural Learnings." In R. C. Lafayette, ed., *The Cultural Revolution in Foreign Languages: A Guide for Building the Modern Curriculum.* Lincolnwood, IL: National Textbook Company, 1975.

Lafayette, Robert and L. Strasheim. "Foreign Language Curricula and Materials for the Twenty-First Century." In *Proceedings of the National Conference on Professional Priorities.* Hastings-on-Hudson, NY: ACTFL, 1981.

Lalande, John. "The Quasi-Business Letter: Passport to Foreign Culture." *The Modern Language Journal* 63 (1979): 17–20.

———. "Teaching German Culture in the German Language Classroom: Toward Achieving a Balanced Perspective." *Schatzkammer* 11, ii (1985a): 70–80.

———. "Making a Connection: Telephone Books, Culture and Language Instruction." *Die Unterrichtspraxis* 18 (1985b): 313–18.

———. Personal communication, 2000.

Lange, Dale L. "Planning for and Using the New National Culture Standards." Chapter 3 (pp. 57–135) in June K. Phillips and Robert M. Terry, eds., *Foreign Language Standards: Linking Research, Theories, and Practices.* The ACTFL Foreign Language Education Series. Lincolnwood, IL: National Textbook Company, 1999.

Lett, John. "Basic Mechanisms for Presenting Culture." Workshop handout, presented at Indiana State University, March 1977.

Lord, Richard. *Culture Shock! Germany.* Portland, OR: Graphic Arts Center Publishing Company, 1996. [Reprinted 1997, 1998.]

Mantle-Bromley, Corinne. "Preparing Students for Meaningful Culture Learning." *Foreign Language Annals* 25, ii (1992): 117–27.

Meade, B. and G. Morain. "The Culture Cluster." *Foreign Language Annals* 6 (1973): 331–38.

Miller, J. D. and M. Loiseau. *USA—France: Culture Capsules.* Rowley, MA: Newbury House, 1974.

Mollica, Anthony. "Cartoons in the Language Classroom." *Canadian Modern Language Review* 32 (1976): 424–44.

Moorjani, Angela and Thomas T. Field. "Semiotic and Sociolinguistic Paths to Understanding Culture." Pp. 25–45 in A. J. Singerman, ed., *Toward a New Integration of Language and Culture.* Reports of the Northeast Conference on the Teaching of Foreign Languages. Middlebury, VT: Northeast Conference, 1988.

Morain, Genelle G. "X-raying the International Funny Bone: A Study Exploring Differences in the Perception of Humor Across Cultures." Pp. 397–408 in J. A. Alatis, ed., *Linguistics and Language Pedagogy: The State of the Art.* Georgetown University Round Table on Languages and Linguistics 1991. Washington, DC: Georgetown University Press, 1991.

Muyskens, Judith A. and Alice Omaggio Hadley. *Rendez-vous: An Invitation to French,* 5th ed. New York: McGraw-Hill, 1998.

Muyskens, Judith A., Linda L. Harlow, Michèle Vialet, and Jean-François Brière. *Bravo!* 3rd ed. Boston: Heinle & Heinle, 1998.

Nostrand, Howard L. *Background Data for the Teaching of French. Part A: La culture et la société françaises au XXᵉ siècle.* Seattle: University of Washington, 1967.

———. "Empathy for a Second Culture: Motivations and Techniques." In G. A. Jarvis, ed., *Responding to New Realities.* ACTFL Foreign Language Education Series, vol. 5. Lincolnwood, IL: National Textbook Company, 1974.

———. "The Beginning Teacher's Cultural Competence: Goal and Strategy." *Foreign Language Annals* 22, ii (1989): 189–93.

Nostrand, Howard L. and Frances Nostrand. "Culture-Wide Values and Assumptions as Essential Content for Levels I to III." In C. J. and P. Castle, eds., *French Language Education: The Teaching of Culture in the Classroom.* Springfield, IL: Illinois Title III, NDEA, 1971.

Ortuño, Marian M. "Cross-Cultural Awareness in the Foreign Language Class: The Kluckhohn Model." *The Modern Language Journal* 75, iv (1991): 449–59.

Patrikis, Peter. "Language and Culture at the Crossroads." Pp. 13–24 in A. J. Singerman, ed., *Toward a New Integration of Language and Culture.* Reports of the Northeast Conference on the Teaching of Foreign Languages. Middlebury, VT: Northeast Conference, 1988.

Phillips, June K. and Robert M. Terry, eds. *Foreign Language Standards: Linking Research, Theories, and Practices.* The ACTFL Foreign Language Education Series. Lincolnwood, IL: National Textbook Company, 1999.

Richmond, Edmun B. "Utilizing Proverbs as a Focal Point to Cultural Awareness and Communicative Competence: Illustrations from Africa." *Foreign Language Annals* 20, iii (1987): 213–16.

Rosser, Harry. *Mosaico Cultural: Images from Spanish Speaking Cultures.* (video) Heinle & Heinle, 1992.

Scanlan, Timothy. "Looking up French Language and Culture in the Paris *Pages Jaunes.*" *The French Review* 59 (1986): 355–88.

Seelye, H. Ned. *Teaching Culture: Strategies for Intercultural Communication.* Lincolnwood, IL: National Textbook Company, 1974, 1984, 1993.

Simon, Paul. *The Tongue-Tied American.* New York: Continuum, 1980.

Singerman, Alan J., ed. *Toward a New Integration of Language and Culture.* Reports of the Northeast Conference on the Teaching of Foreign Languages. Middlebury, VT: Northeast Conference, 1988.

———, ed. *Acquiring Cross-cultural Competence. Four Stages for Students of French.* American Association of Teachers of French National Commission on Cultural Competence. Lincolnwood, IL: National Textbook Company, 1996.

Spinelli, Emily and H. Jay Siskin. "Selecting, Presenting, and Practicing Vocabulary in a Culturally-Authentic Context." *Foreign Language Annals* 25, iv (1992): 305–15.

Standards for Foreign Language Learning: Preparing for the 21st Century. National Standards in Foreign Language Education Project, 1996.

Stern, H. H. "Directions in Foreign Language Curriculum Development." In *Proceedings of the National Conference on Professional Priorities.* Hastings-on-Hudson, NY: ACTFL, 1981.

———. "Toward a Multidimensional Foreign Language Curriculum." In R. Mead, ed., *Foreign Languages: Key Links in the Chain of Learning.* Reports of the Northeast Conference on the Teaching of Foreign Languages. Middlebury, VT: Northeast Conference, 1983.

Strasheim, Lorraine. "Establishing a Professional Agenda for Integrating Culture into K–12 Foreign Languages: An Editorial." *The Modern Language Journal* 65 (1981): 67–69.

Taylor, H. D. and J. Sorenson. "Culture Capsules." *The Modern Language Journal* 45 (1961): 350–54.

Tedlock, D. *The Spoken Word and the Work of Interpretation.* Philadelphia, University of Pennsylvania Press, 1983. [Cited in Moorjani and Field, 1988.]

Terry, Robert M. Personal communication, 2000.

Walker, Galal and Mari Noda. "Remembering the Future: Compiling Knowledge of Another Culture." Chapter 8 (pp. 187–212) in Diane W. Birckbichler and Robert M. Terry, eds., *Reflecting on the Past to Shape the Future.* The ACTFL Foreign Language Education Series. Lincolnwood, IL: National Textbook Company, 2000.

9 NINE Classroom Testing

Introduction

The language teaching profession has made significant progress over the past several decades in articulating the goals of language study and reorienting the curriculum to reflect a stronger focus on proficiency. There is no doubt that communicative language teaching has had a substantial effect on classroom instruction and materials development. Classroom goals are increasingly articulated in communicative and functional terms. Foreign language textbooks and ancillaries are including more communicative activities, authentic materials, and culturally authentic lesson content than ever before, encouraging learners to use language in context for real-world purposes. Yet how are classroom testing practices changing in response to this focus on proficiency?

Magnan (1991) maintains that classroom tests are still largely focused on discrete points of grammar and mastery of isolated components of knowledge and skill, despite the fact that the profession has been advocating communicative language teaching practices for years. She attributes the lack of discourse-driven, functional language testing to three main causes: "(1) students or teachers may prefer more familiar discrete-point testing (Bacon and Finneman 1990), as it may seem more straightforward and hence more accessible and objective; (2) teachers may find it difficult and time-consuming to design and grade discourse-based and functional tests; and (3) the profession has not yet developed a widely accepted, practical model of what communicative testing should entail" (Magnan 1991, p. 136).

Walz's (1991) research, in which he analyzed 12 commercial testing programs that are provided with college elementary French texts, indicates that some of these tests do have integrative sections or blend grammar and communicative language use, although some still have a significant grammatical component or focus. Walz's overall assessment is that these commercial tests are "markedly better" than tests that were examined in a previous study (Rea 1985, cited in Walz 1991), most of which were "predominantly grammar tests" (p. 183).

It is possible that, in the ten years since Magnan's and Walz's studies appeared, classroom tests have continued to evolve to include more integrative formats and communicative item types. However, the retention of some focus on grammar in classroom tests may be due to the continuing interest among language teachers and students to incorporate a focus on form in the curriculum (see the discussions on this issue in Chapters 3, 6, and 7). While the emphasis on strengthening the communicative content of language courses is of primary importance, it is counterbalanced, in many contemporary foreign language programs, with a concern that learners accomplish communicative objectives with some degree of formal accuracy. Thus many language courses continue to blend a concern for developing communicative proficiency with learning how to use the language more accurately and precisely as students' skills develop.

There is no doubt that careful articulation of course goals and the choice of materials and activities are crucial to the success of any language program. Equally important, however, is the design of classroom tests and assessment procedures that accurately reflect course goals and provide needed information about students' progress toward attaining them. This chapter explores the issue of classroom testing and discusses ways in which tests and other types of assessment can be designed to reflect course goals most effectively. Before examining models of classroom test formats, however, it would be useful to clarify some basic terms associated with test design and understand how different types of assessments can be created for different purposes.

Some General Concepts in Language Testing: Assessment Measures and Item Types

One of the important issues to consider when choosing or creating a language test is the purpose for which the test is going to be used. Cohen (1994) distinguishes tests according to their primary function and describes the specific reasons for using each type of assessment (see Illustration 9.1, p. 392). For example, placement tests and general proficiency tests are often used for *administrative* purposes. Classroom tests would fall into the *instructional* category in Cohen's model, as their purpose is to diagnose students' progress, provide feedback, and serve as a means of evaluating performance. Well designed instructional tests also provide important information to teachers about the effectiveness of their teaching and of the curriculum. Tests designed for *research* projects can include those used in evaluation of programs or in experimental designs to investigate specific effects of treatments on learning.

An important distinction that is commonly made among test types is the contrast between *achievement* and *proficiency* tests. Classroom tests are often referred to as *achievement* tests, as they are used to evaluate students' acquisition of certain specified course content. Strictly speaking, a valid achievement test will test only material that has been "covered" during the course of instruction (Clark 1972). *Proficiency* tests, on the other hand, are used to measure an individual's general competence in a second language, independently of any particular curriculum or

Illustration 9.1
The Purpose of
Assessment

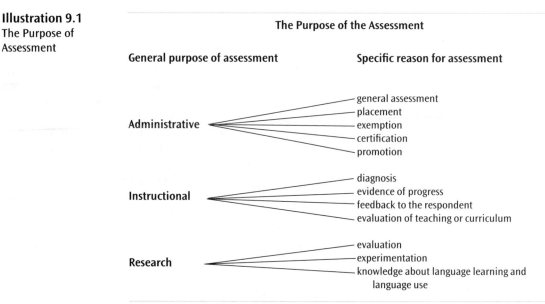

The Purpose of the Assessment

General purpose of assessment   Specific reason for assessment

Administrative
- general assessment
- placement
- exemption
- certification
- promotion

Instructional
- diagnosis
- evidence of progress
- feedback to the respondent
- evaluation of teaching or curriculum

Research
- evaluation
- experimentation
- knowledge about language learning and language use

Source: Cohen 1994, p. 23.

course of study. (An example of a general proficiency test is the ACTFL Oral Proficiency Interview, which will be discussed later in this chapter.) Dandonoli (1987) points out that proficiency tests are appropriate for measuring general progress in the acquisition of language skills, although they should not be used *per se* as classroom achievement tests because they are not meant to sample from a particular course syllabus. This is not to say, however, that there can be no relationship between proficiency testing and classroom achievement testing. As we will see later in this chapter, classroom tests can be designed so that they reflect proficiency goals, presenting language in context and requiring students to use the language beyond the sentence level to carry out realistic tasks. When properly constructed, classroom tests can sample course material in a manner that is consistent with the principles of proficiency testing, while limiting the domain of content to be tested to the material that has been indicated on the course syllabus.

Dandonoli (1987) maintains that while general proficiency tests should not be used in lieu of classroom tests for the purposes of assigning course grades, they can be quite appropriately used for entrance or graduation requirements, "providing the requirements are stated appropriately and relate to the curriculum content instructional goals" (p. 78). (For descriptions of projects using proficiency-based measures for entrance and/or graduation requirements or for articulation and placement into undergraduate language programs, see Freed 1984, 1987; Barnes, Klee, and Wakefield 1991; and Chalhoub-Deville 1997, 1999.)

Liskin-Gasparro (1996) discusses another important classic distinction in test design—the contrast between "direct measures" and "indirect measures" of performance. *Direct* tests are those that "incorporate the contexts, problems, and solution strategies that students would use in real life," whereas *indirect* tests " 'represent competence' by extracting knowledge and skills out of their real-life contexts" (p. 171). She contrasts more traditional paper-and-pencil tests consisting of collections of items (i.e., a type of indirect measure) with newer types of assessments, sometimes called "authentic assessment," "alternative assessment," and "performance assessment" (p. 170). Liskin-Gasparro characterizes "authentic" assessments as more direct types of tests, which include such measures as portfolios, oral proficiency tests, and task- or project-based performance assessments. More will be said about these types of assessments later in this chapter.

Cohen (1994) describes test items on a set of intersecting axes that represent two types of contrasts: *direct* versus *indirect* assessment, discussed above, and *discrete-point* versus *integrative* test formats. Discrete-point items are those that test "one and only one point at a time" (p. 161). Cohen gives the following example of a multiple-choice completion format that tests for a particular verb form:

(Written elicitation)
"Did you go to the frisbee tournament last night?"
(Written multiple-choice completion)
"No, I _____."
    (a) didn't go
    (b) haven't gone
    (c) hadn't gone
(Cohen 1994, p. 161)

He adds that discrete-point tests can be used to test not only isolated grammar points or vocabulary items, but also sociocultural knowledge (as in a multiple-choice item where students choose the appropriate form of a refusal for an invitation from among four options). Although items of this type serve to isolate particular forms for evaluation, they also isolate lexical, grammatical, or pragmatic features from the wider context of natural language use, a point that will be explored further in the next pages.

An *integrative* approach to item design involves testing more than one point at a time, such as in giving a talk (a *"direct integrative* measure") or completing a cloze passage where a number of words have been deleted and must be restored (p. 163). Cohen characterizes this latter type of test as an *"indirect integrative measure"* (p. 163) since it indirectly tests one's reading ability as one completes the task.

Cohen suggests that there is a continuum ranging from the most discrete-point items on one end to the most integrative items on the other, with many test items falling somewhere in between. He adds that it is difficult to find **"truly discrete-point items"** (p. 163) that isolate one point without testing anything else; for example, in the discrete-point grammar example given above, the student has to read the stem and choose among the options to find the appropriate rejoinder. Thus the test item combines the skills of reading and grammar. Valette (1977) calls such mixed tasks "hybrid" test items, as opposed to "pure" test items, given that they assess several skills at once.

Illustration 9.2 provides sample decontextualized, discrete-point test items that are representative of the type of items seen on traditional classroom achievement tests that can still be found in some classrooms today. Of the four-part criteria used in proficiency testing—global tasks/functions, context/content, accuracy, and type of discourse—only one (accuracy) is represented to any extent on this exam. Functional considerations are clearly absent, as students are required to fill in blanks with pieces of discourse for no other purpose than to prove that they know how they work. Items are presented in single-sentence frames, out of context, rendering the content of the text virtually meaningless. There is no evidence of a concern for sociolinguistic considerations, and, in the absence of continuous discourse beyond the sentence level, no opportunity to test discourse competence in any fashion whatsoever.

One might argue that the *individual* test sentences do have meaningful content. Yet research by Hosenfeld (1976) has revealed that students do not even have to process the meaning of the individual sentences on the test to do the tasks that are required of them. Many students have learned to "short-circuit" grammatical exercises of this type, a fact that contributes further to the impression that success on language tests involves learning a few grammatical "tricks" rather than

---

Illustration 9.2
Typical Grammar
Test Items

A. Fill in the blanks with the appropriate form of the verb in the present tense.
   1. Je _____ mes devoirs avant 10 heures du soir. (finir)
   2. Nous _____ un bon restaurant ce weekend. (choisir)
   3. Tu _____ à tes problèmes avec ton camarade de chambre. (réfléchir)
   Etc.

B. Complete the following translations using an expression of quantity.
   1. Nous avons _____ de sucre. *We have enough sugar.*
   2. Marie a _____ de bons amis. *Marie has a lot of good friends.*
   3. J'ai _____ de devoirs ce soir. *I have little homework tonight.*
   Etc.

C. Fill in the blanks with the correct form of the partitive article.
   1. J'aime manger ____ pizza, ____ pain, et _____ salade.
   2. Michel boit _____ lait mais Marie boit _____ café.
   3. Nous prenons ____ thé au café après le film.
   Etc.

* * * * * * * * * * * * * *

(Translation of test items in English for parts A and C)
A. 1. I _____ my homework before 10 P.M. (to finish)
   2. We _____ a good restaurant this weekend. (to choose)
   3. You _____ about your problems with your roommate. (to reflect)
   Etc.

C. 1. I like to eat _____ pizza, _____ bread, and _____ salad.
   2. Michel drinks _____ milk but Marie drinks _____ coffee.
   3. We are having _____ tea at the cafe after the movie.
   Etc.

processing language for some authentic purpose. Tests such as the one in Illustration 9.2 hardly represent real language use and serve to widen the gap between course goals and testing procedures in the classroom. As Valette pointed out in 1978, "the content of the tests and the method in which grades are assigned, reflects more accurately than any lengthy statement of aims and purposes, the real objectives of instruction" (p. 90).

In this chapter, alternative formats for classroom achievement testing are proposed based on many of the previously discussed principles for designing language-practice activities. These formats are suggested as a possible starting point for revising classroom tests to reflect language proficiency goals more directly. One basic principle to be observed throughout the discussion is that classroom tests, like general proficiency tests, should focus not only on the accuracy of the learners' language, but also on language use in context for particular purposes. By including items that encourage learners to use the language they know to accomplish some communicative purpose, achievement tests begin to tell us more directly how students are progressing toward the development of usable levels of proficiency.

The idea of testing language in context is certainly not new. Bondaruk, Child, and Tetrault (1975) advocated contextual testing more than twenty-five years ago, presenting models for embedding test items "in natural discourse-length contexts rather than single-phrase or single-sentence frames" (p. 89). They illustrate their approach with a number of adaptations of the cloze procedure, in which authentic texts are presented with planned deletions that the learner must restore. The authors add that "the use of such testing methods appears to be rare in the United States" (p. 89). Subsequent work on testing continued to argue for the inclusion of more contextualized and communicative formats on classroom tests, if only to bring testing practice more in line with developments in teaching (see, for example, Bartz 1976; Valette 1978; Cohen 1980, 1994; Omaggio 1980, 1983; and Magnan 1991, among others). However, Walz's (1991) study of commercial testing programs revealed that only half of the testing programs he reviewed used contextualized formats for all items, even though the accompanying textbooks provided contextualized exercises.

Walz (1989) makes an important point in discussing the relative effectiveness of "contextualization" in textbooks that can apply to classroom tests as well: Exercises and test items should be designed so that students need to understand the meaning being conveyed in order to accomplish the task. Illustration 9.3 (p. 396) shows a contextualized cloze-type passage designed two ways.

In the first example, students need not process the meaning of the passage in order to complete the task; the task can be done by simply conjugating the verb in parentheses and disregarding the rest of the sentence. In the second example, however, students must first make a semantic choice and then provide the correct form of the verb to complete the passage. The second sample is preferable because the context that has been created must be used to perform the task. Note that this particular sample item represents a structured format that requires a specific answer and focuses on a formal aspect of language use. In designing a classroom test,

Illustration 9.3
Two Ways of
Contextualizing
Test Items

Sample 1

Complete the following passage by giving the appropriate present-tense form of the verbs provided next to the blanks.

Je _____ (aller) souvent au cinéma le weekend avec mes amis. Nous _____ (préférer) les films d'aventure, mais quelquefois nous_____ (choisir) un film d'amour. Les films français _____ (être) très intéressants, mais un peu difficiles à comprendre. . . . (text continues)

Sample 2

Complete the following passage by choosing from the box at the right a verb that makes the most sense in the context. Be sure to give the appropriate form of the verb in the present tense. (Each verb is used only once.)

Je _____ souvent au cinéma le weekend avec mes amis.
Nous _____ les films d'aventure, mais quelquefois nous
_____ un film d'amour. Les films français _____ très
intéressants, mais un peu difficiles à comprendre. . . . (text continues)

| aller |
| choisir |
| être |
| préférer |

(Translation of passages above)

I often _____ to the movies on the weekend with my friends.
We _____ adventure films, but sometimes we _____ a love story.
French films _____ very interesting, but a little difficult to understand. . . .
(text continues)

| to go |
| to choose |
| to be |
| to prefer |

teachers should consider balancing such items with others that are more open-ended and communicative in nature. By creating achievement tests that require meaningful processing, even for more focused items, we can encourage students to develop skills that relate more directly to the proficiency-based goals of the curriculum. Because classroom tests are constructed to elicit those aspects of language that have been the object of recent study in class, they tend to be more *limited in scope* than are proficiency tests. By providing the teacher and students with feedback about the mastery of specific material learned during the course of instruction, they constitute *formative evaluation*—a type of evaluation that enables teachers to alter instruction in progress to better address the needs of the learners. Proficiency tests, on the other hand, are *summative evaluation* measures in that they characterize the language abilities of individuals at a given point in time without regard to a specific course of instruction. Clearly, both types of measures are useful in providing feedback to second-language learners, and the classroom teacher needs to be aware of the characteristics of both kinds of tests and the situations for which they are most appropriate.

The Case for Hybrid Classroom Tests

In order to revise our traditional classroom tests to make them more oriented towards communicative goals, it is not enough to simply add a few "global" or "communicative" items to the basic instrument represented in Illustration 9.2. Nor can we satisfy our testing needs by periodically administering a few proficiency-type tests in speaking, listening, reading, or writing and somehow averaging those results into a final course grade. An additive approach such as this may only serve to reconfirm the students' hypothesis that learning the vocabulary, phonology, morphology, and syntax of the language is one thing and learning to communicate with those features is quite another.

Instead of an additive strategy, the use of a "hybrid" approach (as suggested by Valette's 1977 discussion of test items) is recommended here. Such an approach combines the concern for assessing specific features of language with a focus on communicative language use in context. That is, tests can be constructed to integrate specific lexical, grammatical, sociolinguistic, and discourse features so that they are assessed *as they operate in naturalistic discourse contexts* throughout the test. This means that there is little place for single-sentence items on course exams or quizzes. Rather, language use must be tested beyond the level of the sentence, a point that Wesche (1981) considers essential in communicative language testing:

> Language testing which does not take into account propositional and
> illocutionary development beyond the sentence level, as well as the interaction
> between language behaviour . . . and real-world phenomena, is at best getting at
> only a part of communicative competence. Small wonder that we often find that a
> student's success at second-language classroom exercises and tests appears to bear
> little relationship to his or her ability to use the language effectively in a real-
> world situation (pp. 552-53).

Because natural language *always* occurs in both a discourse context and an extralinguistic, situational context, it makes sense, just in terms of face validity, to give tests that embed the second-language features to be tested in situational formats. In addition, students are more motivated when language-learning materials seem relevant to their communicative needs and interests and resemble authentic language use. Shohamy (1982) found that students had a favorable attitude toward oral interviews, for example, for this reason.

Working on the premise that contextualized testing is both preferable and necessary in a proficiency-oriented approach, it is clear that alternatives must be found for the single-sentence formats typically used on achievement tests. Teachers still need to be concerned, however, that their test instruments enable them to analyze students' performance in terms of specific course objectives; that is, the specific grammar, vocabulary, and cultural items treated in a given unit of study need to be *elicited* directly on the test instrument in order to provide diagnostic information on mastery of the material. A test instrument that elicits strictly open-ended responses to questions may not provide the type of targeted feedback teachers need in this regard. The skill, then, to be mastered in designing achievement tests is to create an examination that will require students both to show how well they can use specified features of the language and to demonstrate that they understand how such features function within naturalistic discourse.

The hybrid test attempts to do this by "artfully combin[ing] grammar and context, structure and situation" (Slager 1978, p. 74).[1] A blend of open-ended, or divergent, responses with specific, convergent items seems preferable when testing a given unit of material. Some sections of the test, for example, can focus on discrete points of grammar, vocabulary, discourse, or pragmatic features while other sections allow students to respond more freely, using whatever language they know to complete the task. In light of the insights of Tarone (1983) and Ellis (1985, 1990) regarding the variable performance of learners, such a blend of testing strategies is further supported. If, for example, it is true that student performance varies depending on the degree of attention paid to form and the nature of the language task in which students are engaged, a testing program that elicits samples of students' work using a variety of formats and task requirements will be more revealing, as well as more representative of their true underlying competence.

In addition to administering proficiency-based achievement tests and quizzes of a formal nature, teachers can broaden the range of assessment procedures to include collections of students' work in portfolios (Shohamy 1991; Magnan 1991; Liskin-Gasparro 1996); samples of oral performance taken during classroom communicative activities; exposés on various topics, including cultural information; and videotaped or audiotaped role-plays or skits. In this way, teachers can determine how well students have synthesized a wide range of material at various junctures along the course of instruction. It also makes sense for teachers to schedule an oral interview or other summative measure at the end of a given course or course sequence to determine the students' overall level of competence. The information gleaned from such summative tests can be of use in program evaluation and in improving articulation, both horizontally and vertically, i.e., between and among curricular offerings.

The following section presents some of the characteristics of test items and formats for classroom quizzes and tests, which constitute the focus of this chapter. The remaining sections of the chapter present samples of testing formats derived from the activity types discussed in Chapters 5 through 8, as well as ways to facilitate the test creation process.

Characteristics of Test Items and Item Types

A classification of test items along the two dimensions depicted in Illustration 9.4 (p. 400) enables us to make useful comparisons and contrasts when considering the characteristics of traditional achievement test items and those to be proposed in the following pages. The intersecting axes resemble in some ways the ones proposed by Cohen (1980, 1994), described earlier, but conceptualize the two continua somewhat differently.

The vertical axis in Illustration 9.4 represents a continuum relating to the nat-

---

[1] Slager was referring here to the design of an "ideal lesson," but his comments are just as applicable to the process of test creation.

uralness or authenticity of the language used on the test. Items that would fall along the upper portion of the continuum would consist of drill-like, traditional "textbook" language that bears little resemblance to genuine language use; those items falling along the lower portion would be excerpted from natural discourse or would approximate authentic communicative exchanges. If one considers the typical achievement test in Illustration 9.2, for example, the series of single-sentence frames that show no logical relationship to one another represent a rather stilted, "textbook" approach to language use and would therefore fall close to the upper end of the vertical axis. If, on the other hand, the test items had been derived from natural discourse, with each sentence following the others in a logical progression, they would have fallen within the lower portions of the continuum.

The horizontal axis in Illustration 9.4 represents the degree of specificity of the test items, ranging from those on the left that require the most convergent, or discrete-point, answers to those on the right that require more global comprehension and/or divergent responses. A few examples should serve to clarify this distinction. Suppose the teacher wanted to test the students' control of past-tense narration in the second language. One of the discrete features necessary in narration might be past-tense verb forms; another feature that might be tested could be the use of adverbial connectors, time expressions, and the like. The teacher might construct several test-item formats to determine how well students can handle the function of narration, ranging from formats in which specific linguistic or lexical features are elicited to those in which free response is encouraged. If, for example, a cloze passage were constructed in which specific parts of speech, such as verbs in the past tense, were deleted and students were asked to fill in the gaps of the passage using a set of vocabulary cues, then the item format would fall along the left-hand portion of the horizontal axis. If, on the other hand, the teacher asked students to write a brief paragraph recounting what they did last weekend, reminding them to use appropriate past tenses in their narration, the item format would fall along the right-hand portion of the continuum. Note that the latter testing format, although global in nature, could be *scored* in either a global fashion or in a discrete-point fashion; that is, points could be awarded for the comprehensibility and quality of the communication in a general sense, or they could be awarded for particular features of the message (such as the appropriate use of tense and the correct forms of the verbs). A scoring scheme that awards credit for both the general comprehensibility of the answer and specific discrete features is another viable option.

It is probably best to construct classroom tests that include items from various points along the horizontal axis, since this represents a blend of communicative and linguistic concerns. All of the test items, however, should fall within the lower ranges of the vertical axis if the test is to represent natural language use. The bottom two quadrants of the schema, then, are the province of proficiency-oriented classroom testing. Contexts for test items should be chosen to reflect the themes of the lessons or units under study, as well as a variety of functional and communicative purposes.

Illustration 9.4
Schema for Assessing
Characteristics of
Test Items

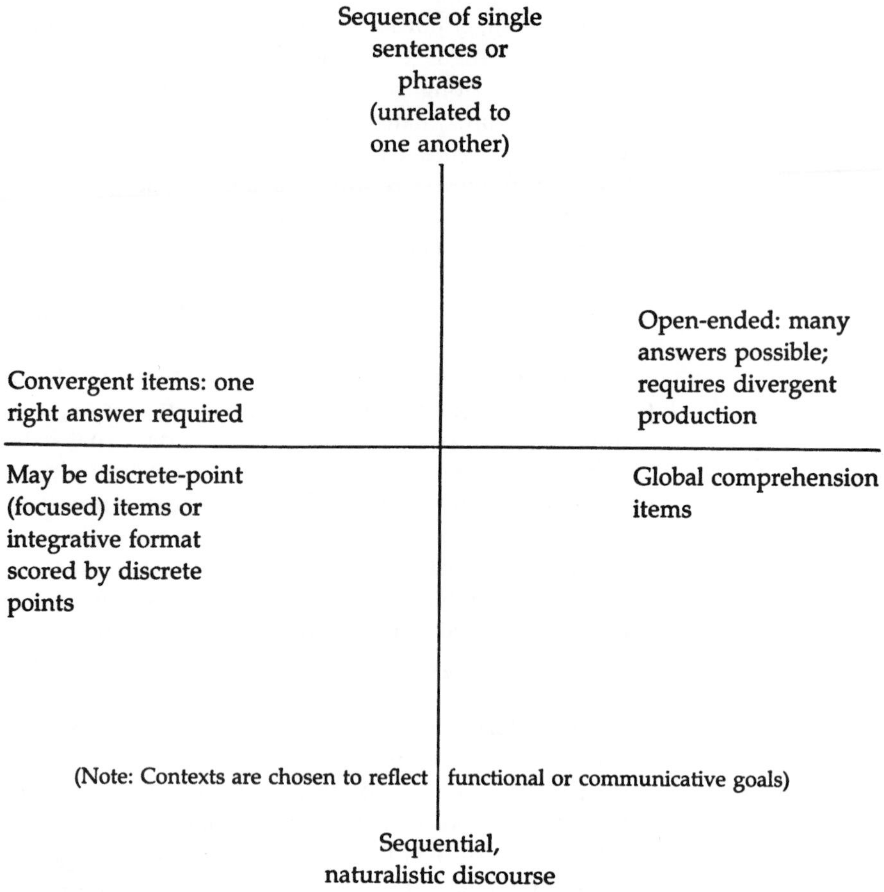

Sequence of single
sentences or
phrases
(unrelated to
one another)

Convergent items: one
right answer required

Open-ended: many
answers possible;
requires divergent
production

May be discrete-point
(focused) items or
integrative format
scored by discrete
points

Global comprehension
items

(Note: Contexts are chosen to reflect | functional or communicative goals)

Sequential,
naturalistic discourse

Source: Adapted from Omaggio 1983.

Consider again the traditional test items in Illustration 9.2. It is clear that virtually all of the sample items are enclosed within the upper left-hand quadrant of the schema represented in Illustration 9.4. If the whole test could thus be characterized, it would not reflect real language use to any extent. Students are not asked to synthesize the bits and pieces of language they have been learning for any real-world purpose, and the testing program, therefore, misses the mark entirely, regardless of what the programmatic goals statements might be.

In the next three sections, various formats for testing listening, reading, and writing skills, both separately and in an integrative fashion, are illustrated, along with suggestions for grading these kinds of items.

Listening Comprehension Formats

The diagram in Illustration 9.5 shows how a variety of listening comprehension formats might fall along the horizontal axis of the schema presented earlier for test-item classification. These are only a few of the formats that could be developed using the basic listening comprehension activity types described for Novice, Intermediate, Advanced, and Superior levels in Chapter 5 (see pp. 192–203).

The teacher, in designing the listening portion of a unit exam, might want to include items from several points along the continuum. For learners who are in the Novice and/or Intermediate ranges, for example, a short passage might be read describing a visual of some type, and students might be asked to identify various pictured items as they hear them mentioned. This section can be scored in a discrete-point fashion, with points awarded for each item correctly identified. A more global, integrative listening passage might require students to listen to a set of directions and follow a map, tracing a route with their pencils as the directions are given. If there is not enough time to do both kinds of items, the teacher may want to use one type on one exam and switch to the other type for the next exam. Another alternative would be to give students a test that includes one pure listening comprehension section and one section in which listening is combined with another skill (such as writing) in a mixed format.

The next section examines some sample test items for listening comprehension, arranged from the most convergent types to the most global formats.

Listening for Specific Grammatical or Lexical Features

In this type of listening item, a passage is read and students are required to listen for specific lexical or grammatical features embedded in the selection. Students might be asked, for example, to listen for cues to tense, gender, or number. If the embedded cues are lexical, they might be asked to listen for numbers, colors, objects in a room, parts of the body, foods, or items in some other lexical category.

In presenting the listening items, the short passage or conversational exchange is read or played on tape once. For Novice or Intermediate listeners, the sentences might then be read more slowly a second time, one by one, with pauses inserted to allow time for writing answers.

Although the following tasks require listening for discrete features of discourse, the fact that students are hearing a passage in context means that the results might be somewhat less diagnostic than if the passage were not contextualized. This is due to the fact that natural language is redundant and thus often provides multiple cues to meaning. If students are listening for cues to tense, for example, they might well use nonmorphological information, such as time words or overall situational constraints in the passage that would not be available in a single-sentence format. However, the contextualized format has the advantage of encouraging students to derive meaning from all of the available cues, both con-

Illustration 9.5
Positions of
Sample Listening
Comprehension
Formats on the
Assessment Schema

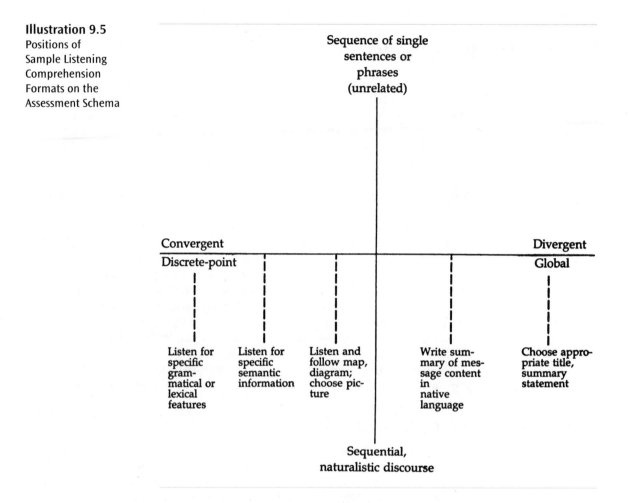

textual and structural—a skill that is of great value in processing natural language outside of the classroom context.

SAMPLE 1 (NOVICE)

Listening for time of day

Context: International train travel

Function: Listening for specific information

Student Task: Students listen to a recorded message giving times of arrivals and departures for trains. As they listen they fill in the schedule given below. (Students are directed to use numbers to designate times rather than write them out.)

Numéro du train_____		
Ville	**Arrivée**	**Départ**
Paris		
Cologne		
Berlin		
Varsovie		
Moscou		

Text: Bonjour. Ici les services SNCF à la Gare du Nord. Le train numéro 241, Paris/Moscou, quitte la Gare du Nord à 17h12 à destination Cologne. Le train arrive à Cologne à 22h36 et quitte la gare à 22h42. Il continue à Hagan, à Hamm, et à Hanovre et arrive à Berlin à 7h06. Le train quitte Berlin à 8h25 et va directement à Varsovie, où il arrive à 18h04. De Varsovie, le train numéro 241 continue à Moscou, où il arrive en gare à 14h45. Je répète . . . **[read twice]**

Translation: *Hello. This is the SNCF train service at the Gare du Nord. Train number 241, Paris/Moscow, leaves the Gare du Nord at 5:12 P.M. for Cologne. The train arrives in Cologne at 10:36 P.M. and leaves the station at 10:42 P.M. It continues to Hagen, Hamm, and Hanover and arrives in Berlin at 7:06 A.M. The train leaves Berlin at 8:25 A.M. and goes directly to Varsovie, where it arrives at 6:04 P.M. From Varsovie, train number 241 continues to Moscow, where it arrives in the station at 2:45 P.M. To repeat . . .*

Follow-up item: As a follow-up to this listening task, a test item can be designed asking students to add appropriate prepositions before the names of the cities and countries in which the train stops, as in the following passage:

Le train Paris/Moscou quitte Paris, va d'abord

_____ Allemagne, _____ Cologne, une jolie ville. Puis il

continue _____ Berlin. Après Berlin, le train va directement

_____Pologne—_____ Varsovie, la capitale—et enfin il arrive

_____Moscou, _____ Russie.

Source: Terry 2000.

SAMPLE 2 (NOVICE)

Recognizing vocabulary in context

Context: Advertising

Function: Recognizing relevant items in a radio advertisement

Student Task: Students imagine that their host family in Guadalajara has decided to buy a larger house and has made a list of items they need to buy to furnish it. As they listen to the test passage, students are directed to check off the items mentioned in the ad that are on the family's list.

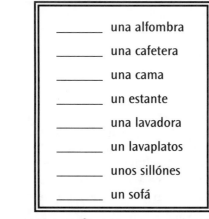

todo en venta

_____ una alfombra

_____ una cafetera

_____ una cama

_____ un estante

_____ una lavadora

_____ un lavaplatos

_____ unos sillónes

_____ un sofá

¡QUÉ OFERTAS!

Passage: Liquidación de muebles este fin de semana. Vendemos todo a la mitad del precio, ¡y menos! Tenemos camas, armarios, y cómodas. Hay juegos de muebles de dormitorio para niños, para niñas y para adultos. Sí, tenemos juegos de dormitorio para toda la familia desde un millón de pesos. Para su sala tenemos 150 sofás, y 200 sillónes de todos los colores y gustos. Cómpre una mesa para el comedor, y otra para la cocina. Con una visita a Muebles San Miguel, se puede decorar toda la casa. Vendemos alfombras, lámparas, y todo tipo de cuadros a precios imposibles de creer. Visítenos en Muebles San Miguel este fin de semana en la Plaza Tapatía.

Translation: *Furniture sale this weekend! We're selling everything at half price, and less! We have beds, armoires, and dressers. There are bedroom sets for boys, for girls and for adults. Yes, we have bedroom sets for the whole family from $300. For your living room, 150 sofas and 200 easy chairs in all colors and styles. Buy a table for the dining room, and another for the kitchen. With one visit to San Miguel Furniture you can decorate your whole house. We're selling area rugs, lamps and all kinds of paintings at hard-to-believe prices. Visit us at San Miguel Furniture this weekend in Tapatía Plaza.*

una alfombra = area rug

una cafetera = coffee maker

una cama = bed

un estante = book shelf

una lavadora = washing machine

un lavaplatos = dishwasher

unos sillónes = easy chairs

un sofá = sofa

Source: McMillen Villar and Meuser Blincow 1993.

SAMPLE 3 (INTERMEDIATE)

Listening for cues to tense

Context: End-of-semester activities

Function: Understanding simple narration of events

Student Task: Students listen to a series of statements about the end-of-semester activities of several students. Some of the students have finished certain tasks; others are planning to do things that still need to be done. Students are asked to indicate on their test papers whether the activity described constitutes something the student (1) will do or (2) has done already.

> **Example:** As you listen to the activities of various students at the end of the semester, indicate whether the activity is something they *will do* or something they *have already done:*

	WILL DO	**HAVE DONE**
1.	[ ]	[ ]
2.	[ ]	[ ]
3.	[ ]	[ ]
4.	[ ]	[ ]
5.	[ ]	[ ]

Passage:

1. Jean-Michel vient de passer l'après-midi à la bibliothèque.
2. Son camarade Etienne étudiera la plupart du week-end chez ses parents.
3. Margarite a déjà passé son examen de chimie à l'amphithéâtre.
4. Karim et Salima feront leurs exposés le dernier jour de classe.
5. Suzanne compte partir samedi matin après son examen de maths.

1. *Jean-Michel has just spent the afternoon at the library.*
2. *His friend Etienne will study most of the weekend at his parents' house.*
3. *Margarite already took her chemistry exam in the amphitheater.*
4. *Karim and Salima will present their exposés the last day of class.*
5. *Suzanne is planning on leaving Saturday morning after her math exam.*

Source: Adapted from Terry 1985.

▨ Listening for Specific Semantic Information

In this type of listening item, students extract specific semantic information from a passage. The information requested can consist of details or may involve a synthesis of several cues or the drawing of inferences.

SAMPLE (INTERMEDIATE)

Recording semantic detail

Context: Student housing

Function: Extracting relevant information from a description

Student Task: A passage is read in which a student is describing an apartment she has just rented, including information about location, price, number and size of rooms, utilities, etc. Students are told to listen to the passage and fill in the information on the chart below, based on the passage content.

1. Location _____
2. Rent/month _____
3. Number and type of rooms _____
4. Name of roommate _____
5. Furnishings (check one):
   [ ] furnished   [ ] unfurnished
6. Utilities (check one):
   [ ] included   [ ] not included
7. Phone number of landlord _____

Passage: Ich bin so glücklich, Mutter, weil meine Wohnung in einer schönen Straße liegt sehr nah zu den Geschäften und nur zwei Blocks von den Park entfernt. Und sie kostet nur DM 640 im Monat! Anna wird sie mit mir teilen. Dafür können wir die Miete und andere Kosten teilen. Wir haben zwei Schlafzimmer, eine kleine Küche und ein kleines Wohnzimmer, aber es ist sehr hell. Ich habe sie gern. Anna bringt ihre eigenen Möbel, und ich habe ein Bett, ein Tisch und alles, und so können wir nächsten Dienstag einziehen. Wenn du mich anrufen willst, sollst du die Hauswirtin anrufen. Ihre Nummer ist 428985.

Monika is describing her new apartment to her mother on the phone. Listen to the following excerpts from her conversation. As you listen, fill in the chart on your test copy.

> *I am so lucky, Mom, because the apartment is on a pretty street right near the shops and only two blocks from the park. And it only costs $400 per month! Anna is going to share it with me. That way we can both divide the rent and the utilities. We have two bedrooms and a little kitchen, and a very small living room, but there's lots of light. I really like it! Anna is bringing her own furniture, and I have my bed and desk and everything, so we're ready to move in next Tuesday. If you want to call me then, just call the landlord. Her number is 428985.*

Source: Activity format adapted from Omaggio 1983, p. 15.

Listening and Following a Map or Diagram, or Choosing or Completing a Picture

In listening items of this type, students are required to synthesize a series of cues in order to complete a task. They might be asked, for example, to follow a set of directions with a penciled line on a map. Another map activity might involve filling in the names of stores or other buildings according to a descriptive passage read to them. A set of names might be entered onto a diagram of a family tree, or a room plan might be completed according to a description of the objects in it. Students might be asked to select from a series of similar pictures the one that is described most accurately in detail, or, alternatively, they might be asked to draw a simple sketch from a description. For other ideas of listening activities of this type, see Chapter 5 (pp.196–200).

Comprehension Questions

For years, classroom teachers and test developers have used conventional formats such as true/false, multiple choice, and completion questions to assess listening comprehension. All of us have taken these types of tests, so there is little need to elaborate on these techniques here. A few comments, however, seem warranted about the use of such questions. If these formats are to be used to test pure listening comprehension, answers should be elicited in the students' native language in order to avoid mixing skills. Questions written on the students' test copies should also be in the native language, unless the teacher wishes to combine reading and listening comprehension in this section of the test. Ideas for mixed-skills formats will be treated later in this chapter for those teachers wishing to test several modalities at once.

When designing comprehension questions for listening passages, teachers should keep in mind the *purposes* for which one might normally be listening to the type of material chosen. For example, when people listen to a news broadcast, they often pay attention to the main ideas of most of the stories and might only listen carefully to details if the story is of special interest to them. Although some instructors may feel that they haven't really tested comprehension unless they create questions relating to all the details of the passage, this kind of comprehensive testing of the facts may not always be the best way to develop listening competence. A more useful comprehension check in the case of the news broadcast example might involve asking a question or two about the global meaning or main ideas of a particular story, and asking detail questions only about those points that would be relatively salient or likely to be retained by native listeners. If, on the other hand, students were listening to a weather report in order to make a decision about what clothes to wear, it might be appropriate to design questions about the details, since they would constitute the most important aspect of the message for the specified listening purpose.

Writing a Summary of a Message in the Native Language

Formats in which students are asked to write, in the native language, a summary of the facts and/or inferences they were able to understand and retain from a listening passage allow somewhat more freedom in answering, and thus tend to fall along the right-hand portion of the horizontal axis depicted in Illustration 9.5. Because students can select whatever information they want to, these kinds of items may be somewhat difficult to grade. It is clear, however, that grading must be done in some objective fashion.

Bernhardt and James (1987) recommend the use of summaries, or "immediate recall protocols," in both listening and reading comprehension and suggest scoring such protocols using a list of the "idea units" (Bernhardt 1983) of which the passage is composed. Because the ideas of a text are hierarchically arranged, with some more central to comprehension and meaning than others, Bernhardt and James propose differential point values for the various facts and inferences in the passage, with a greater number of points for main ideas or statements that show global comprehension and fewer points for minor details or specific facts.

Alternative scoring procedures that are somewhat less complex can also be used when rating student summaries on classroom tests. One option is to award points strictly on the basis of the number of legitimate facts and inferences recorded by the student, deducting points for wrong information and setting a limit on the total number of possible points that can be earned. Another option is to ask students to write down at least X number of facts and/or inferences gleaned from the passage and to award points for any information that legitimately represents the text, regardless of the nature of the particular facts recorded. This second idea may present the least scoring difficulty and allows the greatest flexibility to the students. It also has the advantage of rewarding students for *whatever* information they got from the passage, rather than penalizing them for something they missed that the teacher considered important.

Global Classification and Gisting

On the extreme right-hand portion of Illustration 9.5 are items that require students to report the gist of a listening passage or classify it globally in some way. Possibilities include asking students to give a title to a passage or to choose from multiple-choice options the best paraphrase of the main idea or the best summary statement. A variety of formats for global-classification items can be derived from the global listening comprehension activities suggested in Chapter 5.

Reading Comprehension Formats

The formats suggested for listening comprehension in the previous section can be quite easily adapted for testing reading comprehension. Illustration 9.6 shows the way in which various item types fall along the schema's horizontal axis, ranging from convergent or discrete-point formats to those that are more global in nature. The section that follows presents a few ideas to illustrate the range of formats one might use in testing reading skills. This small sample of ideas can be supplemented by consulting Chapter 5.

Illustration 9.6
Positions of
Sample Reading
Comprehension
Formats on the
Assessment Schema

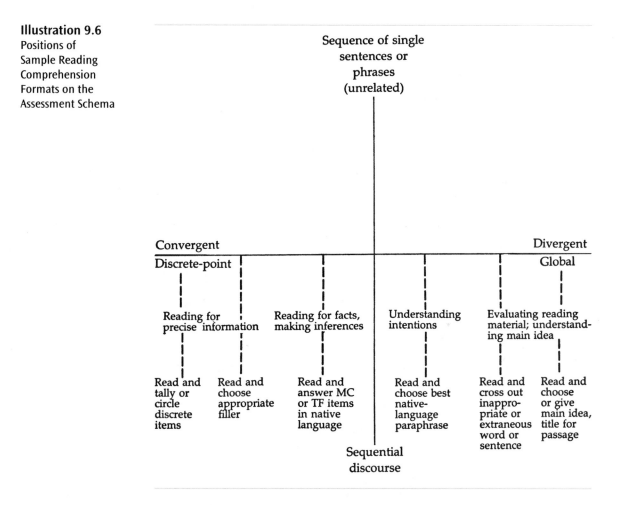

Reading for Precise Information

Filling in charts through semantic matching

Context: Household tasks

Function: Understanding simple descriptions; word associations

Student Task: Students supply the names of the parts of an apartment associated with the activities described in the chart.

> **El apartamento.** Your friend Luis has finally found an apartment which he will share with Pierre Legault, a student from Quebec. Both are very busy since Luis has a job and Pierre is studying, so they decide to draw up a chore schedule. Fill in the chart with the names of the parts of the apartment listing each part only once. (6 points)

CUARTO	RESPONSABILIDAD	NOMBRE
_____	lavar los platos y limpiar el horno	*Pierre*
_____	servir la comida para cenas especiales	*Pierre*
_____	limpiar la ducha y el lavabo	*Luis*
_____	tender las camas y pasar la aspiradora	*Pierre*
_____	sacudir los meubles (¡y no te olvides encima del piano!)	*Luis*
_____	cuidar las plantas fuera *(outside)* de la ventana o la puerta	*Luis*

Source: McMillen Villar and Meuser Blincow 1993.

SAMPLE 2 (NOVICE/INTERMEDIATE)

Reading for specific details

Context: Invitations to parties/social functions

Function: Reading for information about a party

Student Task: Students read the handwritten invitation in Illustration 9.7 (Invitation A) on page 412 and answer questions such as the following:

You have received an invitation to a party! Answer the questions below, based on the information given:

1. What is the occasion for the party?
2. Where is it being held?
3. What is the date and time of the party?
4. What two things does the invitation ask you to do?

(Note that the comprehension questions are designed to elicit the kinds of details that would be important to retain in order to properly respond to the invitation.)

Reading for Sociocultural/Pragmatic Cues to Meaning

SAMPLE (NOVICE/INTERMEDIATE)

Making stylistic distinctions

Context: Invitations to social events

Functions: Understanding conventional expressions; detecting formal vs. informal style

Student Task: Students examine the three invitations to social functions given in Illustration 9.7. They then answer the following questions:

1. Rank the invitations in terms of formality, from least formal to most formal. In one or two sentences, explain why you ranked them as you did.
2. What is the occasion for each of the invitations?
   Invitation A: _____
   Invitation B: _____
   Invitation C: _____
3. For each of the following expressions or ideas in English, give the Spanish equivalent or near equivalent, as represented in the invitations indicated:
   "Dear" _____ (Invitation A)
   _____ (Invitation B)
   "Please come . . ." _____ (Invitation A)
   _____ (Invitation B)
   "RSVP" _____ (Invitation A)
   _____ (Invitation B)
   _____ (Invitation C)
   "Yours truly" _____ (Invitation A)
   _____ (Invitation B)

Source: Adapted from Gutiérrez and Rosser 1992, pp. 233-34.

Reading and Choosing the Best Paraphrase

In this type of format, students are given several options and are asked to choose the best paraphrase of the main idea of a passage, paragraph, or series of paragraphs. Multiple-choice options can be in either the native language (for testing pure reading comprehension) or the target language. In the latter case, compre-

A

Querida amiga,

Eduardo y Carmelita salen para los Estados Unidos dentro de quince días. Para darles una despedida y desearles un buen viaje, estoy organizando una pequeña fiesta en mi casa... el viernes, 4 de septiembre, a las 20:30.

Cuento contigo. Contéstame cuanto antes. Y sobre todo... ¡no les digas nada a nuestros invitados de honor! La fiesta será una sorpresa para ellos.

Afectuosamente,

Mercedes

B

Estimada señorita:

En la ocasión de la quinceañera de nuestra hija Marisol, la familia está organizando una fiesta en nuestra casa, Calle Sur Nº 112, el sábado 17 de julio a las 21:00.

Nos daría mucho gusto tenerles a usted y a su hermano Carlos entre nosotros esa noche para la celebración.

Tenga la bondad de responder tan pronto como le sea posible.

Sin más por ahora, reciba los mejores deseos

C

El señor y la señora Rafael Bolaños de la Garza

invitan cordialmente a Rosario Vega Arroyo a disfrutar de

la celebración del segundo aniversario de su boda que

ofrecerán en su residencia el sábado 17 de febrero

a las 20:00   R.S.V.P.

Calle Jardín 87   Tel. 28 03 94

Illustration 9.7
Invitations to Parties

Source: Gutiérrez and Rosser 1992, pp. 232–33.

hension of the multiple-choice options is also necessary for answering correctly. Another possibility is to ask students to provide a paraphrase of a segment of discourse, in either the native or the target language. In the following example, given four options in the target language, students choose the best paraphrase of the main idea in the test paragraph.

SAMPLE (INTERMEDIATE)

Choosing the best paraphrase of the main idea

Context: Greetings and Leave-takings

Function: Understanding intentions

Student Task: Students read the paragraph in Illustration 9.8 and then choose the best paraphrase of the main idea.

Illustration 9.8 Greetings and Leave-takings

Arrivées et départs

Les Français ont une manière particulière de marquer l'existence des autres. Cela se manifeste parce que l'on pourrait appeler un sens approfondi des arrivées et des départs. Lorsque les Français voient des amis pour la première fois de la journée, ils leur serrent la main ou ils les embrassent. En les quittant, ils leur donnent à nouveau une poignée de main ou ils les embrassent.

La coutume de s'embrasser est la norme entre amis et membres de la même famille. Les hommes se serrent plus souvent la main. La tradition exige *(demands)* souvent trois bises. Quelquefois c'est quatre bises ou deux seulement. C'est une question de région ou d'habitude personnelle. Le plus souvent on commence par la joue *(cheek)* droite.

Que ferait un Américain en retrouvant un groupe d'amis qu'il voit pour la première fois de la journée?

Passage: "Liens culturels: Arrivées et départs"

Choisissez la phrase qui représente le mieux l'idée centrale du passage:

1. Les Français sont, en général, plus affectueux que les Américains.
2. La façon dont les gens se saluent est bien ancrée dans leurs traditions culturelles.
3. Les hommes et les femmes en France suivent des coutumes différentes en se saluant.
4. La tradition exige que les Français s'embrassent quand ils se rencontrent, même s'ils ne se connaissent pas.

Choose the sentence that best represents the main idea of the passage:

1. *The French are generally more affectionate than Americans.*
2. *The manner in which people greet one another is firmly anchored in their cultural traditions.*
3. *Men and women in France follow different customs in greeting one another.*
4. *Tradition demands that French people kiss when they meet one another, even if they don't know each other.*

Source: Illustration 9.8 is from Muyskens, Harlow, Vialet, and Brière 1998, p. 10.

When writing multiple-choice items of this type, care must be taken to design the distractors (wrong answers) so that each one is plausible to students who have only partially understood the passage. Note, in the above example, how elements of the passage have been worked into the distractors and how each might make sense to the student who has not synthesized all of the information. Distractor 1 attracts students who infer too much from the passage or who may be prone to form stereotypic impressions of the other culture. The second alternative, which is the correct answer, captures the main idea of the passage in paraphrase form. The second distractor (response #3) is implied in the passage but does not represent the main idea. The third distractor (#4) is wrong factually, but may be attractive because it combines various elements that were in the passage, albeit incorrectly.

Test writers need considerable practice in writing integrative comprehension items of this type, and any items they write should be tested first on colleagues and/or native speakers so that potential areas of difficulty are eliminated. It is also useful to have someone read the items without looking at the passage, as inexperienced test writers sometimes produce items that have unintentional extraneous cues, allowing the test-taker to choose the correct answer without having read or understood the passage itself.

Writing and Mixed-Skills Formats

The diagram in Illustration 9.9 shows how a variety of writing and mixed-skills formats fall along the horizontal axis of the test classification schema, ranging from the most convergent, or controlled, writing exercises on the left to the most open-ended on the right. The following samples, all of which require written responses in the target language, illustrate the range of formats a teacher might use on a classroom test. These sample items can be supplemented by using some of the ideas for teaching writing presented in Chapter 7.

■ Sentence Cues

Items of this type consist of "telegraphic" sentences or informal notes: Students combine the sentence elements provided into complete and meaningful discourse, adding necessary function words and making necessary changes. To contextualize this type of format, sentences in the section should be logically linked to one another to form a paragraph, or all the sentences should be related thematically in some way.

Illustration 9.9
Positions of
Sample Writing and
Mixed-Skills Formats on
the Assessment Schema

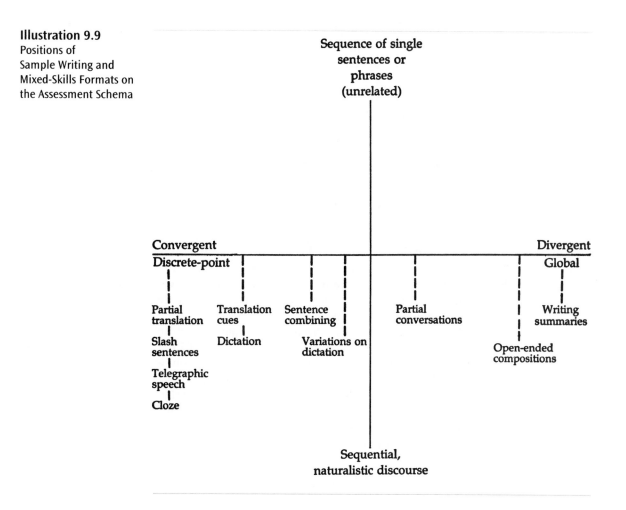

Slash sentences

Context: Impressions of life in an American town

Function: Description, giving opinions

Student Task: Karin is a student from France studying in the United States. She's telling you her impressions of the campus and the town you live in. Here are the elements of the statements she makes. Make complete, correct sentences to reconstruct what she said.

1. Je/aimer/beaucoup/université/campus/et/ville.
2. Les étudiants/ici/être/sympathique/mais/pas/sérieux.
3. Ils/passer/trop/temps/à/bars.

4. Ville/être/petit/mais/charmant.
5. Il/y/avoir/bon/magasins/et/beaucoup/théâtres.
6. Je/aller/cinéma/parce que/je/adorer/films/américain.

1. *I/to love/very much/university/campus/and/town.*
2. *The students/here/to be/nice/but/not/serious.*
3. *They/to spend/too much/time/in/bars.*
4. *Town/to be/small/but/charming.*
5. *There are/good/stores/and/many/theaters.*
6. *I/to go/movies/because/I/to adore/American/films.*

A variety of discrete elements recently learned in class have been embedded into this set of sentences. For example, students show their mastery of present-tense verb forms, including the irregular verbs *avoir* and *être,* as well as the use of adjectives and certain impersonal constructions as they complete the task. This type of integrative format allows the teacher to combine a variety of discrete points of vocabulary and/or grammar into one exercise and thus avoid setting aside a whole section of a test for a single grammatical topic. This latter procedure is quite prevalent in more traditional achievement tests.

The slash sentence format, above, has the advantage of helping students whose proficiency in writing is quite limited to create fuller discourse from very structured sets of cues. The disadvantage, however, is that the format is rather stilted and the stimulus for writing does not resemble natural language use. In the sample below, the cues for writing take the form of simple notes that are expanded by the student into fuller discourse. The "notes" format resembles authentic language use a little more closely, yet retains the advantages of structuring the writing activity to elicit certain features that the teacher would like to test.

Note that Sample 2 below tests the same essential features and content as were tested in Sample 1. However, the format allows for greater flexibility in testing. For example, if the notes are given to the student in the native language, the writing task is an indirect translation activity, and the student must recall necessary vocabulary as part of the test item. If the notes are given in the target language, as shown, they provide key vocabulary and a framework for the written paragraph, which changes the nature of the task and lowers the difficulty level considerably. Choice of native- or target-language stimuli will thus depend on the testing purpose and the proficiency level of the students who are being tested.

SAMPLE 2 (INTERMEDIATE)

Creating full discourse from notes

Context: Impressions of life in an American town

Function: Description, giving opinions

Student Task:

(10 pts.) Vous venez d'interviewer Karin, une étudiante d'échange de Nancy, au sujet de ses impressions des Etats-Unis. En utilisant les notes ci-dessous, écrivez un résumé de ce qu'elle a dit. Ajoutez tous les mots nécessaires pour créer un bon paragraphe intéressant.

- aime beaucoup l'université, campus, ville
- trouve étudiants sympathiques
- étudiants pas trop sérieux, trop de temps—bars
- ville—petite, charmante, bons magasins, beaucoup de théâtres
- cinéma souvent, voir films

Student Response:

Je viens de parler avec Karin, une étudiante de Nancy. Elle dit qu'elle

aime beaucoup l'université, le campus, et la ville. Elle trouve les étudiants ici très sympathiques. Elle pense que les étudiants ne sont pas trop sérieux parce qu'ils passent trop de temps aux bars. Karin trouve la ville un peu petite, mais charmante. Il y a beaucoup de bons magasins et beaucoup de théâtres. Elle va souvent au cinéma parce qu'elle adore voir les films.

(10 pts.) You have just interviewed Karin, an exchange student from Nancy, about her impressions of the United States. Using the notes below, write a resume of what she said. Add any necessary words to make a good, interesting paragraph.

- *likes the university, campus, town very much*
- *thinks students nice*
- *students not too serious, too much time—bars*
- *town—small, quaint, good stores, lots of theaters*
- *movies often, see films*

Student Response:

I just spoke with Karin, a student from Nancy. She says that she

likes the university, the campus, and our town very much. She thinks the students here are nice. She thinks the students are not too serious, since they spend too much time in bars. Karin thinks the town is a little small, but charming. There are a lot of good stores and lots of theaters. She often goes to movies because she loves to watch films.

Scoring: An item such as this might be graded using discrete-point or component scoring. For discrete-point scoring, teachers might deduct 1/2 point for each error in targeted features such as verbs, adjective agreement, prepositions of place, and/or connectors, up to a total of 10 points maximum. For component scoring, teachers might award points for comprehensibility, grammaticality, and ease of expression (i.e., the flow of the discourse), distributed among the 10 points as the teacher sees fit. In either case, it is important to write out criteria for scoring very clearly, especially if more than one teacher will administer and score the test.

Contextualized Partial Translation (Reading and Writing)

In partial translation, elements of discourse are deleted from a short story or dialogue, and students attempt to restore these elements using a native-language version of the text as their guide. This format is an adaptation of a cloze task, but the ambiguity of possible fillers is eliminated through the use of the parallel translation. Like straight translation, this format elicits specific features of the language in a controlled fashion and therefore has high diagnostic power. Partial translation has the further advantage of allowing the teacher to focus on particular parts of the discourse and is generally less time-consuming than full translation because less of the text needs to be produced by the student.

In the sample that follows, a dialogue at a restaurant has been constructed, where students restore the text on the left using the native-language cues given on the right. Items to be restored include grammatical and vocabulary features that have been targeted in the unit being studied, as well as pragmatic features such as culturally appropriate conventional phrases used in ordering a meal.

SAMPLE (NOVICE)

Partial translation using parallel native-language text

Context: Two people eating in a restaurant

Functions: Ordering foods, asking and answering questions about the menu

Student Task: Students complete the dialogue on the left using the native-language text given on the right.

Janine: _____ ! Où est le _____ ?

I'm hungry. Where's the waiter?

Marie: Le voilà. Il arrive avec les _____ .

There he is. He's coming with the menus.

Le serveur: Bonsoir, mesdemoiselles. _____ ce soir?

Good evening, ladies. Would you like an apéritif this evening?

Marie: Pas moi. Et toi, Janine? Qu'est-ce _____ ?

Not me. What about you, Janine? What are you having?

Janine: Moi, je voudrais _____ un _____ .

I'd like to order an appetizer.

Le serveur: Et qu'est-ce que _____ ce soir? Le pâté est _____ . (etc.)

And what are you having tonight? The pâté is excellent. (etc.)

Cloze Adaptation

Another way to provide cues to cloze deletions is to list possibilities in a box next to the paragraphs of a dialogue or story. If cues are provided in alphabetical or random order, students must read the surrounding discourse to know which word fits the context and to produce the correct form. The sample item below is given in English and shows how verbs in the past tense can be elicited through this kind of format.

SAMPLE 1 (INTERMEDIATE)

Verb deletions

Context: Writing in a travel journal

Function: Narrating in the past

Student Task: Marisa is writing in her journal about her day in the city of Chicago. Complete the journal entry using the cues to the right. Be sure to use appropriate past tenses.

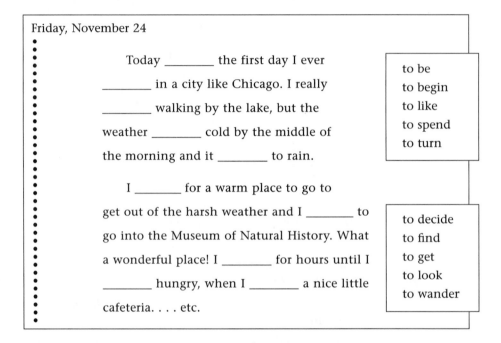

Friday, November 24

Today _____ the first day I ever

_____ in a city like Chicago. I really

_____ walking by the lake, but the

weather _____ cold by the middle of

the morning and it _____ to rain.

    I _____ for a warm place to go to

get out of the harsh weather and I _____ to

go into the Museum of Natural History. What

a wonderful place! I _____ for hours until I

_____ hungry, when I _____ a nice little

cafeteria. . . . etc.

to be
to begin
to like
to spend
to turn

to decide
to find
to get
to look
to wander

SAMPLE 2 (NOVICE)

Personalized cloze passage

Context: Writing a letter to a pen pal

Function: Simple description

Student Task: Students complete the following letter as they wish, using the cues given below the blanks to guide them.

Firenze, l'otto febbraio

Caro Marco,

    Ho letto il tuo anuncio nella rivista *Ciao!* cercando corrispondente. Ho

_____ e sto studiando _____, _____, e _____ a _____.
    (age)   (subject) (subject)   (subject)   (place)

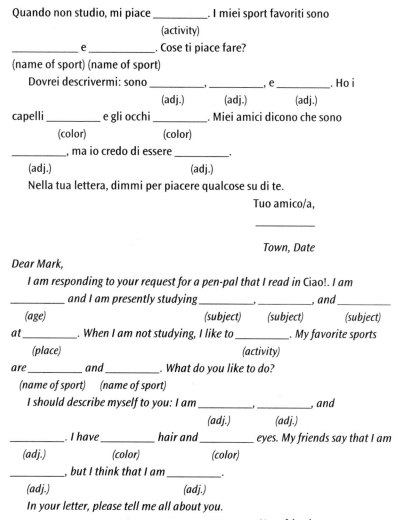

Quando non studio, mi piace _____. I miei sport favoriti sono
                        (activity)
_____ e _____. Cose ti piace fare?
(name of sport) (name of sport)
        Dovrei descrivermi: sono _____, _____, e _____. Ho i
                                    (adj.)   (adj.)   (adj.)
capelli _____ e gli occhi _____. Miei amici dicono che sono
            (color)   (color)
_____, ma io credo di essere _____.
    (adj.)   (adj.)
        Nella tua lettera, dimmi per piacere qualcose su di te.

                                                    Tuo amico/a,

                                                    _____

                                                    Town, Date
Dear Mark,
    I am responding to your request for a pen-pal that I read in Ciao!. *I am*
_____ *and I am presently studying* _____, _____, *and* _____
    (age)   *(subject)*   *(subject)*   *(subject)*
at _____. *When I am not studying, I like to* _____. *My favorite sports*
        (place)   *(activity)*
are _____ *and* _____. *What do you like to do?*
    (name of sport)   *(name of sport)*
    I should describe myself to you: I am _____, _____, *and*
                                            (adj.)   *(adj.)*
_____. *I have* _____ *hair and* _____ *eyes. My friends say that I am*
    (adj.)   *(color)*   *(color)*
_____, *but I think that I am* _____.
    (adj.)   *(adj.)*
In your letter, please tell me all about you.
                                                    Your friend,

▧ Discourse Transformation

In order to test discourse competence in conjunction with grammatical competence, teachers can design test items in which students are asked to transform the discourse in some way. For example, students might be asked to modify a test passage by replacing any repeated nouns with pronouns, to show that they know both the form and the function of these cohesive elements. Another test item might ask students to elaborate on a passage by adding adverbial elements, relative clauses, connectors and link words, or other details that would make the discourse flow more easily. In the following sample, the discourse is transformed by changing the time element: The original passage is in present time, whereas the transformed passage is in the past.

SAMPLE (INTERMEDIATE)

Discourse transformation

Context: Vacation and travel

Function: Writing letters, recounting events

Student Task:

Dominique et Marie-France sont en vacances aux Etats-Unis. Dominique écrit une lettre à leur amie Odile. Mais elle oublie de la mettre à la poste. Retournée en France, elle doit récrire la lettre au passé. Récrivez la lettre au passé pour elle.

> Chère Odile,
>
> Nous passons la première semaine de nos vacances à Los Angeles. Moi, je trouve la ville de Los Angeles très intéressante, mais je crois que Marie-France ne l'aime pas. Les musées et les restaurants sont excellents, mais après une semaine dans une grande ville, elle a envie d'aller à la plage. Alors, nous y allons la semaine prochaine.
>
> Nous pensons faire du camping une semaine, mais ce weekend une jeune Américaine nous a invitées à rester chez elle. Elle nous sert des repas délicieux et nous aimons beaucoup la cuisine californienne. Elle pose beaucoup de questions sur la France et les Français. Elle ne nous croit pas quand nous lui disons que le Français moyen a quatre semaines de vacances payées. Notre visite chez elle nous plaît beaucoup!
>
> Grosses bises,

Dominique and Marie-France are on vacation in the United States. Dominique writes a letter to their friend Odile. But she forgets to put the letter in the mail. On her return to France, she has to rewrite the letter in the past. Rewrite the letter in the past tense for her.

> *Dear Odile,*
>
> *We are spending the first week of our vacation in Los Angeles. I think the city of Los Angeles is really interesting, but I think that Marie-France doesn't like it. The museums and restaurants are excellent, but after a week in a big city, she wants to go to the beach. So we are going there next week.*
>
> *We were thinking about going camping for one week, but this weekend a young American has invited us to stay at her house. She serves delicious meals and we really like California cooking. She asks a lot of questions about France and the French people. She doesn't believe us when we tell her that the average French person has four weeks of paid vacation. We're really enjoying our visit with her!*
>
> *Hugs and kisses,*

In order to save writing time, the teacher may want to provide a partial text on the student's test paper below the original, leaving spaces for the verbs and/or other discourse features that might change as the text is transformed to the past.

▨ Partial Conversations (Reading and Writing)

A somewhat more creative and open-ended format is one in which students supply the other half of a conversation based on the half that they see. This format is especially useful for testing question formation, as in the following example.

Partial conversation

Context: Courses and schooling

Function: Asking for information

Student Task: *Ein Interview.* Brigitte, a German student, is studying at the University of X and meets Mark, an American student who is studying German. She begins to ask him about himself and his studies. Below are Mark's answers. Write an appropriate question for each answer you see.

Brigitte:_____?
Mark: Ich heiße Mark.
Brigitte:_____?
Mark: Dieses Semester belege ich zwei Kurse: Deutsch und Architektur.
Brigitte:_____?
Mark: Weil ich nächstes Jahr in Deutschland Architektur studieren will.
Brigitte:_____?
Mark: In einer Wohnung in Schwabing, in der Nähe von der Technischen Hochschule.
Brigitte:_____?
Mark: Ich fahre im Oktober nach München.

Brigitte:_____?
Mark: My name is Mark.
Brigitte:_____?
Mark: I'm taking two courses this semester: German and architecture.
Brigitte:_____?
Mark: Because I'm going to study architecture in Germany next year.
Brigitte:_____?
Mark: In an apartment in Schwabing, close to the school of architecture.
Brigitte:_____?
Mark: I'm going to Munich in October.

▨ Translation Cues

Another way to test interrogative constructions is to give students a set of cues to guide them in formulating questions that could be used in sustaining a conversation with a native speaker. In the following example, students are given a set of ideas in English and are asked to formulate appropriate questions to get the information they are seeking. This item gives students cues for asking a set of specific questions and then asks them to make up two more questions of their own.

SAMPLE (INTERMEDIATE)

Translation cues for asking questions

Context: Making a new friend

Function: Asking for information, engaging in conversation

Student Task: You and your roommate just met a new French student on campus. You both want to learn something about him. You'll find below a set of things that your roommate would like to find out, but they're written in English. Since you speak French, and since he is a French student, you need to ask these questions in French. For the last two boxes, make up questions that you yourself would like to ask .

> *Modèle:* I wonder if he likes American food.
>
> Your question: *Est-ce que vous aimez la cuisine américaine?*

Questions your roommate wants to ask	Vos questions en français . . .
Hmmm. I wonder how old he is!	
I wonder just where he's from.	
I'd like to know if he can speak English.	
Does he know anybody here at school?	
I wonder if he needs to buy anything for class.	
I wonder if he'd like to go to a party with us Saturday.	
Questions you want to ask yourself	
?	
?	

Source: Adapted from Terry 2000.

▦ Open-Ended Completions (Reading and Writing)

The example that follows shows one way in which completion exercises, in which students must supply a logical ending for a set of partial statements, can be related to a short reading passage. At the same time, personal reactions to that passage can be elicited.

SAMPLE (INTERMEDIATE)

Open-ended completion

Context: Clubs and social activities

Function: Expressing opinions and points of view

Student Task:

Une société secrète. Voici une série de pratiques d'une société secrète sur le campus. Comment réagissez-vous à ces pratiques? Complétez les phrases sous la liste en choisissant une pratique de la société. Choisissez une pratique différente pour chaque opinion que vous complétez.

Les Pratiques de la Société Secrète

A. Chaque membre de la société sait le mot secret.
B. Les femmes doivent porter un chapeau pendant les réunions.
C. Nous dormons pendant les présentations du président.
D. Nous choisissons nos membres dans l'annuaire.
E. Tout le monde prend les réunions au sérieux.
F. Le président de la société a 70 ans.
G. Les membres vont à toutes les réunions.

1. Il est curieux que . . .
2. Il est naturel que . . .
3. Je suis étonné(e) que . . .
4. Mon ami doute que . . .
5. Je suis furieux(-se) que . . .
6. Il est dommage que . . .
7. Il est bon que . . .

A Secret Society. Here is a series of practices of a secret society on campus. How do you react to these practices? Complete the sentences under the list of practices, choosing a different practice for each sentence you complete.

The Practices of the Secret Society

A. *Every member of the society knows the secret word.*
B. *Women have to wear hats during the meetings.*
C. *We sleep during the president's speeches.*
D. *We choose our members from the phone book.*
E. *Everyone takes the meetings seriously.*
F. *The president of the society is 70 years old.*
G. *Members go to all the meetings.*

1. *It is curious that . . .*
2. *It's natural that . . .*
3. *I'm surprised that . . .*

4. *My friend doubts that . . .*
5. *I'm angry that . . .*
6. *It's a shame that . . .*
7. *It's good that . . .*

The test item formats that have been illustrated thus far have been constructed to elicit specific structural and lexical elements in a fairly controlled fashion in order to assess students' mastery of certain features of language. Magnan (1991) expresses several reservations, however, about the extensive use of dialogue or paragraph frames in which grammatical features are embedded on classroom tests. First, if the items are not well constructed there is a danger that students will not need to read the surrounding context in order to perform the task. This can be avoided by constructing the paragraph or dialogue so that students must supply missing elements by making both a semantic and a structural choice among possible options. For example, if a story has been constructed in which verbs in the past tense have been deleted, teachers should not provide cues by simply indicating a verb in the infinitive form beneath each blank. In an item constructed in this way, students would only need to look for the subject and conjugate the verb. There would be no need to read the surrounding story, and the contextualization of the passage would not serve any real function. If, on the other hand, the cues are provided in random order in a box to the right of the passage, as in the first sample cloze adaptation on page 420, students must read the surrounding discourse in order to determine (1) what semantic choice among the options is appropriate and (2) what form the verb should take.

A second limitation of paragraph frames is that they can lack naturalness and authenticity. Certainly this is the case for many Novice-level items, since students' ability to produce original discourse is extremely limited. One way to alleviate this problem is to construct passages that are more personalized in nature, such as the second sample cloze adaptation on pages 420–421. Magnan (1991) suggests that one might personalize an item such as the partial conversation illustrated on page 423 by adding a set of personalized questions that follow the fictitious conversation and are related to the topic. For example, the following personalized questions could be added as a second task following the German conversation between Mark and Brigitte:

1. Was ist dein Lieblingskurs dieses Semester?
2. Gib zwei Gründen, warum du Deutsch studierst.
3. Was tust du ger, wenn du nicht studierst?

1. *What is your favorite course this semester?*
2. *Give two reasons why you are studying German.*
3. *What do you like to do to relax from your studies?*

Care must be taken, however, that the follow-up task does not provide the same structures that are being elicited in the primary task, as the validity of the items would then be compromised.

As was pointed out at the beginning of this chapter, test items need to sample students' competencies through the use of a blend of focused and open-ended tasks, allowing teachers to elicit specific features of language for diagnostic purposes as well as allowing students to create their own discourse in order to communicate personal meaning. This is true for tests designed for learners at every level of proficiency, including the Novice level. Later in this chapter, a form for evaluating test items on a variety of dimensions is given. Use of a form such as this can help teachers achieve an appropriate balance of focused and open-ended activities.

The two remaining sample writing formats in this section represent a move toward the more creative, open-ended portion of the continuum depicted in Illustration 9.9. As students develop in their productive skills, the portion of the test that provides opportunities for open-ended and personalized response might be increased to allow for more creative communication. (See also Chapter 7 for open-ended writing tasks that can be used for testing purposes.)

Responding to a Target-Language Text (Reading/Writing)

One way to combine reading and writing skills in a realistic communicative task is to provide students with a target-language text to which they then write a response. In the first sample below, students are asked to write a letter in response to one received from a French pen-pal.

SAMPLE 1 (INTERMEDIATE)

Responding to a letter

Context: Personal letter

Function: Describing oneself, sharing interests, asking for information

Student Task: Students read the brief letter provided on their test copies (See Illustration 9.10 on p. 428–429) and then respond as they like, answering the questions posed in the letter. Students are directed to ask several questions of their own to obtain more information from their correspondent.

Text of Letter: See Illustration 9.10.

Scoring: A variety of scoring options can be used to score open-ended compositions of this type (see, for example, the suggestions given in Chapter 7, as well as Terry 1992). A suggestion for holistic scoring is given below:

> *9-10 points:* Letter is well written, answers all questions posed, asks appropriate questions, is well organized, and shows excellent control of linguistic features.

> *7-8 points:* Letter is reasonably well written, answers questions posed, asks appropriate questions, shows good control of linguistic features, with some patterned errors.

Illustration 9.10
Letter from a French
Pen Pal (Sample 1)

mardi 24 novembre 1992

Cher(e) _____,

    Mon prof de géographie vient de me donner ton adresse et je m'empresse de t'écrire.

    Je m'appelle Marie-Aline Poilrat, j'ai 17 ans et j'habite à Hendaye au Pays Basque. Je suis en classe de Terminale au Lycée de Saint-Jean-de-Luz. Je fais des langues. Et toi, en quoi te spécialises-tu?

    A Hendaye, pendant la saison, il y a trois fois plus de touristes que d'habitants. Tu devrais voir les embouteillages! Notre maison ne donne pas sur la plage, mais on y est vite en voiture. La plage est à deux kilomètres.

    Mon père travaille pour l'Administration des Douanes et ma mère est infirmière à domicile. J'ai un frère Mathieu; il a 14 ans et on ne s'entend pas très bien. Il est nul! Il est toujours en train de se plaindre!

    Ma meilleure copine s'appelle Sylvie. Le mercredi après-midi, on joue aux jeux vidéos. C'est super-génial! Nous aimons aussi la piscine et le tennis. Est-ce que tu fais partie d'un club sportif? Quelles sortes de choses est-ce qu'on fait pour s'amuser chez toi? Est-ce que tu habites une grosse ville? Vas-tu souvent à la plage?

    Tu dis que tu recherches une correspondante qui aime la musique. Tu tombes bien! Je joue de la guitare depuis 5 ans. J'aimerais bien pouvoir jouer les airs qu'on entend à la radio, surtout les chansons de Patrice Bruel. Je l'adore! Il est super-mignon! Qui est-ce que tu aimes comme chanteur, toi? Réponds-moi vite et dans ta prochaine lettre raconte-moi un peu ta vie. Envoie aussi une photo récente si tu en as une.

    A bientôt te lire.

Ton amie
Marie-Aline

Source: Coulont-Henderson 1992.

5-6 points: Letter is somewhat disorganized, fails to ask or answer questions as directed, shows fair control of linguistic features, with some major errors in common structures.

0-4 points: Letter is poorly written, student fails to follow directions and/or shows poor control of many linguistic features.

    Another way to assign points for this item is to use a componential scoring scheme. For example, points can be awarded for comprehensibility, accuracy, organization, fluency, and/or style, with each component receiving a certain proportion of the total point value.

Source: Letter in Illustration 9.10 provided by Françoise Coulont-Henderson 1992. Idea for format from Terry 1985.

SAMPLE 2 (INTERMEDIATE)

Responding to a short cultural reading

Context: Greeting and leave-taking behavior

Function: Writing about cultural conventions and customs, making comparisons

Illustration 9.10
Translation

Tuesday, November 24, 1992

Dear _____ ,

My geography teacher just gave me your address and I hurried to write to you.

My name is Marie-Aline Poilrat, I'm 17 and I live in Hendaye in the Basque country. I'm a senior in the Lycée de Saint-Jean-de-Luz. I'm majoring in languages. What about you? What is your major?

In Hendaye, during the summer, there are three times as many tourists as there are residents. You should see the traffic jams! Our house isn't on the beach, but you can get there quickly by car. The beach is two kilometers away.

My father works for the Customs Service and my mother is a home-care nurse. I have a brother Matthew; he's 14 and we don't get along that well. He's worthless! He's always complaining!

My best friend's name is Sylvie. Wednesday afternoons, we play video games. It's really great! We also like swimming and tennis. Do you belong to a sports club? What kinds of things do you do to have fun where you live? Do you live in a big city? Do you often go to the beach?

You said that you're looking for a pen pal who likes music. You're in luck! I have been playing the guitar for 5 years. I'd like to be able to play the songs on the radio, especially the songs by Patrice Bruel. I love him! He's super! What singers do you like? Answer quickly and in your next letter tell me a little about your life. Send a recent photo too if you have one.

Hope to hear from you soon!

Your friend,
Marie-Aline

Student Task: Students are asked to read the text about French greeting behavior in Illustration 9.8 (p. 413). They then write a similar paragraph explaining greeting and leave-taking behavior in their own culture, including several points of comparison and contrast with French customs.

Scoring: Points can be awarded for both writing performance and for the cultural comparisons and contrasts students identify in their response.

Guidelines for Creating Contextualized Paper-and-Pencil Tests

Many teachers may see the value of contextualized achievement tests but feel that they do not have the time or the expertise to create such exams on a regular basis. Although creating test items such as those in the previous sections may seem at first glance to be a much more difficult task than creating conventional items, teachers will find that the process becomes much easier with practice. Because the contextualized test integrates so many linguistic and lexical features in a few well-chosen passages, its creation is actually much simpler than when the instrument consists of unrelated items.

A few guidelines should help the teacher who would like to try to write quizzes and tests after the models presented in this chapter. When the steps below are followed, preparation of classroom tests should be relatively easy and should not take an inordinate amount of time. Perhaps the best plan is to begin with a short quiz or unit exam rather than a long test.

Step 1. Take an inventory of the material to be covered on the test or quiz that is planned for the unit or lesson. List the major grammatical features, new vocabulary, discourse features, and cultural content you would like to include.

Step 2. Decide which skill areas you would like to emphasize. Choose some formats from among the samples given in this chapter or in Chapters 5, 6, and 7.

Step 3. Divide the content listed in Step 1 among the item types you have chosen. Be sure to place appropriate emphasis on each aspect of the language you wish to test across skill areas. To do this, construct a testing grid such as the one in Illustration 9.11.

Step 4. Create a simple story, dialogue, or paragraph that includes the features you've identified for each part of your exam. You may find that you can create your own context from models in your text, being sure to keep the themes and cultural content of the lesson in mind. For inspiration, you might want to look at reading passages, cultural commentaries, or passages from a supplementary reader at the same level of difficulty as the material you are testing. Some teachers may want to use authentic texts and design reading or mixed-skills items or item sets based upon them. Before using authentic materials on tests, teachers should make certain that students have had multiple opportunities to deal with such materials in the course of instruction. Classroom tests should not present students with tasks that are significantly different from those with which they are familiar, and questions or activities designed around authentic materials should elicit the same kinds of performance that students have practiced in class.

In creating tests, consider including some global and divergent-production items as well as items that are more discrete-point in nature. If you are not a native speaker of the language you are teaching, have a colleague who is native check the test for the authenticity and accuracy of the language.

◼ Evaluating the Test Draft

Once a preliminary version of a test has been drafted, it is important to look at the way the test as a whole samples the students' use of the language and how credit is awarded for the various tasks that have been created. A form such as the one presented in Illustration 9.12 can be useful in evaluating tests for authenticity of language use, balance of discrete-point versus more global or integrative formats, balance of skills being tested, clarity of directions, and general interest level. In using this particular form, teachers who are preparing a test evaluate it first on a section-by-section basis and then rate it overall using a five-point scale. The first part of the evaluation is done by placing the letter or numeral designating each test section on each of the continua provided on the form. For the test evaluation depicted in Illustration 9.12, the four parts of the sample French quiz in the Ap-

Illustration 9.11
Testing Grid*

Functions/Structures to be Sampled on Quiz 3	Listening	Reading/ Writing	Writing
Understanding descriptions	X		
Describing places/people		X	X
Describing activities		X	X
Vocabulary related to housing	X	X	X
Descriptive adjectives	X	X	X
Colors		X	
Possessive adjectives			X
Numbers above 100	X		
Quantity expressions		X	
Part of Test	A. Listening with English answers	B. Partial translation	C. Describing town
			D. Describing life at the university
Point Values	5	6	14

* Used to create the sample French quiz in the appendix to this chapter

pendix to this chapter have been charted, using the letters A, B, C, and D to designate the test sections.

If a group of teaching assistants in multisection university courses share in the preparation and evaluation of tests, it is a good idea to plan course meetings to review the proposed tests and look over previous evaluations for tests that covered the same material. As each exam is prepared by one or more teaching assistants, a grid similar to the one provided in Illustration 9.11 can be completed and attached to the test draft. The draft can then be evaluated by the teacher(s) who created it together with the course coordinator/director of language instruction, using a form such as the one in Illustration 9.12. Comments can be made on the draft, and a revised form of the test can be prepared for the course meeting. At the course meeting, the tests that have been prepared can be timed, and any final changes that are deemed necessary can be made. A team approach such as this encourages every member of the teaching staff to take responsibility for the testing program while allowing for an efficient division of labor in order to save staff time.

Testing Oral Skills

Many classroom teachers feel that oral exams are among the most difficult types of exams to create, schedule, administer, and grade, especially when they have large classes or many classes in the course of a day. For these reasons, some classroom teachers consider oral tests impractical and do not attempt to test oral skills

Illustration 9.12
Criteria for Test
Evaluation

1. **The Parts of the Test.** For each section of the test, place the letter of the part (A, B, C, D, etc.) on the continua below.

   a. How would you rank the task on a continuum ranging from artificial to authentic language use?

	$\mathcal{B}$		$\mathcal{A}$ C	$\mathcal{D}$
Artificial				Authentic

   b. How would you rank the task on a continuum ranging from discrete-point to open-ended?

$\mathcal{B}$ $\mathcal{A}$		C	$\mathcal{D}$
Discrete-point			Open-ended

   c. How would you rank the task in terms of the focus of the activity, ranging from a focus on minor points to a focus on major points in the chapter or unit?

	$\mathcal{ABCD}$
Minor points	Major points

   d. How would you characterize the task in terms of the components of language use being tested? (Place the letter of the section on the line above the main component(s) tested.)

$\mathcal{BCD}$	$\mathcal{ABCD}$		$\mathcal{B}$
Grammar	Vocabulary	Culture	Reading Comprehension

$\mathcal{A}$		
Listening Comprehension	Pragmatics	Other (specify)

   e. How would you rank the clarity of the task and of the directions?

	$\mathcal{ABCD}$
Confusing	Clear

   f. How would you characterize the general level of interest of the task for your students?

	$\mathcal{B}$	$\mathcal{A}$ C	$\mathcal{D}$
Boring			Fun/Interesting

2. **The Test as a Whole.** Based on your analysis of the sections of the test, how would you rate the test overall (on a scale of 1 to 5, with 5 being the best score) on the following criteria?

1. Authenticity of language use	1	2	③	4	5
2. Relevance to language proficiency development	1	2	3	④	5
3. Clarity of tasks and directions	1	2	3	4	⑤
4. Interest level of test	1	2	3	④	5
5. Balance of skills/components	1	2	3	④	5

   What would you do to improve this test?

   1. Include at least one more item on numbers above 100.

   2. Include more on culture and pragmatics.

in any regular or consistent fashion. Yet it is clear that one of the priorities in the language teaching profession in recent years has been the development of oral proficiency. If we hope to convince learners via our testing program that communicative language use is a major goal of instruction, we will need to administer some type of oral test, if only once or twice in a semester.

Harlow and Caminero (1990) conducted a study that examined the problems and practices associated with oral testing in Spanish, French, and German at 67 large universities in the United States. Responses were obtained from 106 language program directors and coordinators, representing all three language groups. The results indicated that 57% of the language programs surveyed did administer at least one oral test per term/semester to beginning students, with slightly more than half of the respondents indicating that more than one such test was typically given. There were some differences in oral testing practices by language: 67% of the French respondents reported giving oral tests, while 61% of the Spanish and 50% of the German respondents said that they tested oral skills. Overall, 43% of the language programs represented in the sample did no oral testing of their beginning students, stating that such testing was problematic because of lack of time, large classes, and heavy teaching loads. Among the programs that reported administering oral tests, approximately one-half assigned 10–19% of the final grade for this purpose, while another 27% of the respondents assigned between 20 and 50% of the grade on the basis of oral test results. The authors note that this is an encouraging indication that oral skills are considered important in most large institutions, even though they can be difficult to test.

Perhaps one solution to the practical difficulties of oral testing lies in using such tests at different times during the school year with different groups or classes, so that teachers responsible for large numbers of students can reduce their testing load at any one point in time to a manageable level. Tests lasting ten to fifteen minutes might be administered outside of class in the instructor's office, or students can be tested individually or in small groups during class while other class members work on small-group activities. Teachers might also consider administering taped exams in a language laboratory, although this format is the least flexible and has limited potential for testing interactive communication skills.

Various suggestions for oral testing are presented in the following pages, some of which are based on the principles of the ACTFL Oral Proficiency Interview (OPI). A brief description of the structure of the ACTFL Oral Interview precedes the adaptations. This description is intended to introduce the reader to the *nature* of the procedure, but it is not sufficient for training in the administration of such a test. The teacher interested in oral proficiency interviewing should attend a full-day familiarization workshop first and follow that with a four-day intensive workshop sponsored either by ACTFL or by an organization working under its auspices. Only after an intensive training period, including several months of monitored testing and rating, is one certifiable as a tester. For more information on familiarization and tester workshops, write to ACTFL, whose address is provided in the notes at the end of the chapter.

It is important to distinguish, at this point, between the administration of an oral proficiency interview and an oral achievement test. As was pointed out at the beginning of this chapter, oral proficiency testing should be reserved for summative evaluation purposes rather than for testing midcourse or end-of-course achievement. As we have already mentioned, oral proficiency interviews, in order to be valid and reliable, must be administered by trained testers and raters. Normally, a teacher should not test his or her own students when giving "official" oral interviews. In addition, a rating is not considered official until a second trained rater has verified the results. For these reasons, most teachers will probably not be using the procedure *per se* to test their students. However, an understanding of the structure of the oral interview should help teachers design valid and reliable *achievement* tests for oral skills to use with their classes.

The Structure of the ACTFL Oral Proficiency Interview

The ACTFL Oral Proficiency Interview is a face-to-face conversation lasting anywhere between 10 and 25 minutes, depending on the level of the person being tested. An untrained observer might think that this "conversation" does not differ markedly from one a teacher might have with a student taking an oral achievement test, or even from an ordinary conversation one might have with a native speaker. However, the structure of the interview is quite complex and purposeful. The tester needs to know at every point in the process what should be elicited from the interviewee and why it should be elicited. If the interview is not structured properly, a ratable sample may not be obtained, and the interview will have to be repeated at some later date.

All oral interviews must be taped for future verification, both by the tester and by a second tester. The interview consists of four phases, all of which fulfill three functions: (1) psychological, (2) linguistic, and (3) evaluative. Illustration 9.13 presents the structure of the interview in graphic form.

The following description of the conduct of the Oral Proficiency Interview (OPI) is synthesized from *The ILR Handbook on Oral Interview Testing* (Lowe 1982), *The ETS Oral Proficiency Testing Manual* (Liskin-Gasparro 1982), and *The ACTFL Oral Proficiency Interview Tester Training Manual* (Buck, Byrnes, and Thompson 1989; Swender 1999).

Phase 1: Warm-up. The warm-up portion of the interview is very brief and consists of greeting the interviewee, making him or her feel comfortable, and exchanging the social amenities that are normally used in everyday conversations. Typically, the warm-up lasts less than three minutes, but it serves a variety of purposes. First, on the psychological plane, it allows the interviewee to begin thinking in the language and sets him or her at ease. On the linguistic plane, it reorients the person being tested to hearing and using the language while giving the tester an opportunity to determine where the next phase of the interview should begin. This relates to the evaluative function of the warm-up, which is to allow the tester to get a preliminary idea of the rating that will eventually be assigned. Once the warm-up is completed, the tester moves on to Phase 2.

PHASES AND PLANES OF THE OPI

	WARM UP	**ITERATIVE PROCESS** THE LEVEL CHECKS $\rightleftarrows$ THE PROBES		WIND DOWN
PSYCHOLOGICAL PLANE	Puts interviewee at ease.	Shows interviewee what s/he can do.	Shows interviewee what s/he cannot do.	Returns interviewee to level at which s/he functions most accurately; gives interviewee sense of accomplishment.
LINGUISTIC PLANE	Reacquaints interviewee with language; provides transition into language. Provides opportunity for tester to build database of information about interests and experiences of interviewee.	Identifies the functions and content areas that the speaker can handle with greatest ease, accuracy, and fluency.	Identifies the functions and content areas that result in linguistic breakdown.	Provides opportunity for tester to check that all functions have been proven and that the interview is complete.
EVALUATIVE PLANE	Gives tester preliminary indication of skill level.	Finds highest level of sustained performance (floor).	Finds lowest level at which performance can no longer be sustained (ceiling).	

Illustration 9.13
General OPI Structure: Phases and Planes of the OPI

Source: E. Swender, ed., *ACTFL Oral Proficiency Interview Tester Training Manual.* New York: ACTFL, Inc., 1999, p. 38. Reprinted by permission.

Phase 2: Level Check. This phase consists of establishing the highest level of proficiency at which the interviewee can sustain speaking performance—that is, the level at which he or she can perform the functions and speak about the content areas designated by the ACTFL Guidelines with the greatest degree of accuracy. On the psychological plane, this phase of the interview allows the person being tested to demonstrate his or her strengths and converse at the level that is most comfortable for him or her. Linguistically, the level check is designed to elicit a speech sample that is adequate to prove that the person can indeed function accurately at the level hypothesized by the interviewer during the warm-up phase. If during the level check, the interviewer can see that his or her hypothesis was incorrect, the level of questions is adjusted upward or downward accordingly. On the evaluative plane, the level check allows the interviewer to get a better idea of the actual proficiency level of the interviewee, establishing the floor of his or her performance. This phase of the interview is repeated several times throughout the entire testing process and alternates with the probe phase, described next.

Phase 3: Probes. Probes are questions or tasks designed to elicit a language sample at one level of proficiency higher than the hypothesized level in order to establish a ceiling on the interviewee's performance. Psychologically, this allows the tester to show the person being tested what he or she is not yet able to do with the language, verifying the rating that will eventually be assigned to the speech sample. On the linguistic plane, the probes may result in *linguistic breakdown*—the point at which the interviewee ceases to function accurately or cogently because the task is too difficult. If a probe is successfully carried out, the interviewer may begin level checking at this higher level to see if his or her hypothesis about the true proficiency level is wrong. If the interviewee does demonstrate during the probe phase that he or she does not have the language to carry out the task, then the probe can be considered a valid indicator that the hypothesized level is correct. Several probes should be used during the interview, alternated with level checks, to establish beyond any question the appropriate rating. Once the process of level checks and probes has been completed, a role-play (which is required for the Novice-High through Advanced-Mid levels) is introduced. This allows the tester to elicit a more complete speech sample, checking to see if the interviewee can carry out linguistic functions not normally elicited in the conversational portion of the exam. For the Intermediate level, role-plays can be used to encourage the interviewee to ask questions and to initiate, sustain, and bring to a close a simple social situation or transaction. At the Advanced level, a more complicated social or transactional situation is used, and at the Superior level, role-plays can be used to demonstrate that interviewees can handle a situation that is unfamiliar and that requires more complex linguistic abilities to perform (Swender 1999, p. 56).

Phase 4: Wind-down. When a ratable sample has been obtained, the tester brings the interviewee back to the level at which he or she functions most comfortably for the last few minutes of the interview. This serves to make individuals feel successful and allows them to leave the test with the echo of their own voice still in their ears, reminding them that they functioned well in the language. Linguistically, the wind-down portion of the interview represents the most accurate use of the language of which the person is capable. On the evaluative plane, this last phase gives the tester one more opportunity to verify that his or her rating is indeed correct. The tester may end the interview by thanking the person who was interviewed, saying what a pleasure it has been talking with him or her, and wishing the person a pleasant day. Again, the termination of the conversation should resemble as much as possible the way in which conversations normally end in authentic language-use situations.

Formats and Elicitation Techniques for the Novice through Superior Levels

Novice. The test at the Novice level will last for about ten minutes and will consist of attempts at conversation of a simple nature. Often, test candidates at this level cannot sustain a natural conversation because they cannot yet create with the language they have and are unable to produce much beyond isolated words, short memorized phrases, or simple sentences on a limited number of topics. If conversation fails, the interviewer can use props and ask interviewees to name various objects they see in a picture or in the test room. Among the content areas that Novice-level speakers might be able to handle are such things as colors, names of basic objects, names of family members, articles of clothing, days of the week, dates, and telling time. Essentially, the Novice-level interview is like an oral achievement test, since the learner can produce little more than what he or she has learned in the course of his exposure to the target language, either in a natural setting or in class, if there has been some formal learning involved in the acquisition of the language.

Intermediate. Ideally, the test at this level consists of a conversation, usually quite simple in nature, in which the person being tested also asks some questions and demonstrates some ability to "survive" in a common situation likely to be encountered in visiting the target culture. The tester will probe for narration and description in past and future time (i.e., Advanced-level functions) and will be able to show during the course of the interview that the interviewee is still not able to sustain performance at this level. Intermediate-level speakers can create with the language simply to express their own point of view. Generally, they can speak in short sentences rather than in isolated words or phrases. The Intermediate-level interview must elicit questions from the person being tested, since getting information and sustaining one's own half of the conversation are hallmarks of speech at this level. The interviewee must also be considered intelligible to native speakers used to dealing with foreigners in order to obtain a rating of Intermediate.

Advanced. The interviewer will check to see how the person being tested can handle routine social demands, survival situations with a complication, and narration and description in past, present, and future time. In addition, the tester will probe to see how the interviewee can support an opinion, talk about abstract topics, and hypothesize (Superior-level functions). Speakers at this level will typically speak in paragraphs, rather than in short sentences, and will demonstrate a high degree of accuracy in handling basic structures and vocabulary. They would be able to live on the economy of the target culture and carry out schoolwork or basic job requirements with little difficulty. Speakers at the Advanced level are able to participate fully in casual conversations and are understandable to native speakers *not* used to dealing with foreigners.

Superior. The conversation at the Superior level is geared toward abstract topics and discussions about issues of current interest. Interviewees need to show that they can hypothesize and support an opinion, defending their point of view on some controversial issue. In addition, the person being interviewed is asked to handle an unfamiliar situation (such as explaining that he's just lost his contact lens in the trap of the sink in the bathroom of his hotel room and needs a plumber, or that he's locked himself out of his apartment and the doorknob has just dropped off into the shrubbery). This last activity is used to demonstrate that the interviewee is capable of circumlocution in the absence of specialized or unfamiliar vocabulary and can work his way out of a difficulty. The Superior level speaker can describe and narrate in detail, and uses most structures of the language accurately and with facility.

Although OPI interviews are carefully structured, every interview is unique, since the person being interviewed often leads the discussion by his or her answers. The art of interviewing consists of eliciting a ratable sample in a way that seems natural conversationally and that is flexible enough to conform to the needs and abilities of each interviewee. The course of the interview is negotiated by both the interviewee and the tester, but it is the tester, ultimately, who must structure the conversation properly in order to obtain a speech sample that can be rated.

Recent Adaptations of the OPI

Because the Oral Proficiency Interview requires a face-to-face interview on an individual basis, it can be impractical to administer, especially in settings where large numbers of people need to be tested in a relatively short time period. In order to accommodate diverse needs for oral proficiency testing, various alternative testing methods that can be correlated with the OPI have been developed or are currently being explored. Stansfield and Kenyon (1992, 1996) report on the development at the Center for Applied Linguistics of a tape-mediated procedure called the simulated oral proficiency interview, or SOPI. This procedure differs from earlier tape-mediated procedures, including the Recorded Oral Proficiency Exam (ROPE) described by Lowe and Clifford (1980), by combining the following characteristics: (1) a format similar to the OPI, including a warm-up and a variety of tasks at different proficiency levels; (2) the use of both aural and visual (print) stimuli in the elicitation of speech; and (3) the use of a scoring system based on the ACTFL Guidelines (Stansfield and Kenyon 1992, p. 129). First developed to accommodate oral assessment needs in uncommonly taught languages like Chinese, the test is also now available in Arabic, Japanese, Hebrew, Hausa, Indonesian, French, German, Spanish, and Portugese (Stansfield and Kenyon 1996). The SOPI consists of a master tape with test directions and questions, a printed booklet with pictures and other materials used in responding, and a cassette for recording the examinee's responses. Stansfield and Kenyon (1996) describe the prototypical SOPI as including several parts: (1) personalized questions simulating an initial encounter with a native speaker; (2) performance-based tasks, such as those based on a picture to elicit questions, directions, descriptions, or narrations; and (3) topic- and situation-based tasks that elicit such things as stating advantages and disadvantages, supporting an opinion, apologizing, or giving an informal talk (p. 1). They add that the format of the SOPI is adaptable; for example, if examinees are at lower levels of proficiency, the test can be ended midway. The authors report high correlations between the ratings given to samples elicited by the various language-specific SOPI and the OPI, supporting the use of this type of test as a valid alternative for testing proficiency with a face-to-face interview format. (See also Kuo and Jiang 1997, for a detailed comparison of the SOPI and the OPI, with particular reference to testing in Chinese.)

Higgs (1992) describes a pilot project under development at the Language Acquisition Resource Center at San Diego State University called the VOCI (The

Visual-Oral Communications Instrument), which uses video stimuli instead of a face-to-face interview to test oral proficiency. This test, like the SOPI, is designed to accommodate the assessment needs associated with large-scale testing. While the OPI is administered to individuals, the VOCI is designed to be used with groups of students in a laboratory setting.

Adaptations for Classroom Testing: Some Possible Formats for Oral Achievement Tests

Taped Exams. Oral test formats can vary from those in which students respond to taped materials in a laboratory setting to those in which face-to-face interviews are used. Valdman (1981) describes a taped oral exam called the Indiana University French Communicative Ability Test (IUFCAT) designed for first-semester French students. The test includes three tasks: (1) pictorially cued responses; (2) personal questions; and (3) situational responses. Responses are scored using three criteria: (1) semantic and pragmatic appropriateness; (2) grammaticality and correct form of lexical items; and (3) fluency and accuracy, with greater weight given to the first two categories. Although there are opportunities for students to give open-ended, creative answers on some parts of the IUFCAT, it seems that some of the other options available for achievement testing of oral skills are somewhat more integrative and interactive in nature. However, such alternatives require individual or paired interviews, which can be very time-consuming.

Conversation Cards and Interviews. One type of oral achievement test consists of a set of conversation cards that serve as a focal point for the exam. Students may be interviewed individually or in pairs, depending on (1) time constraints; (2) the desire to provide native or near-native input to the interview (when done with one student) versus the desire to provide students with the security and comfort of working with a partner; and (3) the teacher's individual preference for a one-on-one interview format versus a format in which he or she can be observer and note-taker without active participation. Individual instructors should choose a format that meets their own needs as well as those of their students, but the sample test provided here will serve just as well for individual or paired interviews.

Individual Interviews. The teacher sets up an appointment with each student (or sets aside in-class time while others are doing group work) for about 10 to 15 minutes. A set of situationally based conversation cards (see Bonin and Birckbichler 1975) serve as a stimulus for the student/teacher interview. Illustration 9.14 presents four sample cards created for the exam. The interview begins with the teacher selecting one of these cards at random and using it to interview the student. Then the student selects another card at random and uses it to ask questions of the teacher.

The conversation cards should serve as a stimulus for conversation and should not be used as a translation task. Teachers should feel free to expand the interview, asking additional questions that are based on the course material and taking care not to push students far beyond their current level of competence. Students should also be encouraged to expand the interview by asking any follow-up ques-

Illustration 9.14
Oral Test Interview
Cards

French 101
Oral Test I

Situation A

You are discussing your room at the university. Ask the following questions. Ask one or two other questions as well, using appropriate interrogative expressions such as *comment? combien? pourquoi? où? quand?* etc.

Ask your partner . . .
* how s/he is today
* whom s/he lives with at the university
* if there is a telephone in his/her room
* if friends like to visit his/her room
* how old his/her roommate is

Situation B

You are a landlord and you have a student room for rent. You're talking with a potential renter. Ask the following questions. Ask one or two other questions as well, using appropriate interrogative expressions such as *comment? combien? pourquoi? où? quand?* etc.

Ask your partner . . .
* how s/he is today
* where s/he is a student
* if s/he has any animals
* if s/he has a television, radio, or stereo
* if s/he is a good, serious student

Situation C

You are a student looking for a room to rent. Ask the landlord the following questions. Ask one or two other questions as well, using appropriate interrogative expressions such as *comment? combien? pourquoi? où? quand?* etc.

Ask your partner . . .
* how s/he is today
* if s/he has a room to rent
* if there is a shower or sink in the room
* if there is a telephone or TV
* if the room has curtains and a rug
* if the room is expensive

Situation D

You are talking with a friend about your favorite activities. Ask your friend the following questions. Ask one or two other questions as well, using appropriate interrogative expressions such as *comment? combien? pourquoi? où? quand?* etc.

Ask your partner . . .
* how s/he is today
* if s/he plays tennis a lot
* if s/he likes to go to the movies
* if s/he watches TV sometimes
* if s/he needs a new stereo (use an expression with *avoir*)

tions that come to mind. Note that ideas for expanding the interview are provided on the cards themselves.

The whole interview process is taped so that the speech sample can be analyzed and scored at a later time. To enable students to keep a record of their speech, they may be asked to provide their own tape. Over the course of several semesters, the oral tests can be recorded on the same tape so that students can hear their progress over time. Often, the progress is quite dramatic, even when the actual proficiency level of the sample has not changed markedly.

When listening to the taped interview later, the teacher can take notes on a score sheet such as the one in Illustration 9.15. This score sheet will be explained in more detail in the next section.

Paired Interviews. In this variant of the oral achievement test, the teacher sets up a 20- to 30-minute time slot for each pair of students. Each student chooses a conversation card at random, and one student is asked to begin the exam. The student reads the situation aloud to his or her partner and starts to ask questions based on the cues. As the second student answers, the teacher records the conversation on the score sheet by noting questions on the left and answers on the right (see Illustration 9.15). The students then change roles, with the second student using his or her conversation card to ask questions of the first student. The teacher uses the reverse side of the score sheet, which is lined in the same manner, to take notes again: This time, the second student's questions are recorded on the left and the first student's answers are recorded on the right. When the exam is finished, the teacher can cut the score sheet in half and hand it back to the students individually.

During the conversation the teacher does not intervene, unless the speech of one student is incomprehensible to the other. If this should happen, the teacher can ask the student to repeat the question or answer, or can provide some help, noting down on the score sheet that help was needed. When students have had regular, in-class practice on such conversational activities, they often understand one another quite well and seek little help from the instructor during the interview.

Scoring the Interview Test. On the basis of the speech protocol of each student, the instructor assigns a global grade of A through F for each of the four categories on the lower portion of the score sheet: pronunciation, vocabulary, grammar, and fluency. The score sheet also includes a conversion table that allows for some variability in the letter-grade categories. For example, a very good performance might be given an A or 5.0 grade, whereas a slightly less impressive performance, though still meriting an A in the instructor's judgment, might be given a 4.5, or A- grade. The instructor can check one box for each category and then convert each letter grade into a number. The number obtained is entered in the first space to the right of the box and multiplied by the weight provided: pronunciation, 4; vocabulary, 7; grammaticality, 6; and fluency, 3. The sum of the weighted scores will add up to 100 if all categories receive a grade of 5.0.

The weighting scheme depicted on this scoresheet is appropriate for Novice and Intermediate students, based on research done by Higgs and Clifford (1982)

Illustration 9.15
Score Sheet for Oral
Tests

FRENCH 101 & 102 SPEAKING TEST: STUDENT SCORE SHEET

Name _____   Name _____

NOTES: NOTES:

Pronunciation			Pronunciation	
F D C B A	__ x4 = __		F D C B A	__ x4 = __
Vocabulary			Vocabulary	
F D C B A	__ x7 = __		F D C B A	__ x7 = __
Grammar			Grammar	
F D C B A	__ x6 = __		F D C B A	__ x6 = __
Fluency			Fluency	
F D C B A	__ x3 = __		F D C B A	__ x3 = __

A = 4.5 - 5.0   Total = __   A = 4.5 - 5.0   Total = __
B = 4.0 - 4.4   B = 4.0 - 4.4
C = 3.5 - 3.9   C = 3.5 - 3.9
D = 3.0 - 3.4   D = 3.0 - 3.4
F = 2.0 - 2.9   F = 2.0 - 2.9

Source: Adapted from Omaggio 1983.

which shows that speech profiles of learners in this range reflect primarily knowledge of vocabulary and grammar. Pronunciation and fluency, as well as sociolinguistic factors, contribute much less to the overall rating at these levels of competence. The score sheet can also be adjusted to reflect weightings that are more suitable for Advanced-level learners: More weight might then be assigned to grammatical accuracy and fluency, as well as to sociolinguistic features, especially when these goals are emphasized in the program. A variation on the scoresheet (Terry 2000) that includes an overall score for communication as a fifth component, together with a detailed description of the scoring criteria used, is provided in Illustration 9.16. Teachers should develop their own sets of criteria for scoring the various components of the scales using descriptions that are appropriate to the expected levels of speaking ability for students in their course.

At the end of the semester at the University of Illinois, French students in first- and second-year courses come in individually for a final oral achievement test, consisting of an interview much like the ACTFL Oral Proficiency Interview, but limited to topics and structures covered in the course. The interview for first-semester students has varied over the course of several years. One model we have used consists of four parts: (1) a *warm-up,* in which students respond to greetings, questions about the weather, questions about how they are feeling, or about how their day is going; (2) a brief section involving *simple description and information-sharing in the present,* in which students are asked to talk about their families, studies at the university, and/or favorite pastimes; (3) a *description of a familiar drawing or picture,* derived from the textbook or ancillary materials; and (4) a brief *interview* of the instructor, prompted by a situation card that asks students, for example, to create their own questions for a fictitious interview for the school newspaper. All of these topics are related directly to material studied in the course. In second-, third-, and fourth-semester courses, interview materials are adjusted to allow for other types of tasks that reflect the topics studied in those courses. In all of the oral interview materials, instructors are given ideas for possible starter questions for each section of the test, as well as potential follow-up questions that would allow them to expand the interview if the student is able to elaborate somewhat on the initial topic. Oral tests are recorded, and instructors use a score sheet similar to the one in Illustration 9.15 to assign a grade to the sample elicited.

Oral quizzes and exams can be structured in many different ways: Not all need to be modeled on the OPI. Some instructors prefer to have students describe pictures, engage in role-plays, or perform skits for a grade. Others give oral grades based on the evaluation of a selection of interactive tasks that take place in the classroom over a period of several weeks. McPherson (1992) describes an oral assessment procedure that involves in-class interviews with native speakers, after which students provide an oral summary of what they learned on audiotape for a grade. Haggstrom (1992) gives students an interactive task, such as making dates and appointments with others in the classroom, and videotapes each student several times during the activity. She then assesses the samples collected and assigns grades based on the students' performance.

Illustration 9.16   Oral Test Scoresheet with Detailed Scoring Criteria

NAME_____ DATE_____ /_____ /_____

ORAL GRADING COMPONENTS

COMMUNICATION

A Displays communicative ease within context(s); creative, resourceful; easily understood; takes risks.

B Topics handled adequately; ideas clearly conveyed; requires little effort to be understood; some creativity.

C Topics handled adequately but minimally; ideas conveyed in general; basically on-task but no more.

D Requires extra-sympathetic listening; parts of message still not understood; minimally successful.

F Topics handled in totally unsatisfactory manner; unsuccessful communicative effort.

ACCURACY

A Shows exceptional control of required grammar concepts and correctness in a variety of contexts.

B Makes some grammar mistakes that do not affect meaning (agreement, partitive *vs.* definite articles, wrong past participles, etc.); reasonably correct.

C Makes more serious mistakes that often give unintended meaning (conjugation, tense inconsistency, word order mistakes, etc.); although generally adequate.

D Meaning frequently obscured by grammar mistakes; very poor control of a wide range of concepts.

F Meaning completely obscured by grammar mistakes; totally inadequate control.

FLUENCY

A Normal, "thoughtful" delay in formulation of thought into speech; language flows; extended discourse.

B Takes longer than necessary to organize thoughts; says more than required.

C Speech somewhat disjointed because of pauses; language very halting.

D Painful pauses make speech hard to follow; says less than required.

F Speech totally disjointed; long pauses interrupt flow of thought and meaning.

VOCABULARY

A Very conversant with vocabulary required by given context(s); excellent control and resourcefulness.

B Vocabulary mistakes generally do not affect meaning (wrong gender, wrong preposition, etc.); attempts at resourcefulness.

C Adequate, although more serious mistakes give unintended meaning (wrong preposition, incorrect word choice, mangled words, etc.).

D Meaning frequently obscured by minimal/inadequate mastery of vocabulary.

F Meaning totally obscured; inadequate vocabulary.

PRONUNCIATION

A Correct pronunciation and intonation; very few mistakes; almost native-like.

B Some mispronunciation; meaning still clear; tries to "sound French."

C Pronounced foreign accent requiring extra-sympathetic listening; comprehensible.

D Meaning frequently obscured by poor pronunciation; minimally comprehensible; very "American."

F No effort at all to "sound French;" often incomprehensible.

WEIGHTING OF GRADES		
A = 4.5–5.0	Communication	_____ x 5 = _____
B = 4.0–4.4	Accuracy	_____ x 5 = _____
C = 3.5–3.9	Fluency	_____ x 3 = _____
D = 3.0–3.4	Vocabulary	_____ x 4 = _____
F = below 3.0	Pronunciation	_____ x 3 = _____
	TOTAL/SCORE:	

COMMENTS:

Source: Terry 2000.

The research referred to earlier in this chapter by Harlow and Caminero (1990) reveals that various oral testing formats are used in the large universities they surveyed. Eighty-seven percent of the respondents reported that oral tests involved answering questions, 55% reported using role-play, 28% had students describe a picture or something they do, 25% had students read a passage for the purpose of grading pronunciation, 23% reported having students ask the instructor questions, and one department asked students to interpret into English an instructor's responses (pp. 492-493). According to the survey results, most oral tests lasted from 10 to 20 minutes, and for 45% of the programs, all testing was done outside of class, usually in the instructor's office. Fifty-five percent of the respondents indicated that they used class time to administer at least some of their oral tests, and several departments indicated that they set aside a day or more of the course syllabus just for oral testing.

It is clear from the Harlow and Caminero study that many instructors consider oral testing to be an important part of an overall assessment program, especially when communicative language proficiency is the stated goal of instruction. As is the case for the other skill areas, tests of oral performance need to resemble authentic language use as much as possible. Formal exams can, of course, be supplemented with informal assessment throughout the semester to allow for the evaluation of student performance in a variety of language-use situations.

Some Recent Innovations in Test Design

Computer-Adaptive Testing. A number of projects have been undertaken at several universities to develop computer-adaptive measures as placement and/or proficiency tests. In a computer-adaptive test, the test itself adapts to the test taker's performance by selecting the next item to be presented based on answers given for preceding items. This adaptation may be either up or down, depending on successful performance (the next item is at a slightly higher level of difficulty) or unsuccessful performance (the next item is at a slightly lower level of difficulty). The program stops testing once the performance at a given level is shown to be the test taker's highest sustainable performance (Center for Advanced Research on Language Acquisition [CARLA] 1999). Computer-adaptive tests have been used successfully at the University of Minnesota to evaluate the students' target language proficiency in reading, writing, listening, and speaking. The use of such tests and computer-based technology greatly facilitate "test administration, scoring, data analysis and data management, and score reporting" (CARLA 1999). Computer-assisted testing (CAT) is also quite useful in administering placement tests such as those produced by Brigham Young University and the University of Minnesota, as well as the MultiCAT test being developed at The Ohio State University. Given that computer-adaptive tests generally allow the evaluation of convergent-type items where responses have one right answer, other means of evaluating variable interpretive/global responses, such as oral interviews and the evaluation of writing samples, must still be used.

Alternative Assessment Measures. With greater emphasis being placed on performance-based testing, particularly in response to the national and state standards initiatives, new ways to assess performance are now being developed. Liskin-Gasparro (1996) discusses various innovative assessment procedures that have been described in the literature as "authentic assessment," "alternative assessment," and "performance assessment" (p. 170). She notes that "absent from the new assessments are norms, large-scale administrations, right-or-wrong responses, and machine scoring" (p. 170). Some of the new assessments Liskin-Gasparro reviews include portfolios, oral proficiency measures, and other performance-based tasks. Examples of short performance-based tasks are writing a letter, describing a picture, recounting a story, or engaging in a debate. Longer, more complex tasks include group projects such as developing a newscast or creating a newspaper over the course of several weeks or longer. Some of the sample learning scenarios provided in the *Standards for Foreign Language Learning* (1996, 1999) could also be used as a basis for a performance assessment, involving several of the five national standards goals.

The use of portfolios has been discussed by a number of scholars. Donato and McCormick (1994) report on a project in which students in a fifth-semester university conversation course provided documentation of their growth and development in oral skills and reflected on their performance through the use of a portfolio assessment procedure. The authors explain that portfolios are significantly different from diaries or journals because, "in addition to being reflective, they require students to supply concrete self-selected evidence of their growing language abilities" (p. 457). Liskin-Gasparro (1996) describes portfolios as collections of students' work over time, which often include students' own reflections on their work as well as multiple drafts of projects. The contents "can be creative or analytical, written or oral, visual or manipulable" (p. 177). Liskin-Gasparro adds that the student-initiated component in portfolio assessment is considered by some scholars to be central, but also challenging. According to Hart (1994, cited in Liskin-Gasparro 1996), students should develop their own personal standards for evaluating their work and then make selections for their collection on the basis of these standards. In addition to selecting the work to be placed in the portfolio, students can be asked to write reflections about each sample they have included. Liskin-Gasparro notes that the way in which portfolios are evaluated should depend on the teacher's purpose in using them. Student self-evaluation can be a good choice when portfolios are used within a single classroom; however, if this type of assessment is used widely within a school, or across a district or state, then more formal standards would be necessary (p. 178).

Kevorkian and Delett (1998) describe various techniques for designing classroom portfolios based on a research project being conducted at the National Capital Language Resource Center (NCLRC). (Cooperating institutions for this project include Georgetown University, The George Washington University, and the Center for Applied Linguistics.) Kevorkian and Delett describe portfolio assessment as "the systematic, longitudinal collection of student work created in response to specific, universally-known instructional outcomes and evaluated in relation to the same criteria" (p. 2). Steps they identify in designing portfolio assessments include: (1) setting the assessment purpose; (2) identifying objectives or goals that students will work toward; (3) matching tasks that students will carry out to the objectives/goals that have been designated; (4) setting criteria to determine student progress; (5) determining the way portfolios should be organized and managed; and (6) monitoring the collection of language tasks and artifacts in the portfolio to assure that they are assessing the skills specified in a valid and reliable manner.

Liskin-Gasparro (1996) suggests that, despite the potential benefits of new forms of assessments, there are a number of "thorny issues" (p. 181) that need to be addressed, including validity and reliability issues. While alternative assessments may have a high degree of face validity since they represent tasks that are reflective of performance in the world outside the classroom, it is still unclear what level of construct validity they have. She adds that the issue of reliability is also important to consider, as it may be difficult to establish that students' work is being evaluated in a consistent manner from task to task and among judges assigning grades: "The new assessment formats—designing and evaluating portfolios, multistage projects, global measurement of language skills in a performance context—are time-consuming to learn, require continuous attention and refinement, and must be undertaken by groups of teachers working cooperatively" (p. 182). Liskin-Gasparro rightly points out that these considerations represent important challenges that need to be met before authentic assessment programs can be implemented (p. 181). For more information on alternative assessments, readers should consult the sources and bibliographies provided in the references in this section.

Summary: Classroom Testing

The suggestions for classroom testing presented in this chapter are offered as an alternative to achievement tests based mainly on discrete points of grammar and isolated-sentence formats. As our knowledge and expertise in the field of testing increases over the next years, new ideas for classroom testing will be discovered and disseminated that will help us bridge the gap between our statement of course goals in communicative terms and their measurement. A list of professional priorities that should be addressed in the coming years might include the following points:

1. Professional conferences and workshops should be organized to help teachers devise model testing techniques that incorporate natural language as much as possible into their course exams.
2. Local and regional in-service training workshops should be encouraged to disseminate these models to classroom teachers and to stimulate discussion and idea sharing.
3. The possibility of using computerized item banks should be explored as a way of making the development of new or parallel tests less time-consuming. When model test items are stored for a given unit, it should be a relatively simple matter to retrieve old items, change the contexts slightly, and thus

create new tests for a subsequent semester. However, if such item banks are created, there should be an on-going evaluation of the validity and reliability of the items to assure that what is being tested has been taught in the semester for which the test is being created. Changes in textbooks will necessitate a careful reexamination of the items in the test bank.

4. Teacher education programs should include a course on test development among the requirements for certification.

5. Textbook publishers should consider using contextualized formats for any test instruments provided with their programs. Test instruments that are provided by publishers to accompany a textbook should be carefully examined before test items are adopted or adapted for a specific course. The usefulness and success of test items in such ancillaries are predicated on the way in which the instructor has used the course text and accompanying materials, and it is important to verify that the goals reflected on the test are the same as those selected by the instructor for emphasis in the course (Walz 1991). Walz suggests that commercial tests might be useful as models for test design, as a point of departure for discussing testing issues in pedagogy courses, or as makeup tests or written assignments in preparation for a classroom examination.

The five recommendations above parallel some of those made by Woodford (1980) in his "plan for action" for foreign language testing. We cannot afford to continue to ignore the problems inherent in conserving our more traditional methods of achievement testing. The means by which we evaluate our students' skills in the classroom today will determine, in large part, the success of our programs in the future.

Notes
1. This chapter is based, in part, on *Proficiency-Oriented Classroom Testing* (1983) by Alice C. Omaggio. See references for the full bibliographic citation.
2. For readers interested in obtaining information about the training opportunities in oral proficiency testing, write to ACTFL, 6 Executive Plaza, Yonkers, NY 10701-6801, or consult the ACTFL Web site: http://www.actfl.org

Appendix

Sample Test: Quiz for a first-year French course
The following sample quiz is provided to illustrate how some of the formats and testing ideas described in this chapter might be combined to create a classroom test. The sample is not offered as an "ideal" test, but rather is provided for purposes of discussion (see Question 1 in the "Activities for Review and Discussion" section on page 451). The construction of this test is described in Illustration 9.11, and a sample evaluation of its strengths and weaknesses is provided in Illustration 9.12.

French 1
Quiz 3 (25 points)
Instructor's Copy

A. *Un appartement idéal!* Read the passage describing Jeanne's new apartment three times. The first time, read at normal speed. The second time, pause after each sentence so students can complete the form on their test copy. The third time, read at normal speed so students can check their work. (5 points: 1/2 point for each piece of information recorded correctly)

Passage: J'ai de la chance, Maman, parce que l'appartement est dans une jolie rue près d'une petite patisserie/boulangerie et pas loin du campus. Et l'appartement n'est pas trop cher—le loyer est de $400 par mois. J'ai une camarade de chambre très sympa—elle s'appelle Anne-Marie et elle est étudiante en philosophie. Nous avons un salon, deux chambres à coucher, une salle de bains et une petite cuisine. Je l'adore—c'est un appartement idéal! Tu viens le voir?

(Passage: I'm lucky, Mom, because the apartment is on a pretty street near a little pastry shop/bakery and not far from campus. And the apartment isn't too expensive—the rent is $400 a month. I have a really nice roommate—her name is Anne-Marie and she's a philosophy student. We have a living room, two bedrooms, a bathroom and a little kitchen. I love it—it's an ideal apartment! Are you coming to see it?)

B. *Une description détaillée.* (6 pts: 1/2 point per blank)

C. *Une ville universitaire.* (6 pts: 3 points for content/vocabulary; 3 points for grammar)

Content/Vocabulary
    3 pts: all required information is used; vocabulary correct
    2 pts: most information required is used, but a few key words are missing or wrong
    1 pt: much information missing and/or many wrong
        vocabulary words
    0 pts: no answer, or totally incomprehensible

Grammar:
    3 pts: excellent control of grammar
    2 pts: good control of grammar, but some significant errors
    1 pt: poor control of grammar, though answer is partially comprehensible
    0 pts: no answer, or totally incomprehensible

D. *Ma vie à l'université.* (8 pts: 3 points for content, 3 points for grammar, 2 points for cohesive paragraph) Use scales above for content/vocabulary and grammar. Cohesiveness scale is given below.

Cohesiveness:
    2 pts: Student has written full sentences and has linked ideas in a logical manner
    1 pt: Some partial sentences and/or stilted, unnatural style; poor organization
    0 pts: no answer, or totally incomprehensible

French 1
Quiz 3 (25 points)
Student Copy

A. Un appartement idéal! You will hear an excerpt from a telephone conversation in which Jeanne, a student from France, is describing her new apartment to her mother. As you listen, fill in the blanks on the form below in English. You will hear the passage three times. (5 points: 1/2 point for each piece of information recorded correctly)

Information Requested	Answer (in English)
Location of apartment (give at least two details) (1 pt.)	
Cost of apartment (1/2 pt.)	
Number and type of rooms (2 pts.)	
Name of roommate (1/2 pt.)	
Roommate's personality (1/2 pt.)	
Roommate's major (1/2 pt.)	

B. **Une description détaillée.** Jeanne is writing a note to her friend in France describing her new apartment. Complete the description in French below, using the translation on the right as your guide. (6 points: 1/2 point per blank)

Chère Nathalie,
    Je suis enfin chez moi! Je suis très contente, parce que j'ai un_____ appartement dans une_____rue très près du campus. C'est assez _____, mais il y a_____de lumière naturelle. Les murs sont _____ et les chaises sont _____, avec des fleurs _____. J'ai une camarade de chambre très_____—elle étudie la philosophie. Elle a_____de travail, et elle n'a pas_____de temps libre. Mais elle est toujours_____. C'est une_____ amie.
    Tu vas venir nous voir?
                    Bisous,
                        Jeanne
	Dear Nathalie,
	    I'm finally at home! I'm really happy because I have a beautiful apartment on a pretty street very near the campus. It's somewhat small, but there is a lot of natural light. The walls are yellow and the chairs are blue with white flowers. I have a very intelligent roommate—she's studying philosophy. She has too much work, and she doesn't have enough free time. But she is always happy. She's a good friend.
	    Are you coming to see us?
	                    Love,
	                        Jeanne

C. **Une ville universitaire.** Write a brief paragraph describing what Jeanne thinks of our town, using the information below. Add any necessary words to make a good, interesting paragraph.(6 points: 3 for content/vocabulary; 3 for grammar. Be sure to include all the information in your answer.)

- Jeanne likes the university very much.
- She thinks that her professors are very nice, but the students are not too serious.
- Her classes are difficult but interesting.
- She likes to go to Italian restaurants and thinks the food is very good.
- There are a lot of theaters and she adores American movies.

D. **Ma vie à l'université.** Write a brief composition about your life here at the university. Describe the place you live, giving as many details as you can. Talk about your classes and what you are studying. Then talk about what you like to do on the weekends with your friends. (8 points: 3 points for content/vocabulary; 3 points for grammar; 2 points for cohesiveness and logical organization)

Activities for Review and Discussion

1. Examine the sample French quiz given in the Appendix to this chapter. Using the form in Illustration 9.12, discuss the characteristics of the test with others in a small group. Do you agree with the assessment given on the form in Illustration 9.12? What are the strengths and weaknesses of this exam, in your opinion? How would you change the exam to improve it? (Keep in mind that this exam was designed for a first-semester course.)

2. Obtain copies of classroom quizzes and tests that (a) you have taken as a language student yourself or (b) are being given in a language program with which you are familiar. Examine these tests using the schema for assessing characteristics of test items presented in Illustration 9.12. How would you characterize the various items on each of the tests? Discuss how well these tests seem to match course goals. What, if anything, would you do to improve the tests you have analyzed?

3. Using one of the suggested format types in this chapter, design an original listening comprehension test item or item set for a particular chapter or unit in an appropriate textbook (either one that you are using or one that your instructor provides). Be sure to write clear directions and explain how the item is to be scored.

4. Find an authentic text appropriate for students reading at the Intermediate level of proficiency. Design a reading comprehension test item or item set based on this text. You may want to use a fairly simple prose passage or choose an advertisement, brochure, or other appropriate text from an authentic source.

5. Based on a particular chapter or unit in an appropriate language textbook, design two original test items or item sets that involve mixed skills. Feel free to use formats described in this chapter, or design your own formats based on the examples presented here.

6. Develop a testing grid, such as the one presented in Illustration 9.11, for a chapter or unit in the language textbook you are using or in a textbook provided by your instructor. Be sure to include skill emphases, item format types, and point values for your exam.

7. Discuss various options for oral testing that you might use in your own language program. How might oral testing be done efficiently in a teaching situation where you have several classes, each with 25 students or more?

References: Chapter 9

Bacon, Susan M. and Michael D. Finneman. "A Study of the Attitudes, Motives, and Strategies of University Foreign-Language Students and Their Disposition to Authentic Oral and Written Input." *The Modern Language Journal* 74 (1990): 459–73.

Barnes, Betsy K., Carol A. Klee, and Ray M. Wakefield. "Reconsidering the FL Requirement: From Seat-Time to Proficiency in the Minnesota Experience." Pp. 55–69 in S. Magnan, ed., *Challenges in the 1990s for College Foreign Language Programs. Issues in Language Program Direction*. Boston: Heinle & Heinle, 1991.

Bartz, Walter H. "Testing Communicative Competence." Pp. 52–64 in Renate Schulz, ed., *Teaching for Communication in the Foreign Language Classroom*. Report of the Central States Conference on the Teaching of Foreign Languages. Skokie, IL: National Textbook Company, 1976.

Bernhardt, Elizabeth B. "Testing Foreign Language Reading Comprehension: The Immediate Recall Protocol." *Die Unterrichtspraxis* 16 (1983): 27-33.

Bernhardt, Elizabeth B. and Charles J. James. "The Teaching and Testing of Comprehension in Foreign Language Learning." Chapter 5 (pp. 65–81) in D. W. Birckbichler, ed., *Proficiency, Policy, and Professionalism in Foreign Language Education*. Report of the Central States Conference on the Teaching of Foreign Languages. Lincolnwood, IL: National Textbook Company, 1987.

Bondaruk, John, James Child, and E. Tetrault. "Contextual Testing." Pp. 89-104 in Randall L. Jones and Bernard Spolsky, eds., *Testing Language Proficiency*. Arlington, VA: Center for Applied Linguistics, 1975.

Bonin, Thérèse and Diane W. Birckbichler. "Real Communication through Conversation Cards." *The Modern Language Journal* 59 (1975): 22–25.

Buck, Kathryn, Heidi Byrnes, and Irene Thompson, eds. *The ACTFL Oral Proficiency Interview Tester Training Manual*. Yonkers, NY: ACTFL, 1989.

Center for Advanced Research on Language Acquisition (CARLA). "Frequently Asked Questions about Computer-Adaptive Testing (CAT)." Office of International Programs, University of Minnesota. [http://carla.acad.umn.edu/CATFAQ.html]

Chalhoub-Deville, Micheline. "The Minnesota Articulation Project and its Proficiency-Based Assessments." *Foreign Language Annals* 30, iv (1997): 492–502.

———. "Investigating the Properties of Assessment Instruments and the Setting of Proficiency Standards for Admission into University Second Language Courses." Pp. 177–201 in L. Kathy Heilenman, ed., *Research Issues and Language Program Direction*. Boston, MA: Heinle & Heinle, 1999.

Clark, John L. D. *Foreign Language Testing: Theory and Practice*. Philadelphia: Center for Curriculum Development, 1972.

Cohen, Andrew D. *Testing Language Ability in the Classroom*. Rowley, MA: Newbury House, 1980.

———. *Assessing Language Ability in the Classroom, 2nd ed.* Boston: Heinle & Heinle, 1994.

Coulont-Henderson, Françoise. Personal communication, 1992.

Dandonoli, Patricia. "ACTFL's Current Research in Proficiency Testing." Chapter 3 (pp. 75–96) in H. Byrnes and M. Canale, eds., *Defining and Developing Proficiency: Guidelines, Implementations and Concepts*. The ACTFL Foreign Language Education Series. Lincolnwood, IL: National Textbook Company, 1987.

Donato, Richard and Dawn McCormick. "A Sociocultural Perspective on Language Learning Strategies: The Role of Mediation." *The Modern Language Journal* 78, iv (1994): 453–464.

Ellis, Rod. *Understanding Second Language Acquisition.* Oxford: Oxford University Press, 1985.

_____. *Instructed Second Language Acquisition.* Oxford: Basil Blackwell, 1990.

Freed, Barbara. "Proficiency in Context: The Pennsylvania Experience." Chapter 14 (pp. 211–40) in S. J. Savignon and M. S. Berns, eds., *Initiatives in Communicative Language Teaching.* Reading, MA: Addison-Wesley Publishing Company, 1984.

_____. "Preliminary Impressions of the Effects of a Proficiency-Based Language Requirement." *Foreign Language Annals* 20 (1987): 139–46.

Gutiérrez, John R. and Harry Rosser. *Ya verás! Segundo nivel.* Boston: Heinle & Heinle, 1992.

Haggstrom, Margaret. "Using a Videocamera and Task-Based Activities to Make Classroom Oral Testing a More Realistic Communicative Experience." Presentation at the 1992 ACTFL Annual Meeting, Rosemont, IL, November 20, 1992.

Harlow, Linda and Rosario Caminero. "Oral Testing of Beginning Language Students at Large Universities: Is It Worth the Trouble?" *Foreign Language Annals* 23, vi (1990): 489–501.

Heilenman, L. Kathy, ed. *Research Issues and Language Program Direction.* Boston: Heinle & Heinle, 1999.

Higgs, Theodore V. "Group Oral Proficiency Testing Using the VOCI (Visual/Oral Communication Instrument)." Presentation at the 1992 ACTFL Annual Meeting, Rosemont, IL, November 21, 1992.

Higgs, Theodore V. and Ray Clifford. "The Push Toward Communication." In Theodore V. Higgs, ed., *Curriculum, Competence, and the Foreign Language Teacher.* ACTFL Foreign Language Education Series, vol. 13. Lincolnwood, IL: National Textbook Company, 1982.

Hosenfeld, Carol. "Learning about Learning: Discovering Our Students' Strategies." *Foreign Language Annals* 9 (1976): 117–29.

Jones, Randall L. and Bernard Spolsky, eds. *Testing Language Proficiency.* Arlington, VA: Center for Applied Linguistics, 1975.

Kevorkian, Jennifer and Jennifer Delett. "Portfolio Assessment in the Foreign Language Classroom." Presentation at the Northeast Conference on the Teaching of Foreign Languages. New York, 1998.

Kuo, Jane, and Xixiang Jiang. "Assessing the Assessments: The OPI and the SOPI." *Foreign Language Annals* 30, iv (1997): 503–512.

Lafayette, Robert C., ed. *National Standards: A Catalyst for Reform.* The ACTFL Foreign Language Education Series. Lincolnwood, IL: National Textbook Company, 1996.

Liskin-Gasparro, Judith. *The ETS Oral Proficiency Testing Manual.* Princeton, NJ: Educational Testing Service, 1982.

———. "Assessment: From Content Standards to Student Performance." Pp. 169–196 in Robert C. Lafayette, ed., *National Standards: A Catalyst for Reform.* The ACTFL Foreign Language Education Series. Lincolnwood, IL: National Textbook Company, 1996.

Lowe, Pardee Jr. *The ILR Handbook on Oral Interview Testing.* Washington, DC: Defense Language Institute/Language School Interview Transfer Project, 1982.

Lowe, Pardee Jr. and Ray T. Clifford. "Developing an Indirect Measure of Overall

Oral Proficiency." Pp. 31–39 in James R. Frith, ed., *Measuring Spoken Language Proficiency.* Washington, DC: Georgetown University Press, 1980.

Magnan, Sally S. "Just Do It: Directing TAs toward Task-Based and Process-Oriented Testing." Pp. 135–161 in Richard V. Teschner, ed., *Assessing Foreign Language Proficiency of Undergraduates.* Issues in Language Program Direction. Boston: Heinle & Heinle, 1991.

McMillen Villar, Susan and Fran Meuser Blincow. Personal communication, 1993.

McPherson, Elina. "Enhancing Linguistic Spontaneity through Interviews with Native Speakers." Presentation at the 1992 ACTFL Annual Meeting, Rosemont, IL, November 20, 1992.

Muyskens, Judith A., Linda L. Harlow, Michèle Vialet, and Jean-François Brière. *Bravo! Communication et grammaire,* 3rd ed. Boston: Heinle & Heinle, 1998.

Omaggio, Alice C. "Priorities in Classroom Testing for the 1980s." Pp. 47–53 in *Proceedings of the National Conference on Professional Priorities.* Hastings-on-Hudson, NY: ACTFL Materials Center, 1980.

———. *Proficiency-Oriented Classroom Testing.* Washington, DC: Center for Applied Linguistics, 1983.

Schulz, Renate, ed. *Teaching for Communication in the Foreign Language Classroom.* Report of the Central States Conference on the Teaching of Foreign Languages. Skokie, IL: National Textbook Company, 1976.

Shohamy, Elana. "Affective Considerations in Language Teaching." *The Modern Language Journal* 66 (1982): 13–17.

———. "Connecting Testing and Learning in the Classroom and on the Program Level." Pp. 154–78 in June K. Phillips, ed., *Building Bridges and Making Connections.* Reports of the Northeast Conference on the Teaching of Foreign Languages. Middlebury, VT: Northeast Conference, 1991.

Slager, William R. "Creating Contexts for Language Practice." In E. Joiner and P. Westphal, eds., *Developing Communication Skills.* Rowley, MA: Newbury House, 1978.

Standards for Foreign Language Learning: Preparing for the 21st Century. Yonkers, NY: National Standards in Foreign Language Education Project, 1996.

Standards for Foreign Language Learning in the 21st Century. Yonkers, NY: National Standards in Foreign Language Education Project, 1999.

Stansfield, Charles W. and Dorry M. Kenyon. "The Development and Validation of a Simulated Oral Proficiency Interview." *The Modern Language Journal* 76, ii (1992): 129–41.

———. "Simulated Oral Proficiency Interviews: An Update." *ERIC Digest* (May 1996). Washington, DC: Center for Applied Linguistics.

Swender, Elvira, ed. *ACTFL Oral Proficiency Interview Tester Trainer Manual.* Yonkers, NY: ACTFL, Inc., 1999.

Tarone, Elaine. "On the Variability of Interlanguage Systems." *Applied Linguistics* 4 (1983): 143–63.

Terry, Robert. Personal communication, 1985.

———. "Improving Inter-rater Reliability in Scoring Tests in Multisection Courses." Pp. 229–62 in J. C. Walz, ed., *Development and Supervision of Teaching Assistants in Foreign Languages.* Issues in Language Program Direction. Boston: Heinle & Heinle, 1992.

———. Personal communication, 2000.

Teschner, Richard V., ed. *Assessing Foreign Language Proficiency of Undergraduates.* Issues in Language Program Direction. Boston: Heinle & Heinle, 1991.

Valdman, Albert. "Testing Communicative Ability at the University Level." *ADFL Bulletin*13 (1981): 1–5.

Valette, Rebecca M. *Modern Language Testing, 2nd ed.* New York: Harcourt Brace Jovanovich, Inc., 1977.

———. "Developing and Evaluating Communication Skills in the Classroom." In E. Joiner and P. Westphal, eds., *Developing Communication Skills.* Rowley, MA: Newbury House, 1978.

Walz, Joel. "Context and Contextualized Language Practice in Foreign Language Teaching." *The Modern Language Journal* 73, ii (1989): 160–68.

———."A Survey and Analysis of Tests Accompanying Elementary French Textbooks." Pp. 163–186 in Richard V. Teschner, ed., *Assessing Foreign Language Proficiency of Undergraduates.* Issues in Language Program Direction. Boston: Heinle & Heinle, 1991.

Wesche, Marjorie B. "Communicative Testing in a Second Language." *Canadian Modern Language Review* 37 (1981): 551–71.

Woodford, Protase E. "Foreign Language Testing." *The Modern Language Journal* 64 (1980): 97–102.

Planning Instruction for the Proficiency-Oriented Classroom: Some Practical Guidelines

In Chapters 1 through 9, a variety of methodological approaches and theories of language learning and acquisition were considered using proficiency as the organizing principle. A rationale was given for teaching language in a culturally authentic context and for personalizing language practice as much as possible. Sample formats for proficiency-oriented classroom activities were illustrated, as were ideas for infusing cultural materials into the curriculum.

If the accumulation of a repertoire of teaching strategies were enough to ensure effective instruction in the classroom, it might seem reasonable to end the discussion of methodology here. But planning and delivering effective instruction involves much more than understanding language acquisition theories and knowing some appropriate techniques. Just what makes instruction or a given teacher "effective" is still open to some debate. And characterizing the "perfect" teacher is like trying to develop the "perfect" method: Just as there is no "one true way" to teach, there is no one definitive profile of the effective teacher.

Yet there are certain elements that are common to good teaching, even when individual personalities and styles vary considerably. First, effective teachers *plan* instruction carefully and efficiently. They have a clear idea of what the programmatic and course goals are, and they try to reach those goals by actively involving students in their own learning and appealing to their interests and needs. Obviously, daily planning must be related to an overall curricular plan if it is to be effective. Therefore, teachers need to be concerned with long-range curricular goals, and, ideally, should be involved in both the planning and the evaluation of the curriculum in their own institutions.

Because curriculum planning involves such things as the setting of goals (for both the whole sequence of instruction and each individual course), the selection of materials and teaching approaches, the design of the testing program, and the appropriate use of program-evaluation procedures, effective teachers need to be familiar with all aspects of program design. To evaluate outcomes of instruction, teachers need efficient strategies for record keeping and clearly delineated criteria for assigning grades. On a regular basis, they should solicit student input in course evaluations, using that input to alter and improve instruction.

This brief epilogue presents some practical suggestions for some of the essential components of program design, with particular attention to goal setting, text selection, and lesson planning. These suggestions are not meant to be prescriptive; rather, they are offered as a point of departure for further discussion and reflection about how instruction can be organized around the concepts presented in this book. As was mentioned in the first chapter, there are many different approaches that can lead to the development of proficiency, and each instructor needs to select those ideas that seem best suited to his or her own situation.

Setting Goals for a Proficiency-Oriented Program

As we have seen throughout the chapters of this book, the foreign language teaching profession has made a concerted effort in the last twenty years to outline, in general terms, realistic and attainable goals for classroom language learning. With the development of the proficiency guidelines in the early 1980s, language practitioners sought to define and measure communicative language proficiency in terms that would be meaningful across programs and levels of instruction. During the 1980s alone, approximately 2,000 language teachers in French, Spanish, German, and Russian obtained training in administering oral tests and rating student speech samples using the ACTFL Oral Proficiency Interview (Stansfield and Kenyon 1992), and many more teachers in both the commonly and uncommonly taught languages have received such training in the last decade. Practitioners have also become familiar with the guidelines for other skill areas, and ACTFL is currently undertaking a revision of the guidelines in listening, reading, and writing to reflect the newest developments in research in these areas. The focus on proficiency has had an enormous impact on the design of contemporary classroom texts and materials, and continues to influence many teachers and curriculum planners as they outline program and course goals.

A second major initiative relating to the articulation of goals for language study is the development of standards for foreign language learning, both at the state and national levels. These standards-setting projects have envisioned goals for language study all along the curriculum, from kindergarten through the end of undergraduate study (K–16). In addition to articulating general goals for communicative language use (goals that can be measured, at least for adult learners, using instruments such as the OPI and other proficiency-based assessments), the national standards outline goals in four additional areas: cultures, connections, comparisons, and communities. Many of the state standards initiatives include goal areas similar or identical to those of the national standards. The national standards also include sample progress indicators that reflect the thinking of a large group of foreign language practitioners about realistic goals for language study at various junctures in the curriculum.

As teachers consider appropriate goals for their courses, these initiatives can provide helpful guidance, at least in general terms, about what one might expect language learners to be able to do at the various levels of study. For example, the

ACTFL guidelines can be useful in discussing expectations for adult learners in terms of the communications goal (Goal 1) outlined in the national standards. Although the proficiency guidelines are designed for assessment purposes and are not goal statements, they can be used as an articulation device between holistic proficiency assessment and goal-oriented curriculum design (Galloway, cited in Medley 1985). Medley describes the development process as follows:

> *The task of the curriculum developer is to somehow translate these broad level descriptions [i.e., the ACTFL Guidelines] first into general goal statements, and then into much more specific performance outcome statements for each year or semester of instruction (Medley 1985, p. 25).*

The descriptions of functions and content areas typically handled by learners at a given level of proficiency can be translated in various ways into goal statements and performance outcomes. For instance, one might generate goal statements for developing oral proficiency in a four-year sequence as follows:

> *Upon completion of the prescribed four-year sequence of study, the student will be able to:*
> 1. *ask and answer questions related to personal needs, familiar topics and current events, as well as work, family and autobiographical information;*
> 2. *narrate and describe in past, present, and future time;*
> 3. *initiate and sustain a conversation, observing basic courtesy requirements and social demands of the culture (Medley 1985, p. 27).*

This set of statements relates to the attainment of goals derived from (but not identical to) the Intermediate and Advanced level descriptions of the ACTFL Guidelines. One might also use the sample progress indicators in the national standards, as well as other guidelines provided in state or local standards documents, to articulate goals for the various communicative modes (interpersonal, interpretive, and presentational). More specific performance outcome statements can be generated from these overall goal statements, with specific course goals outlined in greater detail for all aspects of communication.

Medley explains that there are two possible approaches that can be taken in the goal-setting process. One might be to look first at the total curriculum and establish some optimum desired performance level as an ultimate goal, and then plan the individual course outlines for each year so that this ultimate goal can be reached. Medley points out, however, that this type of procedure often "results in courses that are unrealistically cluttered with items that 'have to be taught before next year'" (p. 25). He cites Strasheim (1984), who believed that we need to rethink each instructional level in the sequence of courses that make up a total curriculum, reconciling what we know about language learning with both student needs and realistic expectations.

Rather than trying to achieve some kind of "curricular fit" within an idealized master plan for the entire curriculum, a second approach that Medley describes would begin by setting goals for the first course and continuing course by course until realistic goals have been established for the whole sequence. For example, a college course coordinator for the first two years of instruction in Language X may, after several semesters of testing and observation, in cooperation with colleagues and/or teaching assistants, determine that a realistic expectation for oral proficiency at the end of the second-semester course is Intermediate Low. Some students might be better in oral skills than that, while others who complete the course may still be in the Novice-High range. Knowing, however, that most students are able to attain the Intermediate level of proficiency in oral skills enables the coordinator to set realistic goals for the next semester, and so on. Similar objectives can be set for each of the goal areas until the overall expected outcome of the four-semester sequence can be described in a satisfactory manner (Medley 1985, p. 27). Such a procedure facilitates articulation between courses and levels of instruction, including the high school to college transition—a problem that has challenged the language teaching profession for years.

In addition to developing goals for the assessment of communication skills (Goal 1 of the standards), teachers should consider realistic and attainable goals for the remaining four areas: knowledge and understanding of other cultures (Goal 2), connecting with other disciplines and learning about content that is relevant to learners' interests (Goal 3), developing insights into the nature of language and culture (Goal 4), and using the language beyond the classroom (Goal 5). Again, the sample progress indicators in the national standards document can be helpful as teachers consider appropriate objectives to include in their courses.

It would be helpful, when designing a course syllabus, to write out objectives for the course that blend the communication goal with some or all of the other goal areas outlined in the standards. For example, in developing oral proficiency, students can talk about content that relates not only to their personal experiences and interests, but also to the cultural framework of the society or societies whose language they are studying. They can find information about other disciplines (such as art, music, history, etc.) that interests them and report back what they have learned either orally or in writing, sharing what they have found with others in the class. Obviously, the level of language proficiency that learners have attained thus far in their studies will determine to some extent the types of content and the levels of discourse that they can access. In addition, the purpose of the course will be important to consider when designing the curriculum. However, by thinking in terms of cultural understanding and content as integral to language study, we can begin to work toward designing courses that more successfully teach language in context.

Guidelines for Text Selection

Once a set of goal statements is generated for a given course, instructional materials that are congruent with the specified goals can be selected. Not all classroom teachers have the opportunity to choose their textbook for a given course, but for those who do have a say in the selection, some of the guidelines that follow may be helpful. It is important to bear in mind that the textbook does not, in and of itself, constitute the curriculum, for curriculum includes much more than the set of materials used to deliver instruction. In addition, the text cannot guarantee successful language learning. Only the students and the teacher can determine how effective the course will be in enhancing language proficiency. An excellent teacher working with unmotivated learners and mediocre materials may be able to generate some enthusiasm for learning in spite of the text. On the other hand, a mediocre teacher working with an excellent text may fail to do so. It seems evident, however, that it is much easier for teachers and students to attain proficiency goals when text materials are designed to reflect those goals directly.

Just as there is no one "proficiency method," there are no "proficiency textbooks" per se. However, some textbooks can be more proficiency-oriented than others in terms of their design and general approach to language learning. If the hypothesized principles of proficiency-oriented instruction that were listed in Chapter 3 were applied to textbook selection, a list of optimal features could be generated. For example, a good textbook should include:

1. Contextualized language-practice activities, affording abundant practice in a range of contexts likely to be encountered in the target culture
2. Personalized and creative practice activities that encourage students to express their own meaning in their own words as early in the program as possible
3. Suggestions for group work and active communicative interaction among students
4. Authentic language in exercises, readings, and dialogues, as well as abundant visuals and realia throughout the text, integrated with language-practice activities
5. Functional/notional concepts, together with ample opportunities to practice a range of tasks using these concepts
6. Clear and concise grammatical explanations that enable students to work toward accuracy goals from the beginning of instruction
7. Appealing topics, themes, readings, and activities that respond to the needs and interests of students and incorporate content from other disciplines
8. Well-conceptualized writing instruction that helps students engage in the process of writing to present their ideas effectively, coherently, and accurately
9. Cultural material integrated with language-practice activities, selected to reflect both deep and surface culture phenomena, and incorporating both "hearthstone" and "Olympian" culture in a balanced fashion that will appeal to students' interests
10. Ancillaries such as video programs, CD-ROMs, and Web sites with links coordinated to chapter themes that allow students to access authentic language and content beyond the textbook

Many contemporary textbooks include features such as these, offering teachers a wider range of choices than ever before of materials that can help students work toward the goals discussed earlier.

Bragger (1985) suggests that teachers look at textbooks with questions such as the following in mind. Her inventory of questions is summarized and presented in a somewhat modified form below:

1. To what extent are the exercises, including the simple transformational variety, contextualized and personalized?
2. To what extent are the exercises organized to move from structured practice to open-ended activities? Are the creative practice activities optional, or are they an important part of the text?
3. Are the communicative activities designed to help students accomplish specific functional tasks in a variety of contexts?
4. Are students made responsible for their own learning?
5. Are dialogues in the book and tape program contrived, or do they reflect authentic language use?
6. How varied is the vocabulary? Are students given the opportunity to express likes and dislikes, or is the vocabulary "generic"? Is the vocabulary recycled throughout the text? Is it functional, high-frequency, and current?
7. Are structures presented within a functional orientation and integrated with the themes of the chapter in which they occur?
8. Are the communicative situations simulations of what is likely to happen in a target-culture setting? (Based on pp. 61-62.)

Bragger's set of questions, like the set of features presented earlier, is not meant to be exhaustive, but provides some guidance for the teacher seeking a text that will support proficiency goals and enable students to learn language in context. It is important, when selecting a textbook program, to examine the ancillary materials (workbooks, tapes, computer software, etc.) with these same criteria in mind. (See Appendix B for a sample set of guidelines for evaluating multimedia foreign language programs.) If a testing program is included, the tests should be examined and compared to the testing principles suggested in Chapter 9. Obviously, no perfect program exists, but textbook publishers are anxious to satisfy the demands of classroom teachers, and it is important to let them know, on a regular basis, what our needs and expectations are.

■ Designing the Course Syllabus

A well-designed course syllabus is a necessary component of a successful language program, from both the teacher's and the students' points of view. For teachers, the course syllabus provides direction and guidance in the scope, sequence, and pacing of classroom activities; for students, the syllabus provides at a glance the profile of the semester's work and the expectations for successful completion of that work. It is strongly recommended that teachers distribute course syllabi and any accompanying information sheets on the first day of class so that students will know what is expected of them.

The syllabus itself should include information about course goals, daily reading, and homework assignments, as well as quizzes and tests. Syllabi can range from very simple ones, in which page numbers indicate reading assignments to be completed for each class day, to more complex formats in which the content of each class day is more completely described.

Guidelines for Planning Lessons

Many of the same principles that apply to the selection of materials can be used in designing daily lesson plans: That is, lessons should be planned to include contextualized and personalized practice, small-group interaction, creative language use, culturally authentic listening and reading practice, and functional tasks similar to those that might be encountered in the target culture.

Teachers may find that the following guidelines will help them plan more effective lessons:

1. *Develop a plan that is contextualized and encourages students to use the language actively to explore a particular theme.* Plan a lesson that flows logically within the contexts you have identified, integrating the grammatical concepts, functions, vocabulary, and cultural information that relate to the central theme of the lesson or unit. Avoid exercises that consist of non sequiturs or unrelated sentence-length frames. Choose, instead, to embed the practice activities in larger discourse units: focused or open-ended conversational exchanges on topics that are related to the chapter theme, communicative tasks that require students to exchange information in order to complete the activity, writing of paragraph-length discourse, role-plays, and the like. Plan transitions that either make each activity a logical continuation of the one before it or make it clear that there will be a shift in focus.

   In order to contextualize your lesson activities, think of how the language structures and vocabulary you are teaching relate to the chapter theme. For example, if you plan to teach interrogative words and expressions, consider how students can use questioning strategies to accomplish a real-world task that is coordinated with the chapter content. In a unit on travel, students can use the new interrogative structures in a role-play to ask about train or plane schedules, obtain directions, or request hotel accomodations. In a unit relating to foods, students can practice asking about items on a restaurant menu, requesting prices in making purchases, or finding out about the culinary preferences of their classmates.

2. *Plan activities that will help students reach functional objectives.* Activities that involve only question/answer exchanges or that focus exclusively on grammatical manipulation will not afford sufficient opportunities for developing functional skills in the language. It is best to plan activities that are primarily student-centered rather than teacher-centered; that is, plan practice activities that involve *all* students actively during the class hour. Avoid lengthy explanations or one-to-one exchanges that involve only a

single student at a time. Small-group work, board work where everyone participates, comprehension activities where everyone is responsible for noting down information, dictations, paired interviews, and the like are a few of the strategies that require all students to participate simultaneously and actively. In such activities, students should be given opportunities to practice a range of functions, such as asking questions, giving descriptions, narrating a story, making comparisons, expressing opinions, and so on. When possible, classes can be scheduled in a computer lab several times a semester so that students can engage in activities using multimedia applications or the Internet. Teachers can plan lessons that ask students to find information on a given Web site and report back their findings, impressions, and opinions in a subsequent class session. Teachers may also want to explore the use of computer conferencing sessions several times throughout the course to increase the opportunities for active interaction among students.

3. *Plan a variety of activities to accommodate learner differences.* Students are individuals whose preferences and styles of learning differ. Some people learn best in social-interaction activities; others prefer to work alone. Some need visual support for learning, while others learn best by listening or engaging in conversational exchanges. Students sometimes need focused language practice activities with clear objectives and corrective feedback, but will also benefit from more global comprehension and production activities that allow them to create with the language. Having students work on a variety of tasks, both in whole-class and small-group activities, adds interest to a class hour and gives the impression of a faster pace, which tends to enliven instruction for most learners.

4. *Plan activities that are appropriate to the proficiency level of your students.* Students will not experience success and will be frustrated if they are asked to engage in language practice activities for which they don't have the prerequisite knowledge or skills. Teachers should carefully consider the level of proficiency that is necessary for carrying out tasks that they choose for a given lesson. For listening and reading tasks, plan to use advance organizers and/or prelistening and prereading practice. For small-group work, plan guidelines, as well as clear directions for the activity for students to use as they work together. Supplying students with key vocabulary and expressions to help them carry out a task is also recommended, particularly for learners at the lower levels of proficiency. Keep in mind that students are bound to make numerous errors, especially when creating with the language. By circulating among students who are working in groups, teachers can note common errors, using them as a means for diagnosing what learners need in terms of feedback and further instruction.

5. *For each lesson that you plan, prepare a brief outline of what you intend to do during the class period.* It is helpful to write down the set of activities that you are planning to use, as this can help you evaluate your plan in terms of the considerations listed above. It may also be helpful to write down an estimated time for each activity so that the lesson flows at a reasonable pace. Beginning

teachers may want to include detailed notes on their lesson plans, while more experienced teachers may function well with just a brief outline. Using index cards or small slips of paper enables teachers to consult their plans easily and unobtrusively during the lesson.

6. *Evaluate your plan after the class is over.* Decide whether you would do the same things if you were to reteach the lesson, or if you would want to make some changes. Ask yourself how well students responded to the activities you planned and try to diagnose the cause of problems you encountered.

7. *Over the course of the semester, plan lessons to include the full range of course goals.* Obviously, no one lesson can include activities that will address all of the course goals at once. However, over the course of the semester, lessons should be planned in a balanced fashion to ensure that the objectives for the course are being adequately met.

Increasing Focus on Students' Interests

To plan lessons that will appeal to students' interests and needs, teachers need to ask students for their input and involve them in shaping instruction. This can be accomplished on the first day of class by having students fill out an information sheet that inquires into their backgrounds and interests in second-language learning.

Another way to create a student-centered atmosphere early in instruction is to use a get-acquainted activity the first day of class. If this is the first course in the language, students can begin by learning how to greet one another and introduce themselves and then practice in small groups. The teacher, in introducing and having students practice phrases like "What is your name?" or "Where are you from?", can then ask students to recall information about their classmates as a follow-up activity. In the first few weeks of instruction, much can be learned about students' preferences and interests in paired interviews and report-back activities.

For students who have had previous courses in the language, a good first-day activity is an interview with a classmate in the target language, followed by a report-back phase. The pairs can then introduce each other to the rest of the class.

A third way to get to know students is through short individual interviews, either when students come in for extra help or when they take oral tests. Many teachers find that students are much more motivated and cooperative after an informal visit, especially if the teacher and student both share information about themselves and their interests.

Another essential way in which teachers can obtain student input is through course evaluation. Most course evaluations are solicited at the end of the term and filled out anonymously so that students feel free to express their true opinions. Sometimes, however, it is a good idea to ask students for an informal evaluation earlier in the term, especially when the course or the materials are new. A brief survey instrument can be designed, for example, asking students which classroom activities they consider most helpful, most interesting, least helpful, and least interesting, with room for open-ended commentary.

To respond to students' interests in content from other disciplines, teachers might also ask them at the beginning of a course to list the kinds of topics they would like to explore on the Web, and then locate appropriate sites that would be most easily accessible to them from a linguistic perspective. For students at beginning and intermediate levels of proficiency, worksheets with the Web address, vocabulary helps, guidelines, and/or questions can be prepared for learners to use as they explore the site. Brief synopses and reactions to the material can be prepared for oral or written presentation. (Of course, content-based projects such as these can be done using a variety of print materials as well.) In college courses at higher levels of proficiency, students might be asked to do a research project on a topic of their choice using print sources and/or the World Wide Web and prepare a written or oral presentation for the rest of the class. The goal of this type of activity is to help students become aware of the types of materials that are readily available for them to read in the foreign language and to encourage them to use the language to learn about things that interest them.

In Conclusion

There is no doubt that the focus on proficiency as an organizing principle has stimulated a great deal of interest among theorists and practitioners in the language teaching profession in the last several years. As we saw in Chapter 1, the *ACTFL Guidelines* and associated assessment procedures such as the OPI have been enthusiastically received by some, and challenged by others. The same is undoubtedly true of the standards initiatives at the state and national levels. But these movements have energized the profession of language teaching and serve to foster its continued growth and development in the years ahead.

It is through responsible discussion and debate, as well as through data-based research studies, that inadequacies in the present frameworks can be brought to light and improvements can be made. Some possible directions for research in the coming years include further studies to validate the newest form of the guidelines and develop standards-based curricula and assessments; we also need research projects to investigate outcomes of various programs—including study-abroad experiences—and further research into language acquisition and learning processes, all of which should shed additional light on appropriate ways to develop and assess language proficiency.

It is our hope, as language teaching professionals, that each successive stage in this process will bring us closer to our goal of developing a common understanding of our overall goals for language study, along with assessment procedures for measuring student progress, thereby allowing us to communicate more clearly with one another and with the public about what our programs offer. As we learn more about language proficiency through concentrated research and development efforts, we will undoubtedly discover better ways to teach and test language skills. Our work on developing more effective ways to infuse significant cultural content into the curriculum must also continue, so that American students leave their language learning experience with a greater understanding of other peoples and cultures. In recent years, when accountability and excellence in education have received so much public attention, foreign language teachers are regaining greater visibility, respect, and support in the eyes of the nation. We must continue to strive for excellence as we refine and interpret our approaches to language teaching in the years ahead.

Activities for Review and Discussion

1. Discuss how instructors might go about setting goals for a language program at either the secondary or postsecondary level.
2. What are some of the instructional factors that need to be considered in curriculum planning? How might these factors be articulated from course to course, both horizontally (i.e., among courses at the same level) and vertically (among courses at different levels)?
3. Using the guidelines for text selection presented in this chapter (see pp. 459–461), or using guidelines you have developed yourself, evaluate one or several foreign language textbooks that you might consider using in a course you teach or will be teaching soon.
4. If possible, obtain a course syllabus for a beginning- or intermediate-level language course with which you are familiar. Based on your understanding of the concepts presented in this book, would you design the syllabus differently? If so, how would you change it? Give a rationale for your answer.
5. Using a textbook with which you are familiar, write out a lesson plan for a given day. Begin with a statement of objectives that you want your students to accomplish by the end of the hour. Then design activities that you feel will best accomplish these goals. Be sure to indicate how much time each activity would take, in your estimation. Check for flow and integration of activities, as well as for thematic and/or contextual unity in your lesson. Be sure to include a variety of activities to ensure a good pace and a high level of interest. You may want to compare your lesson plan with the ones other members of your class have prepared for the same material.
6. Make a list of characteristics you think are typical of effective language teachers. Base your list on your own personal experience, as well as on principles of teaching you have learned in this book. Compare your list of characteristics with those of others in your class.

References: Epilogue

Bragger, Jeannette D. "The Development of Oral Proficiency." In A. Omaggio, ed., *Proficiency, Curriculum, Articulation: The Ties That Bind.* Middlebury, VT: Northeast Conference, 1985.

Galloway, Vicki. Personal communication. [cited in Medley 1985.]

Medley, Frank W., Jr. "Designing the Proficiency-Based Curriculum." In A. Omaggio, ed., *Proficiency, Curriculum, Articulation: The Ties That Bind.* Middlebury, VT: Northeast Conference, 1985.

Stansfield, Charles W. and Dorry M. Kenyon. "The Development and Validation of a Simulated Oral Proficiency Interview." *The Modern Language Journal* 76, ii (1992): 129–41.

Strasheim, Lorraine A. "Achieving Curriculum Fit for that 'Horrible' Second Year." In P. Westphal, ed., *Strategies for Foreign Language Teaching.* Report of the Central States Conference on the Teaching of Foreign Languages. Lincolnwood, IL: National Textbook Company, 1984.

APPENDIX A

ACTFL PROFICIENCY GUIDELINES—SPEAKING
Revised 1999

The *ACTFL Proficiency Guidelines—Speaking* (1986) have gained widespread application as a metric against which to measure learners' functional competency; that is, their ability to accomplish linguistic tasks representing a variety of levels. Based on years of experience with oral testing in governmental institutions and on the descriptions of language proficiency used by Interagency Language Roundtable (ILR), the *ACTFL Guidelines* were an adaptation intended for use in academia (college and university levels particularly) in the United States. For this reason, the authors of the *Provisional Guidelines* (1982) conflated the top levels (ILR 3–5), expanded the descriptions of the lower levels (ILR 0–1), and defined sublevels of competency according to the experience of language instructors and researchers accustomed to beginning learners. Their efforts were further modified and refined in the *ACTFL Proficiency Guidelines* published in 1986.

After additional years of oral testing and of interpretation of the *Guidelines,* as well as numerous research projects, scholarly articles, and debates, the time has come to reevaluate and refine the *Guidelines,* initially those for Speaking, followed by those for the other skills. The purposes of this revision of the *Proficiency Guidelines—Speaking* are to make the document more accessible to those who have not received recent training in ACTFL oral proficiency testing, to clarify the issues that have divided testers and teachers, and to provide a corrective to what the committee perceived to have been possible misinterpretations of the descriptions provided in earlier versions of the *Guidelines.*

An important example is the treatment of the Superior level. The ILR descriptions postulate a spectrum of proficiency abilities from 0 which signifies no functional competence, to 5 which is competence equivalent to that of a well-educated native speaker. Due to the language levels most often attained by adult learners, the *ACTFL Guidelines* do not include descriptions of the highest ILR levels. The ACTFL Superior level, roughly equivalent to the ILR 3 range, is thus to be seen as a baseline level; that is, it describes a particular set of functional abilities essential to that level, but not necessarily the whole range of linguistic activities that an educated speaker with years of experience in the target language and culture might attain. Keeping this distinction in mind reduces the tendency to expect the Superior speaker to demonstrate abilities defined at higher ILR levels.

For this reason, among others, the committee has broken with tradition by presenting this version of the Speaking Guidelines—in **descending** rather than ascending order. This top-down approach has two advantages. First, it emphasizes that the High levels are more closely related to the level above than to the one below, and represents a considerable step towards accomplishing the functions at the level above, not just excellence in the functions of the level itself. Second, it allows for fewer negatives and less redundancy in the descriptions when they refer, as they must, to the inability of a speaker to function consistently at a higher level.

Another significant change to the 1986 version of the *Guidelines* is found in the division of the Advanced level into the High, Mid, and Low sublevels. This decision reflects the growing need in both the academic and commercial communities to more finely delineate a speaker's progress through the Advanced level of proficiency. The new descriptors for **Advanced Mid and Advanced Low** are based on hundreds of Advanced-level language samples from OPI testing across a variety of languages.

The committee has also taken a slightly different approach to the presentation of these *Guidelines* from previous versions. The full **prose descriptions** of each level (and, when applicable, its sub-levels) are preceded by clearly delineated **thumb-nail sketches** that are intended to alert the reader to the major features of the levels and to serve as a quick reference, but not in any way to replace the full picture presented in the descriptions themselves. Indeed, at the lower levels they refer to the Mid rather than to the baseline proficiency, since they would otherwise describe a very limited profile and misrepresent the general expectations for the level.

This revision of the *ACTFL Proficiency Guidelines—Speaking* is presented as an additional step toward more adequately describing speaking proficiency. Whereas this effort reflects a broad spectrum of experience in characterizing speaker abilities and includes a wide range of insights as a result of ongoing discussions and research within the language teaching profession, the revision committee is aware that there remain a number of issues requiring further clarification and specification. It is the hope of the committee that this revision will enhance the *Guidelines'* utility to the language teaching and testing community in the years to come.

▨ Acknowledgments

ACTFL is indebted to the following individuals who contributed to the original *ACTFL Proficiency Guidelines Project* of 1986: Heidi Byrnes, James Child, Nina

Patrizio, Pardee Lowe, Jr., Seiichi Makino, Irene Thompson, and A. Ronald Walton. Their work was the foundation for this revision project.

We would also like to thank the following committee members and reviewers who generously gave of their time and expertise during the current revision process: Lucia Caycedo Garner, Helen Hamlyn, Judith Liskin-Gasparro, Arthur Mosher, Lizette Mujica Laughlin, Chantal Thompson, and Maureen Weissenreider.

Finally, ACTFL wishes to acknowledge the work of the *Guidelines'* editors, and authors of the Explanatory Notes that accompany the *ACTFL Proficiency Guidelines—Speaking* (Revised 1999).

Karen E. Breiner-Sanders
Pardee Lowe, Jr.
John Miles
Elvira Swender

The Revision of the *ACTFL Proficiency Guidelines—Speaking* was supported by a grant from the United States Department of Education International Studies and Research Programs.

SUPERIOR

Speakers at the Superior level are able to communicate in the language with accuracy and fluency in order to participate fully and effectively in conversations on a variety of topics in formal and informal settings from both concrete and abstract perspectives. They discuss their interests and special fields of competence, explain complex matters in detail, and provide lengthy and coherent narrations, all with ease, fluency, and accuracy. They explain their opinions on a number of topics of importance to them, such as social and political issues, and provide structured argument to support their opinions. They are able to construct and develop hypotheses to explore alternative possibilities. When appropriate, they use extended discourse without unnaturally lengthy hesitation to make their point, even when engaged in abstract elaborations. Such discourse, while coherent, may still be influenced by the Superior speakers' own language patterns, rather than those of the target language.

Superior speakers command a variety of interactive and discourse strategies, such as turn-taking and separating main ideas from supporting information through the use of syntactic and lexical devices, as well as intonational features such as pitch, stress and tone. They demonstrate virtually no pattern of error in the use of basic structures. However, they may make sporadic errors, particularly in low-frequency structures and in some complex high-frequency structures more common to formal speech and writing. Such errors, if they do occur, do not distract the native interlocutor or interfere with communication.

ADVANCED HIGH

Speakers at the Advanced-High level perform all Advanced-level tasks with linguistic ease, confidence and competence. They are able to consistently explain in detail and narrate fully and accurately in all time frames. In addition, Advanced-High speakers handle the tasks pertaining to the Superior level but cannot sustain performance at that level across a variety of topics. They can provide a structured argument to support their opinions, and they may construct hypotheses, but patterns of error appear. They can discuss some topics abstractly, especially those relating to their particular interests and special fields of expertise, but in general, they are more comfortable discussing a variety of topics concretely.

Advanced-High speakers may demonstrate a well-developed ability to compensate for an imperfect grasp of some forms or for limitations in vocabulary by the confident use of communicative strategies, such as paraphrasing, circumlocution, and illustration. They use precise vocabulary and intonation to express meaning and often show great fluency and ease of speech. However, when called on to perform the complex tasks associated with the Superior level over a variety of topics, their language will at times break down or prove inadequate, or they may avoid the task altogether, for example, by resorting to simplification through the use of description or narration in place of argument or hypothesis.

ADVANCED MID
Speakers at the Advanced-Mid level are able to handle with ease and confidence a large number of communicative tasks. They participate actively in most informal and some formal exchanges on a variety of concrete topics relating to work, school, home, and leisure activities, as well as to events of current, public, and personal interest or individual relevance.

Advanced-Mid speakers demonstrate the ability to narrate and describe in all major time frames (past, present, and future) by providing a full account, with good control of aspect, as they adapt flexibly to the demands of the conversation. Narration and description tend to be combined and interwoven to relate relevant and supporting facts in connected, paragraph-length discourse.

Advanced-Mid speakers can handle successfully and with relative ease the linguistic challenges presented by a complication or unexpected turn of events that occurs within the context of a routine situation or communicative task with which they are otherwise familiar. Communicative strategies such as circumlocution or rephrasing are often employed for this purpose. The speech of Advanced-Mid speakers performing Advanced-level tasks is marked by substantial flow. Their vocabulary is fairly extensive although primarily generic in nature, except in the case of a particular area of specialization or interest. Dominant language discourse structures tend to recede, although discourse may still reflect the oral paragraph structure of their own language rather than that of the target language.

Advanced-Mid speakers contribute to conversations on a variety of familiar topics, dealt with concretely, with much accuracy, clarity and precision, and they convey their intended message without misrepresentation or confusion. They are readily understood by native speakers unaccustomed to dealing with non-natives. When called on to perform functions or handle topics associated with the Superior level, the quality and/or quantity of their speech will generally decline. Advanced-Mid speakers are often able to state an opinion or cite conditions; however, they lack the ability to consistently provide a structured argument in extended discourse. Advanced-Mid speakers may use a number of delaying strategies, resort to narration, description, explanation or anecdote, or simply attempt to avoid the linguistic demands of Superior-level tasks.

ADVANCED LOW

Speakers at the Advanced-Low level are able to handle a variety of communicative tasks, although somewhat haltingly at times. They participate actively in most informal and a limited number of formal conversations on activities related to school, home, and leisure activities and, to a lesser degree, those related to events of work, current, public, and personal interest or individual relevance.

Advanced-Low speakers demonstrate the ability to narrate and describe in all major time frames (past, present and future) in paragraph length discourse, but control of aspect may be lacking at times. They can handle appropriately the linguistic challenges presented by a complication or unexpected turn of events that occurs within the context of a routine situation or communicative task with which they are otherwise familiar, though at times their discourse may be minimal for the level and strained. Communicative strategies such as rephrasing and circumlocution may be employed in such instances. In their narrations and descriptions, they combine and link sentences into connected discourse of paragraph length. When pressed for a fuller account, they tend to grope and rely on minimal discourse. Their utterances are typically not longer than a single paragraph. Structure of the dominant language is still evident in the use of false cognates, literal translations, or the oral paragraph structure of the speaker's own language rather than that of the target language.

While the language of Advanced-Low speakers may be marked by substantial, albeit irregular flow, it is typically somewhat strained and tentative, with noticeable self-correction and a certain 'grammatical roughness.' The vocabulary of Advanced-Low speakers is primarily generic in nature.

Advanced-Low speakers contribute to the conversation with sufficient accuracy, clarity, and precision to convey their intended message without misrepresentation or confusion, and it can be understood by native speakers unaccustomed to dealing with non-natives, even though this may be achieved through repetition and restatement. When attempting to perform functions or handle topics associated with the Superior level, the linguistic quality and quantity of their speech will deteriorate significantly.

INTERMEDIATE HIGH

Intermediate-High speakers are able to converse with ease and confidence when dealing with most routine tasks and social situations of the Intermediate level. They are able to handle successfully many uncomplicated tasks and social situations requiring an exchange of basic information related to work, school, recreation, particular interests and areas of competence, though hesitation and errors may be evident.

Intermediate-High speakers handle the tasks pertaining to the Advanced level, but they are unable to sustain performance at that level over a variety of topics. With some consistency, speakers at the Intermediate High level narrate and describe in major time frames using connected discourse of paragraph length. However, their performance of these Advanced-level tasks will exhibit one or more features of breakdown, such as the failure to maintain the narration or description semantically or syntactically in the appropriate major time frame, the disintegration of connected discourse, the misuse of cohesive devises, a reduction in breadth and appropriateness of vocabulary, the failure to successfully circumlocute, or a significant amount of hesitation.

Intermediate-High speakers can generally be understood by native speakers unaccustomed to dealing with non-natives, although the dominant language is still evident (e.g. use of code-switching, false cognates, literal translations, etc.), and gaps in communication may occur.

INTERMEDIATE MID

Speakers at the Intermediate-Mid level are able to handle successfully a variety of uncomplicated communicative tasks in straightforward social situations. Conversation is generally limited to those predictable and concrete exchanges necessary for survival in the target culture; these include personal information covering self, family, home, daily activities, interests and personal preferences, as well as physical and social needs, such as food, shopping, travel and lodging.

Intermediate-Mid speakers tend to function reactively, for example, by responding to direct questions or requests for information. However, they are capable of asking a variety of questions when necessary to obtain simple information to satisfy basic needs, such as directions, prices and services. When called on to perform functions or handle topics at the Advanced level, they provide some information but have difficulty linking ideas, manipulating time and aspect, and using communicative strategies, such as circumlocution.

Intermediate-Mid speakers are able to express personal meaning by creating with the language, in part by combining and recombining known elements and conversational input to make utterances of sentence length and some strings of sentences. Their speech may contain pauses, reformulations and self-corrections as they search for adequate vocabulary and appropriate language forms to express themselves. Because of inaccuracies in their vocabulary and/or pronunciation and/or grammar and/or syntax, misunderstandings can occur, but Intermediate-Mid speakers are generally understood by sympathetic interlocutors accustomed to dealing with non-natives.

INTERMEDIATE LOW

Speakers at the Intermediate-Low level are able to handle successfully a limited number of uncomplicated communicative tasks by creating with the language in straightforward social situations. Conversation is restricted to some of the concrete exchanges and predictable topics necessary for survival in the target language culture. These topics relate to basic personal information covering, for example, self and family, some daily activities and personal preferences, as well as to some immediate needs, such as ordering food and making simple purchases. At the Intermediate-Low level, speakers are primarily reactive and struggle to answer direct questions or requests for information, but they are also able to ask a few appropriate questions.

Intermediate-Low speakers express personal meaning by combining and recombining into short statements what they know and what they hear from their interlocutors. Their utterances are often filled with hesitancy and inaccuracies as they search for appropriate linguistic forms and vocabulary while attempting to give form to the message. Their speech is characterized by frequent pauses, ineffective reformulations and self-corrections. Their pronunciation, vocabulary and syntax are strongly influenced by their first language but, in spite of frequent misunderstandings that require repetition or rephrasing, Intermediate-Low speakers can generally be understood by sympathetic interlocutors, particularly by those accustomed to dealing with non-natives.

NOVICE HIGH

Speakers at the Novice-High level are able to handle a variety of tasks pertaining to the Intermediate level, but are unable to sustain performance at that level. They are able to manage successfully a number of uncomplicated communicative tasks in straightforward social situations. Conversation is restricted to a few of the predictable topics necessary for survival in the target language culture, such as basic personal information, basic objects and a limited number of activities, preferences and immediate needs. Novice-High speakers respond to simple, direct questions or requests for information; they are able to ask only a very few formulaic questions when asked to do so.

Novice-High speakers are able to express personal meaning by relying heavily on learned phrases or recombinations of these and what they hear from their interlocutor. Their utterances, which consist mostly of short and sometimes incomplete sentences in the present, may be hesitant or inaccurate. On the other hand, since these utterances are frequently only expansions of learned material and stock phrases, they may sometimes appear surprisingly fluent and accurate. These speakers' first language may strongly influence their pronunciation, as well as their vocabulary and syntax when they attempt to personalize their utterances. Frequent misunderstandings may arise but, with repetition or rephrasing, Novice-High speakers can generally be understood by sympathetic interlocutors used to non-natives. When called on to handle simply a variety of topics and perform functions pertaining to the Intermediate level, a Novice-High speaker can sometimes respond in intelligible sentences, but will not be able to sustain sentence level discourse.

NOVICE MID

Speakers at the Novice-Mid level communicate minimally and with difficulty by using a number of isolated words and memorized phrases limited by the particular context in which the language has been learned. When responding to direct questions, they may utter only two or three words at a time or an occasional stock answer. They pause frequently as they search for simple vocabulary or attempt to recycle their own and their interlocutor's words. Because of hesitations, lack of vocabulary, inaccuracy, or failure to respond appropriately, Novice-Mid speakers may be understood with great difficulty even by sympathetic interlocutors accustomed to dealing with non-natives. When called on to handle topics by performing functions associated with the Intermediate level, they frequently resort to repetition, words from their native language, or silence.

NOVICE LOW

Speakers at the Novice-Low level have no real functional ability and, because of their pronunciation, they may be unintelligible. Given adequate time and familiar cues, they may be able to exchange greetings, give their identity, and name a number of familiar objects from their immediate environment. They are unable to perform functions or handle topics pertaining to the Intermediate level, and cannot therefore participate in a true conversational exchange.

Sample Foreign Language Media Evaluation Criteria

The materials that follow are part of a "Taxonomy of Features for Evaluating Foreign Language Multimedia Software"(NFLRC 1999), a set of criteria for evaluating foreign language media. The foreign language multimedia evaluation criteria were developed at an invitational Symposium funded by the U.S. Department of Education and held at the National Foreign Language Resource Center of the University of Hawai'i on February 26–28, 1998. In addition to outlining the general criteria, depicted in chart form on the following pages, the taxonomy also contains pedagogical criteria by skill. These skill-based criteria include the specification of input, activities, strategy instruction, tools, and interface for speaking, reading, listening, writing, script (or writing system), vocabulary, and pronunciation. The reading and listening criteria are also given here. The full set of materials can be accessed on the Web at *http://nts.lll.hawaii.edu/flmedia*.

GENERAL CRITERIA

Program Description	Program Operation	Program Features

Intended Users
Age group
  elementary school
  junior high school
  high school
  college
  adult
Year or semester of language study
Proficiency level
Learners with special interests (tourists, business, etc.)
	Ease of Installation
	Are the installation instructions clear?
	Is the program easy to install/uninstall?
	How often does the system crash?
	Is there a particular action that causes regular crashes?
		Program Goals
		Are the goals and objectives for the following clearly defined?
		  the program as a whole?
		  each unit?
		  each activity?

Intended Use For self-instruction As a textbook supplement As a classroom supplement Combination of above	**Quality of the Media** Do graphics, video and audio help users to concentrate on content? Is the text easy to read? Is the audio clear? Are the colors and graphics crisp and clear? Does the video run smoothly? Do the hypertext links work well? Does animation serve a pedagogical purpose?	**General Content** Is the content of interest to intended users? Are the instructional units logically sequenced? Do lessons build on materials presented earlier? Are the explanations clearly worded? Are explanations tailored to the user's level?

Scope
Equivalence in terms of
  hours
  semesters
  years of instruction
Number of lessons or instructional units
	Interface Design
	Is the program user-friendly?
	• the meaning of icons and symbols is easy to understand and remember
	• options, choices, and menus are easily found
	• information is available through links to other parts of the program
	• the screen indicates what part of the program the learner is working on
	• users can move easily between different parts of the program
	• users can enter the program at different points
	• users can start off where they ended
	• an easy exit from the program is available at all times
		Tests
		What is the frequency of the tests?
		  for each individual exercise or activity
		  at the end of each instructional unit
		  at the end of each session
		What type of scores are made available to users?
		Is there an explanation of test scores?
		Is there a cumulative log of scores to track progress?
		Are recommendations for remedial action given?
		Can the tests be printed out?
		Can the test scores be printed out?

GENERAL CRITERIA (continued)

Program Description	Program Operation	Program Features

	Are the instructions helpful?
	• demonstrations of various activities are available
	• instructions can be reviewed
	• type of requested response is clearly indicated
	• place for requested response is clearly indicated
	• guidance is provided through each stage of an activity
	• instructions pop up at any time if users forget what to do
	• user can skip instructions if desired
	• there is a "help" key
	Is the speech interface intuitive and easy to use (i.e., push to talk, hands-free)?
	Is the interface used throughout the program consistently?
	   colors
	   fonts
	   screen layout	

Hardware Requirements
Type of computer
Version of operating system
Memory (RAM)
Disk space
CD-ROM drive
DVD-ROM drive
Speakers
Microphone
Monitor
Sound card
Video card
Network requirements
Other
	Customization
	Are there choices depending on user's level?
	Does the program include authoring features?
	Can users customize the operation of the program?
	Is there a variety of options to support different types of learners?
		Feedback
		Does the user receive quick feedback to responses?
		Is level of feedback language appropriate for intended users?
		What is the availability of feedback?
		   item-by-item
		   logical content break
		   end-of-unit or session
		   learner-controlled
		What type of feedback is available?
		   indication as to whether response is correct or incorrect
		   correct response
		   instructions to repeat the correct response
		   hints leading to correct response
		   invitation to try again
		   explanation of why a particular response is incorrect

GENERAL CRITERIA (continued)

Program Description	Program Operation	Program Features
		a "give-up" option directions to relevant part of program for review intelligent feedback depending on learner response history Can the software track learner interaction with the program?

Documentation
Is there a discussion of program's goals, design, and contents?
Is there a tutorial on program's operation?
Is a demonstration lesson included?
Are there lesson plans for use in a course or guidance for individual use?
Is there information about independent reviews of the program?
		Special Features: Speech Recognition
		Does the system require initial training?
		What does the user need to do to train the system?
		How extensively is speech recognition/processing utilized in each unit of the program?
		   1-2 times
		   3-5 times
		   more than 5 times
		What is the function of speech recognition/ processing in this program?
		   voice navigation
		   pronunciation instruction
		   speaking practice
		How frequently does the system recognize a range of native speech?
		   most of the time
		   some of the time
		   seldom
		How does the system react to nonnative speech?
		   recognizes it despite mistakes
		   asks for repetition
		   does not recognize it

Adapted from "Taxonomy of Features for Evaluating Foreign Language Multimedia Software," *http://nts.lll.hawaii.edu/flmedia/evaluation/general/gencriteria.htm*

LISTENING CRITERIA

Listening Input

Audio
- Are the conditions against which the audio is played authentic?
- Is the tempo of the sound track natural?
- Is there a variety of voices and dialects?
- Is the sound track supported by video or graphics?

Listening Passages
- Are the passages authentic?
- Are the topics of interest to intended users?
- Is there a variety of topics?
- Can the user choose among several passages on the same topic?
- Is there a variety of genres?
- Are the passages of an appropriate length for intended users?
- Is the vocabulary appropriate for the intended level?
- Is the syntax appropriate for the intended level?

Listening Activities

Pre-listening Activities
- Does the program adapt to different levels of users' prior knowledge?
- Are there pre-listening activities that activate prior knowledge?

Listening Activities
- Do listening activities emphasize comprehension of the passage?
- Are the listening activities authentic?
- Is there a variety of listening activities?
- Do users have a choice of listening activities?
- Do the activities motivate learners to keep listening?

Post-listening Activities
- Are there post-listening activities based on selected features of passages?
- Are the features selected for special attention well chosen?
- Do post-listening activities promote acquisition of vocabulary?

Listening Strategy Instruction

Is there an explanation about the benefits of using listening strategies?

Is there systematic practice in the use of listening strategies?

Can the user see that certain tasks are more easily accomplished when strategies are used?

Is there a choice of listening strategies depending on learning style?

Is there feedback on the effectiveness of strategy use?

LISTENING CRITERIA (continued)

Listening Tools	Links to the written version of passage • the whole passage • sentence-by-sentence • word-by-word Spoken glosses • monolingual • bilingual • hint-type Written glosses • monolingual • bilingual • hint-type Visual glosses • images • graphics • videos What kinds of additional resources are available? • on-line talking dictionary • on-line written dictionary • on-line reference grammar • background information • cultural notes

Listening Interface	Ease of navigation
	• Is navigation between audio, activities, glosses, and tools simple?
	• Is navigation between screens fast?
	Playback control
	• Can listeners control the speed of audio playback?
	• Can playback be stopped
	  • after each phrase?
	  • after each sentence?
	Timing
	• Is there enough time to complete activities?
	Archiving
	• Can user's work be saved?
	• Can user's work be printed out?

Adapted from "Taxonomy of Features for Evaluating Foreign Language Multimedia Software,"
http://nts.lll.hawaii.edu/flmedia/evaluation/listening/listen_criteria.htm

READING CRITERIA

Reading Activities

Pre-reading Activities
- Does the program adapt to different levels of users' prior knowledge?
- Are there pre-reading activities that activate prior knowledge?

Reading Activities
- Do reading activities emphasize comprehension of the passage?
- Are the reading activities authentic?
- Is there a variety of reading activities?
- Do users have a choice of reading activities?
- Do activities motivate learners to keep reading?

Post-reading Activities
- Are there post-reading activities based on selected features of passages?
- Are the features selected for special attention well chosen?
- Do post-listening activities promote acquisition of vocabulary?

Reading Strategy Instruction

Is there an explanation about the benefits of using reading strategies?
Is there systematic practice in the use of reading strategies?
Can users see that certain tasks are more easily accomplished with strategy use?
Is there a choice of reading strategies depending on learning style?
Is there feedback on the effectiveness of strategy use?

Reading Tools

What kinds of links are available to the spoken version of the passage?
- the whole passage
- sentence-by-sentence
- word-by-word

What kinds of written glosses are available?
- monolingual
- bilingual
- hint-type

What kinds of spoken glosses are available?
- monolingual
- bilingual
- hint-type

What kinds of visual glosses are available?
- images
- graphics
- videos

What kinds of additional resources are available?
- topical glossaries
- background information
- cultural information
- on-line dictionary
- on-line reference grammar

READING CRITERIA (continued)

Reading Interface

Ease of navigation
- Is navigation between text, activities, glosses, and tools simple?
- Is navigation between screens fast?

Appearance of the text
- Do texts preserve their original format?
- Are texts presented in a variety of fonts and typefaces?
- Are fonts and typefaces attractive and easy to read?
- Do illustrations and graphics aid in text comprehension?

Glosses
- Is there equal access to different types of glosses?
- Are glossed items marked unobtrusively?
- Do glosses cover up text or make it disappear?
- Can different types of glosses be customized by users?

Timing
- Is there enough time to complete activities?

Archiving
- Can user's work be saved?
- Can user's work be printed out?

Adapted from "Taxonomy of Features for Evaluating Foreign Language Multimedia Software," *http://nts.lll.hawaii.edu/flmedia/evaluation/reading/reading_criteria.htm*

APPENDIX C

Samples of Error Coding Procedures for Written Work

Studies by Kulhavey (1977), Higgs (1979), and Lalande (1982) tend to support the use of discovery procedures and coding devices in the correction of written work. Hendrickson (1980), in reviewing numerous studies on feedback, concludes that error correction of some type is valuable for adult learners in that it increases their awareness of the exact environment for applying grammatical rules and for discovering the precise semantic range of lexical items. However, more research on the correction of written work has to be done to clarify the role of various feedback mechanisms in this domain.

There is general agreement among researchers and practitioners that having the teacher straightforwardly correct every error on students' written work is not the most useful way of providing corrective feedback. This approach is time consuming and resembles editing more than it does correcting. Students may feel extremely discouraged if papers are continually returned to them with as many red marks as there are words on a page. There is also good reason to believe that by supplying the corrections themselves, teachers might actually be hindering the learners' progress in building proficiency in writing.

An alternative to overt correction of all errors is a selective approach and the use of discovery techniques, such as those discussed in Chapter 7. Hendrickson (1980) believes that the students' proficiency level should be considered when choosing error-correction strategies: Lower-level students may not be able to find their own errors and correct them, whereas students at higher levels of proficiency may be better able to do so. As Lalande's (1982) study shows, students whose proficiency in writing is intermediate or advanced may profit best from a cuing system whereby their errors are located for them but they are held responsible for finding solutions.

In using Lalande's system of cuing, teachers tally and record students' errors on successive writing assignments, thereby providing them with an individualized profile of their progress over time (see Lalande 1982 for a detailed description of the system used for charting errors and the codes used for German).

The system for French depicted on the following page is somewhat less complex than the system used by Lalande. It is adapted from a charting system described by Brown (1979) to help students analyze and track their composition errors in English. Students record their own performance by counting up the number of errors in each category on a given written assignment and entering the numbers in the appropriate boxes. Teachers correct students' work using the error codes, underlining the error, and placing the code in the margin. In the sample given on p. 487, the student has done three compositions thus far and has recorded the number of errors in each category for each assignment. For example, on Composition 1, the student made 7 accent errors, 8 elision errors, 12 spelling errors, and so forth. In subsequent compositions, the number of errors is slowly decreasing as the student begins to monitor the work more closely. Teachers can collect error charts periodically and, by glancing through them, identify common trends within a class. Using this information, the teacher can then design more targeted language-practice activities and review those concepts that seem to present the most difficulty.

An alternative set of codes for French is provided below. These codes include abbreviations signifying problems relating to both grammar and style.

ERROR CODES FOR FRENCH: GRAMMAR AND STYLE

Evaluation des compositions

Grammaire

AA	adjective agreement wrong
AC	accent wrong or missing
ADV	adverb wrong or misplaced after negative or expression of quantity
AUX	auxillary verb problem
CONJ	conjunction wrong or missing
E	failure to make elision, or inappropriate elision
GN	gender wrong
MD	mood incorrect (indicative, imperative, or subjunctive)
NB	number wrong—sing./plur.
NEG	negative wrong, misplaced, or missing
OP	object pronoun wrong or missing
POS	possessive adjective wrong or missing, lacks agreement
PR	preposition wrong or missing
PRO	y or en wrong or missing
REL	relative pronoun wrong or missing
RP	reflexive pronoun wrong or missing
SP	spelling error
SPN	subject pronoun problem
SVA	subject/verb agreement lacking
TN	tense incorrect
VC	vocabulary wrong, wrong word choice
VF	verb form (e.g., stem) wrong or missing words
WO	word order wrong

Style

AWK	acceptable, but awkward
COM	combine sentences
INC	incomprehensible, due to structure or vocabulary choice that makes it difficult to pinpoint the error
NC	not clear
NL	not logical in terms of paragraph development
POL	incorrect level of politeness (make more or less polite)
PP	past participle in wrong form or has wrong agreement
REP	use pronoun to avoid repetition
RS	repetitive structure
SYN	find synonym to avoid repetition

Source: Muyskens, Harlow, Vialet, and Brière 1998, p. 415.

Error Tracking System: French

Nom _____

Assign-ment # →	Comp. #1	Comp. #2	Comp. #3	(etc.)												
AC	7	6	6													
E	8	4	1													
SP	12	9	6													
GN	4	2	0													
NB	0	1	0													
NEG	7	4	2													
VC	3	2	2													
ART	6	4	4													
SVA	9	7	5													
VF	1	3	1													
TN	/	/	/													
MD	/	/	/													
PP	/	/	/													
AA	7	7	5													
POS	/	3	3													
DOP	/	/	/													
IOP	/	/	/													
RP	/	/	/													
PRO	/	/	/													
ADV	2	/	1													
PR	4	5	5													
CONJ	2	/	1													
WO	5	4	4													
INC	2	1	1													

Key to Abbreviations

AC Accent missing or wrong
E Elision, failure to elide or inappropriate elision
SP Spelling error
GN Gender wrong
NB Number wrong—singular/plural
NEG Negative wrong, misplaced, missing
VC Vocabulary wrong, word choice, missing words
ART Article missing, wrong form used, wrong after negative, expression of quantity
SVA Subject/verb agreement lacking
VF Verb form-stem incorrect
TN Tense incorrect
MD Mood incorrect (indicative, imperative, or subjunctive)

PP Past participle wrong—form or agreement
AA Adjective agreement wrong
POS Possessive adjective wrong or missing, lacks agreement
DOP Direct object pronoun wrong or missing
IOP Indirect object pronoun wrong/missing
RP Reflexive pronoun wrong or missing
PRO Other Pronoun—*y* or *en*
ADV Adverb wrong or misplaced
PR Preposition wrong or missing
CONJ Conjunction wrong or missing
WO Word order wrong
INC Incomprehensible, due to structure or vocabulary choice that makes it difficult to pinpoint the error

Source: Omaggio 1981 (Adapted from Brown 1979).

References: Appendix C

Brown, Cheri. "Individualizing Error Analysis in the Composition Class." Paper presented at the Rocky Mountain Modern Language Association meeting, Albuquerque, NM, 1979.

Hendrickson, James M. "The Treatment of Error in Written Work." *The Modern Language Journal* 64 (1980): 216-21.

Higgs, T. V. "Coping with Composition." *Hispania* 62 (1979): 673-78.

Kulhavey, R. W. "Feedback in Written Instruction." *Review of Educational Research* 47 (1977): 214.

Lalande, John F. "Reducing Composition Errors: An Experiment." *The Modern Language Journal* 66 (1982): 140-49.

Muyskens, Judith A., Linda L. Harlow, Michèle Vialet, and Jean-François Brière. *Bravo!* 3rd ed. Boston: Heinle & Heinle, 1998.

Omaggio, Alice C. *Helping Learners Succeed: Activities for the Foreign Language Classroom.* Language in Education: Theory and Practice, no. 36. Washington, DC: Center for Applied Linguistics, 1981.

Text Permissions

The author is grateful for permissions granted by the following publishers and individuals to reprint the materials below.

p. 8: L. Bachman, *Fundamental Considerations in Language Testing*. Oxford: Oxford University Press, 1990, p. 87.

p. 13: E. Swender, ed., *ACTFL Oral Proficiency Interview Tester Training Manual*. Yonkers, NY: American Council on the Teaching of Foreign Languages, 1999, p.12.

p. 14: E. Swender, ed., *ACTFL Oral Proficiency Interview Tester Training Manual*. Yonkers, NY: American Council on the Teaching of Foreign Languages, 1999, p.31.

p. 26: J. Liskin-Gasparro, *ETS Oral Proficiency Testing Manual*. Princeton, NJ: Educational Testing Service, 1982.

p. 37: *Standards for Foreign Language Learning: Preparing for the 21st Century*. Yonkers, NY: National Standards in Foreign Language Education Project, 1996, p. 9.

p. 183: *Standards for Foreign Language Learning: Preparing for the 21st Century*. Yonkers, NY: National Standards in Foreign Language Education Project, 1996, p. 33.

p. 186: R. J. Lund, "A Taxonomy for Teaching Second Language Listening," *Foreign Language Annals* 23, ii, 1990, p. 111.

pp. 193–194: S. Bacon, "Listening for Real in the Foreign Language Classroom," *Foreign Language Annals* 22, vi, 1989, p. 548.

p. 194: M. Weissenrieder, "Listening to the News in Spanish," *The Modern Language Journal* 71, i, 1987, p. 24.

pp. 197–198: R. Terry, personal communication, 2000.

p. 213: Tylène Transports Tourisme, "Excursions au départ d'Aix-en-Provence," illustration by Michel Palmi, Aix-en-Provence, France, 1987.

p. 214: Comité Régional de Tourisme du Limousin, "Les séjours en campagne," Centre Impression: Limoges, France, 1980.

pp. 216, 218, 219: R. Terry, personal communication, 2000.

p. 221: Comité Régional de Tourisme du Limousin, Centre Impression: Limoges, France, 1980.

p. 223: G. Guntermann, personal communication, 1993.

p. 234: R. Ellis, *Understanding Second Language Acquisition*. Oxford: Oxford University Press, 1985, p. 76.

pp. 241–242: A. Golato, personal communication, 2000.

p. 251: A. Omaggio, "Using Games and Simulations for the Development of Functional Proficiency in a Second Language," *Canadian Modern Language Review* 38, 1982, pp. 529–530.

pp. 251–252: A. Golato, personal communication, 2000.

p. 259: *Standards for Foreign Language Learning in the 21st Century*. Yonkers, NY: National Standards in Foreign Language Education Project, 1999, pp. 313–314.

p. 272: (Note) A. Omaggio, "The Proficiency-Oriented Classroom," in T. Higgs, Ed. *Teaching for Proficiency, The Organizing Principle*. Lincolnwood, IL: National Textbook Company, 1984, pp.43–84.

p. 285: R. Terry, personal communication, 2000.

p. 286: R. Terry, personal communication, 1985.

p. 287: R. Terry, personal communication, 2000.

p. 289: R. Terry, personal communication, 2000.

p. 299: R. Terry, personal communication, 2000.

p. 300: R. Terry, personal communication, 1985.

p. 328: H. Jacobs, S. Zingraf, D. Wormuth, V. Hartfiel, and J. Hughey, *Testing ESL Composition: A Practical Approach*. Rowley, MA: Newbury House, 1981, p. 22.

p. 334–335: C. Gaudiani, *Teaching Composition in the Foreign Language Curriculum*. Language in Education: Theory and Practice Series, no. 43. Washington, DC: Center for Applied Linguistics, 1981, pp. 20–21.

p. 336: H. Jacobs, S. Zingraf, D. Wormuth, V. Hartfiel, and J. Hughey, *Testing ESL Composition: A Practical Approach*. Rowley, MA: Newbury House, 1981.

p. 369: J. Lalande, personal communication, 2000.

p. 370: J. Lalande, personal communication, 2000.

pp. 372–373: J. Lalande, personal communication, 2000.

p. 377: S. Hague, "Vocabulary Instruction: What L2 Can Learn from L1," *Foreign Language Annals* 20, iii, 1987, p. 222.

p. 382: E. Richmond, "Utilizing Proverbs as Focal Point to Cultural Awareness and Communicative Competence: Illustrations from Africa," *Foreign Language Annals* 20, iii (1987), p. 214.

p. 400: A. Omaggio, *Proficiency-Oriented Classroom Testing*. Language in Education: Theory and Practice Series, no. 52. Washington, DC: Center for Applied Linguistics, 1983, p.10.

pp. 402–403: R. Terry, personal communication, 2000.

p. 404–405: S. McMillen Villar and F. Meuser Blincow, personal communication, 1993.

p. 405: R. Terry, personal communication, 1985.

pp. 409–410: S. McMillen Villar and F. Meuser Blincow, personal communication, 1993.

p. 424: R. Terry, personal communication, 2000.

p. 428: F. Coulont-Henderson, personal communication, 1992.

p. 429: F. Coulont-Henderson, personal communication, 1992.

p. 435: E. Swender, ed., *ACTFL Oral Proficiency Interview Tester Training Manual*. Yonkers, NY: American Council on the Teaching of Foreign Languages, 1999, p. 38.

p. 442: A. Omaggio, *Proficiency-Oriented Classroom Testing*. Language in Education: Theory and Practice Series, no. 52. Washington, DC: Center for Applied Linguistics, 1983, p.73.

p. 444: R. Terry, personal communication, 2000.

pp. 469–476: *The ACTFL Proficiency Guidelines-Speaking*. Yonkers, NY: American Council on the Teaching of Foreign Languages, revised 1999.

pp. 477–484: "Taxonomy of Features for Evaluating Foreign Language Multimedia Software", National Foreign Language Resource Center, University of Hawaii, 1999, (*http://nts.lll.hawaii.edu/flmedia*).

p. 487: A. Omaggio, *Helping Learners Succeed: Activities for the Foreign Language Classroom*. Language in Education: Theory and Practice, no. 36. Washington, DC: Center for Applied Linguistics, 1981, p. 14.

Index